Mini Study INDONESIAN Dictionary

WENDY SAHANAYA
AND ALBERT TAN

OXFORD
UNIVERSITY PRESS

OXFORD
UNIVERSITY PRESS

253 Normanby Road, South Melbourne, Victoria 3205, Australia

Oxford University Press is a department of the University of Oxford. It furthers the University's objective of excellence in research, scholarship, and education by publishing worldwide in

Oxford New York

Auckland Cape Town Dar es Salaam Hong Kong Karachi Kuala Lumpur Madrid Melbourne Mexico City Nairobi New Delhi Shanghai Taipei Toronto

With offices in

Argentina Austria Brazil Chile Czech Republic France Greece Guatemala Hungary Italy Japan Poland Portugal Singapore South Korea Switzerland Thailand Turkey Ukraine Vietnam

First published 2005

This dictionary is based on the *Oxford Study Indonesian Dictionary*, by Wendy Sahayana and Albert Tan, © Oxford University Press 2001.

National Library of Australia
Cataloguing-in-Publication data:

Sahanaya, Wendy, 1940–.
The mini study Indonesian dictionary.

ISBN 0 19 555308 X.

1. Indonesian language—Dictionaries—English.
2. English language—Dictionaries—Indonesian.
I. Tan, Albert, 1937–. II. Title.

99.2203

et by Promptset Pty Ltd (Stephen Chan)
by Sheck Wah Tong Printing Press Ltd

INTRODUCTION

Learning a new language involves more than just learning the words and grammar. It means gaining insights into the way in which people from another culture perceive the world and express those perceptions. For this reason it can be an exciting experience. However, it can also sometimes seem confusing and difficult. Feeling secure and at ease in using a bilingual dictionary is essential to the building of confidence in understanding and using a foreign language.

This dictionary has been specially compiled for students of Indonesian whose mother tongue is English as well as for students of English whose mother tongue is Indonesian. Students at both the secondary level and the tertiary level of study will find the dictionary helpful. We have paid particular attention to making the dictionary user friendly. With the help of bolded headwords, easy-to-follow signposts and examples, the best translation can quickly be found.

We have adopted a simplified version of traditional bilingual entry layout. This means that the dictionary is ideal for learning basic dictionary skills, which can subsequently be built upon as the student moves towards larger, more sophisticated dictionaries. We have done our best to make this dictionary a practical, easy-to-use tool for learning and understanding Indonesian.

Throughout the writing of this dictionary we have worked in close consultation with students and teachers. We acknowledge the help of consultants who have read and commented on the dictionary text, in particular Katharina Sukamto, Linda Hibbs, Roswita Khaiyath and Foong Ling Kong.

And, last but not least, we would also like to thank our spouses for their great patience and support in the compilation of this dictionary.

HOW A BILINGUAL DICTIONARY WORKS

A bilingual dictionary is a dictionary that has two languages in it. The two languages in this dictionary are English and Indonesian. When you look up a word in one of the languages, the dictionary gives the translation for that word in the other language. However, it is important for you to remember that not every word can be directly translated from one language to another. The most obvious examples of this will be words for concrete objects which are not found in both the countries where the languages are spoken. An example of this in English is **lamb chop**, which can really only be translated as **potongan daging domba**, a cut of sheep's meat. In Indonesian some fruits such as **durian** and **salak** have no English equivalents. Sometimes the word has been taken from one language and used in the other; for example, the Indonesian words **sate** and **gado-gado** are used for those dishes in English.

You will also find that sample sentences in the English language that attribute responsibility to someone (that is, sentences that are in the active voice) will not do so in Indonesian (they will be in the passive voice). For example, **Fauzi missed the ball** in English says that Fauzi couldn't catch the ball but the Indonesian – **bola tidak tertangkap oleh Fauzi** – says that the ball wasn't caught by Fauzi.

Another example is the way the verb **hurt** is used. It would be quite strange in Indonesian to say something like **did you hurt yourself?** as if it were deliberate. In Indonesian you would say **apakah Anda terluka?** which translates literally as **did you be hurt?** You should take special note of examples like these when you look up words.

This dictionary is divided into two halves, separated by grey-edged pages in the middle. In the first half you look up Indonesian words to find out what they mean in English and in the second half you look up English words and find out how to say them in Indonesian. An attempt has been made to give these two halves the 'feel' of the language. For example, in the Indonesian-to-English section the examples tend to be taken from Indonesian life and in the English-to-Indonesian section the examples tend to be taken from Australian life.

The words you look up are in **this typeface** and in the first half of the dictionary you will find **Indonesian** words in alphabetical order from a to z, with the exception of x (there are no words beginning with x in Indonesian). In the second half you will find **English** words from a to z. In a dictionary, these are called **headwords** because each of them comes at the head of an **entry**. In the entry you can find **translations** and other sorts of information you can use to make sure you get the correct translation. The information has been presented in different ways to help you see clearly which is which. Here is a guide to the different things you will find in an entry:

headword	a word you look up in the dictionary
translation	translations are the only things that are in 'ordinary' type in the dictionary. They are always typed like this, and something that is typed in a different way can never be a translation.
noun, verb, adjective	part of speech tells you if the word you are looking up is a noun, a verb, an adjective or another part of speech. One headword can have more than one part of speech. For instance, **book** can be a noun *(she was reading a book)* or a verb *(I'll book the seats).* Parts of speech are only given in the

	English section of this dictionary, because Indonesian parts of speech are made from base words that cannot always be categorized in this way.
(signpost)	this is information printed in *italics* and within parentheses to guide you to the right translation, to show you how to use the translation, or to give you extra information about either the headword or the translation.
example	a phrase or sentence using the word you have looked up. If these appear in the entry you are looking at, you should read through them carefully to see if they are close to what you want to understand or say.
•	indicates a compound verb such as *to carry on.*
(...)	indicates that the word or group of letters in parentheses is optional. For example, **bandar udara (bandara)** shows you that for **airport** you can use the words **bandar udara** or just **bandara**; **(se)tiap hari** for **every day** indicates you can use **setiap hari** or **tiap hari**; and **mem(per)bandingkan** can be used with or without the **per** for **to compare**.

You can think of a dictionary entry as being made out of different sorts of building bricks. In the entries below you can see how they fit together to help you to find what you need. The more you use your dictionary, the more confident you will feel about finding your way around it.

INDONESIAN–ENGLISH

indicates very different meanings

headword

translation

(*signpost*)

example

example

kabur[1] **1** blurred, hazy, vague; **2** fading; **3** haze; **mengabur, menjadi kabur** to become hazy or blurred; **mengaburkan 1** to make blurred, foggy or hazy; **2** to obscure; **kekaburan** haziness, vagueness; **pengaburan** blurring of.

kabur[2] **1** (*a horse*) bolt; **2** escape, flee, run off; **Edi kabur dari penjara** Edi ran off from prison.

kabut haze, fog, mist; **kabut sudah lenyap** the fog's cleared away; **berkabut** foggy, hazy, misty; **sering berkabut di gunung** it's often misty in the mountains.

ENGLISH–INDONESIAN

part of speech

less *pronoun, adjective, adverb* **1** lebih sedikit; **Rukmana eats less** Rukmana makan lebih sedikit; **2** kurang; **less interesting** kurang menarik; **3 less than** kurang dari; **less than three hours** kurang dari tiga jam; **less than a kilo** kurang dari sekilo.

example

headword

lesson *noun (class)* pelajaran; **a history lesson** pelajaran sejarah; **that accident is a lesson for Helen** kecelakaan itu adalah suatu pelajaran bagi Helen.

(signpost)

let[1] *verb* **1** *(allow)* membiarkan; **the police let us through** polisi membiarkan kami lewat; **2** *(as a suggestion or a command)* mari; **let's go** mari kita pergi; **let's eat out** mari makan di luar; **let me see** *(show me)* mari saya lihat; **3** *(negative)* **don't let** jangan sampai; **don't let the fire go out** jangan sampai api itu mati; **4** *(better not)* sebaiknya; **let's not talk about it** sebaiknya kita tidak membicarakannya.

• compound verb

translation

- **to let off 1** *(fireworks, a bomb)* meletuskan, meledakkan; **2** *(to excuse from)* membebaskan (*homework, for example*).

A STEP-BY-STEP GUIDE TO FINDING THE TRANSLATION YOU NEED

Finding a word in the dictionary

You will be using this dictionary to do one of the following things:

1 look up an Indonesian word or phrase to find out what it means.
2 look up an English word or phrase to find out how to say it in Indonesian.

There have been several spelling reforms of Bahasa Indonesia. We have attempted to keep up-to-date with the latest spelling, but have given some old spellings for some words, such as **film**, which is now spelled the same as the English. In the past it has been spelt as both **filem** and **pilem**, so these words have been included, though the sample sentences all use the latest spelling.

1 Finding out what an Indonesian word means

INDONESIAN-ENGLISH

First of all, look for the word in the first half of the dictionary where you can find the Indonesian words and expressions with their English meanings. You will see the top of every page is marked like this.

No matter what you are using the dictionary to find out, you will always start by looking up a headword. Here are some Indonesian headwords – **mutakhir, mutasi, mutiara** and **mutlak** – with their entries.

mutakhir most up-to-date, state-of-the-art, the very latest.

mutasi 1 *(biology)* mutation; **2** transfer *(of official to new post or student to new school)*; **memutasikan** to make such a transfer.

mutiara pearl; **itu mutiara asli** it's a real pearl.

mutlak absolute, unconditional; **kuasa mutlak** absolute power; **memutlakkan** to make a thing totally essential; **kemutlakan** absoluteness.

Suppose you want to find out what the Indonesian word **tamah** means.

If you look down the first column on page 319 you will find **tamah** between **tali** and **tamak**.

talang gutter *(on a roof)*.

tali cord, rope, string.

tamah, ramah-tamah friendly; **keramah-tamahan** friendliness.

tamak 1 greed; **2** greedy; **ketamakan** greed.

taman garden, park; **taman bacaan** reading room; **taman sari** pleasure park; **taman bibit** nursery *(for plants)*.

When you look at the entry for **tamah** you will find the meaning you are looking for, but you also find that **tamah** is normally used together with the word **ramah**, and this becomes a compound word, **ramah-tamah,** meaning **friendly**. In fact there are quite a few Indonesian words that cannot be used in their base form, but must always be used either in combination with another word, as in the case of **ramah**, or with a prefix. For example, look at the entries for **jamu** and for **ulas** shown here.

jamu[1]**, menjamu** to receive or entertain a guest; **penjamuan, perjamuan** **1** banquet, party, reception; **jamuan, perjamuan makan malam** holding a dinner party; **2** a call, a visit.

jamu[2] herbal medicine, herbal tonic; **jamu-jamuan** medicinal herbs.

ulas, mengulas **1** to review, to comment on; **2** to analyse, to explain; **mengulaskan** to divide into sections; **ulasan** **1** commentary, review; **2** analysis; **pengulas** commentator, reviewer; **pengulas olahraga** sports commentator.

It often happens that an Indonesian word has more than one meaning in English, as is the case of **jamu** above. If you look at the entry for **alamat** on page 6 you will see that it is divided into sections numbered **1** and **2**.

alamat 1 address; **alamatnya ada di muka** the address is on the front; **2** omen, sign; **ini adalah alamat buruk** this is a bad omen; **beralamat** have an address; **mengalamatkan 1** to address; **ke mana saya harus mengalamatkan surat ini?** where should I address this letter?; **2** to indicate; **awan hitam itu mengalamatkan hari akan hujan** the black clouds indicate rain.

The first translation is **address** and the second is **omen** or **sign**. You will need to look at both translations and work out which one fits in best in the Indonesian sentence you are trying to understand. So:

Surat ini dikembalikan oleh karena alamatnya salah *means* 'this letter was returned because the address is wrong'.

But:

Kata orang, burung hantu adalah alamat buruk *means* 'people say an owl is an evil omen'.

Sometimes the two meanings are so different that there are two separate entries for the Indonesian word, as in the case of **jamu**. If you look at the entry for **anggur** on page 11 you will see that there are separate numbered entries.

anggur[1], **menganggur** **1** to be out of work, to be unemployed; **2** to be idle; **penganggur** unemployed person.

anggur[2] wine; **buah anggur** grape.

The first translation is **to be out of work** and the second is **wine**.

Often an Indonesian base word cannot be used alone. In such cases the entry still appears under the base word, but is immediately followed by the affixed form. For example, you will find the entry: **kemis, mengemis** to beg; **pengemis** beggar. This is a case where you cannot use **kemis**, but will always have to use an affixed form of the word.

Often you will have to apply the Indonesian rule of affixation before you can look up the word you need. For example:

to look up these words	you will have to find
berakibat	**akibat** under **a**
terbalik	**balik** under **b**
mempercepat	**cepat** under **c**
pertambahan	**tambah** under **t**

The middle section of this dictionary gives you a more complete explanation of this system of affixation.

2 Finding an English word and how to say it in Indonesian

ENGLISH–INDONESIAN

You can see that it might take you a while to learn how to look up words in Indonesian. However you will find it much easier to look up the word you want in English. But remember to always read the complete entry to make sure you are choosing the right Indonesian word for what you want to say. Suppose you want to know how to say **bathroom** in Indonesian. Look up the word in the second part of the dictionary where the top of every page is marked like this.

If you follow the same method of going through the alphabetical order of the headwords as you did when you were looking up an Indonesian word, you will find **bathroom** on page 422.

bath *noun* **1 to have a bath** mandi; **she's in the bath** dia sedang mandi; **2** *(bathtub to hold water, not for bathing in)* bak mandi; **the bath's empty again** bak mandinya kosong lagi.

bathe *verb* **1** *(a person, animal)* memandikan; **2** *(a wound)* membersihkan; **3** *(go swimming)* berenang.

bathroom *noun* kamar mandi.

baths *plural noun* kolam renang.

bath towel *noun* handuk.

Now you can see that the Indonesian word for **bathroom** is **kamar mandi**.

Sometimes there will be more than one Indonesian word for the English word you are looking up. You will also need to be aware that there may be a change in the part of speech in translation. For example, look how the noun **bath** in the English expression **to have**
a bath is not translated into a similar Indonesian expression. Instead you will have to use the Indonesian verb **mandi** for this meaning. When the dictionary entry gives you more than just one translation, take the time to read through the whole entry.

If you look up **faint** the entry looks like this:

> **faint** *adjective* **1** lemah; **to feel faint** merasa lemah; **2** *(slight)* sedikit; **a faint smell of gas** bau gas sedikit; **3** *(low in volume)* kecil; **4 I haven't the faintest idea** saya sama sekali tidak dapat membayangkan, saya tidak tahu sama sekali.

You can see that **1** tells you that the Indonesian word for feeling **faint** is **lemah**, **2** tells you that the word for **faint** meaning slight is **sedikit**, **3** tells you that the word for **faint** meaning low is **kecil** and **4** gives you an example of **faint** in a common idiomatic English expression. The Indonesian phrase that has a similar meaning would translate literally into English as something like: 'I absolutely cannot imagine'. Remember the information that is either in brackets or in italics or both, like *(slight)* and *(low in volume)*, is there to help you choose the best translation for what you want to say, but such information *will never be* the translation.

Often it is not enough to find the translation of one word. This dictionary also gives you a selection of helpful phrases you will often want to use. In the entry for **accident** you can find out how to use the translation in different expressions.

accident *noun* **1** kecelakaan; **to have an accident** mendapat kecelakaan; **a road accident** kecelakaan di jalan, kecelakaan lalu lintas; **a car accident** kecelakaan mobil; **2** (*by chance*) kebetulan; **I found it by accident** saya menemukannya secara kebetulan; secara tidak sengaja; **I broke the plate by accident** dengan tidak sengaja saya memecahkan piring itu.

About the middle section of this dictionary

The middle section of the dictionary gives you two kinds of information. First, it gives you a brief explanation of the system of affixation in Indonesian. Second, it gives you a pronunciation guide.

A a

abad century; **berabad-abad** many centuries, centuries and centuries.

abadi eternal, lasting; **hidup abadi** eternal life; **perdamaian abadi** lasting peace; **mengabadikan** perpetuate, immortalize; **mengabadikan Soekarno** perpetuate Soekarno's name; **mengabadikan Soekarno dalam bentuk tulisan** immortalize Soekarno in writing.

abai, mengabaikan ignore, disregard; **kita tidak boleh mengabaikan masalah itu** we mustn't disregard the problem.

abdi servant, slave; **mengabdi kepada** to serve; **mengabdi kepada rakyat** to serve the people; **mengabdikan** to appoint, to subjugate; **mengabdikan diri kepada partai** to devote oneself to the party.

abjad alphabet; **menyusun nama menurut abjad** arrange names in alphabetical order.

abon shredded meat that has been boiled and dried, often sprinkled over a meal or vegetable dish to add flavour.

abonemen subscription; **berabonemen** to subscribe.

absen absent; **daftar absen** attendance roll; **mengabsen** to call the roll.

abstrak abstract.

abu ashes; **abu-abu** grey.

acak disordered; **mengacak-acak** mess up; **lemari pakaian dan semua lacinya diacak-acak oleh pencuri** the cupboard and all its drawers were messed up by a thief; **acak-acakan** chaotic, in disorder.

acapkali often, repeatedly.

acar pickles.

acara **1** agenda, program; **acara televisi** TV program; **2** judicial procedure; **pengacara** attorney, lawyer.

acu having reference to; **mengacu pada** to refer to; **mengacukan** to point at using a thing; **dia mengacukan tongkatnya kepada seorang anak** he pointed his walking stick at a child.

a b c d e f g h i j k l m n o p q r s t u v w x y z

acuh, acuh tak acuh indifferent; **saya tidak suka dengan sikapnya yang acuh tak acuh** I don't like her/his indifferent attitude; **mengacuhkan** to care, to heed *(usually used with a negative)*; **Nasrul tidak mengacuhkan permintaan saya** Nasrul didn't care about my request.

ada 1 there is, there are; **ada tikus di dapur** there's a mouse in the kitchen; **tidak ada roti** there was no bread; **ya, ada cukup** yes, there's enough; **2** to be, to be present; **gedung itu tidak ada di situ lagi** that building isn't there any longer; **ada acara apa di televisi?** what's on on TV?; **ada apa?** what's the matter?; **ada yang mudah, ada yang sulit** some are easy, some are difficult; **adalah** am, is, are; **Canberra adalah ibu kota Australia** Canberra is the capital of Australia; **berada** to be (in a place); **dia berada di Menado minggu ini** he's in Menado this week; **keberadaan** presence; **mengadakan** to arrange, to hold, to organize; **mengadakan rapat** to hold a meeting; **keadaan** condition, situation; **dalam keadaan itu** under the circumstances; **keadaan darurat** an emergency.

adab courteousness, good manners, politeness; **beradab** civilized, cultured, polite; **keberadaban** being civilized, having good manners; **peradaban** civilization.

adakalanya sometimes.

adat 1 custom, tradition; **adat istiadat** customs and traditions; **2** manners, proper behaviour.

adegan act, scene in a play.

adik younger brother or sister, younger sibling; **adik-kakak** brothers and sisters/siblings.

adil just, fair; **itu tak adil** that's not fair; **mengadili** to try a case, to bring to justice; **keadilan** justice; **pengadilan 1** the court; **2** trial; **3** courthouse.

administrasi administration; **administrasi negara** public administration.

adonan batter, dough.

adu¹, beradu to collide, to compete; **mengadu** to bump against, to set in competition against; **mengadu domba** to play one against the other.

adu², mengadu(kan) 1 complain about; **Hamid**

mengadukan perkaranya kepada polisi Hamid reported the matter to the police; **2** to sue; **3** to inform on, to report, to tell on.

aduh ouch! ow! *(expression of pain, disappointment, surprise)*; **mengaduh** moan; **anak itu mengaduh kesakitan** the child was moaning with pain.

aduk, mengaduk to mix, to stir; **mengaduk telur** beat eggs; **adukan** mixture; **pengaduk** one who stirs/mixes, stirring implement.

advokat barrister, lawyer.

aerobika aerobics.

agak rather, quite; **saya agak senang di sini** I'm fairly happy here.

agama religion; **beragama** to have a religion, to be religious; **Ahmad beragama Islam** Ahmad is a Muslim.

agar in order that, in order to; **kami berjalan cepat agar tiba tepat pada waktunya** we hurried in order to be on time.

agar-agar a seaweed-based gelatine, a setting agent.

agen 1 agent; **2** agency, branch.

agenda 1 agenda; **2** diary.

agresi aggresion.

agung 1 exalted, high; **2** impressive, prominent; **mengagungkan** to glorify, to praise; **mengagungkan diri** to glorify yourself; **dalam doa kita mengagungkan nama Tuhan** we glorify the name of God in prayer; **keagungan** grandeur, loftiness.

Agustus August.

Ahad, hari Ahad Sunday

ahli expert, specialist; **ahli bedah** surgeon; **ahli waris** heir; **mengahlikan dirinya** to specialize, to become an expert; **keahlian** expertise.

air water, liquid, juice; **air asin** brackish water, salt water; **air mata** tears; **air minum, air putih** drinking water; **air pasang** rising tide; **air tawar** fresh water; **air jeruk** orange juice; **air sumur** well water; **air ledeng** reticulated water; **air terjun** waterfall; **air surut** falling tide; **tahan air** waterproof; **permukaan air** water level; **tanah air** homeland; **buang air besar** defecate; **berair 1** to have water; **2** to be juicy; **mengairi** to irrigate; **mengairi sawah** to flood the rice fields; **pengairan** irrigation; **perairan** territorial waters.

ajaib astonishing, miraculous, remarkable.

ajak, mengajak **1** to invite, to ask, to urge; **dia mengajak saya berjalan-jalan** she's asked me to [illegible] **ajakan** invitation; **Hikmah menolak ajakan saya untuk makan siang bersama** Hikmah rejected my invitation to have lunch together.

ajal death, end; **menemui ajalnya** to die.

ajar, belajar to study, to learn; **kami sedang belajar Bahasa Indonesia** we're studying Indonesian; **mengajar** to teach, to train; **dia mengajar di SMU** he teaches in senior high school; **mengajarkan** to teach; **ibunya mengajarkan matematika** her mum teaches maths; **mengajari** to teach someone, to train someone; **dia mengajari saya** she's teaching me; **ajaran** teaching; **tahun ajaran** school year; **pelajar** student, learner; **pelajaran** lesson, course; **mata pelajaran** school subject; **pengajar** instructor, teacher; **pengajaran** instruction, teaching; **terpelajar** educated; **mempelajari** study carefully, in depth; **sebaiknya Anda mempelajari adat-istiadat negeri itu sebelum berangkat** it's better if you study the customs of the country before you l[illegible]

akademi academy; **akademi militer** military academy; **akademis** academic; **tahun akademis** the academic year.

akal **1** intellect, mind, reason; **akal budi** intelligence, reason; **akal sehat** common sense; **masuk akal** makes sense; **penjelasan itu tidak masuk akal** that explanation doesn't make sense; **2** way, tactics; **cari akal** find a way; **3** deceit, trickiness; **akal busuk** a dirty trick; **berakal** to be intelligent, resourceful or sensible; **mengakali** to double-cross, to play a trick on a person.

akan **1** *(can be used to show future)* will, about to; **ayah akan menjemput saya** my father's coming for me, my father will pick me up; **dia akan senang berjumpa dengan Anda** he'll be pleased to see you; **tidak akan ada masalah** there won't be a problem; **2** about, regarding; **mereka lupa akan kewajibannya** they forgot their duty; **akan tetapi** however; **seakan-akan** as if, as though; **Komang terus membaca seakan-akan tidak tahu saya sudah tiba**

a b c d e f g h i j k l m n o p q r s t u v w x y z

Komang kept on reading as if he didn't know I had arrived; **yang akan datang (yad)** next; **minggu yang akan datang** next week.

akar root, source; **akar kata 'memasang' adalah 'pasang'** the root of the word 'memasang' is 'pasang'; **akar-akarnya** source, origin; **sampai ke akar-akarnya** thorough, drastic; **korupsi harus dibasmi sampai ke akar-akarnya** corruption must be rooted out, corruption must be thoroughtly eliminated.

akhir end, finish; **pada akhir bulan Mei** at the end of May; **akhir-akhir ini** recently; **akhirnya** eventually; **akhirnya saya pulang** eventually I went home; **akhirnya!** at last!; **yang tidak ada akhirnya** endless; **berakhir** to end; **kalau rapat sudah berakhir** when the meeting's over; **berakhir seri** it ended in a draw; **mengakhiri** to close, to conclude, to end; **mengakhiri nyawa** to end a life; **terakhir** final, latest, last, ultimate; **cicilan yang terakhir** the final instalment; **Rob yang terakhir tiba** Rob arrived last; **saya terakhir bertemu dengan mereka pada bulan Mei** I last saw them in May; **sebagai usaha terakhir** as a last attempt; **akhiran** suffix, word ending.

aki car battery.

akibat consequence, result; **akibatnya** as a consequence, finally; **berakibat** to have consequences; **mengakibatkan** to cause, to result in; **kerusuhan itu mengakibatkan kerusakan besar di Jakarta** the riots caused a lot of damage in Jakarta.

akomodasi accommodation.

akrab close, intimate; **teman/kawan akrab** a close friend; **keakraban 1** intimacy; **2** solidarity.

aksara letter, character *(of the alphabet)*.

aksen accent.

akses access; **jalan akses** access road.

aksi action; **aksi politik** political campaign; **beraksi 1** to be in action; **2** to show off; **aksi-aksian** to carry on to get attention.

akte official document; **akte kelahiran** birth certificate; **akte perkawinan, akte pernikahan** marriage certificate.

aktif active, energetic.

a b c d e f g h i j k l m n o p q r s t u v w x y z

aktivitas activity.

aktor actor.

aktris actress.

aktual, aktuil actual, current, recent, topical.

aku 1 I, me; **2 mengaku** to admit, to confess; **Fina mengaku salah** Fina admitted she was wrong; **mengakui 1** acknowledge, admit, confess; **mengakui kekalahan** to concede defeat; **2** to acknowledge, to recognize; **mengakui hak mogok mereka** to acknowledge their right to strike; **pengakuan 1** confession of faith; **2** acknowledgement; **3** admission of guilt.

akuarium aquarium.

akuntan accountant.

akupungtur acupuncture.

akur agree; **mereka tidak akur** they can't stand each other; **mengakurkan** to reconcile; **Fahmi mengakurkan kedua anaknya yang sering bertengkar** Fahmi reconciled her two children who often quarreled.

a.l. (antara lain) among others.

alam, alam baka 1 the eternal world; **alam hewan** animal kingdom; **alam tumbuh-tumbuhan** plant kingdom; **alam khayal** fantasy world; **2** nature, natural; **sumber daya alam** natural resources; **mengalami** to experience; **pengalaman** experience; **berpengalaman** experienced.

alamat 1 address; **alamatnya ada di muka** the address is on the front; **2** omen, sign; **ini adalah alamat buruk** this is a bad omen; **beralamat** have an address; **mengalamatkan 1** to address; **ke mana saya harus mengalamatkan surat ini?** where should I address this letter?; **2** to indicate; **awan hitam itu mengalamatkan hari akan hujan** the black clouds indicate rain.

alami natural, concerned with nature.

alang-alang a tall coarse grass, weeds.

alangkah what a/an . . . *(exclamation)*; **alangkah leganya!** what a relief!; **alangkah sayangnya!** what a pity!

alas 1 base, foundation; **2** layer, lining, covering; **beralas(kan)** to be based on; **Nurdin tidur hanya beralaskan tikar** Nurdin sleeps only on (grass) matting; **beralasan** to have a base or foundation; **mengalasi** to put something down as a base; **Lakshmi mengalasi tempat tidurnya dengan tikar** Lakshmi placed matting on her bed base; **3 alasan** base, excuse, reason; **Mehmet punya alasan yang baik** Mehmet has a good excuse.

alat appliance, device, equipment, implement, instrument, tool; **memperalat** to manipulate, to treat or use as an instrument; **peralatan** equipment, tools.

album album.

alfabet alphabet.

algojo executioner, hangman.

alhasil consequently, eventually, in the end; **mereka sering bertengkar dan alhasil bercerai** they often argued and consequently divorced.

alias 1 in other words, namely; **2** alias, also known as.

alih, mengambil alih to take over; **beralih, mengalih pada** to turn, to move; **perhatiannya beralih pada Tutut, perhatiannya mengalih pada Tutut** his attention turned to Tutut; **mengalihkan** to change, to move; **dia mengalihkan perhatiannya pada Tutut** he turned his attention to Tutut; **peralihan** change, transition, transformation; **daerah peralihan** transition zone.

alir, beraliran to have an ideology; **mengalir 1** flow; **air mengalir** running water; **2** pour, stream, flow; **ratusan orang mengalir ke lapangan itu** hundreds of people streamed onto the field; **3** stream down *(for example, tears)*; **mengaliri** flow through; **sungai itu mengaliri Cirebon** the river flows through Cirebon; **mengalirkan 1** to channel; **2** to drain, to siphon; **3** to shed (tears); **air mata Supri mengalir** Supri burst into tears; **aliran 1** current; **aliran air** water circulation; **aliran darah** blood circulation; **2** trend, ideology; **3** political grouping, school of learning; **aliran musik** music school; **4** pipeline; **5** conduit, wiring; **pengaliran** trend, drift.

alis eyebrow; **penghitam alis** eyebrow pencil.

aljabar algebra.

Alkitab the Bible.

alkohol alcohol.

a b c d e f g h i j k l m n o p q r s t u v w x y z

a b c d e f g h i j k l m n o p q r s t u v w x y z

Allah God; **Allahu akbar** God is great.

almarhum the late, the deceased.

altar altar.

aluminium aluminium.

alumni alumnus, alumna.

alun-alun town square; **alun-alun desa** the village square.

amal charity, good deed; **badan amal** charitable organization; **amal bakti** dedication, service; **beramal** to do a good deed; **mengamalkan 1** to accomplish, to apply, to put into practice; **2** to carry out devotedly; **pengamalan** doing good deeds.

aman 1 calm, peaceful; **2** safe, secure; **mengamankan 1** to arrest, to make safe, to pacify; **polisi sudah mengamankan daerah ini** the police have already pacified this area; **2** place in protective custody; **polisi mengamankan mahasiswa-mahasiswi** the police arrested the uni students; **pencuri itu diamankan** the thief was placed in protective custody; **3** place in safekeeping; **kami mengamankan lukisan-lukisan itu** we've safeguarded those paintings; **4** reassure; **keamanan 1** peacefulness, tranquillity; **2** safety, security; **Dewan Keamanan** Security Council; **pengaman 1** peacemaker; **2** safeguard; **pengamanan** pacification.

amanat instruction, mandate, message, order, trusteeship.

amandel tonsil.

amat very; **amat penting** very important; **amat sulit** extremely difficult; **mengamati 1** to keep track of, to watch closely; **amati jam** watch the time; **polisi mengamati tersangka itu** the police watched the suspect closely; **2** to observe; **Ratna mengamati ternaknya** Ratna observed her farm animals; **3** to guard, to monitor; **pengamat** observer; **pengamat lingkungan** environmentalist; **pengamatan** monitoring, observation, supervision.

amatir amateur.

ambang threshold, sill; **ambang pintu** doorstep; **ujian sudah di ambang pintu** the exam is approaching.

ambil to take; **silahkan ambil sendiri!** help yourself!; **mengambil 1** to take; **siapa mengambil kursi itu?** who took that chair?; **2** to get, to fetch; **Gary sedang mengambil Esky™** Gary's fetching the Esky™; **mengambil keputusan** to make a decision; **ambillah sendiri!** fetch it yourself!; **3** subtract; **4** adopt; **mengambilkan** to get or fetch something for someone; **tolong ambilkan mangkuk itu!** please fetch me that bowl!; **Keti mengambilkan saya buah anggur** Keti fetched some grapes for me; **pengambilan** removal, withdrawal.

ambisi ambition.

amblas disappear, vanish.

ambruk collapse, fall down; **jembatan itu ambruk** the bridge collapsed.

ambulans ambulance.

amin amen.

amis to have the taste or smell of fish; **baju ini bau amis** this dress stinks.

amnesti amnesty.

ampas waste, dregs; **ampas kelapa** coconut shreds after the milk is squeezed out.

ampelas sandpaper.

amplop envelope.

ampuh to have magical powers, be powerful.

ampun forgiveness, pardon; **minta ampun!** have mercy!; **macetnya minta ampun!** good lord! what a traffic jam!; **mengampuni 1** to forgive someone; **dia akan mengampuni saya** she'll forgive me; **2** to pardon, to commute; **pengampunan** amnesty, mercy.

amuk, mengamuk to go berserk, to run amok; **amukan** fight; **pengamuk** person who runs amok; **pengamukan** running amok, raging.

anak child, young of an animal; **anak kucing** kitten; **anak angkat** adopted child; **anak kapal** ship's crew; **anak asuh(an)** protégé; **anak cucu** children and grandchildren, descendants; **anak mas** favourite child; **anak buah** member of a group; **anak tiri** stepchild; **anak sungai** tributary; **beranak** to give birth *(animals)*; **kucing itu beranak lima** the cat had five kittens; **kekanak-kanakan** childish, childlike; **peranakan** of mixed ethnic origin, womb.

analisa, analisis analysis.

ancam, mengancam to threaten; **'awas kalau dekat lagi dengan adik saya,' ancam Fahmi** 'watch out if you have anything to do with my sister again,' threatened

a b c d e f g h i j k l m n o p q r s t u v w x y z

Fahmi; **Iris mengancam akan mengunci pintu** Iris threatened to lock the door.

Anda you, your, yours; **Anda boleh masuk sekarang** you can come in now; **ini minuman Anda** this is your drink; **apakah pena ini kepunyaan Anda?** is this your pen?

andai, andaikata, seandainya supposing that, suppose that; **mengandaikan** to suppose.

andong four-wheeled carriage pulled by two horses, common in central Java.

anduk, handuk towel.

aneh peculiar, strange; **kumbang yang aneh** an unusual beetle; **bunyi yang aneh** a strange noise; **anehnya** the strange thing is.

aneka all sorts of, various; **aneka guna** versatile; **aneka ragam** varied; **beraneka** all kinds, mixed; **beraneka warna** variegated, multicoloured; **keanekaan** variety.

anemer building contractor.

angan, angan-angan **1** idea, thought; **2** daydreaming, fantasy, illusion; **berangan-angan** **1** to dream, to fantasize; **2** to have ideals; **mengangan-angankan** **1** to contemplate, to recall; **2** to fantasize, to imagine; **Bambang mengangan-angankan masa depan yang bahagia** Bambang is dreaming of a happy future.

anggap, berangapan **1** to have the belief; **2 menganggap** to consider, to count, to regard as; **saya menganggap dia bodoh** I consider him stupid; **anak-anak yang berumur di atas dua belas tahun dianggap dewasa** children over twelve are considered adults.

anggota **1** member; **saya menjadi anggota perkumpulan judo** I've joined the judo club; **Shanty seperti anggota keluarga** Shanty's like one of the family; **Anggota MPR** Member of the Consultative Assembly; **2** component, part; **3** limb; **bagian kiri anggota tubuhnya lumpuh** his/her left side is paralysed; **beranggotakan** have members; **organisasi itu beranggotakan lebih dari seratus orang** that organization has more than a hundred members; **keanggotaan** membership; **kartu keanggotaan**

membership card; **iuran keanggotaan** membership fee.

anggrek orchid.

angguk, mengangguk to nod; **dia mengangguk tanda setuju** he nodded his agreement; **menganggukkan kepala** to nod your head.

anggur[1], menganggur **1** to be out of work, to be unemployed; **2** to be idle; **penganggur** unemployed person.

anggur[2] wine; **buah anggur** grape.

angin wind; **desir angin** sound of wind; **angin ribut** storm, typhoon; **angin kencang** strong wind; **angin sepoi-sepoi** breeze, light or soft wind; **angin dari Selatan** the South wind; **kabar angin** rumour, gossip.

angka **1** digit, figure, number, numeral; **Ranto kecewa dengan angkanya** Ranto was disappointed with his marks; **Anda mendapat angka berapa untuk biologi?** what mark did you get for biology?; **2** rate; **angka kelahiran** birth rate; **angka kematian** death rate.

angkasa **1** sky; **2** space; **angkasa luar** outer space.

angkasawan, angkasawati astronaut.

angkat **1** lift, raise; **angkat besi** weightlifting; **angkat telepon** answer the phone; **angkat tangan!** raise your hand! *(in surrender or in the classroom)*; **anak angkat** adopted child; **2** take away, remove; **tolong angkat piring-piring dari meja** please clear the table; **berangkat** to depart, to leave, to set out; **besok pagi kita harus berangkat jam lima** tomorrow morning we have to leave at five; **memberangkatkan** to dispatch, to send; **keberangkatan** departure; **pemberangkatan** dispatching, sending off; **mengangkat** **1** to lift, to raise; **dia mengangkat anak itu** she lifted the child; **2** to appoint; **harap dia tidak diangkat sebagai kepala** I hope he's not appointed head; **angkat sumpah** take an oath; **3** to take up; **mengangkat senjata** take up arms; **4** to adopt *(a child)*; **mengangkat(kan)** to lift, to raise; **angkatan** **1** branch of the armed forces; **angkatan laut** the navy; **angkatan darat** army, infantry; **2** age group, class, generation;

a b c d e f g h i j k l m n o p q r s t u v w x y z

para jenderal itu adalah angkatan tahun 1945 those generals belong to the 1945 generation.

angklung musical instrument constructed of bamboo tubes which are shaken.

angkuh arrogant, proud.

angkut, mengangkut 1 to carry, to transport; **2** to carry away; **angkutan 1** transport, transportation; **2** load, shipment; **pengangkut 1** carrier, transport; **pesawat pengangkut** cargo plane; **2** transporter, truck, van; **pengangkutan** transportation, transport.

anglo brazier.

angsa goose.

angsur, berangsur-angsur 1 little by little; **2** gradually; **Ruli berangsur-angsur sembuh** Ruli's gradually recovering; **mengangsur 1** to do gradually; **2** to pay in instalments; **Sarwono membeli mobil itu dengan cara mengangsur** Sarwono is buying his car by instalments; **angsuran** instalment payment; **pengangsuran** paying by instalments.

angus burnt, scorched

ani-ani small hand knife for harvesting rice.

aniaya ill treatment, injustice; **menganiaya(i) 1** to beat viciously, to torture; **2** to persecute, to tyrannize; **penganiaya** torturer, tyrant; **penganiayaan 1** cruel treatment; **2** oppression; **3** battering.

animis animist; **animisme** animism.

anjing dog; **anjing geladak** a stray dog; **anjing gila** mad dog; **anjing gembala** sheep dog; **anjing ras** pedigree dog; **anjing teraniaya** a mistreated dog.

anjur, menganjurkan 1 to propose, to recommend, to suggest; **Ibu menganjurkan saya supaya mencoba lagi** Mum suggested I try again; **2** to extend, to push something out; **anjuran 1** proposal, suggestion; **2** advice, recommendation; **penganjur** advocate, promoter.

antar[1], mengantar(kan) 1 to deliver, to bring something; **2** to accompany or take a person to a place; **apakah bisa mengantarkan saya ke toko video?** could you take me to the video store?; **antaran** something delivered; **pengantar**

1 companion, escort; **2** delivery person; **pengantar pizza** pizza delivery person; **3** porter, bellboy; **4 kata pengantar** introduction *(in a book)*.

antar[2] inter- *(used in compound words)*; **antar agama** inter-religion; **antar bangsa** international, interracial; **antar budaya** intercultural; **antar daerah** interregional.

antara[1] between; **jarak antara dua titik** the distance between two points; **antara kita** between us; **di antara** between, among; **antara lain** among others; **banyak yang gagal, antara lain Hadi dan Tomo** there were many who failed, among them Hadi and Tomo; **perantara, pengantara** go-between, intermediary; **perantaraan 1** mediation; **2** intermediary.

Antara[2] Indonesian News Agency.

antariksa outer space, interplanetary space.

antena antenna, aerial.

anti 1 anti, opposed to; **anti perang** antiwar; **2** resistant to.

antik antique, funny, unusual.

anting-anting earrings.

antre to queue, to stand in line.

anu, si anu so and so, such and such, what's his name, er, um *(hesitation form)*.

anugerah favour, grace, gift from God; **menganugerahi** to bestow on someone; **menganugerahkan** to bestow, to confer *(a degree, for example)*; **penganugerahan** conferral, presentation.

anut, menganut 1 to follow, to submit to; **2** *(a religion)* to practise; **penganut 1** follower, adherent; **2** person who goes along without sticking up for her/his own views; **penganutan** taking up *(a political philosophy, for example)*.

anyam, menganyam to plait; **menganyam tikar** to plait a straw mat; **anyaman** cane work; **topi anyaman** a straw hat.

apa 1 what, which; **apa ini? ini apa?** what's this? what is it?; **ada acara apa di televisi?** what's on TV?; **ada apa?** what's the matter?; **tidak apa(-apa)** it doesn't matter; **apa ya?** what could it be?; **'apa kabar?'** 'how are you?' *(literally, what's the news?)*; **apa lagi? apa pula?** what else?; **apa yang Putri**

lakukan di ruang guru? what's Putri doing in the teacher's office?; 2 *(colloquial)* or; **mau pergi apa tidak?** do you want to go or not?; 3 *(hesitation marker)* eh; **apa pun** no matter what; **apa pun yang kami lakukan** no matter what we do; **apakah** *(a question marker)* whether; **apakah dia sudah berangkat?** has s/he already left?; **apakah Presiden sudah disumpah?** has the president been sworn in yet?; **saya tidak tahu apakah dia sudah kembali** I don't know whether he's back; 4 **mengapa** why; **mengapa dia tidak mau ikut?** why doesn't s/he want to come along?; **mengapakan** *(colloquial)* to do what to; **anjing itu Anda apakan berteriak begitu?** what did you do to that dog to make it yelp like that?

apabila when, if.

apalagi 1 above all, especially; 2 even less, let alone; 3 moreover.

aparatur apparatus.

apartemen apartment.

apati apathy.

apek musty, mouldy, sweaty; **tas itu bau apek** the bag smells mouldy.

apel apple.

api 1 fire; **menyalakan api** to light a fire; **alat pemadam api** fire extinguisher; **kembang api** fireworks; 2 flame, blaze; **berapi** have fire; **gunung berapi itu meletus lagi** the volcano erupted again; **berapi-api** 1 furious, raging; **dia berpidato dengan berapi-api** he gave a fiery speech; 2 glitter, shine, sparkle; **perapian** 1 fireplace; 2 ignition; 3 oven, range; 4 furnace.

apik *(colloquial)* attractive, neat and nice.

apit hemmed in, wedged in; **berapit** 1 to be hemmed in, be wedged in; 2 to be close to each other; **mengapit** 1 to flank; 2 to clamp, to press between; 3 to hold by pressing between; 4 to staple; 5 to enclose on either side; **mengapitkan** to move close together; **pengapit** 1 clamp; 2 paperclip; 3 bride's or groom's attendant *(at a wedding)*.

apotek, apotik chemist shop, pharmacy; **apoteker** pharmacist.

April April.

apung float; **mengapung, terapung** 1 to float; 2 to floa upward, to soar; **mengapungkan** to set or keep afloat; **pengapung** **1** buoy; **2** float; **pengapungan** floating *(of a boat, etc.)*.

Arab Arab, Arabic.

arah **1** course, direction; **2** aim, direction, purpose; **searah** in the same direction, of the same purpose; **mengarahkan** **1** to aim, to direct; **2** to aim at; **arahan** directive; **pengarah** person who indicates the directions; **pengarahan** **1** briefing; **2** guidelines, instruction.

arak, berarak-arak(an), mengarak to go in a procession; **arak-arakan** procession; **pengarak** person in a procession; **pengarakan, perarakan** procession.

aral hindrance, obstacle.

arang charcoal.

ararut arrowroot.

arbei strawberry.

arca image, statue.

aren sugar palm, **gula aren** palm sugar.

arena arena.

arif **1** learned; **Pak Nasution adalah orang yang arif bijaksana** Pak Nasution is a wise and learned man; **2** capable, clever; skillful; **kearifan** **1** learning, wisdom; **2** ability, cleverness.

arisan a regular social gathering where a kind of lottery is conducted and members take turns to win an amount of money previously deposited by all members.

arit **1** sickle; **2** knife for tapping rubber trees; **3** grass knife; **mengarit** to cut grass.

Arjuna **1** the hero of the *Mahabharata*; **2** handsome man.

arloji watch; **arloji tangan** wrist watch.

armada armada, fleet.

arsip **1** archives, **2** files; **kearsipan** records; **pengarsipan** filing system.

arsitek architect.

arti **1** meaning; **apa artinya?** what does it mean?; **2** sense; **3** significance; **artinya** that is, meaning; **searti** of the same meaning; **berarti** **1** to mean; **2** to be significant; **hal-hal yang berarti** the things that matter; **mengerti** to comprehend, to understand.

artikel article.

artis artist.

arung, mengarungi **1** to cross; **beranikah dia mengarungi samudra itu seorang diri?** was she brave

a b c d e f g h i j k l m n o p q r s t u v w x y z

enough to sail across the ocean alone?; **2** to ford, to wade across or through; **pengarungan** action of crossing.

arus 1 current, stream; **2** flow; **arus barang** commodity flow; **arus dana** cash flow.

arwah soul; **misa arwah** requiem mass.

A.S. (Amerika Serikat) the United States of America.

asa *(not used alone)* **putus asa** to be desperate, to lose hope.

asah, mengasah 1 to sharpen; **2** to file, to grind; **3** to polish; **asahan** shavings; **pengasah 1** sharpener; **2** whetstone; **3** grinder; **pengasahan** grinding, sharpening.

asal[1] **1** origin, source; **2** beginning, cause; **asal kata** word stem, base; **asal mula sejarah** dawn of history; **asal usul** origin, source, pedigree, descent, history; **seasal** related; **asalnya** initially, originally; **berasal 1** to be of good family; **2** to come from; **Wayan berasal dari Bali** Wayan comes from Bali.

asal[2] **1** as long as, provided that; **asal Anda dapat membantu** as long as you can help; **asal bapak senang** as long as the boss is happy; **2** to do something just because one feels like it; **asal saja** perfunctory; **seasalnya** perfunctorily; **asal-asalan** done any old way; **asalkan** provided that; **asalkan itu tidak hilang** provided that you don't lose it.

asam 1 sour; **muka asam** a sour look; **menjadi asam** to turn into acid; **2** tamarind; **mengasami 1** to add acid; **2** to put tamarind into your cooking; **mengasamkan** to pickle, to preserve; **keasaman** acidity; **keasam-asaman** sour(ish), acidic.

asap fumes, smoke; **berasap 1** producing smoke or vapour; **2** *(of food)* smoked, cured; **3** fumigated; **4** *(of clothes)* scented, perfumed; **pengasapan 1** fumigation; **2** curing; **rumah pengasapan daging** smokehouse; **perasapan 1** incense burner; **2** fumigator.

asas 1 basis, principle; **2** base, foundation; **berasas(kan) 1** to be based on; **2** to have principles; **mengasaskan** to base, to establish, to found.

asasi basic, fundamental; **hak asasi** basic right, **hak asasi manusia** human rights.

asbak ashtray.

asbes asbestos.

ASEAN (Association of South-East Asian Nations) ASEAN.

asese agreed, approved; **mengasesekan** to approve.

Asia Asia.

asimilasi assimilation; **berasimilasi** assimilated.

asin briny, salty; **ikan asin** salted fish; **telur asin** salted eggs; **mengasinkan 1** to salt; **2** to pickle; **asinan** pickled vegetable or fruit; **pengasinan** pickling, salting.

asing alien, foreign, strange; **orang asing** foreigner; **mengasingkan 1** to isolate, to separate; **mengasingkan diri** to isolate yourself; **2** to exile, to banish; **3** to segregate; **terasing 1** secluded, isolated; **2** exotic, very foreign; **pengasingan, perasingan 1** banishment, exile; **2** isolation; **3** internment; **4** alienation, estrangement.

asisten assistant.

asli 1 original; **versi yang asli lebih baik** the original version was better; **2** authentic, genuine; **berlian yang asli** a genuine diamond; **3** indigenous, native; **orang asli Kalimantan** a native of Kalimantan; **4** innate; **keaslian 1** authenticity, genuineness; **2** originality.

asmara romantic love.

asoi *(colloquial)* fantastic, fun.

aspek aspect.

aspirasi aspiration.

asrama dormitory, barracks; **asrama pemuda** youth hostel.

assalaamualaikum peace be on you.

astaga heaven forbid, for heaven's sake.

astronot astronaut.

asuh, mengasuh 1 to bring up, to care for, to take care of, to rear *(a child)*; **anak asuh** foster child; **2** to bring up, to educate; **3** to prepare, to train; **4** to maintain, to lend support; **asuhan 1** upbringing; **2** education; **3** leadership; **4** sponsorship; **pengasuh 1** nursemaid; **2** guardian; **pengasuhan** care.

asuransi insurance; **asuransi perjalanan** travel insurance; **mengasuransikan** to insure something; **perasuransian** insurance system.

asyik 1 passionate; 2 be infatuated; 3 busy, occupied; 4 absorbed; 5 fantastic, great; **mengasyikkan** 1 to absorb, to engross, to preoccupy; 2 to fascinate; 3 fascinating, absorbing; **cerita yang mengasyikkan** a fascinating story; **keasyikan** obsession, infatuation, preoccupation.

atap roof; **beratap** to have a roof; **beratapkan** covered with; **rumah itu beratapkan rumbia** the house is roofed with palm thatch; **mengatapi** to cover; **Abdul mengatapi kandang ayam itu dengan daun pisang** Abdul covered the chicken coop with banana leaves; **pengatapan** roofing.

atas 1 on, on top of, upon; **di atas meja tulis** on the desk; **naik ke atas** to go up; 2 over, in addition to; 3 for, because of; **terima kasih atas pertolongan Anda** thank you for your help; **atas dasar** on the basis of; **atas nama** in the name of, on behalf of; **mengatasi** 1 to exceed, to surpass; 2 to overcome; **mengataskan** to put higher; **teratas** highest, uppermost; **teratasi** can be overcome; **atasan** superior.

atase attache.

atau or; **hari ini atau besok** today or tomorrow; **saya akan menelepon atau mengirim email** I'll either phone or e-mail; **ataukah** *(in questions)* or; **hari ini ataukah besok?** today or tomorrow?

ateis atheist, atheistic; **ateisme** atheism.

atlas atlas.

atlet, atlit athlete; **atletik** athletic.

atom atom.

atraksi attraction.

atur, mengatur 1 to put in order, to tidy up; 2 regulate, organize; **lampu lalu lintas mengatur arus lalu lintas** traffic lights regulate the traffic flow; 3 to arrange; **mengaturkan** to put in order for someone; **teratur** 1 in order, tidy; 2 regular, arranged; **keteraturan** orderliness, regularity; **aturan, peraturan** 1 arrangement; **peraturan gaji** salary scale; 2 regulation, rule; **aturan-aturan permainan** the rules of the game; **peraturan presiden** presidential regulation; **peraturan sekolah** the school rules; **taat kepada peraturan** to obey the rules; 3 directions, instructions; 4 behaviour, manner; **tidak**

a b c d e f g h i j k l m n o p q r s t u v w x y z

tahu aturan to have no manners; **5** routine; **aturannya, peraturannya** **1** the rules; **2** in fact, as a matter of fact; **pengatur** regulator, controller; **pengaturan** arrangement; **pengaturan kembali** re-arranging.

aula auditorium, hall.

aum **1** roar of a lion; **2** raging of a storm; **mengaum 1** to bellow, to roar; **2** to buzz; **auman** buzzing, roaring.

avokad, apokat *(old spelling)* avocado.

awak crew; **awak pesawat** flight crew; **perawakan** **1** figure, shape; **2** build, physique; **berperawakan** to have a certain build; **berperawakan kecil** to have a small build.

awal **1** beginning; **pada awal minggu ini** at the beginning of this week; **2** early, first, initial; **kami seharusnya berangkat lebih awal** we should have left earlier; **Randy suka datang awal** Randy likes to be early; **awalan** prefix; **berawalan** prefixed; **mengawal(i)** to be first, to precede; **Sumarlin mengawali sambutannya dengan ucapan 'Selamat Datang'** Sumarlin prefaced his speech with 'Welcome'; **pengawal** escort, pioneer.

awam **1** common, general; **2** lay, non-expert; **orang awam** layperson.

awan cloud; **berawan** cloudy, overcast; **cuaca berawan** dull weather; **mengawan** to climb into the sky *(for example, aircraft)*.

awang-awang **1** atmosphere; **2** air, space; **mengawang 1** to go up into the air; **2** to indulge in fancies; **pikirannya mengawang jauh, pikirannya jauh di awang-awang** her/his thoughts are far away.

awas careful, watch out; **awas, ada lobang di situ** watch out, there's a hole there; **mengawasi** to control, to oversee, to supervise; **pengawas 1** overseer, supervisor, superintendant; **2** caretaker, keeper; **pengawasan 1** care, supervision; **2** checking, control; **3** surveillance.

awet durable, lasting; **awet muda** staying young; **mengawetkan 1** to can, to preserve *(food, for example)*; **makanan yang diawetkan** preserved food; **2** *(animals)* to stuff; **keawetan 1** shelf life; **2** preservation; **pengawet** preservative;

pengawetan conservation, preserving.

ayah father *(as a term of address)*; **ayah Nicole** Nicole's dad; **ayah saya bekerja di pabrik** my dad works in a factory; **berayah** to have a father.

ayak sieve, sifter; **mengayak** to sift; **ayakan, pengayak** **1** sieve, sifter; **2** a person who wobbles or waddles.

ayam chicken; **ayam aduan** fighting cock; **ayam belanda, ayam kalkun** turkey; **ayam jago** cockerel, rooster; **ayam kampung** free-range chicken; **ayam-ayaman** toy chicken.

ayan, orang ayan an epileptic; **penyakit ayan** epilepsy.

ayat **1** verse *(in the Bible or Koran)*; **2** article *(legal)*; **3** clause.

ayo come along! come on let's go!; **ayolah!** come on then!; **ayo duluan!** go ahead!

ayun swing, sway; **berayun** to oscillate, to sway, to swing; **mengayun** to rock, to swing; **mengayunkan 1** to swing something at; **2** to throw something by swinging it; **ayunan 1** cradle; **2** swing; **3** oscillation, swaying; **pengayun** pendulum; **pengayunan** action of swaying.

azas principle; **azasi** essential, fundamental; **hak azasi manusia** human rights.

azimat **1** amulet, charm, talisman; **2** mascot.

B b

bab chapter *(of a book)*.

babak **1** phase, stage; **2** *(sport)* round.

babat[1] tripe.

babat[2], **membabat** to clear, to cut away; **membabat tumbuh-tumbuhan** to clear away bushes.

babi pig; **babi hutan** wild pig.

baca, membaca to read; **membaca keras** to read aloud; **bacaan 1** reading; **2** reading material, literature; **pembaca** reader; **pembacaan** reading.

bacin, bau bacin smelling rotten.

bacok, membacok 1 to hack with a machete; **2** to chop up; **pembacok** person who hacks others with a machete.

badai gale, hurricane, storm.

badak rhinoceros; **berkulit badak** thick-skinned, unfeeling.

badan 1 physical body; **2** group, institution; **badan perwakilan rakyat** parliament, representative body; **berbadan** to have a body; **berbadan kuat** to have a strong body; **berbadan dua** to be pregnant.

badut clown; **membadut** to behave like a clown.

bagai, bagaikan as if, like; **gelap bagai tengah malam** it's as dark as midnight; **sebagai** as; **Dadang bekerja sebagai juru masak** Dadang works as a chef; **dan sebagainya** and so on, etc.; **berbagai** all sorts of, various; **berbagai jenis makanan** various kinds of food.

bagaimana 1 how; **bagaimana kabarnya?** how are things?; **2** how about, what about?; **bagaimana dengan bagian saya?** what about my share?; **bagaimana pun juga** no matter what, anyway; **bagaimana pun juga dia tidak mau datang** no matter what, he does not want to come; **sebagaimana** as, like; **sebagaimana Anda katakan tadi** as you said earlier.

bagasi 1 luggage; **2** luggage rack; **3** *(of a car)* boot.

bagi 1 for; **bagi dia** for him; **2** divide; **bagi dua** divided into two; **bagi rata** shared equally; **membagi 1** to divide; **2** to distribute, to share; **ayo, bagi dong!** come on, share it with me!; **membagi-bagi** to divide into sections; **membagi-bagikan**; to share, to distribute; **Endang membagi-bagikan kertas ujian itu** Endang handed out the tests; **bagian 1** part, share; **bagian utama** the main part; **2** division, section; **bagian resepsionis** the reception desk; **bagian gawat darurat** casualty department; **pembagi 1** *(person or thing)* divider; **2** distributor; **pembagian** distribution, division, sharing.

bagus beautiful, fine; **hari bagus** a beautiful day; **itu sangat bagus!** that's fantastic!; **memperbagus** to make more beautiful.

bahagia blessed, happy; **berbahagia** to be happy; **semoga berbahagia** all the best; best wishes; **membahagiakan** to make happy; **kebahagiaan** happiness, well-being.

a b c d e f g h i j k l m n o p q r s t u v w x y z

a b c d e f g h i j k l m n o p q r s t u v w x y z

bahan material, substance; **bahan bakar** fuel; **bahan baku, bahan mentah** raw material; **bahan makanan** foodstuff, provisions; **bahan pokok** staple supplies; **bahan bangunan** construction material.

bahas, membahas to discuss; **pembahasan** discussion.

bahasa language; **berbahasa** to speak *(a language)*; **saya berbahasa Indonesia** I speak Indonesian.

bahaya danger; **bahaya banjir** danger of flood; **tak ada bahaya lagi** there's no danger any more; **berbahaya** dangerous, risky; **tidak berbahaya** harmless; **membahayakan** to endanger; **kita tidak boleh membahayakan orang lain** we must not endanger others.

bahkan 1 even, in fact; **2** moreover.

bahu shoulder; **bahu-membahu** shoulder to shoulder, to help each other; **kita harus bekerja bahu-membahu** we must work together.

bahwa that; **dia berkata bahwa dia akan datang** he said that he would come.

baik 1 good, kind; **orang baik** good person, kind person; **2** healthy; **3** yes, all right, OK; **baiklah, saya akan membantu** OK, I'll help; **baik-baik 1** fine, well; **'apa kabar?' 'baik-baik saja'** 'how are you?' 'fine, thanks'; **2** carefully; **3** good, respectable; **keturunan orang baik-baik** a descendant of respectable people; **sebaik** as good as; **sebaiknya** better, preferable; **sebaiknya dia diundang juga** it would be better to invite her/him too; **sebaik-baiknya** as well or as good as possible; **kita harus berusaha sebaik-baiknya** we have to try the best we can; **membaik** to improve; **cuaca makin membaik** the weather is improving; **memperbaiki 1** to repair; **memperbaiki karangannya** to improve her essay; **kebaikan 1** goodness, kindness; **2** advantage, benefit; **perbaikan** repair, improvement, upgrading; **perbaikan jalan** road repairs.

baja steel; **berlapis baja** steel-plated; **membaja** to become strong like steel.

bajaj mini-taxi with three wheels.

bajak[1] plow; **membajak** to plow a field; **bajakan** plowing.

bajak[2], **bajak laut** pirate; **membajak 1** to commit piracy; to hijack; **membajak pesawat terbang** to hijack a plane; **2** to pirate books, songs, etc.; **bajakan** loot, plunder; **kaset bajakan** pirated cassette; **pembajak 1** pirate; **2** hijacker; **pembajakan 1** hijacking; **2** pirating *(of books etc.)*.

bajing squirrel; **bajingan** rascal.

baju upper clothing; **baju dalam** underwear; **baju kaos** singlet, T-shirt; **mengenakan baju** to put on a dress; **berbaju** to wear clothing.

bak 1 basin; **2** large container; **bak mandi** tub of water in the bathroom *(full of water that you pour over yourself while standing beside the tub)*.

bakal 1 future; **bakal guru** student teacher; **bakal istri** future wife; **bakal suami** future husband; **2** shall, will; **pemilihan umum bakal diadakan pada bulan Maret** the election will be held in March.

bakar 1 burn, set fire to; **bahan bakar** fuel; **2** barbecued, roasted; **ayam bakar** barbecued chicken; **membakar 1** to burn, to set fire to; **jangan bakar sampah di situ** don't burn the rubbish there; **membakar habis** to incinerate, to burn completely; **membakarkan** to burn something for someone; **terbakar 1** on fire; **2** *(accidental)* to catch fire; **tiba-tiba terbakar** to burst into flames suddenly; **3** burned down; **kebakaran** to be on fire; **kebakaran hutan** forest fire; **pemadam kebakaran** fire brigade; **pembakar** arsonist; **pembakaran** burning, incineration; **pembakaran mayat** cremation *(in Bali)*.

bakat talent; **bakat seni** artistic; **berbakat** talented, gifted.

baki tray.

bakmi noodles; **(bak)mi goreng** fried noodles.

bakso meatball; **mi bakso** noodles with meatballs.

bakti devotion, service; **berbakti** to serve; **membaktikan** to dedicate, to devote; **membaktikan seluruh waktu dan tenaga kepada olahraga** to devote all your time and energy to sport; **kebaktian** religious service.

baku 1 standard; **bahasa baku** standard language;

a b c d e f g h i j k l m n o p q r s t u v w x y z

2 basic; **bahan baku** raw material; **membakukan** to standardize; **pembakuan** standardization.

balai 1 public building; **balai kota** town hall; **2** bureau, office; **balai dagang** chamber of commerce.

balap, balapan racing; **balapan mobil** automobile racing; **mobil balap** racing car; **pembalap** racer.

balas, membalas 1 *(a letter)* to answer; **saya sudah membalas suratnya** I have answered his letter; **2** to retaliate; **membalas budi** to show gratitude; **membalas dendam** to take revenge; **balas membalas** to reciprocate; **baru enam bulan kami balas-membalas dengan email** we've only been exchanging e-mails for six months; **balasan 1** answer, reply; **saya belum mendapat balasan dari Dharsono** I haven't had a reply from Dharsono yet; **2** retaliation, revenge; **pembalas 1** avenger; **2** replier; **pembalasan 1** reply, replying; **2** revenge, retaliation.

balet ballet.

balik 1 return; **Marianne belum balik dari pertemuan** Marianne hasn't returned from the meeting; **2** the other side, behind; **di balik pintu** behind the door; **sebaliknya** on the contrary; **persis sebaliknya** the exact opposite; **berbalik, membalik** to turn over, to turn upside down, to turn around, to turn back; **Jeremy berbalik ketika namanya disebut** Jeremy turned around when his name was mentioned; **membalikkan 1** to turn something; **membalikkan badan** to turn around; **2** to turn upside down; **memutar balikkan fakta** to twist the facts; **terbalik 1** to be upside-down; **kura-kura itu terbalik** that tortoise is upside-down; **2** to capsize; **kapalnya terbalik** the ship capsized; **kebalikan** the contrary, the opposite.

baling, baling-baling propeller.

Balita (Bawah Lima Tahun) anak Balita children under five.

balkon balcony.

balok bar, beam, girder; **balok es** block of ice.

balon balloon; **balon-balonan** bubbles.

balsam, balsem balm, ointment.

balut bandage; **berbalut** bandaged; **membalut** to bandage.

bambu bamboo.

ban tyre; **ban dalam** inner tube; **ban serep** spare tyre; **ban leher anjing** dog collar; **ban karet** elastic band.

band band *(musical).*

bandar harbour; **bandar udara (bandara)** airport.

bandel stubborn; **anak bandel** stubborn child.

banding equivalent, ratio; **lima banding dua** ratio of five to two; **mem(per)bandingkan** to compare; **kalau kita membandingkan kata bahasa Indonesia dengan kata bahasa Inggris** if we compare the Indonesian word with the English word; **perbandingan 1** comparison; **2** proportion, ratio.

bandit bandit, gangster.

banget *(colloquial)* excessively, very; **panas banget** extremely hot.

bangau egret, stork.

bangga proud; **Megawati bangga sekali akan ayahnya** Megawati is very proud of her father; **membanggakan** to be proud of; **membangga-banggakan** to boast of; **dia selalu membangga-banggakan ayahnya** she's always boasting about her father; **kebanggaan** something you are proud of.

bangkai 1 carcass, corpse; **2** *(car etc.)* wreck.

bangkit arise, get up; **membangkitkan 1** to raise, to resurrect; **2** to generate; **membangkitkan tenaga listrik** to generate electricity; **kebangkitan 1** resurgence; **kebangkitan bangsa Indonesia** resurgence of Indonesian nationalism; **2** awakening, resurrection; **pembangkit** generator; **pembangkit tenaga nuklir** nuclear power plant; **pembangkitan** generation *(of energy).*

bangkrut bankrupt, go broke; **membangkrutkan** to cause bankruptcy; **kebangkrutan** bankruptcy.

bangku bench, seat, stool; **bangku gereja** pew.

bangsa nation, people, race; **bangsa terbelakang** a backward people, underdeveloped nation; **bangsa yang sedang berkembang** developing nation; **sebangsa** of the same nationality; **berbangsa** to be of a certain race; **kebangsaan 1** nationality;

a b c d e f g h i j k l m n o p q r s t u v w x y z

2 nationalism; 3 national; **lagu kebangsaan** national anthem; **berkebangsaan** to have the nationality.

bangsal ward.

bangsawan aristocrat, noble; **kebangsawanan** aristocracy, nobility.

bangun 1 be awake, wake up; **bangun pagi-pagi** get up early; 2 get up, rise; **hadirin bangun dari tempat duduknya waktu presiden masuk** the audience got up when the president entered; **membangun** 1 to build, to construct; **mereka membangun tugu lagi** they're constructing another monument; 2 to develop; **membangunkan** 1 to wake someone up; 2 to arouse, to excite **membangunkan semangat** to arouse enthusiasm; **terbangun** to wake up suddenly; **kebangunan** 1 awakening; 2 revival; **bangunan** building, structure; **pembangun** builder, constructor; **pembangunan** 1 construction; 2 development.

banjir flood; **sungai banjir** the river broke its banks; **membanjir** to come in large numbers; **penonton-penonton membanjir ke lapangan** the spectators came in droves onto the field; **membanjiri** 1 to inundate an area; 2 to flood, to swamp; **film-film barat membanjiri negara-negara Asia** Western films flooded into Asian countries; **kebanjiran** 1 to be hit by floods; **pembanjiran** inundating, flooding.

bank bank; **bank devisa** foreign exchange bank.

bantah argue, deny; **berbantah** argue, quarrel; **jangan berbantah dengan Rachmat** don't argue with Rachmat; **membantah** to argue; **jangan membantahnya** don't argue with him; **tak usah membantah** there's no need to argue the point.

bantal cushion, pillow.

banteng the wild ox of Java.

banting throw down with force; **membanting** to throw down violently; **membanting setir** to veer sharply *(a car)*; **terbanting** knocked to the ground; **pembantingan** drastic reduction; **pembantingan harga** drastic price reduction.

bantu, membantu to aid, to assist, to help; **membantu** to help; **bantuan** aid, help; **bantuan untuk negara yang**

sedang berkembang aid for developing countries; **bantuan untuk korban banjir** aid for the flood victims; **pembantu** assistant, helper; **pembantu menteri** assistant to the minister; **pembantu rumah tangga (PRT)** domestic home help.

banyak a lot of, many, much; **anaknya banyak** he has many children; **banyak juga kesalahannya** there were quite a few mistakes; **banyaknya** amount, quantity, number; **banyaknya orang yang mendaftar tiga ratus enam puluh** three hundred and sixty people registered; **sebanyak** as many as, as much as; **buku saya tidak sebanyak buku Anda** I don't have as many books as you do; **sebanyak-banyaknya** at the most, as many, as much as possible; **memperbanyak** to increase; **kebanyakan** **1** the greater part, majority; **2** too much, too many.

bapa, bapak **1** father; **bapak tiri** stepfather; **2** way of addressing an older man *(generally shortened to 'pak')*; **bapak guru** teacher; **mau bertemu dengan siapa, pak?** who do you want to see, sir?; **bapak-bapak** you gentlemen; **'ibu-ibu dan bapak-bapak'** 'ladies and gentlemen'; **berbapak** to have a father.

bara ember, live coal.

barak barracks.

barang **1** commodity, goods; **barang angkutan** freight; **barang jadi** finished product; **2** article, object; **barang bukti** material evidence; **barang pecah belah** earthenware; **barang tiruan** imitation, reproduction; **sudah barang tentu** for certain, positively; **3** baggage, luggage; **barang-barang** **1** belongings; **barang-barang pribadi** personal belongings; **2** commodities, goods.

barangkali maybe, perhaps.

barat **1** west; **barat daya** southwest; **barat laut** northwest; **2** western; **orang barat** westerner; **kebarat-baratan** to behave like a westerner.

baring, berbaring **1** lie down; **2** be stretched out; **3** be in bed *(in hospital)*; **berbaring-baring** to laze about, to relax; **membaringkan** to put to bed; **terbaring** to be stretched out; **pembaringan** bed, something to stretch out on.

a b c d e f g h i j k l m n o p q r s t u v w x y z

baris line, queue, row; **tempat kami di baris pertama** our place was in the front row; **berbaris 1** to form a queue, to line up; **2** to march; **membariskan** to line things up, to put in rows.

barong a Balinese dance where the dancer wears a mask.

baru 1 new, recent; **mobil baru** a new car; **saya masih baru di Jakarta** I'm still new in Jakarta; **2** just so much; **anaknya baru satu** he has just one child; **3** just now, only now; **baru saja tiba** to have just arrived; **Soeharto baru saja mengundurkan diri** Soeharto has just stepped down; **4** not until, only then; **dia baru tiba jam tujuh** he won't arrive until seven, he just arrived at seven *(depending on context)*; **5** to be doing, to be about to; **saya baru saja mau pergi** I'm just going; **baru-baru ini** recently; **Subagio baru-baru ini menelepon** Subagio recently rang; **mem(per)barui** to renew; **pembaru, pembaharu** renewer; **pembaruan** renewal.

basa-basi a convention of good manners *(for example, you might be offered food, but expected not to take it)*; **berbasa-basi** being polite in this way.

basah 1 soaked, wet; **kaki saya basah** my feet are wet; **basah kuyup** to be soaking wet; **2** damp; **handuk ini basah** this towel is wet; **3** fresh; **ikan basah** fresh fish; **membasahi, membasahkan** to moisten, to make wet.

basi 1 off, spoiled, stale; **makanan ini sudah basi** this food has gone off; **2** out-of-date, stale; **berita itu sudah basi** that news is already out-of-date.

basis 1 basis, principle; **2** base; **berbasiskan** to have as a base.

baskom washbasin.

basmi, membasmi to exterminate; **terbasmi** eliminated, obliterated; **pembasmi** eradicator, exterminator; **obat pembasmi lalat** fly spray; **pembasmian** eradication, extermination.

basuh, membasuh 1 to wash; **Ichsan membasuh tangannya** Ichsan washed his hands; **2** to rinse; **pembasuh 1** washing; **2** preparation; **3** person who washes; **pembasuhan** washing; **upacara pembasuhan kaki** foot-cleansing ceremony.

a b c d e f g h i j k l m n o p q r s t u v w x y z

bata, batu bata brick; **terbata-bata** haltingly; **Sudono menceritakan kejadian itu dengan terbata-bata** Sudono haltingly described what had happened.

batal cancelled; **rapat itu batal** the meeting is cancelled; **membatalkan** to cancel; **membatalkan rapat** to cancel a meeting; **pembatalan** cancellation.

batalyon battalion.

batang 1 stalk, stem; **batang pohon** tree trunk; **2** classifier for cylindrical, rectangular objects; **sebatang rokok** a cigarette; **sebatang emas** a gold bar.

batas 1 limit; **batas kecepatan** speed limit; **batas waktu** deadline; **2** border, boundary; **batas wilayah** district boundary; **berbatas** to have a boundary; **kasih seorang ibu kepada anaknya tidak berbatas** a mother's love for her child is boundless; **berbatasan** border on, to be adjacent to; **Brunei berbatasan dengan Malaysia** Brunei borders on Malaysia; **membatasi 1** to be the boundary or border; **2** to limit, to restrict; **terbatas** limited, restricted; **keterbatasan** limitation, limits; **pembatas** divider; **pembatasan** restriction; **pembatasan kelahiran** birth control; **perbatasan** border; **situasi di perbatasan negara itu sangat berbahaya** the situation at that country's border is extremely dangerous.

baterai battery.

batik batik.

batok coconut shell; **batok kepala** skull.

batu stone; **batu bara** coal; **batu es** hailstone; **es batu** ice block.

batuk cough; **batuk kering** dry cough; **batuk darah** to cough blood, to spit up blood; **terbatuk-batuk** cough continuously.

bau 1 odour, smell; **bau busuk** rotten smell; **harum baunya** it's fragrant; **bau yang harum** fragrant smell; **2** unpleasant odour, stink; **di sini ada bau gas sedikit** there's a faint smell of gas here.

bawa, membawa 1 to carry, to bring along, to take along; **membawa tas** to carry a bag; **membawa mobil** to bring a car; **2** to bring about, to cause; **itu membawa untung** it brings good luck; **membawakan** to bring something for someone; **terbawa** brought, taken along *(accidentally)*; **terbawa-bawa** to get involved; **bawaan** something brought; **pembawa** bearer, porter; **pembawaan** nature, talent; **Fina mempunyai pembawaan yang tenang** Fina has a quiet nature; **berpembawaan** have a talent or gift for; **Dewi berpembawaan seperti seorang pemimpin** Dewi has a talent for leadership.

bawah **1** beneath, under; **di bawah jendela** under the window; **2** below; **jeritan itu dari bawah** that scream came from below; **orang-orang yang tinggal di bawah** the people downstairs; **seperti di bawah** as below.

bawang onion; **bawang putih** garlic; **bawang Bombay** brown onion; **bawang merah** small red onion; **daun bawang** spring onion.

baya, sebaya of the same age; **ibu saya sebaya dengan ibu Anda** my mother is of the same age as your mother.

bayam spinach.

bayang, bayang-bayang **1** shadow; **bayang-bayang tiang bendera panjang sekali** the shadow of the flagpole is very long; **2** silhouette; **membayangkan** to imagine; **Anda tak dapat membayangkan betapa mengerikan kejadian itu** you can't imagine how horrible the incident was; **bayangan** shadow.

bayar, membayar to pay (for); **membayar dengan cek** to pay by cheque; **membayar sopir taksi** to pay the taxi driver; **membayar di muka** to pay in advance; **membayar tunai** to pay cash; **bayaran** payment; **Geoff mendapat bayaran tiga puluh lima dolar untuk satu jam kerja** Geoff earns thirty five dollars an hour; **prajurit bayaran** mercenary; **pembayar** payer; **pembayaran** payment.

bayi baby, infant.

bayonet bayonet.

bea duty, tax, toll; **bebas bea** duty-free; **bea (dan) cukai** customs office.

beasiswa scholarship.

beban **1** load; **beban maksimum** maximum load; **2** burden, responsibility; **membebani** to give responsibility; **Sumarlin membebani saya dengan tanggung jawab** Sumarlin gave me the responsibility;

membebankan to load something on; **Sumarlin membebankan tanggung jawab itu kepada saya** Sumarlin gave me the responsibility.

bebas free; **terjun bebas** free-fall; **bebas gula** sugar-free; **malam ini dia bebas tugas** he's off-duty tonight; **orang yang berjiwa bebas** an independent person; **membebaskan** to set free, to release; **kebebasan** freedom, liberty; **pembebas** liberator; **pembebasan** liberation; **pembebasan tahanan politik** release of political prisoners.

bebek duck.

beber, membeberkan **1** to disclose, to spread, to unfold; **Pak Sembiring membeberkan kasus korupsi di kantornya** Pak Sembiring disclosed the corruption at his office; **2** to explain; **pembeberan** disclosure, explaining; **pembeberan kasus korupsi itu menyebabkan dia dipenjarakan** the disclosure of the the corruption resulted in his imprisonment.

beberapa SEE **berapa**.

becak pedicab, trishaw.

beda difference; **apa bedanya antara durian dan nangka?** what's the difference between durian and jackfruit?; **berbeda** be different; **kamus ini berbeda dengan kamus saya** this dictionary is different from my dictionary; **membeda-bedakan, membedakan 1** to discriminate; to treat differently; **saya membedakan kedua murid itu** I treat the two pupils differently; **2** to tell apart; **pembedaan** **1** differentiation; **2** discrimination; **pembedaan seks** sexual discrimination; **perbedaan** difference; **saya tak mengerti perbedaan di antaranya** I can't understand the difference between them.

bedah surgical operation; **alat bedah** surgical instrument; **bedah mayat** autopsy; **membedah** to perform surgery; **pembedah** surgeon; **pembedahan** operation, surgery.

bedak face powder; **berbedak** powdered.

bedil gun, rifle; **berbedil** armed with a rifle.

begini like this, thus; **begini cara melakukannya** here's how to do it; **begini kabarnya** the news is like

a b c d e f g h i j k l m n o p q r s t u v w x y z

a b c d e f g h i j k l m n o p q r s t u v w x y z

this; **sebegini** *(colloquial)* as (much, many, big, small, etc.) as this; **sebegini lamanya** as long as this; **dibeginikan** *(colloquial)* to be treated in this way; **mengapa kursi saya dibeginikan?** why did you do this to my chair?

begitu 1 like that; **kalau begitu** if so, in that case; **tidak begitu** that's not the case; **2** so, very; **begitu marah** so angry; **dia tidak begitu cerdas** he's not very bright; **3** as soon as; **begitu saya tiba** as soon as I arrived; **begitulah** so it is; **begitupun** and so, also, likewise; **sebegitu** so (much, small, etc.); **sebegitu jauh** so far, until now; **dibegitukan** *(colloquial)* to be treated like that; **saya tidak mau dibegitukan** I don't want to be treated like that.

bekal provisions, supplies; **berbekal** be equipped, have a supply; **berbekalkan** supplied with; **membekali** to supply; **pembekalan** supplying; **perbekalan** supplies, provisions.

bekas 1 trace; **bekas jari** fingerprint; **bekas luka** scar; **2** former, ex; **bekas pacar** ex-boyfriend, ex-girlfriend; **3** secondhand, used; **mobil bekas** secondhand car; **berbekas, membekas, meninggalkan bekas** to leave a trace; **noda darah itu hilang tak berbekas setelah dicuci** the blood washed out without leaving a trace; **peristiwa itu sangat membekas dalam ingatan saya** that event is etched in my memory; **pencuri itu meninggalkan bekas kakinya di halaman** the thief left her/his footprints in the yard.

beku 1 frozen; **dua derajat di bawah titik beku** two degrees below freezing point; **2** congealed; **darah beku** congealed blood; **membeku 1** to freeze over; **2** to clot, to solidify; **membekukan 1** to freeze; **kita harus membekukan daging itu** we should freeze that meat; **2** to put on ice; **pembekuan** freezing.

bel bell; **mengebel 1** to ring a bell; **2** to telephone.

bela, membela to defend; **itulah pengacara yang membelanya** that's the lawyer who defended her/him; **pembela 1** defender; **2** defence lawyer; **pembelaan 1** defence; **2** plea.

belacan shrimp or fish paste.

belah **1** crack, gap; **belahan di pagar itu tambah lebar** the crack in the fence is getting wider; **2** side, party; **kedua belah pihak** both sides (parties); **membelah** **1** to cut in half, to split; **apel itu sudah dibelah dua** the apple has been cut in half; **2** to part (hair); **rambutnya dibelah di tengah** her hair is parted in the middle; **belahan** side, section; **belahan bumi** hemisphere; **sebelah** **1** one half; **2** beside, next; **mereka tinggal di sebelah rumah saya** they live next to my house; **sebelah-menyebelah** **1** side by side; **2** next to each other; **menyebelahi** to take sides, to be partial; **bersebelahan** next to each other; **kami duduk bersebelahan** we sit side by side; **terbelah** cracked, split; **pembelahan** fission, splitting.

belajar to learn, to study. SEE **ajar**.

belakang **1** back; **2** back of, behind; **tempat duduk di bagian belakang mobil** the back seat of the car; **di belakang mobil** behind the car; **dari belakang** from behind; **ke belakang** to the back; **pintu belakang** the back door; **di belakang pintu** behind the door; **musik latar belakang** background music; **belakangan** afterwards, later; **bayar belakangan** pay later; **terbelakang** **1** *(not making progress)* left behind; **2** neglected; **belakang-membelakangi** back to back; **membelakangi** **1** to turn your back on; **2** to have your back towards; **terbelakang** **1** last; **2** latest; **3** backward, retarded; **keterbelakangan** backwardness, underdevelopment.

belalang grasshopper, locust.

Belanda Dutch; **Negeri Belanda** Holland, The Netherlands.

belang **1** spot, stripe; **2** skin blemish; **3** blemished, spotted; **berbelang-belang** striped.

belanja expenses; **belanja mingguan** weekly expenses; **uang belanja** housekeeping money; **berbelanja** go shopping; **membelanjakan** to spend money on; **belanjaan** items bought, shopping; **taruh belanjaan itu di mana saja** put the shopping down anywhere; **perbelanjaan** **1** expenses; **2** financing; **3** shopping; **pusat perbelanjaan** a shopping centre.

a b c d e f g h i j k l m n o p q r s t u v w x y z

belantara, hutan belantara, rimba belantara jungle, primeval forest; **padang belantara** field and forest, wilderness.

belas[1], belas kasihan pity; **berbelas kasihan** be compassionate, have pity.

belas[2] teens; **sebelas** eleven; **enam belas** sixteen; **belasan** **1** between ten and twenty; **2** being in the teens; **anak belasan tahun** teenager.

belasungkawa condolence, sympathy; **berbelasungkawa, menyatakan belasungkawa** to express sympathy.

belenggu handcuff; **membelenggu** to handcuff.

beli, membeli to buy; **saya membeli mobil baru** I bought a new car; **membelikan** to buy something for someone; **Jane membelikan Jenny gelang** Jane bought Jenny a bracelet; **terbeli** affordable; **belian** something bought; **pembeli** buyer; **pembelian** purchasing, buying.

belia, muda belia young, youthful.

beliau he, him, his, she, her *(respectful)*; **beliau akan mengadakan kunjungan muhibah** he/she will make a goodwill visit; **hadiah yang bagus ini untuk beliau** this beautiful gift is for him/her; **kunjungan kenegaraan beliau ditangguhkan** his/her state visit was postponed.

belimbing star fruit.

belok bend, curve; **berbelok** to turn; **mobilnya berbelok ke kiri** the car turned to the left; **berbelok-belok** winding, zigzag; **jalan itu belok-belok** it's a winding road; **membelok** to turn, to veer; **membelokkan 1** to turn something; **membelokkan arah** to change direction; **2** to distract; **Saphie membelokkan pembicaraan Max** Saphie distracted Max from what he was saying; **belokan** bend, curve; **pembelokan** change of front *(politics)*.

belot, membelot to be a traitor, to defect, to desert to the enemy; **Sufni membelot ke pihak lawan** Sufni deserted to the enemy; **pembelot** defector, deserter; **pembelotan** defection, desertion.

beluderu, beludru velvet.

belukar scrub, undergrowth; **semak belukar** bushes.

belum 1 not yet; **dia belum menjawab pertanyaan saya**

he hasn't answered my question yet; **belum lama ini** not long ago, recently; **belum pernah** have never yet; **dia belum pernah mengembalikan apa yang dipinjamnya** he has never returned anything he borrowed; **2** *(colloquial)* not (yet) included; **ongkosnya seratus ribu rupiah, belum makanan** the cost is Rp. 100,000, not counting meals; **sebelum** before, by; **siap sebelum hari Senin** ready by Monday; **saya akan kembali sebelum jam tiga** I'll be back by three; **sebelumnya 1** formerly, previously; **2** beforehand; **harap menelepon sebelumnya** please phone beforehand.

belut eel.

bemo a small motorized vehicle for public transport.

benam, membenam to hide, to sink out of sight; **membenam** to be enveloped; **anak itu membenam dalam dekapan ibunya** the child was enveloped in her/his mother's hug; **membenamkan 1** to immerse; **Hasan membenamkan kepalanya ke dalam air** Hasan immersed his head in the water; **2** to suppress; **3** to sink; **terbenam 1** to disappear, to go down; **matahari sedang terbenam** the sun is setting; **2** to be buried.

benang sewing thread, yarn.

benar 1 correct, right; **jawaban yang benar** the right answer, the correct answer; **2** honest, right, true; **keadaan yang benar** the true situation; **benar-benar** actually, really; **apakah dia benar-benar berkata demikian?** did she actually say that?; **sebenarnya 1** actually, as a matter of fact, in fact; **sebenarnya saya tidak mau pergi** actually I don't want to go; **2** fitting, proper; **pilihan yang sebenarnya** the proper choice; **membenarkan 1** to correct *(a mistake)*; **2** to arrange **membenarkan taplak meja** to arrange the tablecloth; **3** to confirm, to substantiate; **4** to justify; **kebenaran 1** correctness; **2** truth; **pembenaran 1** correction; **2** confirmation; **3** justification.

bencana disaster; **bencana alam** a natural disaster; **bencana nasional** national disaster.

a b c d e f g h i j k l m n o p q r s t u v w x y z

a b c d e f g h i j k l m n o p q r s t u v w x y z

benci, membenci to hate, to dislike; **dia benci akan orang itu** he hates that person; **saya membenci pekerjaan rumah tangga** I hate housework; **kebencian** dislike, hate, hatred, loathing.

benda article, thing; **benda asing** foreign body; **benda hidup** living thing; **harta benda** property, wealth.

bendahara treasurer; **perbendaharaan** treasury; **perbendaharaan kata** vocabulary; **bendaharawan** bursar, treasurer *(especially government officials).*

bendera flag; **bendera merah putih** the Indonesian flag; **berbendera** flying a flag; **semua rumah berbendera merah putih pada tanggal 17 Agustus** all houses fly the Indonesian flag on 17 August.

bendung, membendung **1** to dam up; **2** to check, to contain, to repress; **membendung komunisme** to check communism; **membendungi** to dam up; **terbendung 1** dammed up; **2** held back; **bendungan** dam, dyke, weir; **pembendungan** damming up.

bengek 1 asthma; **2** asthmatic.

bengis cruel, harsh; **kebengisan** cruelty.

bengkak 1 puffy, swollen; **membengkak 1** to swell up; **2** to expand, to increase; **pembengkakan 1** swelling; **2** expansion, increase.

bengkel 1 workshop; **2** repair shop; **bengkel mobil** car repair shop, garage; **membengkel** to operate a workshop; **pekerjaan Ali membengkel** Ali runs a repair shop; **membengkelkan** to send something for repair; **membengkelkan mobil yang rusak** to have your car repaired; **perbengkelan** repair shop.

bengkok 1 bent, warped; **pagar itu bengkok** that fence is crooked; **2** crooked, dishonest; **orang yang bengkok hatinya** a dishonest person; **membengkok** to bend; **membengkokkan 1** to cause something to bend; **2** to warp, to distort; **pembengkokan** bending.

benih 1 seed; **2** germ; **3** semen; **4** origin; **5** cause, **membenihkan 1** to germinate something; **2** to conceive *(women)*; **pembenihan 1** germination **2** seedbed.

bening clear, transparent; **kaca bening** clear glass; **air di pantai bening sekali** the water at the beach is very clear; **membeningkan 1** *(water)* to purify; **2** to clear, to make something clear; **kebeningan** clearness; **pembeningan** purification.

benjol 1 bump, lump; **benjol pada kepala** a bump on the head; **2** bruised, swollen; **berbenjol-benjol** covered with lumps and bruises.

bensin petrol.

bentak, membentak to bawl out, to snap at; **bentakan** bellow, growl.

benteng 1 fortress; **2** fortification; **membentengi 1** to fortify; **2** to be used as a fort; **perbentengan** fortification.

bentrok, bentrokan clash; **bentrokan senjata** armed clash.

bentuk shape; **bentuk tubuh, bentuk badan** body shape; **berbentuk** to have the shape of; **membentuk** to form, to shape; **terbentuk** formed, shaped; **pembentuk 1** maker, shaper; **2** *(politics)* someone who forms a cabinet; **pembentukan** formation.

bentur, berbenturan collide; **becak dan sepeda itu berbenturan** the pedicab and the bicycle collided; **membentur** to crash into, to collide with; **mobil itu membentur pohon** the car hit a tree; **membenturkan** to make something ram into or collide; **sopir gila itu membenturkan bisnya pada pohon** the crazy driver drove the bus into a tree; **kebentur** *(colloquial)*, **terbentur** collide with; **saya terbentur dengan meja itu** I banged into the table; **kepala saya terbentur pada lemari itu** I banged my head on the cupboard.

benua continent.

beranda verandah, balcony.

berandal rascal, scoundrel.

berangasan quick-tempered

berangkat to leave

berangus muzzle; **memberangus** to muzzle.

berani brave, bold; **berani melakukan** to dare to do; **kalau berani, silahkan!** I dare you!; **memberanikan** to make brave; **saya memberanikan diri untuk masuk ke kamarnya** I got up the courage to go into her/his room; **keberanian** bravery, courage, daring; **pemberani 1** courageous person; **2** daredevil.

a b c d e f g h i j k l m n o p q r s t u v w x y z

a b c d e f g h i j k l m n o p q r s t u v w x y z

berantak, berantakan 1 in a mess; 2 fall to pieces; **proyeknya berantakan** his project fell apart; **memberantakkan** to put something into disorder.

berantas, memberantas to fight against, to combat, to eradicate; **terberantas** wiped out, eliminated; **pemberantas** someone or something that wipes out, abolishes; exterminator; **pemberantasan** eradication; **pemberantasan demam berdarah** eradication of dengue fever.

berapa 1 how much, how many; **berapa harganya?** how much (is the price)?; **Anda punya uang berapa?** how much money do you have?; **berapa murid di kelas empat tahun ini?** how many students are in year four this year?; 2 how *(large, small, long, etc.)*; **berapa umur Anda?** how old are you?; **berapa jauh?** how far?; **berapa besar?** how big?; **sudah berapa lama Anda di Australia?** how long have you been in Australia?; **berapa panjang kolam ini?** how long is this pool?; **berapa luas segitiga ini?** what's the area of this triangle?; **seberapa** as much as, that much; **seberapa mungkin** as much as possible; **ongkosnya tidak seberapa** the cost is not that much; **beberapa** several, some, a few; **ada beberapa alternatif** there are several alternatives; **beberapa kali** a couple of times; **keberapa** which; **'anak Anda yang keberapa yang menjadi dokter?' 'yang ketiga'** 'which child of yours became a doctor?' 'the third one' *(This question indicates interest in the the place of the child within the family, not her/his name.)*

beras hulled, uncooked rice; **beras putih** white rice; **beras giling** milled rice; **tepung beras** rice flour.

berat 1 heavy; **gaya berat** force of gravity; **bayi ini sudah terlalu berat untuk digendong** this baby is already too heavy to carry; 2 severe; **hukuman berat** a severe punishment; 3 difficult, hard; **belajar bahasa Indonesia tidak begitu berat** it's not so difficult to study Indonesian; 4 weight; **berapa berat bayi waktu lahir?** what was the birth weight of the baby?; **berat bersih** net weight; **berat kotor** gross weight;

memberat to become heavy; **ransel ini mulai memberat** this backpack is getting heavy; **memberatkan** to make things difficult for, to worsen; **perjudiannya memberatkan gaya hidup keluarganya** his gambling made his family's lifestyle difficult; **memperberat** to make heavier; **keberatan** objection; **berkeberatan** to have objections.

beres 1 in order, well done; **pekerjaan rumah Anda beres** your homework is well done; **2** finished, settled; **semuanya sudah beres** everything is settled; **tahu beres!** have no worry, it will be fine; **memberesi 1** to put in order; **2** to take good care of; **membereskan 1** to clear up, to settle; **saya hanya mau membereskan ini dengan Anda** I just want to clear this up with you; **2** to put in order, to straighten up; **membereskan tempat tidur** to make the bed; **keberesan** order, neatness; **pemberesan** resolution *(of conflict etc.)*.

beri, saling memberi give and take; **memberi** to give; **dia memberi adiknya uang sebagai hadiah** she gave her brother money as a gift; **memberi makan** to feed; **dia memberi komentar yang kasar tentang kemeja saya** he made a rude comment about my shirt; **memberi hati 1** to make happy, to cheer up; **2** to encourage; **3** to give in to someone's wishes; **memberi hormat,** to respect, to salute; **memberi salam** to greet and send good wishes; **memberikan 1** to hand over, to give, to give away; **memberikan makanan** to give food; **dia memberikan semua kasetnya (kepada orang lain)** she's given away all her tapes; **2** to extend; **memberitahu, memberitahukan** to inform; **dia memberitahu saya tentang hal itu, dia memberitahukan hal itu kepada saya** she told me about the matter; **mereka memberitahu kami bahwa ada masalah** they informed us that there was a problem; **pemberi** donor, giver; **pemberi darah** blood donor; **pemberian 1** gift, present; **2** awarding, bestowal; **upacara pemberian nama** christening; **3** act of distributing, distribution; **4** issue; **pemberian izin** licensing; **5** giving, extending; **pemberitahuan** announcement.

a b c d e f g h i j k l m n o p q r s t u v w x y z

a
b
c
d
e
f
g
h
i
j
k
l
m
n
o
p
q
r
s
t
u
v
w
x
y
z

beringas hot-tempered, wild; **keberingasan** wildness, savagery.

beringin, pohon beringin banyan tree.

berita **1** news; **berita luar negeri** foreign news; **pembawa berita** news reader; **2** announcement, report; **berita resmi** official report; **memberitakan** to report something; **pemberitaan** **1** announcement, news release; **2** communication; **3** notification.

berkat **1** blessing, favour; **mereka minta berkat dari dewi Sri** they asked for blessing from the rice goddess Sri; **2** due to, owing to, thanks to; **berkat usaha pemerintah** owing to the government's efforts; **memberkati** **1** to bless; **2** to endow; **terberkati** blessed; **berkatan** food taken home from a ceremony; **pemberkatan** giving of a blessing.

berlian polished diamond.

berontak, memberontak to rebel, to revolt; **Indonesia memberontak terhadap Belanda** Indonesia revolted against the Dutch; **pemberontak** insurrectionist, mutineer, rebel; **pemberontakan** mutiny, rebellion.

bersih clean, neat; **pakaian ini sudah bersih** these clothes are already clean; **berat bersih** net weight; **membersihkan** **1** to clean up; **kami sudah membersihkan mobil** we've cleaned the car; **2** to purify; **kebersihan** **1** cleanliness; **petugas kebersihan** cleaner *(in a public place)*; **kebersihan penting sekali** cleanliness is very important; **2** purity; **pembersih** **1** cleaner, **2** cleanser; **obat pembersih** cleanser, detergent; **pembersihan** cleaning.

bersin sneeze.

beruang bear; **beruang-beruangan** teddy bear.

berudu tadpole.

besan people related through the marriage of their children; **Dr Sumitro adalah besan mantan Presiden Suharto** Dr Sumitro and the former President Suharto are related through the marriage of their children; **berbesan** relationship between parents-in-law; **mereka berbesan** their children are married to eac other.

besar **1** big, huge, large; **peristiwa besar** a big event; **besar hati** proud; happy, pleased; **berbesar hati** to rejoice, to feel happy; **besar kepala 1** conceited; **2** obstinate, stubborn; **2** great; **Duta Besar** Ambassador; **Kedutaan Besar Australia** the Australian Embassy; **sebesar 1** as big as; **2** in the amount of; **bon sebesar tiga puluh lima ribu rupiah** a bill of Rp. 35,000; **sebesar-besarnya** as great as possible; **membesar 1** to expand; **2** to grow up; **kuda itu cepat membesar** the horse is growing quickly; **3** to increase; **membesarkan 1** to enlarge, to increase, to magnify; **yang membesarkan hati** encouraging; **2** to bring up, to raise; **dia dibesarkan oleh neneknya** he was brought up by his grandmother; **membesar-besarkan** to exaggerate; **dia membesar-besarkan itu** he made a big drama out of it; **pernyataan yang dibesar-besarkan** an exaggerated statement; **memperbesar** to enlarge, to increase; **kebesaran 1** *(colloquial)* too big; **2** greatness; **besar-besaran** on a large scale; **ada obral besar-besaran di toko itu** that shop is having a mega-sale; **pembesar 1** an official; **2** a high-ranking person, big shot; **pembesaran 1** expansion, increase; **pembesaran hati** encouragement, incentive; **2** enlargement *(of a photo)*; **perbesaran** process of enlargement, magnification.

besi iron; **besi baja** steel; **besi tua** scrap iron.

besok tomorrow; **besok-besok** *(colloquial)* in the future; **besoknya** *(colloquial)* the next day; **keesokan harinya** the following day.

besuk visit to a patient in hospital; **jam besuk** visiting hour; **membesuk** to pay a visit to a patient.

betah 1 endure, stand; **2** feel at home, like; **saya betah tinggal di Bandung** I feel at home living in Bandung.

betapa how very; **betapa mengejutkannya kabar itu** how very shocking the news was; **betapa lagi, betapa pula** even more, the more so; **betapa pun** however.

betina female *(of animals)*; **ayam betina** hen.

betis calf *(of leg)*.

beton concrete.

betul 1 correct, right; **ya, itu betul** yes, that's correct; **2** true; **3** really, very; **anjing**

a b c d e f g h i j k l m n o p q r s t u v w x y z

itu galak betul that dog is really savage; **betul-betul** really and truly, sincerely; **apakah dia betul-betul berkata demikian?** did she really say that?; **sebetulnya** actually, as a matter of fact; **sebetulnya saya tidak mau pergi** actually I don't want to go; **membetulkan 1** to fix, to repair; **2** to correct *(a mistake)*; **kebetulan 1** by chance, coincidence; **kebetulan saja saya menemukannya** I found it by accident; **suatu penemuan yang kebetulan** an accidental discovery; **2** chance to, happen to; **kalau kebetulan saja Anda bertemu dengan Jill** if you happen to see Jill; **pembetulan 1** repair; **2** improvement; **3** correction.

biadab barbaric, uncivilized; **kebiadaban** barbarism.

biak fertile; **berbiaki, berkembang biak** breed, multiply; **kelinci cepat berbiak** rabbits breed quickly; **membiak** to flourish, to multiply; **membiakkan** to breed, to cultivate, to rear; **pembiakan** breeding, cultivation, rearing.

biar 1 let, permit; **biar saya urus** leave it to me; **biar dia ikut** let her come along; **2** so that; **tolong pasang berangusnya biar dia tidak bisa menggigit** please muzzle it so it can't bite; **3** although; **biar kecil dia suka menggigit** although it's small it likes to bite; **biar begitu** none the less, yet, nevertheless; **biarlah** this will do, all right; **biarpun** although; **membiarkan 1** to allow, to let, to permit; **dengan syarat Anda membiarkan saya membayar** on the condition that you let me pay; **2** to keep; **Kartika membiarkan ibunya menunggu** Kartika kept her mother waiting.

biara monastery; **biarawan** monk; **biarawati** nun.

biasa 1 customary, usual; **yang biasa** the usual one; **(sama) seperti biasa** the same as usual; **lebih panas daripada biasa** hotter than usual; **2** accustomed to, used to; **saya biasa bangun pagi-pagi** I'm used to getting up early; **3** common, ordinary; **keadaan yang biasa** a common situation; **luar biasa** extraordinary; **biasanya** usually, customarily; **membiasakan**

to accustom, to make something usual; **saya tidak bisa membiasakan diri pada sistem baru** I can't adapt to the new system; **terbiasa 1** habitual; **2** have become accustomed to; **kebiasaan 1** usage; **2** habit, custom; **kebiasaan tidur larut malam** to have a habit of going to bed late.

biawak monitor lizard.

biaya cost, expense, fee; **biaya administrasi** administrative fee; **biaya fiskal** departure tax *(at airport)*; **biaya perjalanan** travel expenses; **membiayai** to finance, to fund; **pembiaya** financier; **pembiayaan** financing, funding.

bibi, bibik 1 aunt; **2** form of address to older female domestic helpers, often '**bi**'.

bibir edge, lip; **bibir mangkok** edge of the bowl.

bibit 1 germ, seed; **2** seedling; **membibitkan 1** to transplant seedlings; **2** to yield; **pembibitan** cultivation of seedlings.

bicara speak; **dia bicara bahasa Arab** she speaks Arabic; **(nomor itu) sedang bicara** the line's busy *(telephone)*; **berbicara 1** speak; **dia berbicara dengan gurunya** he's speaking to his teacher; **dia berbicara dengan logat Australia** he has an Australian accent; **membicarakan** to discuss, to talk about; **besok kita akan membicarakan masalah itu** we'll discuss the problem tomorrow; **pembicara** speaker; **pembicaraan** discussion; **apakah Anda mengerti pembicaraan kami?** did you understand our discussion?

bidan midwife; **membidani** to serve as a midwife for someone; **kebidanan** midwifery.

bidang 1 area, field, sector; **bidang penelitian** field of research; **2** level surface, plane.

bihun thin rice noodle.

bijak able, experienced, smart, wise; **kebijakan 1** wisdom; **2** policy.

bijaksana 1 farsighted, wise; **2** prudent, tactful; **kebijaksanaan 1** prudence, wisdom; **2** policy; **3** discretion.

biji 1 kernel, seed; **2** stone; **3** classifier for small round objects.

bijih ore; **bijih besi** iron ore.

a b c d e f g h i j k l m n o p q r s t u v w x y z

a b c d e f g h i j k l m n o p q r s t u v w x y z

bikin *(colloquial)* cause, make; **bikin-bikin** making up; **membikin** to make, to build; **membikinkan** to make something on behalf of someone; **terbikin** made from; **bikinan** product; **pembikin** maker; **pembikinan** construction, manufacture.

bila 1 when; **bila dia datang** when he/she comes; **2** when, if; **tolong belikan saya buku itu bila Anda pergi ke sana lagi** please buy me that book if (when) you go there again.

bilamana if, when *(for the future)*; **tolong belikan saya buku itu bilamana Anda pergi ke sana lagi** please buy me that book if *(*when*)* you go there again.

bilang¹ say; **Anda bilang apa?** what did you say?; **membilangi** *(colloquial)* to say to someone.

bilang², berbilang a few, several, some; **berbilang jam** for several hours; **membilang** to count; **terbilang** be calculated; **bilangan** numeral; **bilangan pokok** cardinal number; **bilangan ganjil** odd number; **enam adalah bilangan genap** six is an even number; **pembilangan** counting.

bilik chamber, room.

bilyar billiards.

bimbang 1 anxious, worried; **2** hesitate; **membimbangkan** to cause hestitation; **kebimbangan 1** doubt, hesitation; **2** anxiety, worry.

bimbing to get guidance; **berbimbingan 1** to hold hands; **2** to cooperate, to help each other; **membimbing 1** to lead by the hand; **2** to conduct, to guide, to lead; **bimbingan** leadership; **pembimbing 1** adviser, counsellor, guide; **2** leader; **3** adviser; **pembimbingan** guiding, leading, leadership.

bina building, construction; **membina 1** to build, to construct; **2** to cultivate, to develop; **terbina** cultivated; **pembina 1** builder, cultivator; **2** elder members of an organization; **3** *(sport)* coach; **pembinaan 1** establishment, founding; **2** creation, construction.

binal disobedient, obstinate, uncontrollable; **kuda binal** uncontrollable horse.

binaraga bodybuilding; **binaragawan** male bodybuilder; **binaragawati** female bodybuilder.

binasa destroyed, wiped out **Hiroshima dan Nagasaki**

binasa karena dijatuhi bom nuklir Hiroshima and Nagasaki were wiped out because nuclear bombs were dropped on them; **membinasakan** to destroy, to wipe out; **pembinasaan** annihilation, total destruction.

binatang animal; **binatang liar** wild animal; **binatang buas, binatang ganas** ferocious animal; **binatang piaraan** domesticated animal; **binatang kesayangan, binatang rumah** house pet.

binatu laundry *(drycleaners)*.

bincang, berbincang-bincang deliberate, discuss; **mem(per)bincangkan** to discuss, to talk about something; **perbincangan** **1** discussion; **2** conference.

bingkai **1** brim, edge, rim; **2** frame; **berbingkaikan** framed with; **membingkaikan** to frame *(a picture)*; **bingkaian** frame.

bingkis, membingkiskan send a gift; **bingkisan** **1** gift, present; **2** souvenir; **3** parcel.

bingung **1** bewildered, confused; **saya bingung tentang tanggal ujian** I'm confused about the exam dates; **2** disoriented; **sekarang dia bingung sekali** now he's completely disoriented; **3** panicky; **membingungkan** **1** to confuse, to bewilder, to fluster; **2** confusing, perplexing; **cerita itu membingungkan** it was a confusing story; **perintah-perintah itu membingungkan** the instructions are confusing; **kebingungan** **1** being disoriented; **2** confusion, bewilderment; **3** panic.

bintang **1** star; **bintang film** film star; **2** medal; **sebintang** born under the same star; **berbintang** starry; **malam berbintang** starry night.

bintik freckle, spot, stain; **bintik hitam** blackhead; **mukanya penuh dengan bintik-bintik** his face was covered in spots; **berbintik-bintik** **1** having small spots; **2** bead *(of sweat)*.

biografi biography.

biokimia biochemistry.

biola violin.

biologi biology.

bioskop cinema, movie theatre.

bir beer.

biri-biri sheep.

biro bureau, office; **biro perjalanan** travel bureau.

birokrasi bureaucracy.

biru blue; **biru muda** light blue; **mata biru 1** blue eyes; **2** a black eye; **membiru** to turn blue; **membirukan** to colour something blue; **kebiru-biruan** bluish.

bis[1] bus; **bis antarkota** intercity bus.

bis[2] **1** box; **2** post-office box; **bis surat** mail box.

bisa[1] be able, can, could; **dia tidak bisa datang** he's not able to come; **kalau bisa, tentu saya membayarnya** if I could, certainly I'd pay; **bisa-bisa** *(colloquial)* possible, quite likely; **bisa-bisa dia melarikan diri** it's quite likely that he'll escape; **sebisanya** where possible; **sebisa-bisanya** as much as possible.

bisa[2] poison; **berbisa** poisonous.

bisik, berbisik whisper; **berbisik-bisik 1** whisper to one another; **2** speak confidentially; **membisiki** to whisper at, to someone; **membisikkan 1** to whisper; **2** to imply, to suggest; **bisikan 1** whisper; **2** whispering.

bising 1 noise, uproar; **jangan bising!** don't make any noise!; **2** noisy; **3** buzzing *(in ear)*; **berbising 1** make noise; **2** be dazed; **membisingkan 1** to deafen, to cause noise pollution; **suara pesawat-pesawat itu membisingkan telinga** those planes create noise pollution; **2** to cause ringing in the ears; **kebisingan 1** noise, uproar; **2** to suffer from buzzing in the ear.

biskuit, biskit 1 biscuit, cracker; **2** Dutch rusk.

bisnis business; **berbisnis** to run a business.

bistik beef steak.

bisu 1 dumb, mute; **2** noiseless, quiet; **bisu tuli** deaf-mute; **membisu** to keep quiet, to say nothing.

bisul boil, carbuncle; **berbisul** have a boil; **bisulan** suffer from boils.

bius drugged, intoxicated, unconscious; **obat bius** anaesthetic, narcotic; **membius** to anaesthetize; **membiusi, membiuskan 1** to drug; **2** to attract, to captivate; **terbius 1** drugged **2** intoxicated; **pembiusan** anaesthetization.

blangko 1 form to be filled in; **2** abstain from voting; **3** blank *(paper)*.

blokir blockade.

blus blouse.

bobol collapse, give way; **membobol** to break into; **memboboli** to tear down; **membobolkan 1** to pierce, to penetrate; **2** to destroy, to ruin; **kebobolan 1** pierced, penetrated; **rumah says kebobolan pencuri tadi malam** my house was broken into by thieves last night; **2** penetration; **pembobolan 1** piercing; **2** making a score.

bobot weight; **berapa bobotnya?** what's the weight?; **bobot mati** dead weight; **berbobot** to have weight, to carry weight; **makalah itu cukup berbobot** that (academic) paper carries weight.

bobrok broken down, dilapidated, old, shoddy; **mobilnya sudah bobrok** his car is shoddy.

bocah child, kid *(2–10 years).*

bocor be leaky, leak; **membocorkan 1** to leak a secret; **2** to cause a leak, to cause a puncture; **kebocoran 1** damaged by leakage; **tempat tidur saya kebocoran** my bed is water-damaged; **2** leakage, divulging; **3** puncture; **pembocoran 1** leaking; **2** divulging *(secrets).*

bodoh dumb, stupid; **saya bodoh sekali dalam mata pelajaran sejarah** I'm completely hopeless at history.

bohong, berbohong to lie, to tell a lie; **membohongi** to lie to; **kebohongan 1** falsehood, lie; **2** lying; **bohong-bohongan** fake, false; **pembohong** liar; **pembohongan** lying.

boikot boycott; **memboikot 1** to boycott; **2** to ostracize; something boycotted; **pemboikotan** boycotting.

bola 1 ball; **bola bulutangkis** shuttlecock; **bola basket** basketball; **2** globe; **bola bumi** globe of the earth; **3** round object; **bola mata** eyeball.

bolak-balik 1 back and forth, to and fro; **2** again and again, frequently; **membolak-balik** to turn something over and over; **membolak-balikkan 1** to turn something again and again; **2** to distort, to twist; **pembolak-balikan** turning back and forth repeatedly.

boleh 1 be permitted, may; **Anda boleh meninggalkan sepeda Anda di sini** you may leave your bike here; **saya tidak boleh menggunakan keterangan itu** I am not allowed to use that information; **2** be able, can;

a b c d e f g h i j k l m n o p q r s t u v w x y z

apa boleh buat? what can be done?; **tak boleh jadi** it cannot be; **boleh juga** **1** fair, not bad; **2** likely, maybe; **bolehlah** all right, OK; **seboleh-bolehnya** as far as possible; **mem(per)bolehkan** to allow, to permit; **kebolehan** ability, skill.

bolong hole; **berbolong-bolong** pierced, perforated all over; **membolongi** to put a hole in something.

bolos 1 truant; **2** a sickie; **membolos 1** to desert, to go AWOL (absent without leave); **2** to play truant; **3** to take a sickie; **4** to escape from captivity; **pembolos** **1** absentee, truant; **2** deserter; **pembolosan** absenteeism.

bolpoin ballpoint pen.

bom 1 bomb; **bom atom** atomic bomb; **membom, mengebom** to bomb; **pesawat pembom, pesawat pengebom** bomber.

bon bill, check.

bonceng get dinked, get a ride on a two-wheeled vehicle; **memboncengkan** to give a ride on a two-wheeled vehicle, to dink; **boncengan** **1** to ride double, to be dinked; **2** something carried on the back of a two-wheeled vehicle; **3** bicycle rack.

boneka 1 doll; **2** puppet; **3** figurehead.

bongkar take apart; **bongkar muat** loading and unloading; **membongkar** **1** to force open, to dig up; **2** to break in; **3** to wreck; **4** to disclose, to uncover, to expose; **membongkar rahasia** to disclose a secret; **5** to unload; **terbongkar** disclosed, uncovered; **bongkaran** unloaded goods; **pembongkar 1** demolisher, wrecker; **2** person who discloses something; **pembongkaran 1** disclosure; **2** demolition, removal.

borgol handcuff; **memborgol** to handcuff.

borok sore, ulcer.

borong the whole stock; **memborong 1** to buy up all of something; **2** to do an entire job; **memborongkan** **1** to sell wholesale; **2** to give the entire contract; **borongan 1** complete sale; **2** work contracted; **pemborong 1** contractor; **pemborong bangunan jalan** road construction contractor; **2** wholesale supplier; **pemborongan** **1** wholesale buying or selling; **2** contracting, chartering.

boros extravagant, wasteful; **memboroskan** to waste; **keborosan** wastefulness; **pemboros 1** wastrel; **2** big spender; **pemborosan** extravagance, wasting.

bosan bored; be fed up; **saya sangat bosan** I'm bored to death; **saya sudah bosan mendengar tentang itu** I'm sick to death of hearing about it; **membosankan 1** to bore; **2** boring, tedious; **film itu membosankan sekali** the film's incredibly boring; **dia orang yang membosankan** he's a bit of a drag; **kebosanan** boredom; **pembosan** someone who gets bored easily.

botak bald(-headed); **membotak** to become bald; **membotaki** to shave off all hair, to shave bald.

botani botany.

botol 1 bottle; **2** bottled; **teh botol** bottled tea; **pembotolan** bottling.

brak! crash!

brandal 1 rascal, scoundrel; **2** bandit, gangster; **membrandal** to be a gangster or bandit, to commit an act of banditry.

brangus muzzle *(for dogs)*; **membrangus** to censor, to muzzle; **pembrangusan** censorship.

brengsek 1 in bad condition, useless; **2** damn! hell! *(exclamation of annoyance or disapproval)*; **kebrengsekan** lousiness.

bros brooch.

brosur brochure.

brutal brutal, very violent; **kebrutalan** brutality

bruto gross; **berat bruto** gross weight; **pendapatan bruto** gross income.

buah 1 fruit; **sari buah** fruit juice; **2** result; **buah keringat** the result of your work; **berbuah 1** to bear fruit; **2** to have results; **berbuahkan** to result in something; **membuahkan 1** to bear *(fruit, child, etc.)*; **2** to produce, to yield; **buah-buah(an)** fruit of all kinds; **campuran buah-buahan** fruit salad; **pembuahan** conception, fertilization.

bual boasting, bragging; **pembual** loudmouth, braggart.

buang throw away; **buang air besar** to defecate; **membuang 1** to throw; **monyet itu membuang buah kelapa ke bawah** the monkey threw the coconut down; **2** to throw away, to discard; **dia membuang nasi yang hangus** he threw away the burnt rice; **3** to banish, to exile; **pemerintah membuang tahanan politik ke pulau Buru** the government exiled the political prisoners to Buru island; **4** to waste; **membuang waktu dan tenaga** to waste time and energy; **membuangkan** to discard; **terbuang 1** exiled; **2** thrown away accidentally; **surat penting itu terbuang tadi pagi** that important document was thrown away this morning; **buangan 1** something thrown away, discarded object; **2** exile, outcast; **pembuangan 1** banishment, exile; **2** elimination, removal.

buas 1 ferocious, savage, wild; **2** cruel, ruthless; **kebuasan** cruelty, ferocity, savagery.

buat 1 do, make; **2** for; **buat apa?** for what?; **buat sementara** for the time being; **tolonglah ambil buku ini dari perpustakaan buat saya** could you collect this book from the library for me?; **berbuat** to do; **saya tak dapat berbuat apa-apa** I can't do anything; **Anda akan berbuat apa kalau mereka datang terlambat?** what are you going to do if they're late?; **membuat 1** to make; **membuat kesalahan** to make a mistake; **membuat janji** to make an appointment; **2** to cause; **letusan itu membuat banyak kerusakan** the explosion caused a lot of damage; **terbuat** made; **'terbuat di Indonesia'** 'made in Indonesia'; **buatan 1** make; **mobil itu buatan Jepang** that car is made in Japan; **2** product; **buatan** artificial, false; **kulit buatan** synthetic leather; **pembuat** maker, producer; **perbuatan 1** act, deed; **2** behaviour, conduct.

buaya 1 alligator, crocodile; **2** scoundrel, villain.

bubar break up, disperse, scatter; **kapan sekolah bubar?** when does school break up?; **membubarkan 1** to disperse something, to break up; **polisi membubarkan orang banyak itu di depan kediaman presiden** the police dispersed the crowd in front of the president's house; **2** to dissolve, to liquidate; **membubarkan parlemen** to dissolve parliament;

pembubaran breaking up, dispersal, dissolution.

bubuh, membubuhkan to place on, to put on; **membubuhkan tanda tangan** to sign; **membubuhi** to add something, to affix to something; **apakah saya harus membubuhi surat ini dengan meterai?** do I have to affix a duty stamp to this document?; **pembubuhan** placing.

bubuk powder; **bubuk kopi** ground coffee; **bubukan** *(colloquial)* something ground up; **pembubukan** pulverization.

bubur gruel, mush, porridge; **bubur ayam** rice gruel with chicken; **bubur havermut** oatmeal porridge.

budak slave; **memperbudak** **1** to treat as a slave; **2** to enslave; **pembudakan** enslaving; **perbudakan** slavery, bondage.

budaya culture; **agama dan budaya orang Bali pada dasarnya Hindu** Balinese religion and culture are basically Hindu; **berbudaya** **1** cultured, **2** to have a certain culture; **membudaya** to be entrenched, to be the culture of the society; **membudayakan** to cultivate, to develop; **kebudayaan** culture; **pembudayaan** cultivation; **budayawan** an expert in culture, a person who made a deep study of culture.

budi **1** mind, reason; **2** character; **budi bahasa** good manners; **baik budi** kind-hearted; **berbudi** **1** to have a good character; **2** wise; **3** well behaved.

budidaya cultivation; **membudidayakan** to cultivate; **Suhasmy membudidayakan bunga-bunga untuk dijual di kota** Suhasmy cultivates flowers for sale in the city; **pembudidayaan** cultivation.

budiman sensible, wise.

bujang **1** bachelor, single, unmarried; **2** male servant; **membujang** **1** to be single; **2** to work as a servant; **bujangan** unmarried person.

bujuk coaxing, persuasion; **bujuk-raya** flattery; **membujuk** to persuade; **terbujuk** talked, tricked into; **bujukan** enticement, flattery; **pembujuk** persuader; **pembujukan** persuasion.

bujur **1** lengthwise, longitudinal; **bujur sangkar** rectangle; **2** longitude; **bujur Timur** East longitude; **membujur** **1** to stretch out;

2 to lie alongside; 3 to run, to stretch; **kali itu membujur dari Timur ke Barat** the river runs East to West; 4 horizontal; **membujurkan** to set out lengthwise; **terbujur** stretched out; **bujuran** length; **bujuran pipa** pipeline.

buka 1 open; **biasanya bank tidak buka pada hari Sabtu** usually the bank is not open on Saturdays; 2 **buka puasa, berbuka puasa** to break fast; **membuka** 1 remove, take off; **membuka baju** take off your shirt; **lebih baik Anda membuka sepatu sebelum masuk ke rumah** you'd better take off your shoes before you enter the house; 2 to open; **membuka pintu** to open the door; **membuka rekening bank** to open a bank account; 3 to clear, to reclaim land; 4 to betray, to disclose, to divulge; **membuka rahasia** to divulge a secret; 5 to begin, to start; **membuka praktek** to open a (medical) practice; **membuka-buka** to go through something *(a magazine, drawer)*; **membukai** to open one after another; **membukakan** to open for someone; **keterbukaan** openness; **bukaan, pembuka** opener; **pembuka kata** introduction, preface; **pembukaan** 1 opening; 2 preamble, preface.

bukan 1 not, no *(used with nouns, pronouns; see also* **tidak***)* **bukan hari Senin tapi hari Selasa** not Monday but Tuesday; **dia bukan aktris favorit saya** she's not my favourite actress; 2 isn't it?, aren't you?, won't she? *(often abbreviated to* **kan***)*; **kemarin dia kan mampir di sini?, kemarin dia mampir di sini kan?** she dropped by yesterday, didn't she? **bukan-bukan** nonsense, impossibility; **jangan bicara yang bukan-bukan!** don't talk nonsense!; **bukannya** it is not that; **bukannya saya tidak mau, tetapi saya tidak punya uang** it's not that I don't want, but I don't have the money; **bukan main...nya** really extraordinary; **bukan main ceritanya** it's an extraordinary story; **bukan main cantiknya pacar Anda** how beautiful your girlfriend/boyfriend is.

buking *(informal)* reservation; **membuking** to program, to schedule; **membukingkan** to reserve something for someone.

bukit hill.

bukti evidence, proof; **bukti kesaksian** evidence, testimony; **terbukti** proved, verified; **membuktikan** to demonstrate, to prove, to show; **pembuktian** authentication.

buku book; **buku pintar** a reference book; **buku acara** agenda, program; **buku agenda** datebook, diary; **membukukan** to make into a book.

bulan 1 month; **Bulan Mei** May; **2** moon; **bulan purnama** full moon; **datang bulan** menstruation, to menstruate; **berbulan-bulan** for months; **bulanan** monthly; **majalah bulanan** monthly magazine.

bulat spherical, round; **bulat lonjong** oval; **diterima dengan suara bulat** received unanimously; **membulat** to become round or spherical; **membulati** to draw a circle around something; **membulatkan** to round off, to complete something; **kebulatan 1** roundness; **2** unanimity; **bulatan 1** circle, sphere; **2** roundness; **pembulatan 1** rounding off; **2** completion, integration.

buldoser, buldozer bulldozer.

bule 1 albino; **2** *(derogatory)* white person.

buletin bulletin.

bulu 1 body hair; **bulu mata** eyelash; **2** fur; **3** feather; **bulutangkis** badminton; **berbulu** to have body hair, fur, feathers; **membului** to remove fur or feathers.

bumbu cooking spices; **membumbui** to season something; **bumbu-bumbuan** various kinds of spices.

bumi 1 earth; **kehidupan di bumi** life on earth; **2** soil; **bumi Indonesia** Indonesian soil; **bumi hangus** scorched earth; **membumihanguskan** to implement a scorched earth policy, to reduce to ashes; **pembumihangusan** total destruction; **membumiratakan** to level an area to the ground; **membumi** to return to earth; **membumikan** to cause something to return to earth; **mengebumikan** to bury, to inter; **pengebumian** burial; **bumiputera** native of a country.

buncis French bean, string bean.

buncit bloated, puffed up; **perutnya buncit** his abdomen is bloated;

a b c d e f g h i j k l m n o p q r s t u v w x y z

membuncitkan to puff out the abdomen.

bunda mother.

bundar circular, round; **membundar** to be rounded, to form a circle; **membundarkan** to make something round; **bundaran** **1** circle; **2** roundabout, traffic circle; **pembundaran** rounding.

bung **1** buddy, fellow; **2** brother.

bunga **1** flower; **seikat bunga** a bunch of flowers; **2** floral design; **3** interest; **bunga sebesar delapan belas persen** an interest rate of eighteen per cent; **berbunga** **1** to flower; **2** to bear interest; **berbunga-bunga** patterned *(fabric)*; **membungai** **1** to decorate with flowers; **2** to place a wreath; **3** to pay interest; **mem(per)bungakan** to lend at interest; **bunga-bungaan** **1** artificial flowers; **2** floral decoration.

bungkam **1** quiet, silent; **2** speechless, struck dumb; **3** not explode, not go off; **membungkam** to remain silent; **membungkamkan** to gag, to silence; **kebungkaman** silence, stillness; **pembungkam** gag, muzzle, silencer; **pembungkaman** gagging, muzzling, silencing.

bungkuk bent, crooked, humped.

bungkus **1** pack, parcel; **sebungkus rokok** a packet of cigarettes; **2** wrapper; **berbungkus** wrapped up; **berbungkus daun** wrapped in leaves; **membungkus** to wrap up; **bungkusan** parcel, package; **pembungkus** **1** wrapping, wrapping paper; **pembungkus mayat** shroud; **2** packer, wrapper; **pembungkusan** packing, packaging.

bungsu youngest child in a family.

bunting **1** *(of animals)* pregnant; **2** filled out, full; **membuntingi, membuntingkan** to impregnate *(animals)*.

buntu **1** blocked, stopped; **jalan buntu** blind alley, cul-de-sac, dead-end street; **usus buntu** appendix; **2** clogged up, dead-locked; **membuntukan** to block, to cause a block.

buntung amputated, lopped off.

buntut **1** tail; **sop buntut** oxtail soup; **2** rear end; **buntut kapal** ship's stern; **3** aftermath; **berbuntut**

1 have a tail; **2** have consequences; **membuntuti** **1** to follow; **2** to follow at the rear.

bunuh, berbunuh-bunuhan, bunuh-membunuh to kill one another; **bunuh diri** to commit suicide; **membunuh** to kill; **pembunuh** killer, murderer; **pembunuhan** murder, killing; **pembunuhan adalah suatu kejahatan** murder is a crime.

bunyi **1** noise, sound; **2** contents; **bunyi ceritanya begini** the story goes like this; **sebunyi** of the same sound; **berbunyi** **1** to make a noise; **2** to sound; **bel tanda masuk berbunyi** the bell to go in has rung; **membunyikan** **1** to cause something to make a noise; **membunyikan bel** ring the bell; **2** to sound; **3** to read aloud; **bunyi-bunyian** **1** music; **2** musical instruments.

bupati government officer in charge of a regency, regent.

buru, buru-buru, terburu-buru hurried, in a hurry, in a rush; **berburu** go hunting, hunt; **berburu babi** go pig-hunting; **binatang berburu** predator; **memburu** **1** to chase, to pursue *(wealth, fame, etc.)*; **polisi memburu perampok itu** the police chased the robber; **2** to hunt; **memburu-buru** to make someone hurry up; **buruan** **1** game, prey; **2** fugitive, hunted person; **pemburu** hunter; **perburuan** **1** the hunt; **2** game, prey.

buruh labourer, worker; **buruh borongan** piece worker; **buruh tani** farmhand; **buruh tambang batu bara** coal miner; **upah buruh** wages as a labourer; **memburuh** to work as a labourer; **perburuhan** labour; **Partai Buruh** the Labor Party.

buruk **1** worn out; **2** decayed, rotten; **3** bad, foul, nasty; **cuaca buruk** foul weather; **sikap yang buruk** a bad attitude; **seburuk-buruknya** at the worst; **memburuk** to deteriorate, to worsen; **cuaca makin memburuk** the weather is getting worse; **memperburuk, memburukkan** to make worse; **memburuk-burukkan** to defame, to say nasty things about other people; **keburukan** **1** badness; **2** evil, wickedness.

burung bird.

busa foam, lather, scum; **busa sabun** soapsuds; **berbusa** to be full of foam; **membusa** to become foam.

busana clothing.

busi spark plug.

busuk 1 decomposed, putrid, rotten, spoiled, **daging busuk** bad/rotten meat; **bau busuk** to smell putrid; **membusuk** to become infected, to decay, to go bad, to rot; **membusukkan 1** to cause to rot; **2** to defame, to slander; **kebusukan 1** decomposition, rottenness; **2** badness, evil, wickedness; **pembusukan 1** decaying; **2** putrefaction, spoiling.

busung 1 bloated, edema; **busung lapar** bloating because of starvation; **2** bulging, packed full; **membusung** to be bloated, to be distended, to be puffed up; **membusungkan 1** to inflate, to pump up; **2** to puff up; **Anda boleh bangga dengan prestasi Anda tapi jangan terlalu membusungkan dada** you may be proud of your achievement but don't get too conceited.

busur 1 archer's bow; **2** arc, arch.

buta blind, sightless; **buta ayam 1** near-sighted; **2** twilight blindness; **buta warna** colour blind; **buta huruf** illiterate; **buta tuli** blind and deaf; **membabi buta** rage; **kebutahurufan** illiteracy; **membutakan** to make blind; **kebutaan 1** blindness, sightlessness; **2** darkness.

butir 1 grain, granule, pellet; **butir padi** grain of rice; **2** small object.

butuh necessity, need; **membutuhkan** to need, to require; **saya tidak membutuhkan apa-apa** I don't need anything; **kebutuhan** necessity, need; **kebutuhan pokok** basic necessities.

butut not in a good condition, old, worn and faded.

buyar spread, vanish into thin air *(hope)*; **harapan saya buyar** my hopes have vanished; **membuyarkan** to disperse; **sentuhan tangan Fitri membuyarkan lamunan saya** the touch of Fitri's hand scattered my daydreams.

buyut great grandchildren; **Pangeran William dan Pangeran Harry adalah buyut Raja George VI** Prince William and Prince Harry are the great grandchildren of King George VI.

C c

cabai chilli; **cabai merah** red chilli; **cabai rawit** small, very hot chilli; **kecil-kecil cabai rawit** small but brave or tough.

cabang 1 branch, bough; **2** *(office)* branch; **cabang kita di Blitung** our Blitung branch; **3** *(in the road)* fork; **4** *(club)* affiliate; **bercabang 1** to have branches; **2** to branch off.

cabik 1 ripped, torn; **2** piece, strip; **tercabik-cabik 1** ripped, torn; **cobak-cabik** in rags; **mencabik** to tear to pieces; **mencabik-cabik** to shred; **tercabik** to be torn, to get ripped; **cabikan** rip, snag, tear.

cabut yank out, take out; **cabut kartu** draw a card; **mencabut 1** to extract, to pull out; **dokter gigi mencabut semua gigi Firman** the dentist extracted all Firman's teeth; **Nyoman mencabut pistolnya dari sarungnya** Nyoman drew his pistol from its holster; **2** to revoke; **mencabuti** to pluck; **mencabutkan 1** to have someone extract, to pull out; **Firman ke dokter gigi untuk mencabutkan semua giginya** Firman had the dentist extract all his teeth; **2** to extract, to pull; **pencabut** something or someone that pulls things out; **pencabut bulu** tweezers; **pencabutan 1** annulment, cancellation; **2** extraction.

cacah amount, number; **cacah jiwa** census; **cacah, cacahan** cut up; **daging cacah, cacahan daging** minced meat; **mencacah** to chop into bits *(for example, food)*.

cacar smallpox; **cacar air** chicken pox; **mencacar** to vaccinate.

cacat 1 deformity; **cacat mata, cacat penglihatan** impaired eyesight; **penderita cacat, penyandang cacat** invalid; **2** flawed; **bercacat 1** disabled, handicapped; **2** defective; **mobil bercacat** defective car; **mencacat** to criticize, to find fault; **mencacati** to damage, to injure; **cacatan** criticism, **pencacat** critic; **pencacatan** disfigurement.

caci abuse with words; **cacimaki** curses and

a b c d e f g h i j k l m n o p q r s t u v w x y z

a b c d e f g h i j k l m n o p q r s t u v w x y z

obscenities; **mencacimaki** to curse, to scold.

cacing maggot, worm; **bercacing, cacingan** to have (intestinal) worms.

cadang, suku cadang spare parts; **mencadangkan** to reserve; **mencadangkan tempat untuk presiden** to reserve a place for the president; **cadangan** backup, spare; **kami ada beberapa disket sebagai cadangan** we have some spare disks; **pemain cadangan** reserve player *(for a match)*; **pencadangan** putting by as a reserve.

cadok *(colloquial)* myopic, near-sighted.

cagar guarantee, security; **cagar alam** nature reserve.

cahaya 1 glow; **mengeluarkan cahaya** to radiate; **2** light; **3** ray; **cahaya kilat** flash of lightning; **berkas cahaya** a band of light; **cahaya silau** glare; **bercahaya** gleaming, luminous, shining,; **bercahayakan** reflect light; **mencahayai 1** to illuminate, to shed light on; **2** to expose *(film)*; **pencahayaan 1** illumination, lighting; **2** exposure *(of a film)*.

cair 1 fluid, liquid; **2** diluted, thin; **mencair** to dissolve, to melt; **permen itu mencair dalam mulut** the sweet just melts in your mouth; **gula mencair dalam air** sugar dissolves in water; **mencairkan 1** to melt; **dia mencairkan mentega dalam panci** he melted the butter in a saucepan; **2** to dilute, to water down; **cairan** liquid; **pencair** solvent; **pencairan** liquefying.

cakap¹ 1 able, capable, clever; **2** good-looking; **kecakapan** ability, skill.

cakap², bercakap to speak, to talk; **bercakap-cakap** to have a conversation, to have a chat; **mempercakapkan** to discuss, to talk about; **percakapan 1** conversation; **2** discussion.

cakar 1 claw, talon; **2** paw; **bercakar-cakaran** to claw each other; **mencakar** to claw, to scratch; **cakaran 1** scratches; **2** clawing; **pencakar** rasp, scraper; **pencakar langit** skyscraper.

cakram 1 disk; **2** *(sport)* discus; **lempar cakram** discus throw.

cakrawala 1 heavens, sky; **di bawah cakrawala** under the sky; **2** rotation of planets and stars.

cakup, mencakup 1 to seize, to snap at; **2** to arrest, to round up; **3** to embrace, to include; **mencakupi** to embrace, to include; **tercakup 1** rounded up; **2** caught up in; **3** covered, protected; **tercakup oleh asuransi** covered by insurance; **cakupan 1** scope; **2** low quality because randomly selected; **pencakup** trap; **pencakupan** coverage.

calo 1 person who looks for passengers for public vehicles; **2** ticket scalper; **3** parking attendant *(using standover tactics)*.

calon 1 candidate, prospective; **calon istri, calon suami** prospective wife/husband; **2** applicant; **calon prajurit** military recruit; **mencalonkan** nominate for office; **pencalonan** nomination.

cam, mencamkan to note, to observe carefully; **dia mencamkan nasihat gurunya** he/she paid close attention to his/her teacher's advice.

camat subdistrict head; **kecamatan** subdistrict.

campak measles.

camping, compang-camping in rags, tattered.

campur 1 blended, mixed; **campur aduk** confused, mixed up; **campur baur** associated with, mixed up with; **bercampur baur** associate with; **mencampurbaurkan** to mix up; **pencampurbauran** mixing up; **2** to get involved; **turut, ikut campur** interfere; **jangan ikut campur!** mind your own business!; **bercampur** mixed with; **mentega bercampur gula** butter mixed with sugar; **mencampur** to mix together, to blend; **mencampuri 1** to adulterate, to mix into; **2** to interfere; **mencampurkan** to blend, to adulterate; **tercampur** to get something mixed into it; **kelihatan cat putih ini tercampur cat kuning** it looks as if there's some yellow paint mixed in with the white; **campuran 1** intervention, interference, meddling; **2** alloy, mixture; **3** medley; **percampuran 1** interference, meddling; **2** social intercourse; **3** blending, mixing.

canda, bercanda to joke, to tease

candi Hindu shrine or ancient Buddhist temple.

candu opium; **kecanduan** addicted; **kecanduan rokok**

a b c d e f g h i j k l m n o p q r s t u v w x y z

a b c d e f g h i j k l m n o p q r s t u v w x y z

addicted to smoking; **pecandu 1** opium addict; **pecandu narkotika** a drug addict; **2** fan, follower; **dia pecandu sepak bola** she's a fanatical football fan.

canggung 1 awkward, clumsy; **2** ill at ease; **kecanggungan** awkwardness, clumsiness.

cangkir cup, small mug.

cangkuk graft, transplant; **cangkuk ginjal** kidney transplant; **mencangkukkan** to transplant, to graft; **cangkukan** a transplant; **pencangkukan** transplanting.

cangkul hoe, mattock; **mencangkul** to hoe; **mencangkuli** to break up with a hoe; **pencangkul** someone who hoes; **pencangkulan** hoeing.

cantik beautiful, pretty; **perempuan cantik** a beautiful woman; **cantik molek** very beautiful or attractive; **mempercantik** to beautify; **kecantikan** attractiveness, beauty; **salon kecantikan** beauty salon

canting 1 small dipper for applying wax when making batik; **2** water scoop made of bamboo.

cantol *(colloquial)* hook; **mencantolkan** to hook, to attach to.

cantum, mencantumi dengan to add on to; **mencantumkan 1** to include; **Pak Rudi mencantumkan nama saya di dafter itu** Pak Rudi put my name on the list; **2** to attach, to pin on; **tercantum pada 1** added to, included; **nama Murdani tercantum pada artikel ini** Murdani's name is in this article; **2** attached, inserted; **pencantuman** attachment, inclusion.

cap 1 seal, stamp; **cap jari** fingerprint; **2** brand name, trademark; **cap dagang** trademark; **3** printed; **batik cap** printed batik; **mengecap 1** to place a seal on, to stamp; **2** to brand, stigmatize; **mengecapi 1** to attach a seal or label; **2** to label as; **mengecapkan 1** to have something stamped on; **2** to stamp.

capai[1], mencapai 1 to reach out for and touch; **2** to attain, to reach; **mencapai tujuannya** to achieve the aim; **mencapai keputusan** to reach a decision; **mencapai puncak** to reach the top; **pencapaian** achievement, achieving.

capai², **cape** *(colloquial)* exhausted, tired; **kecapaian** **1** fatigue, weariness; **2** fatigued, worn out.

capcai **1** chop suey; **2** hodge-podge, mish-mash.

caping cone-shaped bamboo sun hat used by farmers working in the rice fields.

caplok, mencaplok **1** to gobble up, to gulp down; **adik saya mencaplok kembang gula saya** *(colloquial)* my brother gobbled up my candy; **2** to annex; **pada masa lampau Uni Sovyet mencaplok Latvia, Lithuania dan Estonia** in the past the Soviet Union annexed Latvia, Lithuania and Estonia.

capung dragonfly.

cara **1** manner, method, way; **cara berbicara,** a way of talking; **dia mengerjakannya menurut caranya sendiri** he does it his way; **2** fashion, style; **cara hidup yang sehat** a healthy lifestyle; **secara** **1** in a ... manner; **secara damai** in a peaceful way; **secara resmi** officially; **2** on a ... scale; **secara kecil-kecilan** on a small scale.

cari look for; **cari gampang** looking for the easiest way; **mencari** to hunt, to look for, to seek; **saya sedang mencari arloji baru saya** I'm searching for my new watch; **mencari kata dalam kamus** to look up a word in the dictionary; **mencarikan** to look for or seek something for someone; **tolong carikan anjing itu** could you look for the dog (for me) please? **pencari** seeker; **pencari pekerjaan** job seeker; **mata pencarian** livelihood; **peternakan adalah mata pencarian yang penting bagi orang Timor** raising livestock is an important way of making a living for the Timorese.

carik ripped, torn *(of paper, cloth)*; **secarik kertas** a piece of paper; **carikan** a piece torn off; **carikan kertas** a scrap of paper.

carter, mencarter to charter; **carteran** chartered; **bis carteran** chartered bus.

cat paint; **cat air** watercolours, water-based paint; **'cat basah'** 'wet paint'; **cat rambut** hair dye; **mengecat** to paint; **saya mau mengecat rambut saya merah muda** I'm going to dye my hair pink.

catat note, record; **mencatat** to make a note of, to record; **saya mencatat namanya**

a b c d e f g h i j k l m n o p q r s t u v w x y z

a b c d e f g h i j k l m n o p q r s t u v w x y z

I wrote down her name; **tercatat 1** noted down, recorded; **2** registered; **surat tercatat** registered letter; **hari terpanas yang pernah tercatat** the hottest day on record; **catatan** note, documentation; **pencatat** registrar; **pencatatan** registration.

catur chess; **main catur** to play chess; **pecatur** chess player; **percaturan** game of chess.

cebol dwarf.

cecap, mencecap to taste.

cedera 1 be faulty, flawed; **2** injured; **kakinya cedera** he has a crook leg; **mencederai** to do irreparable damage, to injure.

cegah, mencegah to prevent; **pencegah** preventative; **pencegahan** prevention; **pencegahan kerusuhan** prevention of riots.

cegat, mencegat to intercept, to hail, to stop *(a person or taxi)*; **pencegatan** interception.

cek[1] cheque; **membayar dengan cek** to pay by cheque.

cek[2], mengecek to check.

cekatan agile; **kecekatan** agility.

cekcok, bercekcok to quarrel, to squabble; **bercekcokan** squabble with each other; **mempercekcokkan** to bicker about; **percekcokan** quarrel.

cekik, mencekik to strangle; **tercekik** strangled; **cekikan** strangulation; **pencekik** strangler; **pencekikan** strangling, throttling.

cekok medicine given by force; **mencekok** to force a child to take medicine; **cekokan** medicine forced into the throat of a child.

cela disgrace, shame; **bercela** to have shortcomings; **hanya Tuhanlah yang tidak bercela** only God is perfect; **mencela** to blame; **tercela** blameworthy, disgraceful, shameful; **pencela** critic, fault-finder; **pencelaan** blaming, fault-finding.

celah gap, space; **celah gigi** gap between the teeth.

celaka 1 bad luck, unlucky; **2** damnit!; **mencelakakan** to bring misfortune; **kecelakaan** accident, mishap; **kena kecelakaan** to have an accident; **kecelakaan di jalan** a road accident; **kecelakaan mobil** a car accident; **kecelakaan serius** a serious accident.

celana pants, trousers; **celana dalam** panties, underpants; **celana jeans** jeans; **celana renang, celana mandi** bathers, swimming trunks; **bercelana** to wear trousers.

celeng boar; **menyelengi uang** to put money in a piggybank; **celengan** **1** savings; **2** money box, piggy bank.

celup, mencelup **1** to dip, to immerse; **teh celup** teabag tea; **2** to dye; **celupan** **1** dyed article; **2** dyeing; **pencelupan** **1** immersion; **2** dyeing.

cemar **1** dirty, filthy; **2** *(reputation)* blackened; **mencemari** **1** to soil, to stain; **2** to defile, to desecrate; **mencemarkan** **1** to make dirty, to soil; **mencemarkan udara** to pollute the air; **2** to cast aspersions; **mencemarkan nama baik** to stain a reputation; **tercemar** dirtied, polluted; **seluruh masyarakat marah karena candi itu tercemar** the whole community was angry because the temple was desecrated; **pencemaran** **1** pollution; **pencemaran udara** air pollution; **2** vilification.

cemas **1** disturbed, worried; **kami merasa cemas tentang Putri** we're worried about Putri; **2** discouraged; **mencemaskan** **1** to alarm, to disturb; **apa yang mencemaskan anjing itu?** what's alarmed the dog?; **2** to worry about, to fear; **tidak ada apa-apa yang mencemaskan** there's nothing to cause worry; **kecemasan** anxiety,worry.

cemberut glum, sullen.

cemburu envious, jealous; **pencemburu** jealous person.

cemerlang **1** shine, sparkle; **bersih cemerlang** squeaky clean; **2** bright, dazzling; **kemeja yang kuning cemerlang** a bright yellow shirt; **mencemerlangkan** to brighten, to dazzle; **kecemerlangan** **1** glitter, glow, lustre; **2** glory; **3** brilliance.

cemeti whip; **mencemeti** to whip.

cemooh, cemoohan ridicule, scorn; **mencemoohkan** to mock, to jeer at.

cendana yellow sandalwood.

cendekia **1** educated; **2** clever, shrewd; **kaum cerdik cendekia** the educated people, the intellectuals; **cendekiawan** **1** an intellectual; **2** the educated class.

a b c d e f g h i j k l m n o p q r s t u v w x y z

cenderamata souvenir, memento.

cenderawasih bird of paradise.

cenderung disposed, inclined; **dia cenderung untuk berbicara banyak** he tends to talk a lot; **kecenderungan 1** inclination, preference; **2** tendency, willingness; **3** trend.

cengang, tercengang astonished, surprised.

cengeng be a crybaby, to snivel or whine; **kecengengan** sentimentality, soppiness.

cengkeram, mencengkeram to grip, to seize; **di lambang negara RI burung Garuda mencengkeram pita** in the state emblem of the Republic of Indonesia the eagle grips the tape; **cengkeraman** grip.

cengkeh, cengkih clove; **bercengkeh** spiced with cloves.

centong 1 ladle; **2** dipper with handle; **mencentong** to ladle out.

cepat fast, quick, speedy; **mobil cepat** a fast car; **makin cepat makin baik** the faster the better; **cepat-cepat** very quickly; **Pandu dibawa cepat-cepat ke rumah sakit** Pandu was rushed to hospital; **secepat** as quickly as; **secepat mungkin** as quickly as possible; **Ron membuat salad secepat kilat** Ron made a salad in a flash; **mencepatkan, mempercepat** to accelerate, to speed up; **Yahya mempercepat mobilnya untuk melewati truk** Yahya speeded up to overtake the truck; **mempercepat tanggal berangkat** to advance the date of departure; **kecepatan 1** speed, velocity; **batas kecepatan** speed limit; **melampaui batas kecepatan** to exceed the speed limit, speeding; **pada kecepatan tertinggi** at top speed; **2** too fast; **percepatan 1** acceleration, speeding up; **2** velocity.

cepret clicking sound *(for example, a camera)*; **mencepret** to take a photo.

cerah 1 bright and clear; **cuaca cerah** fine weather; **masa cerah** a sunny spell; **masa depan Australia cerah** Australia has a bright future; **2** beaming, happy; **ketika mendengar bahwa dia lulus dengan gilang-gemilang, dia keluar dengan wajah cerah**

when he heard that he had a brilliant pass, he came out with a beaming face; **mencerahkan** to brighten, to illuminate; **mencerahkan suasana** to brighten the atmosphere; **kecerahan** **1** brightness, radiance; **2** sharpness *(of a photo)*; **pencerah** brightening agent; **pencerahan** enlightenment.

cerai **1** divorce; **2** separate; **bercerai** **1** to be divorced; **2** to part, to separate; **menceraikan** **1** to divorce; **2** to separate something from something else; **tercerai** separated; **anak ayam itu tercerai dari induknya** the chicken has become separated from its mother; **perceraian** divorce, separation.

ceramah public lecture, talk; **saya mendengarkan ceramahnya semalam** I heard her lecture last night; **berceramah** to give a public lecture; **menceramahkan** to lecture on; **dia akan menceramahkan tarian Bali** she'll be giving a talk on Balinese dance.

cerdas **1** intelligent; **2** clever, mentally agile, shrewd; **dia tidak begitu cerdas** he's not very bright; **mencerdaskan** to develop your mind; **kecerdasan** **1** intelligence; **2** shrewdness.

cerdik clever, cunning,tricky; **kecerdikan** cleverness, cunning, shrewdness.

cerek, ceret kettle, watering can.

cerewet **1** fussy, hard to please; **orang cerewet** grumbler; **2** talkative; **orang cerewet** talkative person.

ceria **1** clean, pure; **2** cloudless; **3** cheerful; **bersifat ceria menghadapi suatu kejadian** cheerful in the face of an incident; **menceriakan** to cleanse, to purify; **keceriaan** happiness, purity.

cerita, ceritera narrative, story; **cerita bersambung** serial story; **cerita burung** gossip, rumour; **cerita pendek (cerpen)** short story; **bercerita** to relate, to tell a story; **orang yang bercerita** narrator, storyteller; **menceritai** to tell; **apakah Anda sudah menceritai Sara tentang Rudi?** have you told Sara about Rudi?; **menceritakan** to narrate, to tell; **apakah Sara sudah menceritakan hal itu kepada Achmad?** has Sara told Achmad about that matter?

cermat accurate, neat; **mencermati** to attend closely to; **kecermatan** accuracy, neatness.

cermin mirror; **saya lihat wajah saya di cermin** I looked at myself in the mirror; **bercermin 1** to have mirrors; **2** to look in the mirror; **mencerminkan** to mirror, to reflect; **tercermin** mirrored, reflected; **cerminan** reflection; **pencerminan** mirroring, reflecting.

cerna digested; **mencerna** to absorb, to digest, to take in; **mencernakan banyak informasi dalam waktu yang pendek** to take in a large amount of information in a short time; **tercerna** digestible; **pencernaan** digestion.

cerutu cigar.

cetak form, mould; **bercetak** printed; **huruf yang bercetak miring** printed in italics; **mencetak 1** to print *(books, etc.)*; **2** to cast, to mould; **3** to score *(in sport)*; **Goenawan mencetak gol** Goenawan scored a goal; **mencetakkan** to print; **cetakan 1** printing; **2** mould; **pencetak** printer; **pencetakan** printing process; **percetakan** printing house, press.

cetus, mencetus to burst out, to flash; **hanya kata-kata itu yang mencetus dari mulut Syariffudin** only those words came out of Syariffudin's mouth; **mencetuskan** to ignite, to light; **tercetus** sparked; **gagasan itu tercetus dengan tiba-tiba** the idea came suddenly; **cetusan** spark, flash; **pencetus** impetus, originator of an idea; **pencetusan** kindling.

cewek *(colloquial)* girl.

cicak house lizard.

cicil, mencicil to pay in instalments; **cicilan** instalment; **cicilan bulanan** a monthly payment; **pencicilan, penyicilan** paying in instalments.

cicip, mencicip to taste *(when preparing food)*; **mencicipi** to nibble, to taste; **cicipan** sample for tasting; **pencicip, penyicip** taster.

cicit great grandchild.

ciduk, menciduk 1 to arrest; **mereka menciduk aktivis itu** they arrested the activists; **2** to scoop up; **menciduk nasi** to scoop up rice; **cidukan** scoop; **cidukan nasi** rice spoon.

Cina China, Chinese; **bahasa Cina** Chinese *(language)*;

makanan khas Cina a specifically Chinese meal.

cincang to chop, to mince; **daging cincang** minced meat; **mencincang** to chop up; **cincangan** something minced, chopped up.

cincin 1 ring; **cincin kawin** wedding ring; **cincin pertunangan** engagement ring; **tukar cincin** to get engaged; **2** washer for bolts, taps, etc.

cingcong fuss; **jangan banyak cingcong** don't be difficult, don't make a fuss.

cinta love; **cinta kasih** fondness; **cinta monyet** puppy love; **jatuh cinta** to fall in love; **bercinta-cintaan** to love each other; **mencintai** to love; **Brendon mencintai Danielle** Brendon loves Danielle; **pecinta** lover; **percintaan** love.

cipta 1 creativity; **daya cipta** creation; **2** idea, thought; **mencipta 1** to compose; **2** to be creative; **menciptakan 1** to create, to conceive, to produce; **menciptakan rekor** to set a record; **ciptaan** creation, composition; **pencipta 1** creator, maker; **2** author, composer; **penciptaan** creating, composing.

ciri 1 characteristic; **ciri khas** specific characteristic; **2** identifying mark; **ciri-ciri** identity; **bercirikan** to be characterized by; **mencirikan** to characterize.

cita feeling, sense; **cita rasa** flavour, taste; **cita-cita** ambitions, goals; **bercita-citakan** to desire, to long for, to have as a goal.

citra image.

cium 1 smell; **2** kiss; **bercium-(cium)an, cium-ciuman** to kiss each other; **mencium 1** to kiss; **dia mencium adiknya** she/he gave her/his little brother/sister a kiss; **2** to smell, to sniff; **saya tidak dapat mencium apa-apa** I can't smell anything; **saya bisa mencium bau melati** I can smell jasmine; **menciumi** to kiss repeatedly; **ibu menciumi anaknya yang baru lahir** the mother kissed her newborn baby over and over; **tercium** kissed, sniffed *(accidentally)*; **ciuman** kiss; **penciuman** act of kissing.

ciut, menciut to shrink; **kaos kaki saya menciut, kaos kaki saya menjadi ciut** my socks shrank.

coba 1 attempt, try; **2** try out; **3** *(colloquial)* please; **coba dengarkan! lagu apa ini?** please listen! what song is

a b c d e f g h i j k l m n o p q r s t u v w x y z

this?; **4** *(as a challenge, colloquial)* just try; **coba! yakinkan saya!** go on! convince me!; **mencoba 1** to attempt, to try; **2** to test; **mereka mencoba mobil baru** they tested the new car; **mencoba-coba** to try over and over; **cobaan 1** test; **2** ordeal, trial; **pencoba 1** someone who tests; **2** tempter; **percobaan 1** trial, experiment; **melakukan percobaan** to do an experiment; **2** temptation; **3** attempt; **pada percobaan pertama** at the first attempt **percobaan nekat** a desperate attempt.

cobak-cabik in rags; **bajunya cobak-cabik** his clothes were in rags.

cocok 1 compatible, fit, suitable; **mebel itu tidak cocok dengan gorden** the furniture clashes with the curtains; **itu kurang cocok** they don't combine well; **kunci ini tidak cocok dengan gembok ini** the key doesn't fit the padlock; **2** correct; **apakah jam itu cocok?** is that clock right?; **3** like, be happy with; **kalau cocok, pakai saja** if you like it, just wear it; **4** agree; **cocok!** agreed!, OK!; **mencocokkan 1** to compare; **2** to adjust; **mencocokkan tingginya** to adjust the height; **3** to correct; **mencocokkan jam** to set the clock right; **mencocokkan arlodji-arlodji** to synchronize watches; **kecocokan** agreement, compatibility, harmony; **pencocokan** checking, verification.

cokelat, coklat 1 brown; **coklat muda** light brown; **coklat tua** dark brown; **2** chocolate; **kecoklat-coklatan** brownish.

coleng, mencoleng to hold up, to steal; **pencoleng** a thief.

colok[1], mencolok, menyolok striking; **persamaan yang menyolok** a striking resemblance.

colok[2], mencolok to poke with your finger, to poke your finger into; **kecolok** to get something poked into it; **mata kucing itu kecolok kayu** the cat got poked in the eye with a stick.

compang-camping in rags.

congkak arrogant, proud.

contoh 1 sample, specimen; **2** design, pattern; **3** example; **sebagai contoh** as an example; **memberikan contoh yang baik** to set a good example; **mencontoh 1** to copy, to imitate; **ada banyak orang yang mencontoh Elvis** there are many Elvis imitators; **2** to copy *(an essay, for example).*

copet pickpocket; **mencopet** to pick pockets; **kecopetan** to have your pocket picked; **dia kecopetan dompetnya** he had his wallet picked out of his pocket; **pencopet, tukang copet** pickpocket; **pencopetan** pickpocketing.

copot 1 dislodged; **semua orang mentertawakannya karena kondenya copot** everyone laughed at her because her hairpiece was dislodged; **2** detached; **mencopot 1** to take off *(shoes, for example)*; **2** to pull out, to extract; **3** to remove, to take away; **Presiden mencopot Menteri Penerangan dari kedudukannya** the President removed the Minister of Information from his position; **mencopotkan** to take something off; **pencopotan** dismissal, firing, removal.

corak design, pattern; **bercorak** to have the design of; **rumah bercorak Dayak** a Dayak-style longhouse.

coret 1 scratch; **2** smear, streak; **coret-coret** doodling, graffiti; **mencoret** to scratch out, to strike through; **mencoret-coret** to jot down, to scribble; **mencoreti 1** to streak repeatedly; **2** to scribble on; **tercoret** marked, streaked; **coretan 1** line, scratch, stripe; **2** graffiti; **pencoretan** scratching out.

corong 1 *(for pouring things)* funnel; **2** *(for ventilation)* shaft; **corong pengeras suara** microphone.

cowok *(colloquial)* boy.

cuaca weather; **prakiraan cuaca, ramalan cuaca** weather forecast; **menurut prakiraan cuaca akan hujan** the weather forecast says it will rain.

cubit, mencubit to pinch; **mencubit bayi** to pinch the baby; **bercubitan** to pinch each other; **cubitan** a pinch.

cuci wash; **mencuci 1** to do the washing, to wash; **mencuci tangan** to wash your hands; **mencuci piring** to do the washing up; **mencuci pakaian** to do the washing; **2** to develop *(a film)*; **mencucikan** to wash; **cucian 1** laundry; **2** washing; **pencuci 1** laundry person; **2** washing agent; **pencuci mulut** dessert.

a b c d e f g h i j k l m n o p q r s t u v w x y z

a b c d e f g h i j k l m n o p q r s t u v w x y z

cucu grandchild; **bercucu** to have a grandchild or grandchildren; **anak cucu** descendants.

cucur, bercucuran to flow, to gush; **bercucuran darah** bleeding; **air bercucuran dari rambutnya** the water streamed off her hair; **mencucurkan** to cause to flow; **mencucurkan darah** to shed blood.

cucut, ikan cucut shark.

cuil, mencuil to break up food using your hand; **secuil ikan** a piece of fish.

cuka vinegar.

cukai customs duty, excise.

cukup 1 enough, sufficient; **makanan itu cukup untuk semua orang** there's enough food for everyone; **cukuplah!** that's enough!; **sudah cukup, terima kasih** thank you, that's plenty; **2** quite; **hawanya cukup panas** it's quite hot; **secukupnya** sufficient; **tambah garam secukupnya** add salt to taste; **mencukupi 1** to make up a lack; **2** to fulfil; **3** to be sufficient; **mencukupkan 1** to make sufficient; **2** to make do with; **mencukup cukupkan** to try to make ends meet; **kecukupan 1** sufficiency; **2** having enough to live on.

cukur, alat cukur razor, shaver; **tukang cukur** barber; **bercukur 1** shave; **2** have a shave; **dia sedang bercukur** he's having a shave; **mencukur** to shave; **mencukur bulu kaki** to shave your legs; **mencukur habis jenggotnya** to shave off your beard; **pencukuran** shaving, trimming down.

culik, menculik to kidnap; **penculik** kidnapper; **penculikan** abduction, kidnapping.

cuma 1 merely, only; **saya cuma membeli satu** I only bought one; **2** but, only; **saya ingin jalan, cuma sekarang hujan** I'd walk, only it's raining; **percuma** in vain, useless; **percuma saya datang** there's no point in my coming; **cuma-cuma** free, free of charge; **saya mendapatkan karcis cuma-cuma** I got a ticket for free.

cumi-cumi squid.

cungkil crowbar, lever; **cungkil gigi** toothpick; **mencungkil** to prise up or off; **ia mencungkil akar pohon besar itu** he prised up the root of the big tree.

cupet narrow-minded.

curah hujan rainfall; **mencurahkan 1** to pour

something on; **dia mencurahkan minjak ke badan sendiri** he poured oil on himself; **2** to expend, to lavish; **anak saya mencurahkan perhatian kepada pelajarannya** my child is devoting her/his attention to her/his studies; **Sukirah mencurahkan isi hatinya kepada saya** Sukirah confided in me; **tercurah(kan) 1** poured; **2** focused; **perhatiannya hanya tercurah(kan) pada bayinya** all his attention was focused on his baby; **curahan 1** precipitation; **2** outflow, outpouring; **pencurahan 1** outpouring; **2** giving.

curam precipitous, sheer, steep; **kecuraman** steepness.

curang deceitful, dishonest; **kecurangan 1** deceit, fraud; **2** corruption; **3** *(of sport)* foul.

curi, mencuri to rob, to steal; **ada yang mencuri makan siang saya** somebody's pinched my lunch; **dia dituduh mencuri** she was accused of theft; **kecurian** be robbed; **Afandi kecurian lukisannya** Afandi was robbed of his paintings; **barang curian** stolen goods; **pencuri** thief; **pencurian** robbery.

curiga suspicious; **Meity merasa curiga ketika tamunya pergi ke belakang** Meity became suspicious when her visitor went to the toilet; **mencurigai** to distrust, to suspect; **mencurigakan** to arouse suspicion; **gerak-gerik tamu itu mencurigakan Meity** her guest's movements aroused Meity's suspicions; **paket yang mencurigakan** a suspicious parcel; **kecurigaan** distrust, suspicion.

cuti leave, holidays; **cuti dinas** official leave; **cuti sakit** sick leave; **cuti tahunan** annual leave; **cuti hamil** maternity leave.

D d

dada breast, chest; **buah dada** breasts.

dadak, mendadak sudden; **meninggal dengan mendadak** to die suddenly.

dadar fry a mixture *(for example, an omelette or a pancake)*; **telur dadar** omelette; **mendadar telur** to make an omelette.

a b c d e f g h i j k l m n o p q r s t u v w x y z

dadu **1** dice; **dadu putar** roulette; **bermain dadu** to throw the dice; **2** cube; **3** pink, light red.

daerah **1** area, region, territory; **daerah istimewa** special administrative territory *(for example, DIY Daerah Istimewa Yogyakarta)*; **DKI, Daerah Khusus Ibukota** municipality of Jakarta; **daerah mewah** an expensive area; **daerah kumuh** slum area; **2** outlying district; **di daerah pinggiran Jakarta** on the outskirts of Jakarta; **sedaerah** of the same region.

daftar list, roster; **daftar abjad** alphabetical list; **daftar absensi** roll, roster; **daftar hitam** blacklist; **mendaftarhitamkan** to blacklist; **daftar kelahiran** registry of births; **daftar penunjuk** index; **daftar barang yang dapat dipesan melalui pos** a mail-order catalogue; **membuat daftar** to make a list, to register a large number; **mendaftar** to enrol, to register; **saya ingin mendaftar untuk kursus itu** I want to enrol in the course; **mendaftarkan 1** to register; **2** to enrol; **saya ingin mendaftarkan diri untuk kursus itu** I want to enrol in the course; **terdaftar** enrolled, registered; **pendaftar** registrar; **pendaftaran 1** registration process; **2** registry.

dagang commerce, trade; **surat dagang** a business letter; **berdagang** be in business, deal, trade; **dia berdagang tekstil** she's in the textile business; **dia sedang berdagang di Dubbo** she's on business in Dubbo; **memperdagangkan, mendagangkan** to trade in; **Makmur mendagangkan saham** Makmur trades in stocks and shares; **dagangan** merchandise; **pedagang** business person, merchant, trader; **perdagangan** commerce, trade.

daging **1** meat; **2** flesh; **mendarah-daging** to run in your blood.

dagu chin.

dahaga thirsty, to be thirsty; **dahaga akan** to thirst for; **dia sangat dahaga akan ilmu pengetahuan** he is thirsty for knowledge.

dahak phlegm; **berdahak, mendahak** to cough up phlegm and spit it out.

dahan bough, branch.

dahi forehead.

dahsyat 1 horrifying, terrifying; **2** awe-inspiring, enormous, powerful; **menjadi dahsyat** to get worse, become terrifying; **kedahsyatan** awesomeness.

dahulu (dulu) previous, used to; **kemarin dulu** the day before yesterday; **dulu dia merokok** she used to smoke; **dahulu (dulu) mereka tinggal di Surabaya** they used to live in Surabaya; **lebih dahulu** before; **dia berangkat lebih dahulu** she left before (us or anyone else); **dahulu-mendahulu(i)** to race each other; **mendahului 1** to precede; **regu kita mendahului dengan sepuluh angka** our team is ten points ahead; **2** to pass by; **dilarang saling mendahului** forbidden to overtake one another; **mendahulukan** to give precedence to; **terdahulu 1** first; **2** earlier; **kedahuluan 1** to be outstripped; **2** to be late; **pendahulu** pioneer, predecessor; **kata pendahuluan** introduction *(in a book)*; **pemeriksaan pendahuluan** preliminary investigation.

daki[1] dirt on the skin.

daki[2], **mendaki** to climb (a hill or mountain); **pendaki** climber; **pendakian 1** pass; **2** path or steps; **pendakian di gunung Bromo** the steps up Mt Bromo; **3** climbing; **cukup perlengkapan untuk pendakian itu** well equipped for the climb.

dakwa accusation, charge, indictment; **surat dakwa** summons, writ; **mendakwa 1** to accuse, to charge; **2** to sue; **terdakwa** the accused, defendant; **dakwaan** accusation; **pendakwa** plaintiff, accuser; **pendakwaan** accusation, charge, indictment.

dalam 1 inside, interior; **bagian dalam oven** the inside of the oven; **di dalam ruang kelas** inside the classroom; **kami semua masuk ke dalam mobil** we all got into the car; **2** in, within; **dalam surat kabar** in the newspaper; **menerjemahkan ke dalam bahasa Indonesia** to translate into Indonesian; **dalam bulan Mei** in May; **dalam foto** in the photo; **3** deep; **sungai ini dalam sekali** this river is very deep; **4** serious, thoughtful; **dalam-dalam** very deep; **dalamnya, kedalaman** depth; **berapa dalamnya kolam renang ini?** how deep is the swimming pool?; **mendalam 1** to become deep; **rasa dukacita yang mendalam** a deep feeling of sorrow; **2** to sink in, to penetrate; **3** to deepen, to intensify; **rasa sakitnya makin mendalam** the pain got worse; **mendalami** to obtain a deeper understanding; **memperdalam, mendalamkan 1** to deepen; **memperdalam got** to deepen the drain; **2** to broaden your knowledge; **pedalaman** back country, interior; **tinggal di daerah pedalaman** to live in the country; **pendalaman** deepening; **pendalaman suatu ilmu** deepening of knowledge.

dalang 1 narrator and puppet master of traditional shadow plays; **2** mastermind; **berdalang, mendalang** to perform a shadow play; **mendalangi** to mastermind, to manipulate; **pedalangan 1** relating a shadow play story; **2** puppetry for shadow play.

dalih excuse; **berdalih pada** to look for an excuse.

dalil argument; theorem; **berdalil** valid; **tak berdalil** groundless, without foundation.

dam dam.

damai peace, peacefulness; **berdamai 1** to be peaceful, be at peace, to make peace; **2** to come to an agreement; **memperdamaikan, mendamaikan** to resolve peacefully, to reconcile; **kedamaian** peacefulness; **pasukan perdamaian** peacekeeping troops; **pendamai** peacemaker.

damba, mendambakan to long for, to yearn; **anak itu mendambakan kasih seorang ibu** the child longed for a mother's love.

dampak impact; **laporan dampak lingkungan** environmental impact report; **berdampak pada** to have an impact or influence on; **kebakaran hutan itu berdampak buruk pada lingkungan** the forest fire had a terrible impact on the environment.

dampar, terdampar to go aground; **kapal itu terdampar di pulau kecil** the ship ran aground on a small island; **mendamparkan** to cause to go aground; **ombak yang besar telah mendamparkan kapal itu pada batu karang** the huge waves drove the ship onto the coral reef.

damping close, near; **berdamping(an)** side by side; **mendampingi 1** to accompany; **mereka didampingi oleh anak-anaknya** they were accompanied by their children; **2** to stand beside; **3** to closely assist; **anak-anak itu mendampingi bapaknya** the children are at their father's side; **mendampingkan** to move close; **pendamping** associate, colleague, partner; **pendampingan** assistance.

dan and.

dana 1 donation; **2** fund; **dana sosial** social fund; **pendanaan** financing, funding.

danau lake; **di tepi danau** at the edge of the lake.

dandan clothing, grooming, outfit; **berdandan 1** to put on make-up; **2** decorated; **mendandani 1** to dress someone; **ibu mendandani saya dengan pakaian Jawa** mother dressed me up in Javanese dress; **2** to equip; **3** to repair; **dandanan 1** clothing, outfit, **2** make-up; **3** equipment.

dandang rice steamer.

dangau a little shed in the rice paddy where a youngster sits and guards the paddy.

dangkal 1 shallow; **airnya sangat dangkal di sini** the water's very shallow here; **2** superficial; **mendangkalkan 1** to make shallow; **2** to consider trivial; **kedangkalan** shallowness, superficiality; **kedangkalan suatu teory itu** the superficiality of the theory; **pendangkalan 1** silting up; **2** making trivial.

dansa Western-style dancing; **berdansa** to dance; **mari kita berdansa** let's go dancing; **kelas dansa** dancing class; **mendansakan** to dance a certain kind of dance.

dapat 1 to be able to, can; **Eva dapat mengemudi sepeda motor** Eva can ride a motorbike; **laci ini tidak dapat dibuka** the drawer won't open; **2** can, may; **apakah saya dapat membantu Anda?** may I help you?; **dia tak dapat menolong saya** she couldn't help me; **3** to get, to obtain; **sudah dapat pekerjaan, belum?** have you got a job yet?; **4** be found, be obtained; **belum dapat kuncinya** the key hasn't been found; **sedapat-(dapat)nya** as much as you are capable

a b c d e f g h i j k l m n o p q r s t u v w x y z

of; **berusaha sedapat mungkin, berusaha sedapat-dapatnya** to do as much as possible; **dia berusaha sedapat-dapatnya untuk membantu saya** he/she did as much as possible to help me; **mendapat 1** to get, to receive; **mendapat hadiah** to get a prize; **apakah Anda sudah mendapat kabar dari Yanti?** have you heard from Yanti?; **2** to experience, to have; **mendapat kecelakaan** to have an accident; **mendapati 1** to discover, to find; **polisi mendapati kebun ganja** the police found the marijuana plantation; **2** to catch red-handed, to meet up with unexpectedly; **mendapatkan 1** to obtain, to produce; **2** to discover, to invent; **terdapat** to be found, to exist; **gedung itu terdapat di Jalan Thamrin** the building is on Thamrin Street; **kedapatan** be found, be uncovered as; **Mick kedapatan mencuri uang** Mick was caught stealing money; **pendapat** opinion; **menurut pendapat saya** in my opinion, in my view; **pendapat umum** public opinion; **pengumpulan pendapat umum** opinion poll; **sependapat** of the same opinion; **saya tidak sependapat dengan dia** I disagree with her; **berpendapat** to be of a certain opinion; **Didin berpendapat bahwa saya yang salah** Didin thought that I was wrong; **pendapatan 1** earnings, income; **pendapatan tahunan** annual earnings; **2** output, yield; **pendapatan ikan** catch *(of fish)*; **3** *(mathematics)* product, result.

dapur 1 kitchen; **2** kiln, stove.

dara, anak dara virgin, young girl; **burung dara** dove.

darah blood; **darah daging** blood relative; **darah mati** blood clot; **pemeriksaan darah** a blood test; **berdarah 1** to bleed; **hidung saya berdarah** my nose is bleeding; **dia ketularan demam berdarah** he's caught dengue fever; **2** to be of a certain ethnic background; **kami berdarah Indonesia** we have Indonesian blood, we are of Indonesian origin; **3** bloody, gory; **mendarah** to be like blood, to become dark red; **mendarah daging** to run in the blood; **perdarahan** bleeding, haemorrhaging.

darat land, shore; **mendarat** to land, to reach the shore; **kapal terbang mendarat dengan sentakan** the plane landed with a bump; **pilot itu mendarat pada kapal induk** the pilot landed on the aircraft carrier; **mendaratkan 1** to put ashore; **2** to cause to land; **penerbang mendaratkan pesawat terbang di bandara Soekarno Hatta** the pilot landed the plane at Soekarno Hatta airport; **daratan** mainland; **pendaratan** disembarkation, landing; **pendaratan darurat** emergency landing.

dari 1 from; **seratus meter dari kolam renang** 100 metres from the swimming pool; **dia dari Cairns** he comes from Cairns; **di seberang saya** across from me; **2** out of (a series); **tiga dari lima murid** three out of five pupils; **3** starting from or at; **dari jam lima** from five o'clock; **4** than; **lebih dari dua puluh tahun** more than twenty years; **sedari** since; **sedari tadi** since just then.

daripada 1 from; **selain (daripada) Adrie semua orang ada di situ** apart from Adrie everyone was there; **2** than; **lebih panas daripada biasa** hotter than usual; **3** instead of; **daripada main tenis kita lebih baik pergi ke pantai** instead of playing tennis we had better go to the beach.

darma 1 duty, obligation; **2** good deed, service; **darmabakti** volunteer work.

darmawisata excursion, field trip, outing; **berdarmawisata** to go on an excursion.

darurat emergency; **dalam keadaan darurat, pecahkan kaca** in an emergency, break the glass; **pintu darurat** emergency exit; **pendaratan darurat** emergency landing; **bagian gawat darurat** casualty department *(in a hospital)*.

dasa ten; **dasa lomba** decathlon; **dasa sila** ten principles; **dasawarsa** a decade.

dasawarsa decade.

dasar 1 base, basis, foundation, principle; **dasar gedung** building foundation; **dasar danau** the bottom of the lake; **pengetahuan dasar** basic knowledge; **fakta-fakta dasar** the basic facts; **2** nature; **itu sudah dasarnya** that's the way it is; **dasar**

laki-laki! just like a man!, what do you expect of a man!; **3** background; **dasar potret itu kabur** the background of the photo is blurry; **berdasar** having a basis, background; **berdasarkan** based on; **film itu berdasarkan dongeng dari India** the film is based on an Indian legend; **mendasar** to be basic to; **hal-hal yang mendasar** basic things; **mendasari** to be a basis for; **mendasarkan** to base one thing on something else.

dasi necktie; **dasi kupu-kupu** bow tie; **berdasi** wearing a tie.

datang 1 come; **Nick datang naik sepeda** Nick came by bike; **apakah Jason datang ke sekolah kemarin?** did Jason come to school yesterday?; **saya datang!** coming!; **2** arrive; **mereka datang ke Perth kemarin** they arrived in Perth yesterday; **mendatang, yang akan datang** coming, future, next; **mendatangi 1** to pay a call, to visit; **2** to come to; **mendatangkan 1** to have brought in; **2** to import; **3** to cause; **kedatangan 1** arrival; **2** to be unexpectedly visited; **pendatang** outsider, stranger; **pendatang baru** newcomer.

datar 1 flat, level, smooth; **daerah di bagian barat kota Melbourne datar** the area on the western side of Melbourne is flat; **permukaan danau di Altona datar** the surface of the lake at Altona is smooth; **2** superficial; **mendatar** to be level, horizontal; **mendatarkan 1** to make level, to smooth out; **2** to ease *(feelings)*; **kedataran** being level; **dataran** plain; **dataran tinggi** plateau; **dataran rendah** lowland; **pendataran** levelling, smoothing.

datuk 1 headman, oldest male of a clan title; **2** grandfather; **3** respectful term of reference and address for persons of high rank.

daulat, berdaulat 1 sovereign; **Indonesia adalah negara berdaulat** Indonesia is a sovereign nation; **2** to become dominant; **mendaulat 1** to elect by popular choice; **2** to force someone to do; **dia mendaulat saya untuk menari** she forced me to dance; **kedaulatan** sovereignty; **daulat-daulatan**

passing the buck; **pendaulatan** dismissal, firing.

daun **1** leaf; **daun bawang** spring onion; **2** a flat thing; **daun pintu** door, **daun rokok** cigarette paper; **berdaun** to be leafy, have leaves; **daun-daunan** foliage; **daun telinga** ear lobe.

daur, daur ulang recycle.

dawet a kind of cold drink.

daya[1] **1** capacity, energy, power; **barat daya** southwest; **daya atom** atomic energy, atomic power; **daya batin** inner strength; **daya gaib** supernatural power; **daya kuda** horsepower; **daya guna** efficiency; **berdayaguna** efficient, useful; **mendayagunakan** using something efficiently; **kedayagunaan** efficiency, usefulness; **pendayagunaan** making efficient use of; **daya tarik 1** attraction; **2** gravitational force; **2** effort; **memberi daya** to provide power; **berdaya** to exert oneself, to strive for, to do one's best.

daya[2] trick; **mendayakan, memperdayakan, memperdayai** to cheat, to deceive, to fool, to trick; **teperdaya** cheated, deceived, fooled; **saya teperdaya oleh janjinya yang manis itu** I was taken in by his nice promise.

dayung **1** oar; **perahu dayung** rowing boat; **2** *(bicycle)* pedal; **berdayung 1** to row; **giliran Anda untuk berdayung** it's your turn to row; **2** to pedal; **mendayung 1** to go rowing, to row; **saya senang mendayung kano** I enjoy canoeing; **2** to pedal; **pendayung 1** rower; **2** oar.

debar feeling a pulse beat; **debar jantung** heartbeat, pulse; **berdebar-debar** to beat rapidly; **mendebarkan hati** to set the heart beating rapidly; **debaran** beat; **debaran jantung** palpitating.

debat debate; **berdebat** to debate; **mereka berdebat selama tiga jam** they debated for three hours; **memperdebatkan** to debate on; **perdebatan** debate, discussion.

debit debit, overdraft.

debu dust, grit; **berdebu** dusty.

dedak bran.

dedaunan leaves.

defile parade; **berdefile** to parade; **angkatan bersenjata berdefile di depan Istana Merdeka** the armed forces paraded in front of the Freedom Palace.

definisi definition.

degap, berdegap-degap to beat, to palpitate, to pound; **jantungnya berdegap-degap karena takut** his heart pounded with fear.

degar, berdegar to boom, to thunder; booming.

dekadensi decadence.

dekap, berdekap tangan with folded arms; **berdekapan** embracing each other; **mendekap** to embrace, to enclose.

dekar, pendekar 1 expert at sword-fighting or in martial arts; **2** champion.

dekat 1 close by, near; **duduklah dekat saya!** sit by me!; **dekat laut** by the sea; **tidak begitu dekat** not very close; **2** in the vicinity; **apakah ada WC dekat sini?** is there a toilet around here?; **berdekat-dekat 1** be close to each other; **2** to associate; **berdekatan** adjacent; **sekolah kami berdekatan** our schools are nearby; **berdekat-dekatan** side by side; **mendekat** to approach, to come near; **ulang tahun saya sudah mendekat** my birthday is nearly here; **mendekati** to come up to; **mereka mendekati kami** they came close to us; **mendekatkan** to bring close; **memperdekatkan 1** to bring things close to each other; **2** to reconcile; **terdekati** approachable; **kedekatan 1** nearness; **2** too close; **dekatan** *(colloquial)* come closer; **pendekatan 1** approach; **2** reconciliation.

dekil *(colloquial)* dirty.

deking cover, shelter; **mendeking** to defend, to protect; **pemerintah Malaysia mendeking usaha pribumi yang lemah** the Malaysian government is protecting the native enterprises which are weak.

deklamasi declamation.

deklarasi 1 declaration; **2** customs declaration.

dekolonisasi decolonization.

dekor decor, scenery.

dekrit decree.

delapan eight, eighth; **delapan belas** eighteen; **Sarah berumur delapan belas tahun** Sarah's eighteen; **delapan puluh** eighty; **delapan puluh lima** eighty-five; **pada jam delapan** at eight o'clock; **tanggal delapan Juni** the eighth of June; **pada lantai delapan** on the eighth floor;

kedelapan 1 all eight; **2** the eighth; **buku yang kedelapan** the eighth book.

delapan belas eighteen.

delapan puluh eighty.

delegasi delegation; **mendelegasikan** to delegate; **pendelegasian** delegating authority.

delima, buah delima pomegranate.

delman two-wheeled horse-drawn carriage.

demam 1 fever, feverish; **dia ketularan demam berdarah** he's caught dengue fever; **2** fad.

demi 1 for the sake of; **demi kepentingan diri Anda sendiri** for your own sake; **2** *(in oaths)* by; **demi Tuhan** I swear by God; **satu demi satu** one by one; **demi kepentingan nasional** in the national interest; **demi hari depan kita** for our future.

demikian such, such was the case, thus; **saya ingin anjing yang demikian** I want a dog of that sort; **demikianlah ceritanya** that's how her/his story goes; **demikian juga** likewise; **dengan demikian** in such a way, so, thus; **sedemikian** of this sort, of that sort; **sedemikian rupa** in such a way or manner.

demisioner outgoing (cabinet, government).

demokrasi democracy; **berdemokrasi** democratic; **mendemokrasikan** democratize; **pendemokrasian** democratization.

demokrat democrat.

demokratis democratic; **mendemokratiskan** democratize.

demonstrasi **1** demonstration, protest; **2** demonstration *(of equipment etc.)*; **berdemonstrasi** to participate in a demonstration; **berdemonstrasi menentang kenaikan harga** to demonstrate against price rises; **para mahasiswa berdemonstrasi di depan gedung MPR** the students demonstrated in front of the People's Consultative Assembly building; **mendemonstrasi** to demonstrate; **mendemonstrasikan** to demonstrate *(quality etc.)*.

dempet to be attached to, stuck together; **rumah dempet** terrace house; **berdempet** stick together; **berdempet-dempetan** jammed together;

a b c d e f g h i j k l m n o p q r s t u v w x y z

mendempetkan to press together.

dempul caulking, putty; **mendempul** to apply caulking or putty.

denah blueprint, ground plan, sketch.

denda fine; **mendenda** to fine.

dendam 1 revenge; **2** grudge, resentment; **menaruh dendam** to bear a grudge; **Amat menaruh dendam pada saya** Amat bears a grudge against me; **Mahatir saling dendam dengan Asril** Mahatir and Asril have hard feelings towards each other; **mendendam** to resent; **kedendaman** resentment; **pendendam** person who bears a grudge.

dendang, berdendang **mendendangkan** to sing; **pada malam itu kami mendendangkan nyanyian lama** that night we sang old songs

dendeng biltong, jerky meat.

dengan 1 with; **mari pergi dengan kami** come on, go with us; **dengan ini** herewith; **dengan begitu** in that way; **dengan segala senang hati** with pleasure; **dengan tak sengaja** by mistake, not deliberately or intentionally; **2** and; **Rusli dengan teman-temannya** Rusli and his friends; **3** by, with, using; **datang dengan bis** to come by bus; **dengan mobil** by car; **mengocok telur dengan garpu** beat the eggs with a fork; **dengan telepon** by telephone; **4** in a particular way; **dia berbicara dengan logat Australia** he speaks with an Australian accent.

dengar hear; **saya dengar bahwa dia sudah kawin** I heard that she's already married; **mendengar** to hear; **saya tak bisa mendengar apa-apa** I can't hear anything; **saya tidak bisa mendengar Anda** I can't hear you; **mendengarkan 1** to listen to; **mendengarkan musik** to listen to music; **saya mendengarkan ceramahnya semalam** I listened to her lecture last night; **2** to pay attention to; **dengarkanlah dengan teliti** listen carefully; **dengarkanlah dia!** listen to him!; **kedengaran 1** can be heard; **2** seems; **itu kedengarannya benar** that seems right; **pendengar** audience, listener; **pendengaran** hearing, sense of hearing.

denging, berdenging, mendenging to ring, to tingle *(of the ears)*; **telinga saya berdenging** my ear is ringing.

dengki angry or unhappy when someone else is more successful, envy, jealousy, spite; **dengki akan** envious of, to be full of hatred or spite; **kedengkian 1** spite, spitefulness; **2** jealousy; **pendengki** one who is envious and spiteful.

dengking scream, squeal, yelp; **berdengking, mendengking** to scream, to squeal, to yelp.

dengkul knee.

dengkur 1 snore, snoring; **2** grunt; **3** purr; **mendengkur 1** to snore; **2** to grunt; **3** to purr.

dengung buzzing, droning, purring sounds; **dengung, berdengung, mendengung 1** to wail *(siren)*, to drone *(plane)*; **2** to reverberate; **mendengungkan 1** to sound *(a siren or gong)*; **2** to tout, propagandize; **dengungan** wail, drone.

dentam, dentum sound of gunfire, firecrackers, etc.; **berdentam 1** to produce a sound like a shot; **kaca etalase pecah berdentam** the shop window broke with a loud crack; **2** to beat *(for example, heart or drum)*; **mendentamkan** to pound with; **dentaman 1** pounding; **2** sound like shots; **dentaman kaca pecah** a crash of broken glass.

denyut beat, throb; **denyut jantung** heartbeat; **denyut nadi** pulse; **berdenyut** to beat, to throb; **denyutan** beat, throb.

deodoran deodorant.

depak, mendepak 1 to kick; **Carmel mendepak bola ke gawang** Carmel kicked the ball to the goal; **2** to dismiss, to fire, to kick out; **pelatih didepak** the coach was kicked out; **depakan** a kick; **pendepakan 1** kicking; **2** dismissal, expulsion.

depan 1 front; **berdiri di (bagian) depan** standing in the front; **ada tempat duduk di jajaran depan** there's a seat in the front row; **2** coming, next; **minggu depan** next week; **hari Kamis depan** next Thursday; **tahun depan** next year; **3** ahead; **perlahan, jembatan sedang diperbaiki di depan** slow down, bridge repairs ahead.

departemen *(often abbreviated to Dep and attached to other abbreviations)* department, ministry; **Departemen Kesehatan (Depkes)** Department of Health; **Departemen Dalam Negeri (Depdagri)** Department of Internal Affairs; **departemen bahasa Indonesia** Indonesian language department.

depot depot, refreshment stand.

depresi depression *(financial, economic, emotional, mental).*

depresiasi depreciation.

derajat 1 degree; **dua puluh dua derajat Celsius** twenty two degrees Centigrade; **2** rank, level; **3** standard; **sederajat** of the same level or degree.

deras fast-flowing; **hujan deras** heavy rain; **menderas 1** to flow quickly; **2** energetic; **menderaskan** to increase speed of flow; **penderasan** rapids.

derek crane, hoisting machine.

deret line, row; **sederet buku** a row of books; **sederet 1** abreast; **berbaris sederet** to march abreast; **2** a line of; **berderet** in a row, in rows; **berderet-deret** lined up; **orang-orang berderet-deret untuk melihat pawai itu** people lined up for the parade; **mendereti** to line; **jalan itu didereti warung** the road was lined with food stalls; **menderetkan, memperderetkan** to line things or people up; **deretan** line, row; **deret-deretan rumah** lines of houses.

dering 1 tinkling like bells; **2** *(crickets)* sound of chirping; **berdering, mendering 1** to ring, to tinkle; **telepon berdering-dering** the phone was ringing; **2** to clink; **3** to chirp; **deringan** tinkling, clinking noise.

derita suffering; **menderita** to suffer; **menderita kekalahan** to suffer defeat; **menderita kejang di kaki** to have cramp in the leg; **terderitakan** bearable *(of suffering)*; **penderita** sufferer, victim; **penderita cacat** disabled person, invalid, physically handicapped; **penderitaan** suffering.

derma alms, donation; **derma korban kebakaran** donation for the fire victims; **berderma** to give a donation; **mendermakan** to donate; **penderma** donor; **penderma darah** blood donor; **pendermaan** act of donating; **dermawan** donor, philanthropist; **kedermawanan** charity, philanthropy.

dermaga pier, quay.

deru sound made by thunder, planes, etc.; **berderu, menderu** to howl, to roar *(wind)*.

desa village; **desa teladan** model village; **alun-alun desa** the village square; **kepala desa** village head; **pedesaan** rural.

desak, berdesak-desak(an) to crowd, to jostle; **mereka semua berdesak-desak(an) ke dalam ruang itu** they all crowded into the room; **mendesak 1** to push, to shove; **2** to insist, to urge; **waktu sudah mendesak** time is running out; **kebutuhan mendesak** urgent need; **kemendesakan** urgency; **mendesaki** to crowd; **mendesakkan 1** to press something against; **2** to force someone to accept; **terdesak** awkward, difficult; **dalam keadaan terdesak** in an awkward situation; **desakan 1** push, shove; **2** pressure, request; **pendesak** one who presses; **golongan pendesak** pressure group.

desas-desus rumour; **pemerintah sendiri menyangkal desas-desus itu** the government itself denies the rumours; **mendesas-desuskan** to spread rumours about.

desau soft rustling sound; **desau daun** the rustling of leaves.

Desember December.

desentralisasi decentralization.

desersi desertion.

desing, berdesing, mendesing to buzz, to rustle *(wind)*, to whistle *(bullet)*.

destar Javanese headcloth like a turban; **berdestar** to wear such headcloth.

detasemen detachment.

detik 1 *(clock)* sound of ticking; **2** *(unit of time)* moment, second; **sepuluh detik** ten seconds; **sedetik** one moment, second, momentary.

devaluasi devaluation; **mendevaluasikan** to devaluate.

devisa foreign exchange.

dewa god, idol; **dewa-dewi** gods and goddesses; **mendewa-dewakan, memperdewakan 1** to deify; **2** to idolize; **banyak orang mendewakan Elvis** many people idolized Elvis.

dewan 1 council; **dewan gereja** church council, synod; **Dewan Keamanan**

Security Council; **Dewan Perwakilan Rakyat** Indonesian Legislative Assembly; **Dewan Mahasiswa** Student Representative Council; **Dewan Rakyat** People's Council; **2** board; **dewan redaksi** editorial board; **dewan menteri** cabinet; **dewan pimpinan** board of directors; **dewan pengurus** board of management.

dewasa **1** adult; **penduduk dewasa** the adult population; **2** time; **dewasa ini** at present, nowadays; **kedewasaan** adulthood, maturity; **mendewasakan** to mature; **pendewasaan** **1** becoming mature; **2** raising the age limit.

dewata gods; **pulau Bali disebut juga Pulau Dewata** Bali is also called the Isle of the Gods.

dewi **1** goddess; **dewi Sri** goddess of the rice crop; **2** beloved, darling.

di *(preposition showing location)* at, in, upon; **di Jayapura** in Jayapura; **di sekolah** at school, in school; **di dapur** in the kitchen; **di pedalaman** in the country; **apartemen di bawah** the flat downstairs; **di atas meja tulis** on the desk; **di jalan** on the road; **di pantai** at the beach, on the beach; **di televisi** on TV; **di kantor** at the office.

di- verbal prefix showing the passive; **semua sudah dimakan habis** all has been eaten.

dia **1** she, her, he, him, it; **dia anjing saya** it's my dog; **saya berjumpa dengan dia kemarin** I met him yesterday; **2** it; **itu dia** that's it.

diagnosa diagnosis.

dialektika dialectics.

diam[1] **1** quiet, silent; **diam!** quiet!; **kenapa anak-anak semua begitu diam?** why are all the children so quiet?; **2** idle, motionless; **Fitri duduk diam saja** Fitri just sat motionless; **diam-diam** quietly, secretly; **mereka diam-diam pergi ke Jepang** without saying anything they went to Japan; **berdiam** to be silent, to say nothing; **berdiam-diaman** not speaking to each other; **berdiam diri** to be silent; **mendiami** to not speak to a person; **mendiamkan** **1** to keep quiet about; **2** to ignore; **3** to silence; **saya berusaha mendiamkan anjing saya** I tried to keep my dog quiet; **4** to keep motionless.

diam², **berdiam** live, reside; **Heru berdiam di Kelapa Gading** Heru lives in Kelapa Gading; **mendiami 1** to live at; **2** to inhabit; **kediaman** residence; **daerah kediaman** a residential area.

didih, **mendidih 1** to boil; **air sudah mendidih** the water's boiling; **2** to boil, to rage; **mendidihkan** to boil liquid; **titik didih** boiling point.

didik, **anak didik** pupil; **mendidik 1** to educate; **2** to bring up, to raise (children); **didikan 1** education, upbringing; **2** pupil of a certain teacher, alumnus; **pendidik** educator; **pendidikan** education; **pendidikan masyarakat** mass education; **berpendidikan** to have an education.

diesel 1 diesel motor; **2** diesel fuel.

diet diet; **diet bebas garam** a salt-free diet; **mengikuti diet** to be on a diet; **berdiet** to diet.

diktat lecture notes, lecture summary

diktator dictator; **mendiktatori** to rule over as a dictator; **diktator-diktatoran 1** to act like a dictator; to be domineering; **2** a false dictator; **kediktatoran** dictatorship.

dikte dictation; **mendikte 1** to dictate to; **2** to order; **mendiktekan** to dictate.

dinamik dynamic.

dinamit dynamite.

dinamo dynamo.

dinas 1 official; **2** agency, department; **dinas penerbangan** department of aviation; **3** government service, official duty; **urusan dinas** official matters; **dinas malam** night duty; **berdinas** to serve in a certain office; **mendinaskan** to put a person into service; **kedinasan** service.

dinding 1 wall, partition; **2** buttress; **berdinding** walled, to be partitioned off; **berdindingkan** to be walled with; **banyak rumah di kota yang berdindingkan batu bata** many houses in towns often have brick walls; **mendindingi 1** to wall in; **2** to block, to shut off; **pendindingan 1** partition; screen; **2** cover; **3** hindrance, restraint.

dingin cold; **susu dingin** cold milk; **hari ini dingin** it's cold today; **saya merasa dingin** I'm cold; **dingin-dingin** being cold; **dingin-dingin begini**

a b c d e f g h i j k l m n o p q r s t u v w x y z

a b c d e f g h i j k l m n o p q r s t u v w x y z

lebih baik tinggal di rumah saja it's so cold it's better to just stay home; **berdingin-dingin** to enjoy cool weather; **mendingini** to make cool; **mendinginkan 1** to chill, to refrigerate; **2** to cool down; **3** to calm down; **kedinginan 1** coldness; **anak itu menggigil kedinginan** the child shivered with cold; **2** to be very cold; **3** too cold; **pendingin 1** cooler; **2 pendingin suasana** peacemaker; **pendinginan** refrigeration, cooling off.

dini early; **dini hari** early dawn.

dipan divan, sofa.

diploma diploma; **berdiploma** to have a diploma.

diplomasi diplomacy; **berdiplomasi** to engage in diplomacy.

diplomat diplomat; **diplomatik** diplomatic.

direksi management.

direktorat 1 directorate; **2** department, division.

direktur director, head of school; **direktur perusahaan** company director.

dirgahayu long live, long life.

diri self; **bunuh diri** to commit suicide; **menyakiti dirinya sendiri** to hurt yourself; **seorang diri saja, sendirian** all alone; **dia kurang percaya pada dirinya sendiri** she doesn't have much self-confidence, **berdiri** to stand; **mereka berdiri di halte bis** they're standing at the bus stop; **berdiri tegak lurus** to stand upright; **berdiri sendiri 1** to be on your own; **2** to be independent; **2** to exist; **Borobudur masih berdiri** Borobudur is still standing; **memberdirikan** to help to stand again; **mendirikan 1** to make stand; **2** to build, to erect; **3** to establish, to found; **terdiri** suddenly stand up; **terdiri atas, terdiri dari** to be composed of, to consist of; **keluarga terdiri-dari empat orang** a family of four; **pendiri** founder, organizer; **pendirian 1** building, founding; **2** standpoint; **sependirian** of the same opinion; **3** *(military)* installation; **berpendirian** to be of the opinion.

dirigen conductor, musical director.

disenteri, disentri dysentery.

disertasi dissertation.

disiplin discipline; **berdisiplin** disciplined; **mendisiplin**

to discipline; **orang tua harus mendisiplin anak-anaknya sejak mereka kecil** parents must discipline their children from the time they are small.

disket floppy disk.

disko disco.

diskotek discotheque.

diskredit discredit; **mendiskreditkan** to discredit.

diskriminasi discrimination; **diskriminasi ras** racial discrimination; **mendiskriminasikan** to discriminate against.

diskusi discussion; **mendiskusikan** to discuss.

distribusi distribution *(food etc.)*; **mendistribusikan** to distribute.

distrik administrative district.

dll (dan lain lain) and others.

doa prayer; **doa restu** blessing; **berdoa** to pray, to say prayers; **mendoakan** to pray that something will happen, to pray for someone else.

doane customs; **biaya doane** customs duty.

dobel double.

dobrak torn; **mendobrak** to break open, to break through *(for example, a door)*; **mobil pemadam api mendobrak pintu gerbang itu** the fire truck battered the gate down; **pendobrak** batterer, destroyer; **pendobrakan** act of battering or breaking open.

dodol a delicacy made from glutinous rice.

dok dock.

dokar two-wheeled cart pulled by a horse.

dokter doctor, physician; **memanggil dokter** to call the doctor; **dokter gigi** dentist; **membuat janji dengan dokter gigi** to make a dental appointment; **kedokteran** medical; **fakultas kedokteran** medical faculty.

Doktor person who has a doctorate in an academic discipline; **Doktor sejarah** a PhD in History.

doktoral doctoral studies.

doktrin doctrine; **mendoktrinkan** to indoctrinate.

dokumen document.

dokumentasi documentation; **mendokumentasikan** to document; **pendokumentasian** system of documentation.

dolar dollar.

a b c d e f g h i j k l m n o p q r s t u v w x y z

a b c d e f g h i j k l m n o p q r s t u v w x y z

domba sheep; **mengadu domba** to play off one against another; **Domba Allah** congregation, the Lamb of God.

dominasi domination; **mendominasi** to dominate.

domine clergyman, minister of religion *(in Protestant churches).*

dompet purse, wallet.

donasi donation.

donat doughnut.

donatur donor.

dong *(colloquial)* a mild way of emphasizing something, used at the end of a sentence; **'Anda lulus?' 'ya, dong'** 'did you pass?' 'yes, of course'; **'jangan begitu dong'** 'don't do that, mate'; **pikir dulu dong** please think first; **beri saya sedikit dong** give me some, will you.

dongak to look up; **mendongakkan kepala** to lift up your head.

dongeng 1 fable, fairytale; **film itu berdasarkan dongeng India** the film is based on an Indian fable; **2** nonsense; **Ah itu dongeng saja**! what nonsense!; **mendongeng 1** to tell a story; **2** to tell a lie; **mendongengi** to tell stories to; **mendongengkan 1** to narrate; **dongengan 1** myth; **2** false story; **pendongeng 1** narrator, storyteller; **2** person who tells tall stories.

dongkel jack, lever; **dongkelan, pendongkel** lever; **mendongkel 1** to lift up, to loosen; **2** to let out.

dongkerak, dongkrak jack *(for a car)*; **mendongkrak 1** to jack up; **2** to help someone achieve their aim.

dongkol irked, resentful; **mendongkol** to be angry, annoyed or furious; **mendongkolkan** annoying, irksome; **kebiasaannya yang jelek itu sangat mendongkolkan (saya)** her/his bad habits are very annoying, her/his bad habits really annoy me.

dorong, mendorong 1 to push; **mendorong mobil** to push a car; **2** to encourage, to motivate, to urge; **Moerti mendorong Insyiria supaya belajar di Australia** Moerti encouraged Insyiria to study in Australia; **terdorong** pushed, shoved; **dorongan 1** pushing; **2** urging; **3** motivation, encouragement; **pendorong 1** organizer, promoter; **2** incentive; **pendorongan** stimulus.

dos cardboard, cardboard box, carton.

dosa sin; **berdosa** commit a sin; **pendosa** sinner.

dosin, lusin a dozen.

dot soother, teat *(for babies)*.

doyan *(slang)* to be fond of, like; **saya tidak doyan keju** I don't like cheese.

drama drama; **dramatisasi** dramatization; **dramatis** dramatic.

drastis drastic.

dsb (dan sebagainya) etc., and so on.

dua two, second; **dua belas** twelve; **dua puluh** twenty; **dua kali** two times; **tanggal dua Juni** the second of June; **dua bulanan** bimonthly; **menduakalikan** to double something; **dua-duanya, kedua-dua(nya)** both of them; **berdua** both, the two; **mereka berdua pergi** they both went; **berdua-dua 1** two by two; **2** both; **berdua-(dua)an** be or do something together; **mendua** to become two; **kemenduaan** indecisiveness; **menduakan** to double, to duplicate; **memperdua(kan)** to halve, to divide in two; **kedua 1** second; **Perang Dunia Kedua** the Second World War; **anak kedua mereka seorang dokter** their second child is a doctor; **2** two, both; **kedua tante saya ada di situ** both my aunts were there; **untuk kedua kalinya** for the second time; **seperdua** half.

duda divorced man, widower.

duduk 1 sit; **semua harus duduk!** everybody has to sit down!; **Anda boleh duduk di atas bangku itu** you can sit on that bench; **Fitri duduk bersila** Fitri was sitting cross-legged; **2** situation, state; **duduknya candi di tengah pulau** the temple is situated in the middle of the island; **3** live, reside; **4** to go to the bottom, to settle; **menduduki 1** to sit on; **2** to occupy a territory; **mendudukkan** to get someone seated; **terduduk 1** to get seated; **2** sedimented; **kedudukan 1** situation, state; **2** position; **3** status; **sekedudukan** of the same status; **berkedudukan 1** to be located; **2** to hold the job or position; **penduduk** inhabitant; **penduduk setempat** the locals; **penduduk dewasa** the adult population; **pendudukan 1** inhabiting; **2** occupation; **ilmu kependudukan** demography.

a b c d e f g h i j k l m n o p q r s t u v w x y z

a b c d e f g h i j k l m n o p q r s t u v w x y z

duga estimate, guess, suspect; **menduga 1** to take depth bearings; **2** to expect, to presume; **saya tak menduga akan terjadi begini!** I never expected it would be like this!; **dugaan 1** hunch, guess; **2** assumption.

duit money; **berapa duit?** *(colloquial)* how much does this cost?; **berduit** wealthy, well-to-do; **mata duitan** grasping, greedy.

duka grief, sorrow; **berduka** be sorrowful, grieve; **ikut berduka cita, turut berduka cita**; offer condolences; **turut berduka cita atas meninggalnya ibu Anda** I offer my condolences on the death of your mother; **kedukaan** misery, sorrow.

dukacita profound sorrow; **merasa dukacita mendalam** a deep feeling of great sorrow; **berdukacita** to grieve.

duku lanseh tree, lanseh fruit.

dukun shaman; **dukun bayi, dukun beranak** woman who helps in child delivery *(usually in villages)*; **dukun pijat** masseur; **berdukun 1** receive treatment from a shaman; **2** serve as a shaman.

dukung be carried on the back or hip *(like a child)*; **mendukung 1** to carry on your back or hip; **2** to support; **sebagian besar penduduk Indonesia mendukung Megawati** the majority of Indonesians support Megawati; **dukungan** endorsement, support; **dia mendapat banyak dukungan** he/she has a lot of support; **pendukung** supporter.

dulu, dahulu 1 formerly, previously; **dulu dia tinggal di New York** he formerly lived in New York; **dulu kala** long ago; **2** first before you do something else; **mari kita berenang dulu sebelum pulang** let's go for a swim first before we go home; **3** before, first, prior; **lebih baik Anda berangkat dulu, nanti saya menyusul** you should leave first, I'll catch up later; **4** for the time being; **tunggu dulu** hang on for a moment; **dulu-dulu** *(colloquial)* **1** former, previous; **2** earlier; **dulunya** *(colloquial)* formerly; **berdulu-duluan, dulu-mendului** to race each other; **mendului, mendahului** to be ahead of, to precede; **Mansyur mendului saya** Mansyur went ahead of me; **mendulukan, mendahulukan** to give precedence or priority; **lebih baik kami mendulukan orang lanjut usia** we should give priority to older people; **keduluan** be preceded; **duluan** first *(before others)*; **saya duluan!** me first!

dungu 1 mentally slow, stupid; **dia sungguh-sungguh dungu** he's a real dope; **2** gullible; **kedunguan** stupidity.

dunia 1 world; **dunia rohani** spiritual world; **dunia olahraga** sports world; **juara dunia** world champion; **dunia Barat** the western world; **Piala Dunia** World Cup; **2** *(biology)* kingdom; **sedunia** the whole world.

duniawi secular, temporal *(power)*, worldly; **kekayaan duniawi** earthly riches; **keduniawian** worldliness, worldly mindedness, materialistic.

dupa incense; **mendupai** to burn incense.

durhaka insubordinate, rebellious, treacherous; **anak durhaka** rebellious child.

duri 1 burr, spine, thorn; **2** fish bone; **berduri** prickly, thorny; **berduri-duri 1** very thorny, prickly; **2** have many difficulties.

durian durian fruit and tree.

durjana evil, wicked; **kedurjanaan** evil crime.

dusta 1 lie; **2** tell a lie; **berdusta** to tell a lie; **mendustai** to lie; **mendustakan** to deny.

dusun 1 orchard; **2** village far from the city; **kepala dusun** head of a village; **pedusunan** cluster of villages.

duta ambassador, envoy; **duta istimewa** special envoy; **duta keliling** ambassador-at-large; **Duta Besar** ambassador; **kedutaan** embassy; **Kedutaan Besar Australia** the Australian Embassy.

duyun, berduyun-duyun in throngs; **mereka datang berduyun-duyun ke stadion** they thronged to the stadium.

duyung dugong.

dwi two; **dwi bahasa** bilingualism; **dwi kewarganegaraan** dual citizenship, dual nationality; **dwi warna** bicoloured.

dwidasawarsa two decades.

dwifungsi dual function.

dwiguna having dual use or benefit.

dwiperan playing two roles.

dwitunggal duumvirate, two working as one.

a b c d e f g h i j k l m n o p q r s t u v w x y z

dwiwarna the Indonesian red-and-white flag.

E e

ecer, mengecer to retail; **eceran** retail; **harga eceran** retail price; **pengecer** retailer.

edan *(colloquial)* crazy, insane.

edar, beredar, mengedarkan 1 to revolve, to turn; **2** *(money)* to circulate; **banyak uang palsu beredar sekarang** a lot of counterfeit money is circulating at present; **mengedarkan 1** to circulate, to pass around; **tolong edarkan pengumuman ini** please circulate this announcement; **2** *(money)* to circulate, to issue; **edaran 1** something circulated; **2** cycle, orbit; **pengedar** circulator, dealer; **pengedaran** circulating, circulation; **peredaran 1** rotation; **2** orbit, **3** circulation; **peredaran darah** blood circulation.

edisi edition.

efek effect; **efek sampingan** side-effect.

efektif effective; **mengefektifkan** to make effective; **keefektifan** effectiveness; **pengefektifan** trying to make effective.

efisien efficient; **mengefisienkan** to make efficient; **keefisienan** efficiency; **pengefisienan** trying to make efficient.

eja, mengeja to spell; **bagaimana mengejanya?** how do you spell it?; **bagaimana mengeja nama keluarga Anda?** how do you spell your surname?; **mengejakan** to spell out; **ejaan, pengejaan** spelling; **salah ejaan** a spelling mistake.

ejek, mengejek to make fun of, to ridicule; **mengejek** to make fun of something because of the way it is; **mengejek topinya yang berbulu** to make fun of a hat with feathers on it; **ejekan 1** mockery, ridicule; **2** a laughing stock, something made fun of.

ekonomi 1 economics, **2** economy; **ekonomi bebas** free economy; **ekonomi berencana** planned economy; **ekonomi terpimpin** guided economy;

3 household economy; **ekonomis** economical, thrifty; **perekonomian** economy, economic matters.

ekor 1 *(animals)* tail; **ekor kuda** horse's tail, ponytail; **2** classifier for animals; **tiga ekor kucing** three cats; **3** tail end of; **ekor layangan** kite tail; **berekor** to have a tail; **mengekor 1** to hang like a tail; **2** to follow, to tail, to walk behind; **mengekor-ekor** to follow for no particular reason; **pengekor**, follower, hanger-on.

eksakta exact; **mata pelajaran eksakta** the exact sciences.

eksekutif executive.

eksema eczema, rash.

eksentrik eccentric.

ekses excess.

ekshibisi, eksibisi exhibition.

ekspansi expansion.

ekspedisi 1 forwarding, freight, shipping; **2** mailroom; **mengekspedisikan 1** to send by dispatch; **2** to expedite; **pengeskpedisian** forwarding, shipping.

ekspedisi expedition.

eksploitasi 1 development, working; **2** exploitation, operation, use; **mengeksploitasi** to exploit; **mengeksploitasi(kan) 1** to operate, to use for profit; **2** to exploit *(people)*; **pengeksploitasian 1** using, working something; **2** exploiting.

eksplorasi exploration.

eksponen exponent.

ekspor export; **mengekspor** to export; **pengekspor** exporter; **barang-barang ekspor** export goods.

eksportir exporter.

ekspres express.

ekspresi expression.

ekspresionis expressionist.

eksternal external.

ekstrak extract.

ekstrim extreme; **ekstrimis** extremist.

elak, mengelak 1 to evade, to get out of the way; **2** to get out of doing; **dia mengelak dari tanggung jawab** he avoided taking responsibility; **mengelak dari** evasive *(answer)*; **mengelakkan 1** to dodge, to push to the side; **Murtopo berhasil mengelakkan pertanyaan wartawan** Murtopo succeeded in evading the journalists' questions; **2** to shirk.

elang eagle, hawk.
elastik, elastis elastic.
elektrifikasi electrification.
elektrik electrical.
elemen element.
elok 1 beautiful, lovely; **2** good; **semua hadiahnya elok** all her gifts were lovely; **mengelokkan, memperelok** to make beautiful; **lampu hiasan itu memperelok kota Jakarta** the decorative lighting beautifies Jakarta; **keelokan** beauty.
elpiji (LPG) liquid propane gas.
email[1] enamel.
email[2] e-mail.
emang uncle.
emansipasi emancipation.
emas gold; **emas hitam** oil; **emas putih** platinum; **tukang emas** jeweller; **beremas** to have gold; **mengemas** to become golden, to be like gold; **keemasan, keemas-emasan 1** golden; **2** gilded.
embargo embargo.
embel-embel appendage, small addition, trifle.
ember bucket.
embik bleat *(of sheep, goat)*; **mengembik** to bleat; **embikan** bleat.
embun 1 dew; **2** haze; **berembun** dewy; **mengembun 1** to be like dew; **2** to condense; **pengembunan** condensation.
embus, berembus, mengembus 1 to breathe out, to exhale; **2** *(wind)* to blow; **mengembuskan 1** to exhale; **mengembuskan napas yang terakhir** to die; **2** to blow; **embusan 1** bellows; **2** *(wind)* blowing, blast; **3** suggestion; **pengembusan** exhalation.
emis, mengemis to beg for; **pengemis** beggar.
emoh *(colloquial)* reluctant, unwilling; **dia emoh membicarakan hal itu** he's unwilling to discuss the matter.
emosi emotion.
empang 1 fish pond; **2** dam, embankment.
empas, mengempas to be tossed about, to throw; **mengempaskan 1** to hurl, to throw something against something else; **2** to slam *(a door)*; **terempas** flung, hurled, tossed; **empasan** violent crashing.
empat four, fourth; **empat belas** fourteen; **Lucie berumur empat belas tahun** Lucie's fourteen; **empat puluh** forty; **mengadakan selamatan empat puluh hari** to hold a religious meal

a b c d e f g h i j k l m n o p q r s t u v w x y z

forty days after someone's death; **berempat** to be four; **kami berempat** the four of us; **keempat 1** fourth; **harimau yang keempat** the fourth tiger; **2** all four; **keempat harimau itu** all the four tigers; **seperempat** a quarter, one-fourth; **tiga perempat** three-quarters; **perempatan 1** crossroad, intersection; **2** a fourth.

empelas, ampelas sandpaper; **mengampelas** to sandpaper, to scour.

emper, emperan 1 porch, verandah; **2** awning, overhang.

emping crackers made from nuts called '*belinjo*'.

empu master craftsman.

empuk 1 soft; **tempat tidur yang empuk** a soft bed; **2** tender, well-cooked *(food)*; **3** easy to cheat or defeat; **4** soft and attractive *(sound)*; **mengempukkan** to make something soft; **pengempuk 1** softener; **2** padding, stuffing.

enak 1 delicious, tasty; **makanan yang enak** a tasty dish; **2** nice, pleasant; **malam yang enak** a pleasant evening; **3** well; **saya merasa tidak enak badan** I don't feel so good; **4** at ease, comfortable; **saya tidak pernah merasa enak bersama Nurdin** I'm never really comfortable with Nurdin; **enaknya** the easy way, so nice; **seenak** as delicious; **seenak-enaknya** as you wish, as you please; **Firdaus selalu melakukan segala sesuatu seenak-enaknya** Firdaus always does just whatever he feels like; **berenak-enak** to enjoy; **mengenakkan** to put at ease, to reassure; **mengenak-enakkan** to make your mouth water; **memperenak** to make more comfortable; **keenakan 1** pleasantness; **2** have too much fun; **enakan** *(colloquial)* comfortable, more pleasant, preferably; **enak-enakan** relax, take it easy.

enam six, sixth; **enam belas** sixteen; **enam puluh** sixty; **sekarang jam enam** it's six o'clock; **tanggal enam Maret** the sixth of March; **di tingkat enam** on the sixth floor; **berenam** six together; **keenam 1** sixth; **kancil yang keenam** the sixth mousedeer; **2** all six; **keenam kodok itu** all the six frogs.

enau sugar palm.

encer 1 liquid, thin, watery, weak; **teh encer** weak tea; **2** quick-witted, smart;

otaknya encer he's smart; **mengencerkan** to dilute; **memperencer** to make something more dilute; **pengencer** thinning agent, thinner; **pengencer cat** paint thinner; **pengenceran** dilution, thinning.

encok rheumatism.

endap[1], **mengendapkan** to precipitate, to settle; **mengendapkan kotoran** let the dirt settle; **endapan** deposit, sediment.

endap[2], **mengendap, mengendap-endap** to creep in a crouching position, to move stealthily, to slip; **lihatlah kucing itu mengendap di antara semak-semak!** look at that cat creeping through the bushes!; **pencuri mengendap-endap di antara rumah-rumah** the thief moved stealthily between the houses.

engah, terengah 1 panting for breath; **2** excited, nervous; **terengah-engah 1** gasping, puffing; **2** hurrying; **engahan** panting, puffing.

enggak, nggak, kagak *(Jakarta slang)* no, not.

enggan dislike, reluctant, unwilling.

enggang hornbill.

engkau 1 *(formal, may be abbreviated to* **kau***)* you; **2** your; **berengkau** to be on familiar terms with.

engkol crank, handle.

engsel 1 hinge; **2** switch.

ensiklopedi encyclopaedia.

entah who knows, I don't know; **saya pernah bertemu dengannya, tapi entah di mana** I've seen her before but I don't know where; **entah bagaimana** don't know how; **entah bagaimana, saya kira mereka tidak jadi datang** I somehow think they won't come; **entah ... entah ...** whether ... or ...; **entah sudah selesai entah belum, Anda tak mungkin tahu** whether it's finished or not, you can't possibly know; **entahlah 1** do not know; **2** or perhaps ... I don't know.

enteng 1 *(weight)* light; **2** easy; **dianggap enteng** considered unimportant; **3** *(cigarettes)* mild; **mengentengkan 1** to ease, to lighten, **2** to alleviate; **obat itu dapat mengentengkan sakitnya** that medication can alleviate the pain; **entengan** *(colloquial)* easier, lighter.

a b c d e f g h i j k l m n o p q r s t u v w x y z

eram, mengeram, mengerami to brood, to sit on eggs; **induk ayam itu sedang mengeram** the hen is sitting on the eggs; **induk ayam itu mengerami telurnya** the hen is sitting on the eggs; **mengeramkan** to hatch eggs; **pengeram** incubator; **pengeraman** hatching.

erang groaning, moaning from pain; **mengerang** to groan, to moan; **erangan** groaning, moaning.

erat 1 firm, tight; **2** *(promise)* firm; **3** *(relationship)* close; **mereka bersahabat erat** they have a close friendship; **erat-erat, seerat-eratnya** as tightly as possible; **mengeratkan, mempererat** to tighten, to firm up, to strengthen; **keeratan** closeness.

ercis peas.

Eropa, Eropah Europe, European.

erti, (me)ngerti understand; **saya tidak mengerti** I don't understand; **apakah Anda mengerti pembicaraan saya?** do you understand my discussion?; **dimengerti** be understood; **dapat dimengerti** understandable; **mengertikan 1** to cause to understand, to explain; **dia mengertikan maksud kata-kata Mira kepada saya** he explained the meaning of Mira's words to me; **2** to understand, to explain to oneself; **pengertian** understanding, way you understand; **itu terlalu sulit bagi pengertian saya** it's beyond me; **salah pengertian** misunderstanding.

es ice; **es batu** ice block; **balok es** block of ice; **es campur** shaved ice mixed with fruit and syrup; **es kopi** iced coffee; **es krim** ice-cream; **es lilin** ice lollypop; **es teler** iced fruit mix topped with condensed milk; **hujan es** hail.

esa one, single; **Tuhan yang maha esa** the one and only God; **keesaan** oneness, unity.

esok, besok tomorrow; **esok hari** tomorrow; **hari esok** the future; **esok lusa** the day after tomorrow, in the future; **esoknya** the next day; **keesokan (harinya, paginya)** the following *(day, morning)*; **surat itu tiba keesokan harinya** the letter arrived the following day; **keesokannya** the following day.

a b c d e f g h i j k l m n o p q r s t u v w x y z

a b c d e f g h i j k l m n o p q r s t u v w x y z

estafet, lari estafet relay race.

estetika aesthetics.

etalage, etalase shop window.

eter ether.

etika ethics, label.

etiket etiquette.

etnologi ethnology.

evakuasi evacuation; **mengevakuasi** to evacuate.

evaluasi evaluation; **mengevaluasi** to evaluate.

evolusi evolution; **berevolusi** to evolve.

F f

faal *(medical)* function; **faal usus** digestive function; **ilmu faal (alat tubuh)** physiology.

faedah benefit, profit, use; **berfaedah** advantageous, beneficial, useful.

faham, paham comprehension, understanding; **memahami** to understand.

fajar dawn.

fakir destitute, miserable, poor; **fakir miskin** the poor.

fakta fact; **fakta-fakta dasar** the basic facts.

faktor factor.

faktur invoice.

fakultas faculty; **fakultas kedokteran** medical faculty.

falak 1 heavenly sphere; **2** outer space; **ilmu falak** astronomy.

falsafah, falsafat philosophy; **berfalsafah** to philosophize.

famili 1 relative; **2** family; **berfamili 1** have a family; **2** be related.

fana 1 lasting only a short while, transitory; **dunia fana** our present world; **2** perishable; **kefanaan** impermanence.

fanatik fanatic.

fantasi 1 fantasy, illusion; **2** imagination; **berfantasi** to fantasize; **memfantasikan** to imagine.

farisi hypocrite, Pharisee.

farmasi pharmacy.

fasal 1 chapter; **2** concerning, regarding; SEE **pasal**.

fasih 1 fluent; **2** eloquent, glib; **kefasihan** fluency.

fasik 1 atheistic, godless; **2** sinner.

fasilitas facilities.

fatal fatal.

fatsal, pasal article, clause, section.

fatwa **1** a binding rule in religion; **2** instructions, guidance by someone older; **berfatwa** to give advice, instructions on or about religious matters; **memfatwakan** to advise, to instruct.

Februari, Pebruari February.

federal federal.

federasi federation.

feminin feminine.

feminisme feminism.

feodal feudal.

fihak direction, side. SEE **pihak**.

fikir idea, thought; **ahli fikir** thinker, philosopher. SEE **pikir**.

fiksi fiction.

fiktif fictitious, **kefiktifan** fictitiousness.

film, filem **1** film for a camera; **2** film, movie; **memfilmkan** to film; **perfilman** the movie industry.

filsafah, filsafat philosophy; **berfilsafat** to philosophize; **memfilsafatkan** to philosophize about.

filsuf philosopher.

Fira'un **1** pharaoh; **2** tyrant.

firdaus paradise.

firma company, firm.

firman the word of God, God's order, God's command; **berfirman** to decree, to speak (of God); **memfirmankan** to decree, to say, to proclaim.

fisika physics; **fisika inti** nuclear physics.

fiskal **1** fiscal; **tahun fiskal** the fiscal year; **2** departure tax.

fitnah slander; **memfitnah** to libel, to slander; **pemfitnah** detractor, slanderer; **pemfitnahan** slandering, defamation.

fitrah, zakat fitrah *(Islam)* offering in rice or cash paid at the end of the fasting month; **memfitrahkan** to give away as an offering.

fokus **1** *(lens)* focus; **2** *(of attention)* focus; **berfokuskan pada** to focus on; **memfokuskan** to focus; **pemfokusan** focusing.

folio folio.

fondasi foundation.

fonem phoneme.

formal formal; **memformalkan** to formalize; **formalitas, keformalan**

a b c d e f g h i j k l m n o p q r s t u v w x y z

a b c d e f g h i j k l m n o p q r s t u v w x y z

formality; **formal-formalan** *(colloquial)* to do in a formal way, be formal.

formasi **1** formation; **2** position, line item in a budget.

format format, form.

formulasi formulation; **memformulasikan** to formulate.

formulir form; **mengisi formulir** to fill in a form; **formulir pesanan** order form.

forsir, memforsir to compel, to force.

fosfat phosphate.

fosfor phosphorous.

foto photograph, picture; **mengambil foto** to take a photo.

fotokopi photocopy.

foya, (ber)foya-foya to be extravagant, to enjoy yourself, to throw money around.

fraksi **1** *(in parliament)* faction; **2** *(of a political party)* section.

frekwensi frequency.

front **1** front; **2** *(military)* front line.

frustrasi **1** frustration; **2** frustrated; **kefrustrasian** frustration.

fungsi **1** function, job; **2** function, purpose; **berfungsi sebagai** to function as; **memfungsikan** to make function.

fungsional, fungsionil functional.

fungsionaris functionary, official.

fusi **1** *(physics)* fusion; **2** *(politics)* coalition; **berfusi** coalesce, fuse; **memfusikan** to merge; **perfusian** coalescence, state of being merged.

futbal footbal, soccer.

fuyonghai egg fooyong *(Chinese omelette with meat and vegetable and sweet and sour sauce).*

G g

gabah unhulled rice grain.

gabuh empty, infertile, sterile; **karena lama tidak hujan, padi di sawah gabuh** because there has been no rain for a long time, the rice kernels are empty.

gabung bunch, bundle; **bergabung 1** to come

together, to gather together; **anak-anak telah bergabung di pantai** the children have gathered at the beach; **2** to fuse, to merge; **kedua perusahaan itu bergabung menjadi satu** the two companies have merged into one; **menggabungkan 1** to bale, to bundle; **2** to fuse, to join a thing to something else; **sekolah kami menggabungkan tiga kelas menjadi satu** our school has combined three classes into one; **gabungan** combination, federation, fusion, merger; **gabungan buruh se-Indonesia** the Indonesian Federation of Labour; **tergabung** joined together, united; **penggabungan** combination, union.

gada club, cudgel; **bersenjatakan gada** to be armed with a club; **gada-gada** weather-vane, windsock.

gadai 1 pawning; **2** security; **menggadai, menggadaikan 1** to accept as security; **2** to pawn; **dia telah menggadaikan arloji bapaknya** he pawned his father's watch; **pegadaian, rumah gadai** pawnshop; **penggadaian** mortgaging, pawning; **tergadai** pawned.

gadang, bergadang to stay awake; **bergadang semalam suntuk** stayed awake all night long.

gading ivory, tusk.

gadis unmarried girl, virgin; **gadis tua** old maid, spinster; **menggadis** to stay single or unmarried.

gado, menggado to eat side-dishes only with no rice; **gado-gado** salad of raw and lightly cooked vegetables with a peanut sauce, jumbled-up things.

gaduh commotion, noisy, uproar; **jangan gaduh, ayah sedang tidur** don't be noisy, dad is sleeping; **menggaduh(kan)** to cause a commotion, to disturb; **gerombolan pro-integrasi menggaduhkan keamanan di Timtim** pro-integration gangs disturbed the peace in East Timor; **kegaduhan** commotion, uproar, disturbance.

gadungan fake, false; **polisi gadungan** bogus police officer, impostor.

gaet hook; **menggaet** to hook, to snatch; **tergaet** to get hooked, to get involved in.

gagah 1 brawny, muscular, strong; **gagah berani** strong and brave; **2** handsome; **3** brave; **menggagahi** to rape; **menggagahkan** to make brave and strong; **kegagahan 1** courage, valour; **2** firmness, strength; **3** handsomeness; **4** conceitedness.

gagak crow, raven.

gagal fail; **regu kami gagal lagi** our team failed again; **menggagalkan 1** to cause to fail, to defeat; **2** to frustrate; **kegagalan** abortive attempt, failure.

gagang handle, holder; **gagang pintu** door handle.

gagap, menggagap to stammer, to stutter; **tergagap-gagap, menggagap-gagap 1** to stammer, to stutter; **2** hastily, hurriedly.

gagas, menggagas to consider, to reflect on, to think of; **gagasan** idea, opinion.

gagu dumb, mute.

gaib 1 mysterious **2** hidden, invisible; **3** belonging to the invisible or supernatural; **ilmu gaib** supernatural power; **kegaiban** mystery; **menggaibkan** to make invisible.

gairah passion, strong desire; **gairah kerja** a passion for work; **bergairah** passionate, very enthusiastic; **menggairahkan 1** to arouse, to stimulate; **bau bawang goreng menggairahkan nafsu makan saya** the smell of fried onions makes me hungry; **2** to excite, to delight; **konser yang betul-betul menggairahkan** a really exciting concert; **3** to encourage, to stimulate; **kegairahan** enthusiasm, passion; **kegairahan main gitar** enthusiasm for playing the guitar.

gajah elephant.

gaji salary, wage; **gaji bersih** net wages; **gaji bulanan** monthly pay; **mendapat gaji** to be getting a wage; **menggaji 1** to employ, to hire; **perusahaan itu menggaji lebih dari seratus orang pekerja** that company employs more than a hundred people; **2** to pay a salary or wage; **hari gajian** payday.

galak 1 fierce, vicious; **anjing galak** a vicious dog; **2** sharp and mean; **matanya galak** its eyes are mean; **3** cheeky, forward; **anak yang galak** a bully; **menggalakkan 1** to incite, to stir up; **ia menggalakkan kerusuhan itu** she incited the riot; **2** to encourage; **kegalakan** **1** ferocity; **2** audacity, cheekiness; **penggalakan** encouragement.

galaksi galaxy.

gali, menggali **1** *(a hole, mine, well)* to dig; **menggali batu bara** to mine for coal; **2** to dig up *(carrots etc.)*, to excavate, to exhume; **galian** the result of digging; **penggali** **1** digger, excavator; **2** shovel, spade; **penggalian** **1** quarrying; **2** excavating, digging.

gambar design, drawing, figure, illustration, image, picture; **gambar coret** pen sketch; **gambar hidup** movie film; **bergambar** illustrated *(magazine etc.)*; **menggambar** to draw; **Desi pandai menggambar tumbuh-tumbuhan** Desi's skilled at drawing plants; **menggambari** to illustrate; **Ani menggambari bukunya dengan bunga-bunga** Ani drew flowers in her book; **menggambarkan** **1** to explain by using a sketch; **2** to depict, to describe; **cerita Lupus menggambarkan hidup kaum muda** the Lupus stories depict the life of teenagers; **penggambaran** description, drafting; **gambaran** illustration, picture; **penggambar** draftsperson.

gamblang **1** clear, easy to understand **2** explicit; **Fauzi bilang secara gamblang bahwa dia tidak puas** Fauzi explicitly stated that he wasn't satisfied; **menggamblangkan** make clear and explicit; **kegamblangan** clarity, explicitness.

gamelan orchestra of gongs and xylophones *(Bali, Java and Sunda)*.

gampang easy, simple; **gampang memutuskannya** it's easy to decide; **menggampangkan** **1** to facilitate; **pesawat terbang menggampangkan perjalanan** planes facilitate travel; **2** to take lightly, treat something which is hard as being easy; **jangan menggampangkan pelajaranmu** don't take your study lightly; **mempergampang** to alleviate, to make easy.

gampar, menggampar to slap someone's face.

ganas **1** ferocious, savage, vicious; **komodo adalah binatang yang ganas** the komodo is a ferocious animal; **2** malignant

a b c d e f g h i j k l m n o p q r s t u v w x y z

(tumour); **mengganas 1** to rage, to rampage, to storm; **penjahat-penjahat itu mengganas di seluruh kota** those criminals raged through the whole city; **2** to be ferocious, vicious.

ganda multiple, times; **sejak krisis ekonomi harga barang-barang naik berlipat ganda** since the economic crisis the price of goods has increased massively; *(in sport)* a doubles partnership; **berganda** doubled; **main berganda, bermain ganda** to play a game of doubles; **mempergandakan, menggandakan** to double, to multiply; **regu kita menggandakan hasil golnya musim ini** this season our team doubled its goals; **pergandaan** multiplication; **pergandaan lima** five-time increase.

gandeng, bergandeng, bergandengan 1 arm in arm, side by side; **mereka berjalan bergandengan** they walked arm in arm; **2** coupled; **gerbong kereta api bergandeng** railway carriages are coupled together; **menggandeng 1** to pull, to tow; **2** to hold hands; **menggandengkan** to join together.

gandrung 1 crazy about, infatuated; **Rita gandrung pada Ranto** Rita's crazy about Ranto; **2** devoted to a cause; **menggandrungi** to be crazy about; **Russell menggandrungi Nicole Kidman** Russell's crazy about Nicole Kidman; **menggandrungkan** to be keen on having; **Jessie menggandrungkan rambut warna ungu** Jessie's keen on having purple hair; **kegandrungan** craze for, infatuation with.

gandum wheat.

gang 1 alley, lane; **2** corridor, passageway.

ganggu, mengganggu 1 to disturb; **pestanya mengganggu lingkungan sepi** their party disturbed the quiet environment; **2** to disturb, to interfere with, to intrude on; **jangan ganggu saya, saya sedang sibuk** don't disturb me, I'm busy; **terganggu** disturbed; **Carl terganggu kesehatannya** Carl's health is impaired; **gangguan** interference, disturbance; **gangguan keamanan** disturbance of the peace; **pengganggu** disturber of the peace, intruder, teaser;

pengganggguan annoying, interfering, teasing.

gangsa, angsa goose.

ganja 1 hemp plant; 2 hashish, marijuana; **pengganja** drug addict.

ganjil 1 *(of numbers)* odd, uneven; **bilangan ganjil** an odd number; 2 abnormal, odd, queer; **mengganjilkan** to make a number odd; **keganjilan** peculiar nature, strangeness.

ganteng good-looking, handsome.

ganti 1 replacement, substitute; **ganti rugi** compensation, indemnity; **sebagai ganti** in lieu of, in place of, instead of; **sebagai ganti daging kami makan tahu** in place of meat we ate tofu; 2 to change *(name, clothes, etc.)*; **karena basah, dia ganti baju** because she was wet, she changed her clothes; **kita harus ganti kereta di Strathfield** we have to change trains at Strathfield; **bergantian** to take turns; **kami bergantian menyetir mobil** we took turns driving the car; **mengganti** to make up for, to replace; **mengganti vas yang pecah** replace the broken vase; **menggantikan** to come after, to succeed, to take the place of; **Ibu Rusman akan menggantikan Pak Harmon** Ms Rusman will take over from Mr Harmon; **tergantikan** replaceable; **tidak tergantikan** irreplaceable; **pengganti** replacement, substitute, successor; **pengganti ratu** the queen's successor; **penggantian** change, compensation, replacement, substitution.

gantung, bergantung 1 hang, hanging; **gantung diri** to hang oneself; **gambar Anda bergantung di kamar tidur saya** your sketch hangs in my bedroom; 2 to depend on; **hal itu bergantung pada keadaan** that depends on the situation; **menggantung** 1 *(a person)* to hang; 2 *(clothes)* to hang up; **menggantungkan** 1 to hang out; **Yati menggantungkan pakaiannya** Yati hung her clothes out (to dry); 2 to make dependent; **tergantung** depend(ent) on; **itu tergantung pada cuaca** it depends on the weather; **gantungan** 1 hanger, hook; 2 gallows.

ganyang to crush, to destroy; **Sukarno ingin mengganyang Malaysia** Sukarno wanted to crush Malaysia.

a b c d e f g h i j k l m n o p q r s t u v w x y z

gara-gara 1 commotion, turbulence; **Lupus selalu cari gara-gara** Lupus is always looking for trouble; **2** just because of; **gara-gara saya terlambat** just because I was late.

garam salt; **garam bata** block salt; **garam halus** table salt.

garansi guarantee, warranty; **bergaransi** having a guarantee.

garap, menggarap to cultivate, to work on; **menggarap tanah** to cultivate, to till the land; **garapan** assignment, task.

garasi garage.

gardu 1 guardhouse, sentry post, ticket booth *(on toll road)*; **gardu jaga** guard house; **2** relay station; **gardu listrik** electrical relay station.

garing dry and crisp, crunchy.

garis line; **garis batas** border, finish line *(sport)*, frontier; **menggarisbawahi 1** to underline; **2** to emphasize; **menggaris 1** to scratch; **2** *(a page)* to draw lines, to rule; **bergaris** lined *(of paper)*; **garisan** line drawn; **penggaris** ruler.

garpu fork; **bergarpu** to use a fork.

garuda eagle, Indonesian national symbol, mythical bird.

garuk, bergaruk-garuk to scratch; **anjing ini selalu bergaruk-garuk** this dog is always scratching (itself); **menggaruk** to scratch *(the body)*.

gas 1 gas; **gas air mata** tear gas; **gas alam, gas bumi** natural gas; **2** petrol fumes.

gatal itch; **tangan saya gatal** my hand is itchy; **menggatalkan** to cause an itch; **ulat bulu itu menggatalkan** those hairy caterpillars make you itchy.

gaul, bergaul to associate, to mix with; **Meiti lebih suka bergaul dengan anak muda** Meiti prefers to mix with young people; **menggauli** to have sexual intercourse with; **pergaulan** social interaction.

gaun gown.

gawang goal, hurdles.

gawat 1 critical, grave, serious; **unit gawat darurat** emergency room; **2** dangerous, risky.

gaya 1 energy, force; **gaya berat** gravity; **2** fashion, style, way; **gaya baru** the latest style; **gaya bebas** *(sport)* freestyle; **gaya kupu-kupu** *(sport)* butterfly stroke;

bergaya 1 energetic, powerful, strong; **2** to be in a certain style; **dia selalu bergaya** he's always (dressed) in style.

gayung scoop, water dipper.

gedek woven sheets of bamboo for house walls.

gedung building; **gedung bertingkat** multi-storey building.

geger commotion, noise, uproar; **menggegerkan** to cause a commotion or stir.

gejala indication, sign, symptom; **bintik merah itu adalah salah satu gejala demam berdarah** these red spots are a sign of dengue fever.

gejolak, bergejolak to flare up, to fluctuate.

geladak deck of a ship.

gelagat aspect, indication, sign; **gelagat buruk** bad signs.

gelandang *(sport)* half-back; **bergelandangan** to laze about, to loiter, to wander around without purpose; **menggelandang** to be a tramp; **gelandangan** tramp, vagrant; **pergelandangan** vagrancy.

gelang bangle, bracelet; **gelang karet** rubber band; **bergelang** to wear a bracelet.

gelanggang 1 arena, boxing ring, forum; Gelanggang Olah Raga (GOR), stadium; **2** round area surrounding something.

gelanting, gelantung, bergelanting to dangle, to hang down; **anting-anting Ibu Subroto selalu bergelanting** Mrs Subroto's earrings always dangle.

gelap 1 dark; **2** obscure, unclear; **3** illicit, secret; **pasar gelap** black market; **menggelapkan 1** to darken, to obscure; **2** to embezzle; **kegelapan 1** darkness, obscurity; **kegelap-gelapan** fairly dark; **penggelap** embezzler; **penggelapan 1** *(as a precaution)* blackout; **2** embezzling.

gelar 1 title; **2** academic title; **gelar sarjana** a university degree; **bergelar** to have a title; **menggelari 1** to name; **2** to give a title; **mempergelarkan** to stage, to present *(a play)*; **pegelaran, pergelaran** performance, presentation; **pergelaran wayang kulit, pegelaran wayang kulit** a shadow play presentation.

gelas glass *(for drinking)*.

geledah, menggeledah to search *(a building)*, to frisk

a b c d e f g h i j k l m n o p q r s t u v w x y z

(a person); **penggeledahan** search.

geledek thunder; **menggeledek** to thunder; **suaranya menggeledek di gelanggang** his voice thundered through the arena.

geli 1 amused, tickled; **saya geli melihat anak-anak kucing itu bermain** I was amused to see the kittens playing; **2** ticklish; **3** to set your teeth on edge; **menggelikan 1** absurd, ridiculous; **2** to tickle; **kegelian** amused, tickled; **penggeli hati** a joke.

gelimpang, bergelimpangan, tergelimpang to lie on the ground, sprawled; **korban penembakan di Dili itu bergelimpangan di jalan** the victims of the Dili massacre lay sprawled on the road.

gelisah 1 anxious, nervous, restless; **sebelum ujian tidur saya selalu gelisah** I always sleep restlessly before exams; **kucing tampaknya menjadi gelisah waktu ada banyak angin** cats seem to get restless when it's windy; **2** concerned, worried; **menggelisahkan** to alarm, to make restless, to upset; **kabar itu menggelisahkan mereka** the news upset them; **kegelisahan 1** nervousness, restlessness; **2** anxiety, concern, worry.

gelombang movement of large rolling waves; **bergelombang 1** to billow, to surge; **2** to fluctuate; **suku bunga bergelombang naik turun** interest rates fluctuate; **3** bumpy, corrugated, wavy.

gelora enthusiasm, passion; **gelora perjuangan bangsa** enthusiasm for national struggle; **bergelora** enthusiastic, impassioned; **sorak sorai untuk kemenangan Rudi bergelora** the cheering for Rudi's win became more enthusiastic; **menggelorakan** to incite, to whip up; **menggelorakan semangatnya untuk menang** whip up the spirit to win.

GELORA, GOR (GELanggang Olah RAga) sports stadium.

gema echo; **bergema, menggema** to echo, to reverberate; **suaranya bergema di balai yang kosong** his voice echoed in the empty hall.

gemar to be fond of, to enjoy; **gemar akan pacuan kuda** fond of horse-racing; **kegemaran** hobby, the thing you like doing; **kegemaran menusuk tubuh** the craze for body-piercing; **menggemari** to be fond of; **kelihatan Anda menggemari musik rok** it seems you're fond of rock music; **menggemarkan** to please, to satisfy; **penggemar** fan; **dia penggemar tinju** he's a boxing enthusiast; **Kevin penggemar Spice Girls** Kevin's a Spice Girls fan.

gemas to eat them up because they are so adorable.

gembala shepherd.

gembar-gembor, menggembar-gemborkan to brag about, to make a big noise about.

gembira cheerful, happy, pleased, proud; **saya gembira ketemu lagi dengan Ita** I'm glad to meet you again, Ita; **dia sangat gembira mendapat anak anjing baru itu** she's delighted with the new puppy; **Nyonya Prayitno sangat gembira puterinya mendapat gelar** Mrs Prayitno is very happy that her daughter has been awarded a degree; **bergembira** to be cheerful, to rejoice; **menggembirakan 1** to cheer up, to make happy; **hadiah itu menggembirakan Tuti** getting that prize made Tuti happy; **kegembiraan** happiness, cheerfulness; **penggembira 1** cheerful character; **Agus seorang penggembira** Agus is a cheerful person; **2** *(sports)* supporter.

gembok padlock; **bergembok** to be locked with a padlock; **menggembok** to lock with a padlock; **tergembok** padlocked.

gembung puffed up, swollen; **menggembung** to fill up, to swell up; **balon menggembung** the balloon filled up; **menggembungkan** to inflate.

gemerlap, gemerlapan to glitter, to shine; **bergemerlapan** to be gleaming or shining.

gemetar to quiver, to shake, to tremble; **Abdul gemetar kedinginan** Abdul shook with cold; **bergemetaran** to tremble; **tangannya bergemetaran** her hand trembled; **menggemetarkan** to make tremble; **gemetaran** trembling, tremor.

gempa shaking; **gempa bumi** earthquake.

gempar commotion, uproar; **menggemparkan** to cause an

a b c d e f g h i j k l m n o p q r s t u v w x y z

uproar or commotion; **insiden yang menggemparkan** sensational incident; **kegemparan** sensation, tumult, uproar.

gempur, menggempur **1** to attack and destroy, to hit hard; **musuh menggempur desa itu** the enemy attacked and destroyed the village; **2** *(an argument or idea)* demolish; **pers menggempur rencana-rencana pemerintah** the press demolished the government's plans; **gedung baru itu akan digempur karena dibangun tanpa ijin** the new building will be torn down because it was constructed without a building permit; **penggempur** destroyer; **penggempuran** destruction.

gemuk **1** fat, obese; **menjadi gemuk, bertambah gemuk** to become fat; **2** fat, grease; **3** *(of soil)* fertile, rich; **4** fertilizer; **menggemuki** to grease, to lubricate; **menggemukkan badan** to fatten; **kegemukan** overweight, too fat.

genang, bergenang, menggenang to be stagnant; **menggenangi** to flood, to inundate; **air hujan menggenangi perumahan itu** the rainwaters flooded the housing estate; **genangan** flooded area, puddle; **penggenangan** flooding, overflowing.

genap even *(of numbers)*, complete, full; **bilangan genap** even number; **segenap** entire, whole; **segenap anggota keluarga** the whole family; **menggenapi, menggenapkan** to (make) complete.

gendong, menggendong to carry on the hip *(usually with a cloth sling)*, to piggyback; **sambil menunggu kereta, para ibu itu menggendong anak-anaknya** while they were waiting for the train the mothers carried their children on their hips.

gendut potbellied.

generasi generation.

generator generator.

genetik genetic.

genetika genetics.

gengsi prestige; **bergengsi** prestigious.

genit flirtatious, vain; **gadis genit** a flirtatious girl.

genius genius.

genteng roof tile.

genting **1** critical, precarious; **2** roof tile.

geografi geography.

gerak movement; **gerak tubuh Lina agak kaku** Lina's body movements were rather stiff; **bergerak** to move, to be in motion, to be active; **tidak bergerak-gerak** to not make any movement at all; **menggerakkan 1** to move, to set in motion; **2** to activate, to motivate; **Yanti menggerakkan semua temannya** Yanti motivated all her friends; **gerakan** movement; **gerakan politik** political movement.

gerbang, pintu gerbang entrance gate.

gerbong railway carriage.

gereja church.

gergaji saw; **menggergaji** to saw.

gerhana eclipse; **gerhana total** total eclipse; **gerhana matahari** solar eclipse; **gerhana bulan** lunar eclipse.

gerimis drizzle, rain lightly *(spitting)*.

gerobak cart, wagon.

gersang arid, barren, dry.

gesa, tergesa-gesa hasty, in a hurry; **Dodi tergesa-gesa keluar dari ruang** Dodi hurried out of the room.

geser, bergeser to move, to shift; **meja bergeser** the table moved; **menggeserkan 1** to rub against; **kucing suka menggeserkan diri pada orang** cats like to rub themselves against people; **2** to shift, to move; **Sri menggeserkan peti berat pada pintu** Sri pushed the heavy box up against the door.

giat active, energetic; **Harmin selalu main dengan giat** Harmin always plays energetically; **menggiatkan, mempergiat(kan) 1** to activate; **2** to encourage; **kegiatan 1** energy; **2** activity.

gigi 1 tooth; **dokter gigi** dentist; **pemeliharaan gigi** dental care; **2** gear; **masukkan gigi** to put the car in gear; **tukar giginya** to change gear.

gigit, menggigit to bite; **anjing itu suka menggigit orang** that dog often bites people; **tergigit** bitten *(accidentally)*; **gigitan** a bite.

gila 1 crazy, insane, mad; **2** infatuated, obsessed; **bergila-gilaan** to fool around; **jangan bergila-gilaan saja** don't just fool around; **menggila** to drive someone mad; **pesta di rumah tetangga saya makin menggila** the noise from my neighbour's party was

a b c d e f g h i j k l m n o p q r s t u v w x y z

a b c d e f g h i j k l m n o p q r s t u v w x y z

maddening; **menggilai** to be very fond of, to be crazy about; **Keti menggilai Tom Cruise** Keti's crazy about Tom Cruise; **kegilaan** insanity, madness; **gila-gilaan** **1** foolish; **2** frantic; **3** crazy; **keadaan ekonomi yang gila-gilaan** the economic situation is crazy.

gilas, menggilas 1 to crush, to pulverize; **2** to run over; **mobil itu menggilas kucing saya** that car ran over my cat; **tergilas** to be run over; **gilasan** something crushed or run over; **penggilas** crusher, pulverizer; **penggilas jalan** steam roller.

gilir, bergilir in turn, to take turns; **giliran** turn; **giliran siapa sekarang?** whose turn is it now?

ginjal kidney.

girang cheerful, glad, happy.

gitar guitar.

gizi nutrient; **bergizi** nutritious, nourishing.

global global, overall; **keadaan global** the overall situation; **secara global** broadly, globally.

goblok stupid, **kegoblokan** stupidity.

godok, menggodok 1 to boil; **2** to train intensively; **3** to consider, to debate, to discuss; **sudah lama mereka menggodok rencananya** they've been discussing their plans for a long time; **godokan 1** boiled food; **2** someone who trained intensively; **penggodokan** boiling; intensive training.

gol *(sport)* goal, point, score.

golf golf; **pegolf** golfer.

Golkar (Golongan Karya) the Functional Group, under Soeharto the political group for civil servants.

golong, menggolongkan to classify, to group; **menggolongkan makanan menurut gizinya** classify food according to its nutritional value; **tergolong 1** classified; **2** belonging to; **golongan** category, class, group; **penggolongan** classifying, grouping.

goncang 1 shaky, swaying; **2** changeable, unstable; **iman yang tidak akan goncang** an unshakable faith; **bergoncang 1** to move, to shake violently; **gedung itu bergoncang** the building was shaking; **2** to fluctuate, to be unstable; **menggoncangkan 1** to shake; **gempa bumi kemarin menggoncangkan kota ini** yesterday's earthquake shook this city; **2** to make something fluctuate; **keadaan ekonomi menggoncangkan suku bunga** the economic situation has caused interest rates to fluctuate; **tergoncang** shaken; **kegoncangan** jolt, shock.

gondrong long-haired *(men)*; **kegondrongan** *(colloquial)* too long *(of hair)*.

gorden curtain.

goreng fried; **pisang goreng** fried banana; **menggoreng** to fry; **penggorengan** wok.

gores scratch; **menggores** to scratch; **menggoreskan** to scratch with; **cucunya menggoreskan paku pada meja** her grandchild scratched the table with a nail; **tergores** scratched; **goresan** scratch; **goresan pena** a pen sketch.

gosok, menggosok 1 to brush, to rub, to scrub; **(meng)gosok gigi** to brush the teeth; **2** to incite, to instigate; **3** to polish, to shine; **menggosoki** to rub repeatedly; **Ayah menggosoki kaca spion dengan sapu tangannya** Dad kept polishing the rear-view mirror with his handkerchief; **menggosokkan** to rub something onto something; **Bambang menggosokkan obat salep pada gigitan nyamuk itu** Bambang rubbed the ointment onto the mosquito bite.

got drain, gutter.

gotong, menggotong to carry a heavy thing together; **gotong-royong** community self-help, mutual cooperation; **bergotong-royong** to co-operate, to share work.

goyah loose, not stable, shaky; **gigi ini goyah** this tooth is loose; **menggoyahkan** make something wobble or shake.

goyang shaky, unsteady, wobbly; **setelah minum alkohol semalam badan Budi goyang** after last night's binge Budi was shaky; **bergoyang** to rock, to sway, to wobble; **menggoyang 1** to jolt, to rock, to shake; **2** to make a thing wobbly; **menggoyangkan** to shake, to swing; **menggoyangkan pemerintah** destabilize a government; **tergoyang** shaken; **goyangan 1** staggering; **2** fluctuation, oscillation.

grafik graph.

a b c d e f g h i j k l m n o p q r s t u v w x y z

a b c d e f g h i j k l m n o p q r s t u v w x y z

gratis at no cost, free; **menggratiskan** to give away for free.

gua cave.

gubernur governor.

gudang **1** warehouse; **2** storeroom; **menggudangkan** to store in a warehouse; **penggudangan** storage, storing; **pergudangan** warehousing.

gudeg vegetable and chicken dish cooked in coconut milk, specific to central Java.

gugat, menggugat **1** to accuse, to charge; **pengadilan menggugat Tommy mengenai penggelapan uang negara** the court charged Tommy with embezzlement; **2** to criticize, to judge; **3** to claim, to demand; **mereka menggugat tindakan perdana menteri** they criticized the action of the prime minister; **gugatan** **1** accusation; **2** claim; **3** criticism; **penggugat** litigant, plaintiff.

gugur **1** to fall *(of leaves, hair, etc.)*; **musim gugur** autumn; **2** to die in battle; **3** to abort; **berguguran** to fall *(several things)*; **rambutnya berguguran** all her hair fell out; **menggugurkan** to make fall prematurely; **menggugurkan pemerintah** to topple the government; **menggugurkan kandungan** to abort an unborn child; **keguguran** to have a miscarriage; **guguran** something fallen; **guguran nuklir** nuclear fallout; **pengguguran** abortion.

gula sugar; **gula-gula** candy, sweets; **menggulai** to sweeten.

gulai Indonesian curry; **gulai kambing** curry of goat; **menggulai** to prepare a curry.

gulat, bergulat to wrestle; **pegulat** wrestler; **pergulatan** **1** wrestling; **2** encounter, struggle.

guling roll; **bantal guling** bolster; **berguling** **1** to roll; **kuda itu berguling di pasir** the horse rolled in the sand; **2** to sleep with a bolster; **menggulingkan** **1** to roll; **3** to defeat, to topple; **regu kita menggulingkan semua regu lain** our team defeated all the others; **terguling** **1** rolled; **2** overthrown.

gulung **1** roll; **segulung karton** a roll of cardboard; **2** *(of rope)* coil; **bergulung** **1** by the roll; **2** to keep rolling in; **3** *(sleeves)* be rolled up; **menggulung** **1** to come in rolls or waves; **2** to roll; **dia menggulung rokok** he rolled a cigarette; **3** *(sport)* to defeat; **menggulungkan** to wind or to roll up; **tergulung** **1** rolled, wound; **2** *(sport)* defeated; **gulungan** something that is wound or rolled up; **penggulung** roller; **penggulungan** rolling up.

guna **1** purpose, use; **apa gunanya bekerja keras begini?** what's the use of working so hard?; **2** for, in order to; **saya hanya bekerja guna dapat uang** I only work in order to get money; **berguna** useful; **cari sesuatu yang berguna** find something useful; **menggunakan, mempergunakan** to make use of, use, utilize; **kegunaan** purpose, use; **kegunaannya sangat tinggi** it's extremely useful.

gundul **1** bald; **2** leafless; **3** barren; **menjadi gundul** to become bald or barren; **menggunduli** **1** to shave bald; **2** to make barren; **kegundulan** baldness; **penggundulan** **1** shaving bald; **2** becoming barren *(of land)*.

gunting clippers, scissors; **menggunting** to cut with scissors; **guntingan** **1** clipping; **2** cut, style of cutting; **jas ini bagus guntingannya** this coat has a good cut.

guntur thunder.

gunung mountain; **gunung (ber)api** volcano; **bergunung-gunung** mountainous; **menggunung** **1** to pile up; **2** to be like a mountain; **gunungan** mountain figure representing the universe *(in Javanese wayang)*; **pegunungan** mountain range.

gurih delicious, tasty.

guru teacher; **berguru** to be a student of a particular person; **Kepi berguru pada Prof. Ardan** Kepi is studying with Prof. Ardan; **menggurui** to act like a teacher; **kenapa Flora suka menggurui saya?** why do you always have to lecture me? *(speaking to Flora)*; **keguruan** matters relating to teachers; **fakultas keguruan** education faculty; **perguruan** institution, school; **perguruan tinggi** tertiary institution.

guruh thunder.

gurun wilderness; **gurun pasir** desert.

gusar angry; **menggusarkan** to make angry.

gusi gum*(s)*.

a b c d e f g h i j k l m n o p q r s t u v w x y z

H h

habis 1 finished, used up; **apakah bir sudah habis?** is the beer finished?; **2** end; **habis bulan** the end of the month; **3** after that, then *(colloquial)*; **kami berenang, habis itu kami bersantai** we went for a swim and then relaxed; **4** completely, entirely; **rumah sakit itu habis terbakar** the hospital burned down completely; **habis tempo** due date, use-by date; **waktu sudah habis!** time's up!; **sehabis** after; **sehabis berenang kami bersantai** after swimming we relaxed; **menghabisi 1** to finish, to end; **2** to finish off; **3** to spend time; **menghabisi hari dengan membaca** to spend the day reading; **menghabiskan 1** to finish; **2** to spend time; **3** to consume, to use up; **apakah Anda sudah menghabiskan sisa makanan?** have you finished the leftovers?; **saya telah menghabiskan seluruh uang saya** I've spent all my money; **4** to finish off; **kehabisan** run out of; **kehabisan bensin** run out of petrol; **habis-habisan** completely; **pemerintah yang baru ini dikritik habis-habisan** this new government has been severely criticized; **penghabisan** conclusion, end; **ujian penghabisan** final exam.

hadap, hadapan façade, front side; **di hadapan ibunya** in front of her/his mother; **berhadapan 1** front on, opposite; **rumah mereka berhadapan dengan mesjid** their house is opposite the mosque; **2** be faced with; **3** face to face; **berdiri berhadapan dengan musuh** to stand face to face with your enemy; **berhadap-hadapan** face to face, opposite each other; **menghadap 1** to face, to front; **sekolah itu menghadap ke pantai** the school faces the beach; **2** to make a formal appearance; **menghadapi** to be up against, face (difficulties); **Craig menghadapi masalahnya** Craig faced up to his problems; **menghadapkan 1** to aim; **menghadapkan senapan** to aim a rifle; **2** to point something; **3** to bring face to face; **4** to present formally; **terhadap 1** about, concerning; **pemeriksaan terhadap insiden** an investigation into the incident; **2** to, toward; **tidak adil terhadap pemuda** not fair to young people.

hadiah 1 prize; **memenangkan hadiah besar** to win the jackpot; **2** reward; **3** gift; **mereka membawa hadiah** they brought a gift; **berhadiah** with a gift; **undian berhadiah** raffle; **menghadiahi dengan** to give a gift; **Budi menghadiahi pacarnya jam tangan** Budi gave his girlfriend a watch; **menghadiahkan** to donate, to present; **Budi menghadiahkan jam tangan kepada pacarnya** Budi gave his girlfriend a watch.

hadir be present; **menghadiri** to attend, to be present at; **menghadiri kelas** to attend a class; **menghadirkan** to cause someone or something to be present; **kehadiran** attendance, presence; **hadirin** audience, those present.

hafal 1 know by heart; **2** know very well; **menghafal(kan)** to memorize.

hai 1 *(exclamation to get attention)* hey!; **2** *(greeting)* hi.

haid menstruation.

haji 1 someone who has made the pilgrimage to Mecca; **naik haji** pilgrimage to Mecca; **2** term used for addressing someone who has been on the pilgrimage to Mecca, for example, 'Pak Haji'.

hak 1 right; **hak azasi** basic rights; **hak azasi manusia** human rights; **hak mogok** the right to strike; **hak milik** property rights; **2** rightful authority; **berhak** have the right to; **Anda tidak berhak berkata begitu** you have no right to say that.

hakekat, hakikat reality, truth; **pada hakekatnya** in essence, properly speaking.

hakim judge; **menghakimi** to judge; **kehakiman** judicial affairs; **penghakiman** judging, judgment.

hal 1 matter, thing; **dia memberitahu saya hal-hal yang aneh** she told me some strange things; **pada hal** even though, while, whereas, in fact, **dia tidak lulus, pada hal dia pintar sekali** he didn't pass even though he's very intelligent; **2** case; **dalam hal itu** in that case.

a b c d e f g h i j k l m n o p q r s t u v w x y z

halal **1** allowed, kosher, permitted; **makanan halal** kosher food; **2** legal, rightful; **menghalalkan** to allow, to permit.

halal bihalal to ask and give forgiveness at the end of the fasting period *(for Muslims).*

halaman **1** *(of a building)* yard; **halaman sekolah** schoolyard; **halaman belakang** the backyard of the house; **2** *(of a book)* page.

halang, halangan obstacle; **berhalangan** unable to do; **menghalangi** to block, to hinder, to prevent; **mereka menghalangi polisi masuk** they prevented the police entering; **menghalangi 1** to be in the way, to hamper; **menghalangi jalan** to block the road or way; **menghalang-halangi** to prevent; **penghalang** hindrance, obstacle.

halau expel; **menghalau 1** to chase, to drive away; **2** to drive, to herd; **penghalau** driver, herder; **anjing penghalau domba** sheep dog; **penghalauan 1** driving, expelling; **2** herding.

halilintar **1** flash of lightning; **2** thunderbolt.

halte, halte bis bus stop.

haluan **1** bow, prow *(of a boat)*; **2** course, direction, policy; **sehaluan** of the same course or policy; **berhaluan** follow a course or a policy.

halus **1** cultured, refined, sensitive; **2** delicate, soft; **3** *(of spirits)* invisible, unseen; **orang halus** a spirit; **4** small; **5** finely milled; **menghaluskan, memperhalus** to refine, to touch up; **kehalusan** **1** refinement; **2** gentleness; **3** smoothness, softness; **penghalus** refiner; **penghalusan** refining.

hama **1** plant disease, pest; **2** infection.

hamba **1** servant, slave; **2** I, yes *(when talking to high-ranking people)*; **berhamba** to be a servant; **menghambakan** to domineer, to treat as a servant; **memperhamba** to enslave a person.

hambar **1** tasteless; **2** trite; **menghambarkan** to make tasteless; **kehambaran** having no flavour.

hambat, menghambat **1** to hamper, to impede, to obstruct; **2** to head off; **terhambat** blocked, obstructed; **hambatan** barrier, hindrance, obstacle, obstruction.

hambur, berhambur(an) scattered about; **menghambur 1** to be scattered; **domba-domba menghambur ke mana-mana** the sheep were scattered everywhere; **2** to move suddenly; **menghambur(kan) 1** to scatter, to spread about; **Renaldy menghambur(-hambur)kan uangnya untuk membeli rokok dan bir** Renaldy used his money just to buy cigarettes and beer; **2** to cast a net; **terhambur** scattered all about; **hamburan** something scattered about; **penghamburan 1** dispersal; **2** waste; **penghamburan dana** wasting of funds.

hamil pregnant, pregnancy; **hamil muda** early stage of pregnancy; **menghamili** to impregnate, to make pregnant; **kehamilan** pregnancy; **pil pencegah kehamilan** the contraceptive pill.

hampa 1 empty; **dengan tangan hampa** empty-handed; **2** without result.

hampar, berhamparan be spread out; **menghampar** to be spread out evenly; **menghampari** to spread something on something; **menghamparkan 1** *(a rug)* to spread; **2** to explain, to clarify; **terhampar** spread out evenly; **hamparan 1** carpet, rug; **2** spread out area; **penghamparan** spreading.

hampir 1 close, near; **2** almost; **hampir setiap hari** almost every day; **hampir setiap orang** almost everybody; **hampir tidak** hardly; **saya hampir tidak dapat mendengar Anda** I can hardly hear you; **hampir-hampir** very nearly; **hampir-hampir saja kami mendapat kecelakaan** we very nearly had an accident; **menghampiri** to approach, to come near to.

hancur 1 shattered, smashed; **hatinya hancur ketika mendengar berita itu** he/she was shattered upon hearing the news; **2** dissolved; **menghancurkan 1** to destroy, to smash, to shatter; **mereka menghancurkan jendela** they smashed a window; **masyarakat tidak akan menghancurkan dokumen seperti itu** the people are not going to destroy such documents; **2** to dissolve; **3** to crush; **kehancuran** destruction; **tingkat kehancuran** the scale of the damage; **penghancur** agent

a b c d e f g h i j k l m n o p q r s t u v w x y z

a b c d e f g h i j k l m n o p q r s t u v w x y z

causing destruction; **penghancuran 1** crushing, smashing of; **2** annihilation, total destruction; **3** disintegration, dissolving.

handuk towel.

hangat warm; **berita hangat** current news; **sambutan hangat** a warm welcome; **menghangat** to get warm; **menghangati 1** to warm up; **2** to incite; **menghangatkan** to heat, to warm up; **kehangatan 1** heat, warmth; **2** tenseness; **3** eagerness; **penghangat** warmer.

hanggar aeroplane hangar.

hangus 1 burnt, scorched; **nasinya hangus lagi!** you've burnt the rice again!; **2** singed; **menghanguskan 1** to roast until burnt; **2** to burn, to singe, to scorch; **kehangusan** state of being burnt.

hantam, berhantam 1 fight, scuffle; **2** collide with; **3** infringe on; **menghantam 1** to hit hard; **2** to pound; **3** to attack strongly; **menghantamkan 1** to hit; **2** to hit with something; **hantaman** blow, punch.

hantu 1 ghost; **2** evil spirit; **berhantu** haunted; **menghantui 1** to frighten; **2** to haunt, to obsess.

hanya 1 just, only; **yang tinggal hanya tiga** there are only three left; **hanya beberapa saat sesudah magrib** just after evening prayer; **hanya berkelakar saja** just joking; **2** however, only; **saya ingin ikut, hanya tidak mempunyai cukup uang** I'd like to come along, only I don't have enough money.

hanyut 1 adrift, carried, washed away by water; **2** drift, wander; **3** lose yourself *(as in daydreams)*; **hanyut dalam angan-angan** lost in daydreams; **4** drag on *(a talk or conversation)*; **hanyut dalam pembicaraan** to get carried away in the conversation; **menghanyutkan** to carry away *(floods etc.)*.

hapus, menghapus 1 to completely remove; **ada virus baru yang dapat menghapus isi file** there's a new virus that can wipe the contents of files; **2** to clean, to wipe off *(a whiteboard etc.)*; **menghapus** to rub out; **menghapuskan** to eliminate, to wipe out; **penghapus** eraser, rubber; **penghapusan** erasing, wiping out.

haram 1 forbidden; **daging babi haram bagi orang Islam**

dan Yahudi pork is forbidden to Muslims and Jews; **anak haram** illegitimate child; **2** on no account, under no circumstances; **3** never! *(exclamation of strong denial)*; **mengharamkan 1** to forbid, to prohibit; **2** to abstain from.

harap 1 hope; **2** *(as part of a command)* please; **harap diam!** please be quiet!; **harap diperhatikan!** please pay attention!; **harap berhubungan dengan kami** please contact us; **berharap** hope, expect; **kami berharap Anda akan datang** we hope that you'll come; **mengharap(kan) 1** to hope for; **2** to expect; **kami mengharapkan kedatangan kira-kira lima ratus orang** we're expecting about five hundred people; **harapan 1** hope; **hilang harapan** to give up hope; **mempunyai harapan** to have hope; **2** expectation; **pengharapan 1** hope; **2** expectation, reliance.

harga price; **berapa harganya?** what is the price?; **harga buku itu tiga puluh dolar** the price of the book is thirty dollars; **harganya terlalu mahal** it costs too much; **separoh harga (karcis)** half-fare; **harga karcis seorang** fare per person; **harga karcis pulang-pergi ke Kempsie** the return fare to Kempsie; **berharga 1** cost; **kamera ini berharga delapan ratus dolar** this camera costs eight hundred dollars; **2** valuable; **cincin itu berharga sekali** that ring is very valuable; **menghargai** to appreciate, to value; **saling menghargai** to appreciate one another; **cincin ini dihargai sepuluh juta rupiah** this ring is valued at ten million rupiah; **menghargakan** to price, value; **penghargaan 1** appreciation, respect; **2** valuation.

hari day; **sepanjang hari** all day long; **empat hari sesudahnya** four days later; **hari libur** holiday; **hari besar, hari raya** a public holiday; **hari Senin adalah hari raya** Monday's a holiday; **sehari** a day; **sehari sesudah** the day after; **sehari sebelum** the day before; **sehari-hari** daily, every day; **bahasa Indonesia sehari-hari** spoken Indonesian; **sehari-harian** all day long; **berhari-hari** many days, for several days; **harian** daily; **surat kabar harian** daily newspaper.

a b c d e f g h i j k l m n o p q r s t u v w x y z

a b c d e f g h i j k l m n o p q r s t u v w x y z

harimau tiger; **harimau kumbang** black panther; **harimau tutul** leopard.

harmonika harmonica, mouth organ.

harmonis 1 harmonious; **2** harmonic.

harta property, wealth; **harta benda** property, riches, wealth; **berharta** propertied; **hartawan** wealthy person.

haru, mengharukan to move, to reach your emotions; **sandiwara itu sangat mengharukan (orang)** it's a very moving play; **terharu** affected, moved.

harum 1 aromatic, fragrant; **2** fragrance, perfume; **3** have a good reputation; **mengharumkan** to give a scent to; **keharuman 1** fragrance; **keharuman melati** the fragrance of jasmine; **2** fame.

harus have to, must; **kami harus berangkat sekarang** we must leave now; **saya harus menelepon ke rumah** I have to phone home; **Anda harus sudah ada di sini jam delapan** you must be here by eight; **seharusnya 1** should, ought to, **seharusnya kita berangkat besok** we're due to leave tomorrow; **kami seharusnya berangkat lebih awal** we should have left earlier; **2** proper; **mengharuskan** to compel, to require; **diharuskan membayar sebelumnya** payment in advance is required; **keharusan 1** necessity, requirement; **2** imperative, must.

hasil 1 crop, yield; **hasil utama** staple crop; **2** product; **hasil kotor** gross output; **3** result, outcome; **dia mendapat hasil yang baik** she's achieved good results; **berhasil** succeed; **dia berhasil menurunkan kucing itu** he managed to get the cat down; **kami tidak berhasil menghubungi Handoko** we didn't manage to get in touch with Handoko; **dengan berhasil** successfully; **berhasil-guna** effective; **keberhasilan** success; **keberhasilan yang hebat** a great success; **menghasilkan 1** to produce; **2** to produce results; **penghasil** producer; **penghasilan 1** production, yield; **2** income, earnings; **Liana mendapat penghasilan sebanyak empat puluh ribu dolar setahun** Liana makes forty thousand dollars a year; **mendapat penghasilan** to make a living.

hasrat desire, longing; **berhasrat** desire, wish.

hasut, menghasut to incite, to stir up; **polisi menuduh mereka menghasut kerusuhan** the police accused them of starting the riot; **hasutan 1** instigation, provocation; **2** agitation; **penghasut** agitator, provocateur; **penghasutan** instigating, provoking.

hati 1 liver; **2** centre of the emotions; **jantung hati** sweetheart; **dengan senang hati** gladly; **sedang murung hati** to be in a bad mood; **baik hati** kind-hearted; **yang membesarkan hati** encouraging; **hati-hati 1** be careful, be on your guard; **hati-hati ada tangga!** mind the step!; **2** carefully; **dia mengangkat jambang itu dengan hati-hati** she carried the vase carefully; **sehati** like-minded; **berhati-hati** to be careful, take care; **memperhatikan 1** to pay attention, to take note; **Anda tak memperhatikan** you weren't paying attention; **jangan perhatikan dia!** don't take any notice of her!; **2** to observe, to watch; **pemerhati** observer; **perhatian 1** attention, notice; **menjadi pusat perhatian umum** to be in the spotlight; **mencurahkan perhatian kepada** to devote one's attention to; **2** interest.

haus 1 thirsty; **saya haus** I'm thirsty; **2** thirst, thirstiness; **kehausan 1** be thirsty; **2** thirst.

havermut oatmeal.

hawa[1] **1** air; **2** climate, weather.

Hawa[2] Eve; **kaum Hawa** women.

hayat life; **ilmu hayat** biology; **menghayati 1** to experience fully; **2** to perceive; **penghayat** someone who understands or who practises something; **penghayatan** complete understanding, comprehension.

hayati biological, vital; **keanekaragaman hayati** biodiversity.

hebat extremely intense; **hebat!** terrific!; **pakaian Anda hebat!** your outfit is amazing!; **dengan kecepatan yang hebat** at a terrific speed; **perjalanan yang benar-benar hebat** a simply fantastic trip; **menghebat** to increase in intensity; **memperhebat(kan)** to intensify; **kehebatan 1** intensity; **2** furore, fuss;

hebat-hebatan intense; **penghebatan** intensification.

heboh 1 commotion, fuss, uproar; **2** sensational; **menghebohkan** to create a fuss or commotion; **kehebohan** fuss, stir.

hela, menghela to drag, to haul, to pull; **terhela** dragged along; **penghela** person or thing that pulls or tows.

helai 1 sheet *(of paper etc.)*; **2** a classifier for paper, cloth, etc.; **tiga helai kertas kado** three sheets of gift wrap; **berhelai-helai** a number of sheets; **Mustafa menulis surat berhelai-helai** Mustafa wrote a letter of several pages; **helaian** sheet *(of paper etc.)*.

hemat economical, thrifty; **lebih hemat membeli sepuluh sekaligus** it's more economical to buy ten at a time; **berhemat** to be thrifty, to save; **menghemat** to economize, to save; **saya berjalan ke sekolah untuk menghemat biaya** I walk to school to save money; **kita akan naik taksi untuk menghemat waktu** we'll take a taxi to save time; **penghematan 1** economizing; **2** economy.

hendak 1 wish; **hendaklah Anda maklum, hendaknya Anda maklum** I hope you understand; **2** intend, be going to, have the intention to do; **hendaknya** to be better that, should; **menghendaki 1** to wish for; **2** to demand, to require; **kehendak** desire, wish; **sekehendak-hati** to the heart's desire; **berkehendak** intend to do; **menghendaki** to desire, to want.

hening silent, quiet; **malam yang hening** a quiet night; **mengheningkan 1** to clear; **2** to silence; **3** to concentrate your thoughts; **mengheningkan cipta** to observe a moment of silence; **mengheningkan pikiran** to clear your thoughts; **keheningan** silence, stillness; **keheningan malam** silence of the night.

hentak, menghentak 1 to stamp on hard; **2** to stab; **3** to pound, to throb; **menghentakkan** to pound or stamp; **menghentakkan kaki** to stamp your feet; **terhentak** to be thrown down; **hentakan** pounding, stamping; **penghentak** pestle.

henti tak henti-hentinya ceaselessly, incessantly;

berhenti 1 stop; **apakah kereta api ini berhenti di Cirebon?** does this train stop in Cirebon?; **2** end; **musiknya berhenti** the music stopped; **memberhentikan 1** *(a vehicle)* to stop; **2** to sack; **pemberhentian 1** discharge, dismissal; **2** stoppage; **pemberhentian buruh** work stoppage; **menghentikan 1** to stop, to halt; **tidak ada yang dapat menghentikan Amin untuk berbuat sesukanya** there's nothing to stop Amin doing what he wants; **2** to end; **mereka sudah menghentikan pemogokan itu** they've ended the strike; **terhenti 1** stopped; **2** broken off; **penghentian** bringing to a stop, ceasing; **perhentian 1** stopping, closing down; **2** stopping place *(for example, for a bus)*.

heran amazed, surprised; **saya heran melihat besarnya buaya itu** I was amazed at the size of the crocodile; **mengherankan 1** to cause amazement; **besarnya buaya itu mengherankan saya** what amazed me was the size of the crocodile; **2** to be surprised; **sangat mengherankan!** what a surprise!; **tidak mengherankan Anda lelah** it's no wonder you're tired; **terheran-heran** extremely amazed; **keheranan** amazed.

hewan 1 animal, beast, cattle; **hewan piara(an)** pet animal; **2** *(as a class)* animal; **dokter hewan** veterinarian; **kehewanan** relating to animals; **fakultas kehewanan** faculty of veterinary science.

hias, berhias 1 decorated; **2** dressed up; **berhiaskan** decorated with; **menghias(i) 1** to decorate; **menghiasi pohon natal** to decorate the Christmas tree; **2** to garnish; **3** to illustrate *(a book or magazine)*; **hiasan 1** decoration; **lampu hiasan yang berkilauan** sparkling fairy lights; **2** illustration; **penghias** decorator, illustrator; **penghiasan** decorating, ornamentation; **perhiasan** jewellery.

hibah bequest, donation, gift, grant; **menghibahkan** to donate, to grant; **Pak Haji menghibahkan tanahnya untuk mesjid** Pak Haji donated his land for a mosque.

hibur amuse yourself; **menghibur 1** to cheer up, to comfort; **2** to entertain; **carilah sesuatu untuk menghibur anak-anak itu** find something to entertain those children; **hiburan** **1** consolation, comfort; **2** entertainment.

hidang, menghidangi **1** to serve with; **Lisa menghidangi tamunya teh dan kue** Lisa served her guest tea and cakes; **menghidangkan** to serve (food, drink); **mereka menghidangkan ikan dengan saos jeruk nipis** they served the fish in a lemon sauce; **2** *(entertainment)* to present; **hidangan** something served.

hidung nose; **hidung mancung** sharp, pointed nose; **hidung pesek** pug nose.

hidup **1** be alive, to live; **kelelawar hidup dengan makan buah-buahan** bats live on fruit; **harimau itu ditangkap hidup-hidup** the tiger was captured alive; **2** life; **seluruh hidupnya** all her life; **3** *(machines)* run, go; **mesin mobil ini tidak mau hidup** this car won't start; **4** long live!; **menghidupi** to support; **dia tidak mampu menghidupi anak-anaknya** he can't support his children; **menghidupkan 1** to bring back to life, to revive; **2** *(a light, TV, etc.)* to turn on, *(an engine)* start; **3** *(fire, lamp, etc.)* to light; **4** *(interest)* to revive; **kehidupan 1** life; **begitulah kehidupan!** that's life!; **2** existence; **penghidupan 1** lifestyle; **2** livelihood.

hijau **1** green; **hijau daun** leaf green, **hijau tua** dark green; **2** inexperienced; **menghijau** to be or to turn green; **menghijaukan 1** to make green; **2** to plant; **3** to reforest, to replant; **penghijauan 1** greening; **2** planting; **3** reforesting, reforestation.

hikmah, hikmat **1** philosophy, wisdom; **2** magical power; **3** power in general; **berhikmah 1** to have wisdom; **2** to have magical power.

hilang **1** be lost, vanished; **hilang ingatan** insane, crazy; **mata-rantai yang hilang** the missing link; **2** to go missing; **beberapa barang hilang** several things have gone missing; **asalkan tidak hilang** as long as you don't lose it; **menghilang** to disappear; **pelan-pelan air itu menghilang** the water slowly disappeared; **menghilangkan 1** to lose, to make disappear; **obat ini dapat menghilangkan sakit gigi** this medicine relieves the pain of toothache; **2** to leave out, to omit; **kehilangan 1** suffer from a loss; **Sari kehilangan gelangnya** Sari's lost her bracelet; **2** loss; **kehilangan keseimbangan** to lose your balance; **kehilangan kesempatan** to miss an opportunity; **penghilang** eliminator, remover; **obat penghilang nyeri** an analgesic; **penghilangan 1** removal; **2** elimination, eradication.

hilir lower section of a river, downstream; **berhilir-mudik** go up and down; **Morhazlin berjalan hilir-mudik di kamarnya** Morhazlin was pacing his room.

himpun, berhimpun to assemble, to gather; **berhimpun-himpun** collect all together; **menghimpunkan 1** to assemble, to gather; **2** to accumulate, to collect; **terhimpun** assembled, collected; **himpunan 1** association, club; **2** collection; **penghimpun 1** collector; **2** compiler; **penghimpunan** accumulation, collection; **perhimpunan 1** association, organization; **2** gathering place.

hina contemptible, mean; **menghina 1** to humiliate, to insult; **dia dituduh menghina presiden** he was accused of insulting the president; **2** to offend; **terhina** degraded, insulted; **kehinaan 1** insignificance; **2** humiliation; **hinaan 1** insult; **2** gibe, taunt; **penghinaan** causing humiliation.

hindar, menghindar to pull to one side; **sepeda itu menghindar supaya saya dapat mendahuluinya** the bicycle pulled over to the side so I could overtake it; **menghindari** to avoid; **Mariam selalu menghindari dia** Mariam always keeps away from him; **menghindarkan** to place out of the way.

Hindia The Indies; **Hindia Belanda** the Dutch East Indies.

Hindu Hindu; **Hindu Dharma** Balinese Hinduism.

hingga until, up to; **hingga sekarang, hingga kini** up to now, so far; **hingga kini semuanya berjalan baik** so far everything's going well; **hingga hari Senin** until Monday; **sehingga 1** until; **2** with the result that; **dia terlambat bangun sehingga ketinggalan kereta api** he got up so late that he missed

a b c d e f g h i j k l m n o p q r s t u v w x y z

the train; **tak terhingga** unlimited.

hinggap 1 alight, perch; **2** *(infection)* attack; **menghinggapi 1** to alight, to perch on; **2** to descend on; **3** to get attacked by; **dia dihinggapi kolera** she got cholera.

hipotek mortgage; **menghipotekkan** to mortgage.

hirau, menghiraukan to note, to pay attention to; **saya harus menghiraukan nasihat orangtua saya** I have to heed the advice of my parents; **tidak menghiraukan** does not take any notice, to ignore.

hiruk-pikuk fuss, hullabaloo; **jangan hiruk-pikuk!** stop making such a din!; **kehiruk-pikukan** racket; noise, din; **semalam saya tidak bisa tidur oleh karena kehiruk-pikukan pesta di rumah tetangga saya** I couldn't sleep last night because of the racket from my neighbour's house.

hit a hit, extremely popular; **lagu hit** a very popular song.

hitam 1 black; **2** dark, swarthy; **hitam manis** dark and attractive; **menghitamkan 1** to blacken; **2** *(reputation)* to denigrate; **kehitaman 1** blackness; **2** very black.

hitung, ilmu hitung arithmetic; **berhitung** count; **anak itu sudah dapat berhitung** that child can already count; **menghitung 1** to count, to do sums; **2** to calculate; **saya akan menghitung buku-buku di kelas** I shall count the books in the class; **3** to count in, to reckon; **terhitung** counting, countable; **jumlahnya lima belas tidak terhitung anak-anak** fifteen not counting the children; **bintang-bintang di langit tak terhitung banyaknya** the stars in the sky are uncountable; **memperhitungkan 1** to calculate, to estimate; **memperhitungkan jumlah bahan-bahan yang diperlukan untuk membangun sebuah rumah** to estimate the amount of materials needed to build a house; **2** to take into consideration when calculating; **jangan lupa memperhitungkan kemungkinan hujan** don't forget to take into consideration the possibility of rain; **3** to count on; **penghitungan** counting, enumeration; **perhitungan**

1 calculation;
2 consideration.

hiu, ikan hiu shark.

hobi 1 hobby; **2** like to do; **saya hobi membaca** I like to read.

honor, honorarium
1 honorarium, stipend; **2** payment for services; **menghonor** to pay an honorarium.

honorer 1 honorary; **2** be paid an honorarium because not officially in the job.

hormat 1 honour, respect; **2** respectful; **dengan hormat** yours faithfully, with respect; **menghormat** to salute *(military)*; **menghormati** to honour, to respect; **terhormat** respected; **Bapak yang terhormat** Dear Sir; **Saudara Henry yang terhormat** Dear Henry; **kehormatan 1** honour; **2** honorary; **penghormatan** giving honour, respecting.

hostes 1 bar waitress; **2** call-girl.

hot 1 sexy; **2** very popular.

hotel hotel; **perhotelan** hotel affairs; **sekolah perhotelan** hotel, hospitality school.

hubung, berhubung connected, related; **berhubung dengan** in connection with, with regard to; **berhubungan 1** related to; **2** be in contact, get in touch with; **kami tidak berhasil berhubungan dengan Handoko** we didn't manage to get in touch with Handoko; **menghubungi** to contact, to get in touch with; **dia belum menghubungi saya** he hasn't contacted me yet; **menghubungkan 1** to connect, to join; **2** to put someone in contact with someone else; **hubungan 1** connection, relationship; **apa hubungan antara mereka berdua?** what's the link between the two?; **2** contact; **kami sudah tidak ada hubungan lagi** we've lost contact; **3** context; **sehubungan dengan** in connection with.

hujan rain; **hujan batu, hujan beku, hujan es, hujan kerikil** hail; **hujan deras** downpour; **hujan gerimis** drizzle; **musim hujan** rainy season; **menghujani 1** to rain on; **2** to shower someone with; **mereka menghujani Yuliana dengan hadiah** they showered Yuliana with prizes; **kehujanan** to get caught in the rain.

hujat blasphemy.

hukum law; **hukum adat** customary, traditional law;

a b c d e f g h i j k l m n o p q r s t u v w x y z

a b c d e f g h i j k l m n o p q r s t u v w x y z

berhukum have rules, follow laws; **menghukum 1** to punish someone; **2** to criticize, to judge; **3** to sentence to; **hukuman 1** punishment; **hukuman yang seberat-beratnya** the maximum penalty; **dijatuhi hukuman seumur hidup** to be sentenced to life; **2** someone who has been sentenced; **orang hukuman** prisoner.

hulu 1 headwaters, upper section of a river; **2** beginning of; **berhulu** have upper reaches; **penghulu** chief, headman.

huma 1 field where rice is cultivated without irrigation; **2** land recently cleared for agriculture; **berhuma 1** to grow rice without irrigation; **2** clear land ready for cultivation.

huni, berhuni inhabited, occupied; **menghuni** to occupy, to reside in; **menghunikan** to inhabit; **program transmigrasi menghunikan orang dari satu pulau ke pulau lain** through the transmigration program people from one island are settled on another; **penghuni 1** inhabitant, occupant; **2** guardian spirit; **penghunian** occupancy.

huru, huru-hara 1 disturbance; **2** riot.

huruf character, letter; **huruf hidup** vowel; **huruf mati** consonant.

hutan forest, woods; **hutan lindung** protected forest; **hutan suaka** sanctuary; **menghutankan 1** to reforest; **2** to let the jungle take over; **kehutanan** forestry; **penghutanan** forestation; **perhutanan 1** forestry affairs; **2** forestry service.

hutang debt, obligation; **hutang nasional** national debt; **berhutang budi 1** to be greatly obligated; **2** credit; **berhutang** to owe; **saya berhutang Rp. 5.000 pada Rizal** I owe Rizal Rp. 5,000; **menghutangkan** to lend; **penghutang** debtor.

I i

ia[1], **dia** he, she.

ia[2] yes; **ialah** are, is; **Pak Gus Dur ialah Presiden Indonesia yang baru** Pak Gus Dur is the new President of

Indonesia; **beria** assent, say yes; **beria-ia** to say yes to everything; **seia-sekata** unanimous; **mengiakan** to agree to, to answer yes to.

iba, iba kasihan **1** compassion, pity; **2** compassionate.

ibadah, ibadat devotion, religious service; **beribadah** **1** devout, pious; **2** worship; **peribadahan** carrying out religious duties.

ibarat **1** like; **anjing itu ibarat iblis** that dog is like a devil; **2** metaphor, simile; **mengibaratkan** **1** to compare things; **2** to treat like a thing; **pembantunya mereka ibaratkan anjing** they treat their servant like a dog.

iblis devil, Satan.

ibni, ibnu son of.

Ibrani Hebrew.

ibu mother; **ibu tiri** stepmother; **ibu bapak** parents; **keibubapakan** parental; **ibu kandung** birth mother; **ibu-ibu** **1** mothers; **2** Ladies; **Ibu-ibu dan Bapak-bapak** Ladies and Gentlemen; **seibu** having the same mother; **keibuan** maternal, motherly; **keibu-ibuan** feminine, motherly.

ibunda courteous term for mother, my old lady.

idam **1** craving, desire; **2** aspiration; **mengidam** to crave, to long for; **mengidam-idamkan** to crave, to desire greatly; **idaman** **1** what you crave for; **tempat idaman untuk bertamasya** the perfect place for a picnic; **2** what you aspire to; **idam-idaman** aspirations.

idap, mengidap **1** to be ill, to suffer (a disease) for a long time; **2** to contract (a disease).

ide idea.

ideal ideal; **idealisme** idealism.

ideologi ideology; **berideologikan** to have an ideology; **berideologikan demokratis** to have a democratic ideology; **mengideologikan** to make a certain thing the ideology.

Idul Adha feast of the sacrifice of Ismael by Abraham.

Idul Fitri feast at the end of the fasting period *(Islamic)*.

iga rib.

igau, mengigau **1** to talk in your sleep; **2** to be delirious, to rave; **mengigaukan** to talk about something while asleep or delirious; **igauan** **1** what is said during sleep or

a b c d e f g h i j k l m n o p q r s t u v w x y z

delirium; **2** delirium; **3** nonsense.

ijasah, ijazah 1 diploma; **2** professional certificate or licence; **berijazah** licensed, certified.

ijin permit, permission.

ikal curl, curly, wavy; **mengikal** to curl (hair); **mengikalkan** to curl a person's hair for him/her.

ikan 1 fish; **ikan asin** salted fish; **2** meat; **ikan ayam** chicken meat; **perikanan** fishery.

ikat 1 cord for tying,; **2** bunch, bundle; **3** band; **ikat pinggang** belt; **4** method of tying and dying yarn into a design before it is woven; **kain ikat** weavings made from yarn that has been tie-dyed; **seikat** a tied-up bunch; **seikat bunga** a bunch of flowers; **seikat kunci** a bunch of keys; **mengikat 1** to tie, to fasten; **2** to bind; **3** to compose *(for example, a poem)*; **4** to mount *(for example, a gem)*; **mengikatkan** to tie one thing to something else; **ikatan 1** something bound; **2** union; **3** bond, knot, tie; **4** binding tie; **ikatan darah** blood ties; **seikatan** belonging to the same organization; **pengikat** binder, fastener.

ikhlas sincere; **mengikhlaskan 1** to accept absolutely; **2** to sacrifice for a cause; **keikhlasan** sincerity, wholeheartedness.

ikhtiar 1 initiative; **2** effort; **berikhtiar** endeavour; **mengikhtiarkan 1** to endeavour, to try hard; **2** to arrange for; **pengikhtiaran** trying hard.

ikhtisar abstract, summary, synopsis.

iklan advertisement; **iklan baris, iklan mini** the classified ads; **mengiklankan** to advertise; **mengiklankan barang bekas di koran** to advertise secondhand goods in the newspaper; **pengiklan** advertiser; **pengiklanan** advertising; **periklanan** the advertising business.

iklim climate; **iklim panas** hot climate; **iklim politik** political climate.

ikrar promise, vow; **berikrar** promise; **mengikrarkan** to promise.

ikut 1 follow, go along; **silahkan ikut main** won't you join the game?; **ikut serta** accompany, go along, participate; **Herman tidak pernah ikutserta** Herman

a b c d e f g h i j k l m n o p q r s t u v w x y z

never joins in; **mengikutsertakan** to allow someone to join in, to include a person; to join in, to participate; **ikut campur 1** intervene; **2** meddle in things not your business; **ikut-ikut(an)** be a hanger-on; **jangan ikut-ikut!** mind your own business!; **berikut 1** accompanying; **2** as follows, following; **kami akan naik pesawat terbang yang berikut** we're catching the next plane; **di halaman berikutnya** on the next page; **berikut-ikut** consecutively, successively; **mengikut 1** to follow, to obey; **2** to act like, to follow after; **mengikuti 1** to follow; **2** to take *(a course)*; **saya ingin mengikuti kursus itu** I want to take the course; **3** to obey; **4** to keep up with *(news or information)*; **5** to be a part of the group; **mengikutkan 1** to include, to send with; **2** to follow; **ikutan** something to be followed; **ikut-ikutan** a follower of whatever is going on; **pengikut 1** follower; **2** participant.

ilah a god; **tidak berilah** atheistic, godless; **mengilahkan** to deify.

ilham 1 divine inspiration; **2** brainstorm, inspiration; **mengilham** to prompt, to suggest; **mengilhami** to inspire.

ilmiah scientific.

ilmiawan scholar, scientist.

ilmu 1 knowledge; **2** science, branch of science; **ilmu jiwa** psychology; **3** esoterik knowledge; **ilmu batin** mysticism, spiritualism; **ilmu gaib** magic; **berilmu** learned, scholarly; **ilmuwan** scientist.

imam 1 communal prayer leader *(Islam)*; **2** title of chief of Islamic state; **3** Catholic priest; **keimaman** priesthood.

iman 1 belief, creed, faith; **2** confidence; **beriman** believing, faithful.

imbang 1 balance; **2** match, equal; **seimbang** balanced; **daya jual dan daya beli tidak seimbang** the selling power and the purchasing power are not balanced; **keseimbangan** balance, equilibrium; **keseimbangan kekuatan** balance of power; **hilang keseimbangan** to lose your balance; **berimbang 1** balanced; **2** matched; **3** comparable; **mengimbangi** to equal; **imbangan** balance, counterweight, equal in weight; **pengimbang, perimbang** counterpart, opposite number; **pengimbangan** equalization; **perimbangan 1** balance; **2** proportion, ratio.

imbuh extra, supplement; **mengimbuh** to give extra; **imbuhan 1** something given extra; **2** affix.

imigran immigrant.

imigrasi immigration; **Kantor Imigrasi** Immigration Office; **keimigrasian** matters relating to immigration.

iming, mengiming-iming to entice, to tantalize.

imlek Chinese calendar; **Tahun Baru Imlek** Chinese New Year.

imperialis imperialist.

impi, bermimpi, mengimpi to dream, to hope; **mengimpikan** to dream of; **impian** dream, vision, wish; **taman impian** amusement park, dreamworld; **semalam impian saya sangat indah** I had a wonderful dream last night.

impor import; **mengimpor** to import; **pengimpor** importer; **pengimporan 1** import business; **2** importation; **importir** importer.

inap, menginap to sleep over, to stay overnight; **kita akan menginap di Bromo** we're going to stay at Bromo overnight; **menginap di rumah teman** to stay with a friend; **penginapan** lodging for the night; **penginapan itu agak sederhana** the accommodation's a bit basic.

incar drill; **mengincar 1** to aim *(a gun etc.)*; **2** to have your eye on a thing or person; **saya mengincar mobil itu** I'd like to get that car; **incaran 1** aim *(of a gun etc.)*; **2** target.

indah 1 attractive, beautiful, handsome; **gambar indah** a beautiful picture; **dengan indah** beautifully; **2** precious, valuable; **intan yang indah** a valuable diamond; **memperindah** to beautify, to embellish; **keindahan** beauty; **mengindahkan** to pay attention.

indekos room and board; **mengindekoskan** to have someone rent a room somewhere; **orangtua saya mengindekoskan saya di rumah guru** my parents made me board at the teacher's house.

indera[1] **1** exalted, the God Indra; **2** the Gods; **keinderaan** where the Gods live.

indera[2], **panca-indera** the five senses; **indera cium**

the sense of smell; **penginderaan** sensation, sensory perception.

Indo a Eurasian.

Indonesia Indonesia, Indonesian; **Bahasa Indonesia** Indonesian language; **mengindonesiakan 1** to Indonesianize; **2** to put into Indonesian; **keindonesiaan 1** Indonesian; **2** Indonesianized; **pengindonesiaan** Indonesianization.

induk 1 *(usually for animals)* mother; **2** chief, main; **kapal induk** aircraft carrier; **perusahaan induk** parent company; **3** something that can be considered as a mother; **induk kereta api** locomotive.

induksi induction; **menginduksikan** to induce.

industri industry; **industrialisasi** industrialization; **perindustrian** industrial affairs.

infeksi infection; **infeksi mata** an eye infection; **infeksi tenggorokan** a throat infection.

inflasi inflation.

informan informant.

informasi information.

informal informal; **keinformalan** informality.

infus to give an infusion or feed intravenously.

ingat recall, remember; **ingatlah pada saya!** remember me!; **ingat akan diri(nya)** to become conscious, to be in control of yourself; **tak ingat diri** to lose consciousness; **saya tidak ingat** I don't remember; **ingat-ingat** be careful or attentive; **seingat** as far as you can remember; **seingat saya** as I recall; **mengingat 1** to recall, to recollect, to remember; **2** to think of, to keep in mind; **mengingat ongkosnya** to bear the cost in mind; **kami akan mengingat masalah itu** we will take that problem into account; **kami harus mengingat rakyat dulu** we should consider the people first; **3** considering; **mengingat kondisi kesehatannya** considering her health; **mengingat bahwa dia sendiri yang melakukannya** considering he did it himself; **mengingat-ingat 1** to keep in mind; **2** to keep thinking about; **mengingatkan 1** to remind you about; **tolong ingatkan ibu Anda untuk**

menjemput saya please remind your mother to pick me up; **2** to keep in mind; **3** to warn; **4** to record; **memperingati 1** to commemorate; **2** to note down, to record; **memperingatkan** to warn, to caution; **saya memperingatkan Anda bahwa itu mahal** I warn you, it's expensive; **dia memperingatkan saya supaya mobil dikunci** he warned me to lock the car; **teringat** enter your mind, occur to you; **ketika menonton film itu saya teringat akan kejadian yang terjadi dua puluh tahun yang lalu** while watching the film I suddenly remembered the incident that occurred twenty years ago; **teringat-ingat** be constantly reminded; **ingatan 1** memory; **daya ingatan saya kurang baik** I have a bad memory; **nama itu mengbangkitkan ingatan** that name rings a bell; **2** idea, thought; **ingatan Anda baik** your idea is a good one; **pengingat 1** someone who has a very good memory; **2** reminder; **peringatan 1** remembrance, memory; **upacara peringatan** memorial service; **2** warning, admonition.

Inggris England, English; **apakah Anda berbahasa Inggris?** do you speak English?; **harap bicara dalam bahasa Inggris** please speak English.

ingin desire, wish; **Anda ingin apa?** what will you have?; **saya ingin mandi** I'm going to have a bath (shower); **saya ingin menjadi insinyur** I would like to become an engineer; **apakah Anda ingin ke pantai?** do you fancy going to the beach?; **ingin tahu** curious; **keingintahuan** curiosity; **menginginkan,** to desire; **sangat menginginkan** to be desperate to; **dia sangat menginginkan ijazah dari Universitas Melbourne** he's desperate to have a degree from Melbourne University; **keinginan** desire, longing, wish; **berkeinginan** to have a desire.

ingkar 1 refuse, reluctant; **2** not keep your word; **mengingkari 1** to go back on (your word); **2** to deny (a fact); **keingkaran 1** denial, **2** refusal; **pengingkaran 1** negation; **2** denial.

ingus nasal mucus, snot; **membuang ingus** to blow

your nose; **beringus** to have a runny nose; **ingusan** **1** runny-nosed; **2** inexperienced.

ini 1 these, this; **kuas ini** this paintbrush; **yang ini** this one; **apakah Anda dapat pegang buku-buku ini sebentar?** can you hold these books for a moment?; **apa ini?** what's this?; **ini Sukra** this is Sukra speaking *(on the phone)*; **ini nomor telepon saya** here's my phone number; **2** this *(coming period of time)*; **pagi ini** this morning; **sore ini** this afternoon.

inisiatif, inisiatip initiative; **berinisiatif 1** to take the initiative; **2** to have initiative.

injak, menginjak 1 to stamp, to step on; **dilarang menginjak rumput** keep off the grass, do not step on the grass; **2** to enter a certain age or status; **menginjak-injak 1** to trample down, to tread under foot; **2** to be disrespectful of, to disobey, to ignore; **menginjakkan kaki** to set foot on; **terinjak** stepped or trampled on; **terinjak-injak 1** trampled on; **2** disregarded, ignored; **injak(-injak)an** pedal, stirrup.

Injil Gospel; **penginjil** evangelist, preacher.

insaf, insyaf akan realize, understand; **apakah Anda insyaf sudah jam berapa sekarang?** do you realize what time it is?; **menginsafkan 1** to make a person aware or realize; **2** to be aware of.

insinyur (Ir) engineer.

inskripsi inscription.

inspeksi inspection; **menginspeksi** to inspect.

inspektur inspector.

instansi 1 level of a court's jurisdiction; **2** agency, institute.

instruksi 1 directive, instruction; **Inpres** *(**Instruksi Presiden**)* Presidential Directive; **2** briefing; **menginstruksikan** to instruct.

instruktur instructor.

instrumen instrument; **instrumen gesek** stringed instrument.

insya Allah God willing.

intai, mengintai 1 to spy on; **2** to lie in wait; **intaian** place to spy from; **pengintai** observer, scout; **pengintaian 1** observation, reconnaissance; **2** espionage.

intan diamond.

intelek intellect.

intelektual intellectual.

intensif intensive; **mengintensifkan** to intensify.

intensifikasi intensification; **mengintensifikasikan** to intensify, to step up.

interlokal long-distance call, make a long-distance call; **menginterlokal** to make a long-distance call.

internasional international.

interviu interview, **menginterviu** to interview.

inti **1** kernel, nucleus; **2** core, gist; **inti pembicaraan saya** the subject of my talk; **3** contents, filling; **intisari** abstract, essence; **mengintisarikan** to make an abstract of; **berintikan** to have as a core.

intim close, intimate; **teman intim** close friend; **hubungan intim** very close relationship.

intip, mengintip to spy on, to peep at; **pengintipan** spying, surveillance.

introduksi introduction.

intuisi intuition.

ipar brother-in-law, sister in-law; **adik ipar, kakak ipar** brother/sister-in-law; **beripar** be a brother or sister-in-law of.

Ir (insinyur) engineer.

irama rhythm; **seirama** in rhythm with; **berirama** rhythmical; **mengiramakan** to provide a rhythm.

iri envious of a person's status or achievements, full of jealousy; **iri-hati** be jealous; **melakukan karena beriri hati** to do out of spite.

Irian New Guinea; **Irian Jaya** Indonesian New Guinea, now West Papua *(Papua Barat)*.

irigasi irrigation; **mengirigasikan** to irrigate.

iring, seiring **1** in a row; **2** of one mind, unanimous; **3** together or along with; **beriring** consecutive, successive; **beriring-iring(an)** in single file, one after the other; **mengiring(i)** **1** together with; **2** to join in, to accompany, to escort; **teriring** accompanied; **iringan** **1** follower; **2** accompaniment; **iringan musik** backing group; **3** procession; **iring-iringan** procession; **pengiring** **1** escort, follower, retinue; **2** accompanist; **pengiringan** escorting.

iris slice very thinly; **seiris** a slice; **mengiris** to slice; **irisan** slice, section; **pengirisan** act of slicing.

a b c d e f g h i j k l m n o p q r s t u v w x y z

irit economical; **mengirit** to economize on, to save; **pengiritan** economizing.

Isa Jesus; **Nabi Isa** Jesus Christ *(Islam).*

isap, mengisap 1 to suck; **ke luar mengisap udara** to go out for a breath of air; **2** to smoke; **mengisap rokok** to smoke a cigarette; **3** *(liquid)* to absorb; **isapan** something inhaled; **pengisap 1** something that sucks; **alat pengisap debu** vacuum cleaner; **2** extortionist; **3** someone who smokes; **pengisapan 1** exploitation; **2** smoking.

iseng do for fun; **iseng-iseng 1** do something just to amuse yourself; **saya sedang iseng-iseng saja** I do it for the hell of it; **2** casually, leisurely.

isi 1 contents; **2** capacity, volume; **3** substance; **4** the people who live in a building; **seisi** the entire contents, the entire population; **berisi 1** to have contents; **2** to have substance; **berisikan** to contain a particular thing; **mengisi** to fill up; **mengisi formulir** to fill in a form; **mengisikan 1** to fill for someone; **2** to put something in as contents; **isian** filler, stuffing; **pengisi 1** filler; **2** fill-in; **pengisian** filling up.

Islam Islam; **mengislamkan** to convert to Islam, Islamize; **keislaman** Islamic; **pengislaman** Islamization.

isolasi insulation, insulating tape; **mengisolasi** to insulate.

isolir, mengisolir to isolate.

istana castle, palace.

istilah technical term; **mengistilahkan** to provide a term for; **peristilahan** terminology.

istimewa different, extraordinary, special; **cabe yang istimewa pedasnya** extra hot chillies; **istimewa besarnya** extra large; **mengistimewakan** to regard or treat as special; **keistimewaan 1** peculiarity, special feature; **2** special treatment.

istirahat 1 rest; **istirahat sakit** sick leave; **2** break, pause; **jam istirahat** recess *(in school)*; **beristirahat** take a break, rest; **tempat beristirahat di pantai** a seaside resort; **mengistirahatkan** to give a person a break or rest; **pengistirahatan 1** giving a person a rest; **2** retiring someone; **peristirahatan**

a b c d e f g h i j k l m n o p q r s t u v w x y z

vacation resort provided for members of a group; **peristirahatan terakhir** cemetery.

istri married woman, wife; **sepasang suami-istri** *(husband and wife)* a married couple; **sudah bertahun-tahun mereka hidup sebagai suami-istri** they've been married for many years; **memperistrikan** to take someone as a wife.

isu **1** issue, problem; **2** rumours; **mengisukan** **1** to make an issue of; **2** to gossip about.

isyarat sign, signal; **mengisyaratkan** to beckon, to signal.

itik kind of duck.

itikad **1** conviction; **2** determination, will; **beritikad** have conviction or faith; **beritikad baik** to have goodwill.

itu **1** it, that, those; **apa itu?** what's that?; **siapa itu?** who's that?, who is it?; **di mana itu?** where's that?, where is it?; **apakah itu Mustafa?** is that Mustafa?; **itu tidak benar** that's not true; **laki-laki itu** that man; **yang itu** that one; **anjing-anjing itu** those dogs; **'Anda ingin kue yang mana?' 'yang itu'** 'which cake would you like?' 'that one, please'; **ya, itu benar** yes, it's true; **2** the; **orang itulah yang saya perlukan** the very person I need!; **itu alat yang cocok untuk pekerjaan ini!** the right tool for the job!; **3** there; **itu mereka** there they are; **itu dia** there she is; **4** hesitation word; **5** clause marker: when, if, in that case.

iur to contribute; **iuran** **1** contribution; **2** subscription; **3** premium for insurance; **4** dues, levy; **iuran keamanan** dues for local security service.

izin **1** permission; **2** franchise, licence, permit; **Surat Izin Mengemudi (SIM)** driver's licence; **seizin** with the permission of; **mengizinkan** **1** to allow, to permit; **gurunya mengizinkan mereka pulang** the teacher allowed them to go home; **2** to license; **perizinan** **1** permission; **2** licensing.

J j

jabar, menjabarkan **1** to clarify, to spell out; **2** to convert a fraction; **3** to announce; **penjabaran** spelling out.

jabat, berjabat(an) tangan shake hands; **jabatan 1** duty, function; **2** position, post; **dipecat dari jabatan** to be axed from a positon; **pejabat** functionary, official; **pejabat presiden** acting president.

jadi 1 be, become, work as; **jadi polisi** to be or become a police officer; **2** so, therefore; **jadi nama Anda siapa?** so what's your name?; **jadi apa yang akan kita kerjakan** so what shall we do?; **3** end up doing; **pertandingan itu tak jadi diadakan** the match wasn't held as planned; **4** finished; **program itu sudah jadi** the program is finished; **jadinya 1** outcome; **begitulah jadinya kalau terlalu boros** that's what happens if you're too extravagant; **2** consequently; **jadinya, bagaimana? bagaimana jadinya?** so what happened? how did it end?; **menjadi 1** to become; **Anisah ingin menjadi guru** Anisah wants to become a teacher; **menjadi buta** to go blind, **2** be; **uang tidak menjadi alasan** money is not the reason; **menjadi-jadi** to increase, to worsen; **tingkahnya makin menjadi-jadi** his/her behaviour is getting worse; **menjadikan** make into something; **terjadi** happen, occur, take place; **apa yang terjadi?** what's happening?; **gejolak moneter yang terjadi pada tahun 1997** the monetary fluctuations that occurred in 1997; **kejadian 1** creation, Genesis; **2** event, incident; **berada pada lokasi kejadian** to be on the scene; **kejadian berurutan** a sequence of events; **jadi-jadian** an imaginary being having supernatural powers, apparition, ghost.

jadwal 1 schedule, timetable; **2** list, table; **jadwal perjalanan** itinerary; **menjadwalkan** to plan, to timetable; **penjadwalan** scheduling.

jaga 1 wake up; **2** guard, watchman; **jaga malam** night watch; **3** be on duty; **dokter jaga** the duty doctor; **4** preserve; **jagalah kebersihan!** do not litter!; **berjaga-jaga** be on the safe side, be on your guard; **berjaga 1** to stay awake; **2** to stand guard; **3** to be on your guard; **menjaga 1** to keep an eye on, to watch over; **ayah sedang menjaga anak-anak** Dad's looking after the kids; **2** to guard against; **3** to guard; **4** to keep, to maintain; **tolong jaga tempat duduk saya** will you keep my seat?; **menjagai 1** to watch over; **ibu menjagai adik yang demam** mother is keeping watch over my brother who is feverish; **2** to guard for someone; **penjaga** guard; **penjagaan 1** guarding, security; **penjagaan yang ketat** surveillance; **2** guardpost.

jagal butcher, slaughterer; **menjagal 1** to butcher, to slaughter; **2** to be a butcher; **penjagal, tukang jagal** butcher; **penjagalan 1** abattoir, slaughterhouse; **2** butchering, slaughtering; **3** murder.

jagat world; **jagat raya** the universe; **sejagat** universal, worldwide.

jago 1 cock, rooster; **2** champion; **3** charismatic leader; **menjagoi 1** to back, to support *(a sports team)*; **2** to lead; **menjagokan 1** to sponsor, to back; **2** to put forward as a candidate; **jagoan** champion.

jagung corn, maize.

jahat bad, evil, wicked; **bermaksud jahat** to have evil intention; **lingkungan yang jahat** a dangerous neighborhood; **kejahatan 1** evil, wickedness; **2** crime; **pembunuhan adalah suatu kejahatan** murder is a crime; **berjuang melawan kejahatan** to fight against crime; **penjahat** criminal.

jahe ginger.

jahit sewing; **jahit-menjahit 1** sewing, tailoring; **2** needlework; **menjahit 1** to sew, to stitch; **saya menjahit baju untuk Sri** I sewed a dress for Sri; **2** to tailor; **menjahitkan** to sew; **saya menjahitkan baju di tukang jahit** I had a dress made at the dressmaker; **jahitan 1** sewn item; sewing to be done; **2** seam, stitch, suture; **penjahit, tukang jahit** seamstress, tailor; **penjahitan** sewing.

jaja, berjaja to hawk, to peddle; **menjajakan** to peddle, to hawk things; **jajaan** items peddled; **penjaja** hawker, peddler.

jajah, menjajah 1 to colonize; **2** to cross, to tour; **terjajah** colonized; **jajahan 1** colony; **2** district; **penjajah** colonizer; **penjajahan 1** colonialism; **2** colonization.

jajan, berjajan to buy sweets, to eat snacks; **jajan-**

jajanan, jajanan various kinds of snacks.

jajar line, row; **sejajar** **1** parallel; **2** in a row; **3** at the same level; **membuat sejajar 1** to make parallel; **2** to put on a par; **kesejajaran** parallelism; **berjajar** to be in a row or line; **berjajaran 1** side by side; **2** in rows; **menjajarkan 1** to put in a row; **2** to make parallel; **jajaran 1** line, row; **2** series.

jaksa district attorney, public prosecutor; **jaksa agung** attorney general; **kejaksaan 1** prosecuting counsel's office; **2** attorney; **3** judiciary.

jala net, especially a casting net for fishing; **jala-jala** hair net; small net; **menjala** to use a casting net; **penjala** person who fishes with a casting net.

jalan 1 path, road, street; **jalan raya** highway, main road; **jalan satu arah** one-way street; **lampu jalan** streetlamp; **peta jalan** street map; **menyeberang jalan** to cross the road; **jalan ke Sidoardjo** the road to Sidoardjo; **2** course; **jalan pesawat terbang** flight path; **3** way, manner; **4** pass, go on; **jalan-jalan** go for a stroll; **sejalan 1** parallel; **2** be in accordance with; **berjalan 1** to walk; **jangan berjalan di pinggir kali** don't walk on the edge of the river; **berjalan dengan tidak bersepatu** to walk barefoot; **2** to go, to run, to work; **mesin ini tidak mau jalan** this engine won't run; **semuanya berjalan dengan baik sekali** everything went really well; **3** to be almost at an age; **umur Angela sudah berjalan lima tahun** Angela is going on for five; **berjalan-jalan 1** to take a stroll; **kami berjalan-jalan di taman** we went for a walk in the park; **2** to take a pleasure trip; **menjalani 1** to walk on; **2** to undergo, to endure; **3** to go through a period of your life; **4** to travel through somewhere; **menjalankan 1** to drive, to operate; **apakah Anda bisa menjalankan video ini?** can you work the video?; **2** to start, to put into operation; **3** to carry out, to perform; **jalanan 1** pathway; **2** road, track; **pejalan** walker; **pejalan kaki** pedestrian; **penyeberangan pejalan kaki** pedestrian crossing; **perjalanan 1** journey, trip, tour; **2** course.

jalang untamed, wild.

a b c d e f g h i j k l m n o p q r s t u v w x y z

jalar creeping; **ubi jalar** sweet potato; **menjalar 1** to crawl, to creep *(for example, snake, plants)*; **ular hanya bisa menjalar karena tidak mempunyai kaki** snakes can only crawl because they have no legs; **2** to spread *(for example, disease, fire)*; **flu adalah salah satu penyakit yang mudah sekali menjalar** flu is one of the diseases that spread easily; **penjalaran 1** climbing, creeping; **2** spreading; **3** stake for climbing plants.

jalin 1 *(hair)* plait, intertwined, tied; **berjalin** tied together; **menjalin 1** to plait, to weave together; **2** to make a thing closer *(for example, a relationship)*; **Australia sudah menjalin hubungan diplomatik hampir dengan semua negeri di dunia** Australia has established diplomatic relations with nearly all countries in the world; **3** *(stories)* to compose; **menjalinkan** to include, to interweave; **terjalin 1** tied in; **2** involved; **keterjalinan** entanglement, involvement; **jalinan 1** something plaited, wickerwork; **2** combination.

jalur 1 strip, stripe; **2** traffic lane; **jalur lambat** slow lane; **3** space between two columns, lines or rows; **berjalur-(jalur) 1** striped; **2** be evenly spaced.

jam 1 hour; **dua jam kemudian** two hours later; **setengah jam** half an hour; **2** o'clock; **jam dua** two o'clock; **3** time for doing; **jam kerja** work hours; **digaji menurut jumlah jam kerjanya** to be paid by the hour; **jam karet** not on time *(literally rubber time)*; **jam kuliah** class hours *(lecture time)*; **4** watch; **jam tangan** watch; **jam beker, jam weker** alarm clock; **berjam-jam** for hours and hours; **jam-jaman** *(colloquial)* on an hourly basis.

jamak[1] plural.

jamak[2] customary, ordinary; **menjamakkan** to see as customary.

jaman age, epoch, era, period; **sejaman** in the same period.

jamban lavatory, toilet.

jambang(an) 1 pot, vase; **2** whiskers.

jambret, menjambret to grab, to seize, to snatch; **pencuri menjambret tas wanita tua itu** the thief snatched the old lady's bag; **jambretan** thing snatched.

a b c d e f g h i j k l m n o p q r s t u v w x y z

jamin guarantee, security; **menjamin** to guarantee; **terjamin** guaranteed; **jaminan 1** guarantee; **2** bail, collateral, security; **penjamin** guarantor; **penjaminan** giving a guarantee.

jamrud emerald.

jamu^1, menjamu to receive or entertain a guest; **penjamuan, perjamuan 1** banquet, party, reception; **jamuan, perjamuan makan malam** holding a dinner party; **2** a call, a visit.

jamu^2 herbal medicine, herbal tonic; **jamu-jamuan** medicinal herbs.

jamur fungus, mushroom, toadstool; **berjamur** mouldy; **menjamur** to mushroom; **gedung bertingkat menjamur di Jakarta** multi-storey buildings are mushrooming in Jakarta; **penjamuran** mushrooming.

janda 1 widow; **janda kembang** young widow; **2** divorcee; **menjanda 1** to be widowed; **2** divorced.

jangan 1 *(negative imperative)* do not, don't; **jangan beli mobil itu** don't buy that car, **jangan ikut campur** mind your own business!; **2** should not; **kita jangan pergi ke Bogor hari ini** we should not go to Bogor today; **jangan mau** be sure not to; **jangan mau bayar sebelumnya** be sure not to pay in advance; **jangan tidak** have to, must; **Anda jangan tidak mengundang Gai** you must invite Gai; **jangan sampai** otherwise; **hati-hati, jangan sampai terpeleset** be careful you don't slip; **jangan-jangan 1** let's hope not; **jangan-jangan Rachmi sudah berangkat** let's hope Rachmi hasn't left yet; **2** I'm afraid that, it could be that, maybe, perhaps *(something bad)*; **jangan-jangan ada krisis moneter lagi** I'm afraid that there'll be another monetary crisis; **jangankan** let alone; **jangankan uang, pakaian saja Kim tak punya** Kim has no clothes, let alone money.

janggal 1 awkward, clumsy; **2** discordant, displeasing; **3** *(behaviour)* improper, indecent; **kejanggalan** awkwardness, impropriety.

jangka 1 compass for drawing circles; **2** length of time; **dalam jangka panjang** in the long run; **jangka waktu dua tahun** a two-year period; **3** phase; **berjangka 1** to be a particular length; **tabungan berjangka** term

a b c d e f g h i j k l m n o p q r s t u v w x y z

deposit; **2** to be spaced; **2** to plan, to work out; **menjangkakan** to fix, to plan; **penjangkaan** planning out.

jangkau, menjangkau **1** to reach to, to reach for; **2** to reach out, to extend to; **menjangkaukan** to reach something out; **dia menjangkaukan tangannya ke saya** she reached out her hand to me; **terjangkau** **1** achieved, reached; **2** achievable; **tidak terjangkau** out of reach; **jangkauan 1** extent, range, reach, scope; **2** what you hope to reach.

jangkerik, jangkrik, jengkerik cricket *(insect).*

jangkit, berjangkit, menjangkit **1** spread (of disease); **penyakit demam berdarah sedang berjangkit di daerah itu** dengue fever is spreading in that area; **2** to spread contagion all around; **menjangkiti** to infect a person; **terjangkiti, kejangkitan 1** contaminated, infected; **2** smitten by; **penjangkitan** passing on of disease; **perjangkitan** outbreak of disease; **perjangkitan kolera** an outbreak of cholera.

jangkung tall *(a person).*

janji 1 promise; **dia melanggar janjinya** he broke his word; **2** appointment; **membuat janji dengan dokter gigi** to make a dental appointment; **menepati janji** to keep an appointment or a promise; **berjanji** to promise to do; **saya sudah berjanji** I've already given my word; **menjanjikan** to promise; **dia juga menjanjikan oleh-oleh** he also promised me a gift; **perjanjian 1** agreement; **2** pact.

jantan 1 *(for animals)* male, masculine; **2** bold, brave; **3** dashing; **4** macho, virile; **kejantanan** machismo, virility; **pejantan** stud.

jantung heart; **sakit jantung** heart disease; **serangan jantung** heart attack; **jantung hati** sweetheart.

Januari January.

jarah, menjarah to loot; **barang jarahan** goods looted; **penjarah** looter; **penjarahan** looting.

jarak distance between, gap; **jarak dekat** short distance; **jarak jauh** long distance; **membuat jarak** to keep at a distance from; **jaraknya dapat ditempuh dengan jalan kaki** it's within walking distance; **berjarak 1** to be at a distance of; **rumah harus**

berjarak satu meter dari batas tanah the house must be one metre from the land boundary; **2** to put distance between.

jarang 1 rare, scarce; **barang tenunan demikian jarang** such textile is rare; **2** infrequently, rarely; **Tracy jarang pulang** Tracy rarely comes home; **3** spaced wide apart, sparse; **4** coarse in texture; **jarang-jarang** rarely, seldom; **menjarangkan, memperjarang 1** to space, to thin out; **2** to dilute; **kejarangan** infrequency, rarity, sparseness; **penjarangan** spacing, thinning out.

jari 1 digit; **jari tangan** finger; **jari kaki** toe; **ibu jari** thumb; **2** digit-like projection; **jari-jari 1** radius; **2** spokes of a wheel.

jaring dragnet or seine fishing net *(not a casting net)*; **jaring-jaring 1** web; **2** mesh, sports net; **menjaring 1** to catch in a net; **2** to encompass a large area; **terjaring** caught, snared; **tiga penjahat terjaring polisi** three criminals were caught by the police; **jaringan 1** net; **2** network; **penjaring** thing used as a net; **penjaringan** act of netting.

jarum 1 hypodermic or sewing needle; **2** hand of clock, pointer; **jarum panjang** the minute hand; **jarum pendek** the hour hand; **jarum-jarum 1** needle on scales; **2** nettles; **jarum pentol** pin.

jas coat, jacket; **jas hujan** raincoat.

jasa 1 merit; **2** service; **biro jasa angkutan** travel bureau; **berjasa 1** to do a good turn; **2** *(person)* deserving.

jasmani body; **latihan jasmani** physical exercise; **kesehatan jasmani dan rohani** physical and mental health.

jati[1] teak *(tree and wood)*.

jati[2]**, sejati** genuine, real, true; **teman sejati** a true friend; **cinta sejati** true love.

jatuh 1 fall; **genteng jatuh dari atap** the tile fell off the roof; **jatuh harga** fall in price; **jatuh cinta, jatuh hati** fall in love; **2** fail; **Rumeena jatuh dalam ujian matematika** Rumeena failed the maths exam; **berjatuhan** fall *(many things)*; **korban-korban berjatuhan akibat perang** many victims fell as a result of the war; **menjatuhi** to impose; **pembunuh sadis itu dijatuhi hukuman mati**

a b c d e f g h i j k l m n o p q r s t u v w x y z

the sadistic murderer was given the death sentence; **menjatuhkan 1** to drop, to let fall; **Alison menjatuhkan panci panas** Alison dropped the hot saucepan; **2** *(government)* to overthrow, to topple; **3** to ruin a good name; **korupsi menjatuhkan nama baik Soeharto** corruption ruined Soeharto's good name; **4** *(fine, sentence)* to impose, to pass; **hakim menjatuhkan hukuman mati pada pembunuh** the judge passed the death sentence on the murderer; **menjatuhkan veto** cast a veto; **kejatuhan 1** downfall, fall *(of a government)*; **2** be hit by a falling object; **Wulandari tewas kejatuhan kelapa** Wulandari died because he was hit by a falling coconut; **penjatuhan** dropping.

jauh 1 distant, far, remote; **berapa jauhnya?** how far away is it?; **jauh sekali ke kolam renang yang terdekat** it's a long way to the nearest swimming pool; **tidak jauh lagi** not far away, it's already quite near; **dari jauh** from a distance; **terlalu jauh** too far; **2** far, by far; **sepeda Anda jauh lebih bagus dari sepeda saya** your bike is much better than mine; **jauh lebih cepat** much faster; **orangnya jauh terlalu banyak** far too many people; **jauh hari** long beforehand; **jauh-jauh** when you are far; **sejauh** as far as; **sejauh-jauhnya** as far as possible; **berjauhan** to be far from each other; **jauh menjauhi** to keep at a distance from each other; **menjauh** to be or become distant; **menjauhi 1** to avoid, to keep away from; **2** be far from; **kejauhan 1** distance; **2** *(colloquial)* too far.

Jawa Java, Javanese **bahasa Jawa** Javanese *(the language)*; **menjawakan** to Javanize; **kejawaan 1** being Javanese; **2** Javanism.

jawab, jawaban answer, reply; **jawab(an) yang salah** the wrong answer; **berjawaban** to reply to each other; **menjawab** to answer, to respond; **jawablah aku!** answer me!; **dia sama sekali tidak menjawab** she didn't even bother to reply.

jaya 1 victory; **2** glorious, victorious; **Indonesia jaya** glorious Indonesia; **3** prosperous; **berjaya 1** victorious; **2** successful; **menjayakan** to glorify; **kejayaan 1** fame, glory; **2** prosperity.

jazirah peninsula.

jebak trap; **menjebak** to frame, to trap; **jebakan** snare, trap; **penjebak** **1** trapper; **2** snare, trap; **penjebakan** snaring, trapping.

jeblos give way; **menjebloskan 1** to throw into; **2** to throw into prison; **Edi dijebloskan ke dalam penjara** Edi was thrown into jail; **kejeblos** drive, step into a ditch or hole.

jeda(h) interval, rest; **berjeda(h)** to rest, to take a rest.

jejak 1 *(animal)* trail, track; **2** footprint; **berjejak 1** step, tread on; **2** leave tracks; **menjejaki 1** to step, to tread on; **2** to trail, to track down; **3** to investigate; **menjejakkan** to set down *(your foot)*.

jejal, berjejal 1 crowd; **2** be crowded, jam-packed; **menjejal** to stuff full; **menjejali** to crowd, to fill; **penonton sepak bola menjejali stadion itu** the soccer spectators packed the stadium.

jejer line, row, series; **berjejer** in a row; **menjejer(kan)** to arrange in a row; **jejeran** line, row, series.

jelajah, menjelajah(i) 1 to cruise overseas; **2** to explore (an area); **menjelajahkan** to analyze, to examine, to investigate; **penjelajah** **1** explorer; **2** examiner; **penjelajahan** exploration.

jelang, menjelang 1 *(for addressing mail)* to; **2** approaching, around; **menjelang ajal** approaching the end of life; **menjelang Natal** approaching or around Christmas; **kesibukan menjelang Hari Natal** the Christmas rush.

jelas clear, distinct, explicit; **perintah yang jelas** clear instructions; **apakah jelas? sudah jelas?** is that clear?; **dengan jelas** obviously; **jelas sekali** very clear; **menjelaskan** to clarify, to explain; **memperjelas** to clarify; **kejelasan** clarity; **penjelasan** explanation; **dalam rapat menteri memberikan penjelasan tentang pembinaan dan pengembangan radio dan film** in the meeting the minister explained the founding and growth of radio and film.

jelek 1 ugly; **2** bad, horrible; **dia betul-betul jelek** he's really horrible; **3** poor in quality; **pekerjaan yang jelek**

a b c d e f g h i j k l m n o p q r s t u v w x y z

poor work; **jeleknya** the trouble is ...; **kejelekan** **1** ugliness; **2** badness, evil; **3** poorness of quality.

jelita *(for people)* beautiful, charming, graceful, lovely, sweet; **kejelitaan** loveliness.

jelma, menjelma to take on a form; **menjelma menjadi** to appear, to assume a form; **jelmaan 1** creation, incarnation; **2** what a thing has been changed into; **penjelmaan 1** incarnation; **2** transformation; **3** materialization, realization.

jemaah assembly, community; **jemaah gereja** church congregation; **jemaah haji** Muslim adherents making a pilgrimage to Mecca.

jembatan 1 bridge; **2** bond between; **menjembatani** to bridge.

jempol 1 thumb; **2** first-rate, tops; **jempolan** top quality.

jemput, menjemput to call for, to collect, to pick up; **mobil antar-jemput** limousine service, pick-up service, shuttle service; **sudah waktunya untuk menjemput anak-anak dari sekolah** it's time to collect the children from school; **saya akan menjemput Anda jam enam** I'll pick you up at six; **jemputan** pick-up service, limousine; **penjemput** person who comes to meet others; **penjemputan 1** *(at airport, station)* pick-up service; **2** picking up of.

jemu 1 tired; **2** bored, fed up with, sick of; **menjemukan 1** to bore, boring; **2** tiresome; **kejemuan 1** boredom; **2** be very bored.

jemur 1 sunbathe; **2** dry in the sun; **3** dried rice plant; **berjemur** sunbathe; **menjemur** to dry in the sun; **menjemurkan** to spread out to dry; **jemuran 1** items being dried; **2** the wash, laundry; **penjemuran 1** clothesline, rack for drying clothes; **2** drying in the sun.

jenaka funny, humorous; **cerita jenaka** joke; **kejenakaan** facetiousness, humour, joke.

jenazah body, cadaver, corpse.

jendela window.

jenderal general *(rank)*.

jenggot beard.

jengkal span of the hand

jengkel annoyed, irritated; **apakah Anda jengkel pada saya?** are you cross with me?; **menjengkelkan** to annoy, to irritate, annoying, irritating; **kejengkelan** annoyance, irritation.

jenis 1 kind, sort, genre; **Anda suka musik jenis apa?** what sort of music do you like?; **2** species, race; **3** gender; **jenis kelamin** gender, sex; **sejenis** of one kind, race or type; **berjenis-(jenis), bermacam jenis** various.

jentik-jentik mosquito larva.

jenuh 1 having had too much of; **2** saturated; **menjenuhkan 1** to satiate; **2** to saturate; **kejenuhan 1** saturation; **2** overfull.

Jepang Japan, Japanese.

jepit, jepitan, penjepit 1 pincers, tongs, tweezers; **2** clamp, clip; **jepit rambut, jepitan rambut** hairclip, hairpin; **menjepit** to hold something by clamping or pinching; **menjepitkan 1** to pinch, to squeeze; **2** to clip; **terjepit, kejepit** *(colloquial)* **1** be squeezed; **2** be in a fix; **jepitan** clip; **jepitan pakaian** clothes peg.

jera frightened; **Marcia pernah hampir tenggelam karena itu dia sekarang jera berenang di kolam lagi** because she was nearly drowned Marcia is now frightened to swim in the pond again; **menjerakan** to frighten, intimidate.

jerapah giraffe.

jerami straw; **topi jerami** a straw hat.

jerat 1 lasso, snare; **2** ruse, trick; **menjerat 1** to snare, to snarl, to tangle; **2** to deceive, to round up, to trick; **3** to entice; **terjerat** trapped; **jeratan** noose, trap; **penjerat** a person who entraps; **penjeratan** garroting, strangulation.

jerawat acne, blackhead, pimple; **berjerawat** to be pimply; **mukanya berjerawat** her/his face is pimply; **jerawatan** pimply; **mukanya jerawatan** her/his face is pimply.

jerih exhausted, tired, weary; **jerih payah** effort; **berjerih payah** to make a great effort.

jerit scream, shriek; **jerit tangis** to scream and cry; **menjerit** to scream; **menjerit-jerit** to yell out at the top of your voice; **jeritan** screams.

Jerman German, Germany.

jernih 1 clear; **2** pure; **air jernih** clear water; **menjernih** to clear up by itself; **air sungai itu sudah menjernih lagi** the river water is clear again now; **menjernihkan**

a b c d e f g h i j k l m n o p q r s t u v w x y z

a b c d e f g h i j k l m n o p q r s t u v w x y z

1 to make clear, to clear up; **obat itu dipakai untuk menjernihkan air** that chemical is used to clarify water; **2** to purify, to cleanse; **kejernihan** clarity, purity; **penjernih** purifier; **penjernih air** water purifier; **penjernihan** purification.

jeruk citrus fruit; **jeruk bali** pomelo; **jeruk manis** mandarin; **jeruk nipis** lime.

jidat forehead.

jihad, jihat holy war.

jijik 1 nauseating, repugnant; **2** disgusting; **menjijikkan 1** to abhor, to abominate, to loathe; **2** loathsome, nauseating; **kejijikan 1** filthiness; **2** disgust, repugnance.

jika, jikalau 1 if; **jika hujan** if it rains; **jika saya menang lotere** if I won the lottery; **jika saya Anda, saya akan melupakannya** if I were you I'd forget it; **2** *(future)* when; **jikalau Anda datang, tolong bawa CD baru itu** when you come bring the new CD; **jika kiranya** supposing, if by chance.

jilat, menjilat to lick; **kucing itu menjilat badannya sendiri** the cat's licking itself; **menjilat-jilat** to lick again and again; **penjilat, penjilat pantat** a crawler.

jilbab covering or shawl worn over the head by Moslem women.

jilid volume; **tiga jilid** three volumes; **jilid ketiga** the third volume; **berjilid-jilid** in volumes; **menjilid** to bind *(books)*; **buku yang dijilid** a bound book; **penjilid** book-binder.

jimat amulet, charm, talisman.

jin 1 genie; **2** evil spirit.

jinak 1 domesticated, tame; **2** docile, gentle; **kuda jinak** a docile horse; **3** benign; **(ber)jinak-jinak merpati** acting coy; **menjinakkan** to tame; **penjinak** (animal) tamer; **penjinakan** domestication, taming.

jingga orange *(colour)*.

jingkat, berjingkat-jingkat, menjingkat to stand or walk on tiptoe.

jintan, jinten caraway seed; **jintan hitam** cumin.

jitu accurate, exact, precise, spot-on.

jiwa soul, spirit; **jiwa raga** spirit and body; **menyelamatkan jiwa** to save a life; **orang yang berjiwa bebas** an independent person.

jodoh 1 marriage partner, mate; **2** match, be a mate.

joget dance; **berjoget** to dance.

jok 1 seat of a car; **2** car upholstery.

joki jockey.

jongkok, berjongkok to squat.

jual sell; **jual-beli** selling and buying; **menjual** to sell; **Supri menjual sayuran di pasar** Supri sells vegetables at the market; **saya menjual sepeda saya kepadanya** I sold him my bike; **terjual** sold out; **karcis pertandingan itu telah terjual habis** tickets for the game are sold out; **jualan** merchandise, goods for sale; **penjual** seller, vendor; **penjual eceran** retailer; **penjualan** selling, turnover.

juang struggle; **berjuang** fight, struggle; **kira-kira seperempat abad lamanya bangsa Timtim berjuang untuk kemerdekaannya** the East Timorese fought for their independence for about a quarter of a century; **memperjuangkan** to struggle for; **pejuang** fighter, warrior; **perjuangan** struggle, fight; **perjuangan kemerdekaan** the struggle for independence.

juara 1 champion; **juara dunia** world champion; **2** referee in a cockfight; **kejuaraan** championship.

jubah long flowing robe.

jubel, berjubel-jubel to crowd; **orang berjubel-jubel di dalam bis** the bus is packed with people.

judes cruel, vicious; sharp or venomous *(with words).*

judi gambling; **berjudi** to gamble; **penjudi** gambler; **perjudian** gambling.

juga 1 also, too; **di rumah dan di sekolah juga** both at home and at school; **pada musim kering dan musim hujan juga** both in the dry season and the wet season; **'saya tidak makan daging' 'saya juga tidak'** 'I don't eat meat' 'neither do I'; **'saya tinggal di Kebayoran' 'saya juga'** 'I live in Kebayoran' 'so do I'; **'saya tidak suka akan film itu' 'saya juga'** 'I hated that film' 'me too'; **2** even if; **3** anyway; **biar capek, saya masih juga mau ikut** even though I'm tired I want to come along anyway.

jujur honest; **jujur belaka** fair and square; **tidak jujur** insincere; **kejujuran** honesty.

Juli July.

juling cross-eyed.

Jumat Friday; **hari Jumat depan, hari Jumat yang akan**

a b c d e f g h i j k l m n o p q r s t u v w x y z

datang next Friday; **hari Jumat yang lalu** last Friday; **tutup hari Jumat** closed on Fridays.

jumlah **1** amount, sum, total; **jumlah uang yang tepat** the right amount of money; **2** number, quantity; **jumlahnya** in the amount of; **jumlahnya lima belas tidak termasuk anak-anak** the total is fifteen not counting the children; **uang insentif yang lumayan besar jumlahnya** an incentive payment that is quite large; **sejumlah** as much as, to the amount of; **sejumlah uang** a sum of money; **sejumlah besar** a large sum; **menjumlah** to add; **menjumlahkan** to add or count up; **dia sedang menjumlahkan uang itu** he's just counting the money; **terjumlah** **1** added up, totalled; **2** considered to be among; **penjumlahan** adding.

jumpa meet; **sampai jumpa lagi** till we meet again, see you; **berjumpa** run into; **saya berjumpa dengan Suci di depan perpustakaan** I met Suci outside the library; **menjumpai** **1** to find; **2** to go to meet; **saya akan menjumpai Cheryl di perpustakaan** I'm going to meet Cheryl at the library; **3** to meet with, to encounter; **Kevin menjumpai Siraj** Kevin encountered Siraj; **perjumpaan** meeting, encounter.

jungkal, menjungkalkan to overthrow, to overturn; **terjungkal** tumble forward.

Juni June.

junjung, menjunjung **1** to carry on your head or shoulders; **2** to respect; **junjungan** someone who is respected.

junta junta.

juntai, berjuntai to dangle.

jurang chasm, gorge, ravine; **tebing jurang** the edge of the cliff.

juri jury.

jurnalis journalist, reporter.

juru skilled worker; **juru bahasa** interpreter; **juru ulas olahraga** a sports commentator; **juru bicara** spokesperson; **jururawat** nurse *(old term, now perawat)*; **kejuruan** vocational, trade; **sekolah kejuruan** vocational school.

jurus movements, steps in martial arts; **menjurus** to go, to lead, to point in a particular direction; **jurusan** **1** direction; **jalan satu jurusan** one-way street;

jurusan berlawanan the opposite direction; **2** *(academic)* department, field; **jurusan Bahasa Indonesia** the Indonesian Department.

jus 1 *(tennis)* deuce; **2** juice; **jus avokad** avocado juice.

justru exactly, precisely; **ya, justru begitu** yes, exactly.

juta million; **sejuta orang** a million people; **lima juta Rupiah** five million Rupiah; **jutaan** millions of, by the millions; **jutawan** millionaire.

K k

kak (kakak) elder brother or sister.

kabar message, news, report; **kabar hari ini** today's news; **surat kabar** the newspaper; **'halo! apa kabar?' 'kabar baik'** 'hello! how are you?' 'I'm fine'; **apakah ada kabar?** any news?; **kabarnya** people say; **kabarnya Anda akan berhenti kerja** they say you're resigning; **berkabar 1** relate, tell; **2** send news about; **mengabari** to inform, to let a person know; **mengabarkan** to report.

kabel cable.

kabinet 1 *(government)* cabinet; **2** *(for storage)* cabinet.

kabisat, tahun kabisat leap year.

kabul answered, granted *(for example, prayer)*; **mengabulkan 1** to grant *(a wish)*; **2** to answer a prayer; **pengabulan** approval, consent, fulfilment, grant.

kabung white mourning headband; **berkabung** mourn, be in mourning for a death in your family; **masa berkabung** mourning period; **misa berkabung** funeral mass; **perkabungan** grieving, mourning.

kabur[1] **1** blurred, hazy, vague; **2** fading; **3** haze; **mengabur, menjadi kabur** to become hazy or blurred; **mengaburkan 1** to make blurred, foggy or hazy; **2** to obscure; **kekaburan** haziness, vagueness; **pengaburan** blurring of.

kabur[2] **1** *(a horse)* bolt; **2** escape, flee, run off; **Edi kabur dari penjara** Edi ran off from prison.

kabut haze, fog, mist; **kabut sudah lenyap** the fog's

a b c d e f g h i j k l m n o p q r s t u v w x y z

cleared away; **berkabut** foggy, hazy, misty; **sering berkabut di gunung** it's often misty in the mountains.

kaca glass; **kaca bening** clear glass; **kacamata** eyeglasses, spectacles; **kacamata hitam, kacamata gelap** sunglasses.

kacang bean, nuts; **sele kacang** peanut butter.

kacau chaotic, in disorder; **kacau balau** in utter confusion, topsy-turvy; **mengacaukan, memperkacaukan** to cause chaos, to confuse, to stir; **kekacauan** confusion, riots, unrest; **pengacau** terrorist; **pengacauan** rebellion, revolt.

kacoa, kacua cockroach.

kacung *(derogatory)* boy labourer, houseboy.

kadal lizard.

kadaluarsa, kadaluwarsa, kedaluwarsa barred by statute of limitaton, expired; **waktu kadaluarsa** use-by date.

kadang, kadang-kadang, terkadang now and then, occasionally, sometimes; **kadang-kadang saya naik kereta** I sometimes take the train; **saya terkadang naik kereta** now and then I take the train; **kadang-kala** occasionally, once in a while.

kadar content, degree; **ada buah yang kadar gulanya tinggi** there are fruits with high sugar content; **ala kadarnya** whatever is available; **kita harus makan ala kadarnya** we have to eat what's available.

kader cadre.

kadet cadet.

kado gift, present.

kafeteria cafeteria.

kafilah caravan.

kafir heathen, unbeliever.

kaget shocked, startled; **saya kaget mendengar bahwa ibunya meninggal dalam kecelakaan** I was shocked to hear that her mother had died in a car accident.

kagum 1 amazed, 2 impressed; **mengagumi, kagum akan** to admire; **saya mengagumi kecerdasannya, saya kagum akan kecerdasannya** I admire his cleverness; **mengagumkan** 1 to amaze; amazing, astonishing; **cerita yang mengagumkan** an amazing story; 2 to give rise to admiration; **kekaguman** admiration, surprise; **pengagum** admirer.

-kah question particle; **maukah Anda pergi ke Jepang?** do you want to go to Japan?; **tinggikah guru Anda?** is your teacher tall?

kaidah norm, principle, rule.

kail hook and line, fish hook; **mengail ikan** to catch fish with a hook; **pengail** angler.

kain cloth; **kain kebaya** sarong and blouse.

kais, mengais to scratch, to scrape.

kaisar emperor, caesar; **kekaisaran** empire.

kait barb, hook; **berkait** to be hooked on; **berkaitan** interlaced, related; **mengaitkan** to hook on; **kaitan, pengait** hook.

kaji, mengkaji examine, investigate, inspect, go over thoroughly, study; **mengaji Koran** to recite verses from the Quran; **pengkajian** investigation or research, study.

kakak elder sister, elder brother; **kakak sulung** eldest sister, eldest brother; **kakak perempuan saya** my older sister; **kakak laki-laki** older brother.

kakatua **1** cockatoo; **2** pincers.

kakek grandfather.

kaki **1** leg; **duduk bersilang kaki** sit cross-legged; **2** foot; **di kaki bukit** at the foot of the hill; **pergelangan kaki saya keseleo** I sprained my ankle.

kaku **1** stiff; **merasa kaku** to feel stiff; **2** awkward; **anak itu tampaknya kaku** that child appears awkward.

kakus lavatory, toilet, water closet; **menyiram kakus** to flush the lavatory.

kaktus cactus.

kala era, time; **kadang kala** sometimes; **dahulu kala** in former times; **dari dahulu kala orang percaya akan inkarnasi** people have believed in incarnation for ages; **pada kala Sukarno berkuasa, ekonomi Indonesia sangat buruk** during the Sukarno era the Indonesian economy was very bad; **ada kalanya dia berbohong** sometimes she lies; **berkala** periodically; **kinerja perusahaan itu dievaluasi secara berkala** the company's performance is evaluated periodically.

kalah defeated, lose; **regu kita kalah** our team lost; **mengalahkan** to beat, to defeat; **dia mengalahkan lawannya** she defeated her opponent.

kalang-kabut confused, disordered, chaotic; **sewaktu terjadi kerusuhan di Jakarta seluruh penduduk menjadi kalang-kabut** during the Jakarta riots all citizens were confused.

kalangan circle, group; **pembicaraan itu hanya untuk kalangan ekonomi atas** that discussion is only for the rich.

kalau if; **kalau Garin ada di situ** if Garin's there; **kalau hujan** if it rains; **kalau saya menang undiannya** if I won the lottery; **kalau tidak** or else, otherwise; **ayo cepatlah, kalau tidak kita akan ketinggalan** hurry up, or else we'll be left behind; **saya ingin menelepon ke rumah dulu, kalau tidak mereka akan khawatir** I'll phone home first, otherwise they'll worry; **kalau saja Anda memberitahu saya** if only you'd told me.

kalbu heart, mind.

kaldu broth.

kaleng can, tin; **sekaleng tomat** a can of tomatoes.

kali 1 time; **kali ini** this time; 2 times; **dua kali waktunya** twice the time; **tiga kali harganya** three times the price; **cobalah sekali lagi** try once more; **sekali sehari** once a day; **tanda kali** multiplication sign; **sekaligus** at the same time, simultaneously; **lebih hemat membeli sepuluh sekaligus** it's more economical to buy ten; **mengalikan** multiply; **perkalian** multiplication.

kalian you all, you yourselves; **kalian harus bekerja keras, bukan saya** you all should work hard, not me; **silakan putuskan hal itu antara kalian sendiri** you can decide among yourselves.

Kalimantan Borneo *(an island in Indonesia)*.

kalimat sentence; **tulislah suatu kalimat dalam bahasa Indonesia** write a sentence in Indonesian.

kalung necklace.

kalut confused; **pikiran Agnes sangat kalut** Agnes's thinking is very confused.

kamar room; **kamar mandi** bathroom; **kamar tunggu** waiting room; **kamar belajar** study; **kamar bicara, kamar periksa** consulting room; **kamar kecil** toilet.

kambing goat; **kambing hitam** scapegoat.

kamera camera.

kami we, us *(excluding the listener)*; **mari ikut bersama kami** why don't you come with us?; **kami tidak akan ada di rumah** we won't be home; **rumah Anda lebih kecil dari rumah kami** your house is smaller than ours; **kami mengenalkan diri kepadanya** we introduced ourselves to her.

Kamis Thursday; **pada hari Kamis** on Thursday; **hari Kamis yang lalu** last Thursday; **hari Kamis depan** next Thursday.

kampak axe.

kampanye campaign.

kamper camphor.

kampret bat.

kampung **1** village; **2** residential area; **sekampung** of the same village, the entire village; **perkampungan yang miskin dan kotor** slum.

kamu you *(informal, used only among peers or by a superior to a subordinate)*; **kamu tidak boleh pergi ke sana** you mustn't go there; **–mu** *(the first syllable of 'kamu' is dropped when it is used as the object of a verb or when it is used as a possessive pronoun and it is then joined to the relevant word)*; **siapa yang memukulmu?** who hit you?; **itu bukumu** that book is yours.

kamus dictionary.

Kanada Canada.

kanak-kanak child, children, kids; **taman kanak-kanak** kindergarten.

kanan right; **di sebelah kanan** on the right; **belok kanan di lampu lalu lintas** turn right at the traffic lights.

kancil mouse deer.

kancing button; **mengancingkan** to button up.

kandang pen, stable; **kandang kelinci** rabbit hutch; **kandang anjing** doghouse, kennel; **kandang ayam** chicken coop.

kandas run aground, stranded; **kapal itu kandas dekat Krakatau** that ship ran aground near Krakatau.

kandidat candidate.

kandung bag, bladder, womb; **saudara kandung** sibling of same parents; **kandung empedu** gallbladder; **kandungan** **1** womb; **2** content; **mengandung** **1** to be pregnant; **Mariam sedang mengandung lagi** Mariam is pregnant again; **2** to contain; **buah itu mengandung vitamin apa?** what vitamin does that fruit contain?

kangkang, mengangkang to straddle.

kangguru kangaroo.

kan(g)ker cancer.

kanji starch.

kantin canteen.

kantong, kantung 1 sack; **satu kantong beras** one sack of rice; 2 pocket.

kantor office; **kami bekerja sekantor** we work in the same office; **gedung kantor** office block, office building; **kantor pos** post office; **kantor cabang** branch office.

kantuk, mengantuk to be sleepy; **saya mengantuk** I feel sleepy; **Anda kelihatan mengantuk** you look sleepy; **saya mulai mengantuk** I'm getting sleepy.

kanvas canvas.

kaos 1 sock, stocking; 2 singlet, T-shirt.

kap top cover; **kap lampu** lampshade; **kap mobil** roof of the car.

kapak axe.

kapal boat, ship, vessel; **kapal tambang** ferry; **kapal penumpang** a passenger ship; **kapal barang** cargo ship; **kapal layar** sailing boat; **kapal selam** submarine; **kapal tangki** tanker; **kapal udara** airplane; **pembuatan kapal** shipbuilding.

kapan when; **kapan Chelsea akan tiba?** when is Chelsea arriving?; **kapan ulang tahun Anda?** when's your birthday? **kapan-kapan** one of these days; **telepon saya kapan-kapan** give me a ring sometime; **kapan pun** forever, whenever; **sampai kapan pun saya tidak akan lupa peristiwa itu** I'll never forget that event forever.

kapas cotton.

kapasitas capacity.

kapital capital; **kapitalis** capitalist; **kapitalisme** capitalism.

kapten captain.

kapuk kapok.

kapur calcium, lime; **kapur tulis** chalk.

karam sink; **kapal tangki itu karam di Selat Malaka** that tanker sank in the Malacca Straits.

karang[1], mengarang 1 to arrange; 2 to write an essay; **karangan** composition, essay; **karangan tentang polusi** an essay on pollution; **karangan bunga** bouquet; **pengarang** author, composer, **hak pengarang** copyright.

karang[2] coral; **terumbu-karang** coral reefs; **bunga**

karang sponge; **udang karang** lobster.

karantina quarantine.

karat[1] rust; **berkarat** rusty.

karat[2] carat; **emas dua puluh dua karat** twenty-two-carat gold.

karate karate.

karburator carburettor.

karcis ticket; **karcis kereta api** train ticket; **karcis masuk** admission ticket; **karcis pulang-pergi** round-trip ticket.

karena because, on account of, since; **karena hujan, pertandingannya dibatalkan** since it was raining, the match was cancelled; **oleh karena tidak ada kereta api, kami terpaksa naik bis** because there were no trains, we took the bus; **kami tidak bisa sampai ke sana oleh karena banjir** we couldn't get there because of the floods.

karet rubber; **jam karet** flexible time, rubber time; **gelang karet** a rubber band; **kasur karet busa** a foam mattress, **kebun karet** rubber plantation; **pipa karet** rubber tube.

kari curry.

karib close, intimate; **sahabat karib** best friend, close friend.

karikatur caricature.

karton carton.

kartu card; **permainan kartu** a game of cards.

karung bag, sack; **karung beras** rice bag.

karunia gift, reward; **mengaruniai** to favour, to reward; **kami dikaruniai seorang anak perempuan** we've been blessed with a daughter.

karya work; **karyawan** male employee, male worker; **karyawati** female employee, female worker.

kas cash, cashier desk.

kasar rough, rude, vulgar; **komentar yang kasar** a rude comment; **perkiraan secara kasar** a rough idea.

kasasi **1** the highest court; **2** appeal to the supreme court.

kaset cassette; **kaset pop** a pop cassette; **kaset video** a video cassette.

kasih affection, love; **terima kasih** thank you; **kasih sayang** affectionate love; **kasih tahu** inform; **mengucapkan terima kasih** to thank; **mengasihi** to like to love; **berkasih-kasihan** to love each other; **kekasih** beloved, sweetheart; **kasihan** **1** mercy, pity; **merasa**

kasihan terhadap to feel sorry for; **2** poor thing, what a pity!; **mengasihani** to pity somebody.

kasip *(colloquial)* too late.

kasir cashier.

kassa cashier's desk.

kasta caste.

kasur mattress.

kasut slippers.

kata word; **kata bilangan** numeral; **kata benda** noun; **kata depan** preposition; **kata kerja** verb; **kata keterangan** adverb; **kata majemuk** compound word; **kata sambung** conjunction; **kata sandang** article; **kata yang searti** synonym; **kata sifat** adjective; **apa kata Indonesianya untuk 'control'?** what's the Indonesian word for 'control'?; **dengan kata lain** in other words; **kata demi kata** word for word; **kata pengantar, kata pendahuluan** introduction *(in a book)*; **berkata** say; **Rudi berkata bahwa sudah malam** Rudi remarked that it was night time already; **mengatakan** to say something, to say that; **saya sendiri yang mengatakannya** I said it myself; **mengatakannya kembali** to say something again; **boleh dikatakan** it can be said, you could say; **tak perlu dikatakan** that goes without saying; **kata orang** they *(people)* say.

katai dwarf.

katak frog, toad.

katalog catalogue.

kategori category.

Katolik Catholic.

katulistiwa Equator.

katup 1 valve; **mesin mobil itu katupnya perlu diganti** the valve of that car engine needs to be replaced; **2** closed, shut.

kau (engkau) you, thee, thou.

kaum 1 group; **kaum muda** young people; **kaum kerabat** relatives; **kaum tani** farmers; **kaum terpelajar** intellectuals; **kaum kolot** conservatives; **2** class; **kaum elit** elites or upper classes; **kaum kaya** the rich; **kaum miskin** the poor; **kaum buruh** labourers, workers.

kawah 1 crater; **2** cauldron.

kawal, mengawal 1 to guard; **2** to escort; **pengawal** guard, watchman; **barisan pengawal** life guard.

kawan friend; **lingkungan kawan-kawan saya** my circle of friends; **kawan akrab**

a b c d e f g h i j k l m n o p q r s t u v w x y z

close friends; **kawan hidup** life partner.

kawasan district, region; **kawasan Asia-Pasifik** Asia-Pacific region.

kawat 1 cable, wire; **kawat penyambung** extension cable; **kawat (ber)duri** barbed wire; **2** telegram; **apakah kawatnya sudah dikirim?** has the telegram been sent?

kawin marry, married *(subject can be male or female)*; **dia kawin dengan laki-laki Indonesia** she married an Indonesian man; **mereka kawin tahun lalu** they got married last year; **Susi kawin dengan Rudi** Susi married Rudi; **mengawinkan 1** to marry; **Pak Budi mengawinkan putri sulungnya kemarin** Pak Budi married off his youngest daughter yesterday; **2** to mate; **anak singa yang dikawinkan dengan harimau disebut 'liger'** the offspring of a lion crossed with a tiger is called a 'liger'; **mengawini** to get married, to marry *(subject must be male)*; **Rudi mengawini Susi** Rudi married Susi; **perkawinan** marriage.

kaya rich, wealthy; **kami tidak begitu kaya** we're not very rich; **yang kaya dan yang miskin** the rich and the poor; **kekayaan** wealth; **kekayaan perusahaan** company's assets.

kayak as if, like; **dia berjalan kayak orang pusing** he walks as if he is dizzy.

kayu log, timber, wood.

kayuh oar, paddle; **mengayuh** to paddle, to row, **mengayuh becak** to pedal a becak.

ke to, towards; **dia turun ke bawah ke ruang belajar** he went down to the study; **ke kota** to go into town; **Irwan pergi ke kantornya** Irwan's gone into the office.

kebal immune, invulnerable; **kekebalan** immunity, invulnerability; **kekebalan diplomatik** diplomatic immunity.

kebaya long-sleeved blouse for women (national costume).

kebiri castrated; **mengebiri** to castrate, to sterilize.

kebun garden, park, plantation; **kebun karet** rubber plantation; **kebun raya** botanical garden; **kebun binatang** zoo.

kecam, mengecam to criticize; **kecaman** criticism.

kecap[1] soy sauce.

a b c d e f g h i j k l m n o p q r s t u v w x y z

a b c d e f g h i j k l m n o p q r s t u v w x y z

kecap², mengecap to taste; **mengecap kenikmatan** to enjoy pleasure.

kecapi harp, lute.

kecele cheated, disappointed, fooled.

kecewa disappointed; **dia kecewa dengan angkanya** he was disappointed with his marks; **mengecewakan** to disappoint, disappointing.

kecil little, small; **kecil hati** discouraged; **hati kecil** conscience; **dengan suara kecil** in a low voice; **mengecilkan** to make small, to reduce, to turn down; **mengecilkan hati** to discourage, to frighten; **tolong kecilkan suaranya** could you turn down the volume please?; **memperkecil** to make smaller, to reduce.

kecoh cheat, deceive; **mengecoh** to deceive.

kecuali except; **apa saja kecuali itu** anything but that; **semua anak kelas lima kecuali Toni** everyone from the fifth form but Toni; **kecuali yang terakhir** except the last one; **kecuali pada waktu hujan** except when it rains; **kecuali kalau dia yang melakukannya** unless he does it; **pengecualian** exception; **dengan pengecualian, kecuali** with the exception of.

kecup kiss; **mengecup** to kiss.

kedai small shop.

kedaluwarsa barred by statute of limitation, expired; **tanggal kedaluwarsa** expiry date.

kedelai soy bean.

kedip wink; **mengedipkan mata** to wink; **Ratna mengedipkan mata kepada saya** Ratna winked at me.

kejam brutal, cruel; **kekejaman** cruelty; **seperti kekejaman Hitler** like Hitler's cruelty.

kejang convulsed, cramp, stiff; **menderita kejang di kaki** to have a cramp in your leg; **kejang-kejang** an epileptic fit; **kejang mulut** lock-jaw.

kejap blink, moment; **dalam sekejap mata** in a moment; **mengejapkan mata** to blink the eyes.

kejar, mengejar, berkejar-kejaran to chase one another.

keji despicable, nasty; **itu kelakuan yang keji** that was a nasty thing to do.

keju cheese.

kejut startled; **mengejutkan** to shock; **sangat**

mengejutkan it was a shock; **saya terkejut mendengar berita itu** I was shaken by the news.

kedok mask.

kekal eternal, everlasting.

kekang bit, rein; **mengekang** to bridle, to curb.

kekar firm, solid, strong.

kekasih darling, sweetheart.

kekeh laugh loudly; **tertawa terkekeh-kekeh** to roar with laughter.

keker binoculars.

kelabu grey.

kelahi fight; **berkelahi** to fight; **mereka berkelahi** they were fighting; **perkelahian** a fight.

kelak *(formal use)* some day, soon, one day; **kelak kita akan bertemu lagi** we'll meet again one day.

kelakar joke; **berkelakar** to joke; **saya hanya berkelakar saja** I was only joking.

kelam dark; **kelam-kabut** dusky, hazy; **kekelaman** darkness.

kelambu mosquito net.

kelamin gender, sex; **penyakit kelamin** venereal disease; **alat-alat kelamin** sexual organs; **jenis kelamin** gender.

kelana wanderer.

kelantang, mengelantang to bleach.

kelapa coconut.

kelas class; **menghadiri kelas** to attend a class; **dia selalu bepergian kelas satu** he always travels first class.

kelasi sailor.

kelasik, klasik classical.

keledai donkey.

kelelawar bat.

kelengkeng lychee.

kelenteng Chinese temple, joss-house.

kelereng marbles; **main kelereng** to play marbles.

keliaran, berkeliaran to prowl, to roam, to walk about.

keliling, sekeliling around; **di sekeliling Istana Bogor ada kebun yang indah** around the Bogor Palace there is a beautiful garden; **di sekeliling kota** around the city; **berkeliling** go around; **berkeliling kota** to wander around town; **berkeliling mengunjungi toko-toko** to go round the shops; **mengelilingi** to surround; **Jasmin dikelilingi oleh teman-temannya** Jasmin's surrounded by friends.

kelilip speck of dust in the eye; **kelilipan** get dust in the eye.

a b c d e f g h i j k l m n o p q r s t u v w x y z

kelinci rabbit.

kelingking little finger.

kelip, berkelip-kelip to flicker, to glitter, to twinkle.

keliru to be wrong or mistaken; **saya keliru menangkap maksudnya** I misunderstood the meaning; **guru pun bisa keliru** even the teacher can be wrong; **kekeliruan** mistake.

kelok, berkelok-kelok bend, curve; **jalan itu sangat berkelok-kelok** that's a really winding road.

kelola, mengelola to carry out, to manage, to organize; **dia mengelola suatu biro perjalanan** she manages a travel agency; **pengelolaan** management.

kelompok group, party; **kelompok anak sekolah** a party of schoolchildren; **mengelompokkan** to group.

kelontong hawker, peddler; **barang-barang kelontong** small wares; **toko kelontong** a small shop that sells all the basic needs.

kelopak sheath; **kelopak mata** eyelid.

keluar come or go outside; **karena asap itu semua orang lari keluar** because of the smoke everyone ran outside; **mengeluarkan 1** to take or put outside; **2** to expel; **3** to issue; **edisi baru majalah itu sudah keluar** a new edition of the magazine has been issued.

keluarga family; **keluarga yang terdiri atas empat orang** a family of four; **Shanty seperti anggota keluarga** Shanty's like one of the family; **perencanaan keluarga** family planning; **keluarga berencana** a planned family.

keluh, mengeluh to complain; **keluhan** complaint.

keluyur, mengeluyur, berkeluyuran to hang around, to loiter; **mereka selalu ngeluyur di disko itu** *(colloquial)* they always hang around that disco.

kemah, berkemah go camping; **minggu depan kami akan berkemah di daerah Albany** we're going camping near Albany next week.

kemenakan nephew, niece.

kemarau, musim kemarau dry season.

kemari come here, this way.

kemarin yesterday; **kemarin sore** yesterday afternoon; **kemarin pagi** yesterday morning; **kemarin dulu** the day before yesterday; **kemarin saya lihat dia** I saw her yesterday.

kemas, berkemas-kemas pack, put in order, tidy; **peti kemas** container; **mengemas** to pack, to tidy.

kembali to come back, to go back, to return; **uang kembali** change; **kembali ke sekolah** go back to school; **Lucy sudah kembali ke Denpasar** Lucy's gone back to Denpasar; **dia belum kembali ke kantor** she's still not back at the office; **kami pergi naik bis dan kembali jalan kaki** we went by bus and walked back; **mengembalikan** to give back, to return; **mereka mengembalikan uang saya** they gave me my money back *(in a shop)*.

kembang flower; **kembang api** fireworks, sparkler; **berkembang 1** to bloom, to grow; **bagaimana anak-anak berkembang menjadi besar** how children develop; **2** to develop, to expand; **negara berkembang** developing country; **mengembangkan** to cause to develop; **mengembangkan industri** to develop an industry; **perkembangan** development; **film itu memperlihatkan perkembangan atau kemajuan suatu bangsa** that film shows the development or progress of a nation.

kembar twins; **anak kembar satu telur** identical twins; **kembar tiga** triplets.

kembara, mengembara to roam, to wander; **pengembara** vagabond, wanderer; **kembara, mengembara(i)** to wander about; **mereka mengembarai Siberia** they roamed over Siberia; **pengembara** traveller, wanderer; **pengembaraan** wandering; **pikirannya mengembara kemana-mana** her/his thoughts were wandering.

kembung bloated, filled with air, puffed; **mengembung** to puff up.

kemeja shirt.

kemelut crisis.

kemenyan incense.

kemilau shining, shiny.

kemis, mengemis to beg; **pengemis** beggar.

kempes, kempis deflated, flat; **ban sepeda saya kempes** my bicycle tyre is flat; **mengempeskan** to deflate.

kemucing feather duster.

a b c d e f g h i j k l m n o p q r s t u v w x y z

a b c d e f g h i j k l m n o p q r s t u v w x y z

kemudi 1 steering wheel; 2 reins; 3 rudder; **mengemudikan** to pilot, to steer; **dia mengemudikan mobil dengan cepat sekali** she drives very fast; **surat ijin mengemudi (SIM)** driving licence; **pengemudi** driver, pilot.

kemudian later, then; **beberapa waktu kemudian** after a while; **saya ke bank kemudian ke kantor pos** I went to the bank and then the post office.

kena be affected by, be hit by, suffer from; **kena kecelakaan** have an accident; **kena flu** have flu; **mengenakan** 1 to fasten, to put on; **mengenakan pakaian** to put your clothes on; 2 to impose *(a tax or fine)*.

kenal be acquainted with, know; **apakah Anda kenal Tasem?** do you know Tasem?; **berkenalan dengan** get acquainted with; **mengenal** to know, to recognize; **Hitler dikenal sebagai diktator** Hitler is known as a dictator; **mengenalkan, memperkenalkan** to introduce; **dia mengenalkan saya kepada bapaknya** she introduced me to her father; **kenalan** acquaintance; **semua kenalan saya** all the people I know; **pengenal** identification; **kartu pengenal** identification card; **pengenalan** identification, introduction; **terkenal** famous, familiar, well-known; **wajahnya terkenal** his face is familiar.

kenang, terkenang be reminded of, to remember; **mengenang** to recall, to remember; **kenang-kenangan** memento, memories, souvenirs; **saya mempunyai kenang-kenangan yang indah dari perjalanan saya ke Lombok** I have good memories of my visit to Lombok; **mengenangkan** to remember, to remind.

kenapa how come, why; **kenapa Anda terlambat?** why are you late?

kenari kind of nut; **burung kenari** canary.

kencang 1 fast, quick; **biasanya kereta api lebih kencang daripada mobil** a train is usually faster than a car; 2 tight; **tangannya terikat kencang** her hands were tightly tied; **mengencang** 1 to increase in speed; 2 to become tighter; **mengencangkan** 1 to speed up; **karena takut terlambat Agus mengencangkan laju kendaraannya** because he was afraid of being late Agus speeded up; **2** to tighten; **kekencangan 1** acceleration; **2** tightness.

kencing to urinate; **air kencing** urine; **kencing manis** diabetes.

kendali bridle, reins; **terkendali** controlled; **mengendalikan 1** to have the reins; **2** to control, to manage; **mengendalikan diri** to control oneself; **tujuan kita ialah mengendalikan polusi** our aim is to control pollution.

kendara, berkendaraan drive, ride; **mengendarai** to drive; **dia mengendarai mobilnya naik ke feri itu** he drove on board the ferry; **mengendarai mobil terlalu cepat berbahaya** it's dangerous to drive too fast; **kendaraan** vehicle.

kendati, kendatipun although, in spite of.

kendi kind of earthenware jug; **kendi itu muat satu liter** that jug holds a litre.

kendur loose, not tight, slack; **mengendurkan** to loosen.

kening eyebrow.

kental thick, strong *(liquid)*; **kopi kental** strong coffee.

kentang potato.

kentara clear, visible.

kenyal 1 elastic; **2** *(for meat)* tough.

kenyang full, satisfied; **saya sudah kenyang** I'm full; **kekenyangan** satiated, too full.

kepada to; **surat ini ditujukan kepada Bapak Presiden** this letter is to be sent to the President; SEE ALSO **pada**.

kepala 1 head; **sakit kepala** to have a headache; **keras kepala** obstinate; **2** leader, chief; **kepala keluarga** head of the household; **kepala sekolah** head (teacher) of the school.

kepalang inadequate, insufficient; **kepalang tanggung** done by halves.

kepang plait; **berkepang** with plaits; **mengepang** to plait.

keping chip, piece, splinter; **berkeping-keping** in pieces, in shreds.

kepingin *(colloquial)* to desire, to long for.

kepiting crab.

kepleset to slip.

kepompong cocoon.

kepung, mengepung to surround; **pengepungan** besiege.

kera monkey.

kerabat relations, relatives; **berkerabat** be related to.

kerah collar.

keramas, berkeramas to shampoo your hair.

keramat 1 holy, sacred; **tempat keramat** sacred place; **2** having miraculous powers, supernatural.

keran tap.

kerangka framework, skeleton.

keranjang basket; **mata keranjang** a flirt; **keranjang sampah** a waste-paper basket; **bola keranjang** basketball.

kerap, kerap kali frequently, often; **saya kerap kali bertemu dengan Setiadi di stasiun** I often meet with Setiadi at the station.

keras 1 firm, hard, tight; **menjadi keras** to become hard; **bekerja keras** to work hard; **keras kepala** obstinate; **2** loud; **suara keras** a loud voice; **3** seriously; **dia sakit keras** she is seriously ill; **berkeras, bersikeras** insist, persist, use force; **mengeras 1** to harden; **2** to increase in volume; **mengeraskan 1** to amplify, to harden, to tighten; **2** to force; **kekerasan 1** hardness, stiffness, volume; **2** force; **pengeras** hardener; **pengeras semen** concrete hardener; **pengeras suara** loudspeaker.

keraton sultan's palace.

kerbau buffalo.

kerdil dwarfish, extremely short; **orang kerdil** a dwarf.

kereta carriage, cart, wagon; **kereta api** train; **perkereta apian** railway *(the system)*.

kerikil gravel.

kering arid, crispy, dry; **makanan kering** crispy, dry food; **mengering** to become dry; **mengeringkan** to dry up; **mengeringkan rambut** to dry your hair; **kekeringan** drought, dryness, too dry; **pengering** dryer; **pengering rambut** hairdryer; **pengeringan** drainage, drying up.

keringat perspiration, sweat; **berkeringat** to sweat.

keris kind of dagger with a wavy blade.

keriting curly; **mengeritingkan** to curl, to perm; **mengeritingkan rambut** to have a perm.

kerja activity, occupation, work; **tenaga kerja** labour

a b c d e f g h i j k l m n o p q r s t u v w x y z

force; **lamaran kerja** a job application; **bekerja** to work; **dia bekerja sebagai akuntan** she's an accountant; **bekerja lembur** to work overtime; **mengerjakan** to do, to perform a task; **apa yang sedang Anda kerjakan?** what are you doing?; **pekerja** employee, worker; **pekerjaan** job, occupation, task, work; **pekerjaan rumah** homework; **pekerjaan rumah tangga** housework; **kami bermaksud menyelesaikan pekerjaan ini pada hari ini** we're aiming to finish the work today.

kerongkongan throat.

kertas paper; **sehelai kertas** a sheet of paper; **kertas bungkus** gift-wrapping paper.

kerucut cone.

keruh **1** muddy; **air yang keruh** muddy water; **2** disturbed, restless; **suasana yang keruh** a disturbed atmosphere.

kerumun, berkerumun crowd, swarm, throng; **pada malam tahun baru biasanya orang berkerumun di kota-kota** on New Year's eve people usually throng into cities; **mengerumuni** to crowd around; **ke mana saja Ratu Elizabeth pergi, beliau selalu dikerumuni orang** no matter where Queen Elizabeth goes, people crowd around her.

kerut frown, wrinkle; **berkerut** frown; **dia sering mengerutkan dahi** he frowns a lot.

kesal cross, fed up.

kesan impression; **berkesan** get an impression, leave an impression; **mengesan** to impress; **mengesankan** impressive, to give an impression.

kesatria high caste, knight, noble.

keseleo sprain; **pergelangan kakinya keseleo** his ankle was sprained.

kesohor famous, well-known.

ketan sticky (glutinous) rice.

ketat tight; **mengetatkan, memperketat** to tighten.

ketawa, tertawa to laugh; **tertawa terbahak-bahak** to laugh very loudly.

ketiak armpit; **berjalan dengan tongkat ketiak** to be on crutches.

ketik ticking or clicking sound; **mengetik** to type; **dia sedang mengetik laporan itu** she's typing the report now; **pengetik** typist.

ketika when, at a point in time; **hari sedang hujan**

a b c d e f g h i j k l m n o p q r s t u v w x y z

ketika saya berangkat it was raining when I left; **seketika** an instant, a moment; **ia bertindak seketika** she acted at once; **sukses seketika** an instant success.

ketimun cucumber.

ketok, ketuk knock, tap; **mengetok, mengetuk** to beat, to knock on; **mengetuk pintu** to knock on the door; **mengetok mobil** to panel-beat a car; **ketokan** knocking or tapping sound; **ada suara ketokan dalam mesin** there's a knocking sound in the engine.

ketombe dandruff.

ketua chairman, chief.

ketumbar coriander.

khas exclusive, special, specific to; **makanan khas Bali** Balinese cuisine.

khayal, khayalan imagination, vision; **mempunyai daya khayal yang hidup** to have a vivid imagination; **mengkhayalkan** to fantasize, to imagine.

khianat treason, treachery; **berkhianat** to commit treason; **katanya dia berkhianat** they say he committed treason; **mengkhianati** to betray; **katanya dia mengkhianati negaranya** they say he betrayed his country; **pengkhianat** traitor.

khidmat loyalty, respect, reverence; **berdoa dengan khidmat** to pray reverently; **kekhidmatan** respect, reverence.

khilaf error, mistake, oversight.

khotbah sermon; **berkhotbah** preach a sermon; **pengkhotbah** preacher.

khusus special; **tidak secara khusus** not specifically; **dekorasinya adalah pilihan yang khusus** the decor has been specially chosen; **khususnya** especially; **saya datang khususnya untuk bertemu dengan Anda** I came especially to see you; **mengkhususkan** to specialize in; **kami mengkhususkan dekorasi Jepang** we specialize in Japanese decor.

kiai religious leader or teacher.

kiamat the end of the world, Judgement Day.

kian more and more; **kian lama harga beras kian mahal** rice is getting more and more expensive; **gadis itu kian besar kian cantik** the girl is more beautiful as she grows up; **sekian** as much as this, a certain amount; **sekian banyak** about this much.

kibar, berkibar fly, wave; **mengibarkan** to display, to wave; **kibarkan bendera!** fly a flag!

kidal left-handed; **petenis kidal** left-handed tennis player.

kikir[1] file; **kikir kuku** a nail file; **mengikir** to file.

kikir[2] miserly, stingy.

kikis, mengikis to erode, to scrape off; **pengikis** scraper; **pengikisan** erosion.

kikuk to feel awkward or clumsy.

kilang mill; **kilang minyak** oil refinery.

kilap, mengkilap to gleam, to glitter, to shine.

kilat 1 flash of lightning; **Mathew menulis jawabannya secepat kilat** Mathew wrote the answer in a flash; **pos kilat** express post; **2** gleam, shine.

kilau glare, shine; **berkilauan** sparkle; **lampu hiasan yang berkilauan** sparkling fairy lights.

kilo, kilogram kilogram.

kilometer kilometre.

kimia chemistry; **ahli kimia** chemist; **kimiawi** chemical.

kini now, the present; **masa kini** the present.

kios kiosk.

kipas fan; **kipas angin** electric fan; **mengipasi** to fan.

kira estimate, guess; **ya, saya kira begitu** yes, I guess so; **apakah Anda kira bahwa mereka akan datang?** do you think they'll come?; **saya kira tidak** no, I don't think so; **saya kira dia sudah berangkat** I think he's already left; **kira-kira** approximately; **sekarang kira-kira jam lima** it's about five o'clock now; **kira-kira sepuluh persen** roughly ten per cent; **mengira** to assume, to guess, to expect; **saya mengira bahwa Anda letih** I guess you're tired; **saya mengira dia akan membawa anak-anak itu** I assume she'll bring those children; **salah mengira** to make a mistake; **perkiraan** calculation, estimate, guess.

kiri left; **mengemudi di sebelah kiri** to drive on the left; **belok kiri di mesjid itu** turn left at the mosque; **jangan memberikan atau menerima apapun dengan tangan kiri** don't give or take anything with your left hand.

kirim, berkirim salam to send greetings; **mengirim** to send; **negeri Inggris mengirim bantuan** the UK is sending aid; **saya mengirim hadiah untuk ulang tahunnya** I sent her a present for her birthday; **kiriman** consignment, something sent; **pengirim** sender; **pengiriman** sending, dispatch.

kisah story; **kisah cinta** love story; **berkisah** narrate a story.

kisar rotation; **berkisar** revolve, rotate, turn; **kisaran** revolution.

kismis raisin.

kisut creased, wrinkled.

kita us, we *(including the listener)*; **kita terlambat! mudah-mudahan kita tidak ketinggalan pesawat** we're late! I hope we don't miss the plane; **dia kenal kita** she knows us; **pemerintah kita** our government.

kitab book; **Alkitab** Bible; **Kitab suci** Holy Bible.

kitar, sekitar about, around, approximately; **kami akan tiba sekitar jam tiga** we'll arrive around three; **umurnya sekitar tiga puluh tahun** she's about thirty; **sekitarnya** environs, surroundings; **daerah Bandung dan sekitarnya** Bandung and its environs; **mengitari** to surround; **musuh mengitari benteng** the enemy encircled the fort.

klakson horn; **membunyikan klakson** to sound your horn.

klep valve.

klien client *(legal term)*.

klimaks climax.

klinik clinic; **klinik bersalin** maternity clinic.

klise negative *(photography)*.

koalisi coalition; **pemerintahan koalisi** coalition government.

kobar in flames, on fire; **berkobar** flare up; **mengobarkan** to inflame, to incite, to stir up; **kobaran** raging fire; **mengobarkan semangat** to rouse enthusiasm; **kobaran api itu tak dapat dikuasai** the fire was out of control.

kocok, mengocok to beat, to mix, to shake; **mengocok telur** to beat eggs.

kode code; **kode untuk menelepon ke Perth adalah 08** the dialling code for Perth is 08.

kodok, katak frog.

kodrat force of nature, omnipotence.

kokoh firm, solid, strong; **meja yang terbuat dari jati kokoh-kuat** a table made of teak is strong and sturdy.

kokok, berkokok to crow *(rooster)*.

kol cabbage; **kembang kol** cauliflower.

kolaborasi collaboration; **berkolaborasi** to collaborate; **kolaborator** collaborator.

kolam pond, pool; **kolam renang tertutup** an indoor swimming pool; **rumah yang berkolam renang sangat sedikit** very few houses have a swimming pool.

koleksi collection; **koleksi yang lengkap** the complete collection.

kolera cholera.

kolonel colonel.

kolonial colonial.

kolonisasi colonization.

kolot old-fashioned.

koma[1] comma; **titik koma** semi-colon.

koma[2] coma; **sudah empat hari dia dalam keadaan koma** she/he's been unconscious for four days now.

komandan commandant, commander.

komando command.

kombinasi combination.

komentar comment.

komedi comedy.

komentator commentator.

komisaris commisioner.

komisi commision, committee.

komodo giant lizard found on Komodo Island (Indonesia).

komodor commodore.

kompas compass.

komplit complete.

komponis composer.

kompor cooker, stove; **kompor gas** a gas cooker; **kompor minyak tanah** a kerosene cooker.

kompromi to compromise.

komputer computer.

komunis communist.

konde bun, coil *(hair)*.

kondektur conductor.

kondensator condensor.

kondisi conditon; **dalam kondisi buruk** in bad condition.

konperensi conference.

konfrontasi confrontation.

konggres congress.

kongsi association, union; **kongsi dagang** trading company.

konperensi conference.

konon however; they say.

a b c d e f g h i j **k** l m n o p q r s t u v w x y z

konsekwen consistent.
konsekwensi consequence.
konser concert; **menonton konser** to go to a concert; **karcis konser** a concert ticket.
konstitusi constitution.
konstruksi construction.
konsul consul; **konsulat** consulate; **konsuler** consular.
konsumen consumer.
kontak contact.
kontan cash; **saya bayar kontan** I paid cash.
kontrak contract.
koper trunk, suitcase.
koperasi a cooperative.
kopi coffee; **secangkir kopi** a cup of coffee; **minta kopi pahit** a black coffee, please *(without sugar, usually also black)*; **kopi susu** a white coffee; **kopi kental** strong coffee; **kopi bubuk** ground coffee.
kopiah cap commonly worn by men in Indonesia.
kopor suitcase; **kopor-kopor saya ada di bagasi** my luggage is in the boot.
kopra copra.
koran newspaper.
korban **1** casualty, victim; **hanya ada seorang korban** there is only one casualty; **mengumpulkan uang untuk korban banjir** to raise money for victims of the floods; **2** sacrifice; **hewan-hewan korban Idul Adha** Idul Adha sacrificial animals; **mengorbankan** to sacrifice; **banyak sekali binatang korban yang dikorbankan pada Hari Raya Idul Adha** many sacrificial animals are sacrificed at Idul Adha.
korek to dig, to niggle; **korek api** matches; **korek telinga** ear pick, ear buds; **mengorek** to bring up, to dig up; **saya sedang berusaha mengorek informasi itu** I'm just trying to dig up that information; **jangan mengorek-ngorek masalah itu lagi** don't bring up that problem again.
koreksi correction.
koresponden correspondence.
kornet corned beef.
korupsi corruption.
kosong **1** empty; **botol kosong** an empty bottle; **'tidak ada kamar kosong'** 'no vacancies'; **pikiran saya menjadi kosong** my mind went blank; **omong kosong** to talk nonsense; **2** nil; **mereka menang empat–kosong** they won

four–nil; **mengosongkan** to empty, to vacate; **apakah Anda bisa menolong saya mengosongkan gudang?** can you help me clear out the storeroom?

kota city; **ibu kota** capital city; **Canberra adalah ibu kota Australia** Canberra is the capital of Australia.

kotak box, casket; **kotak alat-alat** a tool kit; **kotak pos** post box; **kotak surat** letter box.

kotor dirty, filthy; **segala sesuatu cepat menjadi kotor pada musim kering** everything gets dirty quickly in the dry season; **air kotor itu menimbulkan berjangkitnya penyakit kolera** the contaminated water caused an outbreak of cholera; **mengotorkan** to make something dirty; **jangan kotorkan bajunya** don't get your dress dirty; **mengotori** to make dirty.

koyak torn; **koyak-koyak** ragged; **mengoyakkan** to tear.

kran faucet, tap.

kredit credit; **permintaan kredit** credit application; **kredit macet** credit freeze; **secara kredit** instalment plan.

kretek, rokok kretek clove cigarettes.

kriminal criminal; **hukum kriminal** criminal law; **perbuatan kriminal** criminal act.

kriminologi criminology.

krisis crisis; **krisis moneter, krisis keuangan** monetary crisis.

kristal crystal.

Kristen Christian.

Kristus Christ.

kritik(an) criticism; **mengkritik** to criticize.

ksatria knight, nobleman, chivalry, nobility.

kuah gravy, sauce.

kuali frying pan.

kualifikasi fitness, qualification.

kualitas quality, standard; **pekerjaan Dani berkualitas tinggi** Dani's work is of a high standard; **kualitas hidup** the quality of life.

kuas brush *(for painting or shaving).*

kuasa authority, power; **kuasa mutlak** absolute power; **Tuhan Yang Maha Kuasa** Almighty God; **menguasai 1** to control, to take charge of; **polisi tak sanggup menguasai orang banyak itu** the police have lost control of the crowd; **2** to cope with; **saya akan menguasai ini** I'll cope with this; **kekuasaan** power, authority; **penguasa** manager, person in charge.

kuat 1 loud, powerful, strong; **bangunan kuat** a solid structure; **2** be able to; **jangan memilih mobil Saab kalau tidak kuat membayar** don't choose the Saab if you can't pay for it; **kekuatan** force, power, strength; **kekuatan angin** wind force.

kuatir, khawatir afraid, worried, worry.

kubik cubic.

kubis cabbage.

kubur grave, tomb; **mengubur(kan)** to bury; **kuburan** cemetery; **penguburan** burial.

kucing cat.

kuda horse; **kuda jantan** stallion; **kuda betina** mare; **daya kuda** horse power.

kudus holy.

kue cake.

kuil Hindu temple.

kuku nail; **kikir kuku** a nail file; **cat kuku** nail varnish; **mengikir kuku** to file your nails.

kukuh strong, sturdy.

kukus steam; **ketel kukus** steam boiler.

kuli coolie, labourer.

kuliah university lecture.

kulit 1 skin; **orang dari timur jauh berkulit kuning langsat** people from the far east have creamy yellow skin; **2** leather; **3** bark.

kulkas refrigerator.

kuman bacteria.

kumandang, berkumandang, mengumandang to echo, to resound.

kumbang beetle.

kumis moustache.

kumpul, berkumpul assemble, collect together; **mereka berkumpul di depan sekolah** they assembled in front of the school; **mengumpulkan** to accumulate, to collect; **dia mengumpulkan uang logam** she collects coins; **mengumpulkan uang untuk korban banjir** to raise money for flood victims; **perkumpulan** club, association; **dia anggota perkumpulan tenis** he's a member of the tennis club; **pengumpulan** collecting; **pengumpulan pendapat umum** opinion poll.

kumur gargle.

kunang-kunang firefly.

kunci key; **seikat kunci** a bunch of keys; **mengunci** to lock; **saya mengunci jendela-jendela sebelum berangkat** I locked the windows before leaving.

kuning yellow; **kuning cemerlang** bright yellow; **kuningan** brass; **kekuning-kuningan** yellowish.

kunir, kunyit saffron, turmeric.

kunjung, berkunjung visit; **kalau ada kesempatan, berkunjunglah ke Bromo** if you have the chance, go to Bromo; **mengunjungi** to visit; **saya mempergunakan kesempatan itu untuk mengunjungi museum wayang** I took the opportunity to visit the puppet museum; **kunjungan** a visit, a call; **kunjungan ke Lombok** a visit to Lombok.

kuno ancient, old-fashioned.

kunyah, mengunyah to chew.

kunyit, kunir turmeric.

kupas, mengupas to peel.

kuping ear.

kupon coupon.

kupu-kupu butterfly.

kura-kura tortoise.

kurang 1 less; **kurang cepat daripada kita** less quickly than us; **kurang dari tiga jam** less than three hours; **2** minus; **tujuh kurang empat sama dengan tiga** seven minus four is three; **3** not enough; **saya kurang tidur** I didn't have enough sleep; **peta jalan itu kurang baik** the road map is not very good; **kurang ajar** bad-mannered, impudent; **berkurang** decrease; **hujan mulai berkurang** the rain is decreasing; **berat badannya sudah berkurang** the body weight has decreased; **mengurangi 1** to decrease, to cut back on, to cut down on, to lessen; **mengurangi kecepatan** to reduce speed; **2** to subtract from; **mengurangkan** to lessen, to reduce, to subtract; **harganya dikurangkan** they've reduced the price; **kekurangan** lack, shortage; **kami agak kekurangan uang saat ini** we're a bit short of money at the moment; **kami mulai kekurangan waktu** we're getting short of time; **ada kekurangan dalam baju ini** there's a fault in this garment; **pengurangan** decrease; **pengurangan jumlahnya** a decrease in the number of.

a b c d e f g h i j **k** l m n o p q r s t u v w x y z

a b c d e f g h i j k l m n o p q r s t u v w x y z

kurma date *(the fruit).*

kursi chair.

kursus course *(study)*; **kursus lanjutan** an advanced course; **kursus menjahit** a sewing course; **mengikuti kursus** to go on a course.

kurung 1 cage, prison; **2** brackets, parentheses; **tanda kurung** brackets; **berkurung** close off, be shut up; **berkurung diri, mengurung diri** to shut yourself off; **mengurung(kan)** to put in a cage, to put in prison; **mengurungkan niatnya** to cancel your plans; **kurungan** cage, jail; **pengurungan** confinement, incarceration.

kurus thin.

kusir coachman.

kusta leprosy.

kusut rumpled, tangled.

kutil wart.

kutip, mengutip to cite, to quote; **di antara tanda kutip** in inverted commas; **kutipan** quotation.

kutu louse, flea **kutu busuk** bed bugs.

kutub pole, polar.

kutuk curse; **mengutuk** to put a curse on; **terkutuk** accursed; **dari sudut politik dan peradaban apapun, Hitler dianggap terkutuk** from the political angle and any aspect of civilization, Hitler is considered accursed; **kutukan** a curse; **kata kutukan** swearword.

kuyup, basah kuyup soaking wet; **saya basah kuyup dalam perjalanan ke sini** I got drenched on the way here.

kwitansi receipt.

L l

laba 1 profit; **2** advantage, benefit, gain.

labah-labah spider.

laboratorium laboratory.

labuh, berlabuh 1 to anchor, to dock; **kapal itu sedang berlabuh** the ship is docking now; **2** be at anchor; **melabuhkan kapal** to drop anchor; **pelabuhan** anchorage, dock, harbour, port; **pelabuhan udara** airport.

laci drawer *(in a desk).*

lada pepper *(black or white).*

ladam horseshoe.

ladang agricultural field that is not irrigated; **ladang gandum** a field of wheat; **ladang padi** a field of (unirrigated) rice; **berladang** own or cultivate such fields; **peladang** a person who owns or cultivates an unirrigated field.

lagak 1 attitude, behaviour; **2** mannerism; **3** bluff; **berlagak 1** pretend; **berlagak bodoh** pretend to be stupid; **2** put on airs.

lagi[1] **1** again; **coba lagi** try again; **lagi pula** moreover, besides; **lagi pula, sudah terlambat** besides, it's too late; **2** any longer, any more *(with negatives)*; **saya tidak mau belajar itu lagi** I don't want to study that any more; **3** else, more, other; **saya minta sambal sedikit lagi** I'd like a little more sambal; **saya tidak mau lagi** I don't want any more; **lebih memalukan lagi** even more embarrassing; **lebih cepat lagi** even faster; **lagi-lagi** again and again, more and more, over and over.

lagi[2] be doing *(colloquial)*; **Vivi lagi mencari informasi itu di Internet** Vivi's looking for the information on the Internet; **selagi 1** during, while; **Saladin datang selagi saya belajar** Saladin came while I was studying; **2** as long as, while; **selagi saya tinggal di sini, saya tidak pernah bicara dengan tetangga** as long as I've lived here, I've never spoken to the neighbours.

lagu 1 melody, song; **2** manner, way; **3** intonation; **melagukan 1** to carry the melody; **2** to sing.

–lah *(suffix)* **1** suggesting action; **masuklah!** come in!; **cepatlah!** hurry up!; **2** showing agreement; **baiklah, saya akan datang** OK, I'll come; **3** asking for belief; **4** emphasizing; **itulah mesjid yang terkenal** that's the famous mosque; **5** trivializing; **seratus ribu rupiah! berapalah itu?** one hundred thousand rupiah! how much is that anyway?

lahap extremely hungry, ravenous; **melahap 1** to devour, to gobble down; **2** to annexe illegally.

lahar lava.

lahir[1] external, outward; **lahir dan batin** relating to the inner self and the outer world; **maaf lahir batin** forgive my sins *(a greeting for Islamic New Year)*; **2** material, worldly.

a b c d e f g h i j k l m n o p q r s t u v w x y z

lahir² be born; **tanggal lahir** date of birth; **bayi itu lahir semalam** the baby was born last night; **melahirkan** to give birth; **kelahiran** birth; **angka kelahiran** birth rate; **pembatasan kelahiran** birth control.

lain 1 another, other; **lain kali** another time; **orang lain** other people; **di mana yang lain?** where are the others?; **2** different; **di tempat yang lain** somewhere else; **mengambil jalan lain** to take an alternative route; **tak ada pilihan lain, tak ada jalan lain** there is no alternative; **selain (daripada)** besides, apart from; **3** not including; **ongkosnya Rp. 500.000 selain servis** the cost is Rp. 500,000 not including service; **berlainan dengan** different from; **melainkan 1** but (rather); **2** only, except for; **kelainan 1** deviation, difference; **2** abberation, disorder; **kelainan bicara** speech impediment.

laju 1 fast, quick; **lajunya** speed; **2** rate; **melajukan** to accelerate.

lajur 1 row; **2** *(of cloth)* strip; **3** column; **4** lane; **ambil lajur kiri** take the left lane.

laki-laki man, male *(for humans)*; **kelaki-(laki)an 1** manliness; **2** manhood; **laki** *(colloquial)* husband.

lakon 1 drama, play; **2** *(of a play)* act; **3** story; **melakonkan 1** to present *(a play)*; **2** to act out *(a story, play, etc.)*.

laksa 1 fine white noodles; **2** kind of food prepared with fine noodles.

laksamana admiral.

laksana 1 characteristic, quality; **2** like, resembling; **rambut Ida mengkilap laksana sutra** Ida's hair shines like silk; **melaksanakan 1** to bring about; **2** to implement, to carry out; **mereka melaksanakan rencana Sumardi** they implemented Sumardi's plan; **pelaksana 1** organizer; **2** producer; **3** manager; **pelaksanaan** implementation.

laku 1 attitude, behaviour, conduct; **2** in demand, sell well; **selaku 1** as if, like; **2** as, in the capacity of; **selakunya** whatever sells; **berlaku 1** be valid; **itu tidak berlaku untuk siswa** that doesn't apply to students; **2** occur, happen; **3** prevail; **4** behave; **harap semua berlaku baik!** behave yourselves!; **5** act as; **memberlakukan** to put into effect; **keberlakuan** validity *(of a licence, for example)*; **melakukan 1** to carry out, to execute, to perpetrate; **Nathan melakukannya sendiri** Nathan did it by himself; **ada beberapa urusan yang harus saya lakukan** I've got a couple of things to do; **2** to commit *(a crime)*; **memperlakukan** to treat; **kata Siregar dia diperlakukan dengan baik** Siregar says he was treated well; **kelakuan 1** act, deed; **2** behaviour; **dia minta maaf atas kelakuannya** he apologizes for his behaviour; **berkelakuan** to behave; **Kim berkelakuan jelek** Kim behaved badly; **pelaku 1** agent, doer, perpetrator; **2** *(grammar)* subject; **3** cast, performer; **perlakuan** treatment.

lalai 1 careless, negligent; **2** absent-minded; **melalaikan** to neglect; **saya tidak mau melalaikan pekerjaan rumah saya** I don't want to neglect my homework; **kelalaian** carelessness, neglect.

lalap a kind of salad with a spicy sauce; raw vegetables and leaves.

lalat a fly; **tahi lalat** mole.

lalim cruel, tyrannical, unjust; **kelaliman 1** despotism, tyranny; **2** cruelty; **3** oppression.

lalu 1 pass; **lalu lintas** traffic; **peraturan lalu lintas** traffic rules; **2** last, past; **sejam yang lalu** an hour ago; **3** afterwards, then; **saya ke bank lalu ke kantor pos** I went to the bank and then the post office; **selalu** always; **berlalu** pass by; **waktu berlalu dengan cepat** the time passed quickly; **melalui 1** to pass through, via; **kami akan pergi melalui Malang**; we're going via Malang; **2** by means of; **ada virus baru yang menyebar melalui Internet** a new virus is being spread through the Internet; **terlalu** too, exceedingly; **arloji saya terlalu cepat** my watch is too fast; **keterlaluan** excessive, far too much.

lama 1 *(duration)* long; **berapa lama?** how long?; **sudah lama sekali saya tidak bertemu dengan mereka** it's been ages since I've seen them; **2** long-standing, old; **mobil kami yang lama adalah Datsun** our old car was a Datsun; **lama-lama, lama kelamaan** eventually, finally; **lama-lama saya bosan juga** eventually I got bored; **selama** as long as, during, while; **saya belajar**

a b c d e f g h i j k l m n o p q r s t u v w x y z

bahasa Jawa selama tiga tahun I studied Javanese for three years; **selama-lamanya** **1** forever, for good; **2** at the longest.

lamar, melamar **1** to propose marriage to; **2** to apply for a job; **Eri melamar pekerjaan di Hotel Mandarin** Eri applied for a job at the Mandarin Hotel; **lamaran** **1** marriage proposal; **2** job application; **formulir lamaran pekerjaan** job application form; **pelamar 1** suitor; **2** applicant.

lambai, melambai (-lambai) to beckon, to wave; **melambaikan** to wave, to cause to wave; **dia melambaikan tangan dari bis kepada kami** she waved to us from the bus; **lambaian tangan** a wave of the hand.

lamban **1** rather lazy; **2** awkward, clumsy; **murid yang lamban** slow-learner; **kelambanan 1** laziness; **2** awkwardness, clumsiness.

lambang emblem, symbol; **membeli mobil BMW sebagai lambang kekayaan** to buy a BMW as a status symbol; **melambangkan** to symbolize.

lambat leisurely, slow, slowly; **bisa berbicara agak lambat?** can you speak slowly please?; **lambat-lambat 1** very slowly; **2** be slow; **selambat-lambatnya** at the latest; **melambatkan, memperlambat 1** to slow something down; **2** to delay; **karena Yudi sakit kami akan memperlambat perjalanan kami** because Yudi is sick we'll delay our trip; **terlambat** late; **penerbangan itu terlambat satu jam** the flight was an hour late; **kelambatan** delay, slowness; **kelambatan dua jam** a two-hour delay; **perlambatan** **1** retardation; **2** deceleration.

lambung[1] **1** side of, flank; **2** an interior cavity; **lambung kapal** ship's hold.

lambung[2] the bounce *(of a ball, for example)*; **melambung** to bounce, to float upwards, to jump up.

lampau past; **pada masa lampau** in the past; **melampaui 1** *(time)* to pass; **2** to exceed, be excessive; **terlampau 1** overlooked, passed over; **2** exceedingly, too (much); **terlampau sulit** too difficult; **terlampaui** passed over; **masa percobaannya sudah terlampaui** her/his trial period has passed.

lampir, lampiran attachments, enclosure; **melampiri 1** to attach, to append to; **2** to enclose; **surat ini dilampiri poswesel sebesar Rp. 500.000,00** enclosed is a money order for Rp. 500,000.00; **melampirkan** to attach, to append; **keterangan lanjutan dilampirkan pada suratnya** further information is enclosed with the letter; **terlampir** attached, enclosed.

lampu 1 lamp; **2** light; **tolong nyalakan lampu Anda** will you turn your light on?; **lampu jalan** streetlights; **lampu lalu lintas** traffic lights; **lampu besar** headlight.

lampung, melampung to float; **pelampung** buoy, float; **baju pelampung, rompi pelampung** life jacket.

lamun, melamun to daydream; **lamunan** daydream, fantasy; **pelamun** daydreamer.

lancang 1 dare to do something without permission, **lancang mulut** to say things without thinking or without considering other people's feelings; **2** cheeky; **kelancangan 1** presumption; **2** impudence, insolence.

lancar 1 fast, quick; **2** fluent; **dia lancar berbahasa Indonesia** she speaks fluent Indonesian; **3** smooth *(discussion etc.)*; **selancar angin** windsurf; **berselancar** surf with a board; **peselancar** surfer; **melancarkan 1** to accelerate, to speed up; **2** to launch *(an attack, movement, etc.)*; **3** to expedite; **kelancaran 1** smoothness; **2** fluency; **pelancaran** expediting.

landa, melanda to attack violently, to knock someone down; **terlanda 1** knocked down; **2** hit, pounded; **3** overwhelmed.

landas 1 base; **2** substratum; **berlandaskan** be based on, rest on; **negara RI berlandaskan Pancasila** the Republic of Indonesia is based on Pancasila; **melandaskan 1** to rest one thing on something else; **2** to base; **pernyataan ini dilandaskan observasi** this statement is based on observation; **landasan** base; **landasan terbang** runway.

langgan, melanggan to be a customer; **berlangganan 1** to become a customer; **2** to subscribe to; **langganan, pelanggan 1** client, customer; **2** subscriber.

langgar, berlanggar(an) collide; **melanggar 1** to collide with, to run into; **melanggar kangguru** to crash into a kangaroo; **2** to break, to violate; **melanggar janji** to break a promise; **dia melanggar peraturan itu** she broke the rules; **3** *(territory)* to encroach upon; **pelanggar 1** offender; **pelanggar hukum** law breaker; **2** violator; **pelanggaran 1** *(of rule, law)* violation; **2** trespass; **3** *(sport)* foul, penalty.

langit sky; **langit-langit** ceiling; **melangit** to rise into the sky, to soar.

langkah 1 step, stride; **dia maju dua langkah** he moved forward two steps; **dengan langkah-langkah cepat** at a brisk pace; **2** action, step; **langkah yang layak** proper measures; **melangkah 1** to step forward; **2** to stride; **melangkahi 1** to step over, to stride by; **2** to skip, to skip over; **3** to ignore instructions; **4** to overstep.

langsing slender, slim; **menjadi langsing** to become slim; **melangsingkan badan, melangsingkan tubuh** to slim; **pelangsing** tool for slimming; **obat pelangsing tubuh** slimming pills.

langsung 1 direct, straight; **siaran langsung dari Surabaya** a direct broadcast from Surabaya; **dia langsung ke dokter** he went straight to the doctor; **2** immediately, straightaway; **kami akan langsung melakukannya untuk Anda** we'll do it for you straightaway; **berlangsung** take place; **rapat sedang berlangsung** the meeting is under way; **melangsungkan 1** to carry out, to perform; **2** to continue, to keep a thing going; **kelangsungan** continuing; **kelangsungan hidup** survival.

lanjur dragged out, stretched; **te(r)lanjur** too late *(past and irreversible)*; **saya sudah terlanjur membuat janji** the appointment has been made.

lanjut 1 advanced; **yang sudah lanjut usia** the elderly; **2** detailed, long; **3** continue, continued; **selanjutnya** furthermore; **dan selanjutnya** etcetera, and so forth; **untuk selanjutnya** henceforth; **berlanjut** continued; **episode berlanjut** continuing episode; **melanjutkan 1** to continue; **mereka melanjutkan pertandingan** they continued the match; **mereka melanjutkan perjalanannya** they continued (with) their journey; **2** to extend, to lengthen; **lanjutan 1** continuation; **pendidikan lanjutan** advanced education; **sekolah lanjutan** secondary school; **2** sequel.

lantai 1 floor; **2** storey of a building; **lantai kelima** the fifth floor.

lantar[1], lantaran *(colloquial)* because.

lantar[2], terlantar neglected; **unggas semuanya mati karena terlantar** the poultry all died because they were neglected; **menerlantarkan** to neglect; **keterlantaran** state of neglect.

lantas 1 directly, straightaway, then; **2** and so?

lantik, melantik to inaugurate, to install; **Habibie dilantik sebagai presiden ketika Suharto mengundurkan diri** Habibie was installed as president when Suharto resigned.

lap 1 cloth; **lap piring** tea towel; **2** rag; **mengelap** to wipe with a cloth.

lapang 1 open, spacious, wide; **tanah lapang** open field; **lapang dada** relieved; **2** free, unoccupied; **3** roomy; **lapangan 1** field, square; **lapangan sepak bola** soccer field; **2** sphere, range; **lapangan belajar** field of study.

lapar hungry; **saya lapar sekali** I'm starving; **busung lapar** malnutrition, undernourished; **kelaparan 1** hunger; **2** famished; **masyarakat di sana kelaparan** people there are starving.

lapis 1 layer, lining; **lapis baja** steel plating; **2** row; **3** stratum; **4** in layers; **berlapis** have a layer, stratified; **melapis** to coat, to line; **lapisan 1** a layer; **lapisan ozon** ozone layer; **2** stratum, class; **3** coating.

lapor report; **melapor** to report; **saya harus melapor di kantor imigrasi** I have to report to immigration; **melaporkan** to inform, to notify, to report; **kami sudah melaporkan pencurian itu** we've reported the theft; **melaporkan diri** check in, report; **laporan 1** account, report; **2** statement; **pelapor** commentator, reporter.

lapuk 1 mouldy, mildewed; **menjadi lapuk** get mouldy; **2** decayed, putrefied, rotten; **3** obsolete, out-of-date;

kelapukan 1 weathering; **2** corrosion.

larang, melarang to ban, to forbid, to prohibit; **dia melarang saya keluar** he forbade me to go out; **'dilarang merokok'** 'no smoking'; **'dilarang parkir'** 'no parking'; **terlarang** prohibited, forbidden, banned; **larangan 1** prohibition, ban; **larangan kegiatan politik** a ban on political activity; **2** embargo.

laras 1 key, pitch, scale; **2** harmony; **selaras 1** in accordance with; **2** in harmony, harmonious; **3** melodious, tuneful; **keselarasan 1** harmony; **2** conformity; **penyelarasan, pelarasan** adjustment, adaptation; **melaraskan** to adapt, to adjust; **kelarasan** harmony.

lari 1 run; **lari berganti, lari beregu** relay race; **lari santai** jogging; **dia lari melintasi taman itu** he ran across the park; **2** escape, leave; **Edi lari dari penjara** Edi escaped from prison; **melarikan 1** to run off with; **Edi melarikan uang** Edi absconded with the money; **Edi melarikan diri dari penjara** Edi escaped from prison; **2** to abduct, to kidnap; **3** to drive a vehicle; **pelari** jogger, runner; **pelarian 1** escapee, fugitive; **2** refugee; **3** escape, flight, running.

laris in demand, popular, sell well.

larut[1] 1 soluble; **2** fused; **melarut** to become dissolved; **melarutkan** to dissolve; **melarutkan sesendok gula** to dissolve a spoonful of sugar; **pelarut** solvent; **larutan** something dissolved.

larut[2] 1 drawn out, protracted; **2** *(of night)* late, far advanced; **larut malam** late at night; **berlarut-larut** drag on, drawn out; **pertandingan itu berlarut-larut** the match dragged on; **kelarutan** lateness *(of night)*.

latar 1 yard; **2** plane, surface; **3** background; **candi di latar belakang** the temple in the background; **pelataran 1** area, field; **pelataran khusus untuk pejalan kaki** pedestrian precinct; **pelataran parkir** carpark; **2** background.

latih accustomed; **berlatih 1** practise, train; **2** rehearse; **melatih** to train; **melatih calon-calon prajurit** to drill army recruits; **2** to practise; **terlatih 1** skilled, trained; **2** exercised; **latihan** exercise, practice, training; **pelatih**

coach, instructor, trainer; **pelatih panahan** the archery instructor.

lauk pauk side dishes served with rice.

laut sea; **Laut Mati** the Dead Sea; **Laut Timor** the Timor Sea; **timur laut** northeast; **barat laut** northwest; **melaut 1** to go to sea; **2** to head towards the sea; **lautan** ocean, seas; **Lautan Hindia** the Indian Ocean; **Lautan Teduh** the Pacific Ocean; **pelaut** seaman, person who makes a living from the sea.

lawak joke; **melawak** to joke; **pelawak** comedian.

lawan 1 enemy, opponent; **2** the opposite; **3** against; **berlawanan 1** disagree with; **2** be clashing, opposite to; **melawan 1** to oppose, to be against; **2** versus; **berjuang melawan kolera** to fight against cholera; **perlawanan** resistance; **tanpa perlawanan** without resistance.

lawat, melawat 1 to visit; **2** to go on a trip; **pelawat** tourist, visitor; **perlawatan** expedition, trip.

layak 1 decent, proper; **2** fair; **gaji yang layak** a decent wage; **layaknya** properly speaking; rightly; **kelayakan** fit, up to standard, usable; **selayaknya** properly, rightly.

layan, melayani 1 to wait on; **2** to serve; **layanan** service; **pelayan** waiter, waitress.

layang, layang-layang kite; **melayang** to fly, to float in the air; **melayangkan** to fly *(a plane, kite, etc.)*; **Prayitno ingin melayangkan pesawat peluncur** Prayitno wants to fly gliders.

layar 1 sail; **kapal layar** a sailing boat; **2** *(for movies)* screen; **berlayar 1** go by boat, sail; **dia sering berlayar** she does a lot of sailing; **2** have a sail; **pelayaran** navigation.

layu 1 faded, wilted; **2** pale, weak; **cepat sekali bunga ros itu layu** that rose wilted really quickly.

lazim common, ordinary, usual; **kelaziman** the ordinary, usual.

lebah bee.

lebar 1 broad, wide; **pintu terbuka lebar** the door was wide open; **2** width; **lebar meja ini setengah meter** the width of this table is half a metre; **melebarkan, memperlebar** to widen; **perlebaran** expansion, widening.

Lebaran last day of the Islamic fasting month when Muslims celebrate with feasting and visits.

lebat 1 dense, thick; **pohon apel kami lebat buahnya** our apple tree is full of fruit; **hutan lebat** dense jungle, **2** heavy; **hujan lebat** heavy rain.

lebih more, more than *(used for forming the comparative)*; **harganya lebih dari seratus dolar** it will cost over a hundred dollars; **lebih jauh dari kantor pos itu** further than the post office; **pena ini dapat menulis lebih baik daripada yang itu** this pen writes better than the other; **lebih cepat lebih baik** the faster the better; **kurang lebih** more or less; **berlebih 1** left over; **2** too many, too much; **berlebih-lebihan** excessive; **melebihkan** to exaggerate, to increase; **kelebihan** excess, surplus; **lebihnya** leftovers, remainder.

lecet grazed, chafed.

ledak, meledak 1 to explode; **2** to break out; **Perang Dunia Kedua meledak ketika itu** the Second World War broke out at that time; **meledakkan** to blow up; **teroris-teroris meledakkan gedung kedutaan** the terrorist blew up the embassy; **ledakan** an explosion; **peledak 1** explosive; **2** person who explodes things.

lega 1 open, plenty of room; **2** relieved, without worries; **alangkah leganya!** what a relief!; **saya merasa lega mendengar bahwa Anda tidak luka** I was relieved to hear you weren't injured.

legalisasi legalization.

legenda legend; **legendaris** legendary.

legong a Balinese dance performed by young girls.

leher neck.

lekas 1 fast, quick; **2** soon; **lekas-lekas!** hurry up!

lekat, melekat to stick to; **lalat-lalat itu melekat pada kertas lengket itu** the flies stuck to the sticky paper.

lekuk dent, dimple, hollow.

lelah exhausted, tired; **Anda baru tidur jam tiga pagi! Oleh karena itu sekarang lelah!** you didn't go to sleep until three this morning! No wonder you're tired!

lelaki man, male.

lelang auction; **melelang** to sell in an auction.

leleh melt; **meleleh** to melt, to trickle.

a b c d e f g h i j k l m n o p q r s t u v w x y z

leluasa **1** free, unconfined; **2** generous; **keleluasaan** doing whatever you like, freedom to act.

leluhur ancestors.

lem glue.

lemah **1** feeble, weak; **suaranya lemah** her voice was feeble; **2** supple; **melemah** to become feeble; **kelemahan** weakness.

lemak fat, grease; **berlemak** greasy.

lemari cupboard, cupboard-like container; **lemari es** fridge, refrigerator.

lemas **1** faint, limp; **2** flexible.

lembab damp, humid; **melembabkan** to dampen; **kelembaban** humidity, mugginess; **patung itu cepat berlumut oleh karena kelembaban udara** the statue quickly became mossy because of the humidity; **pelembab** moisturizer.

lembaga institute, organization; **Lembaga Bantuan Hukum** legal aid institution; **melembagakan** to institutionalize; **kelembagaan** institutional.

lembar **1** *(paper)* sheet; **2** classifier for paper; **lima lembar fotokopi** five photocopies.

lembek **1** soft; **2** weak; **menjadi lembek** to become weak or soft; **kelembekan** flabbiness, softness.

lembing javelin, spear.

lembu bull, cow.

lembung, melembung to puff up, to swell; **melembungkan** to blow up *(a balloon)*.

lembur overtime; **bekerja lembur** to work overtime; **gaji lembur** overtime pay.

lembut gentle, soft; **melembutkan** to refine, to soften; **kelembutan** gentleness, softness; **pelembutan** softening.

lempar throw; **lempar lembing** javelin-throwing; **melempar** to throw; **melempari** to pelt, to throw at; **dia melempari anjing itu** he threw *(stones or other things)* at the dog; **melemparkan** to throw; **dia melemparkan buku itu ke lantai** he threw the book on the floor; **pelempar** launcher, pitcher, thrower.

lencana badge.

lengah careless, negligent; **kelengahan** **1** forgetfulness; **2** idleness.

lengan **1** arm; **lengan patah** to break your arm *(unintentionally)*; **2** sleeve;

a b c d e f g h i j k l m n o p q r s t u v w x y z

menggulung lengan baju to roll up your sleeves.

lengkap 1 complete; **koleksi yang lengkap** the complete collection; **2** fully equipped; **apartemen yang serba lengkap** a fully furnished flat; **selengkap-lengkapnya** as completely as possible; **perlengkapan** equipment; **bagian perlengkapan pria** the men's department; **perlengkapan laboratorium** laboratory equipment.

lengket sticky; **kertas lengket** sticky paper.

lengkung bend, curve; **melengkung** to bend, to buckle, to curve, to warp; **lengkungan** arc, curve.

lensa lens.

lentera lantern.

lenyap disappear; **melenyapkan** to make disappear, to remove.

lepas 1 free; **burung beo lepas** the mynah bird got free; **2** undone; **ritsletingnya lepas** the zip came undone; **melepas** to remove, to take off; **melepaskan 1** to set free; **Hikmah melepaskan semua burung bapaknya** Hikmah released all her father's birds; **2** to fire; **seratus buruh dilepaskan dari pabrik itu** one hundred workers were fired from that factory; **3** to fire *(a rifle)*; **lepasan** release.

lereng slope *(hill, mountain)*.

les lesson *(not in school)*, take lessons; **les bahasa Indonesia** to take private lessons in Indonesian.

leset, meleset to fail to meet *(target, aim)*; **terpeleset** to slip and fall.

lestari ever-lasting, long-lasting; **melestarikan** to preserve; **melestarikan lingkungan** to preserve the environment; **pelestarian** conservation; **pelestarian hutan** forest conservation.

lesu 1 lacking energy, listless; **2** depressed; **menjadi lesu** to become slow; **perdagangan lesu bulan ini** trade has slowed this month.

letak location; **meletakkan** to put something somewhere; **letakkan buku itu di atas meja** put the book on the table; **terletak** be located or situated; **candi itu terletak di atas bukit** the temple is situated on top of a hill.

letih tired, worn out; **sangat letih** exhausted; **meletihkan** exhausting; **keletihan** exhaustion, over-tired.

letnan lieutenant.

letup sound an explosion makes; **meletup** to explode, to go off; **letupan** explosion.

letus sound a large explosion makes; **meletus** to erupt, to explode; **gunung berapi itu meletus lagi** the volcano erupted again; **letusan** eruption, explosion.

lewat 1 through, via; **kereta api itu lewat Sukabumi** the train goes through Sukabumi; **polisi itu mengijinkan kami lewat** the police let us through; **kami lewat rumah Anda** we passed by your house; **2** *(with time)* past, over; **musim kemarau sudah lewat** the dry season is over; **pukul enam lewat sepuluh** ten past six; **melewati** to exceed, to pass through; **melewatkan** to miss *(an opportunity)*.

lezat delicious.

liang hole, opening.

liar 1 primitive, wild; **binatang liar di Kalimantan** wildlife in Kalimantan **2** illegal, not authorized; **pertambangan liar** unauthorized mining.

liat 1 *(meat, criminal)* tough; **2** *(soil)* clayey; **tanah liat** clay.

libat to wind, to wrap; **melibatkan** to involve; **melibatkan diri** to involve yourself; **sandiwara itu akan melibatkan semua orang** the play will involve everybody; **terlibat** involved; **dua mobil terlibat dalam kecelakaan itu** two cars were involved in the accident; **keterlibatan** involvement.

libur break, holiday, leave; **libur yang luar biasa** a fantastic holiday; **libur sekolah** the school holidays; **berlibur** to go on holidays; **ke mana Anda akan berlibur?** where are you going for your holiday?; **berliburan** take a vacation; **liburan** holiday.

licik sly, tricky; **dia kelihatan licik** he looks shifty; **kelicikan** cunning, slyness, trickiness.

licin 1 slippery; **2** bare, smooth; **permukaan licin** a smooth surface; **3** cunning.

lidah tongue.

lidi rib of a palm leaf; **sapu lidi** broom made of these ribs.

lihat 1 see; **2** refer to; **lihat dalam kamus** refer to the dictionary; **melihat** to observe, to see; **melihat-lihat** to browse, to window-shop; **melihat-lihat di toko-toko** to have a look around the shops; **memperlihatkan** to display, to show; **dia memperlihatkan perangko**

a
b
c
d
e
f
g
h
i
j
k
l
m
n
o
p
q
r
s
t
u
v
w
x
y
z

itu kepada saya he showed me the stamp; **kelihatan** obvious, visible; **laut sudah kelihatan** the sea is already visible; **kelihatannya** apparently; **Melanie kelihatannya senang** Melanie looks pleased; **penglihatan** eyesight; **berpenglihatan lemah** to have poor sight.

lilin candle, wax.

lima five, fifth; **lima belas** fifteen; **lima puluh** fifty; **tanggal lima Desember** the fifth of December; **pada lantai lima** on the fifth floor; **kelima** fifth; **anak yang kelima** the fifth child.

limau citrus fruit.

limbah waste; **air sungai itu berwarna merah karena limbah pabrik batik** the river water is red because of the waste from the batik factory.

limpah lots of, plenty; **berlimpah-limpah, berlimpah ruah** in abundance; **melimpah 1** to flood, to overflow; **2** to be abundant; **melimpahkan 1** to give very generously; **2** to cause to overflow; **limpahan** gift, overflow.

limun lemonade.

lindas, melindas to run over.

lindung, berlindung be protected or sheltered; **berlindung dari hujan** to take shelter from the rain; **melindungi** to protect, to shelter; **pelindung** patron, protector; **perlindungan** patronage; protection; **perlindungan lingkungan hidup** environmental protection.

linggis crowbar.

lingkar circle, circumference, rim, hoop; **Lingkar Pasifik** Pacific Rim; **lingkar pinggul** hip measurement; **melingkar** curled; **berdiri melingkar** to stand in a circle; **melingkarkan** to embrace, to put something around; **lingkaran** circle; **lingkaran setan** vicious circle.

lingkung circle, perimeter; **lingkungan 1** circle; **lingkungan kawan-kawan saya** my circle of friends; **2** area; **lingkungan yang baik** a nice neighbourhood; **3** sphere; **lingkungan hidup** the natural environment.

linglung 1 absent-minded; **2** confused.

lintang 1 across; **2** latitude; **melintang** to lie across, crosswise.

lintas move quickly; **lalu lintas** traffic; **melintas 1** to hurry, to rush past; **2** to take a short cut; **3** to cross over; **kita melintas saja** we'll just take a shortcut; **melintasi** **1** to flash past, to rush by; **dia lari melintasi taman itu** he ran across the park; **2** *(difficulties)* to overcome; **perlintasan** crossing, overpass; **perlintasan jalan kereta api** level crossing.

lipat fold; **berlipat** folded, pleated; **melipat, melipatkan** to fold together; **melipat surat** to fold a letter; **melipatgandakan** to increase many times, to multiply; **berlipat ganda** multiplied.

liput, meliput to cover an event *(in journalism)*; **meliputi** **1** to cover; **2** to comprise, to include; **liputan** coverage.

lirik, melirik to look sideways; **lirikan mata** a peering look.

lisan oral, spoken; **bahasa lisan** colloquial language, spoken language; **ujian lisan** the oral exam.

listrik electricity, electrical; **kompor listrik** an electric stove, **kesetrum listrik** to get an electric shock; **tukang listrik** electrician; **mematikan listrik** to turn off the electricity.

liter litre.

liur saliva.

loak secondhand, used; **pasar loak** flea market; **barang loakan** junk, secondhand goods.

loba greedy.

lobak radish.

lodeh style of cooked food; **sayur lodeh** a vegetable dish cooked with coconut cream.

logam metal.

logat accent, dialect; **berlogat** to have an accent or dialect; **dia berlogat Australia** he has an Australian accent.

lohor midday prayer *(Islam)*.

lokakarya seminar, workshop.

lokal local.

lokasi location, site.

loket ticket window.

lokomotip locomotive.

lolos get away, get out; **dia lolos dari penjara** he got away from jail; **meloloskan** to release, to set free; **meloloskan diri** to escape.

lomba contest, race; **peserta lomba, pengikut lomba** competitor *(in a race)*, athlete; **perlombaan** contest, race; **peserta perlombaan, pengikut perlombaan** competitor.

lombok[1] chilli.

Lombok², pulau Lombok Lombok Island.

lompat jump; **lompat jauh** long jump; **lompat tinggi** high jump; **melompat** to jump; **melompat-lompat** to jump up and down; **melompati** to jump over; **lompatan** hurdle; **pelompat** hurdler; **pelompatan** jumping.

loncat jump, leap; **loncat tinggi** high jump; **meloncat** to leap *(upwards)*; **meloncati** to jump over; **kuda meloncati pagar** the horse jumped the fence.

lonceng bell.

longgar **1** loose; **celana ini longgar** these trousers are loose; **2** not disciplined; **3** *(contract)* not binding; **melonggarkan** to loosen, relax *(discipline)*; **kelonggaran** **1** looseness; **2** concession, dispensation; **3** too loose; **pelonggaran** loosening, relaxing.

longsor slide; **tanah longsor** landslide; **longsoran** **1** landslide; **2** soil erosion.

loreng striped; **kucing loreng** a tabby cat.

lorong **1** lane, path; **2** alley; **3** hallway.

losin, lusin dozen; **selosin, selusin** a dozen; **setengah lusin** a half dozen.

losmen cheap hotel, inn, cheap bed and breakfast *(not in a person's home)*.

loteng attic, upstairs.

lotere **1** lottery, raffle; **2** lottery ticket.

lotot, melotot bulging, goggling, open wide *(eyes)*.

lowong empty, vacant; **lowongan** a vacancy; **lowongan pekerjaan** a job vacancy.

lu *(slang, Jakarta)* you.

luang free, vacant; **pada waktu luang saya** in my leisure time; **meluangkan** **1** to make room for, to vacate; **2** to make time for; **saya tidak dapat meluangkan waktu** I can't spare the time; **terluang** spare, vacant; **peluang** chance, opportunity; **jangan menyia-nyiakan peluang itu** don't waste that opportunity.

luap, meluap **1** overflow; **waktu hujan lebat kali itu meluap ke rumah rumah di pinggirnya** during the heavy rain the river overflowed into the houses along its banks; **2** to flare up, boil over.

luar **1** exterior, outside; **luar negeri** abroad; **tinggal di luar negeri** to live abroad; **dingin di luar** it's cold out there; **dia (pergi) ke luar kamar** he went out of the room; **2** beyond; **luar biasa** extraordinary, unusual; **hujan yang luar biasa banyaknya** an abnormal amount of rain.

luas broad, extensive, wide; **danau yang luas** a large lake; **luasnya** area, width; **berapa luasnya segitiga ini?** what's the area of this triangle?; **meluas** to spread; **hama meluas di desa-desa** the pests spread through the villages; **meluaskan, memperluas** to expand, to extend, to widen; **keluasan** breadth, extent, space; **perluasan** expansion, extension.

lubang burrow, cavity, hole, pit; **berlubang** having a hole; **berlubang-lubang** full of holes, perforated; **melubangi** **1** to dig a hole; **2** to pierce *(as in body piercing)*, to punch a hole; **3** to hollow out.

lucu **1** amusing, funny; **Anda memang lucu** you are really funny; **cerita yang lucu** a funny story; **2** cute; **anak lucu** a cute kid; **3** cuteness.

lucut to slip off; **melucuti** to disarm; **perlucutan** removal; **perlucutan senjata** disarmament.

ludah saliva; **meludah** to spit; **meludahi** to spit at.

luka injury, wound; **luka parah** badly hurt, seriously wounded; **apakah Anda luka?** did you hurt yourself?; **melukai**; to injure, to hurt.

lukis painted; **seni lukis** art of painting; **melukis** to draw, to paint; **dia melukis ayam jantan** he painted a picture of a rooster; **melukiskan** to describe; **lukisan** drawing, painting; **pelukis** painter.

lulus pass *(an exam)*; **apakah Anda lulus?** did you pass?; **meluluskan** to approve, to grant; **meluluskan permintaan** to grant a request; **lulusan** graduate.

lumayan fair, reasonable; **makanan yang lumayan** a decent meal; **bahasa Indonesianya lumayan** her Indonesian is fair; **uang insentif yang lumayan besarnya** a reasonable incentive payment.

lumba-lumba dolphin.

lumbung rice barn.

lumpia Indonesian spring rolls.

a b c d e f g h i j k l m n o p q r s t u v w x y z

lumpuh paralysed; **melumpuhkan 1** to paralyse; **2** to deactivate, to disable; **kelumpuhan** paralysis.

lumpur mud; **berlumpur** muddy; **sepatu Anda berlumpur** your boots are muddy.

lumur, berlumuran have a smear or stain; **berlumuran darah** to have blood stains; **melumurkan** to smear, to stain.

lumut moss; **berlumut** mossy.

lunak 1 *(food)* soft; **2** free and easy, gentle; **melunak** to become soft; **pelunak** softener.

lunas paid off; **melunasi, melunaskan** to pay, to settle; **pelunasan** paying off a debt.

luncur, meluncur to glide, to skim, to slide; **meluncur dengan cepat** to flash by; **meluncurkan** to launch something physical; **peluncur** launcher; **peluncuran** blast off, launching.

luntang-lantung loaf about; **luntang lantung saja sepanjang hari** to bum around all day.

luntur discoloured, faded; **warna-warna itu sudah luntur** the colours have faded; **meluntur** to fade or lose colour; **melunturi** to stain with running colours; **kaos kaki itu melunturi kemeja saya** the socks stained my shirt; **kelunturan** to get stained by running colours.

lupa forget; **ah, sebelum saya lupa!** oh, before I forget!; **lupa ingatan** insane; **jangan lupa menelepon!** don't fail to call!; **melupakan** to forget about a thing; **kelupaan** forgetfulness; **pelupa** forgetful person.

luput 1 escaped, got away; **2** not on target.

lurah village chief; **kelurahan** district administered by the lurah.

lurus straight; **garis lurus** a straight line; **berambut lurus** to have straight hair; **berdiri tegak lurus** to stand upright; **menjadi lurus** to become straight, to stretch out straight; **kelurusan hati** honesty, integrity.

lusa the day after tomorrow.

lutut knee; **berlutut** to kneel.

luwes 1 smooth, sociable; **2** flexible; **meluweskan** to smooth; **keluwesan** smoothness, flexibility.

M m

maaf **1** excuse, forgive, pardon; **maaf Pak Nasri** pardon me, Pak Nasri; **minta maaf** to apologize; **dia minta maaf atas kelakuannya** he apologizes for his behaviour; **2** ask permission to leave; **maaf saya harus pergi sekarang** sorry, I have to go now; **bermaaf-maafan, saling memaafkan** forgive each other; **memaafkan** to forgive; **dia tidak akan memaafkan saya** he'll not forgive me; **kita harus bersedia memaafkan kesalahan orang** we have to be willing to forgive people for their mistakes; **pemaaf** forgiving person, person who forgives, a forgiving person.

mabuk **1** drunk; **2** feel nauseated; **mabuk darat** car sick; **mabuk udara** air sick; **memabukkan** to intoxicate, to make drunk; **pemabuk** a drunk.

macam **1** kind, sort; **2** method, way; **(ber)macam-macam, beraneka macam** all kinds of, various; **ada bermacam-macam tumbuh-tumbuhan di kebun raya** there are all kinds of plants in the botanical gardens; **semacam** a kind of; **semacam bunga** a certain kind of flower.

macan tiger; **macan tutul** leopard.

macet stuck, jammed, out of order; **jendela itu macet** the window is jammed; **memacetkan** to clog or jam up; **kecelakaan itu memacetkan lalu lintas** the accident jammed up the traffic; **kemacetan** **1** jamming, sticking; **kemacetan lalu lintas** a traffic jam; **2** stoppage, shutdown.

madu[1] honey; **berbulan madu** go on a honeymoon.

madu[2] co-wife, concubine, second wife; **saya tidak mau dimadu** I don't want to be a co-wife.

magrib **1** west; **2** sunset; **sembayang magrib** Islamic sunset prayer.

maha great, very; **maha luas** very wide; **maha baik** very good; **maha penting** very, very important; **Tuhan Yang Maha Esa** the one and only God.

a b c d e f g h i j k l m n o p q r s t u v w x y z

mahal expensive; **kemahalan 1** expensiveness; **2** too expensive; **karcis konser itu kemahalan untuk saya** the concert ticket is too expensive for me.

maharaja emperor; **kemaharajaan** empire.

maharani princess.

mahir proficient, skilled; **kemahiran** capability, skill.

mahasiswa university student *(both male and female)*; **mahasiswi** university student *(female)*.

mahkamah court of law; **mahkamah agung** supreme court.

mahkota crown.

mahluk creature; **mahluk halus** supernatural creature.

main 1 play; **main kartu** to play a game of cards; **2** to take part in an activity *(that is not considered respectable)*; **main curang** unfair play; **main judi** gamble; **3** do something without thinking; **main tembak** shoot without good excuse; **main-main 1** in fun, not serious; **2** *(colloquial)* drop by for a visit; **main-main di rumah nanti** drop over some time, **bermain** play; **Petra bermain futbol** Petra plays football; **bermain-main** all in fun; **memainkan 1** to play; **mempermainkan** to make a fool of; **jangan coba mempermainkan saya!** don't try to make a fool of me!; **mainan, main-mainan 1** toy; **2** knickknack; **pemain** actor, player; **permainan 1** game; **permainan kartu** a game of cards; **2** performance, show; **3** acting; **4** tricks.

majalah journal, magazine, periodical.

majelis council, committee; **majelis hakim** court council.

majikan boss, employer; **majikan Anda** your boss.

maju 1 advance, go forward; **maju ke depan** to move forward; **2** thrive, progress; **3** progressive, forward-looking; **memajukan 1** to move something forward; **waktu dimajukan dua jam** the time was put forward two hours; **2** to advance, to improve; **kemajuan** development, progress; **kemajuan yang nyata** a definite improvement; **kemajuan-kemajuan teknologi** advances in technology.

maka 1 so, then; **2** word introducing a clause; **makanya** consequently, because of that, no wonder!; **Anda baru tidur jam tiga**

pagi! Makanya sekarang lelah! you didn't go to sleep until three this morning! No wonder you're tired!

makam burial plot, grave; **memakamkan** to bury; **pemakaman** funeral.

makan 1 eat, eat a meal; **waktu makan** meal time; **makan siang** have lunch; **nafsu makan** appetite; **saya sudah makan** I've already eaten; **2** swallow, take; **makan obat** take medicine; **3** consume, destroy; **4** need, take; **makan waktu** take time; **perjalanan itu akan makan waktu empat jam** the journey will take four hours; **memakan** to consume, to use up; **gempa bumi itu memakan banyak korban** the earthquake claimed many victims; **makanan** food, provisions; **makanan khas Bali** Balinese cuisine; **makanan pokok** staple foods; **pemakan 1** eater; **binatang pemakan daging** a carnivore; **2** consumer.

makhluk creature.

maki, maki-maki abuse; **memaki** to abuse, to use abusive language; **makian** abuse; **kata-kata makian** abusive words.

makin increasingly, the more; **anak itu makin tinggi** that child is growing taller; **makin ... makin** more and more; **makin cepat makin baik** the faster the better; **semakin** more and more; **semakin banyak waktu yang terbuang** more and more time is wasted.

maklum 1 have knowledge, know; **2** be understanding; **maklumlah, orang perempuan!** you know how it is with girls!; **memaklumi** to know, to understand; **memaklumkan, mempermaklumkan 1** to announce, to notify; **dimaklumkan bahwa besok sekolah akan tutup** it was announced that tomorrow the school would be closed; **2** to declare, to proclaim; **negara itu memaklumkan perang dengan negara tetangganya** that country declared war on its neighbour.

maklumat announcement, declaration.

makmur prosperous, rich, wealthy; **kemakmuran** prosperity.

makna 1 meaning; **2** purpose, sense; **bermakna** to have meaning, to be significant.

maknit magnet.

makro large-scale, macro, major.

maksimal, maksimum maximal, maximum; **memaksimalkan** to maximize.

maksud 1 aim, purpose; **untuk maksud yang baik** for a good intention; **2** intention, plan; **3** meaning, sense; **apa maksud Anda?** what do you mean?; **itu bukan maksud saya** that's not what I meant; **bermaksud** intent, plan; **kami bermaksud menyelesaikan pekerjaan ini pada hari ini** we're aiming to finish the work today; **saya bermaksud menelepon ibu** I meant to phone my mother.

malah in fact, instead, on the contrary; **saya sudah belajar terus, malah tidak lulus** I studied consistently and in fact I didn't pass.

malaikat angel.

malam 1 evening, night; **nanti malam** later tonight; **malam ini** this evening; **besok malam** tomorrow evening; **2** *(before the name of a day)* **pada malam Minggu** on Saturday evening; **malam Kudus** holy night; **malam Natal** Christmas Eve; **malam Tahun Baru** New Year's Eve; **3** *(after the name of a day)* **kemarin malam, tadi malam** last night; **Minggu malam** Sunday night; **malam-malam** at night, late at night; **semalam 1** last night; **2** one night; **bermalam 1** to spend the night, to sleep over; **2** to keep overnight; **kemalaman** be caught out by nightfall; **semalaman, semalam-malaman** the whole evening or night.

malang 1 across, transverse; **malang melintang** in the way, to lie across; **2** unlucky; **nasib malang!** bad luck!; **kemalangan** bad luck, struck by disaster.

malapetaka misfortune, great disaster.

malas 1 lazy; **2** not feel like doing, not be in the mood to do; **saya malas pergi ke sekolah** I don't feel like going to school; **bermalas-malas, (ber)malas-malasan** loaf, take it easy; **kemalasan** laziness; **pemalas** lazy person.

maling thief; **kemalingan 1** robbed; **2** robbery, theft.

malu 1 shy, **bicara saja! jangan malu!** speak up! don't be shy!; **2** embarrassed; **saya malu sekali** I was terribly embarrassed; **3** ashamed, shame; **tidak tahu malu**

knows no shame; **malu-malu** be shy or bashful; **malu-malu kucing** coy, pretending to be shy; **memalukan** 1 disgraceful, shameful; 2 shame; **mempermalukan** to disgrace, to shame; **kemaluan** genitals; **kemalu-maluan** very ashamed; **pemalu** shy or timid person.

mamah, memamah to chew.

mampat, mampet 1 compressed, solid; 2 clogged up; **memampatkan** to compress; **kemampatan** condition of being clogged up.

mampir call by, drop in; **apakah Anda dapat mampir untuk berenang?** are you able you to come over for a swim?

mampu 1 able, capable; 2 wealthy; **penyanyi itu orang mampu** that singer is a wealthy person; 3 afford, be able; **kami tidak mampu pergi ke luar negeri** we can't afford to go overseas; **kemampuan** 1 ability, capacity; 2 prosperity; **berkemampuan** have a certain capacity; **ketidakmampuan** lack of ability.

mampus *(colloquial)* 1 to die; 2 darn! damn!

mana 1 where; **di mana toko itu?** where is that shop?; **letakkan barang belanjaan di mana saja** put the shopping down anywhere; 2 which; **Anda pilih yang mana?** which have you chosen?; 3 how *(is it possible)*; **mana bisa!** how come!; **mana tahan!** I cannot stand it, I can't stop myself; 4 what kind, which kind; **Soraya orang mana?** what nationality is Soraya?; **mana-mana** anywhere, everywhere, wherever; **di mana-mana ada lumpur** there was mud everywhere.

mancanegara foreign countries.

mancung pointed, sharp *(nose)*.

mandi bathe, have a bath; **dia sedang mandi** she's in the bath; **bak mandi** tub to hold water *(for bathing by throwing water over yourself but not for immersing yourself in)*; **bak mandi kosong** the bath's empty; **bermandikan** bathed; **tubuhnya bermandikan keringat** he is bathed in sweat; **memandikan** to bathe; **memandikan anjing** to wash the dog; **pengantin itu dimandikan dengan air harum** the bride was bathed in scented water;

mempermandikan 1 to baptize; **2** to bathe according to ritual; **pemandian** bathing place; **permandian 1** bathing place; **2** baptism.

mandor foreman, overseer.

manfaat benefit, use; **manfaat besar** great benefit; **bermanfaat** beneficial; **memanfaatkan** to exploit, to make use of, to utilize.

mangga mango.

manggis mangosteen.

mangkat to pass away *(for nobility)*.

mangkir 1 absent; **mangkir sekolah** absent from school; **2** be missing, lack.

mangkok, mangkuk cup, bowl.

mangsa 1 prey; **2** victim.

manik-manik 1 beads; **2** small droplets.

manikam gem, precious stone.

manipulasi manipulation; **bermanipulasi** to engage in manipulation; **memanipulasi** to manipulate.

manis 1 sweet; **2** talking sweetly; **3** attractive, cute, **memaniskan** to sweeten; **mempermanis 1** to make sweeter; **2** to make more attractive; **kemanisan 1** sweetness; **2** beauty; **3** oversweet; **manisan** candy, sweets; **pemanis 1** sweetener, **2** cosmetics; **3** decoration.

manja 1 spoiled; **anak manja** a spoiled child; **2** attached, friendly; **3** intimate; **bermanja-manja** to be sweet with; **anak itu bermanja-manja dengan ibunya** that child is the apple of her mother's eye; **memanjakan** to baby, to pamper, to spoil; **kemanjaan** comforting closeness.

manjur 1 effective, efficacious; **prosedur itu manjur** that procedure is effective; **2** strong, powerful; **kemanjuran** effectiveness.

mantan former; **mantan presiden** former president.

mantap steady, stable; **memantapkan** to put on a stable basis; **kemantapan** steadiness, stability; **pemantapan** consolidation, stabilization.

mantel cape, coat, cardigan.

mantu, menantu son or daughter-in-law.

manusia 1 human being; **2** human; **kemanusiaan 1** humanity, being a human; **2** human nature; **perikemanusiaan** humanitarianism.

a b c d e f g h i j k l m n o p q r s t u v w x y z

mara danger, disaster; **marabahaya** disasters.

marah be angry, become angry; **marah-marah** irritable; **membuat marah, memarahkan** to infuriate, to make angry; **kegiatan Arya membuat Pak Lurah marah** Arya's activities infuriated the village head; **apa yang membuat Sumardi marah?** what made Sumardi angry?; **memarahi** to reprimand, to scold; **guru memarahi Nasrudin** the teacher reprimanded Nasrudin; **kemarahan** anger, fury; **pemarah** bad-tempered; **dia bersifat pemarah** he's very bad-tempered.

Maret March.

margarin margarine.

mari 1 come; **ke mari** come here; **ke sana ke mari** to go here and there; **2** let us; **mari kita pergi** let's leave!; **mari-mari** goodbye.

markas 1 office, station; **2** army or police post; **markas besar** headquarters.

marmar, marmer marble.

marmot, marmut guinea pig.

martabat 1 grade, rank, status; **2** prestige; **3** value.

martil hammer.

mas[1] sir, brother *(used in Java to refer to or to address men of the same age or older).*

mas[2]**, emas** gold.

masa 1 time period; **masa kini, masa sekarang** these days, nowadays; **pada masa depan, di masa mendatang** in the future; **masa lalu, masa lampau, masa silam** the past; **2** during; **pada masa kecil saya suka main kelereng** when I was little I liked to play marbles; **3** phase; **masa bodoh** I don't care; **semasa 1** during the time; **2** contemporary.

masak 1 mature, ripe; **2** experienced; **3** cook, cooked; **buku masak** cookery book; **masak-masak** carefully, deeply; **pikir masak-masak sebelum melakukan apa-apa** think carefully before you do anything; **memasak** to bake, to cook; **siapa yang akan memasak malam ini?** who's cooking tonight?; **Tjasmadi senang memasak** Tjasmadi likes cooking; **masakan** food, cooking; **4** cooking method, cuisine; **masakan Indonesia** Indonesian cooking.

masalah problem; **menyebabkan masalah** to cause problems;

mempermasalahkan to make a problem out of something; **permasalahan** a set of problems; **permasalahan ini sebetulnya sudah kami laporkan kepada guru** actually we've already reported these problems to the teacher.

masam acid, sour; **memasamkan 1** to make sour, to pickle; **2** to acidify; **kemasaman 1** unfriendliness; **2** acidity.

masehi Christian *(usually Protestant)*; **tahun masehi** the Gregorian calendar.

masih still, yet; **Anda masih tinggal di Sukabumi?** do you still live in Sukabumi?; **semasih** when; **semasih muda dia adalah seorang pekerja keras** when he was still young he was a hard worker.

masing, masing-masing 1 each; **adik perempuan saya masing-masing mempunyai binatang peliharaan** my little sisters each have a pet; **kami masing-masing mendapat hadiah** we each got a prize; **2** respective, respectively.

maskapai company, enterprise; **maskapai pengangkutan** transport company.

masuk 1 enter, go into; **silahkan masuk** please come in; **ijin masuk** admission permit; **dilarang masuk** no admission; **masuk angin** to catch cold; **2** be present at work; **masuk sekolah** attend school; **3** join in, participate; **masuk Islam** become a Muslim; **memasuki** to enter; **Azhar memasuki ruang kelas dengan cepat** Azhar came into the classroom very quickly; **memasukkan 1** to take into, to put into; **Iwan memasukkan anaknya di taman kanak-kanak** Iwan enrolled his child in kindergarten; **tolong masukkan barang-barang ini** please include these items; **2** to import; **3** to enter something in; **4** *(sport)* to score a goal; **regu kami memasukkan lima belas gol dalam pertandingan itu** our team made fifteen goals in that match; **termasuk** counted, included; **ongkos itu termasuk makan malam** dinner is included in the price; **kemasukan 1** possessed; **2** entered accidentally; **bir ini kemasukan lalat** a fly has gotten into this beer; **masukan** input; **pemasukan 1** entry; **2** import.

masyarakat 1 community, society; **ilmu masyarakat** sociology; **2** inhabitants, people; **bermasyarakat** form a group; **memasyarakat, diterima oleh masyarakat** acceptable to society; to spread and become popular in society; **memasyarakatkan** to introduce to society; **kemasyarakatan** social, societal.

masyhur famous, well-known; **memasyhurkan** to make famous, to make well-known; **kemasyhuran** fame.

mata 1 eye; **bulu mata** eyelash; **air mata** tears; **mata-mata** spy; **2** essential part, source of; **mata air** a spring; **mata angin** points of the compass; **mata pelajaran** school subject; **mata pencaharian** means of making a living; **bermata** have a particular kind of eye; **bermata rabun** be almost blind, short-sighted; **memata-matai** to spy on.

matahari the sun; **matahari terbit** sunrise; **matahari terbenam** sunset; **sinar matahari, cahaya matahari** sunshine.

matang 1 ripe; **2** cooked; **telur setengah matang** soft-boiled egg; **kurang matang, belum matang** undercooked; **3** mature, adult; **mematangkan** to let ripen; **kematangan 1** overripe; **2** ripeness; **3** maturity.

mati 1 be dead, die; **mati rasa** numb; **2** go out, stop; **mesin mati** the motor's dead; **listrik mati** power-cut; **3** fixed; **harga mati** fixed price; **mematikan 1** to kill; **mematikan serangga** to exterminate insects; **pukulan yang mematikan** a deadly blow; **2** to extinguish, to put out; **mematikan listrik** to turn off the electricity; **kematian 1** death; **2** have someone die; **anak-anak itu kematian orang tuanya** those children lost their parents; **mati-matian** to do one's utmost, with a great deal of effort; **Rini mati-matian menentang usulan saya** Rini strongly opposed my proposal.

mau 1 shall, will; **ibu mau ke pasar** mum will go to the market; **2** want, wish; **Ijar tidak mau makan** Ijar doesn't want to eat; **mau tahu** curious; **mau tak mau** whether you want or not; **kemauan** desire, wish.

maut death; **yang membawa maut** fatal.

mawar rose *(flower)*.

mayat body, human corpse.

mayor major; **mayor laut** lieutenant commander; **mayor udara** squadron leader.

mbak elder sister *(in Java only, term for addressing women older than yourself).*

mebel furniture; **permebelan** furniture industry.

medali medal.

medan 1 field, plain, square; **medan perang** battlefield; **2** domain, realm.

mega cloud.

megah 1 glorious; **2** fame, glory; **3** luxurious; **memegahkan 1** to brag about; **memegahkan diri** to brag about yourself; **2** to exalt; **kemegahan** glory, greatness.

meja table; **menyiapkan meja** to lay the table; **garam meja** table salt; **tenis meja** table tennis.

Mekah Mecca.

mekanik, mekanika, ilmu mekanik mechanics.

mekanis mechanical; **mekanisme** mechanism; **mekanisasi** mechanization.

mekar 1 open up, blossom; **2** rise; **adonan roti itu mekar** the bread dough is rising; **memekarkan 1** to make blossom or rise; **2** to develop, to spread out.

melar 1 expand, rise, stretch; **baju hangat ini melar** this jumper has stretched; **2** elastic.

melarat miserable, poor; **memelaratkan** to impoverish, to ruin, **kemelaratan** misery, poverty.

melati jasmine.

Melayu Malay, Malayan.

melek open *(for eyes)*; **memelekkan** to open (eyes); **melek huruf** literate.

meleset be wrong, miss the target.

melulu exclusively, only.

memang 1 yes you're right, that's true; **apa memang Dede yang menang?** did Dede really win?; **'Abdul ganteng kan?' 'memang'** 'isn't Abdul good-looking?' 'he sure is'; **2** indeed, in fact, yes that's true, (but ...); **memang tidak mahal, tapi ...** you're right, it's not expensive, but ...; **memangnya 1** actually; **memangnya saya harus ikut?** do I actually have to go along?; **2** actually yes ...

memar bruised.

mena, tidak semena-mena arbitrarily, unfairly, without reason.

menang win; **tak ada kemungkinan menang**

a b c d e f g h i j k l m n o p q r s t u v w x y z

sekarang there's no chance of winning now; **memenangkan 1** to pronounce a contestant the winner; **2** to win; **PDI memenangkan berapa kursi pada tahun 1999?** how many seats did PDI win in 1999?; **kemenangan** victory; **pemenang** winner.

menantu son or daughter-in-law.

menara tower, minaret.

mencong *(colloquial)* askew, crooked; **memencongkan** to twist askew.

mending *(colloquial)* **1** fairly good, mild; **2** average, middling; **3** better, preferable.

mendung cloudy, overcast.

mengapa 1 why; **2** doing what; **sedang mengapa?** what are you doing?

mengenai about, concerning.

menit minute.

mentah unripe, raw; **mangga mentah** unripe mango; **bahan mentah** raw materials; **mentah-mentah 1** raw, uncooked; **ikan mentah** uncooked fish; **2** not thought through, unconsidered; **jangan menerima pendapatnya mentah-mentah** don't take his opinion without question.

mentega butter.

menteri 1 cabinet minister; **Menteri Penerangan** Minister of Information; **2** *(chess)* bishop; **kementerian** department, ministry.

mentimun cucumber.

menu menu.

menung, bermenung meditate, muse; **memenungkan** to think deeply about; **termenung** lost in thought; **Rachmat duduk termenung memikirkan nasibnya** Rachmat sat lost in thought considering his fate.

merah red; **Palang Merah** the Red Cross; **merah putih** the red and white *(the Indonesian flag)*; **memerah** to blush, to redden, to become red; **memerahkan** to make red; **kemerah-merahan** reddish; **pemerah** stuff to make red.

merak peacock.

mercon, mercun fireworks.

mercu summit, top point; **mercu suar** lighthouse; **mercu buana** top of the globe.

mercun, mercon fireworks.

merdeka free, independent, liberated; **negara merdeka** a free country; **memerdekakan**

a b c d e f g h i j k l m n o p q r s t u v w x y z

to make free, to set free, to release; **kemerdekaan** freedom, independence, liberty; **perjuangan kemerdekaan** the struggle for independence; **pejuang kemerdekaan** the independence fighters.

merdu melodious, sweet; **kemerduan** sweetness of voice.

merek brand, trademark.

mereka their, them, they.

meriam big gun, cannon.

merica white pepper, **penghalus merica** pepper mill.

merk 1 brand, make; **merk apa sepeda Anda?** what make is your bike?; **2** label, trademark; **3** quality; **bermerk 1** to have a trademark; **2** to carry a sign on it.

merosot to decline, to drop, to fall, to go, to slide down *(prices)*.

merpati dove, pigeon.

mertua parent-in-law.

mesin engine, machine; **mesin bakar** combustion engine; **mesin jahit** sewing machine; **mesin cetak** printing press; **bermesin** motorized.

Mesir Egypt.

mesjid mosque.

meski, meskipun although, even so, in spite of; **meskipun demikian, kami senang** even so, we are happy.

mesra close relationship *(as between lovers or partners)*, intimate; **bermesraan** be very close with each other; **kemesraan 1** absorption; **2** feeling of intimacy, love; **bermesra-mesraan** in an intimate way.

mesti 1 certain, surely; **kalau Kasim diundang dia mesti datang** if you invite Kasim he'll certainly come; **2** have to, must; **saya mesti ke sekolah hari ini** I must go to school today; **3** should; **lampu itu mestinya di atas meja tulis itu** that lamp should be on the desk; **semestinya** naturally, proper; **sudah semestinya** as a matter of course, naturally.

mestika magic jewel, precious stone.

meter, meteran 1 *(device)* meter; **1** meter; **meteran air** water meter; **membaca meteran** to read the meter; **2** *(length)* by the metre; **dijual meteran** sold by the metre; **3** tape measure; **4** having a meter; **taksi meteran** metered taxi.

meterai stamp duty, payment sticker; **apakah saya harus membubuhkan meterai pada surat ini?** do I have to stick a duty stamp on this document?; **bermeterai** have a seal.

metode method.

mewah extravagant, luxurious; **daerah mewah** a luxurious area, a posh area; **kemewahan** extravagance, luxury.

mi, mie noodles; **mi bakso** noodles with meatballs.

mikrolet medium-sized bus.

mikroskop microscope.

mil mile.

miliar billion; **miliarder** billionnaire.

mili(meter) millimetre.

milik belonging to, property; **milik pribadi** private property; **tanah ini milik Hendratmo** this land is the property of Hendratmo; **hak milik** ownership *(legal term)*; **memiliki** to own; **Fazal memiliki rumah ini** Fazal owns this house; **pemilik** owner, proprietor; **pemilikan** ownership, possession; **kepemilikan** ownership.

milisi militia.

militer **1** soldier; **2** military; **kemiliteran** military.

milyar billion; **milyarder** billionnaire; **milyaran** by the billions.

milyun million; **milyuner** millionaire.

mimbar dais, pulpit, speaker's platform.

mimisan have a nosebleed.

mimpi dream; **mimpi buruk** nightmare; **bermimpi** dream; **memimpikan** to dream about; **Safera memimpikan ibunya** Safera dreamed about her mother.

minat interest; **berminat** to have an interest in; **Oppie berminat masuk regu kita** Oppie has an interest in joining our team; **meminati** be interested in; **Suwandi meminati sejarah film** Suwandi is interested in film history; **peminat** an interested person.

minggu week; **minggu lalu** last week; **minggu depan** next week; **setiap minggu** every week; **akhir minggu** weekend; **hari Minggu** Sunday; **hari Minggu yang lalu** last Sunday; **hari Minggu depan** next Sunday; **berminggu-minggu** many weeks, weeks and weeks; **mingguan** weekly; ***Hai* bukan majalah mingguan** *Hai* is not a weekly magazine; **dua mingguan** bi-weekly.

minim, minimum minimum; **meminimumkan** to minimize.

minoritas minority.

minta ask, beg, request; **saya minta kopi tiga cangkir** may I have three cups of coffee, please, I asked for three cups of coffee; **minta diri** ask permission to leave; **minta-minta** beg for alms; **meminta** to ask for; **meminta-minta** to beg for; **memintai** to request; **memintakan** to ask for on behalf of someone; **peminta-minta** beggar; **permintaan** request; **permintaan kredit** credit application; **atas permintaan** on request.

minum 1 drink; **Farid suka minum teh** Farid likes to drink tea; **2** take in; **minum obat** take medicine; **minuman** a drink; **minuman panas** a hot drink; **minuman keras** alcoholic drinks; **peminum** alcoholic.

minus 1 having little economic potential, poor; **daerah minus** a poor area; **2** minus.

minyak fat, grease, oil; **minyak wangi** perfume; **minyak mentah** crude oil; **minyak bakar** fuel oil; **minyak tanah** kerosene; **berminyak** be greasy, have oil; **meminyaki** to grease, oil; **perminyakan** petroleum or refinery business.

miring 1 at an angle, slanting, sideways; **2** crazy; **memiringkan** to place at an angle; **Fatima memiringkan topinya** Fatima wore her hat at an angle; **kemiringan** slope.

mirip resemble; **wajah Sylvia mirip wajah Ann** Sylvia's face looks like Ann's face; **kemiripan** resemblance; **kemiripan yang menyolok** a striking resemblance.

misal example, instance; **misalnya** for example.

misi mission.

miskin destitute, poor; **yang kaya dan yang miskin** the rich and the poor; **sangat miskin** very poor; **kemiskinan** poverty; **garis kemiskinan** poverty line.

mistar ruler.

mobil automobile, car; **mobil derek** tow truck; **mobil sewa** hire car; **bermobil** go by car.

mobilisasi mobilization.

modal financial capital; **modal tetap** real estate; **bermodal** have capital; **bermodalkan** have as capital; **memodali** to finance; **modalwan, pemodal** capitalist; **permodalan**

a b c d e f g h i j k l m n o p q r s t u v w x y z

capitalization, providing capital.

mode fashion; **sedang mode** in fashion; **pameran mode** fashion show; **ketinggalan mode** out-of-date.

model 1 *(of a plane, car, etc.)* model; **2** the fashion.

modem modem.

modern modern; **memodernkan, mempermodern** to modernize; **kemodernan** modernity.

modernisasi modernization.

modifikasi modification; **memodifikasi(kan)** to modify.

modul module.

moga, moga-moga I hope that, may; **semoga** I hope that; **semoga sukses** I wish you success.

mogok 1 strike, go on strike; **sopir bus sedang mogok** the bus drivers are on strike; **2** break down, stall; **mobil kami mogok di Jalan Thamrin** our car broke down on Thamrin Street; **pemogok** striker; **pemogokan** strike; **bagaimana kalau ada pemogokan sopir bis?** what if there's a bus strike?; **pemogokan pegawai perusahaan kereta api** train strike.

mohon 1 ask, request; **mohon diri** ask permission to leave; **2** beg, implore; **mohon maaf** ask forgiveness; **memohon** to plead for, to request; **memohon pekerjaan** to ask for work; **memohonkan 1** to plead for something; **2** to plead on behalf of someone; **3** to beg from; **pemohon 1** applicant; **2** petitioner; **permohonan 1** appeal, petition, request; **2** application; **permohonan visa** visa application.

molek beautiful, cute, pretty; **mempermolek** to make more beautiful; **kemolekan** beauty.

molekul molecule.

momen moment.

momok 1 ghost, spook; **2** haunting danger; **momok perang** the spectre of war.

Monas (Monumen Nasional) the national monument in Jakarta.

moncong 1 muzzle, snout; **2** spout; **memoncong** to protrude, to stick out; **memoncongkan** to make something stick out.

mondar-mandir, mundar-mandir to move back and forth aimlessly.

a b c d e f g h i j k l m n o p q r s t u v w x y z

monopoli monopoly; **memonopoli** to have a monopoly, to monopolize; **pemonopolian** monopolizing.

montir mechanic, repair person.

monumen monument.

monyet 1 monkey; **2** term of abuse.

moral morality; **bermoral** have high moral standards.

morat-marit in disorder; topsy-turvy.

moril 1 moral, morality; **2** morale.

mortir artillery mortar; **memortir** to shell.

mosi motion, vote; **mosi tidak percaya** vote of no confidence.

motif 1 design, motif; **bermotif** to have a design; **kain batik bermotif bunga dan burung** a batik cloth with a design of flowers and birds; **2** *(intent)* motive; **bermotif(kan)** to have as a motive.

motivasi motivation; **bermotivasikan** to have a motivation; **memotivasi** to motivate.

motor 1 engine, motor; **2** motorcycle; **3** moving force; **bermotor 1** motorized; **kendaraan bermotor** motorized vehicles; **2** to go by motorcycle.

moyang great-grandparent; **nenek moyang** ancestors.

-mu (kamu) you, your.

muak 1 nauseated, revolted; **2** loathe; **saya sudah muak bekerja di sini** I'm fed up with working here; **memuakkan** nauseating, repugnant; **gambar-gambar itu memuakkan siapa saja yang melihatnya** those pictures make whoever sees them feel sickened; **kemuakan** feeling of loathing.

mual 1 queasy; **sesudah makan nasi goreng itu saya mual** I felt queasy after eating that fried rice; **2** feel loathing; **memualkan** sickening.

Muang Thai Thailand.

muara 1 estuary, mouth *(of a river)*; **2** orifice; **bermuara** to empty into.

muat 1 contain, hold, accommodate; **bus ini muat tiga puluh lima orang** this bus holds thirty five people; **2** be contained in a publication; **3** include; **bermuatan 1** contain, have a load of; **satu truk bermuatan batu bara** a truckload of coal; **2** be charged with electricity; **memuat** **1** to contain, to hold; **2** to accommodate, to be able to hold; **3** to load, to take on; **feri itu sedang memuat mobil** the ferry boat is loading cars; **memuati** to load onto; **mereka sudah selesai memuati truk itu** they've finished loading the truck; **memuatkan 1** to load; **memuatkan barang-barang ke truk** to load a truck with goods; **2** to place; **muatan** **1** contents, load; **2** capacity; **3** cargo; **pemuatan** loading, placing.

muda 1 *(age)* young; **kaum muda** young people; **2** deputy; **3** green, unripe; **mangga muda** an unripe mango; **4** light, pale; **biru muda** light blue; **memudakan** to rejuvenate; **pemuda** youth, young man; **kepemudaan** matters relating to youth.

mudah[1] easy, simple; **mudah saja** it's easy; **mudah memutuskannya** it was easy to decide; **memudahkan 1** to ease, to facilitate; **2** to take lightly; **mempermudah** to facilitate, to make easier; **kemudahan** ease.

mudah[2], **mudah-mudahan 1** hopefully, I hope so, may; **mudah-mudahan tidak** I hope not; **mudah-mudahan film itu belum mulai** hopefully, the film won't have started; **2** maybe, perhaps.

mudik 1 inland, upstream, up-country; **2** return to the village; **hilir mudik** to go to and fro.

mufakat 1 to agree; **kami sudah mufakat untuk menunda perjalanan kami** we've agreed to cancel our trip; **2** agreement, consensus; **kata mufakat** word (of agreement).

mujarab effective, efficacious; **obat mujarab** effective medicine; **kemujaraban** effectiveness, efficacy.

mujur 1 straight ahead; **2** luck, lucky; **kami mujur** we were lucky; **kemujuran** luck; **pemujur** lucky person.

muka 1 face; **muka masam** sour face; **2** front; **halaman muka** the front page; **3** surface; **muka laut** surface of the sea; **di muka** in advance, in front of; **harus membayar di muka** you have to pay in advance; **di muka televisi** in front of the TV; **4** face, reputation; **muka tebal** not feeling shame; **bermuka** having a certain kind of face; **bermuka dua** double-faced; **bermuka bulat** having a round face; **mengemukakan 1** to propose, to suggest; **2** to put to the front; **pemuka** leader, promoter; **permukaan** surface; **permukaan licin** a smooth surface.

mula beginning, basis, original cause; **mula-mula** at first, at the beginning; **mula-mula dia agak malu** at first he was shy; **dari semula** at first, from the beginning, originally; **dari semula kami ingin membeli mobil baru** originally we wanted to buy a new car; **pada mulanya** at the beginning; **bermula 1** have a beginning; **bermula dari** starting from; **2** first; **3** before; **mulai 1** begin, start; **film itu mulai jam delapan** the film begins at eight; **semua kata yang mulai dengan huruf 'S'** all the words beginning with 'S'; **2** from, beginning; **mulai kemarin** from yesterday; **memulai** to begin; **saya sudah memulai pekerjaan rumah saya** I've made a start on my homework; **pemula 1** initiator, originator; **2** beginner; **permulaan 1** beginning, outset; **pada permulaan sandiwara itu** at the beginning of the play; **2** basis, origin.

mulas churning, upset *(stomach)*.

mulia glorious, noble, sublime; **orang yang mulia** a noble person; **memuliakan, mempermuliakan** to glorify, to honour deeply; **kemuliaan** glory, magnificence, pomp.

mulur 1 elastic; **2** flexible.

mulut 1 mouth; **mulut busuk** bad breath, saying horrible things; **mulut besar** big mouth; **2** opening; **3** nozzle; **bermulut** to have an opening.

munafik hypocrite, hypocritical; **kemunafikan** hyprocrisy.

muncul appear, emerge, turn up; **muncul di televisi** to appear on television; **bermunculan** to appear in numbers, to spring up; **sesudah hujan jamur bermunculan** after rain hundreds of mushrooms emerge; **memunculkan 1** to bring out of the water; **2** to bring into view; **3** to set in context; **film itu dimunculkan pada masa perjuangan kemerdekaan** the film is set during the struggle for independence.

a b c d e f g h i j k l m n o p q r s t u v w x y z

mundar-mandir, mondar-mandir to move back and forth aimlessly.

mundur 1 back up, go back; **2** decline, decrease, deteriorate; **3** retreat; **memundurkan** to make something back up, to go back; **waktu dimundurkan satu jam** the time was put back one hour; **kemunduran 1** decline, decrease; **2** deterioration.

mungkin possible; **secepat mungkin** as soon as possible; **tidak mungkin dapat menelepon di sini** it's impossible to make a phone call around here; **mungkin dia sakit** she may be ill; **memungkinkan** to enable, to make possible; **kalau cuaca memungkinkan** weather permitting; **kemungkinan** possibility; **sebagai kemungkinan lain kita bisa ke Taman Mini** alternatively, we could go to Taman Mini.

mungkir to deny, to disavow, to go back on *(an agreement)*; **memungkiri 1** to deny; **2** to ignore; **3** to break *(a promise)*.

munisi munitions.

muntah throw up, vomit; **saya muntah beberapa kali** I was sick several times; **memuntahi** to vomit on; **memuntahkan** to vomit up; **muntahan** the vomit.

murah cheap; **murah hati** generous; **bermurah hati** generous; **kemurahan 1** inexpensiveness; **2** generosity; **3** too cheap; **murahan** of a cheap sort; **barang murahan** cheap goods; **pemurah** generous person.

muram depressed, gloomy, sad; **memuramkan** to sadden.

murid 1 pupil, student of lower grades; **2** disciple, follower.

murka 1 anger, fury; **2** angry; **kemurkaan** anger, fury, rage.

murni clean, pure; **susu murni** unadulterated milk; **memurnikan** to cleanse, to purify; **kemurnian** genuineness, purity; **pemurni** cleanser; **pemurnian** cleansing, purifying.

murung depressed, melancholy; **bermurung-murung** to be in a depressed mood; **kemurungan** depression; **pemurung** depressive.

musafir traveller, wanderer.

museum museum.

musik music; **bermain musik** play music; **pemusik, musikus** musician.

a b c d e f g h i j k l m n o p q r s t u v w x y z

musim period, season; **musim bunga, musim semi** spring; **musim dingin** winter; **musim gugur, musim rontok** autumn; **musim panas** summer; **musim kemarau, musim kering** dry season; **musim pancaroba** transitional season; **rambutan belum musim** rambutan are not in season; **bermusim** have a season; **negara yang bermusim dingin** a country that has a winter season; **musiman** seasonal.

muslihat 1 trick; **2** strategy, tactics.

muslim a Moslem; **kaum muslimin** Moslems.

muslimat a Moslem woman.

musnah annihilated, destroyed; **memusnahkan** to annihilate, to destroy; **kemusnahan** destruction, extinction; **pemusnah** agent for destroying, disinfectant; **pemusnahan** annihilation.

mustahil impossible, out of the question; **kemustahilan** impossibility.

musuh adversary, enemy; **bermusuhan** be enemies; **memusuhi** to be hostile towards; **permusuhan** hostility.

musyawarah 1 conference, meeting; **2** deliberation, discussion; **bermusyawarah** engage in deliberations; **memusyawarahkan** to deliberate, to discuss; **permusyawarahan** conference, deliberation, discussion.

mutakhir most up-to-date, state-of-the-art, the very latest.

mutasi 1 *(biology)* mutation; **2** transfer *(of official to new post or student to new school)*; **memutasikan** to make such a transfer.

mutiara pearl; **itu mutiara asli** it's a real pearl.

mutlak absolute, unconditional; **kuasa mutlak** absolute power; **memutlakkan** to make a thing totally essential; **kemutlakan** absoluteness.

mutu quality; **bermutu** excellent, high quality.

N n

naas misfortune, unlucky; **kenaasan** bad luck.

nabi prophet; **Nabi Isa** Jesus Christ.

nada 1 intonation; **2** tone, note; **senada 1** monotonous; **2** in harmony; **bernada** have a tone.

nadi, urat nadi artery.

nafas breath; **bernafas** to breathe; **lukisan yang bernafaskan Islam** a painting with a Moslem touch; **pernafasan** breathing, respiration.

nafkah livelihood, subsistence; **mencari nafkah** to make a living.

nafsu natural appetite or desire; **nafsu makan** appetite; **bernafsu** passionate, desirous.

naga dragon.

nah *(exclamation)* well!, here!, see now!

nakhoda ship's captain, skipper; **nahkoda kapal** captain of a ship; **Nakhoda Agung** Admiral of the fleet.

naik 1 climb, go up; **naik tangga** go up a ladder or stairs; **naik pangkat** be promoted; **naik kelas** to go up a grade in school; **naik haji** go on a pilgrimage to Mecca; **naik turun** ups and downs; **2** ride; **naik bis** go by bus; **menaiki** to climb, to go up into; **monyet itu menaiki pohon kelapa** the monkey climbed the coconut tree; **menaikkan** to put up; **menaikkan gaji** increase the salary; **menaikkan harga** to put up the price; **kenaikan 1** increase, raise; **2** promotion; **kenaikan pangkat** promotion; **3** ascension.

najis dirty, ritually unclean *(Islam)*.

nakal naughty, mischievous; **kenakalan** delinquency, mischief, naughtiness.

nama 1 name; **siapa namanya? namanya siapa?** what's his/her name?; **nama julukan, nama panggilan** nickname; **nama keluarga** surname; **nama kecil** given name; **pemberian nama** naming; **2** fame, title; **bernama** called, named; **dia bernama Dedi** he's called Dedi; **menamai** to give a real name, **menamakan** to call, to give a nickname to; **kami akan menamakannya si Cebol** we'll call her Shortie; **kenamaan, ternama** well known, famous.

nampak evident, visible; **nampaknya** apparently; **menampakkan** to exhibit, to show; **penampakan** appearance *(of spirits)*, vision.

namun however, yet.

nanah pus; **bernanah** to fester.

nanas pineapple.

nangka jackfruit.

nanti **1** later; **2** presently; **nanti dulu** wait a minute; **nanti malam** later this evening, later tonight; **nantinya** eventually; **menanti** to wait for; **mereka menanti sebentar** they waited for a moment; **menanti-nanti 1** to wait for a long time; **2** to look forward to; **menantikan** to watch, to wait for; **dia menantikan orang-orang keluar dari gereja** she/he waited for the people to come out of the church; **penantian** waiting; **masa penantian** a period of waiting.

narapidana convict.

nasi cooked rice; **nasi goreng** fried rice; **nasi kuning** yellow rice, saffron rice *(for ceremonies)*.

nasib destiny, fate; **nasib baik** lucky; **senasib** having the same destiny; **nasib-nasiban** *(colloquial)* at random, depending on luck.

nasihat advice; **saya menghargai nasihat Anda** I appreciate your advice; **menasihati** to advise; **saya menasihatinya supaya berhenti** I advised him/her to stop; **Hermin menasihati Anis agar dia merasa lebih senang** Hermin advised Anis so that she would feel happier; **penasihat** adviser.

nasional national; **kenasionalan, nasionalitas** nationality; **nasionalis** nationalist; **nasionalisme** nationalism; **nasionalisasi** nationalization; **menasionalisasi** to nationalize.

naskah document, manuscript, original text.

nasrani Christian; **menasranikan** to convert to Christianity.

Natal Christmas; **Selamat Hari Natal!** Happy Christmas!; **natalan** Christmas celebration.

naung **1** shadow, shade; **2** protection, shelter; **bernaung** be under shelter, take shelter; **menaungi 1** to shade; **2** to protect, to shelter; **naungan** shelter, protection.

negara state; **warga negara** citizen; **tamu negara** state guest; **negara bagian** state in a federal system; **negara kangguru** Australia; **negara berkembang** developing country; **kenegaraan** matters relating to the state; **negarawan** statesman.

negatif negative.

negeri 1 country, land; **pegawai negeri** civil servant; **pergi ke luar negeri** to go abroad; **negeri merdeka** an independent state; **2** state-owned, state-run; **sekolah negeri** state school.

nekat desperate, prepared to take risks; **percobaan nekat** a desperate attempt; **kenekatan** determination to do; **nekat-nekatan** *(colloquial)* undertake without worrying about the risks.

nelayan fisherman.

nenek 1 grandmother, great aunt; **nenek-moyang** ancestors.

neraca balance, pair of scales.

neraka hell; **di sini rasanya seperti di neraka!** it's like hell here!

netral neutral; **pakai gigi netral** to be in neutral; **menetralkan** to neutralize; **kenetralan** neutrality; **penetralan** neutralization.

ngawur do randomly, do without any reason.

ngeri horrified, horrifying; **mengerikan** to appal, to horrify, blood-curdling; **keadaan gedung itu mengerikan** the condition of the building is appalling.

ngilu sharp or nagging pain; **gigi saya ngilu** my tooth is painful.

niaga commerce, trade; **berniaga** trade; **keniagaan** marketing, trade; **perniagaan** commerce, trade.

niat aim, intention; **berniat** to intend; **niatan** thing intended.

nikah 1 marriage, wedding; **akad nikah** *(Moslem)* marriage ceremony; **2** marry; **menikah** to get married; **mereka menikah kemarin** they got married yesterday; **menikahi** to marry; **Agus menikahi Ami** Agus married Ami; **menikahkan** to marry someone off; **Angie menikahkan puterinya dengan anak temannya** Angie married her daughter to her friend's son; **pernikahan** wedding ceremony.

nikmat 1 comfort, luxury; **2** deeply enjoyable; **makanan yang nikmat** an enjoyable meal; **3 nikmat Allah** God's gift *(Islam)*; **menikmati 1** to enjoy; **apakah Anda menikmati pesta itu?** did you enjoy the party?; **2** to benefit from; **kenikmatan 1**

bliss, enjoyment; **2** amenities, comfort; **3** enjoy the privilege of.

nila blue dye, indigo.

nilai **1** price, value; **nilai gizi** nutritional value; **2** school grades; **nilai tinggi** a good pass; **3** moral value; **bernilai** precious, valuable; **menilai** to appraise, to evaluate; **guru menilai pekerjaan kami** the teacher marks our work; **penilai** **1** appraiser, assessor; **2** grader, judge; **penilaian** **1** judgement; **2** appraisal, evaluation.

ningrat aristocracy, nobility.

nipah nipa palm, thatch palm.

Nipon Japan.

nisan gravestone.

niscaya certainly, surely; **keniscayaan** certainty.

nista **1** abuse, insult; **2** stigma; **3** humiliated, insulted; **kenistaan** **1** insult; **2** indignity.

noda **1** spot, stain; **2** disgrace, shame; **bernoda** disgraced, stained; **menodai** **1** to stain; **2** to disgrace.

nol nought, zero.

nomor **1** number; **nomor lima** number five; **2** *(of a periodical, magazine)* issue; **3** number in a musical show; **menomori** to number things; **senomor** per number, per issue; **penomoran** numbering.

nominal nominal.

nona, Nn miss, term of address for (young) unmarried women.

non-aktif inactive, laid off; **menonaktifkan** to deactivate, to decommission.

nonformal **1** outside the usual system, irregular; **2** *(colloquial)* informal.

November November.

normal normal; **menormalkan** to normalize.

normalisasi normalization; **menormalisasikan** to normalize.

Norwegia Norway.

not musical note.

nota **1** note; **2** statement of account; **3** memorandum.

notaris notary public.

notes, buku notes small notebook, notepad.

nuansa nuance; **nuansa biru yang manis** a pretty shade of blue.

nujum fortune telling; **ahli nujum** fortune-teller; **pernujuman** astrology.

nurani inner; **hati nurani** heart of hearts.

nusa island, native country; **Nusa Tenggara** the Lesser Sunda Islands *(Bali to Timor)*.

nusantara **1** archipelago; **2** the Indonesian archipelago.

-nya *(as a suffix)* her, his, its, their.

nyala flame; **bernyala, menyala 1** to flame, to flare up; **semangatnya bernyala(-nyala), semangatnya menyala(-nyala)** her/his enthusiasm flared up; **2** *(light)* to burn; **semua lampu menyala** all the lights were on; **bernyala-nyala** burn, flare up repeatedly; **api ini tidak mau menyala** this fire won't burn; **menyala-nyala 1** to flare up violently; **2** raging, spirited; **menyalakan 1** to ignite, to set fire to; **menyalakan api** to start a fire; **2** to switch on; **3** to inflame, to stir up.

nyaman comfortable, pleasant; **menyamankan 1** to make fresh, to freshen up; **2** to make pleasant or comfortable; **kenyamanan 1** freshness; **2** pleasure.

nyamuk mosquito.

nyanyi, bernyanyi, menyanyi to sing; **dia menyanyi di paduan suara itu** he sings in the choir; **menyanyikan** to sing; **nyanyian** singing, song; **penyanyi** singer.

nyaring high-pitched, piercing; **suara nyaring** a high voice; **menyaringkan** to make your voice sharp and piercing.

nyaris nearly *(of something bad)*; **nyaris mati** nearly die.

nyata **1** evident, obvious; **perubahan yang nyata** a definite change; **2** real, tangible; **bukti nyata** hard proof; **kemajuan yang nyata** a real improvement; **senyatanya** as it is, as clear as possible; **menyatakan 1** to clarify, to explain; **2** to assert, to declare; **menyatakan perang** to declare war; **ternyata 1** apparently; **2** it turns out; **kenyataan 1** data, fact; **2** truth, reality; **pernyataan 1** declaration; **2** expression; **surat pernyataan terima kasih** a thank you letter.

nyawa life force, soul; **senyawa 1** completely in agreement, of one soul; **2** chemical compound; **bersenyawa 1** agree completely; **2** *(in a chemical reaction)* become a compound; **persenyawaan** fusion of chemicals; **bernyawa 1** to have a soul;

2 alive, animate; **tidak bernyawa** dead.

nyenyak, tidur nyenyak be fast asleep, sleep soundly.

nyonya, Ny **1** Mrs *(generally for non-Indonesians, can be used without the person's name)*; **2** lady; **3** *(colloquial)* wife, **4** term of address for Chinese and Western women.

O o

obat **1** medicine; **obat batuk** cough mixture; **2** toiletry; **obat kumur** gargle, mouthwash; **3** chemical preparation; **obat nyamuk** mosquito repellent; **berobat** to have medical treatment; **mengobati** to treat; **obat-obatan** medicines; **pengobatan** medical treatment.

obeng screwdriver.

obligasi bond, debenture.

obor **1** torch; **2** guide, adviser.

obral clearance sale; **mengobral** **1** to sell out, to sell cheaply; **2** to spend freely; **obralan** sale items; **pengobralan** clearance sale.

obrol, (me)ngobrol to chat; **Susi sedang ngobrol dengan Rudi** Susi is chatting with Rudi; **siaran obrol** chat show; **obrolan** chat, gossip.

obyek[1] **1** thing, object; **2** aim; **obyek wisata** tourist attraction.

obyek[2] earning on the side, moonlighting; **obyekan** sideline business; **pengobyek** person who moonlights or uses employer's supplies and facilities for own gain.

obyektif **1** objective, unbiased; **2** objective, goal.

oceh, mengoceh to babble, to jabber; **ocehan** babble, gossip, twaddle.

odol toothpaste.

ofisial official *(sport)*.

ojeg, ojek motorcycle or bicycle used for public transport; **mengojek** to make a living by using your motorcycle or bicycle to transport people and goods; **pengojek** someone who does such work.

oke, OK OK; **OK-OK** all right, tolerable.

Oktober October.

olah processing; **olah data** data processing; **siap olah** ready for processing; **mengolah** to process, to turn a raw material into a manufactured product; **pengolah** processor; **pengolahan 1** manufacture; **2** processing; **3** tabulation of data.

olahraga 1 sport; **2** physical exercise; **berolahraga** do physical exercise, take part in sport; **Ruth tidak berolahraga** Ruth doesn't exercise.

oleh[1] 1 oleh karena because of; **kami tidak bisa sampai (oleh) karena banjir** we couldn't get there because of the floods; **2** *(passive voice, means of, agency)* by; **dimakan oleh tikus** eaten by a rat; **tak pernah terpikir oleh saya** it never occurred to me.

oleh[2], oleh-oleh souvenir from a trip as a gift; **memperoleh** to get, to obtain; **memperoleh medali emas** to get a gold medal; **perolehan** gain, result.

oles, mengolesi, mengoleskan to lubricate, to spread an oily substance; **tukang pijat itu mengolesi tubuh Abdulkadir dengan minyak kayu putih** the masseur spread eucalyptus oil on Abdulkadir's body; **tukang pijat itu mengoleskan minyak kayu putih pada tubuh Abdulkadir** the masseur spread eucalyptus oil on Abdulkadir's body; **olesan** a smear.

oli lubricating oil.

Olimpiade Olympiad, Olympic Games.

Olimpik Olympics.

olok-olok 1 funny remark, joke; **2** ridicule; **berolok-olok** joke; **mengolok-olok 1** to joke with, to kid someone; **2** to make fun of, to mock; **siapa yang berani mengolok-olok guru kita?** who's game to make fun of our teacher?; **olok-olokan 1** joke; **2** mockery, ridicule.

om uncle, a form of address used by young people to someone older.

ombak wave; **pemecah ombak** breakers; **berombak 1** be choppy or wavy; **2** rolling, undulating; **rambut berombak** wavy hair.

ombang-ambing, terombang-ambing 1 bob up and down, oscillate; **2** to toss about helplessly; **sekoci penolong terombang-ambing di teluk** the lifeboat was drifting about in the bay; **3** be uncertain; **mengombang-ambingkan** to make someone feel uncertain; **jangan mengombang-**

ambingkan perasaan saya don't play on my feelings.

omel, mengomel to grumble and complain at someone; **pembantu saya selalu mengomel** my maid is always grumpy; **omelan** grumbling.

omong, mengomong(kan) to talk; **omong kosong** **1** nonsense; **2** gossip; **3** say, talk; **omong-omong** **1** chat, idle chatter, talk; **2** by the way, speaking of that.

ompong toothless.

onar noisy sensation, stir.

onderdil spare parts.

ongkos charges, cost, expenses; **ongkos pesan** a booking charge; **ongkos tambahan** an additional or extra charge; **mengongkosi** to finance.

ons 100 grams.

opelet a small bus that can carry up to six or seven passengers in the city area.

operasi **1** action, campaign, operation; **2** surgical operation.

operasional operational.

opname hospitalization, be hospitalized; **Leni diopname di rumah sakit** Leni has been hospitalized.

opor meat or chicken cooked with spices and coconut cream.

oposisi opposition.

optik optics.

optimal best, optimum.

optimis optimist.

optimistis optimistic.

orang **1** person; **orang asing** foreigner; **orang besar** dignitary; **seorang** a/one person; **orangtua** parent; **beberapa orang** several people; **orang-orang baik** nice people; **2** one; **orang hanya bisa berusaha sedapat-dapatnya** one can only do one's best; **3** people in general; **kata orang, dia pelit sekali** people say he's really mean; **seorang** **1** **seorang diri** alone; **2** one *(of persons)*; **3** a certain person; **seseorang** someone; **rupanya ada seseorang yang bersembunyi di hutan** it seems someone is hiding in the forest; **perorangan** individual.

orbit orbit.

orde economic or sociopolitical system; **Orde Baru** the New Order, sociopolitical system in Indonesia under Soeharto; **Orde Lama** the Old Order *(under Soekarno)*.

organisasi organization; **organisator** organizer.

orientasi orientation; **berorientasi** be oriented.

orisinal **1** original; **itu cerita yang benar-benar orisinal** it's a really original story; **2** the original *(copy of a document etc.)*.

orkes, orkestra orchestra *(classical music)*.

otak brain.

otomatis automatic; **dengan otomatis** automatically.

otomobil automobile.

otonom autonomous.

otonomi autonomy.

otorita, otoritas authority.

otot[1] **1** muscle; **2** tendon; **berotot** muscled, strong.

otot[2], **mengotot** to persevere, to persist.

ozon ozone; **lapisan ozon** the ozone layer.

P p

pabean customs office *(at the airport)*; **melewati pabean** to go through customs.

pabrik factory, mill; **pabrik gula** sugar mill.

pacar girlfriend or boyfriend; **berpacaran** courting, be boyfriend or girlfriend; **Allison berpacaran dengan Rudi sekarang** Allison's going out with Rudi at the moment.

pacu spur; **berpacu** race; **memacu 1** to spur; **2** to push ahead; **pacuan 1** race; **2** racecourse; **kuda pacuan** race horse; **pacuan kuda** horse race; **ikut serta dalam pacuan kuda** take part in a horse race.

pacul hoe, spade; **memacul** to dig, to hoe.

pada[1] **1** at, on; **pada halaman sepuluh** on page ten; **2** at, in *(with time)*; **pada jam enam** at six o'clock; **pada akhir pekan** at the weekend; **pada malam hari** at night; **pada saat itu** at that time; **pada tahun 1994** in 1994; **pada musim dingin** in winter.

pada[2] enough, sufficient; **memadai** to suffice, be sufficient.

padahal 1 actually, in fact; **2** besides.

padam 1 extinguished; **tiba-tiba lampu-lampu padam** suddenly the lights went out; **2** calmed, suppressed;

a b c d e f g h i j k l m n o p q r s t u v w x y z

a b c d e f g h i j k l m n o p q r s t u v w x y z

memadamkan 1 to extinguish, to put out; **2** to suppress; **pemadam** thing that extinguishes; **alat pemadam api** fire extinguisher; **pemadam kebakaran** fire brigade

padan equal, match; **sepadan** match; **jas itu tidak sepadan dengan celana itu** the coat doesn't go with the trousers; **berpadanan** go together, harmonize; **memadankan** to match; **padan kata** word that becomes part of a compound word.

padang field, plain; **padang pasir** desert; **padang rumput** field, meadow.

padat 1 compact, solid; **acara padat** a full agenda; **2** dense; **lapangan itu padat dengan orang** the field was packed with people; **memadatkan 1** to make solid; **2** to pack tight; **kepadatan 1** density; **kepadatan penduduk** population density; **2** conciseness.

paderi Catholic priest.

padi 1 rice plant, unhusked rice; **2** very small, **padi-padian** grain.

padu 1 compact, solid; **2** in harmony; **berpadu dengan** to be united, to unite with; **memadukan 1** to join, to unite; **2** to forge, to weld; **3** to agree; **terpadu** fused, integrated; **perpaduan** cohesion, unity; **paduan** blend, fusion, synthesis; **paduan suara** choir.

pagar 1 fence; **2** hedge; **memagari** to put a fence around.

pagi morning *(up until about 10 a.m.)*; **pagi ini** this morning; **besok pagi** tomorrow morning; **setiap pagi** every morning; **masih terlalu pagi** it's still too early; **pagi-pagi** early in the morning; **bangun pagi-pagi** to get up early; **paginya** that (same) morning; **keesokan paginya** the following morning; **kepagian** too early, too soon.

paha thigh.

paham 1 understanding; **ada salah paham** there's been a misunderstanding; **2** concept view; **paham politik** political concept; **paham ras** rasial view; **paham akan, memahami** know, understand; **Jordan paham akan masalah itu** Jordan understands that problem; **apakah semua paham akan tugasnya?** does everyone know what they have to do?; **sepaham** like-minded;

memahamkan to explain, to make a person understand.

pahat chisel; **memahat** to carve, to sculpt with a chisel; **pahatan** carving, relief; **pemahat** sculptor.

pahit bitter *(real as well as figurative)*; **kopi pahit** coffee without sugar; **kepahitan** bitterness.

pahlawan hero; **kepahlawanan** heroism.

pailit bankrupt.

pajak tax; **mengenakan pajak** to impose tax; **pajak kekayaan** wealth tax; **pajak pendapatan, pajak penghasilan** income tax; **perpajakan 1** taxation; **2** tax system.

pajang, memajang to decorate, to drape; **pajangan** decoration.

pak 1 package, parcel; **2** pack; **sepak kartu** a pack of cards; **mengepak** to pack, to package; **saya belum mengepak** I haven't packed yet; **pengepakan** packing.

pakai 1 by means of, with; **siap pakai** ready to use; **2** wear; **Anda pakai ukuran berapa?** what size do you take?; **berpakaian 1** get dressed; **apakah Mike sudah berpakaian?** is Mike dressed yet?; **2** wearing clothes; **Lyn sering berpakaian merah** Lyn often wears red; **memakai 1** to wear; **Tamsin sedang memakai sepatu olahraganya** Tamsin's wearing her trainers; **2** to make use of, to use; **saya memakai pisau untuk membuka paket itu** I used a knife to open the parcel; **pakaian** clothes; **pakaian anak-anak** children's wear; **membuka pakaian** to take your clothes off; **mengganti pakaian** to change your clothes; **pemakai** consumer, user; **pemakaian** consumption, use.

pakaian olahraga sports wear.

pakansi holiday, vacation.

pakat, sepakat agreed; **bersepakat** to agree with each other; **menyepakati** to agree.

paket parcel, package.

paksa 1 force; **2** compulsion; **memaksa** to compel, to force; **terpaksa** be forced to; **oleh karena tidak ada kereta api, kami terpaksa naik bis** as there were no trains, we had to take the bus; **paksaan** compulsion.

pakta pact.

paku nail, spike; **paku jamur, paku payung** thumbtack;

memaku to nail; **terpaku** to stand rivetted in amazement.

pala nutmeg.

palang 1 crossbar; **Palang Merah** the Red Cross; **2** barrier; **memalangi** to block, to hamper, to obstruct; **memalangkan** to crucify.

palawija secondary crop.

palem palm.

paling the most; **yang paling tua** the oldest; **paling sedikit** the least; **paling-paling** at the most; **paling paling Mira cuma mau jadi bintang tamu** at the most Mira only wants to be a guest star.

palsu counterfeit, fake; **intan palsu** fake diamond; **memalsukan** to forge *(documents)*; **pemalsu** counterfeiter, forger; **pemalsuan** counterfeiting, forging.

palu 1 hammer; **2** gavel.

paman uncle.

pamer, memamerkan 1 *(clothes)* to model; **2** to display, to exhibit; **keramik dari Bandung dipamerkan** ceramics from Bandung were on display; **3** to show off; **Shanti memamerkan kekayaannya** Shanti was showing off her wealth; **pameran** exhibition; **pameran kerajinan tangan** a handicrafts display; **pameran mode** fashion show.

pamit farewell, say goodbye; **berpamitan** to take leave.

pamrih 1 profit, reward; **2** intent, purpose, what you are aiming for.

panah bow (and arrow); **main anak panah** to play darts; **memanah** to shoot at with an arrow; **panahan** archery; **pemanah** archer.

panas 1 hot; **minuman panas** a hot drink; **merasa panas** to feel hot; **mulai panas** to warm up *(the weather)*; **panas dingin** cold and hot, feverish; **2** tense; **suasana panas sebelum pemilu** a tense atmosphere before the election; **memanas** to heat up; **suhu politik makin memanas** the political climate is heating up; **memanaskan** to heat up; **dia memanaskan makanan itu** he warmed the food; **memanaskan badan** to warm up *(for example, an athlete)*; **kepanasan 1** too hot; **2** heat; **3** suffering from the heat.

panca five; **panca indera** the five senses, **pancalomba** pentathlon; **pancasila** five principles.

pancang 1 pile, pole, stake; **2** boundary marker;

memancang to drive, to ram piles; **terpancang 1** planted, rooted in the ground; **2** *(reputation)* established; **pancangan 1** marker, stake; **2** place to dig in; **pemancangan** marking with a stake.

pancar, terpancar dispersed, scattered; **memancarkan 1** to radiate; **2** to spout, to spray out; **3** to broadcast; **pancaran 1** emission, flow; **2** broadcast; **3** product; **pemancar 1** radio or TV transmitter; **2** fountain; **3** radiator.

pancaroba transition (period).

Pancasila the five basic principles of the Republic of Indonesia.

pancawarsa period of five years.

pancawindu period of forty years.

panci saucepan.

pancing 1 fishing rod; **2** fish hook; **memancing 1** to fish, to go fishing; **saya tidak suka memancing** I hate fishing; **2** to goad, to provoke a reaction; **pancingan** provocation, inducement; **pemancing** something used to get a reaction; **terpancing** provoked to a reaction.

pancung 1 shirt-tail, train of dress; **2** angular, cut off sharply; **hukuman pancung** punishment by decapitation; **memancung** to amputate, to cut off; **pancungan** a cut.

pancur, memancur to gush, to pour out, to spout; **pancuran 1** shower; **2** jet, spray; **pancuran air** fountain, jet of water.

pandai[1] **1** clever, smart; **2** capable; **dia pandai main gitar** she's good at playing the guitar; **kepandaian** cleverness.

pandai[2] crafter of metals; **pandai besi** blacksmith; **pandai emas** goldsmith.

pandang a look; **sekali pandang** at first glance; **berpandangan 1** view each other; **2** have a particular opinion; **memandang** to gaze, to look at; **terpandang** esteemed, highly respected; **Ruli adalah orang terpandang di kotanya** Ruli is a highly respected person in his town; **pandangan 1** opinion, view; **menurut pandangan saya** in my view; **2** something you see; **pemandangan** scenery, view; **pemandangan yang sangat menakjubkan** it was an

a b c d e f g h i j k l m n o p q r s t u v w x y z

astonishing sight; **melihat pemandangan** to see the sights.

pandu guide; **pandu kapal** ship's pilot; **memandu** to guide; **panduan 1** escort; **buku panduan** guidebook; **2** *(project)* pilot; **pemandu** guide; **pemandu wisata** tourist guide.

panekuk pancake.

panen harvest.

pangeran 1 prince; **2** *(cards)* jack.

panggang 1 baked, roasted; **ayam panggang** barbecued chicken; **2** toasted; **memanggang** to bake, to roast, to toast; **memanggang ayam** to barbecue a chicken.

panggil, memanggil 1 to call, to summon; **memanggil taksi** to call a taxi; **memanggil dokter** to call the doctor; **2** to call, to name; **mereka panggil saya tante** they call me aunt; **panggilan** summons.

panggung 1 raised platform, stage; **2** grandstand; **3** scaffolding.

pangkal 1 base, starting point; **pangkal pokok** gist; **2** cause; **3** base point, **berpangkal** to be based; **dia berpangkal di Ubud** she's based in Ubud; **pangkalan 1** place to start out from; **pangkalan taksi** taxi stand; **2** *(military)* base.

pangkas get a haircut; **memangkas 1** to cut or trim hair; **Tony memangkas rambutnya** Tony's had his hair cut; **2** to prune, to trim; **pemangkas, tukang pangkas** barber.

pangkat position, rank; **naik pangkat** be promoted; **berpangkat** to hold an important position; **kepangkatan** ranking.

pangku lap; **memangku 1** to put on your lap; **2** to administer, to manage; **pangkuan** lap.

panglima commander *(military)*.

panik panic.

panili vanilla.

panitia committee; **kepanitiaan** structured as a committee.

panjang length, long; **panjang akal** resourceful; **panjang umur** have a long life; **sepanjang 1** all along; **ada pohon di sepanjang jalan itu** there are trees all along the road; **2** as far as; **sepanjang malam** all night long; **memanjangkan** to lengthen; **memperpanjang** to extend, to lengthen *(a visa,* *vacation, etc.)*; **kepanjangan** **1** too long; **2** length; **perpanjangan** extension *(of a visa etc.)*.

panjat, memanjat to climb.

panji banner, standard.

pantai beach, coast, seashore; **di pantai barat** on the west coast; **pergi ke pantai** to go to the beach.

pantang **1** forbidden, prohibited, taboo; **2** avoiding a taboo thing; **berpantang** to abstain from.

pantas **1** proper, suitable; **2** fair, reasonable; **3** alert, smart; **4** no wonder! of course!; **pantasan** *(colloquial)* no wonder! of course!

pantat behind, bottom, buttock.

Pantekosta Pentecost, Pentecostal.

panti **1** house, residence; **2** institution; **panti asuhan** orphanage; **panti jompo** old people's home; **panti pijat** massage parlour.

pantul, memantul to bounce back or off; **memantulkan** to reflect; **pantulan** **1** reflection; **2** rebound.

Papa, Papi Dad *(particularly in westernized families)*.

papan board, plank; **papan tulis** blackboard, whiteboard; **papan pengumuman** noticeboard; **papan roda** skateboard.

papar, memaparkan to explain, to relate; **Salim memaparkan pengalamannya** Salim described his experience; **paparan** explanation.

papaya pawpaw, papaya.

para indicates plural, a group; **para penumpang** passengers; **para pembaca** readers.

parabola parabolic antenna for receiving satellite television.

parade parade.

paraf initials; **memaraf** to initial; **harap memaraf di sini** put your initials here.

parah in serious condition; **penyakit parah** a serious illness; **luka parah** serious wound, badly hurt; **mobil itu rusak parah** the car was badly damaged.

parang machete, chopping knife.

paras **1** face; **2** appearance, looks.

parasit parasite.

pariwisata **1** tourism; **2** a tour; **berpariwisata** to make

a b c d e f g h i j k l m n o p q r s t u v w x y z

a trip; **kepariwisataan** tourism business; **wisatawan** tourist.

parkir **1** park; **lapangan parkir mobil, pelataran parkir mobil** a carpark; **dilarang parkir** no parking; **tempat parkir** parking space; **2** be placed somewhere; **memarkir** to park; **di mana Anda memarkir mobilnya?** where did you park the car?

parkit budgie, parakeet.

parlemen parliament.

paroh, paruh^{1} half; **separuh** half, a part; **saya memberinya separuh dari uang itu** I gave him half of the money.

paruh^{2} beak.

partai^{1} party *(political)*; **memilih Partai Buruh** to vote for the Labor Party; **berpartai** belonging to a party.

partai^{2} event *(sport)*; **partai ganda** doubles.

partisipasi participation; **berpartisipasi** to participate.

paru-paru lungs.

parut **1** file, rasp; **2** grate, scrape; **kelapa parut** grated coconut; **0** grater, scraper; **parutan** board for scraping or grating.

pas^{1} **1** be the right size or fit; **sepatu ini tidak pas** these shoes don't fit; **ruang pas** fitting room; **2** exact, exactly; **uang pas** the right money; **3** exactly at; **mengepas** to try on; **pas-pasan** just enough.

pas^{2} document, pass; **pas jalan** travel permit.

pasal **1** *(in the Bible)* chapter, section; **2** *(legal)* article.

pasang^{1} pair; **sepasang suami-istri** a married couple; **sepasang pengantin** the bride and groom; **berpasang-pasang** in pairs; **berpasangan** to make a pair; **pasangan** **1** pair; **2** counterpart.

pasang^{2}**, pasang aksi** show off; **memasang** **1** to install, to put on or in; **mereka sudah memasang alat tanda bahaya** they've fitted an alarm; **memasang iklan dalam surat kabar** to put an ad in the paper; **2** to fasten, to pin, to post; **3** to turn on; **memasang televisi** to turn on the television; **4** to set; **memasang weker** to set the alarm clock.

pasang^{3} rise *(tidal)*; **pasang naik** high tide; **pasang surut** rise and fall of the tide

pasanggrahan place for travellers to stay, resthouse.

pasar market; **pasar malam** fair; **pasar modal** capital market; **memasarkan** to market things; **pasaran** market; **pemasaran** marketing.

pasfoto passport photo.

pasien patient *(medical)*.

Pasifik the Pacific.

pasir sand.

Paskah Easter.

paspor passport.

pasrah accept your fate; **memasrahkan** to submit to a thing; **kepasrahan** acceptance, resignation.

pasti 1 certain, definite; **dia pasti terlambat** he's certain to be late; **ilmu pasti** mathematics; **2** confirm, decide; **memastikan 1** to ascertain, to determine; **2** to confirm, to decide; **kepastian 1** certainty; **2** assurance; **3** for sure.

pastor, pastur Catholic priest.

pasukan troops *(military)*.

patah broken; **kakinya patah** his leg is broken; **mematahkan 1** to break; **kami mematahkan dahan kayu kering itu untuk dibakar** we broke those dry sticks for the fire; **2** discouraging; **patahan** broken fragment.

patok pole, stake; **mematok** to determine, to define; **patokan 1** pole; **2** criterion, norm, standard; **3** rule.

patriotik patriotic.

patroli patrol; **berpatroli** to patrol.

patrun dress pattern.

patuh obedient, submissive; **mematuhi** to obey; **mematuhi hukum** to obey (or respect) the law; **kepatuhan 1** obedience; **2** discipline.

patuk, mematuk to bite, to peck with the beak.

patung 1 statue; **2** sculpture; **mematung** to be like a statue; **pematung** sculptor; **patungan** sharing costs.

patut 1 decent, fitting, proper; **2** ought to, should; **sepatutnya** properly, rightly.

pauk, lauk pauk side dishes eaten with rice.

paus[1], **ikan paus** whale.

Paus[2], **Sri Paus** the Pope.

pawai parade, procession.

paya swamp, marsh.

payah 1 tired; **2** difficult, troublesome; **kepayahan 1** fatigue, weariness; **2** exhausted; **3** difficulty; **sakit payah** seriously ill.

payung 1 umbrella; **2** parachute; **terjun payung** a parachute jump.

a b c d e f g h i j k l m n o p q r s t u v w x y z

a b c d e f g h i j k l m n o p q r s t u v w x y z

Pebruari, Februari February.

pecah 1 broken, smashed; **barang pecah-belah** crockery, fragile items; **2** chapped, split open; **kulit pecah** chapped skin; **3** *(war)* broken out; **memecahkan 1** to solve; **memecahkan suatu persoalan** to solve a problem; **2** to split; **3** to break; **dengan tidak sengaja saya memecahkan piring itu** I accidentally broke the plate; **terpecah-pecah** in pieces; **pecahan 1** fragment, piece; **2** fraction; **pemecah 1** a breaker; **pemecah rekor** record breaker; **2** something that breaks things up; **pemecahan 1** answer, solution; **2** fission.

pecat, memecat 1 to discharge, to sack; **dipecat dari jabatan** to be axed from a position; **2** to suspend; **pemecatan 1** discharge, dismissal; **2** suspension.

pecel cooked vegetables with peanut sauce.

peci rimless cap *(usually black)* worn by men in Indonesia.

pedal pedal; **pedal gas** accelerator.

pedang sword.

pedas 1 hot, with a lot of chilli; **sambal ini terlalu pedas buat saya** the sambal's too hot for me; **2** biting, severe.

pedati cart, wagon pulled by a steer or buffalo.

pedih 1 smarting; **2** poignant; **memedihkan** painful, making something smart; **memedihkan mata** irritating to the eyes.

pedoman 1 compass; **2** orientation; **3** directive, manual; **berpedoman 1** be guided by; **2** orient yourself.

peduli care about, pay attention, take notice of; **saya tak peduli** I couldn't care less; **mempedulikan** to pay attention to, to mind.

pegal 1 *(of muscles)* painful, stiff; **2** weary.

pegang, berpegang pada hang, hold on to; **berpegang tangan** holding hands; **berpegangan 1** hold on to each other; **2** hang on to; **memegang 1** to hang on, to take hold of; **Anda memegang apa?** what have you got in your hand?; **peganglah tangan saya** take my hand; **2** to handle; **3** to control, to hold, to occupy; **memegang jabatan** to hold a position; **4** to have on you; **pegangan 1** handle, thing to hold on with; **2** grip; **3** something you can rely on; **4** connection; **5** guide; **pemegang 1** handle, knob; **2** person holding on.

pegawai employee, official, staff; **pegawai negeri** a civil servant.

pejam, terpejam closed *(eyes)*; **memejamkan** to close your eyes.

peka sensitive; **kepekaan** sensitivity.

pekan 1 *(weekly)* market; **2** five-day week; **berpekan-pekan** for weeks; **sepekan** one week.

pekat 1 concentrated, thick; **malam pekat** a dark night; **hitam pekat** pitch black; **2** strong; **kopi pekat** strong coffee; **kepekatan 1** density, thickness; **2** darkness.

pekerti character, nature; **budi pekerti** character.

pekik, pekikan scream, yell; **memekik** to scream, to yell.

pel mop, wipe; **kain pel** floor cloth; **mengepel** to mop; **mengepel lantai dapur** to mop the kitchen floor.

pelan, perlahan slow; **pelan-pelan, perlahan-lahan** slowly.

pelangi rainbow.

pelat metal plate; **pelat nomor** licence plate.

pelbagai all sorts of, various.

peleceh flatterer; **pelecehan** harassment; **pelecehan seksual** sexual harassment.

pelekat 1 placard, poster; **2** glue.

pelesir joy, pleasure; **berpelesir** to take a trip for amusement.

pelihara, memelihara 1 to protect, to take care of; **2** to raise, to rear; **memelihara kambing** raise goats; **3** to keep, to maintain; **peliharaan** things to be protected; **binatang peliharaan** pet, zoo animal; **pemelihara** caretaker; **pemeliharaan 1** care, maintenance; **pemeliharaan gigi** dental care; **2** cultivation, rearing; **3** safeguarding.

pelik complicated; **perkara yang pelik** a complicated case; **kepelikan** complexity.

pelit stingy.

pelita[1] **1** oil lamp; **2** light *(metaphorical sense)*.

Pelita[2] (*Pembangunan Lima Tahun)* five-year development.

pelitur polish, varnish; **memelitur** to varnish.

pelopor 1 pioneer; **2** forerunner, vanguard; **3** ranger, scout; **memelopori**

1 to crusade, to pioneer; **2** to be in advance of; **kepeloporan** pioneering.

pelor bullet.

pelosok 1 remote place; **2** corner.

peluang 1 opportunity; **2** *(wind)* quiet; **berpeluang** have an opportunity.

peluh perspiration, sweat; **berpeluh** to sweat.

peluit flute, whistle.

peluk embrace; **peluk cium** a hug and a kiss; **berpelukan** to embrace each other; **memeluk** to embrace; **Tracy memeluk saya** Tracy gave me a hug.

pelupuk cover, wrapper; **pelupuk mata** eyelid.

peluru 1 bullet; **2** missile, projectile; **3** *(sport)* shot-put.

pematang bund, dyke between rice fields.

pemda (pemerintah daerah) local government.

pemilu (pemilihan umum) general elections.

pemuda young man; **pemudi** young woman.

pena pen.

penalti penalty *(sport)*.

penat exhausted, tired, weary; **kepenatan 1** tired; **2** fatigue, weariness.

pencak system of self-defence; **pencak silat** system of self-defence.

pencar, berpencar to disperse; **memencarkan** to disperse things.

pencet, memencet 1 to crush, to smash; **2** to press; **pencetan** pressure.

pencil 1 isolated, secluded; **2** desolate, remote; **memencilkan** to isolate, to segregate.

pendam, memendam to bury; **terpendam 1** buried; **2** kept in the heart.

pendek short; **pendeknya** in brief, in short; **pendek umur** have a short life; **memendekkan, memperpendek** to abbreviate, to make short; **kependekan 1** abbreviation; **2** shortness; **3** too short.

pendekar fighter, especially a sword fighter.

pendeta Protestant clergyman.

pendopo large-roofed platform without walls in front of Javanese residence.

penetrasi penetration.

pengalaman experience.

penganten, pengantin bride or groom; **penganten baru** newly married couple.

pengap oppressive, stuffy.

pengaruh influence; **pengaruh sampingan** side-effect; **berpengaruh** influential; **mempengaruhi** to influence.

penggal 1 lump, piece; **2** fragment; **memenggal** to cut off, to cut to pieces; **penggalan** bit, piece.

pening dizzy; **pening kepala** headache.

peniti 1 safety pin; **2** brooch for pinning a ***kebaya*** together.

penjahit tailor.

penjara jail, prison; **memenjarakan** to imprison.

penjuru 1 angle, corner; **2** direction something comes from; **penjuru angin** points of the compass; **dari segala penjuru** from all directions.

pensil pencil.

pensiun pension; **pensiunan** retired.

penting important; **mementingkan 1** to emphasize; **mementingkan diri sendiri** selfish; **2** to give importance to, to bring to notice; **3** to consider important; **kepentingan** (self-) interest; **demi kepentingan** in the interest of; **pentingnya** importance.

pentol knob; **pentolan 1** prominent; **2** leader of a gang; **3** bulb.

penuh 1 full; **kecepatan penuh** full speed; **2** complete; **dibayar penuh** paid in full; **memenuhi 1** to fill; **orang banyak memenuhi gelanggang** the crowd filled the stadium; **2** to fulfil, to meet a demand; **memenuhi janji** to keep a promise; **terpenuhi** complied with; **kepenuhan 1** over-full; **2** completeness.

penyek, penyet *(colloquial)* flattened out, squeezed.

penyok *(colloquial)* dented.

penyu 1 turtle; **2** tortoiseshell.

pepatah proverb, saying.

per[1] by the, per; **per kapita** per capita; **per lusin** per dozen.

per[2] spring; **berper** with springs.

perabot 1 utensils; **2** tools; **3** furniture; **perabotan** household furnishings.

peraga, alat peraga audiovisual aids, teaching aid; **memperagakan** to exhibit, to display; **peragaan** show; **peragawan** male model; **peragawati** female model.

a b c d e f g h i j k l m n o p q r s t u v w x y z

perah, memerah 1 to squeeze; **2** to milk; **memerah kambing** to milk a goat; **perahan** something squeezed out; **sapi perahan** dairy cattle; **pemerah** milker.

perahu boat; **perahu dayung** rowboat; **perahu layar** sailboat; **perahu tambang** ferry boat.

perak 1 silver; **2** rupiah.

peran 1 actor; **2** character, role; **peran utama** the main character; **peran ganda** double role; **berperan** to have a role; **memerankan** to play the role of, to portray.

Perancis 1 French; **bahasa Perancis** French *(the language)*; **2 orang Perancis** the French *(the people)*.

perang war; **perang dunia** world war; **perang saudara** civil war; **berperang** have a war.

perangai 1 disposition, nature; **2** attitude, behaviour; **berperangai** have a particular attitude, disposition; **Julie seorang yang berperangai optimis** Julie tends to be optimistic.

perangko postage stamp.

peras, memeras 1 to press, to squeeze; **memeras jeruk** to squeeze oranges; **2** to milk; **3** to blackmail; **perasan** what has been squeezed out; **pemeras 1** press; **2** exploiter; **pemerasan 1** pressing, squeezing; **2** exploitation, extortion.

perawan girl, virgin; **perawan tua** spinster.

perban bandage; **memerban** to bandage.

percaya 1 belief, faith; **percaya akan hantu** believe in ghosts; **tidak percaya akan diri sendiri** to lack self-confidence; **2** believe, trust; **saya percaya kepadanya** I believe her; **mempercayai** to believe in, to rely on; **Jason sama sekali tidak dapat dipercayai** Jason can't be trusted at all; **mempercayakan** to entrust to; **tepercaya 1** reliable, trustworthy; **2** believable; **kepercayaan** faith, trust, confidence, belief; **saya menaruh kepercayaan penuh kepada Anda** I have absolute confidence in you.

percik spot, stain; **bepercikan** to splash; **sepercik** a splatter of; **memerciki** to splatter, to sprinkle; **memercikkan** to spatter with; **percikan** sprinkling.

percuma in vain.

perdana 1 first, principal; **Perdana Menteri** prime minister; **2** inaugural, first introduction; **pertunjukan perdana** premiere.

perdata 1 court of justice; **2** civil cases; **hukum perdata** civil law.

perekat glue.

perempatan crossroads.

perempuan 1 female, woman; **adik perempuan saya** my little sister; **kakak perempuan saya** my older sister; **ipar perempuan** sister-in-law; **2** feminine; **keperempuanan** femininity.

pergi 1 go; **pulang pergi** return trip, there and back again; **2** be out, leave; **saya akan pergi (keluar kota) pada akhir pekan** I'll be away next weekend; **bepergian** to go on a trip, to travel; **bepergian dengan bis** take a bus trip; **kepergian** **1** departure; **2** journey, trip.

pergok, memergoki 1 to catch someone by surprise; **2** to catch red-handed; **saya memergokinya memeriksa surat-surat Dani** I caught him going through Dani's documents; **kepergok** **1** surprised, unexpected; **2** be caught red-handed.

peri-, perihal 1 concerning, having to do with; **2** attitude; **perikemanusiaan** humanity, humanitarianism; **tak terperikan** indescribable.

peribahasa proverb.

perih smarting *(wound)*, bitter *(sorrow)*.

periksa examination, inspection, investigation; **ruang periksa** examination room; **memeriksa 1** to investigate, to look into; **saya akan memeriksa dokumen Anda** I'll just check your documents; **2** to inspect; **dia memeriksa nama-namanya** she checked their names; **3** to cross-examine, to interrogate; **pemeriksa 1** inspector, investigator; **2** cross-examiner; **pemeriksaan** **1** inspection, investigation; **pemeriksaan terhadap insiden** an investigation into the incident; **2** cross-examination, interrogation; **3** check-up, examination; **pemeriksaan darah** a blood test.

perintah command, order; **kita harus taat kepada perintahnya** we must obey her commands; **memerintahkan** to command, to order; **guru itu memerintahkan murid-**

muridnya supaya tetap bersama-sama the teacher instructed the children to stay together; **pemerintah** government; **pemerintahan** government administration.

peristiwa 1 affair, event, incident; **2** phenomenon.

periuk cauldron, cooking pot.

perkakas implements, tools.

perkara 1 case, matter; **2** lawsuit.

perkasa brave, courageous; **gagah perkasa** brave and strong; **keperkasaan 1** courage; **2** power.

perkedel fried, meat-filled ball of potato mash, meat patties.

perkosa 1 violent; **2** violence; **3** rape; **memperkosa** to rape, to violate; **perkosaan** rape.

perlahan 1 slow; **2** soft-voiced; **perlahan-lahan** slowly; **dia bangkit perlahan-lahan** he got up slowly.

perlu 1 be needed, necessary; **apa perlunya menunggu** what's the point of waiting; **2** need to; **tak perlu menunggu** there's no need to wait; **memerlukan** to need; **keperluan** need, necessity, requirement; **keperluan sehari-hari** daily needs.

permadani carpet.

permai beautiful, fine, pretty; **indah permai** beautiful *(for scenery)*.

permaisuri queen consort.

permak altered, changed; **celana yang dipermak** altered trousers; **mempermak** to alter.

permata jewel, precious stone.

permen candy; **permen karet** chewing gum.

permisi 1 permission; **2** ask to be excused, ask permission to leave.

pernah 1 ever, once; **saya pernah ke Dili** I once went to Dili; **2** *(to form perfect tenses in statements and questions)*; **Anda pernah menonton film itu?** have you seen the film?; **3 tidak pernah** never.

peron railroad platform.

pers the press.

persen 1 percentage; **2** tip.

persentase percentage, rate.

persero 1 share; **2** partner, shareholder; **perseroan** company, partnership.

persis exactly, precisely; **persis jam delapan** exactly eight o'clock.

persneling gear, transmission.

personalia personnel.

personel, personil personnel, staff.

pertama first, the first; **Sarah adalah yang pertama** Sarah's the first; **untuk pertama kali** for the first time; **pertolongan pertama** first-aid; **yang pertama** the first; **yang pertama sekali** the very first; **pertama-tama** first of all; **pertama-tama, saya mau minum kopi** first, I'm going to have a coffee.

Pertamina (Perusahaan Pertambangan Minyak dan Gas Bumi Nasional) state-owned oil company of Indonesia.

pertanda sign.

pertiwi earth; **Ibu Pertiwi** country of origin, motherland.

perut belly, stomach.

perwira officer *(military)*.

pesan 1 order; **kami pesan gulai kambing dengan nasi putih** we ordered goat curry and steamed rice; **2** instruction, order; **3** message; **ada pesan dari Ludi** there's a message from Ludi; **memesan** to order goods, to reserve a place; **Anda harus memesan tempat di sana** you'll have to book a table there; **pemesan** buyer, customer.

pesantren school for children and young people to study the Koran.

pesawat 1 instrument, machine; **pesawat uap** steam engine; **2** plane; **pesawat udara** airplane; **3** telephone extension; **minta pesawat 2486** may I have extension 2486 please?

pesek flat-nosed.

pesiar 1 journey, trip; **2** go for a ride, take a trip; **kapal pesiar** pleasure cruiser.

pesisir beach, coast; **daerah pesisir** coastal area.

pesona 1 enchantment, spell; **2** magic formula; **mempesona** to enchant; **mempesonakan 1** to enchant, to enthral; **2** enchanting; **terpesona** enchanting; **Kasim terpesona oleh kecantikan Tuti** Kasim is enthralled by Tuti's beauty.

pesta festivity, party; **pesta Natal** a Christmas party; **pesta ulang tahun** a birthday party; **berpesta** celebrate, have a party.

pestisida pesticide.

peta 1 map; **2** chart.

petak 1 cabin, compartment, partition; **2** garden bed;

a b c d e f g h i j k l m n o p q r s t u v w x y z

petak sawah rice terrace; **berpetak** compartmentalized, partitioned; **pemetakan** breaking up into parcels.

petang 1 afternoon; **2** dark, dusk.

petasan firecracker.

peti box, chest, trunk; **peti jenazah** coffin; **peti kemas** sea container.

petik, memetik pick, pluck; **memetik buah mangga** to pick mangoes.

petir thunderclap, thunderbolt.

petromaks kerosene pressure lantern.

petua, petuah 1 religious advice; **2** advice in general.

piagam charter, contract, deed.

piala cup, goblet.

piano piano.

piatu orphaned; **anak piatu** child who lost his/her mother; **yatim piatu** orphan.

pici type of rimless cap commonly worn by men in Indonesia.

picik 1 narrow; **2** narrow-minded.

pidana criminal; **hukum pidana** criminal law; **perkara pidana** criminal case.

pidato address, speech; **pidato sambutan** welcoming speech; **berpidato** to make a speech.

pigura 1 picture, painting; **2** figure.

pihak 1 side; **2** party; **pihak ketiga** third party; **berpihak, memihak** to take sides.

pijak pedal; **memijak** to step on.

pijat massage; **dukun pijat** masseur; **panti pijat** massage parlour; **memijat** to massage.

pijit, memijit to pinch, to squeeze.

pikat decoy; **memikat** to decoy.

piket 1 picket in a strike; **2** posted guard; **petugas piket** duty officer.

pikir to think; **pikir-pikir** think over carefully; **pikir-pikir dulu!** think first! *(before doing anything)*; **berpikir** think; **dia berpikir sebentar** he thought for a moment; **berpikiran** have a particular thought; **memikirkan** to think about; **terpikir** spring to mind; **tak pernah terpikir oleh saya** it never occurred to me; **pikiran 1** idea, thought; **pikiran saya berubah** I've changed my mind; **2** opinion; **3** intelligence; **pemikiran** consideration, thinking.

piknik picnic.

pikul, memikul to carry on the shoulders; **memikul risiko** to take the risk; **pikulan 1** carrying pole; **2** load; **pemikul** bearer.

pikun senile.

pil pill, tablet.

pilar pillar.

pilek to catch/have a cold.

pilem *(old spelling)* film.

pilih, memilih 1 to choose, to select; **saudara memilih dengan baik** you chose well; **2** to elect, **3** to vote; **memilih Partai Buruh** to vote for the Labor Party; **terpilih 1** elected; **dia telah terpilih** she has been elected; **2** selected; **pilihan 1** choice; **tak ada pilihan lain** there is no alternative; **2** selection; **pemilih** voter; **pemilihan 1** election; **pemilihan umum** general election; **2** poll.

pilon innocent; **berlagak pilon** *(colloquial)* pretending to be innocent.

pilot plane pilot.

pimpin, memimpin to guide, to lead; **siapa yang memimpin di sini?** who's in charge here?; **terpimpin** led by, guided by; **demokrasi terpimpin** guided democracy; **pimpinan 1** guidance, leadership; **2** administration, management; **pemimpin 1** guide, leader; **2** manager; **kepemimpinan** leadership.

pinang areca nut; **peminangan, pinangan** marriage proposal; **meminang** to propose.

pincang 1 crippled, lame; **2** have a defect; **kepincangan 1** lameness; **2** defect; **3** imbalance.

pindah 1 move; **mereka sudah pindah ke Sulawesi** they've moved to Sulawesi; **2** change, transfer; **pindah kereta** change trains; **pindah tangan** change hands, transfer to someone else; **berpindah** move; **berpindah-pindah** move repeatedly.

pinggang waist.

pinggir 1 edge, seam; **2** border; **di pinggir kota** at the edge of town; **pinggiran** coastal area, edges, outskirts; **di daerah pinggiran Jakarta** on the outskirts of Jakarta.

pingpong ping-pong, table tennis.

pingsan 1 unconscious; **2** faint; **dia pingsan di sekolah** she collapsed at school; **Kent jatuh pingsan** Kent fainted.

pinjam, meminjam to borrow from; **bolehkah saya pinjam pena Anda?** may I borrow your pen?; **meminjamkan** to lend; **saya meminjamkan sepeda kepada Sugianto** I lent Sugianto my bike; **pinjaman** loan; **peminjam** borrower.

pinset tweezers.

pintal, memintal to spin, to twine; **pintalan** ball of string.

pintar 1 clever, smart; **2** skilled at; **Tracy pintar berbahasa Indonesia** Tracy speaks Indonesian very well.

pintas, sepintas a second *(of time)*; **jalan pintas** a short cut; **memintas** to take a short cut.

pintu door, gate; **ambang pintu** doorstep, **pintu air** floodgate, locks; **pintu darurat** emergency exit; **pintu masuk** entrance.

pipa 1 pipe for smoking; **2** conduit, pipe, tube.

pipi cheek.

piring plate; **piringan hitam** phonograph record.

pisah, berpisah 1 apart; **2** separated; **dia berpisah dengan pacarnya** she's split up with her boyfriend; **memisahkan** to separate, to set aside; **saya harus memisahkan surat-surat ini** I must sort out these papers; **terpisah 1** separate; **kami tidak suka terpisah** we don't like being apart; **kami ingin kamar yang terpisah** we want separate rooms; **2** get separated accidentally; **pemisah 1** arbiter; **2** referee; **3** thing that separates; **pemisahan 1** separation; **2** isolation; **perpisahan 1** discord; **2** leave-taking, parting; **pesta perpisahan** farewell party.

pisang banana; **pisang goreng** banana fritters.

pisau knife; **pisau bedah** scalpel; **pisau silet** razor blade.

pita 1 ribbon; **2** tape; **pita ukur** measuring tape.

pitam fit; **naik pitam** get mad.

piutang 1 credit; **2** accounts receivable, claim.

piyama pyjamas.

plakat poster.

plang signpost.

planit planet.

plastik plastic.

platina 1 platinum; **2** distributor contact, points.

plestor adhesive plaster, band-aid.

plus 1 plus; **2** having a surplus.

pohon tree.

pojok corner; **di pojok kamar** in a corner of the room; **terpojok** forced into a corner; **pojokan** street corner.

pokok 1 base, basic, fundamental, main, principal; **gaji pokok** basic salary; **2** beginning; **3** capital, stake; **4** subject; **5** reason; **berpokok 1** be based on; **2** have capital.

pola 1 pattern; **pola baju** pattern for sewing; **pola mode** fashion design; **2** model, system.

Polandia Poland.

poles, memoles to polish.

polis policy; **polis asuransi** insurance policy.

polisi police; **polisi lalu lintas** traffic police; **kepolisian** police; **akademi kepolisian** police academy.

politik 1 politics, political; **keyakinan politik** political beliefs; **2** policy; **politik luar negeri** foreign policy; **berpolitik** play at politics; **politikus, politisi** politician.

polos 1 smooth; **2** plain; **3** straightforward.

Polri (Kepolisian Republik Indonesia) Indonesian Police Force.

pompa pump; **pompa air** water pump.

pondok cabin, cottage, hut.

poni fringe *(hair)*.

pop pop culture; **musik pop** pop music.

populer popular.

porak-poranda broken in pieces, disorder, in a mess.

pori pore.

poros axis, axle.

porsi portion.

Portugis Portuguese.

pos 1 mail; **kantor pos** post office; **pos kilat** express post; **pos laut** sea mail; **pos udara** air mail; **poswesel** money order; **2** post, station; **pos polisi** police station; **mengeposkan** to post; **mengeposkan surat** to mail a letter.

posisi position.

positif positive.

pot pot; **pot bunga** flowerpot.

potensi, potensial potential.

potlot pencil.

potong 1 piece; **2** lump; **3** slice; **4** be reduced by; **potong jalan** take a short cut; **memotong 1** to cut off, to slice; **Miriam memotong bawang-bawang itu** Miriam cut the onions; **2** to slaughter; **3** to amputate, to operate on; **4** to cut, to deduct, to reduce; **mereka**

a b c d e f g h i j k l m n o p q r s t u v w x y z

memotong harganya sepuluh dolar they took ten dollars off the price; **tiga juta Rupiah dipotong lima persen** three million Rupiah reduced by five per cent; **potongan 1** deduction from wages; **2** discount; **3** way something is made or built; **4** a cut; **pemotongan 1** butchering; **2** process of cutting.

potret photograph, picture, snapshot; **juru/tukang potret** photographer; **berpotret** to pose for a photograph; **memotret** to take a photo; **saya memotret candi itu** I took a photo of the temple; **pemotretan** photography.

prajurit 1 soldier; **2** a private; **keprajuritan 1** military; **latihan keprajuritan** military exercises; **2** heroism.

prakarsa initiative.

prakarya manual labour.

prakiraan forecast; **prakiraan cuaca** weather forecast.

praktek 1 professional practice; **praktek dokter** doctor's surgery; **2** practise; **berpraktek** to practise *(a profession).*

praktis practical; **dengan praktis** practically.

pramugara steward; **pramugari** stewardess.

Pramuka (Praja Muda Karana) scouts.

prasangka prejudice, **berprasangka** be prejudiced.

preman 1 private, civilian; **2** *(colloquial)* hoodlums.

premi premium.

preseden precedent.

presentasi presentation.

Presiden president.

prestasi achievement, performance.

pria man, male; **bagian perlengkapan pria** the men's department.

pribadi 1 individual, personal; **milik pribadi** personal property; **barang-barang pribadi** personal goods; **2** person; **kepribadian 1** individuality; **2** personality; **3** identity.

pribumi indigenous, native.

pribumisasi process of handing businesses over to the indigenous people.

prihatin apprehensive, concerned; **keprihatinan** concern.

prima first-rate.

primitif primitive.

prinsip principle.

prioritas priority; **memprioritaskan** to give priority to.

prisma prism.

problem, problim problem.

produk product.

produksi production; **berproduksi** to be in production; **memproduksi** to produce; **produktif** productive; **produktivitas** productivity.

profesi profession; **berprofesi** have a profession; **profesional** professional; **profesionalisme** professionalism.

profesor professor.

profil **1** appearance; **2** profile.

program, programa program.

proklamasi proclamation; **memproklamasikan** to announce, to proclaim.

promosi promotion.

propaganda propaganda.

propinsi, provinsi province.

proporsi proportion.

proporsional balanced, proportional.

prosedur procedure.

prosen, persen per cent; **prosentase, prosentasi, persentase** percentage.

proses **1** process; **2** legal action; **memproses** to process.

prosesi procession.

prospek prospect, future chances.

protes protest; **memprotes** to protest.

Protestan Protestant.

protokol protocol; **jalan-jalan protokol** main streets of a city.

provinsi, propinsi province.

proyek project; **proyek contoh** pilot project.

proyeksi forecast, projection; **memproyeksikan** **1** to project; **2** to forecast, to plan.

psikiater psychiatrist.

psikolog psychologist.

psikologi psychology.

puas contented, satisfied; **Marg puas dengan hasilnya** Marg was pleased with her results; **memuaskan** to satisfy, satisfactory, satisfying; **tak ada yang memuaskan bagi Usman** nothing satisfies Usman; **kepuasan** satisfaction.

puasa fast; **buka puasa** to break the fast; **bulan puasa** fasting month *(Islam)*;

a b c d e f g h i j k l m n o p q r s t u v w x y z

a b c d e f g h i j k l m n o p q r s t u v w x y z

berpuasa to fast, to observe the fast.

publik public.

publikasi publication.

pucat pale because of fright or illness; **memucat** to turn pale; **kepucatan** being pale.

pucuk 1 sprout, tip of a leaf; **2** tip of something; **pucuk api** tongue of flame.

pudar 1 faded, pale; **celana jeans yang menjadi pudar** faded jeans; **2** dim, weak; **memudar** to dim, to fade; **kepudaran** fading away.

puisi poetry.

puja worship; **memuja** to adore, to worship; **pujaan 1** adoration, worship; **2** idol.

pujangga man of letters, poet of renown.

puji, memuji to commend, to praise; **pujian 1** praise; **lagu-lagu pujian** songs of praise; **2** recommendation.

pukul 1 strike; **pukul rata** all in all, in general; **2** blow; **3** o'clock; **pukul tujuh** seven o'clock; **memukul 1** to hit, to strike; **memukul bola** to hit the ball; **2** to defeat; **memukulkan** to hit with; **dia memukulkan tinjunya di atas meja** he banged his fist on the table; **pukulan 1** stroke; **2** blow, strike; **pukulan di kepala** a knock on the head; **3** good fortune; **pemukul 1** beater, hammer; **2** person who strikes.

pula 1 as well, likewise; **Fitrah menangis, demikian pula Wayan** Fitrah cried, Wayan did too; **lagi pula** moreover; **mungkin pula** probably also; **2** again; **3** who else, where else, how else, etc.; **siapa pula yang pergi ke Balikpapan?** who else went to Balikpapan?; **4** how in the world, why in the world, what in the world, etc.; **mengapa pula mau ke rumah guru?** why on earth do you want to go to the teacher's house?; **5** still; **belum pula selesai** still not done or completed.

pulang return home; **pulang pergi** return trip, there and back again; **berpulang** die; **memulangkan 1** to bring back, to give back, to return; **2** to reimburse; **pemulangan 1** return, restitution; **2** repatriation.

pulas fast asleep.

pulau island; **Pulau Dewata** Isle of the Gods, Bali; **kepulauan** archipelago.

pulih 1 *(from an illness)* recovered; **2** restored; **memulihkan** to restore; **terpulihkan** can be restored;

pemulihan 1 recovery; **2** restoration.

pulpen fountain pen.

puluh tens; **sepuluh** ten; **tiga puluh** thirty; **berpuluh-puluh** tens; **puluhan** tens.

pun 1 then, subsequently; **2** also, even; **Bambang pun tidak suka itu** even Bambang didn't like it; **meski pun demikian** even so; **bagaimana pun juga** at all events, in any case, in any event, no matter what.

punah extinct; **kepunahan** extinction.

puncak 1 summit, top; **puncak gunung** the summit of the mountain; **2** peak, zenith.

pundak shoulder.

punggung back; **sakit punggung** backache; **tulang punggung** backbone.

pungut adopted; **anak pungut** adopted child; **memungut 1** to pick, to pick up; **2** to collect; **pemerintah memungut pajak jalan** the government collects road taxes; **pungutan 1** harvest; **2** amount collected; **pungutan liar** illegal collection; **pemungut** collector; **pemungutan 1** collection; **2** adoption.

puntung 1 butt, stub, stump; **puntung rokok** a cigarette butt; **2** crippled, maimed.

punya 1 *(colloquial)* have, possess; **yang punya** owner; **2** belonging; **siapa punya jas ini?** whose is this jacket?; **saya tahu siapa yang punya itu** I know whose it is; **3** *(colloquial)* a possessive marker; **4** after, with; **mempunyai** to have, to own, to possess; **Ami mempunyai tiga anak** Ami has three children; **kepunyaan** possession, property; **mobil itu bukan kepunyaan Nora** that's not Nora's car; **itu bukan kepunyaan saya** that's not mine.

pupu relationship; **saudara sepupu** first cousin.

pupuk fertilizer, manure; **pupuk buatan** artificial manure; **pupuk hijau** compost, green manure; **pupuk kandang** fertilizer from animals.

pura-pura pretend, pseudo.

purba ancient; **zaman purba** ancient times.

purbakala olden times; **ilmu purbakala** archeology; **kepurbakalaan** archaeological.

puri 1 castle, royal palace; **2** town; **3** Balinese temple.

a b c d e f g h i j k l m n o p q r s t u v w x y z

purnama, bulan purnama full moon.

pusaka heirloom.

pusar navel; **pusar kepala** crown of the head; **berpusar** revolve, whirl around; **pusaran 1** rotation; **2** crank, handle; **3** vortex.

pusat 1 navel; **2** centre; **di pusat kota** in the town centre; **pusat perbelanjaan** a shopping centre; **menjadi pusat perhatian umum** to be in the spotlight; **3** central; **Jakarta pusat** central Jakarta; **memusatkan** to concentrate on, to focus on; **saya tak bisa memusatkan pikiran saya** I can't concentrate.

pusing 1 dizzy, whirling; **saya pusing kepala** I've got a headache; **2** confused, puzzled; **memusingkan 1** to make dizzy; **2** to confuse, to puzzle; **3** to worry about; **masalah ini memusingkan kepala saya** this problem has worried me.

Puskesmas (Pusat Kesehatan Masyarakat) community health clinic.

pustaka 1 book; **2** divining manual; **kepustakaan 1** literature; **2** documents; **3** bibliography; **perpustakaan** library; **perpustakaan umum** the public library; **pustakawan** male librarian; **pustakawati** female librarian.

putar turning; **putar balik** turn around; **berputar** rotate; **berputar-putar** beat around the bush; **memutar 1** to revolve, to turn; **2** to twist, to wind; **3** *(a film)* to show; **putaran 1** circle; **putaran air** whirlpool; **2** crank, windlass; **3** wheel; **4** showing *(of a film)*.

putra 1 prince; **2** child, son; **putranya berapa?** how many children do you have?; **3** a child of; **putra Yogya** a child of Yogya; **4** male; **berputra** have a child.

putri 1 princess; **2** daughter, girl; **3** female; **keputrian** women's affairs.

putih 1 white; **putih bersih** pure white; **putih telur** egg white; **2** fair-skinned, pale; **3** pure; **memutih 1** to turn white all over; **2** to fade, to turn pale; **memutihkan 1** to bleach; **2** to whitewash; **3** to get legal papers for something; **pemutih** bleach, whitener; **pemutihan 1** bleaching, whitewashing; **2** getting legal papers for something.

putus broken off, severed; **putus sekolah** drop out of school; **putus asa, putus**

harapan lose hope; **berputus asa** be desperate, lose hope; **memutuskan 1** to decide, to resolve; **Mia memutuskan untuk berhenti main film** Mia decided to stop acting in films; **silakan putuskan hal itu antara kalian sendiri** you can decide among yourselves; **2** to break off, to interrupt; **jangan putuskan pembicaraan!** don't hang up on me!; **3** to finish; **4** to break a promise; **5** to sever; **keputusan 1** decision; **keputusan Presiden** Presidential decree; **keputusan yang benar** the right decision; **Peter tak pernah bisa mengambil keputusan** Peter can never make up his mind; **2** conclusion; **mencapai keputusan** to reach a conclusion; **pemutusan** severance; **pemutusan hubungan** severance of relations.

puyuh quail; **telur puyuh** quail's eggs.

Q q

Quran the Koran.

R r

raba, meraba 1 to feel, to grope; **2** to guess; **dia tidak bisa meraba maksud saya** she can't guess my intention; **rabaan 1** groping, touch; **2** estimate, guess.

Rabu Wednesday; **setiap hari Rabu** every Wednesday; **hari Rabu yang lalu** last Wednesday; **hari Rabu depan** next Wednesday.

rabuk fertilizer; **rabuk hijau** compost; **merabuki** to apply manure.

rabun dim, hazy, short-sighted.

racun poison; **meracuni** to poison; **keracunan 1** poisoned; **2** showing symptoms of being poisoned.

radang inflamed, hot; **meradang 1** to become inflamed; **2** to get excited; **peradangan** infection; **radang mata** an eye inflammation; **radang paru-paru** pneumonia; **radang tenggorokan** a throat inflammation.

radiator radiator.

radio radio; **mendengarkan radio** to listen to the radio; **mendengar lagu itu di radio** to hear the song on the radio.

radioaktif radioactive.

radiologi radiology.

radius radius.

raga body; **beraga 1** to boast, to show off; **2** to hold an exhibition; **peragaan 1** ostentation; **2** exhibition, show; **3** modelling; **olahraga** sport; **jiwa raga** body and soul.

ragam 1 melody, tune; **2** kind, manner; **3** caprice, whim; **seragam** of one kind, uniform; **pakaian seragam** uniform, special clothes showing that the wearer is a member of the armed forces or an organization; **berseragam** to be in uniform; **keseragaman** uniformity; **beragam** various; **keragaman** diversity, variety.

ragi yeast.

ragu, ragu-ragu 1 hesitate, uncertain, wary; **saya ragu-ragu** I have my doubts; **2** hesitate to do; **jangan ragu-ragu bertanya** don't hesitate to ask; **3** be doubtful; **meragukan 1** to confuse; **2** to make a thing doubtful; **keraguan 1** hesitancy; **2** doubt.

rahang jaw; **tulang rahang** jaw bone.

rahasia secret; **menyimpan rahasia** to keep a secret; **secara rahasia** in secret; **rencana rahasia** a secret plan; **membuka rahasia** to let the cat out of the bag.

rahib 1 monk; **2** nun.

rahim uterus, womb.

raih, meraih 1 to reach for; **2** to sweep up, to take in; **3** to achieve, to manage to obtain.

raja 1 king; **2** tycoon; **3** person who excels at things; **merajai** to rule over; **merajakan 1** to make into a king; **2** to treat like a king; **3** to consider very important; **kerajaan 1** empire, kingdom.

rajawali a goshawk or white-tailed eagle.

rajin 1 diligent, industrious; **2** frequently; **kerajinan 1** diligence; **2** handicraft; **pameran kerajinan tangan** a handicrafts display; **pengrajin** artisan, craftsperson.

rajuk, merajuk to pout, to sulk; **perajuk** grumbler.

rajut net; **rajut rambut** hairnet; **merajut 1** to make a net; **2** to crochet, to knit;

rajutan crocheted or knitted material.

rak rack, shelf; **rak buku** bookshelf.

rakit raft; **rakit penyelamat** life raft; **merakit** to assemble, to connect, to join; **perakit** assembler; **perakitan** assembling.

raksasa 1 mythical gigantic demon; **2** giant; **3** gigantic; **bangunan raksasa** an enormous structure.

rakus gluttonous, greedy; **kerakusan** gluttony, greed.

rakyat citizenry, people, populace; **rakyat jelata** the common people; **Dewan Perwakilan Rakyat** People's House of Representatives; **merakyat** be close to the people, to spread among the people; **kerakyatan 1** democracy; **2** populist.

ralat error, mistake *(in speech or writing)*; **meralat** to correct the mistake.

Ramadan, Ramadhan fasting month, ninth month of the Islamic calendar.

ramah friendly, easy to get along with; **ramah-tamah** polite and friendly; **pesta ramah-tamah** an informal party; **keramahan** friendliness; informality; **peramah** a very friendly person.

ramai 1 busy, crowded; **toko-toko ramai** the shops were busy; **hari yang ramai sekali** a hectic day; **2** bustling, festive, lively; **disko itu ramai sekali** that disco is really lively; **3** loud, noisy; **jalan ini ramai sekali** this street is really noisy; **meramaikan** to cheer up, to enliven; **keramaian 1** festivity; **2** bustle, noise.

ramal, meramal to tell fortunes; **meramalkan 1** to predict; **2** to portend; **ramalan 1** prediction, prognosis; **ramalan cuaca** weather forecast; **2** fortune-telling; **peramal, tukang ramal** fortune teller.

Ramayana Hindu epic that is the base of many traditional Indonesian stories.

rambah, merambah to clear, to cut down; **mereka merambah hutan** they cleared the forest; **rambahan** what is cut down; **perambah jalan** pioneer.

rambat, merambat to creep and spread; **rambatan** propagation; **perambatan** the process of spreading.

Rambo a character from the film *Rambo*.

rambut hair of the head; **sikat rambut** hairbrush; **sisirlah rambut Anda!** just comb your hair!; **berambut** having hair; **dia berambut pirang** he's blond.

rambutan a tropical fruit that has a red hairy skin and sweet white flesh.

rames 1 mix; **2** provide with a mixture; **nasi rames** rice with various accompaniments.

rampas, merampas to grab, to snatch; **tasnya dirampas orang** she had her bag snatched; **polisi merampas semua barang penyelundupan** the police seized all the contraband; **rampasan** confiscated goods, spoil; **perampas** robber; **perampasan 1** robbery; **2** expropriation.

ramping slender, slightly built, slim.

rampok robber; **merampok** to plunder, to rob; **perampok** robber; **perampokan** robbery.

rampung completed, finished; **merampungkan** to complete, to finish.

ramu, meramu to collect, to gather; **ramuan** ingredients.

rana, merana 1 ailing, suffer chronically; **2** waste away; **3** keep worrying.

rancak, serancak a set; **serancak gamelan** a set of gamelan instruments.

rancang post, stake; **merancang 1** to stake out; **2** to plan, to make a schedule; **rancangan** plan, project; **perancang** designer, planner, planning body; **perancang mode** fashion designer.

rangka 1 framework; **rangka tubuh** skeleton; **2** blueprint, draft.

rangkai bunch *(flowers, fruit)*; **merangkai(kan)** to join, to tie together.

rangkak, merangkak 1 to crawl; **2** to make slow progress; **3** to fawn on; **merangkak-rangkak** to cringe.

rangkap 1 double; **rangkap empat** in quadruplicate; **merangkap 1** to wear double layers; **2** to double as; **perangkap** person who has two jobs.

rangkul, merangkul to cuddle, to embrace; **rangkulan** an embrace.

rangsang 1 exciting, stimulating; **2** pungent; **merangsang** to stimulate;

a b c d e f g h i j k l m n o p q r s t u v w x y z

rangsangan stimulus; **perangsang** incentive, stimulus; **perangsangan** **1** act of exciting, stimulating; **2** incentive, motivation.

rangsum ration; **merangsum** to ration.

ranjang bed.

ranjau **1** bamboo-spiked booby trap; **2** anti-personnel weapon, mine.

rantai **1** chain; **2** necklace; **3** sequence, series; **4** measure of distance; **berantai 1** have a chain; **surat berantai** chain letter; **2** in sequence; **rantaian** chain, sequence, series.

rantang set of stacked containers for carrying ready-to-eat food; **rantangan** system in which you get your food delivered on a regular basis.

rantau **1** shoreline; **2** length of a river; **3** abroad, foreign country; **merantau 1** to leave your home area to make a living, to go overseas; **2** to wander about; **3** to sail along a river; **perantau 1** someone wandering about the country; **2** settled foreigner.

ranting **1** small branch, twig; **2** branch, subsection *(of companies)*.

rapat **1** close, dense, near; **Jawa Tengah rapat penduduknya** the population is dense in Central Java; **2** close, familiar, intimate; **3** assembly, meeting; **rapat umum** a public meeting; **rapat-rapat** very close; **Nani menutup mulutnya rapat-rapat** Nani didn't say a single word; **merapat 1** to move closer; **tolong merapat sedikit** move up a bit; **2** to join together; **3** to moor, to tie up; **kerapatan** density.

rapi(h) neat, orderly; **berpakaian rapi** be neatly dressed; **merapikan** to put in order, to tidy up; **apakah Anda sudah merapikan kamar Anda?** have you tidied up your room?; **kerapian** neatness, tidiness.

rapor, rapot school report card.

rapuh brittle, likely to snap.

ras[1] race; **diskriminasi ras** racial discrimination.

ras[2] thoroughbred; **kuda ras** a thoroughbred horse.

rasa **1** taste, sensation; **rasa coklat** chocolate-flavoured; **2** feeling, sense; **rasa malu** embarrassment; **rasa hormat** feeling of respect; **rasa sentimen** spiteful; **3** have a certain opinion; **saya rasa**

I think; **merasa 1** to feel; **saya merasa lelah** I feel tired; **dia merasa kurang sehat** she doesn't feel well; **2** to think, to believe; **perasaan** feeling, opinion; **rasa tanggung jawab** have a sense of responsibility; **memperlihatkan perasaan** to show one's feelings; **melukai perasaan seseorang** to hurt somebody's feelings.

rasi, serasi harmonious, compatible.

rasial, rasialis racialist, racist; **rasialisme** racism.

rasionalisasi **1** rationalization; **2** reduction in the number of workers in a firm.

rasuk possession by a spirit; **merasuk 1** to possess a person; **2** to pervade completely; **kerasukan** possessed.

rata 1 flat, level; **2** even; **sama rata** as even as; **3** average; **rata-rata 1** on the average, mean; **suhu rata-rata** the average temperature; **2** quite even; **merata 1** to smooth; **2** to be spread evenly; **pemerataan** even distribution; **meratakan** to level.

ratna gem, jewel, precious stone.

ratu queen *(ruling)*.

ratus hundred; **seratus** one hundred; **dua ratus** two hundred; **sekitar seratus** about a hundred; **ratusan** hundreds.

raung sound of a siren, a siren; **meraung 1** to roar; **2** to moan; **raungan 1** roar; **2** moan.

rawa, rawa-rawa swamp, marsh; **berawa** swampy.

rawan 1 emotional, sensitive; **2** disturbed, troubled; **daerah rawan** dangerous area; **kerawanan** unsafe.

rawat, merawat to nurse, to take care of; **perawatan 1** treatment; **perawatan gigi** dental hygiene; **2** nursing care; **di perawatan intensif** in intensive care; **juru rawat, perawat** nurse.

rawit, cabai rawit a kind of very small, very hot chilli.

raya great, large; **Jakarta Raya** greater Jakarta; **Hari Raya/Hari Idul Fitri** main Islamic religious day; **jalan raya** main road; **kebun raya** botanical garden; **merayakan** to celebrate; **mereka merayakan Hari Idul Fitri** they're celebrating Idul Fitri; **perayaan** celebration.

rayap termite; **merayap** to creep, to crawl.

rayon area, district.

rayu emotional, sad; **merayu 1** to try to persuade; **2** to deceive, to flatter; **rayuan** flattery, persuasion.

razia 1 raid by police; **2** surprise checking of documents or licences by police.

reaksi reaction; **bereaksi, mereaksi** to react.

reaktor reactor.

rebah collapse, fall down; **merebahkan 1** to fall down; **2** to lie down, to rest; **merebahkan diri** to lie down; **rebahan** lying down; **dia sedang rebahan di sofa** she/he's lying down on the sofa.

rebung bamboo shoot.

rebus boiled; **kacang rebus** boiled peanuts; **merebus** to boil; **merebus telur** to boil an egg.

rebut, berebut 1 remove forcefully, snatch; **2** struggle to reach a goal; **merebut 1** to seize, to take forcefully; **tas Nina direbut orang di bis** Nina's bag was snatched on the bus; **2** to compete, to fight for; **rebutan 1** fight, struggle; **2** thing fought over; **perebutan** fight, struggle; **perebutan kekuasaan** a power struggle.

reda decrease, subside; **mereda** to calm down, to subside; **hujan sudah agak mereda** the rain has subsided a bit; **peredaan** calming down, slowing down.

redaksi editorial staff; **redaktris** female editor; **redaktur** male editor.

redam 1 dim, faint, vague; **2** hushed, muffled; **meredam** to hush a thing up.

reduksi 1 reduction; **2** discount.

redup overcast, dull.

refleksi reflection; **merefleksikan** reflect.

reformasi reformation; **mereformasi** to reform; **reformis** reformer.

regimentasi regimentation; **meregimentasikan** to regiment.

regional regional; **regionalisasi** regionalization.

registrasi registration.

regu 1 group team; **regu kita menang** our team won; **2** shift; **dua regu pekerja** two shifts of workers.

reguler regular; **meregulerkan** to regularize.

regulasi regulation.

rehabilitasi rehabilitation; **merehabilitasi** to rehabilitate.

a b c d e f g h i j k l m n o p q r s t u v w x y z

a b c d e f g h i j k l m n o p q r s t u v w x y z

rejeki livelihood, luck, subsistence.

reka 1 invention; **2** trick; **mereka-reka 1** to devise, to invent; **2** to plan, to schedule; **3** to imagine things; **rekaan 1** invention, plan; **2** invented story, fiction; **itu hanya rekaan!** that's just a fabrication!; **3** improvization.

rekam, merekam 1 to print, to stamp; **2** to embroider; **3** to record, to note down; **4** to record on tape or record; **saya akan merekam acara itu untuk Anda** I'll record the program for you; **rekaman 1** notes, recorded material; **2** recording of music, film, etc.; **perekam 1** recording instrument; **2** recording technician.

rekan colleague; **rekanan 1** partner; **2** partnership; **3** steady customer.

rekat, merekatkan to glue; **perekat** glue, adhesive.

rekayasa, merekayasa to engineer *(changes etc.)*; **di film *Forrest Gump* Forrest direkayasa bertemu dengan Presiden Kennedy** in the film *Forrest Gump* a meeting between Forrest and President Kennedy was engineered; **perekayasa** person who engineers something; **perekayasaan** engineering *(changes)*; **perekayasaan politik** political engineering.

rekening 1 bill; **2** bank account; **rekening tabungan** savings account; **membuka rekening bank** to open a bank account.

reklame advertisement.

rekomendasi recommendation; **merekomendasikan** to recommend.

rekonstruksi reconstruction *(of a crime, for example)*; **merekonstruksi** to reconstruct.

rekor record *(in sports etc.)*; **rekor dunia** world record; **hasil penjualan CD itu mencapai rekor** record sales for the CD.

rekreasi recreation.

rekrut, merekrut to recruit.

rel railway track.

rela willing; **dengan rela** willingly; **saya akan membantu Anda dengan rela** I'll willingly help you; **merelakan** to allow, to consent to;**Wayan merelakan kepergian anaknya** Wayan consented to the departure of his child; **relawan** volunteer.

elasi relation.

elevan relevant.

em brake; **rem angin** air brakes; **rem cakram** disk brakes; **mengerem** to put on the brakes.

remaja adolescent, teenager; **kaum remaja** the adolescents.

rembes, merembes 1 to leak, to ooze out; **2** to permeate; **rembesan** oozing liquid; **perembesan 1** oozing, leakage; **2** infiltration.

rembet, merembet 1 to creep, to climb up; **2** to hang down; **3** to spread; **perembetan** involvement.

remeh insignificant, trivial; **meremehkan** to belittle, to disparage.

rempah spices *(for commercial purposes)*; **rempah-rempah** various spices.

rempak, serempak all together, in unison.

remuk crushed, shattered; **meremukkan** to crush, to pound to pieces.

renang, berenang swim, **baju renang** swimsuit; **kolam renang** swimming pool; **(pergi) berenang** to go for a swim; **perenang** swimmer.

rencana plan, schedule; **perubahan rencana** a change of plan; **berencana** with a plan; planned; **keluarga berencana** a planned family; **merencanakan** to plan, to project; **para menteri merencanakan strategi pemerintah** the ministers planned the government's strategy; **perencana** planner, planning authority; **perencanaan 1** planning; **perencanaan keluarga** family planning; **2** design; **perencanaan gedung sekolah** school building design.

renda lace.

rendah low; **lebih rendah** lower; **Majelis Rendah** Lower House; **umur yang paling rendah** the minimum age; **merendah 1** to descend; **2** to be modest; **kerendahan 1** too short; **2** lowness; **rendahan** lower; **pegawai rendahan** subordinate.

rendam, berendam 1 submerged; **2** soak; **merendam** to soak; **merendam pakaian** to soak the clothes.

rendang meat cooked in coconut milk and spices.

rengat cracked

renggang 1 wide apart; **2** *(a knot)* loose; **merenggangkan 1** to place wide apart, to space out; **2** to loosen *(a*

a b c d e f g h i j k l m n o p q r s t u v w x y z

knot); **kerenggangan** aloofness, distance.

renggut, merenggut 1 to pull, to tug at; **2** to get with a great effort; **renggutan** a jerk, a tug.

rengut sullen and gloomy; **merengut** to be sullen.

rentak, serentak 1 all at once, simultaneously; **2** all together as a group.

renung, merenung to daydream, to muse; **merenungkan** to meditate on, to reflect on; **renungan** meditation, reflection.

reorganisasi reorganization; **mereorganisasi(kan)** to reorganize; **pereorganisasian** process of reorganizing.

reparasi repairs; **mereparasi** to repair.

repatriasi repatriation.

Repelita (Rencana Pembangunan Lima Tahun) Five-year Development Plan.

repot busy, occupied; **jangan repot-repot** don't go to any trouble; **merepotkan** to cause difficulties, to create a fuss.

representatif representative.

reproduksi reproduction.

republik republic; **Republik Rakyat Tiongkok** People's Republic of China.

reputasi name, reputation.

reruntuh(an) debris, ruins, wreckage; **reruntuhan pesawat terbang** plane wreckage.

resah fidgety, restless; **meresahkan** to make nervous; **desas-desus yang meresahkan** disturbing rumours; **keresahan** restlessness, unrest.

resap, meresap 1 to infiltrate, to penetrate; **2** to ooze out; **3** to be absorbed; **resapan** absorption; **peresapan 1** absorption; **2** infiltration.

resensi book review; **meresensi buku** to review a book.

resep 1 recipe; **2** prescription.

resepsi reception.

resepsionis receptionist.

reserse detective, police investigator.

reses recess of parliament.

resesi recession.

resi 1 receipt; **2** baggage check.

residen head of a residency, resident *(in colonial administration).*

resmi **1** legitimate, official; **2** formal; **meresmikan** **1** to make official; **2** to announce officially open *(something new like a new bridge etc.)*.

resolusi resolution.

resort police, army administrative unit.

restoran restaurant.

restu blessing.

retak **1** crack; **2** cracked; **meretakkan** to crack; **retakan** crack.

retribusi **1** toll or fee to use a public facility; **retribusi pelabuhan** harbour tax; **2** dues.

revisi revision; **merevisi** to revise.

revolusi revolution; **revolusioner** revolutionary; **merevolusikan** to revolutionize.

rewel **1** fussy, hard to please; **dia betul-betul rewel** he's being really unreasonable; **2** troublesome; **kerewelan** fussiness.

rezeki **1** livelihood; **mencari rezeki** to make a living; **2** luck, fortune; **mendapat rezeki** to be in luck by getting someting; **3** blessing of God.

rezim regime.

ria cheerful.

riak **1** ripples; **riak udara** air wave; **2** indication, intention.

rial Saudi Arabian money.

riang **1** cheerful, joyful; **2** dizzy; **meriang** **1** to feel dizzy and feverish; **2** to excite; **keriangan** cheerfulness; **periang** a cheerful person.

rias make-up; **rias wajah** to make up; **berias** made up; **riasan** ornament; **perias** make-up person; **perias rambut** hairdresser.

ribu thousand; **seribu** a thousand; **lima ribu** five thousand; **ribuan** thousands of; **ada ribuan wisatawan di Bali** there were thousands of tourists in Bali.

ribut loud, noisy; **angin ribut** storm; **ribut tentang rekeningnya** to create a fuss over the bill; **tukang ribut** troublemaker.

rimba jungle, forest.

rimbun thick, dense; **pohon yang rimbun** dense vegetation.

rinci detail; **merinci** **1** to plan, to schedule; **2** to break down into separate parts; **rincian** breakdown, details; **perincian** **1** details, the way something is divided up; **2** subsection.

a b c d e f g h i j k l m n o p q r s t u v w x y z

rindang 1 leafy, luxuriant; 2 shady.

rindu 1 longing, yearning; 2 feel homesick for, yearn for; **merindukan** to miss, to yearn for; **saya merindukan Anda** I miss you; **dia merindukan anak perempuannya** she's missing her daughter; **kerinduan** longing, yearning.

ringan 1 light in weight; 2 minor in importance; **minuman ringan** a soft drink; **makanan ringan** snacks; **meringankan** 1 to alleviate, to lighten; 2 to make light of; **keringanan** 1 lightness; 2 relief.

ringgit national currency of Malaysia and Brunei.

ringkas brief, concise; **ringkasnya** in brief, **meringkaskan** to make brief, to shorten, to summarize; **keringkasan** succinctness; **ringkasan** précis, résumé, summary.

ringsek broken in pieces, total write-off.

rintang, merintangi 1 to block a person's way; 2 to hamper, to interfere with; **rintangan** 1 hindrance, obstacle; **ada rintangan kecil** there's been a slight hitch; 2 barrier, restriction.

rintih groan, moan; **merintih** to groan, to whimper; **rintihan** groaning, moaning.

rintik 1 spot; 2 droplet; **rintik-rintik** small spots; **hujan rintik-rintik** it's drizzling.

rintis, merintis 1 to clear a way; 2 to do pioneering work; **rintisan** 1 pioneering effort; 2 path; **perintis** pioneer; **perintisan** pioneering.

risau nervous, restless; **merisaukan** 1 to worry about; 2 to cause worry; **kerisauan** restlessness, worry.

riset research; **melakukan riset** to do research on; **periset** researcher.

risi(h) feel uncomfortable about something taboo; **film itu membuat saya risih** that film made me uncomfortable.

risiko peril, risk; **berisiko** risky.

riuh noisy; **anjing-anjing itu riuh sekali** those dogs make a dreadful din; **keriuhan** din, clamour.

riwayat 1 narrative, story, tale; **riwayat hidup** biography, curriculum vitae; **riwayat singkat** brief account; 2 history.

robek torn; **merobek** to tear; **robekan** something torn.

roboh collapse; **jembatan itu roboh waktu banjir** the bridge collapsed during the floods; **merobohkan 1** to cause to come down, to demolish; **tentara merobohkan jembatan yang satu itu** the army demolished that bridge; **2** to bring down, to overthrow; **konspirator itu tak berhasil dalam usahanya untuk merobohkan pemerintah** the conspirators were unsuccessful in their attempt to overthrow the government; **3** *(sport)* to floor someone.

roda wheel; **beroda** wheeled; **kendaraan beroda dua dilarang di jalan tol** two-wheeled vehicles are forbidden on the toll road.

rodi forced labour; **kerja rodi** to do forced labour.

roh soul, spirit.

rohani spiritual; **kerohanian** spirituality.

rok skirt; **rok sepan** a tight skirt; **rok mini** a mini-skirt.

roket rocket.

rokok cigarette; **rokok kretek** clove-flavoured cigarettes; **merokok** to smoke; **'dilarang merokok'** 'no smoking'; **perokok** habitual smoker.

rolet roulette.

Roma Rome.

roman figure, looks; **beroman halus** having delicate features.

roman novel.

romantis romantic.

romantika romance.

rombak, merombak 1 to tear down; **2** to remodel, to reorganize; **rombakan** result of reorganization; **perombak 1** someone who tears things down; **2** reorganizer; **perombakan 1** reorganizing, making extreme changes.

rombeng tattered, torn; **merombeng** to buy and sell secondhand goods; **rombengan** junk; **barang rombengan** odds and ends.

rombong, berombongan come in large groups; **rombongan 1** entourage, group, party; **rombongan haji** a group going to Mecca; **2** gang.

rompak, merompak to commit piracy.

rompi vest, waistcoat.

ronda 1 beat, patrol, rounds; **2** guard, watch person; **3** to patrol; **meronda** to make the rounds; **ronda malam** night watch; **peronda** patrol, watch person.

ronde a round *(sport)*.

a b c d e f g h i j k l m n o p q r s t u v w x y z

a b c d e f g h i j k l m n o p q r s t u v w x y z

rongga hollow space, hole; **berongga** hollow.

rongrong, merongrong **1** to gnaw at, to nag; **2** to undermine.

ronsen X-ray.

ronta, meronta to struggle to get free; **meronta-ronta** to keep struggling; **tahanan-tahanan itu meronta-ronta dari ikatan** the captives struggled to get free of their bonds.

rontok drop off, fall out, shed; **musim rontok** autumn; **rambutnya rontok semuanya** all her hair fell out; **merontokkan** to cause to fall off or out; **rontokan** thing fallen off.

ros rose.

rosot, merosot to decline, to sink; **harga saham merosot** share prices fell; **merosotkan** to decrease; **krismon merosotkan nilai rupiah** the monetary crises reduced the value of the rupiah.

rotan rattan.

roti **1** bread; **2** bun.

royal extravagant.

ruam rash.

ruang **1** space; **ruang angkasa** outer space; **2** *(in a newspaper)* column; **3** hall, room; **ruang makan** dining room; **ruang keluarga** family room; **ruang tamu** sitting room; **ruang tunggu** waiting room; **ruang kelas** classroom; **ruangan** **1** space; **2** chamber, room.

ruas **1** space between joints; **2** *(mathematics)* parts of an equation.

rubah fox.

rugi **1** suffer loss financially; **2** lose out; **merugi** to suffer losses; **merugikan** **1** to cause a financial loss; **krismon pada tahun 1997 merugikan banyak perusahaan** the 1997 financial crisis inflicted loss on many companies; **2** to damage, to harm; **mereka tidak merugikannya** they did not harm him; **kerugian** financial loss.

rujak a kind of fruit salad with a spicy dressing.

rukun harmonious; **rukun tani** local farmer's cooperative; **rukun tetangga** neighbourhood association; **kerukunan** harmony.

rumah dwelling, house; **pekerjaan rumah** homework; **pekerjaan rumah tangga** housework; **rumah sakit** hospital; **rumah sakit bersalin** maternity hospital; **rumah makan** restaurant;

berumah tangga have a family, to start a family; **perumahan** housing; **perumahan orang kaya** a housing complex for the rich.

Rumawi, Romawi Roman; **angka Rumawi** Roman numerals.

rumit 1 difficult, hard; **2** complex, intricate; **kerumitan 1** complexity, difficulty; **2** complication.

rumpun cluster of plants; **rumpun bambu** a stand of bamboo.

rumput 1 grass; **memotong rumput** to cut the grass; **mesin potong rumput** mower; **2** weeds; **rumput air** swamp grass; **rumputan, rerumputan** weeds.

rumus formula *(chemistry, mathematics).*

runcing pointed; **bambu runcing** bamboo spikes; **memperuncing** to aggravate; **perkembangan ini telah memperuncing keadaan** this development has aggravated the situation; **meruncingkan** to sharpen *(a point).*

runding, berunding confer, deliberate, discuss; **menteri-menteri sedang berunding** the government ministers are conferring; **merundingkan** to discuss; **besok kita akan merundingkan masalah itu** we'll discuss the problem tomorrow; **saya akan merundingkan itu dengan Richard** I'm going to discuss it with Richard; **perunding** negotiator; **perundingan** negotiation.

runtuh 1 collapse; **tanah runtuh** landslide; **2** fall; **meruntuhkan 1** to cause to collapse; **2** to bring down, to overthrow; **keruntuhan** collapse, fall; **runtuhan, reruntuhan** debris, rubble.

runut trace; **merunut(i)** to follow, to investigate, to trail.

rupa 1 appearance, form, shape; **2** kind, sort; **rupanya** apparently, it seems; **rupanya dia sudah pulang** it seems she's already gone home; **rupa-rupa** all sorts, various; **rupa-rupanya** probably, seemingly; **rupa-rupanya dia melarikan uang temannya** apparently he's absconded with his friend's money; **serupa 1** of a kind, similar; **kedua burung itu serupa** the two birds are the same kind; **2** be similar to; **menyerupai** to resemble; **lukisan ini menyerupai lukisan Picasso** this painting resembles a Picasso; **berupa 1** have the shape of, shaped; **2** in the form of; **3** handsome, pretty; **rupawan** good-looking person.

rupiah Indonesian monetary unit; **merupiahkan** to convert to rupiah.

rusa deer.

rusak 1 broken, damaged, out of order; **jam ini rusak** this clock is broken; **mobil saya rusak** my car broke down; **2** depraved; **merusak, merusakkan** to damage, to destroy, to ruin; **dia merusak semua mainan adiknya** she's broken all her little sister's toys; **Anda akan merusak sepeda itu** you'll ruin that bicycle; **kerusakan** damage, flaw; **kerusuhan itu mengakibatkan kerusakan besar di Jakarta** the riots caused a lot of damage in Jakarta; **perusak, pengrusak 1** disturber; **2** destroyer, vandal; **perusakan, pengrusakan** act of damaging.

Rusia Russia.

rusuh disturbed, restless; **merusuhkan** to create a disturbance; **kerusuhan 1** commotion, riot; **2** turbulence, turmoil; **perusuh** rioter; **beberapa perusuh ditembak mati** several rioters were shot dead; **perusuhan** disturbance, riot.

rusuk flank, margin, side; **tulang rusuk** rib.

rutan (rumah tahanan) detention centre.

rute route.

rutin routine; **menjadi rutin** to become ordinary or routine

ruwet complex, complicated **keruwetan** complexity, complication.

RW (Rukun Warga) administrative unit of residents in a city.

S s

saat 1 moment; **pada saat ini** at the/this moment; **2** instant, point; **pada saat itu polisi tiba** at that point the police arrived; **hanya beberapa saat sebelum jam dua belas** just before midday; **sesaat** a moment, one moment.

saban each, every; **saban hari** every day.

sabar calm, patient; **sabarlah!** be patient!; **bersabar** be calm, be patient; **kesabaran** **1** patience; **2** tolerance; **ketidaksabaran** impatience; **penyabar** someone with a patient nature.

sabit sickle; **bulan sabit** crescent moon; **menyabit** to cut grass, rice, etc. with a sickle.

sabot, sabotase sabotage; **menyabot** to sabotage.

Sabtu Saturday; **sampai jumpa hari Sabtu** see you on Saturday; **tiap Sabtu** on Saturdays, every Saturday; **Sabtu lalu** last Saturday; **Sabtu depan** next Saturday.

sabun soap; **sebatang sabun** a bar of soap; **sabun bubuk** soap powder; **sabun cair** liquid soap; **sabun cuci** laundry soap; **sabun mandi** bath soap; **tempat sabun** soap dish.

sadar **1** aware; **2** conscious; **Mytha masih belum sadar** Mytha's still unconscious; **menyadari** to become aware of; **para guru harus menyadari tanggung jawabnya** teachers must be aware of their responsibilities; **menyadarkan** to make someone realize; **tersadar** **1** come to realize; **2** come to, regain consciousness; **kesadaran** **1** awareness, consciousness; **2** realization; **3** come to the realization.

sadis sadist, sadistic; **kesadisan** sadism.

sadur coating of metal; **menyadur** **1** *(metal)* to plate; **2** to adapt; **menyadur cerita** to adapt a story; **saduran** **1** metal coating; **2** adaptation; **penyadur** **1** someone who does metal-plating; **2** adaptor; **penyaduran** **1** act of plating; **2** the adapting of something.

sagu sago *(both the palm and the food)*.

sah legal, valid; **tidak sah** invalid; **mengesahkan** **1** to approve, to confirm, to legalize, to ratify; **2** to authorize; **pengesahan** **1** authorization, confirmation; **2** legalization, ratification.

sahabat friend, mate; **sahabat karib** close friend; **bersahabat** **1** be friends or mates; **2** friendly; **persahabatan** friendship.

sahaja natural, simple; **bersahaja** simple, uncomplicated; **kesahajaan**, **kebersahajaan** simpleness, simplicity.

saham share, stock; **pemegang saham** shareholder.

a b c d e f g h i j k l m n o p q r s t u v w x y z

sahut answer *(orally)*; **bersahut-(sahut)an, sahut-menyahut** to answer back and forth; **menyahut** to answer a call, to reply to; **sahutan** reply.

saing, bersaing compete; **mampu bersaing** competitive; **sayang mereka selalu harus bersaing** it's a pity they always have to compete with each other; **dua puluh orang bersaing untuk mendapat pekerjaan itu** twenty people competed for that job; **menyaingi** to compete with; **tersaingi** get competition from, can be competed with; **saingan** competitor, rival; **persaingan** competition, rivalry; **persaingan sengit** fierce competition.

sains science.

saja 1 only, just, nothing else than; **dia saja** only he, she (him, her); **biasa saja** just as usual; **2** exactly; **apa saja yang harus saya beli?** exactly what should I buy?; **3** emphasizing word; **kalau mau minum bir ambil saja** if you want some beer just help yourself; **apa saja dapat terjadi** anything could happen; **mereka baru saja tiba** they have just arrived; **kalau saja** if only; **kalau saja dia tidak mabuk!** if only he hadn't been drunk!

sajak 1 lyrics, poem, verse; **menulis sajak** to write poetry; **2** rhyme; **bersajak 1** rhyme; **2** be in rhyming form; **3** write poetry; **4** recite poetry; **menyajakkan** to make a poem of, to put into rhyme; **penyajak** poet; **persajakan 1** poetry; **2** rhyme.

saji, sajian dishes served on the table or offered to guests; **menyajikan 1** to dish up, to serve; **dapatkah Anda menyajikan sopnya?** can you serve the soup, please?; **2** to present, to provide, to supply; **penyajian** presentation.

saka, pusaka 1 heritage; **Sang Saka Merah Putih** the Indonesian flag; **2** heirloom.

sakit 1 ill, sick, sickness; **jatuh sakit** to fall ill; **sakit hati** offended; **dia sakit keras** she is seriously ill; **sakit maag** to have indigestion; **rumah sakit** hospital; **2** painful, sore; **punggung saya sakit** my back hurts; **sakit kepala** to have a headache; **sakit tenggorokan** to have a sore throat; **sakit-sakit(an)** ail, be in poor health, be sickly; **menyakiti,** to hurt, to offend;

Fiona suka menyakiti hati orang Fiona often hurts people's feelings; **menyakitkan** to be painful, to hurt; **kesakitan** in pain; **penyakit** disease, illness; **penyakit parah** a serious illness; **penyakit menular** an infectious disease; **kuman penyakit** germs; **berpenyakit** suffer from a disease.

saksi witness; **saksi mata** eyewitness; **bersaksi** testify; **menyaksikan 1** to witness; **2** to watch an event; **3** to testify; **kesaksian** testimony, evidence; **penyaksian** giving evidence.

sakti 1 divine power, supernatural; **2** having magic or divine power; **3** sacred; **kesaktian** supernatural powers.

saku 1 bag, sack; **2** pocket.

salah[1] 1 fault; **siapa yang salah?** who is at fault?; **salah siapa?** who's fault (was it)? **2** mistake; **ejaan yang salah** a spelling mistake; **3** wrong; **jawaban yang salah** the wrong answer; **salah sambung** you've got the wrong number *(on the phone)*; **4** be in the wrong, be mistaken; **saya salah** I was wrong; **salah duga, salah kira** miscalculate, misjudge; **salah mengerti** misunderstand; **menyalahgunakan** to misuse; **penyalahgunaan** abuse, misuse; **penyalahgunaan alkohol** alcohol abuse; **salah kaprah** *(Java)*, **kesalahkaprahan** commonly committed error in word use; **salah-salah** if something turns out wrong; **bersalah** be guilty; **saya yang bersalah** I was the one who was wrong; **menyalahi 1** to conflict with; **2** to violate; **3** to do wrong to; **menyalahkan** to accuse, to blame; **menyalahkan orang** to blame someone for something; **dia yang harus disalahkan** she's to blame for it; **mereka tidak dapat disalahkan** you can't blame them; **mempersalahkan** to blame, to hold responsible; **kesalahan 1** error, mistake; **kesalahan yang sembrono** a careless mistake; **2** fault; **itu kesalahan Susan** it's Susan's fault; **3** guilt.

salah[2], salah satu one, either of the, one of several; **silahkan ambil salah satu** take one (of them); **salah seorang** one of the people.

salak[1], (buah) salak snakefruit, a kind of fruit with skin that looks like snakeskin.

a b c d e f g h i j k l m n o p q r s t u v w x y z

salak² high-pitched bark; **menyalak** to bark; **menyalaki** to bark at.

salam¹ **1** *(in greeting)* peace; **2** greetings; **salam kepada keluarga Anda** say hello to your family; **salam pembuka** salutation; **bersalaman** greet one another; **bersalam-(salam)an** shake hands in greeting; **menyalami** **1** to greet officially; **2** to shake the hand of.

salam², daun salam leaf like bayleaf *(for cooking)*.

saldo balance *(finance)*.

saleh pious, virtuous; **Hamid adalah seorang yang amat saleh** Hamid is very pious; **kesalehan** piety.

salep ointment, salve.

salib Christian cross; **menyalibkan** to crucify; **penyaliban** crucifixion.

salin, bersalin **1** change clothes; **2** bear a child, give birth; **rumah sakit bersalin** maternity hospital; **menyalin** **1** to change; **2** to copy; **saya menyalin semua perinciannya** I copied down all the details; **3** to translate; **salinan** copy.

saling one another, mutual(ly); **mereka saling mencintai** they love each other; **dua pesawat itu saling bertabrakan** the two planes crashed into each other; **saling pengertian** mutual understanding.

salju snow; **bersalju** snow-covered.

salon drawing room; **salon kecantikan** beauty parlour.

salur, saluran **1** channel, duct, gutter; **mengganti saluran** to change channels; **saluran air** canal, drain; **2** *(telephone)* line; **menyalurkan** **1** to channel; **2** *(goods)* to distribute; **menyalurkan bahan baku ke pabrik** to provide raw materials to a factory; **tersalur(kan)** channelled, having an outlet; **penyalur** **1** distributor; **2** conductor; **penyaluran** **1** distribution; **2** channelling.

salut salute.

sama¹ equal, same; **mobilnya sama dengan mobil kita** their car's the same as ours; **sama-sama** same to you; **sama rata** equal, having the same treatment; **sama sekali** absolutely; **saya tidak percaya itu sama sekali** I absolutely don't believe that; **dia sama sekali tidak menjawab** she didn't even bother to reply; **bersamaan** with, together; **menyamai** to equal, to match;

menyamakan, mempersamakan 1 to compare (with); **2** to treat the same as; **3** to place on a par; **kesamaan** sameness, similarity; **persamaan 1** similarity; **tak ada persamaan antara kami berdua** we have nothing in common; **2** comparison; **3** equality; **persamaan hak bagi pria dan wanita** sexual equality.

sama[2] 1 *(colloquial)* together with; **ayo, pergi sama saya saja!** come on, just come (or go) with me!; **satu sama lain** each other; **kami mengenal satu sama lain** we know each other; **2** and; **3** also do, do together; **bersama 1** together with; **2** herewith; **3** collective, joint; **(ber)sama-sama** do together; **saya pergi ke Daimaru bersama-sama Wati** I went to Daimaru together with Wati; **bersamaan** do simultaneously.

samadi, bersamadi to meditate.

samar 1 dim, hidden, vague; **2** disguised, masked; **samar-samar** dimly, vaguely; **menyamar 1** to be in disguise; **2** to be incognito; **menyamarkan** to camouflage, to conceal, to hide; **samaran** disguise; **nama samaran** pseudonym; **penyamaran** camouflage, disguise.

sambal chilli paste; **menyambal** to prepare sambal.

sambar, menyambar 1 to seize from the air; **2** to attack, to strike; **3** to steal; **tersambar 1** to be seized; **2** to be struck; **tersambar kilat** to be struck by lightning; **sambaran** strike, stroke.

sambil at the same time, while; **dia mendengarkan musik sambil belajar** he listened to music while studying; **sambil lalu** in passing; **sambilan 1** sideline; **2** part-time.

sambung 1 continue, go on; **2** be connected; **salah sambung!** wrong number!; **bersambung 1** be connected; **2** continued; **bersambungan** connected; **menyambung** to continue, to connect to; **sambungan 1** continuation, extension; **2** connection; **sambungan yang salah** a faulty connection; **kawat sambungan** extension lead; **penyambung 1** connector, link; **2** someone who connects; **penyambungan** connecting, connection.

sambut, menyambut **1** to receive, to welcome; **2** to accept; **sambutan** reception, welcome; **mendapat sambutan yang hangat** to receive a warm welcome; **penyambut** someone who welcomes; **penyambutan** reception, welcoming.

sampah garbage, rubbish; **tukang sampah** garbage collector; **tempat sampah, keranjang sampah** rubbish bin.

sampai **1** as far as, to, till, until; **sampai hari Senin** until Monday; **sampai jumpa hari Sabtu!** see you on Saturday!; **2** arrive; **mereka sudah sampai** they've arrived; **3** go as far as, get to the point of; **sampai anjingnya pun dibunuh** even his dog was killed; **sesampainya** upon arriving; **menyampaikan 1** to convey, to extend; **menyampaikan kabar** to break the news; **2** to deliver, to hand over; **Esther menyampaikan hadiah itu kepada saya** Esther delivered the gift to me; **kesampaian** accomplished, achieved; **keinginannya tidak kesampaian** his desire is not achieved.

sampan dugout, sampan, small boat; **sampan karet** a rubber dinghy; **bersampan** ride in a small boat.

samping side; **di samping** beside, next to; **di samping bank** next to the bank; **duduklah di samping saya!** sit next to me!; **ke samping** to the side; **menyampingkan, mengesampingkan 1** to put aside; **2** to bypass, to ignore; **terkesampingkan** ignored, shunted aside; **sampingan** side-, secondary.

sampul cover, wrapper; **sampul surat** envelope; **bersampul** covered, in an envelope, wrapped; **menyampul(i)** to place in an envelope, to put a cover on, wrap; **tersampul** wrapped.

samudra ocean; **Samudra Pasifik** Pacific Ocean.

sana there, yonder; **di sana** over there; **sebelah sana** the other side; **seberang sana** the opposite side; **sana sini** everywhere, here and there.

sanak relation, relative; **hanya ada sanak-saudara dan teman-teman akrab** there were just relations and close friends.

sandal sandal, open-toe slipper; **sandal jepit, sandal Jepang** flip-flops, thongs; **bersandal** wear sandals.

sandang clothing; **sandang pangan** basic necessities, food and clothing.

sandar, bersandar 1 lean on; **bersandar pada dinding** to lean on the wall; **bersandar ke depan** to lean forward; **2** be based on, be dependent on; **bersandaran** lean on; **bersandarkan** be based on; **sandar menyandar 1** to lean on each other; **2** to depend on one another; **menyandar** to buttress, to lean against; **dia berdiri menyandar ke tembok** he stood leaning against the wall; **menyandarkan 1** to base something on; **dia menyandarkan nasibnya pada saya** he relies on me for everything; **2** to prop, to lean; **kami menyandarkan tangga itu pada tembok** we leaned the ladder against the wall; **sandaran 1** assistance, support; **2** abutment, prop; **sandaran buku** bookend; **3** basis.

sandera hostage; **menyandera** to take hostage; **penyanderaan** taking of hostages.

sandiwara 1 drama, play; **2** theatrical troupe; **bersandiwara 1** be on the stage; **2** play-act, pretend; **3** dramatize.

sandung, tersandung, kesandung stumble; **kakinya tersandung tas saya** he stumbled against my bag; **batu sandungan** stumbling block.

sang title or article *(also used in a sarcastic way)*; **Sang Merah Putih** the red-and-white flag of Indonesia; **Sang Surya 1** the sun; **2** the Sun God.

sangat extremely, very; **benar? itu sangat bagus!** really? that's fantastic!

sangga prop, support; **menyangga** to prop up, to support; **penyangga** buffer, support.

sanggah, menyanggah to contradict, to protest, to rebut; **sanggahan** protest, rebuttal; **penyanggah 1** opponent; **2** discussant; **3** protester; **penyanggahan** act of opposing.

sanggul hair bun, twist of hair; **bersanggul** wear your hair in a bun; **menyanggul(kan)** to put hair up in a twist; **sanggulan** hair worn in a bun.

sanggup able, capable; **polisi tak sanggup menguasai orang banyak itu** the police have lost control of the crowd; **kesanggupan** capability, power.

a b c d e f g h i j k l m n o p q r s t u v w x y z

a b c d e f g h i j k l m n o p q r s t u v w x y z

sangka **1** idea, supposition; **salah sangka** misinterpretation; **2** suspicion; **menyangka** **1** to consider, to suppose, to think; **tersangka** **1** suspected; **yang tersangka, si tersangka** the suspect; **2** expected; **sangkaan** idea, supposition; **persangkaan** **1** suspicion; **2** estimate, expectation, presupposition.

sangkal, menyangkal **1** to deny; **pemerintah sendiri menyangkal desas-desus itu** the government itself denies the rumours; **2** to reject; **sangkalan** denial; **penyangkal** person who denies; **penyangkalan** denial, refusal.

sangkar[1] bird cage, chicken coop; **sangkar burung** bird cage, chicken coop.

sangkar[2] diagonal; **bujur sangkar** rectangle.

sangkut, bersangkut closely joined, connected; **sangkut-paut** connection, relation; **menyangkutpautkan** to involve, to relate to; **tersangkut paut** be involved; **bersangkut(an)** be concerned with, be involved with, relevant; **kepada yang bersangkutan** to whom it may concern; **menyangkut** to concern, to involve, to relate to; **menyangkutkan** **1** to hang, to hook; **2** to involve someone in something; **tersangkut** **1** involved; **2** to get caught; **ketersangkutan** involvement; **kesangkut** **1** *(colloquial)* dragged into something, involved; **2** be attached to, caught on, stuck; **3** stumble over; **sangkutan** **1** connection, relation; **2** involvement; **3** hook, peg; **mengangkat telepon dari sangkutannya** to take the phone off the hook; **4** obstacle; **persangkutan** **1** connection, relation; **2** involvement.

sangsi doubt, doubtful; **tak ada sangsi lagi** there's no doubt about it; **sangsi akan** be in doubt about; **menyangsikan** to be doubtful about, to question; **saya menyangsikan hal itu** I doubt it; **kesangsian** doubt, skepticism; **penyangsian** doubting.

santai relax, relaxed; **bersantai** relax; **duduk bersantai** to sit relaxed; **bersantai-santai** enjoy your leisure, to relax; **saya akan bersantai-santai menonton televisi malam ini** I'm going to relax and watch telly tonight; **menyantaikan** to cause to relax; **kesantaian** state or quality of being relaxed.

santa *(female)* saint.

santan coconut cream.

santap, bersantap dine, have a meal; **santap malam** have dinner; **menyantap** to eat, to partake of; **santapan** food, meal; **santapan dari Lombok** Lombok cuisine.

santri 1 student at traditional Muslim school; **2** strict follower of Islam.

santun good manners; **dia tidak tahu sopan santun** he/she is bad-mannered; **santunan 1** help, sympathetic care; **2** insurance compensation.

sanubari inner self.

sapa, bersapa-sapaan, saling menyapa, sapa menyapa to greet each other; **tegur-sapa** greetings; **menyapa** to address, to speak to in greeting.

sapi bull, cow, ox.

sapu broom; **sapu lidi** broom of coconut mid-ribs; **sapu tangan** handkerchief; **menyapu** to sweep; **menyapu bersih** to sweep clean, to wipe out; **tersapu** to be swept away; **sapuan** wiper, something to wipe with; **penyapu 1** wiper; **2** sweeper; **penyapuan** cleaning up, reform.

saran suggestion; **menyarankan** to make a suggestion, to propose, to suggest.

sarang 1 lair, nest, web; **sarang madu** honeycomb; **2** hideout; **3** breeding place, hotbed; **bersarang** nest, make a nest.

sarap, sarapan 1 breakfast; **saya mau menyediakan sarapan** I'll get breakfast ready; **2** have breakfast.

sarat full, loaded; **kesaratan 1** overloaded, too full; **2** density.

sarden, sardencis tinned sardines.

sari 1 concentrate, essence; **tolong kasih dua gelas sari buah papaya** two pawpaw juices please; **2** main point, nucleus; **3** pollen.

sariawan mouth ulcer, sprue.

saring, menyaring 1 to filter, to sift, to strain; **2** to distil, to refine; **3** to separate, to sift, to sort; **4** *(people)* to screen; **saringan, penyaring** filter, sieve, strainer; **penyaringan 1** sifting; **2** filtering; **3** screening, selection.

sarjana 1 degree-holder, scholar; **2** title of degree

similar to a bachelor degree; **kesarjanaan** scholarly, scholarship.

sarong, sarung 1 sarong; **2** sheath; **sarung bantal** pillowcase; **bersarung 1** wear a sarong; **2** sheathed; **menyarungi 1** to encase; **2** to put something on; **3** to sheathe; **menyarungkan** to use as a sheath.

sastera, sastra books, literature; **kesusastraan** things relating to literature.

satai, sate satay, skewered meat.

satu one; **satu anak laki-laki** one boy, one son; **saya punya satu kalau Anda mau pena** if you want a pen I've got one; **pada pukul satu** at one o'clock; **kami mengenal satu sama lain** we know each other; **tidak satu pun** not a single one; **satu jalan** one way, having the same orientation; **jalan satu arah** one-way street; **satu-satu** one by one; **satu-satunya** only; **satu-satunya tempat duduk yang kosong** the only free seat; **bersatu** united; **menyatu** to become one, be one; **mempersatukan, menyatukan 1** to unite; **kesatu** *(colloquial)* the first; **kesatuan 1** *(military)* unit; **2** totality; **3** oneness, unity; **negara kesatuan** unitary state; **satuan** unit; **pemersatu** integrationist, unifier; **pemersatuan, penyatuan** unification; **persatuan 1** association, club, union; **2** unity.

satwa, margasatwa fauna, wild animals.

saudagar merchant.

saudara 1 brother, sister, relative; **2** formal term of address for people of equivalent status; **bersaudara 1** be siblings; **2** be related; **persaudaraan 1** relationship; **2** friendship; **3** brotherhood, fraternity.

sauh anchor; **membuang sauh** cast anchor; **membongkar sauh** weigh anchor.

saus 1 gravy, sauce; **2** mixture to give flavour.

sawah paddy, rice field; **mengairi sawah** to flood the rice fields.

sawo 1 sapodilla fruit; **2** brown like the skin of sapodilla.

saya 1 I, me, my, mine; **saya orang Australia** I am Australian; **saya sakit** I am sick; **kakak adik saya** my siblings; **dia memukul saya** he hit me; **2** yes *(Javanese usage, deferential)*.

sayang **1** it's a pity; **2** be very fond of, love; **dia sayang akan adik perempuannya** she's devoted to her little sister; **kasih sayang** affectionate love; **3** darling, dear; **sayang(nya)** it is a pity; **alangkah sayangnya!** what a pity!; **bersayang-sayangan** love each other; **menyayangi** **1** to pity; **2** to be attached to, to love; **menyayangkan** to consider something to be a pity, to regret; **kesayangan** darling, favourite; **Lena adalah kesayangan guru** Lena is teacher's pet; **penyayang** **1** charitable, loving, merciful.

sayap **1** wing; **2** wing of a political party; **bersayap** winged.

sayembara competition, contest *(not sport or a fight)*; **sayembara menulis** a writing competition; **menyayembarakan** to have a competition.

sayur **1** vegetable; **sayur-mayur, sayur-sayuran** all kinds of vegetables; **sayur sop** soup vegetables; **2** a vegetable dish; **sop sayur** vegetable soup; **sayuran** vegetables.

se- **1** one; **seorang** one person; **2** same; **saya rasa kita sekelas** I think you're in the same class as me; **3** as ... as; **dia setinggi kakaknya** he's as tall as his older brother; **secepat mungkin** as soon as possible; **4** as soon as, when; **setiba Anda di negeri itu, harap menulis surat** on your arrival in that country, please write a letter; **5** all; **konperensi se-Australia** all-Australia conference; **sedunia** the whole world; **Organisasi Kesehatan Sedunia** World Health Organization.

sebab **1** because, due to; **penerbangan itu dibatalkan sebab cuaca buruk** the flight's been cancelled due to bad weather; **2** cause, reason; **apa sebabnya Anda terlambat?** how come you're late?; **tiada seorang pun yang tahu apa sebabnya dia melakukan itu** nobody knows why he did it; **menyebabkan** to cause, to give rise to; **menyebabkan masalah** to cause problems; **penyebab** cause; **penyebab kecelakaan itu** the cause of the accident.

sebar, menyebar(kan) to scatter, to spread; **ada virus baru yang menyebar melalui Internet** there's a new virus that spreads through the Internet; **menyebarkan pupuk** to spread fertilizer;

a b c d e f g h i j k l m n o p q r s t u v w x y z

menyebarkan berita to spread the news; **bersebaran** be spread all over, lie all over; **sebaran** something spread; **surat sebaran** leaflets; **penyebar** disseminator; **penyebaran** distributing, spreading.

sebelas 1 eleven; **Roy berumur sebelas tahun** Roy is eleven; **pada jam sebelas** at eleven o'clock; **kesebelasan** a soccer eleven; **kesebelas** all the eleven; **kesebelas orang itu** all the eleven people; **2** eleventh; **orang kesebelas** the eleventh person; **tanggal sebelas Maret** the eleventh of March.

sebentar 1 for, in a moment, minute; **tolong jaga bayinya sebentar** could you mind the baby for a moment?; **tunggu sebentar** just a minute; **2** later in the same day; **sebentar lagi dia akan datang bekerja di halaman** she'll be here to do the garden in a while; **sebentar-sebentar** every now and again.

seberang across, opposite; **rumah di seberang jalan** the house across the street; **biasanya dia duduk di seberang saya** she usually sits across from me; **tanah seberang** foreign *(from another island or overseas)*; **berseberangan** opposite each other; **seberang menyeberang** facing, opposite each other; **menyeberangi** to cross to the other side; **menyeberangi jalan** to cross the road; **menyeberangkan** to take across; **kapal tambang itu dapat menyeberangkan empat puluh mobil** the ferry can take forty cars across; **penyeberangan** crossing; **penyeberangan pejalan kaki** a pedestrian crossing.

sebut, menyebut(kan)
1 to mention; **sebutkan nama barang-barang ini** mention the names of these things; **2** to call, to name; **patung itu disebut Tugu Tani**; the statue is called the Farmer's Monument; **menyebut-nyebut** to keep mentioning, to mention again and again; **dia menyebut-nyebut nama Irwan** she kept mentioning Irwan's name; **tersebut** mentioned; **hal tersebut tidak dapat diumumkan** that matter cannot be made public; **sebutan**
1 expression, term;
2 quotation; **3** designation;
4 comment, predicate;
penyebut 1 person who calls

or mentions; **2** *(in mathematics)* denominator; **penyebutan** addressing, mentioning.

sedak, tersedak, kesedak choke, swallow the wrong way; **Rini tersedak ketika makan kacang goreng** Rini choked while eating peanuts.

sedan, mobil sedan sedan *(car)*; **sedan atap terbuka** convertible.

sedang[1] **1** average, medium; **mobil ukuran sedang** it's a medium-sized car; **2** sufficient.

sedang[2] **1** at the time that, while; **Fitnah suka menyanyi waktu mandi** Fitnah likes singing while bathing; **2** be in the process of; **dia sedang mengetik laporan itu** she's typing the report; **(nomor itu) sedang sibuk** the line's busy; **3** whereas, while; **tempat tidur itu mahal sedang yang ini murah** that bed is expensive while this one is cheap; **sedangkan 1** at the time that, while; **2** but, whereas; **mereka ribut sedangkan kita tidak** they're noisy but we're not.

sedap **1** delicious, nice, tasty; **2** refreshed; **penyedap** something used as flavouring.

sedekah **1** alms, giving of alms; **2** religious meal.

sederhana plain, simple; **masakan sederhana** plain cooking; **diatur dengan sederhana** arranged simply; **menyederhanakan** to simplify; **kesederhanaan** simplicity; **penyederhanaan** simplification.

sedia **1** ready; **2** willing; **sedianya** actually, as a matter of fact, in the beginning; **bersedia 1** be ready, be prepared; **2** willing; **menyediakan 1** to prepare; **David sedang sibuk menyediakan makanan malam** David's busy cooking dinner; **2** to set aside in preparation; **jangan lupa menyediakan waktu untuk makan dulu** don't forget to allow enough time to eat first; **3** to supply; **sekolah menyediakan kertas** the school supplies the paper; **tersedia** available, on hand; **ketersediaan** availability; **kesediaan** readiness, willingness; **penyediaan 1** act of preparing; **2** supplying; **persediaan** stock, supply; **mempunyai persediaan** to have in stock.

sediakala always, at first, former.

a b c d e f g h i j k l m n o p q r s t u v w x y z

a b c d e f g h i j k l m n o p q r s t u v w x y z

sedih distressed, sad; **dia merasa sedih kalau jauh dari pacarnya** he was miserable if his girlfriend wasn't with him; **bersedih hati** be sad; **menyedihkan** to sadden, distressing; **ujian itu menyedihkan saya** I felt really miserable after the exam; **kesedihan** sadness, sorrow.

sedikit 1 a bit, a little, some; **sedikit lagi** a little more; **kurang sedikit** a little less; **kami perlu waktu sedikit lagi** we need a little more time; **sedikit demi sedikit** little by little; **bawangnya tinggal sedikit** there aren't many onions left; **sedikit banyak** more or less; **2** few, little; **rumah yang berkolam renang sangat sedikit** very few houses have a swimming pool; **sedikit yang berpikir bahwa ...** few people think that ...; **kami mempunyai uang sedikit** we have a little money; **sedikit terlambat** it's a little late; **3** a bit, slightly; **sakit kepala sedikit** to have a mild headache; **sedikit-sedikit** little by little; **sedikitnya** at least.

sedot, menyedot to sip, to suck; **sedotan** a straw *(for drinking)*; **penyedot debu** vacuum cleaner.

sedu 1 a sob; **tersedu-sedan, tersedu-sedu** sob, sobbing; **2** a hiccup.

seduh, menyeduh to pour boiling water on.

segala 1 all, all of them; **2** entirely, wholly, **3** *(colloquial)* and all, unnecessarily; **segala-galanya** everything; **segala-galanya sudah siap** everything is ready.

segan be reluctant to do; **saya segan menunggu** I'm reluctant to wait; **segan-segan** be reluctant to; **jangan segan-segan menelepon saya** don't hesitate to call me; **segan menyegani** to have mutual respect; **menyegani** to respect, to be in awe of; **Pak Mursalin adalah orang yang disegani di kampungnya** Mr Mursalin is highly respescted in his village; **keseganan 1** aversion, reluctance; **2** respect.

segar 1 fresh; **2** refreshing; **3** fit; **menyegarkan, mempersegar** to refresh; **kesegaran 1** freshness; **2** fitness; **penyegar** freshener; **penyegar udara** air freshener.

segel 1 seal, stamp; **segel resmi** official seal; **2** ration coupon; **bersegel** sealed;

menyegel to seal, to stamp; **gedung itu telah disegel karena belum ada izin bangunan** the building has been closed because there is no building permit; **penyegelan** act of sealing.

segera immediately, quickly, straightaway; **saya segera menelepon mereka** I rang them immediately; **kami harus segera berangkat** we have to go right now; **segera sebelum** immediately before; **segera sesudah** immediately after; **sesegera mungkin** as soon as possible.

segi 1 side; **segi empat** four-sided figure *(in mathematics)*; **2** angle; **dari segi keamanan** from the security point of view; **3** sector; **bersegi** with sides; **persegi** square; **kotak persegi** a square box; **tiga meter persegi** three square metres.

sehat 1 healthy; **cara hidup yang sehat** a healthy lifestyle; **2** sound; **sehat-sehat** in good health; **Rizal sehat-sehat saja** Rizal is in good health now; **menyehatkan** to make healthy; **Ridwan suka makan makanan yang kurang sehat** Ridwan eats too much junk food; **mempersehat** to make healthier; **kesehatan** health.

sejahtera 1 prosperous; **2** safe; **kesejahteraan 1** prosperity; **2** safety.

sejak since; **hujan turun sejak kemarin** it's been raining since yesterday; **sejak saya lahir** from the time I was born.

sejarah history; **bersejarah** historic; **hari yang bersejarah** an historic day.

sejati genuine, real, true; **cinta sejati** true love; **teman sejati** a true friend; **kesejatian** authenticity.

sejuk chilly, cool; **hari ini hawanya agak sejuk** it's quite chilly today; **menyejukkan** to cool; **kesejukan** coolness; **penyejuk** cooler; **penyejuk udara** air conditioner.

seka, berseka rub yourself clean; **menyeka** to rub, to wipe; **menyekakan 1** to brush away *(for example, tears)*; **2** to use to wipe; **penyeka** something to rub or wipe with.

sekali 1 very; **panas sekali** very hot; **banyak sekali** very many, very much; **kasihan sekali** it's such a pity; **2** absolutely; **Anda benar sekali** you're absolutely right.

sekaligus all at once; **semua anak berteriak sekaligus** all the children screamed at once.

sekap, menyekap **1** to ripen fruit by keeping it warm; **2** to put in jail; **sekapan** **1** ripe fruit; **2** prisoner.

sekarang **1** now; **apakah mereka ada di rumah sekarang?** are they at home now?; **sekarang mereka sudah punya tiga anak** they've got three children now; **2** nowadays; **masa sekarang, zaman sekarang** these days.

sekoci **1** bobbin, shuttle; **2** lifeboat.

sekolah **1** school; **sekolah menengah pertama (SMP)** a junior high school; **sekolah menengah umum (SMU)** high school, secondary school, senior school; **2** attend school; **mengapa dia tidak ke sekolah?** why doesn't she go to school?; **bersekolah** go to school; **menyekolahkan** to send to school; **sekolahan** **1** schooling; **2** *(building)* school.

sekon second *(time)*.

sekop spade.

sekretariat secretariat; **Sekretariat Negara** State Secretariat.

sekretaris secretary.

seks sex; **pendidikan seks** sex education.

seksama accurate, conscientious, exact, thorough.

seksi[1] **1** dissection; **2** section; **3** platoon.

seksi[2] sexy.

seksual sexual; **pelecehan seksual** sexual harassment.

sektor sector.

sekutu ally; **bersekutu** allied; **persekutuan** **1** federation; **2** partnership; **membubarkan persekutuan** to dissolve a partnership; **3** alliance, league; **4** fellowship.

sel **1** *(prison)* cell, cubicle; **2** *(biology and technology)* cell; **3** political cell.

sela **1** crack, gap, opening; **2** interval; **3** interrupt; **4** cash crop; **menyela** to interrupt; **jangan suka menyela orang yang berbicara** don't interrupt people while they're talking; **bersela** with gaps or intervals; **sela menyela** alternate, intermittent; **penyelaan** interruption.

selada lettuce.

selai jam; **selai kacang** peanut butter.

selam, juru selam diver; **menyelam 1** to dive; **2** to be under water; **menyelami 1** to dive into; **2** to dive for; **3** to fathom, to penetrate; **tak terselami** unfathomable; **penyelam** diver; **penyelaman 1** diving; **2** immersion, submersion.

selamat 1 safe; **untung kami selamat** luckily we're safe; **2** congratulations, greeting, wish for good luck; **Selamat Datang di Bali!** welcome to Bali!; **selamat jalan!, selamat tinggal!** bye for now!; **saya mengucapkan selamat kepada Adrian atas hasil ujiannya** I congratulated Adrian on his results; **3** salvation; **Juru Selamat** Redeemer, Saviour; **selamatan** hold a ceremonial meal; **menyelamatkan** to rescue, to save; **keselamatan** safety; **standar keselamatan yang paling rendah** the minimum safety standards; **penyelamat** rescuer; **penyelamatan** redemption, rescuing.

Selandia Baru New Zealand.

selang break, interval; **berselang seling 1** alternating, alternately; **2** intermittent; **menyelang nyeling(kan)** to alternate, to vary; **menyelang nyelingi** to alternate with; **berselang 1** at intervals, at an equal distance from each other, intermittently; **berselang hari** on alternate days; **berselang empat hari** at four-day intervals; **2** ago; **empat hari berselang** four days ago; **berselang-selang 1** alternating; **2** intermittent.

selaput 1 film, membrane; **2** coating; **berselaput** covered with a membrane; **menyelaputi** to form a thin layer around.

Selasa, hari Selasa Tuesday.

selat 1 narrows, straits; **2** passage.

selatan south; **di selatan** in the south; **bagian selatan** the south side; **angin selatan** a south wind; **paling selatan** southernmost.

sele jam.

selederi celery.

seleksi selection; **menyeleksi** to select.

selendang narrow shawl or stole; **berselendang** wear such a shawl; **menyelendangkan** to carry on the shoulder.

selenggara, menyelenggarakan 1 to operate, to run, to take care of; 2 to organize; 3 to carry out, to execute; **terselenggara** carried out; **penyelenggara** 1 caretaker; 2 executor; 3 operator, organizer; **penyelenggaraan** 1 implementation; 2 organization.

selentingan, kabar selentingan gossip, rumours.

selera 1 appetite; 2 taste; **berselera** 1 have appetite; 2 have a taste for.

selesai completed, done, finished; **pekerjaan rumah saya sudah selesai** I've finished my homework; **menyelesaikan** 1 to finish; **saya harus menyelesaikan pekerjaan ini sebelum kita berangkat** I have to finish this work before we leave; 2 *(debt)* discharge, settle; **penyelesaian** 1 arrangement; 2 completion, settlement, solution.

selesma a cold, the sniffles.

seleweng, menyeleweng 1 to deviate, to digress; 2 to engage in improper activity; 3 to be unfaithful to a partner; **menyelewengkan** to deflect, to divert; **terselewengkan** deflected, diverted; **penyeleweng** crook; **penyelewengan** 1 deviation; 2 corruption, irregularity.

selidik 1 accurate, careful; 2 critical, observant; **menyelidiki** 1 to examine carefully, to investigate; 2 to do research; **penyelidik** 1 investigator, research worker; 2 detective, examiner; 3 scout, spy; **penyelidikan** 1 research; **mengadakan penyelidikan** to carry out a study; 2 inquiry, investigation.

selimut 1 blanket; 2 camouflage, cover; **berselimut** 1 covered over; 2 camouflaged; **berselimutkan** covered with; **menyelimuti** 1 to cover with a blanket; 2 to cover; **terselimuti** be blanketed; **penyelimutan** 1 covering; 2 camouflaging.

selinap, menyelinap 1 to move stealthily, to slither; **menyelinap masuk** to sneak in; **menyelinap keluar** to sneak out; **dia menyelinap ke arah saya** he sneaked up on me; 2 to get away, to slip away into.

seling interspace, interval; **berseling** alternate, take turns; **selingan** 1 interlude, something put in between;

2 variation from the routine.

selip[1], menyelip to slip into a place; **menyelipi** to insert between; **menyelipkan** to insert something in between; **terselip 1** enclosed; **2** inserted, slipped in; **selipan** insert.

selip[2] to skid; **terselip** skid.

selisih 1 difference; **selisih harga kedua barang itu tidak besar** the difference in price between those two items is not great; **2** quarrel; **berselisih** to disagree, to have a difference of opinion; **mereka selalu berselisih pendapat tentang hal itu** they always disagree on that topic; **memperselisihkan** to disagree over; **perselisihan** disagreement, dispute, quarrel.

selokan 1 drain, gutter; **2** sewer; **3** ditch.

selop slipper, sandal.

selot bolt, lock; **menyelot** to lock.

selubung 1 cover, veil; **2** wrapper; **berselubung** covered in; **menyelubungi** to cover with a veil or wrapper; **menyelubungkan** to use something as a covering; **terselubung** covered, veiled; **penyelubungan** act of covering.

selundup, menyelundup 1 to duck into, to hide; **2** to infiltrate; **menyelundupi** to infiltrate; **menyelundupkan** to smuggle; **selundupan** contraband; **barang selundupan** things that are smuggled; **penyelundup** smuggler; **penyelundupan** smuggling.

seluruh entire, whole; **seluruh keluarga** the whole family; **seluruh dunia** the whole world; **seluruhnya** all of it; **menyeluruh 1** to spread all over; **2** comprehensive, exhaustive; **keseluruhan** entirety, totality; **secara keseluruhan** on the whole.

semadi 1 meditation; **2** meditate; **bersemadi** meditate, meditating.

semai, semaian seedling; **menyemai(kan)** to raise seedlings; **penyemaian** raising seedlings; **persemaian** nursery, seedbed.

semak bushes, underbrush; **semak belukar** scrub, undergrowth, weeds.

semangat enthusiasm, spirit, morale, zest; **dia mencoba meningkatkan semangat regu itu** he's been trying to boost the team's morale; **menyemangati** to encourage; **bersemangat** energetic, enthusiastic.

a b c d e f g h i j k l m n o p q r s t u v w x y z

semangka watermelon.

semat hook, peg, pin; **menyematkan** to attach, to fasten, to pin; **penyematan** pinning on.

semata, semata-mata merely, simply, solely.

semayam lie down, lie *(for nobility)*; **menyemayamkan** to lay down a corpse; **jenazahnya disemayamkan di mesjid sebelum dimakamkan** the corpse was laid in the mosque before being buried; **bersemayam** reside; **persemayaman** **1** throne; **2** residence *(for nobility)*.

sembah **1** respectful greeting *(made with palms together and fingertips upward touching the forehead)*; **2** homage, obeisance; **3** words *(speaking to royalty)*; **menyembah** **1** to pay homage; **2** to worship; **menyembah-nyembah** to beg or entreat in a polite way; **mempersembahkan** **1** to offer or present something to a high person; **2** to inform or report to a high person; **3** to dedicate; **4** to present a performance; **sembahan** person or thing worshipped; **penyembah** worshipper; **penyembahan** adoration, worship; **persembahan** **1** gift, tribute; **2** dedication.

sembahyang prayer service, prayer; **bersembahyang** pray, praying, worship; **umat Islam bersembahyang lima kali sehari** Muslims pray five times a day; **menyembahyangkan** to pray for.

sembarang of any kind, no particular one; **dengan sembarang** any old way; **kesembarangan** arbitrariness, doing things any old way; **sembarangan** **1** at random; **jangan membuang sampah sembarangan!** don't throw the rubbish just anywhere!; **2** just anyone, anything.

sembelih, menyembelih to slaughter; **sembelihan** an animal to be slaughtered; **penyembelih** butcher; **penyembelihan** butchering, slaughter.

sembelit **1** constipation; **2** constipated.

sembilan nine, ninth; **jam sembilan** nine o'clock; **sembilan belas** nineteen; **sembilan puluh** ninety; **di lantai sembilan** on the ninth floor; **tanggal sembilan Juli** the ninth of July; **kesembilan** the ninth.

semboyan slogan, motto; **bersemboyan** have as a slogan.

sembrono careless, doing things in any way you think of; **pekerjaan yang sembrono!** such careless work!; **kesembronoan** frivolity, recklessness.

sembuh heal, recover; **dia sudah sembuh** she's recovered now; **menyembuhkan** to cure; **kesembuhan** recovery *(from an illness)*; **tersembuhkan** curable; **penyembuh** healer; **penyembuhan** healing.

sembunyi 1 concealed, hidden; **2** hide; **bersembunyi** to hide; **dia bersembunyi di belakang pintu itu** she hid behind the door; **menyembunyikan 1** to hide; **siapa yang menyembunyikan coklat itu?** who's hidden the chocolate?; **2** to conceal, to suppress; **menyembunyikan perasaan** to disguise one's feelings; **tersembunyi 1** hidden; **2** stealthily; **persembunyian** hiding; **tempat persembunyian** hiding place.

sembur spittle; **bersembur-(sembur)an** to spray one another; **menyembur 1** to squirt, to spurt; **2** to spray spit at.

semen cement, **menyemen** to cement.

semena, tidak semena-mena arbitrarily, without reason; **tindakan semena-mena** an arbitrary act.

semenanjung peninsula.

semenda related by marriage; **bersemenda** to be related by marriage.

semenjak since.

sementara 1 while; **sementara menunggu bis dia membaca koran** while waiting for the bus she/he read the newspaper; **2** provisional, temporary; **laporan sementara** interim report; **untuk sementara** for the time being.

semi young shoot; **musim semi** spring; **bersemi** to bud, to sprout.

semir polish; **semir sepatu** shoe polish; **menyemir 1** to polish; **2** to spread something oily or greasy on, to lubricate; **3** to bribe, to grease the palm; **penyemir 1** someone who polishes; **2** something to polish with.

sempat 1 have sufficient time, opportunity; **saya belum sempat menelepon** I haven't had the time to telephone; **2** still be able to do; **menyempati** to find an

a b c d e f g h i j k l m n o p q r s t u v w x y z

a b c d e f g h i j k l m n o p q r s t u v w x y z

opportunity for; **menyempatkan** to take the opportunity; **saya menyempatkan diri untuk mengunjungi mereka** I took the opportunity to join them; **kesempatan** opportunity; **guru memberi kesempatan kepada Mochtar** the teacher gave Mochtar an opportunity; **kehilangan kesempatan** to miss an opportunity.

sempit **1** narrow, tight; **gang yang sempit** a narrow lane; **2** limited, pressed; **menyempit** to constrict, to narrow, to tighten; **jalan menyempit** the road narrows; **menyempitkan, mempersempit** to tighten; **kesempitan** **1** narrowness; **2** being hard-pressed; **3** too narrow; **penyempitan** constriction.

semprot, menyemprot **1** to spray; **2** to scold; **menyemprotkan** **1** to squirt out; **2** to inject, to spray; **semprotan** **1** syringe; **2** scolding; **penyemprot** sprayer, syringe; **penyemprotan** spraying.

sempurna **1** perfect; **dia bicara bahasa Indonesia dengan sempurna** she speaks perfect Indonesian; **2** complete; **menyempurnakan** **1** to perfect; **2** to complete; **kesempurnaan** **1** perfection; **2** completeness; **penyempurnaan** act of perfecting.

semrawut chaotic, disorganized; **lalu lintas di Jakarta semrawut** the traffic in Jakarta is chaotic; **kesemrawutan** **1** chaos, lack of organization; **2** be chaotic or disorderly.

semua all; **semua orang tahu bahwa** everybody knows that; **semuanya** all *(of it/them)*; **semuanya sudah ada di sini** they're all here; **semua yang Anda katakan** everything you said; **semua-muanya** *(colloquial)* anything and everything; **kesemuanya** all of, everything.

semur dish mainly of meat stewed with spices and soy sauce.

semut ant; **menyemut** to swarm; **kesemutan** to have pins and needles, to become numb *(arm, leg)*; **tangan saya kesemutan** my arm has gone to sleep.

sen cent.

senam gymnastics; **bersenam** to do gymnastics; **pesenam** gymnast.

senang **1** contented, happy; **kami merasa sangat senang**

mendengar kabar Anda we're delighted to hear your news; **bersenang hati** be pleased; **2** like; **apakah Anda senang tinggal di Medan?** do you like living in Medan?; **3** comfortable; **bersenang-senang** to have a good time; **menyenangi** to like; **menyenangkan** to amuse, to do someone a favour, to please; **kesenangan 1** contentment, happiness; **2** favourite.

senantiasa always.

senapan gun, rifle; **senapan angin** air rifle; **bersenapan** have a rifle.

senat 1 faculty senate; **2** senate.

senda-gurau joke; **bersenda-gurau** to joke.

sendi 1 hinge, joint; **2** socket; **3** principle; **bersendi** based on, hinged; **bersendikan** be based on; **bersendi-sendi** with joints; **persendian 1** base, pivot; **2** the body joints.

sendiri self; **dia sendiri yang mengatakannya** she said it herself; **2** own; **komputer saya sendiri** my own computer; **saya mempunyai kamar sendiri** I've got my own room; **3** by yourself; **dia mengerjakannya sendiri** she did it by herself; **sendiri-sendiri** individually, separately; **menyendiri 1** to be alone, to be apart; **2** to be aloof or stand-offish; **sendirian** alone; **saya tinggal sendirian di rumah itu** I live by myself in the house; **penyendiri** a loner, liking to be alone.

sendok, senduk 1 spoon; **sendok makan** dessertspoon, tablespoon *(in recipes)*; **sesendok makan tepung** a tablespoon of flour; **2** ladle; **3** spoon-like tool; **menyendok 1** to ladle out; **2** to scoop.

sendratari ballet, dance-drama.

Senen *(old spelling)* Monday; SEE **Senin**.

seng 1 zinc; **2** iron sheeting; **3** roofing.

sengaja intentional(ly), deliberate(ly); **dia melakukan itu dengan sengaja** he did it deliberately; **kesengajaan** intent.

sengat the sting of an insect; **menyengat** to sting; **saya disengat tawon** I was stung by a bee; **sengatan** pain or wound from a sting; **penyengat 1** something that stings; **2** wasp.

sengketa **1** lawsuit, legal action; **2** quarrel; **bersengketa** to have a legal dispute; **mempersengketakan** to dispute, to quarrel over; **persengketaan** conflict, dispute.

sengsara **1** misery, suffering; **2** be miserable, suffer; **menyengsarakan** to cause misery, to torment; **kesengsaraan** misery, suffering.

seni **1** fine, refined; **2** art; **pameran seni rupa** art exhibition; **seni bangunan** architecture; **seni lukis** art of painting; **seni pahat, seni patung** sculpture; **kesenian** art; **seniman** artist.

Senin, hari Senin Monday; **pada hari Senin** on Monday; **sampai hari Senin!** see you on Monday!; **setiap hari Senin** every Monday; **hari Senin yang lalu** last Monday; **hari Senin depan** next Monday.

senior **1** senior, Sr; **2** *(colloquial)* male university seniors.

seniwati female artist.

senja dusk, twilight.

senjata weapon; **senjata api** firearms; **bersenjata, bersenjatakan** to be armed; **mempersenjatai** to arm; **persenjataan** armament, arms; **gudang persenjataan** armory.

senonoh polite, proper; **tidak senonoh** improper, obscene.

sensasi sensation, sensational news.

sensor, sensur censor; **menyensor** to censor; **penyensor** censor; **penyensoran** censoring.

sensus census; **menyensus** to take a census.

sentak pull, pull out; **menyentak, menyentakkan** **1** to jerk at, to pull at; **2** to startle; **menyentak-nyentak** to jerk at something repeatedly; **tersentak** be startled; **sentakan** a jerk; **kapal terbang mendarat dengan sentakan** the plane landed with a bump.

senter, lampu senter flashlight, spotlight; **menyenter** to light, to shine; **senteran** thing shone or projected.

sentimen **1** bad feeling, grudge; **2** hold a grudge.

sentosa **1** quiet, tranquil; **2** safe; **aman sentosa** peaceful, safe; **kesentosaan** **1** peace, rest, tranquillity; **2** safety.

sentral central.

sentuh, menyentuh touch; **bersentuhan** be touching each other; **bersentuh-sentuhan** continually coming into contact with each other; **menyentuh** to nudge, to touch; **tersentuh 1** touched; **2** slightly nudged; **sentuhan, persentuhan** contact, touch.

senyap, sunyi-senyap **1** deserted, very quiet; **2** quiet, silent.

senyum smile; **senyum hambar** forced smile; **senyum-senyum** smile continually; **bersenyum-(senyum)an** smile at each other; **tersenyum** smile; **senyuman** a smile.

sepak a kick; **sepak bola** soccer; **menyepak** to kick; **sepakan 1** kicking; **2** kick.

separuh half.

sepat when food has the effect of putting your teeth on edge or drying your mouth, like green bananas *(explanation only)*.

sepatu footwear, shoe; **sepatu bola** soccer shoes; **sepasang sepatu** a pair of shoes; **sepatu luncur es** ice skates; **sepatu roda** rollerskates; **bersepatu** wear shoes.

sepeda bicycle; **bersepeda** ride on a bike.

seperti as, like; **seperti sudah Anda ketahui** as you know; **seperti biasa** as usual; **sama seperti biasa** the same as ever; **seperti itik** like a duck; **seperti saya katakan** like I said; **itu seperti apa?** what's it like?; **rupa Bambang seperti ayahnya** Bambang looks like his father; **di kota besar seperti Jakarta** in big cities such as Jakarta; **sepertinya 1** as it should be; **2** it seems that, it is as if; **sepertinya saya pernah ke sini** it's as if I've been here before.

sepi 1 quiet, still; **2** desolate, lonely; **3** *(business)* slack; **menyepi, nyepi 1** to become desolate, to grow still; **Hari Raya Nyepi** day of quiet in Bali when you are not allowed to leave your home or hotel; **2** to seclude yourself; **kesepian** **1** loneliness, solitude; **2** deserted, lonely; too quiet; **merasa kesepian** to feel lonely.

seprei bedsheet.

September September.

sepuh plating material; **disepuh dengan emas** gold-plated; **menyepuh** to plate;

a b c d e f g h i j k l m n o p q r s t u v w x y z

sepuhan gilt; **penyepuhan** gilding, plating.

serah, menyerah to surrender; **serah terima** hand over, transfer; **menyerahterimakan** to hand over; **menyerahi** to entrust, to hand over to; **Ahmad diserahi tanggung jawab yang cukup besar oleh atasannya** Ahmad was entrusted with considerable responsibility by his boss; **menyerahkan** to hand, to transfer something over; **saya sudah menyerahkan pekerjaan rumah saya** I've handed in my homework; **terserah** up to you!; **penyerahan 1** delivery, transfer; **2** surrender, yielding.

serai lemongrass.

serak, berserak-(serak) scattered; **berserakan** to be scattered; **menyeraki** to scatter things on; **menyerakkan** to scatter around; **terserak** scattered; **serakan** garbage scattered about.

seram hair-raising, horrible; **menyeramkan 1** to make your hair stand on end; **2** to terrify; **3** frightfulness.

serambi porch, verandah.

serang attack; **serang-menyerang** to attack each other; **menyerang** to attack; **terserang 1** attacked; **2** fell ill; **terserang flu** to get flu; **serangan** attack; **lumpuh karena serangan otak** to become paralysed because of a stroke; **penyerang** aggressor, attacker; **penyerangan** aggression, attack.

serangga insect; **gigitan serangga** an insect bite; **obat pembasmi serangga** insect repellent.

serani Christian; **menyeranikan** to convert to Christianity.

serap, menyerap 1 to absorb a fluid; **2** to pervade; **penyerap 1** absorbent; **2** absorber.

serat[1] fibre; **berserat** fibrous; **mangga Indramayu selalu berserat** Indramayu mango is always fibrous.

serat[2] jammed, tight.

serba completely, fully, wholly; **serba ada** having everything; **serba aku** egoistic; **apartemen yang serba lengkap** a self-contained flat; **serba aneka** all different varieties, diversity; **serba sama** homogeneous; **keserbasamaan** homogeneity.

serbet napkin, serviette.

serbu, menyerbu to invade in a large group; **serbuan 1** invasion; **2** rush, stampede; **penyerbu** attacker, invader; **penyerbuan** attacking, invasion.

serbuk 1 dust; **2** pollen; **3** powder; **penyerbukan** pollination.

serdadu soldier; **serdadu bayaran** mercenary.

sere lemongrass.

serem frightening, horrible.

serempak altogether, in unison.

serempet, (ber)serempetan brush against each other; **menyerempet, nyerempet** to graze, to brush against; **keserempet, terserempet** to get grazed.

serentak 1 at once, jointly, together; **2** all at once.

seret, menyeret to drag; **menyeret-nyeret** to carry away, to drag along; **terseret 1** dragged along; **2** involved *(in something bad).*

seri[1] **1** royal title; **2** shining splendour; **berseri** beam, shine; **berseri-seri** beam, gleam; **wajah Nan tampak berseri-seri** Nan beamed *(with pleasure).*

seri[2] be a tie; **pertandingan itu seri** the match was a draw.

seri[3] series; **film seri** serial film; **berseri** in a series.

serigala jackal, wolf.

serikat 1 united; **Amerika Serikat** the USA; **2** league, union; **berserikat** allied, united; **perserikatan** association, organization, union; **Perserikatan Bangsa-bangsa** the United Nations.

serikaya annona, custard apple, coconut jam.

sering often; **saya ingin bertemu lebih sering dengan Sadikin** I'd like to see Sadikin more often; **sering-sering** often, over and over; **seringnya** frequency; **sesering** as often as; **keseringan** frequency, too frequent.

serius serious; **apakah Anda serius?** are you serious?; **keseriusan** seriousness.

sero a share *(in business)*; **pesero** shareholder; **pe(r)seroan** company, partnership.

serobot, menyerobot 1 to grab, to pinch; **2** to try to get ahead of each other; **serobotan** thing snatched; **penyerobot 1** person who snatches; **2** person who acts

a b c d e f g h i j k l m n o p q r s t u v w x y z

high-handedly; **penyerobotan** annexation, illegal occupancy.

serong 1 slanting; **garis serong** slanting line; **2** unfaithful; **main serong 1** disloyalty, insincerity; **2** adultery; **serong menyerong** to crisscross; **menyerong** to go askew; **menyerongkan** to slant, to tilt.

sersan naval petty officer, sergeant.

serta 1 along with; **2** and, as well as; **beserta 1** along with, as well as; **2** attached *(documents)*; **menyertai** to accompany; **hujan angin ribut disertai petir dan guntur** a thunderstorm *(literally, rain and strong wind accompanied by lightning and thunder)*; **menyertakan** to enclose a thing; **kesertaan** participation; **peserta** participant; **penyertaan** attaching, enclosing.

sertifikat, sertipikat certificate.

seru shout, yell; **perdebatan yang seru** heated debate; **berseru** call out, shout out; **menyerukan 1** to call, to shout out; **2** to proclaim; **seruan 1** call, cry; **2** exclamation; **tanda seru** exclamation mark; **3** appeal; **penyeruan 1** calling, crying; **2** appeal.

seruling flute.

serupa similar.

servis service; **menyervis** to service engines etc.

sesak 1 close, narrow, **sesak napas** short of breath; **2** crowded, tight; **bersesak-(sesakan)** crowd each other, pack yourself in; **menyesakkan** to constrict, to oppress, to tighten.

sesal regret, remorse; **menyesal** to be sorry, to regret; **saya amat menyesal tentang itu** I feel awful about it; **menyesali** to blame something on someone, to regret; **menyesalkan** to deplore, to regret; **penyesalan 1** regret, remorse; **2** reproach.

sesama, sesama manusia fellow human beings; **sesama mahasiswa** fellow students.

sesat 1 lose your way; **2** deviate, go astray; **menyesatkan** to lead astray, to mislead; **itu iklan yang menyesatkan** it's a misleading advertisement.

sesuai 1 appropriate; **2** agree with; **bersesuaian** agree with, be in mutual accord; **menyesuaikan** to adapt, to adjust, to bring into line; **saya tidak bisa menyesuaikan diri pada sistem baru** I can't adapt to the new system; **kesesuaian 1** conformity, uniformity; **2** compatibility, suitability; **penyesuaian** adaptation, adjustment, **persesuaian** agreement, compatibility.

sesudah after.

setan 1 devil, satan; **2** someone evil; **persetan!** damn it!, hell!

setel[1] **1** *(clothes, cards, etc.)* set, suit; **menyetel** to match; **setelan** set, suit of clothes.

setel[2]**, menyetel 1** to adjust, to tune up; **2** to turn on; **menyetel TV** to turn on the television; **penyetelan** installation, tuning; **penyetelan kacamata** fitting of glasses.

setelah after.

setengah half; SEE ALSO **tengah**.

seterika iron; **papan seterika** ironing board; **menyeterika 1** to do the ironing, to iron; **2** *(colloquial)* to flatten, to smash; **seterikaan 1** iron; **2** clothes for ironing.

seteru enemy; **berseteru** hostile; **memperseterukan** to treat as an enemy; **perseteruan** hostility.

setia faithful, loyal; **kesetiaan** allegiance, loyalty.

setia kawan loyal; **kesetiakawanan** solidarity.

setip eraser, rubber.

setir steering wheel; **menyetir** to drive or steer (a car); **menyetir mobil** to drive a car; **saya harus belajar menyetir** I must learn to drive; **menyetirkan** to drive a vehicle for someone.

setop, menyetop to stop; **kesetop** *(colloquial)* have your way obstructed; **setopan** a (bus) stop; **penyetopan** stopping.

setor deposited; **menyetor 1** to make a deposit; **2** to pay a rental fee; **3** to put in storage; **menyetor(kan) 1** to deposit; **2** to deliver something you have made to the person who paid for it; **setoran 1** deposit; **2** rental fee; **penyetor 1** supplier; **2** depositor; **penyetoran** depositing, payment.

setrip 1 line; **2** decorative stripe; **3** *(rank)* stripe; **4** *(golf)* straight; **bersetrip-setrip** with stripes.

setrum electric current; **menyetrum 1** to induce; **2** to charge, to electrify;

kesetrum to get an electric shock.

setrup syrup.

sewa 1 hire, rent; **mobil sewa** car hire; **2** rented; **sewa-rumah** house rent; **menyewa 1** to rent; **Ismail menyewa rumah baru** Ismail's rented a new house; **2** to hire; **mari kita menyewa mobil saja** let's just hire a car; **menyewakan** to hire out, to rent out; **'rumah untuk disewakan'** 'house to let'; **sewaan** hired, rented items; **rumah sewaan** a rented house; **penyewa** lessee, tenant; **penyewaan** renting out; **penyewaan mobil** car hire; **persewaan** rental.

si definite article used with names or nicknames; **di mana si Gunawan?** where's Gunawan?; **pasti itu si gendut!** I bet it's the fat one!

sia, sia-sia 1 in vain, useless; **2** meaningless; **menyia-nyiakan** to frustrate, to neglect, to waste; **kesia-siaan** being in vain, uselessness.

sial 1 be unlucky; **2** bad luck; **kesialan** bad luck, misfortune; **sialan 1** unlucky person or thing; **2** person or thing that brings bad luck; **3** damn it!

siang 1 day, daylight period; **2** period from about 10 a.m. to 3 p.m.; **makan siang** lunch; **sekolah siang** afternoon-school session; **siang-siang** early, in time; **kesiangan 1** caught by daylight; **2** overslept, **3** do something late in the morning when it should have been done earlier; **siangan** *(colloquial)* later in the day.

siap prepared, ready; **makan malam belum siap** dinner's not ready yet; **siap cetak** ready to print; **siap sedia** completely prepared; **siap siaga** prepared and completely alert; finished, done; *(military)* attention; **bersiap 1** get ready, prepared; **2** *(sport)* on your mark; **bersiap-siap** make preparations; **dia sedang bersiap-siap untuk masuk universitas** she's making preparations for entering university; **menyiapkan, mempersiapkan** to get ready, to prepare; **kesiapan** readiness; **persiapan** preparations.

siapa who, whom, whose; **siapa nama Anda?** what's your name?; **siapa (itu)?** who is it?; **siapa lagi?** who else?; **jas siapa ini?, jas ini siapa**

punya? whose is this jacket?; **siapa punya ini?** whose is this?; **siapa saja** anybody; **siapa pun** anybody at all, whoever; **tak ada siapa pun di rumah** there isn't anybody at home; **siapa pun boleh pergi** anybody can go; **siapa-siapa** who *(plural)*.

siar, menyiarkan **1** to spread news; **2** to broadcast; **3** to announce; **tersiar** **1** announced, broadcast; **2** circulated, spread about; **siaran** **1** broadcast; **siaran langsung dari Surabaya** a live broadcast from Surabaya; **2** announcement; **siaran pers** press release; **penyiar** broadcaster; **penyiar berita** newsreader; **penyiaran** broadcasting.

siasat strategy; **bersiasat** have a lot of stratagems, have something as a strategy; **menyiasati** to pry into a person's business; **penyiasat** **1** investigator; **2** strategist, tactician; **penyiasatan** **1** investigation; **2** using tactics or stratagems.

sibuk **1** busy; **saya sibuk** I'm busy; **hari sibuk** a busy day; **waktu sibuk, jam sibuk** rush hour; **2** *(a phone)* engaged; **sedang sibuk** to be in a rush; **menyibukkan** **1** to incite, to stir up; **2** to busy yourself with; **mempersibuk** to cause a person to be busy; **kesibukan** activity, stir; **kesibukan sehari-hari** daily activities.

sidang **1** meeting, session; **2** assembly, council, group; **bersidang** be in session, convene; **menyidangkan** **1** to convene on a matter; **2** to bring to trial; **persidangan** **1** assembly, meeting; **2** court session; **3** summoning of the accused.

sidik examination, investigation; **sidik jari** fingerprint; **menyidik** to investigate; **penyidik** investigating officer; **penyidikan** police investigation.

sifat **1** characteristic; **sifat khas** special characteristic; **2** identifying feature; **3** disposition, nature; **4** attribute of God; **bersifat** to have the characteristic, nature or quality; **dia bersifat pemarah** he's very bad-tempered.

sih *(colloquial)* particle used to soften questions; **ada apa sih?** hmm, what's wrong?; **mau apa sih?** then what do you want?

sihir black magic, witchcraft; **menyihir** to practise black

a b c d e f g h i j k l m n o p q r s t u v w x y z

a b c d e f g h i j k l m n o p q r s t u v w x y z

magic on someone; **sihiran** sorcery.

sikap attitude; **sikap yang tegas** a firm attitude; **bersikap** to have an attitude.

sikat 1 brush; **sikat gigi** toothbrush, **sikat rambut** hairbrush; **2** bunch *(of bananas)*; **menyikat 1** to brush; **saya sudah menyikat gigi saya** I've brushed my teeth; **2** *(colloquial)* to take away; **3** *(colloquial)* to clean out, to wipe out; **4** *(sport)* to defeat completely; **penyikatan** brushing, combing.

siksa torture; **menyiksa 1** to torture; **2** *(colloquial)* to annoy, to irritate; **siksaan** torture; **penyiksa** tormentor, torturer; **penyiksaan** torturing.

siku 1 elbow; **2** right angle; **3** something at right angles; **siku segi tiga** a right-angled triangle; **bersiku** angled or curved; **siku menyiku** to nudge each other.

sila[1] cross-legged; **bersila** sit with the legs crossed; **Fitri duduk bersila** Fitri was sitting cross-legged.

sila[2] principle; **Pancasila** the Five Principles of Indonesia.

silah, menyilahkan, mempersilahkan to ask, to invite; **silakan** please *(use to urge someone to do something, not to ask for something)*; **silahkan masuk** please come in; **silahkan ambil satu** please take one; **silahkan duduk** please take a seat.

silam 1 *(sun)* set; **2** ago, of the past; **tahun yang silam** *(formal)* last year.

silang crosswise, intersecting; **tanda silang** sign of a crossing; **teka-teki silang** crossword puzzle; **silang empat** crossroads; **bersilang 1** crossed; **bersilang tangan** have your arms folded; **duduk bersilang kaki** to sit cross-legged; **2** piled up in a crisscross way; **bersilangan** to cross each other, to pass each other; **silang menyilang** crisscross; **menyilangi** to intersect or cross; **menyilang(kan), mempersilangkan** to place in the form of a cross; **penyilangan** crossing, mutation; **persilangan 1** crossing; **persilangan jalan** road crossing; **2** conflict, contradiction.

silap false, mistaken, wrong; **kesilapan** error, mistake.

silat traditional self-defence arts; **bersilat 1** to practise self-defence; **bersilat lidah** to argue; **2** to mime self-defence; **persilatan** things relating to self-defence.

silaturahim, silaturrahim, silaturahmi, silaturrahmi friendship, good relationship, demonstration of friendship.

silau dazzled, temporarily blinded by glare; **menyilaukan 1** to become dazzling, to cause glare; **2** to blind someone with glare.

silet razor blade; **menyilet** to slice with a razor blade.

silih berganti alternately, in turns, by turns, changing; **bersilih** to change, to turn into.

silinder cylinder.

silsilah family tree, genealogy.

simbol, simbul symbol; **bersimbol(kan)** to have something as a symbol; **menyimbolkan** to symbolize.

simpan, menyimpan 1 to store; **saya menyimpan buku-buku dulu** I'll put the books away first; **2** to keep something in storage; **Anda yang menyimpan surat itu!** you kept the letter!; **menyimpan rahasia** to keep a secret; **menyimpankan** to store for someone; **simpanan 1** goods stored, savings; **2** storage place; **3** mistress; **penyimpan 1** a depositor, person who saves; **2** storage place; **penyimpanan** storage.

simpang branch *(of a road)*, deviation; **simpang empat, simpang jalan** crossroads, intersection; **simpang siur** crisscross; **kesimpangsiuran 1** crisscrossing; **2** confusion, mix-up; **bersimpangan** intersect; **menyimpang 1** to deviate, to diverge; **2** to take a side route; **persimpangan 1** branching off; **2** byway, side route; **3** crossroads; **penyimpangan** deviation, divergence; **persimpangan** branching off, intersection.

simpati sympathy; **bersimpati** sympathize; **Achmad bersimpati kepada Lina** Achmad sympathized with Lina.

simpatik sympathetic.

simpul knot, node; **menyimpul 1** to button clothing; **2** to tie a knot; **menyimpulkan 1** to tie into a knot; **2** to conclude; **tersimpul 1** knotted; **2** implied, included; **kesimpulan** conclusion; **berkesimpulan** to come to a conclusion; **simpulan 1** knot, node; **2** action of buttoning.

sinar 1 beam, gleam, glow, ray; **sinar matahari** sunshine;

a b c d e f g h i j k l m n o p q r s t u v w x y z

2 gleam; **sinar menyinar** glitter and gleam; **bersinar** to radiate, to shine; **menyinari 1** to shine on; **2** to irradiate; **menyinarkan 1** to radiate, to send off; **2** to make shine; **penyinaran 1** illumination; **2** radiation.

sindir, menyindir to allude; **sindir menyindir** to make allusions to each other; **penyindir** teaser; **sindiran** teasing, allusion.

singa 1 lion; **singa laut** walrus; **2** Leo.

singgah, menyinggahi to drop by, to stop over; **persinggahan 1** stopover, transit; **2** port of call.

singgung, bersinggungan to nudge, to touch; **menyinggung 1** to contact, to touch; **2** to insult, to offend; **3** to touch on *(a subject)*; **tersinggung** offended.

singkat 1 brief, concise; **2** short in time; **melakukan sesuatu dalam waktu singkat** to do something at short notice; **singkatnya** in brief, in short; **mempersingkat** to shorten, **singkatan 1** abbreviation; **'PBB' adalah singkatan dari 'Perserikatan Bangsa-bangsa'** 'UN' stands for 'United Nations'; **2** abstract, résumé.

singkir, menyingkir 1 to step aside; **2** to evacuate; **menyingkiri** to avoid, to evade; **menyingkirkan 1** to evacuate; **2** to put away, to remove; **3** to eliminate, to get rid of; **tersingkir 1** prevented, safeguarded; **2** gotten rid of; **tersingkirkan** to be pushed, to be shunted aside.

singkong cassava.

singsing, menyingsing to break clear, to lift, to rise; **fajar sudah menyingsing** it's dawn; **menyingsing(kan)** to roll up.

sini 1 here; **tidak jauh dari sini** not far from here; **ke sini 1** to here; **2** *(colloquial)* come here!; **2** *(colloquial)* I, we.

sinis 1 scornful, sarcastic; **2** cynical; **kesinisan 1** sarcasm, scorn; **2** cynicism.

sinterklas *(colloquial)* Santa Claus.

sinting rather crazy.

sinyal 1 signal; **2** light at a railway crossing.

sipil 1 civil; **2** civilian.

sipir jailer.

sipit slanting *(eyes)*.

sipu, tersipu-sipu bashful, embarrassed, shy.

siput snail.

siram, menyiram to flush, to pour water over; **menyiram kakus** to flush the lavatory; **Dion menyiram kebun itu** Dion watered the garden; **menyirami** to pour water on; **menyiramkan** to pour out; **Dion menyiramkan air ke kebun itu** Dion watered the garden; **siraman 1** a splash of water; **2** bride bathing ceremony *(Java)*; **penyiram** vessel to pour liquids; **penyiraman** pouring of liquids, watering.

sirap[1] raised slightly; **tersirap** scared; **darahnya tersirap melihat kejadian itu** she/he was scared to death at seeing what happened.

sirap[2] shingle; **atap sirap** shingled roof.

sirat mesh, network; **menyiratkan** to imply; **tersirat 1** knotted; **2** implied, implicit.

sirene siren; **sirene kebakaran** fire alarm.

sirih 1 betel vine; **2** a mixture wrapped in betel leaf for chewing; **makan sirih** to chew betel.

sirik to be jealous or envious.

sirip fish fin.

sisa 1 leftovers, remainder; **tidak ada sisanya** there's none left; **2** remnant; **bersisa** left over; **menyisakan 1** to leave behind; **2** to set aside.

sisi side; **ke sisi kiri** to the left side; **dari sisi ke sisi** from side to side; **bersisi** have a side.

sisih, menyisih 1 to get out of the way; **2** to be separate from; **3** to set aside; **menyisihkan 1** to set aside, to separate out; **2** to ignore, to reject; **3** *(in sport)* to eliminate; **tersisih** isolated, set apart; **tersisihkan** *(sport)* eliminated; **regu kita sudah tersisihkan** our team has already been eliminated; **penyisihan 1** isolation; **2** elimination.

sisik 1 scales *(of animals)*; **2** turtle shell; **bersisik** scaly; **menyisiki** to remove scales.

sisip, bersisipan have an insert; **menyisipkan** to insert, to stick in; **tersisip 1** inserted; **2** implied; **sisipan 1** thing inserted; **2** infix; **penyisipan** insertion.

sisir 1 comb; **2** bunch; **sesisir pisang** a bunch of bananas; **menyisir** to comb; **menyisir rambut** to comb your hair; **menyisirkan** to comb for someone; **tersisir** combed.

sistem system.

a b c d e f g h i j k l m n o p q r s t u v w x y z

siswa **1** student *(at secondary school)*; **2** student *(at college but not university)*; **3** student at such institutions.

siswi female student as in **siswa**.

sita, menyita to confiscate, to seize; **sitaan** confiscated goods; **penyitaan** confiscation.

situ there *(not far away)*.

situasi circumstances, situation.

siul sound of whistling; **bersiul** whistle *(people, trains, etc.)*; **siulan** whistling.

skala scale *(of maps etc.)*.

sketsa sketch.

skor score.

skors, menskors **1** to suspend a person; **diskors** to be suspended; **2** to adjourn; **penskorsan** suspension.

skorsing suspension *(student, sportsperson, etc.)*.

skrip script.

slang hose, tube.

soal **1** matter, problem; **soal pendapat** to be a matter of opinion; **2** question; **soalnya** the thing is; **soalnya, alamatnya hilang** the thing is, I've lost her address; **menyoalkan** to set questions; **mempersoalkan** **1** to question a thing; **2** to deal with, to discuss; **persoalan** **1** matter, issue, problem; **persoalan politik** a political issue; **memeriksa persoalan** to look into the matter; **2** debate, discussion.

sobat **1** friend; **2** *(colloquial)* comrade.

sobek ripped, torn; **celana jeans saya sobek** I've got a tear in my jeans; **menyobek** to tear, to rip; **sobekan** a torn piece.

soda soda.

sodor, menyodorkan to hand, to hold something out, to stretch out.

sogok, menyogok to bribe; **dia menyogok polisi** he bribed the police; **sogokan** bribe; **penyogokan** bribery.

sohor, kesohor, tersohor famous.

sokong prop, support; **menyokong** **1** to prop up, to support; **menyokong sebuah keluarga** to support a family **2** to aid; **sokongan** aid, contribution, support; **sokongan uang untuk penderita cacat** benefits for the disabled; **penyokong** contributor, supporter.

sol sole *(shoe)*; sol *(music)*.

solat *(Islam)* **1** prayers performed five times daily;

2 perform the prayers and rituals; **bersolat** to perform prayers and rituals.

solek elegant, stylish,well-dressed; **bersolek 1** put on make-up; **2** dress up *(for women)*; **pesolek 1** person who uses make-up; **2** a woman who likes being well-dressed.

sombong arrogant, conceited; **dia begitu sombong** he's so big-headed; **menyombongkan** to boast, to brag about; **menyombongkan diri** to brag about yourself; **kesombongan 1** arrogance, boasting; **2** conceit, vanity.

songsong, menyongsong to meet, to welcome; **penduduk dunia menyongsong abad ke-dua puluh satu** the world population welcomed the twenty-first century.

sop soup.

sopan 1 respectful; **2** polite; **sopan santun** be correct in behaviour; **sopan santun terhadap majikan** to be polite to one's employer; **kesopanan** good manners, polite behaviour.

sopir chauffeur, driver; **sopir maut** extremely dangerous driver; **menyopir, nyopir** to drive a motor vehicle as a chauffeur; **menyopiri** to drive.

sorak applause, cheering; **bersorak-sorai** cheer, shout; **bersorak-soraklah tiga kali untuk Ken** three cheers for Ken; **menyoraki** to cheer a person; **menyorakkan** to yell out; **sorakan** applause, cheers, yells.

sore afternoon, early evening *(after about 2 p.m. until dusk)*; **sore ini** this afternoon; **besok sore** tomorrow afternoon; **hari Minggu sore** on Sunday afternoon; **jam lima sore** at five o'clock in the afternoon; **setiap sore** every afternoon; **sore-sore** towards evening; **sorenya** the following afternoon; **kesorean** too late *(in the afternoon)*.

sorga heaven.

sorong pushing, sliding; **pintu sorong** sliding door; **menyorong** to push, to slide; **menyorongkan 1** to slide a thing forward; **2** to push forward; **tersorong** put or slid forward; **sorongan** thing pushed or shoved.

sorot beam, ray of light; **sorot balik** flashback; **menyorot 1** to gleam, to shine; **2** *(pictures)* to project; **3** to gaze; **4** to draw attention to; **menyoroti 1** to illuminate; **2** to spotlight; **menyorotkan 1** to radiate a thing; **2** to illuminate with; **tersorot** looked, gazed at; **sorotan 1** beam, ray; **2** radiation, spotlight; **3** attention; **penyorot 1** projector, reflector; **2** commentator, reviewer; **penyorotan 1** illumination, spotlight; **2** elucidation.

sosial 1 social; **jaminan sosial, tunjangan sosial** social security; **2** charitable; **kesosialan 1** friendliness; **2** social; **sosialisasi** socialization.

sosialis socialist.

sosialisme socialism.

sosiologi sociology.

sosis sausage, frankfurter.

soto a kind of soup.

S(e)panyol Spain, Spanish.

spesial special; **spesialis** specialist; **spesialisasi** specialization.

spion spy; **kaca spion** rear-view mirror.

spiritus methylated spirits, rubbing alcohol.

spontan spontaneous; **kespontanan** spontaneity.

stabil stable; **stabilisasi** stabilization.

stabilo highlighter pen.

standar standard; **menstandarkan** to standardize.

stadion stadium.

starter 1 starter *(of a car)*; **2** fluorescent light starter.

stasiun 1 depot, railway station; **2** public transportation terminal.

statistik 1 statistics; **2** statistical; **perstatistikan, kestatistikan** having to do with statistics.

stensil, menstensil to mimeograph; **stensilan** a stencil.

stopkontak electric socket.

sua, bersua 1 to meet, to run into; **2** meet up with, find.

suaka 1 asylum; **2** sancturary; **suaka margasatwa** wildlife sanctuary.

suam feverish, warm; **suam-suam** rather warm; **suam-suam kuku** lukewarm.

suami husband; **suami-istri** married couple; **bersuami** to be married, to have a husband; **bersuamikan** be married to a particular man.

suap mouthful; **uang suap** a bribe; **sesuap** a mouthful; **menyuap 1** to eat with the hand; **2** to bribe a person; **3** to give something as a

a b c d e f g h i j k l m n o p q r s t u v w x y z

bribe; **menyuapi** to feed a person; **menyuapkan** to feed something to a person; **penyuapan 1** feeding or eating with the hand; **2** bribery.

suar flare, signal light; **mercu suar** lighthouse.

suara 1 voice; **suara nyaring** a high voice, a loud voice; **2** sound; **tolong kecilkan suaranya** could you turn down the volume please?; **3** vote; **bersuara 1** have a voice; **2** produce a sound; **menyuarakan 1** to express something; **2** to utter.

suasana ambience, atmosphere.

suatu a certain, unspecified; **pada suatu hari** on a certain day; **sesuatu 1** unspecified; **2** a certain something **ada sesuatu yang perlu saya katakan** I've got something to tell you; **ada sesuatu yang salah** there's something wrong.

subsidi subsidy.

subuh dawn, daybreak; **sholat subuh** morning prayer.

subur 1 fertile; **2** prosperous, thriving; **3** healthy; **menyuburkan 1** to make fertile; **2** to make prosper; **mempersubur** to increase productivity; **kesuburan 1** fertility; **2** prosperity; **penyubur** fertilizer.

subyek 1 subject, topic of discussion; **2** *(grammatical)* subject.

suci 1 pure, purified; **suci hama** aseptic, sterile; **menyucihamakan** to sterilize; **2** holy; **menyucikan 1** to clean, to disinfect, to purify; **2** to sanctify; **tersuci** most pure or holy; **kesucian 1** purity; **2** holiness.

sudah 1 already; **saya sudah selesai** I've (already) finished; **'sudah makan?' 'belum'** 'have you (already) eaten?' 'not yet'; **seperti sudah Anda ketahui** as you (already) know; **2** past, last; **tahun yang sudah** the past year, last year; **3** *(colloquial)* all right, OK; **sudahlah! mari pulang!** all right! let's go home!; **sudah-sudah** bygone; **sesudah** after; **sesudah jam sepuluh** after ten o'clock; **sesudah sekolah selesai** after school; **sesudahnya** afterwards, thereafter; **segera sesudahnya** directly afterwards; **menyudahi 1** to conclude something; **2** to fulfil; **kesudahan 1** conclusion, result; **2** finally, in the end; **berkesudahan** having an end.

a b c d e f g h i j k l m n o p q r s t u v w x y z

a b c d e f g h i j k l m n o p q r s t u v w x y z

sudi **1** prepared, ready, willing; **dia sudi menolong saya** she's willing to help me; **2** *(formal)* please; **kesudian** willingness.

sudut **1** corner; **di sudut jalan** at the corner of the street; **2** angle; **3** point of view; **bersudut** have angles, corners; **menyudut** **1** to form an angle; **2** to go to a corner; **menyudutkan** to put a thing in a corner.

suhu temperature; **suhu rata-rata** the average temperature; **pengukur suhu** thermometer.

sujud **1** from a kneeling position, to bow your forehead to the floor; **2** perform ritual prayers *(Islam)*; **bersujud** **1** perform such a bow; **2** admit you are of a humble station.

suka **1** joy, pleasure; **sesuka hati** as you please; **2** like, be fond of; **saya tidak suka ikan** I don't like fish; **Harjo suka makan** Harjo likes eating; **3** be willing, would like; **sukaduka** having ups and downs, happiness and sorrow; **sukaduka seorang guru** the ups and downs of a teacher; **4** tend to; **suka ribut** tend to be noisy; **sesukanya, sesuka** as you wish, whatever you like; **bersuka-suka** enjoy yourself; **bersuka-sukaan** enjoy yourself; **menyukai** to like, to love; **kesukaan** **1** joy, pleasure; **2** something you like doing, hobby.

sukacita **1** glad, happy; **2** happiness, joy; **bersukacita** rejoice; **kesukacitaan** joy, state of being glad.

sukar difficult, hard; **itu benar-benar sukar** it's really difficult; **sukar sekali memutuskannya** it's difficult to decide; **menyukarkan, mempersukar** to cause difficulty; **kesukaran** **1** difficulty, hardship; **saya mengalami kesukaran mencari nomor telepon Anda** I had difficulty getting your phone number; **2** suffer hardship.

sukarela voluntary; **sukarelawan** a volunteer; **sukarelawati** a woman volunteer.

sukses **1** success; **2** be successful; **mensukseskan** to make successful; **kesuksesan** success; **pensuksesan** making successful.

suku a part; **suku bangsa** ethnic group; **suku bunga** *(bank)* interest rate; **suku minoritas** an ethnic minority; **sesuku** of the same ethnic group; **bersuku-**

suku be grouped in ethnic groups; **kesukuan** tribalism; **Pak Nasution selalu menonjolkan kesukuannya** Mr Nasution made others aware of his ethnic origins.

sulam, bersulam embroidered; **menyulam** to embroider; **menyulamkan** to embroider a design onto; **sulaman** embroidery.

sulap conjuring; **tukang sulap** conjurer; **menyulap** 1 to conjure up; 2 *(colloquial)* to cause to disappear; **sulapan, penyulapan** conjuring; **penyulap** conjurer; .

Sulawesi Sulawesi *(formerly Celebes)*.

suling flute; **bersuling, menyuling** to play the flute.

suling, menyuling to distil; **sulingan 1** distillate; 2 refinery; **penyulingan** distilling, refining.

sulit 1 complicated, difficult, hard; **itu benar-benar sulit** it's really difficult; **pertanyaan yang sulit** a difficult question; **2** hidden, secret; **menyulitkan, mempersulit 1** to complicate; **2** to cause difficulties; **kesulitan** difficulty, trouble.

suluh torch; **bersuluh** light with a torch; **penyuluh 1** person who gives information; **penyuluh lapangan pertanian** agricultural extension worker; **2** investigator, spy; **penyuluhan 1** illumination; **2** information.

sulung first-born, eldest; **anak sulung** first-born child.

sumbang, sumbang saran brainstorming; **menyumbang 1** to contribute; **2** to assist, to help; **menyumbangkan 1** to offer as a contribution; **2** to give as help; **sumbangan** contribution; **penyumbang** contributor, supporter.

sumbat plug, stopper; **menyumbat** to plug, to stop up; **menyumbatkan** to obstruct with; **tersumbat** clogged up, gagged, stopped up; **sumbatan** a thing to plug or close up with; **penyumbat** a plug; **penyumbatan** blockage, clogging, obstruction.

sumber 1 well; **2** source; **sumber penghasilan** source of income; **sumber-sumber alam** natural resources; **bersumber** to be based on, to have as a source.

sumbu¹ 1 wick; **2** fuse.

sumbu² 1 wagon axle; **2** axis, pivot.

a b c d e f g h i j k l m n o p q r s t u v w x y z

sumpah **1** oath; **mengambil sumpah** to take an oath; **2** curse; **bersumpah** swear an oath; **menyumpahi** to curse a person.

sumpit[1] chopsticks.

sumpit[2], **menyumpit** to shoot with a blowpipe; **menyumpitkan** to use as a blowpipe; **sumpitan** blowpipe.

sumsum marrow.

sumur well; **sumur bor** artesian well; **sumur mati** dry well.

sunat circumcision; **menyunat 1** to circumcise a person; **2** to skim money off the top; **menyunati** to circumcise several people; **menyunatkan** to have a person circumcised; **sunatan** circumcision.

sungai river, stream; **anak sungai** tributary stream.

sungguh **1** true; **2** really, truly; **sungguh?** really?; **dia sungguh dungu** he's a real dope; **3** actually, in fact; **sungguh saya capek** I'm very tired indeed; **sungguhpun** although, even; **sungguhpun mereka datang** even if they come; **sungguhpun hujan** even if it rains; **sungguh-sungguh** seriously, wholeheartedly; **sesungguhnya** actually, in truth; **sesungguhnya dia tidak sakit** actually she/he's not sick; **bersungguh-sungguh** make a great effort, try seriously; **kesungguhan** seriousness; **sungguhan** *(colloquial)* in earnest, serious.

sungut, bersungut-sungut complain, grumble; **sungutan** complaint, grumbling.

suntik, menyuntik **1** to inject; **2** to inoculate; **suntikan** injection, vaccination; **penyuntik** **1** person who gives injections; **2** syringe; **penyuntikan** injecting, vaccinating.

sunyi **1** lonely; **2** quiet; **3** deserted, desolate; **bersunyi-sunyi** withdraw; **kesunyian 1** loneliness; **2** quiet, solitude.

supaya **1** so that; **saya menasihatinya supaya berhenti** I advised him to stop; **2** to introduce a polite command.

suram **1** hazy, vague; **2** dark, dull, gloomy; **lampu yang suram** a dim light, **kesuraman 1** indistinctness, vagueness; **2** dullness.

surat **1** letter, note; **surat kilat** express letter;

2 certificate, document, receipt; **surat kawin** marriage certificate; **surat kabar** newspaper; **bersurat 1** inscribed, written; **2** compose a letter; **bersuratan, surat menyurat 1** to correspond, to write to each other; **2** correspondence; **menyurati 1** to inscribe; **2** to write a letter to a person; **suratan 1** destiny, fate; **2** fate lines on the hand; **surat-suratan** *(colloquial)* correspond, write to each other.

surga heaven, paradise.

suruh, menyuruh to order a person to do; **Dadang menyuruh adiknya membeli surat kabar** Dadang told his younger sibling to buy a newspaper; **suruhan 1** message, order; **2** delegate, messenger; **pesuruh** messenger; **penyuruh** person who gives orders.

susah 1 troubled; **2** hard to get; **3** bothersome, difficult; **dengan susah payah** with great difficulty; **susah-susah** go to a lot of trouble; [illegible] make every effort; **menyusahkan 1** to make difficult; **2** to worry about; **mempersusah** to make a thing difficult; **kesusahan 1** difficulty; **tanpa kesusahan** without any bother; **2** grief, worry; **3** be in trouble.

susastra, kesusastraan literature.

susila 1 decent, moral; **nilai-nilai susila** moral values; **2** decency; **bersusila** to have good morals; **kesusilaan** decency, morality.

suster nun, nursing sister.

susu milk; **susu bubuk** powdered milk; **susu murni** pure milk; **susu segar** fresh milk; **menyusu** to suckle on the breast; **menyusui** to give suck.

susul, bersusul-susulan, susul menyusul following each other in succession; **menyusul 1** to come afterward, to follow; **2** to follow and catch up with; **nanti saya menyusul** I'll join you later; **tersusul** be caught up with; **susulan 1** appendix, supplement; **2** continuation.

susun 1 orderly row, stack; **2** row, series; **3** arranged in a stack; **bersusun 1** stacked; **2** in layers, rows or stories; **tempat tidur bersusun** bunk beds; **3** arranged in an orderly way; **menyusun** to arrange in an orderly way; **menyusun acara** to prepare the agenda; **tolong susun**

map-map ini please arrange these files; **tersusun** **1** arranged, stacked; **2** compiled, composed; **susunan 1** compilation, composition; **2** formation, structure; **penyusun** compiler, composer; **penyusunan 1** arranging, compiling; **2** composing.

susup, menyusup 1 to move below a thing; **kucing itu menyusup di bawah mobil** the cat crawled under the car; **2** to infiltrate, to penetrate; **menyusupi** to enter stealthily; **menyusupkan 1** to place a thing below something else; **2** to smuggle; **penyusup** infiltrator; **penyusupan** infiltration, penetration.

susur edge, margin; **menyusur, menyusuri 1** to go along the edge; **2** to follow, to trace; **tersusur, tersusuri** followed, traced; **penyusur** person who follows up; **penyusuran** action of tracing.

susut decrease, shrink; **menyusut 1** to decrease in size, to shrink; **2** to subside; **3** to wipe off; **menyusutkan 1** to decrease, to reduce; **2** to wipe off again and again; **penyusutan 1** contraction, shrinkage; **2** decrease, reduction.

Sutan 1 title for Minangkabau nobility; **2** term of address for this rank.

sutera silk; **sutera tiruan** artificial silk.

swa- self-, a formal prefix.

swadaya self-help; **berswadaya** to operate on a self-supporting basis.

swakarya self-developing.

swalayan self-service; **pasar swalayan** supermarket.

swapraja autonomous region or area.

swasta private; **menswastakan** to privatize; **penswastaan** privatization.

Swedia Sweden, Swedish.

Swis Switzerland, Swiss.

syahbandar harbourmaster, port officer.

syahid Islamic martyr or warrior killed while fighting for Islam; **kesyahidan** martyrdom.

syair 1 story in verse form; **2** poem; **menulis syair** write poetry; **membaca syair** recite poetry; **3** rhyme giving clues to a lottery; **penyair** poet.

syak, syak wasangka distrust, doubt, suspicion.

syal shawl.

a b c d e f g h i j k l m n o p q r s t u v w x y z

syaraf nerve; **gangguan urat syaraf** a nervous breakdown.

syarat condition, requirement; **syarat penjualan** the conditions of sale; **dengan syarat Anda membiarkan saya membayar** on condition that you let me pay; **syarat-syarat** qualifications; **bersyarat** conditional; **bersyaratkan** have as a condition; **mensyaratkan, mempersyaratkan** to set as a condition; **persyaratan** rules and regulations.

syukur 1 thank God; **2** fortunately, happily; **bersyukur 1** thank God; **2** *(colloquial)* be grateful; **mensyukuri 1** to be grateful to God; **2** *(colloquial)* to thank someone; **syukuran** expression of gratitude to God by holding a ceremonial feast.

T t

taat 1 obedient; **2** loyal; **dia taat kepada keluarganya** he was loyal to his family; **menaati 1** to obey; **pegawai menaati perintah majikannya** the employees obeyed their boss's commands; **2** to be faithful; **ketaatan** fidelity, loyalty.

tabah 1 determined; **2** able to endure *(difficulties etc.)*, tough; **dia kelihatan tabah pada upacara pemakaman suaminya** she looked tough at her husband's funeral; **menabahkan hati** to make determined; **mempertabah** to make more determined; **ketabahan** determination, firmness.

tabel list, table; **tabel waktu** timetable.

tabiat 1 character, disposition, nature; **2** attitude, behaviour.

tabib 1 traditional healer; **2** physician.

tabir curtain, partition, screen.

tablet pill, tablet.

tabok slap in the face; **tabokan** a slap.

tabrak, bertabrakan collide; **kedua pesawat terbang itu bertabrakan** the two planes crashed into each other; **tabrak lari** hit and run; **menabrak** to hit against; **sepeda motor itu menabrak pintu gerbang** the motorbike hit the gate; **menabrakkan** to crash, to

a b c d e f g h i j k l m n o p q r s t u v w x y z

run into; **tertabrak** accidentally hit; **siku tangan saya tertabrak kosen pintu** I knocked my elbow on the doorframe; **tabrakan** collision; **penabrak** someone who collides.

tabuh drum at the mosque, **tabuhan** percussion instruments; **menabuh** to strike *(a drum)*.

tabung 1 bamboo tube used for storing things; **tabung gas** gas tank; **2** money box; **menabung** to save, to save up; **saya sedang menabung agar dapat pergi ke Brasil** I'm saving up to go to Brazil; **tabungan 1** money box; **2** savings; **uang tabungan** savings; **penabung** depositer; **penabungan 1** savings; **2** process of saving.

tabur, bertabur(an) scattered, spread; **tabur bunga** sprinkling flowers; **bertaburkan** to be spread over with; **menabur 1** *(seed)* to sow; **2** to scatter; **menaburi 1** to sow *(for exampke, a field)* **2** to spread over, scatter over; **menaburkan 1** to sow with something; **2** to scatter, to spread; **taburan** sowing; **penabur** sower.

tadah 1 receptacle for storing things; **2** cistern; **tukang tadah** receiver of stolen goods; **menadah 1** to catch with the hand or in a cistern; **2** *(colloquial)* to receive stolen goods; **menadahkan** to catch with or in; **tadahan** stolen goods; **penadah 1** receptacle; **2** a fence; **3** *(sport)* catcher.

tadi 1 a while ago, earlier; **majikan Anda menelepon tadi** your boss phoned earlier; **2** just past, last, this *(afternoon, evening, etc.)*; **saya ke kantor pos jam dua tadi** I went to the post office at two o'clock *(just now)*; **tadi malam** last night; **3** the one from before, earlier; **tadinya** at first, earlier.

tafsir, tafsiran **1** interpretation; **2** commentary; **3** explanation of religious scripts with further information; **men(t)afsirkan** to interpret; **penafsiran** interpretation.

tagih 1 addicted to; **2** accustomed to; **ketagihan 1** addiction; **2** addicted to; **ketagihan minuman keras** addicted to alcohol; **3** to demand payment; **uang tagihan** the money collected, the payment.

tahan 1 endure, put up with, stand; **dia tak tahan**

kelembabannya she can't cope with the humidity; **2** hold out, last; **tahan lama** durable; **bertahan** hold out; **Fretilin bertahan di gunung-gunung** the Fretilin held out on the mountains; **bertahan diri** defend yourself; **menahan 1** to hold back, to keep; **menahan diri** to control yourself; **dia ditahan semalam di rumah sakit** they kept her in hospital overnight; **2** to arrest, to detain; **polisi menahan murid-murid yang memprotes** the police detained the students who were protesting; **3** to provide support for; **mempertahankan** to defend; **mempertahankan tanah air** to defend the country; **tertahan 1** endured, stopped; **tidak tertahan** irresistible, unbearable; **2** detained; **ketahanan** staying power; **tahanan** detainee; **penahan** person who restrains or resists; **penahanan 1** restraint; **2** detention, arrest; **pertahanan** defense; **Departemen Pertahanan** Department/Ministry of Defence.

tahap phase, stage; **pada tahap ini sulit untuk mengetahui apa yang akan terjadi** at this stage it's hard to know what will happen; **bertahap-tahap** in stages.

tahi excrement, faeces; **tahi kucing!** bullshit!; **tahi lalat** mole *(on face)*.

tahu[1] know; **tahu diri** self-conscious; **ya, saya tahu** yes, I know; **siapa tahu!** who knows!, you never know!; **tahu adat** well mannered; **tahu-tahu** suddenly and unexpectedly; **setahu** as far as you know; **setahu saya, mereka sudah berangkat** as far as I know they've left; **mengetahui 1** to know, to understand; **saya sama sekali tidak mengetahui hal itu** I haven't a clue about the matter; **2** to detect, to find out; **saya sudah mengetahui ke mana dia pergi** I've found out where he went; **ketahuan** to be found out or detected; **pengetahuan** knowledge; **ilmu pengetahuan** science; **pengetahuan dasar** basic knowledge; **sepanjang pengetahuan saya** to the best of my knowledge; **berpengetahuan** knowledgeable; **memberitahu** to tell someone about something; **mengapa Anda tidak memberitahu saya tentang hal itu?** why didn't you tell

a b c d e f g h i j k l m n o p q r s t u v w x y z

a b c d e f g h i j k l m n o p q r s t u v w x y z

me about the matter?; **memberitahukan** to tell something to someone; **mengapa kamu tidak memberitahukan hal itu kepada saya?** why didn't you tell me about it?; **pemberitahuan** announcement.

tahu² tofu, bean curd; **tahu pong** deep-fried tofu, puffy tofu.

tahun year; **Tahun Baru** New Year; **tahun kabisat** leap year; **enam tahun yang lalu** six years ago; **anak berumur dua tahun** a two-year-old child; **sepanjang tahun** the whole year, all the year round; **bertahun-tahun** years and years; **menahun** chronic, lasting many years; **tahunan** **1** year; **umurnya pasti sudah tiga puluh tahunan** he's certainly in his thirties; **2** annual; **3** perennial.

tajam **1** sharp; **sudut tajam** a sharp bend; **2** incisive; **menajamkan** to sharpen; **mempertajam** to aggravate, to make worse; **ketajaman** **1** too sharp; **2** sharpness; **penajaman** **1** sharpening; **2** aggravation.

tajuk crown; **tajuk gigi** crown of a tooth; **tajuk rencana** an editorial.

tak no, not; **acuh tak acuh** indifferent; **tak akan** will not.

takar, takaran dosage, measurement; **menakar** to measure.

takdir divine decree, fate, predestination.

takhta throne.

takhyul superstition.

takjub astonished; **takjub akan** to be astonished at; **kami takjub akan keindahan alam negeri ini** we're astonished at the the beauty of this country; **menakjubkan** to astonish, to amaze; **pemandangan yang sangat menakjubkan** it was a marvellous sight; **ketakjuban** astonishment, amazement.

taksi taxi, cab; **pangkalan taksi** cab stand; **memanggil taksi** to call a cab; **naik taksi, bertaksi** to take a taxi.

taksir, menaksir to estimate, to value; **saya taksir harganya kira-kira Rp. 60.000** I estimate it will cost about Rp. 60,000; **taksiran** appraisal; **penaksir** appraiser; **penaksiran** evaluation.

taktik tactics

takut be afraid; **dia takut akan ular** he fears snakes; **mengapa Anda takut akan**

anjing? why are you afraid of dogs?; **saya takut!** I'm scared!; **saya takut terjatuh** I'm scared of falling; **menakuti 1** to frighten; **Anda menakuti saya** you gave me a fright; **2** to fear; **menakut-nakuti** to frighten, to scare off; **jangan menakut-nakuti anak kecil itu** don't frighten the little child; **menakutkan 1** to cause someone to fear; **2** to fear; **ketakutan 1** anxiety, fear; **2** frightened; **penakut** coward.

takwa devotion, piety; **bertakwa** devout, God-fearing, pious.

takzim respect.

talak divorce *(according to Islamic tradition).*

talang gutter *(on a roof).*

tali cord, rope, string.

tamah, ramah-tamah friendly; **keramah-tamahan** friendliness.

tamak 1 greed; **2** greedy; **ketamakan** greed.

taman garden, park; **taman bacaan** reading room; **taman sari** pleasure park; **taman bibit** nursery *(for plants).*

tamasya panorama, scenery, view; **bertamasya** go on an excursion; **kami bertamasya di pinggir sungai** we picnicked on the edge of the river.

tamat 1 completed, finished; **2** conclusion, end; **menamatkan** to end, to finish; **menamatkan sekolah** to finish school; **tamatan 1** graduation; **2** a graduate.

tambah 1 add; **sepuluh tambah tujuh sama dengan tujuh belas** ten plus seven is seventeen; **2** additional amount; **minta tambah lagi** I want more; **3** increasing, more; **tambah bagus** to get better; **Bahasa Indonesia saya tambah baik** my Indonesian is getting better; **bertambah** become more, increase; **cuaca bertambah baik** the weather is improving; **bertambah buruk, bertambah jelek** get worse; **segala sesuatu bertambah jelek** things are getting worse and worse; **bertambah-tambah, makin bertambah** keep increasing; **menambah** to add to, to increase; **menambah kecepatan** to increase speed; **menambahkan 1** to add; **lebih baik saya menambahkan garam sedikit** it would be better if I added a little salt; **2** to cause to increase; **tambahan 1** additional, extra;

pekerjaan rumah tambahan extra homework; **tidak ada biaya tambahan** at no extra charge; **2** furthermore; **penambahan** addition; increasing; **pertambahan** growth, increase; **pertambahan penduduk** population increase.

tambak **1** earth dam, embankment; **2** fish pond; **3** dyke.

tambal mend, patch; **tambal ban** patch a tyre; **bertambal** patched; **bertambal-tambal** patched all over; **menambal** to mend, to patch; **menambali** to apply a patch to; **menambalkan** to patch with; **tambalan** patch, repairs; **penambal** **1** someone who patches; **2** something to patch with; **penambalan** patching.

tambang mine; **tambang batu bara** coal mine; **tambang emas** gold mine; **menambang** to dig, to mine; **penambang** miner; **penambangan** mining; **penambangan emas** gold mining; **pertambangan** mining, mine workings.

tambat tether; **bertambatan** be connected with; **menambat(kan)** to tether, to tie up; **tambatan** **1** mooring buoy or tying-up post; **2** tether; **penambat** something to tie with; **penambatan** tethering, mooring; **pertambatan** ship moorings.

tambur drum; **menambur** to beat a drum.

tampak[1] appear, be visible; **tampaknya** apparently, it seems that; **menampakkan** to make visible; **penampakan** appearance.

tampak[2] measles; **sakit tampak** to have measles.

tampan **1** good-looking, handsome *(males)*; **dia kelihatan tampan** he looks handsome; **2** appropriate; **ketampanan** handsomeness.

tampang appearance of a person; **saya tidak tahan melihat tampangnya** I can't stand her/his appearance; **menampang** **1** to look at yourself in the mirror; **2** to show off; **penampang(an)** profile.

tampar slap with the hand; **tampar-menampar** to slap each other; **menampar** to beat, to slap; **Nyoman menampar anaknya** Nyoman spanked her child; **menampari** to slap repeatedly; **menamparkan** to use something to slap; **Firdaus menamparkan buku**

tulisnya ke muka Yuliana Firdaus slapped Yuliana's face with his exercise book; **tamparan** a slap; **penamparan** action of slapping.

tampil 1 step forward; **2** appear *(for example, on stage)*; **menampilkan 1** to put someone or something forward; **2** to bring forward, to show; **penampilan 1** presentation; **2** appearing.

tampung, menampung 1 to catch and hold falling water; **2** to receive, to take in; **menampung** to catch and hold falling water; **tertampung** accommodated, taken in; **penampung** thing or person that catches; **penampungan 1** collecting and saving; **2** place that collects or receives; **3** accommodating, receiving.

tamu guest, visitor; **bertamu** visit as a guest; **kami bertamu ke rumah Tante Koh pada hari Natal** we visited Auntie Koh at Christmas; **ketamuan** be visited by.

tanah 1 land; **tanah milik** land that is private property; **2** country, land; **tanah air** homeland; **bertanah air** to have a homeland; **tanah Jawa** Java; **3** ground, soil; **tanah longsor** landslide; **pertanahan** agrarian matters.

tanam, cocok tanam agriculture; **bercocok tanam** practise agriculture; **bertanam** cultivate, plant; **musim tanam** planting season; **menanam 1** to plant things; **2** to cover with earth; **anjing itu menanam tulangnya di kebun** the dog has buried its bone in the garden; **3** *(money)* to invest; **menanami** to plant; **Odo menanami kebunnya dengan bunga** Odo planted his garden with flowers; **menanamkan 1** to implant; **2** to invest; **tertanam** buried, planted; **tanaman 1** plants; **2** crop; **tanam-tanaman** all kinds of plants, vegetation; **penanam** planter; **penanaman 1** planting; **2** investment.

tanda 1 indication, mark, sign; **tanda terima** receipt; **tanda pengenal** identity card; **tanda bahaya** danger signal; **2** omen; **3** typographic symbol; **di antara tanda kutip** in inverted commas; **bertanda 1** marked, labelled; **2** signified; **menandai** to make a mark; **menandakan** to indicate, to signify; **penanda** something used as a sign or marker; **pertanda** **1** indication, sign; **2** landmark; **penandaan** giving a sign, signalling.

tandan bunch; **setandan pisang** a bunch of bananas.

tandang, bertandang visit.

tandatangan signature; **bertandatangan** signed; **menandatangani** to sign; **menandatangani sebuah cek** to sign a cheque; **penandatangan** signatory; **penandatanganan** the signing.

tanding counterpart, match, equal; **setanding** be equal to, to be comparable to; **bertanding** compete; **ikut bertanding dalam balapan sepeda** to compete in a bicycle race; **menandingi 1** to be equal or comparable to; **2** to compete with; **3** to stand up to; **menandingkan** to compare; **mempertandingkan 1** to compare with; **2** to put into combat; **tertandingi** can be equalled; **tandingan** equal, match; **pertandingan** competition, contest; **pertandingan bola basket** a basketball competition; **pertandingan di kota sendiri** home match; **Pertandingan Olimpiade** Olympic competition.

tandu litter, stretcher; **menandu** to carry on a stretcher.

tanduk horns of an animal; **bertanduk** horned.

tangan 1 arm, hand; **bersilang tangan** to fold your arms; **bergandengan tangan** holding hands; **2** thing that serves for a hand or arm; **tangan pendek** short-sleeved *(of clothing)*; **panjang tangan** person who likes to steal; **buatan tangan** handmade item; **mobil ini sudah berpindah tangan beberapa kali** this car has already had many owners; **bertangan** having hands; **bertangan kosong** empty-handed; **menangani** to handle *(work, problem, etc.)*; **tertangani** handled, taken care of; **penanganan** handling.

tangga 1 ladder; **anak tangga** rung of the ladder; **rumah tangga** household; **ibu rumah tangga** housewife; **2** staircase, stairs; **3** thing arranged in steps; **bertangga** with steps; **bertangga-tangga 1** gradually; **2** graduated, terraced.

tanggal[1] date; **tanggal berangkat** date of departure; **menentukan tanggal** to fix a date; **bertanggal** dated;

tertanggal dated; **surat Anda tertanggal 11 Maret 2000** your letter dated 11 March 2000; **penanggalan** **1** calendar; **2** dating.

tanggal², **menanggalkan** to take off; **dia menanggalkan sepatunya** he took off his shoes.

tangguh¹ **1** difficult to defeat, strong; **2** having integrity; **ketangguhan** **1** strength; **2** integrity.

tangguh² delay, postponement; **menangguhkan** to delay, to postpone something; **penangguhan** delay, postponement.

tanggul dyke, embankment.

tanggung **1** guaranteed; **2** bear, suffer; **3** responsible; **menerima tanggung jawab** to accept responsibility; **bertanggungjawab** be liable or responsible for; **dia yang harus bertanggungjawab atas keterlambatannya** he's responsible for the delay; **dia tidak bertanggung jawab** he's irresponsible; **mempertanggungjawabkan** to account for, to justify; **pertanggungjawaban** **1** responsibility; **2** justification; **menanggung** **1** to bear; **2** to be responsible for; **tanggungan** **1** burden; **2** thing or person you are responsible for; **3** bail, guarantee, security; **4** insurance; **penanggung** **1** guarantor; **2** sufferer; **3** insurer; **pertanggungan** responsibility.

tangis **1** weeping; **2** wail; **bertangis-tangisan** **1** cry for each other; **2** keep on crying; **menangis** to weep; **menangisi** to mourn, to weep for; **tangisan** crying.

tangkai **1** stalk, stem; **2** handle; **3** classifier for slim objects; **setangkai bunga mawar** a single rose.

tangkal amulet, talisman; **menangkal** to avert disaster, to avoid catastrophe; **penangkal** **1** amulet, charm; **2** preventive for; **penangkalan** preventive measure.

tangkap, menangkap **1** to catch; **Anda tak dapat menangkap saya!** you can't catch me!; **2** to arrest, to seize; **apakah Tommy sudah ditangkap?** has Tommy been arrested yet?; **3** comprehend, understand; **saya tidak dapat menangkap maksudnya** I cannot understand what he meant; **tertangkap** to get caught; **tertangkap basah** caught in the act; **dia tertangkap**

basah menerima uang semir he was caught red-handed receiving bribes; **hasil tangkapan 1** catch, haul; **2** prisoner; **penangkap** captor, trap; **penangkap ikan 1** person who catches fish; **2** fish net, trap; **alat-alat penangkap ikan** fishing tackle.

tangkas agile, deft.

tangki tank for liquids; **tangki air** water tank.

tangkis, menangkis 1 to ward off; **2** to repulse, to repel; **tangkisan** defense, resistance; **penangkis** thing that repels; **penangkisan 1** repelling; **2** warding off.

tani, orang tani farmer; **bertani** practise farming; **petani** farmer; **rumah petani** farmhouse; **pertanian** agriculture, farming; **tanah pertanian** farm, farmland.

tanjak sloping upward; **menanjak 1** to slope upward; **2** to ascend, to climb; **menanjakkan 1** to make something slope up; **2** to bring things up; **tanjakan 1** steep grade; **tanjakan terjal** a steep slope; **2** ascent, climb; **penanjakan** ascending, climbing.

tanjung cape, promontory; **Tanjung Priok** the port of Jakarta; **Tanjung Perak** Surabaya port.

tanpa without; **tanpa Anda** without you; **tanpa gula** without sugar; **tanpa perlawanan** without resistance; **tanpa prasangka** without prejudice.

tantang, menantang to challenge; **tantangan** challenge, defiance; **tantangan ide yang baru** the challenge of new ideas; **penantang** challenger; **penantangan** challenging.

tante aunt, ma'am.

tanya 1 question; **tanya-jawab** question and answer; **numpang tanya, bung!** can I ask a question, mate!; **2** inquire; **tanya saja di bagian resepsionis** you can ask at reception; **bertanya** ask a question; **dia selalu bertanya tentang hal yang aneh-aneh** he always asks about strange things; **bertanya-tanya** ask questions repeatedly; **anak itu selalu bertanya-tanya** that child's always asking questions; **bertanya-tanya dalam hati** wonder silently; **menanyai** to question repeatedly; **menanyakan** to ask about; **saya mau menanyakan hal itu kepadanya** I'm going to ask her about that matter;

mempertanyakan to question; **penanya** interrogator, questioner; **pertanyaan** question.

taoco soya bean paste.

taoge, tauge bean sprout.

tapak 1 palm of the hand, sole of the foot; **tapak sepatu** sole of a shoe; **2** footprints, tracks; **setapak 1** a footstep; **2** measure of palm or sole; **jalan setapak** footpath.

tapal paste, plaster; **tapal gigi** toothpaste; **tapal batas** border, frontier.

tapi, tetapi but.

tapis, menapis to filter, to sieve; **tapisan 1** filtered material; **2** a filter or sieve.

taplak meja tablecloth.

tara equal, match; **tidak ada taranya** have no equal; **setara 1** be equal, equivalent; **2** suited for each other.

taraf 1 class, grade, standard; **taraf hidup** living standard; **2** level; **setaraf** equal, equivalent, of the same level; **menyetarafkan 1** to make equal; **2** to consider on a par with; **3** to balance; **penarafan** ranking.

tari a dance; **menari** to dance; **menari-nari** to jump up and down for joy; **tarian** dance; **tarian Jawa** Javanese dance; **tari-tarian** dances, a variety of dances; **penari** dancer.

tarik pull; **tarik tambang** tug-of-war; **bertarik-tarikan** tug each other, tug-of-war; **menarik 1** to attract, to pull; **coba tarik perhatian mereka** try to get their attention; **apa yang menarik perhatian Anda?** what attracted your attention?; **2** to draw out, to extract; **3** to drive; **menarik bis** to drive a bus; **4** to collect; **menarik ongkos** to charge a fee; **5** attractive, interesting; **baju itu menarik** that's a nice outfit; **film kejam tidak menarik bagi saya** violent films don't appeal to me; **menarik-narik 1** to drag, to pull repeatedly; **orang tua itu menarik-narik kereta besinya** the old man dragged his iron cart along; **2** to implicate; **menariki** to pull repeatedly on; **saya menariki tali anjing itu, tapi dia tidak mau bergerak** I pulled and pulled on the dog's leash but she wouldn't move; **menarikkan** to pull or drag; **tertarik 1** extracted; **akhirnya giginya semuanya tertarik** in the end he had all his teeth pulled; **2** attracted, interested; **tampaknya dia tidak tertarik** he doesn't seem to be interested;

tarikan 1 pulling; **2** attraction; **penarik** person or thing that attracts; **penarikan 1** pulling; **2** collection.

tarip fare, tariff; **tarip angkutan** transportation cost; **tarip pesawat terbang** plane fare.

taruh place, put; **bertaruh** bet, wager; **saya berani bertaruh saya tidak akan lulus** I bet I won't pass; **bertaruhkan** to bet; **menaruh 1** to place, to put; **dia menaruh anaknya di atas tempat tidur** she placed her child on the bed; **koran itu ditaruh di mana?** where was the newspaper put?; **2** have, keep; **saya menaruh kepercayaan penuh kepada Anda** I have absolute confidence in you; **menaruhkan** to place, to put; **mempertaruhkan 1** to pawn; **2** to entrust; **3** to risk; **taruhan 1** bet; **2** stake; **3** something saved; **4** security; **pertaruhan 1** things placed somewhere; **2** bet; **3** things entrusted to a person.

tas bag, handbag, briefcase.

tata arrangement, order, system; **tata acara** agenda; **tata bahasa** grammar; **tata buku** accounting, bookkeeping; **tata cara** customs and manners; **mereka menentang tata caranya** they opposed the procedure; **tata guna** the way of using; **penatagunaan** use; **tata laksana** managing; **ketatalaksanaan** management; **tata negara** form of government, state structure **ketatanegaraan** matters relating to form of government or constitution; **tata susila** ethics, good manners; **menata** to organize, to put in order; **tatanan** arrangement, planning; **penata** person or thing that puts things in order; **penataan** ordering; structuring.

tatkala at the time, when; **tatkala itu** at that time.

tauge, taoge bean sprouts.

taut, bertaut 1 close, fit together; **cepat sekali lukanya bertaut** her wound healed really quickly; **2** become one, fuse; **bertautan** be linked with, related to; **mempertautkan, menautkan 1** to combine things; **2** to stitch a wound; **3** to attach a thing; **tautan** link; **penautan** joining up; **pertautan 1** bond, contact; **2** joining, linkage.

tawa, tertawa laugh; **Asrul tiba-tiba tertawa** Asrul suddenly burst out laughing; **tertawa terkekeh-kekeh** giggle; **menertawai, menertawakan** to laugh at; **anak-anak menertawai badut** the children laughed at the clown; **tertawaan** laughing stock; **kalau Anda berbuat begitu, Anda akan menjadi tertawaan orang** if you do that you will be the laughing stock.

tawan, menawan to capture in war; **menawan hati** fascinating; **tertawan** to be captured as a prisoner of war; **tawanan 1** military internee; **2** prisoner of war; **penawanan** capturing.

tawar[1] insipid, tasteless; **air tawar** fresh water *(not salty)*; **roti tawar** plain bread *(not sweet)*.

tawar[2] bargain; **tawar-menawar** haggling; **menawar** to bargain, to offer a price for; **menawari** to offer to a person; **Sumadi menawari Sita pekerjaan itu** Sumadi offered Sita the job; **menawarkan** to offer; **dia menawarkan buku itu kepada saya** he offered the book to me; **saya menawarkan bantuan** I offered to help; **tawaran** bid, offer; **tawaran pekerjaan** a job offer; **penawar** bargainer, bidder; **penawaran 1** bid, deal, offer; **2** bargaining.

tawon bee; **saya tersengat tawon** I was stung by a bee.

tebak, menebak to guess; **tebakan** guess; **penebak** person who guesses.

tebal 1 thick; **2** dense; **3** strong; **4** insensitive; **tebal muka** insensitive, shameless; **bertebal muka** being insensitive or shameless; **menebal** to become thick; **menebalkan 1** to thicken; **2** to reinforce; **mempertebal** to make thicker; **ketebalan** thickness; **penebalan** process of thickening; **pertebalan** thickening.

tebang, menebang to fell *(a tree)*; **tebangan** felled tree; **penebang** someone who chops down trees; **penebangan** felling of trees.

tebar, bertebar(an) scattered about, spread around; **menebari** to scatter; **dia menebari tanah kosong itu dengan benih rumput** she scattered the bare ground with grass seeds; **menebarkan 1** to spread around, to disperse; **2** to spread and throw; **tebaran**

a b c d e f g h i j k l m n o p q r s t u v w x y z

a b c d e f g h i j k l m n o p q r s t u v w x y z

litter, seed; **penebaran** dispersion, spreading.

tebing river bank or mountain side that slopes steeply; **tebing jurang** the edge of the cliff.

tebu sugar cane.

tebus, menebus 1 to redeem; **2** to make up for a wrong; **3** to fulfil; **menebus janji** to fulfil a promise; **menebus hutang** to pay a debt; **tebusan 1** ransom; **membayar uang tebusan** to pay ransom; **2** compensation; **penebus 1** ransom; **2** person who pays a ransom or compensation, redeemer; **penebusan 1** redemption; **2** compensation.

teduh 1 calm; **2** shade, shaded; **pohon yang teduh** a shady tree; **tanaman yang tumbuh di tempat teduh** shade-loving plants; **berteduh** take shelter; **tempat berteduh** shade, shelter; **berteduhkan** make a shelter; **berteduhkan daun pisang** using a banana leaf for shelter; **meneduhi** to give shade or shelter; **meneduhkan 1** to calm a person down; **2** to make sheltered or shaded; **keteduhan 1** calm, quiet; **2** shade(d), shelter(ed); **peneduhan** giving shade or shelter.

tega bear, stand; **apakah Anda tega melihat bayi menangis begitu?** can you stand to see a baby cry like that?

tegak straight up, upright; **prajurit-prajurit berdiri tegak** the soldiers stood upright; **menegak** to become upright; **menegakkan 1** to build, to erect; **mereka menegakkan suatu pondok di halaman** they erected a hut in the (house) yard; **2** to make something upright; **tegakkan itu!** put it upright!; **3** to maintain; **menegakkan hak manusia** to uphold human rights; **ketegakan** uprightness; **penegak** upholder; **penegakan** maintenance; **penegakan hukum** law enforcement.

tegang 1 taut, tight; **2** strained, tense; **perasaan tegang** a tense feeling; **hubungan yang tegang** a strained relationship; **ber(si)tegang** taking a firm stand; **menegang** to become tight, to tighten; **tiba-tiba tali itu menegang** suddenly the rope tightened; **menegangkan 1** to tighten; **2** to make tense; **mempertegang** to make more tense; **campur tangan orangtua Rini mempertegang hubungannya dengan suaminya** interference of Rini's parents made her relationship with her husband more tense; **ketegangan 1** tension; **2** strain, stress; **3** suspense; **tegangan** stress, tension.

tegap 1 robust, sturdy, well-built; **teman saya berbadan tegap** my friend has a well-built body; **2** steady and unshakeable; **menegapkan** to make sturdy, to strengthen; **ketegapan** sturdiness, firmness.

tegas 1 clear, distinct; **dengan tegas** clearly; **2** firm, resolute; **sikap yang tegas** a firm attitude; **tegasnya** explicitly, in other words, that's to say; **menegaskan 1** to clarify, to explain; **kami akan menegaskan tanggalnya** we'll confirm the date; **2** to assert, to insist; **dia menegaskan bahwa hal itu tidak diwajibkan** he emphasized that it wasn't compulsory; **ketegasan 1** firmness, resolve; **2** clearness, explicitness; **meminta ketegasan** to ask for an explanation; **penegasan** confirmation.

teguh 1 firm, solid, strong; **persetujuan yang teguh** a firm agreement; **2** tenacious; **penduduk Bali memegang teguh adat dan kebudayaannya** the Balinese hold firmly to their customs and culture; **berteguh** strengthen yourself; **meneguhkan, memperteguhkan 1** to confirm; **2** to strengthen; **keteguhan** firmness, strength; **peneguhan** strengthening.

teguk gulp, swallow; **seteguk obat batuk** a swallow of cough mixture; **meneguk** to drink, to swallow; **meneguki** to gulp down, to swallow repeatedly; **tegukan** swallow, gulp.

teh tea *(both the drink and the leaves)*; **teh botol** bottled tea; **teh es** iced tea; **teh pahit** unsweetened tea; **teh susu** tea with milk.

tekad 1 determined to do, no matter what; **2** determination, strong will; **bertekad (hati)** being determined; **saya bertekad untuk pergi** I'm determined to go.

tekan pressure; **bertekanan** exerting pressure; **menekan 1** to press, to push down; **menekan tombol** to press a

a b c d e f g h i j k l m n o p q r s t u v w x y z

button; **2** to oppress, to repress, to suppress; **3** to compress; **menekankan 1** to emphasize, to stress; **2** to press with; **kuda itu menekankan seluruh badannya ke pagar** the horse pressed its whole body up against the fence; **tertekan** oppressed, suppressed; **tekanan 1** pressure; **tekanan darah** blood pressure; **2** emphasis, stress; **3** stress, tension; **penekan** something or someone that stresses or emphasizes; **penekanan 1** pressing; **2** stressing, emphasizing.

teka-teki puzzle, riddle; **teka-teki silang** crossword puzzle; **berteka-teki** to ask riddles.

teken 1 signature; **2** sign; **meneken** to sign; **tekenan** registration for military service.

teknik technique, engineering; **teknis** technical; **teknisi** technician.

teknologi technology.

teko teapot.

teks text.

tekstil textile; **pertekstilan** matters to do with textiles and/or the textile industry.

tekuk, bertekuk bent up; **bertekuk lutut** on bended knees, surrender; **menekuk** to bend, to fold.

tekukur large turtledove.

tekun 1 diligent, persistent; **2** diligence; **dengan tekun** diligently, strenuously; **bertekun** hold fast, persevere, stick to; **menekuni** to occupy yourself diligently; **menekuni** to study or do diligently; **ketekunan 1** application, diligence; **2** perseverance.

teladan example, model; **desa teladan** model village; **mahasiswa teladan** model student; **meneladan** to emulate, to follow the example of, to imitate; **meneladani** to set an example.

telaga lake.

telah already *(used to indicate things that have happened)*; **mereka telah tinggal di Ambon** they've lived in Ambon; **telah ada rintangan kecil** there's been a slight hitch; **dia telah bekerja sebentar di sini** she worked here for a while; **setelah** after; **setelah tiba di rumah dia langsung tidur** after arriving home he went straight to sleep.

telan swallow; **menelan 1** to swallow; **menelan obat** to take medication (by swallowing); **2** to swallow up; **kuda-kuda itu tak kelihatan karena ditelan kabut** the horses were swallowed up in the fog; **tertelan 1** accidentally swallowed; **2** swallowed up; **3** be caught up; **penelanan** swallowing.

telanjang bare, naked, nude; **telanjang bulat** to be stark naked; **bertelanjang** being naked; **bertelanjang dada** bare-breasted, bare top; **menelanjangi 1** to strip a person or thing; **2** to strip a person of.

telapak 1 telapak tangan palm of hand; **telapak kaki** sole of foot; **2** bottom part.

teledor careless, negligent; **keteledoran 1** carelessness, negligence; **2** default *(on a payment etc.)*

telegraf telegraph; **telegrafis** telegrapher.

telegram telegram.

telekomunikasi telecommunications.

telekung white praying shawl for Muslim women.

telepon (telpon, tilpon *old spellings***)** telephone, **telepon genggam** mobile; **telepon umum** public telephone; **gardu telepon** telephone booth; **panggilan telepon** telephone call; **buku (petunjuk) telepon** telephone directory; **nomor telepon** telephone number; **kartu telepon** phone card; **telepon berdering-dering** the phone rang; **(ber)telepon-teleponan** telephone each other; **menelepon** to telephone; **nanti saya akan menelepon Anda kembali** I'll ring you back later; **meneleponkan** to phone on behalf of someone; **tolong teleponkan taksi** could you ring for a taxi?; **penelepon** caller; **perteleponan** relating to telecommunications.

telentang lie on your back; **tertelentang** lying on your back.

televisi television; **pidatonya akan disiarkan melalui televisi** they're televising his speech; **acara televisi** television program; **pertelevisian** relating to television.

telinga 1 ear; **telinga tipis** easily offended; **2** ear-shaped handle; **telinga panci** handle of a pan.

teliti careful, thorough; **baca petunjuk pemakaian itu dengan teliti** read the instructions carefully;

dengarkanlah dengan teliti listen carefully; **seteliti-telitinya** as carefully as possible; **meneliti 1** to examine carefully; **2** to research, to do research; **program yang diteliti dengan baik** a well-researched program; **ketelitian** carefulness; **peneliti** researcher, research worker; **penelitian** research.

teluk bay, cove, gulf.

telungkup face down; **menelungkup** to lie face down; **menelungkupi** to lie face down on; **menelungkupkan** to put a thing face down; **tertelungkup** flat on your face.

telunjuk index finger.

telur 1 egg, roe, etc.; **selusin telur** a dozen eggs; **telur asin** salted (duck) egg; **telur setengah matang** soft-boiled egg; **telur mata sapi** a fried egg, sunny side up; **2** ovum; **bertelur** lay eggs.

tema theme.

teman companion, friend; **dia teman saya yang paling akrab** he/she's my best friend; **berteman** be, make friends with *(in a general way)*; **dia berteman dengan Frank** he made friends with Frank; **menemani** to accompany; **anjing itu menemani saya** the dog keeps me company.

tembaga copper.

tembak, menembak to shoot; **menembak mati** to shoot dead; **hukuman tembak** sentence to death by firing squad; **bertembak-tembakan** shoot at each other; **perusuh-perusuh itu bertembak-tembakan** the terrorists were firing at random; **menembakkan** to fire a gun; **saya belum pernah menembakkan pistol** I have never fired a pistol; **menembaki** to fire on something over and over; **tembakan 1** shooting; **tembakan terdengar dari jauh** shooting could be heard in the distance; **2** shot; **tembak-menembak** an exchange of fire; **penembak**, marks person, sharpshooter; **penembakan** shooting.

tembakau tobacco.

tembikar 1 ceramics, glazed porcelain; **2** earthenware.

tembok brick or stone wall; **menemboki** to wall up.

tembus 1 perforate, penetrate, penetrated; **menembus 2** come out, emerge; to break through, to penetrate, to pierce; **pisau**

itu menembus perutnya the knife went into her/his stomach; **air sudah menembus bendungan** the water has broken through the dam; **menembusi** to penetrate; **tertembus** perforated, pierced; **tembusan 1** perforation; **2** penetration; **3** passage, thoroughfare; **4** carbon copy *(for sending to someone)*; **penembusan** penetration.

tempat location, place, site, spot; **tempatnya cukup besar** the place is quite big; **saya telah meletakkan tas saya di suatu tempat** I've put my bag down somewhere; **Pak Rustam tidak ada di tempat** Pak Rustam is out; **di tempat yang sejuk** in a cool place; **tempat tidur** bed; **tempat tinggal** residence; **bertempat tinggal** live, stay; **mereka tidak bertempat tinggal di sini lagi** they no longer live here; **setempat 1** local; **penduduk setempat** the locals; **perpustakaan setempat** the local library; **koran setempat** the local newspaper; **2** of the same place; **bertempat** be located; **gedung itu bertempat di Jalan Cut Mutiah** that building is on Cut Mutiah Street; **menempati** to live in, to occupy; **menempatkan** to put a thing in a certain place; **dia menempatkan cangkirnya di dapur** he placed his cup in the kitchen; **penempatan** appointment, placement.

tempayan a kind of large water jar.

tempe fermented soybean in blocks.

tempel 1 stick; **2** patch; **bertempelan** be next to, stick; **menempel 1** to adhere, to cling; **2** to patch; **menempeli 1** to make something stick to; **2** to freeload, to sponge off; **3** to cover a thing by sticking things on; **4** to bribe; **menempelkan** to stick something on; **tertempel** attached, stuck on; **tempelan 1** poster, sticker; **2** something attached to a person or thing; **penempel** instrument for sticking things up; **penempelan** attachment.

tempeleng slapping on the face or ears; **menempeleng** to slap a person on the face or ears; **tempelengan** a slap given.

tempo time.

tempuh, menempuh to go through, to undergo; **menempuh ujian** to take an exam.

a
b
c
d
e
f
g
h
i
j
k
l
m
n
o
p
q
r
s
t
u
v
w
x
y
z

tempur, bertempur clash, collide; **pesawat tempur** fighter plane; **mempertempurkan 1** to fight for; **2** to cause a person to fight for others; **pertempuran** battle, combat.

tempurung coconut shell.

temu, bertemu (dengan) meet; **saya pernah bertemu dengannya, entah di mana** I've met her before, but can't remember where; **sampai bertemu lagi** until we meet again, see you later; **kedua jalan itu bertemu di sini** the two roads meet here; **ketemu** meet; **menemui 1** to go to meet; **2** to come upon, to run into; **3** to experience; **menemukan 1** to find, to meet with; **apakah Anda sudah menemukan cincinnya?** did you find your ring?; **2** to find, to discover; **siapa yang menemukan Australia?** who discovered Australia?; **3** to invent; **Bill Gates bukan orang yang menemukan komputer** Bill Gates isn't the person who invented the computer; **mempertemukan** to bring together, to cause to meet; **penemu** discoverer, inventor; **Bill Gates bukan penemu komputer** Bill Gates isn't the inventor of the computer; **penemuan 1** invention; **2** discovery; **pertemuan** meeting.

tenaga 1 energy, power; **tenaga atom** atomic energy; **tenaga surya** solar energy; **kehabisan tenaga** exhausted, ran out of energy or power; **2** personnel, staff; **tenaga kerja** human resources, labour force; **ketenagakerjaan** matters relating to the labour force; **bertenaga 1** powerful; **2** equipped with a power source; **ditenagai** powered; **ditenagai angin** wind-powered.

tenang 1 calm, composed; **tenang sajalah!** keep calm!; **dengan tenang** calmly; **2** quiet, still; **(ber)tenang-tenang** calm down; **menenangkan** to calm somebody down; **cobalah tenangkan dia** try to calm her/him down; **ketenangan 1** calm and quiet; **2** composure; **penenang** person or thing that makes calm; **obat penenang** tranquillizer; **penenang saraf** sedative.

tenda 1 tent; **2** awning; **3** hood of a car or pedicab.

tendang, menendang 1 to kick; **Rudi menendang Heru** Rudi kicked Heru;

menendang bola to kick the ball; **2** to expel; **tertendang** kicked; **tendangan** a kick *(sport)*; **tendangan pertama** kick-off; **penendang** person who kicks.

tendensi tendency.

tengadah, menengadah to look upwards; **menengadahkan** to hold up your head, to face upwards.

tengah centre, middle; **pada tengah malam** in the middle of the night; **tengah hari** midday; **tengah-tengah** middle; **di tengah-tengah ruang** in the middle of the room; **2** among; **3** in the process of; **setengah 1** half; **telur setengah matang** soft-boiled egg; **tiga setengah** three and a half; **setengah jam** half an hour; **jam setengah lima** half past four; **setengah-setengah** half-hearted(ly); **menengah 1** to move to the centre; **2** intermediate, middle; **sekolah menengah pertama** a junior high school; **kelas menengah** middle-class; **3** average; **4** to be neutral; **menengahi** to intervene, to mediate; **penengah 1** arbitrator, mediator; **2** person with a neutral attitude; **3** thing used to separate two sections; **pertengahan** the middle; **pertengahan bulan** the middle of the month.

tenggang sensitive, thoughtful; **tenggang waktu** grace period; **bertenggang rasa** considerate; **saling bertenggang rasa** show mutual respect.

tenggara southeast; **Asia Tenggara** Southeast Asia; **Nusa Tenggara** the Lesser Sunda Islands.

tenggelam 1 be under water, sink; **dia mati tenggelam di danau** he drowned in the lake; **2** disappear, sink below the surface; **matahari tenggelam** the sun set; **menenggelamkan** to cause to sink; **musuh menenggelamkan kapal itu** the enemy sank the ship; **penenggelaman** sinking, torpedoing.

tenggorok(an) larynx, throat; **sakit tenggorokan** having a sore throat.

tengkar, bertengkar quarrel, squabble; **mereka selalu bertengkar** they're always squabbling; **saya bertengkar dengan pacar saya** I had a row with my boyfriend; **berteman kembali setelah bertengkar** they've made up after their quarrel;

mempertengkarkan to turn something into the reason for a quarrel; **kedua orang tua itu mempertengkarkan soal ayam jantan** those two old men are fighting over the cockerel; **pertengkaran** dispute, quarrel.

tengkorak cranium, skull.

tengkulak broker, middleman.

tengok, menengok 1 to view; **2** to look; **tengok kiri!** eyes left!; **3** to visit *(usually with the intention of finding out someone's condition)*; **menengokkan** to turn your head to look at a thing or person.

tenis tennis; **tenis meja** table tennis.

tentang about, regarding; **saya amat menyesal tentang hal itu** I feel awful about it; **bertentangan 1** being in contradiction, incompatible; **2** being in conflict; **menentang 1** to oppose; **saya menentang ide itu** I'm against the idea; **mereka menentang tatacaranya** they oppose the procedure; **2** to defy; **siswa-siswa berdemonstrasi menentang peraturan baru** the students are demonstrating against the new regulations; **menentangi** to fight, to go against, to oppose repeatedly; **mempertentangkan** to set against; **penentang** opponent, the opposition; **penentangan** opposition, resistance; **pertentangan 1** conflict, controversy; **2** contradiction, contrast; **3** opposition, resistance.

tentara army; **ketentaraan 1** military; **dinas ketentaraan** military duty; **2** military forces.

tenteram peaceful, quiet, tranquil; **keadaan di Timtim belum tenteram** the situation in East Timor is not yet peaceful; **menenteramkan 1** to pacify; **2** to calm, to reassure; **ketenteraman** calm, tranquillity; **penenteraman** reassurance.

tentu 1 fixed, definite, definitely, without fail; **belum tentu** not yet definite; **'apakah Anda benar-benar lebih suka yang ini?' 'tentu'** 'do you really like this better?' 'definitely'; **2** certain, sure; **saya belum tentu apakah saya akan pergi** I'm not sure if I'll go; **Eva tentu datang terlambat** Eva's bound to be late; **tentunya** certainly, of course; **menentu** certain, stabilized; **keadaan di daerah itu tidak**

menentu the situation in that region is uncertain; **menentukan 1** to determine, to establish; **menentukan tanggal** to fix a date; **pada waktu yang ditentukan** at a set time; **2** to make certain about; **menentukan tempat** to get your bearings; **tertentu** certain, sure; **jumlah tertentu** a certain number; **ketentuan** certain, certainty, clear; **berketentuan** be sure, certain; **penentu 1** person who determines; **2** thing determining; **penentuan** act of determining.

tenun weaving; **kain tenun** woven cloth; **pabrik tenun** textile factory; **bertenun, menenun** to weave; **tenunan** fabric; **penenun** weaver; **penenunan** weaving; **pertenunan 1** textile mill; **2** textiles.

teori theory; **berteori** theorize; **berteori-teorian** theorizing; **menteorikan** to theorize about.

tepat 1 exact, precise; **jam lima tepat** at five on the dot; **dia datang tepat pada waktunya** she arrived dead on time; **jumlah uang yang tepat** the right amount of money; **tepat guna** efficient; **bertepat guna** be efficient; **2** appropriate; **usaha yang tepat** an appropriate effort; **tepatnya** be exact; **bertepatan** coincide; **menepati 1** to head straight for; **2** to fulfil; **menepati janji** to keep a promise or an appointment; **menepatkan 1** to aim, to direct; **2** to adjust, to set; **menepatkan waktu jam** to adjust the clock/watch; **ketepatan** accuracy, precision; **bertepatan** coincidentally, accidentally; **Karim datang bertepatan dengan ulang tahun saya** Karim's arrival coincided with my birthday; **penepatan** adjustment, correction.

tepi border, edge, side; **di tepi danau** at the edge of the lake; **bertepi** be bordered by; **bertepikan** have something along the edge; **rok bertepikan renda** a skirt trimmed with lace; **menepi 1** to move to the side; **2** to go along the side of; **menepikan** to move a thing to one side; **mengetepikan 1** to place something at the side; **mengetepikan perahu** to moor a boat; **2** to ignore, to neglect; **tepian 1** border, edge, hem; **2** place to bathe on the riverbank.

tepuk light blow; **bertepuk tangan** applaud; **semuanya**

a b c d e f g h i j k l m n o p q r s t u v w x y z

bertepuk tangan everyone clapped; **Amir bertepuk sebelah tangan** Amir's love is unrequited; **menepuk** to clap, to slap; **menepukkan** to slap with; **tepukan 1** applause, clapping; **2** beater.

tepung flour; **tepung terigu** wheat flour; **tepung gula** icing sugar; **tepung kanji** cornstarch.

terali latticework, trellis, window bars.

terang 1 bright, clear; **sekitar jam setengah enam sudah terang** it gets light at about five thirty; **menjadi terang** become light; **2** evident; **terang-terangan, terus terang** bluntly, openly, frankly; **katakan secara terang-terangan, katakan secara terus terang** please be frank, please speak openly; **menerangi 1** to light; **2** to remove undergrowth; **menerangkan 1** to clarify, to explain; **nanti akan saya terangkan** I'll explain later; **tolong terangkan kepada saya bagaimana melakukannya** please tell me how to do it; **2** to declare, to state; **3** to illuminate, to light up; **4** to indicate; **keterangan 1** information; **saya tidak boleh mempergunakan keterangan itu** I am not allowed to use the information; **2** explanation; **menanyakan keterangan tentang** to make enquiries about; **3** official statement; **penerangan 1** providing information; **Kementerian Penerangan** the Ministry of Information; **2** explanation, clarification; **bagian penerangan, pusat penerangan** information desk, information office; **teknologi penerangan** information technology, IT; **3** illumination, lighting.

teras porch, terrace; **berteras** with a porch.

terasi shrimp or fish paste.

teratai lotus.

terbang 1 to fly; **kebanyakan burung dapat terbang** most birds can fly; **kami terbang dari Bandara Sukarno-Hatta** we flew from Sukarno-Hatta Airport; **2** disappear; **3** ascending rapidly; **beterbangan** fly in all directions *(of many things)*; **kelelawar selalu beterbangan pada waktu senja** bats always fly in all directions at dusk; **menerbangi** to fly over; **kami menerbangi Uluru** we flew over the Uluru; **menerbangkan** to make a thing fly; **penerbang** aviator, pilot; **penerbangan** flight; **penerbangan dari Darwin terlambat** the flight from Darwin is delayed.

terbit 1 emerge, rise; **matahari terbit** sunrise; **2** appear, come out; **majalah *Hai* terbit kemarin** *Hai* magazine came out yesterday; **menerbitkan** to publish; **menerbitkan majalah *Hai*** to publish *Hai* magazine; **Percetakan Universitas Oxford menerbitkan banyak buku untuk para pelajar** Oxford University Press publishes many books for students; **terbitan 1** publication; **2** edition, issue; **terbitan berseri** serial; **penerbit** publisher; **penerbitan 1** publication; **2** publishing house.

teriak, teriakan, berteriak scream, shout; **jangan berteriak** don't shout; **berteriak-teriak** keep shouting; **korban tanah longsor berteriak-teriak minta tolong** the victims of the landslide kept shouting for help; **meneriaki** to shout at; **tukang sate itu meneriaki sopir taksi yang belum membayar** the sate seller shouted at the taxi driver who hadn't paid; **meneriakkan** to yell out.

terigu wheat.

terik extreme, intense; **panas terik** burning hot, intense heat.

terima acceptance; **terima kasih** thanks, no thanks *(in Indonesian saying* ***terima kasih*** *after an offer always indicates a refusal)*; **'Anda mau minum kopi?' 'terima kasih'** 'would you like a cup of coffee?' 'no thanks'; **terima kasih banyak** thanks a lot; **surat tanda terima** receipt; **terima kasih atas** with thanks for; **terima kasih atas bantuan Anda** thanks for your help; **mengucapkan terima kasih** to say thank you; **berterima kasih** be grateful; **menerima 1** to accept, to approve; **dapat diterima** acceptable; **2** receive; **menerima surat** receive a letter; **menerimakan** to hand over; **penerima** receiver; **penerimaan 1** acceptance; **2** revenue.

terjal sheer, very steep; **lereng terjal** a steep slope.

terjemah, terjemahan translation; **menerjemahkan, menterjemahkan** to translate; **penerjemah, penterjemah** translator; **penerjemahan, penterjemahan** translating.

a b c d e f g h i j k l m n o p q r s t u v w x y z

terjun jump down; **air terjun** waterfall; **terjun ke dalam kolam renang** dive into a pool; **terjun payung** a parachute jump; **beterjunan** jump in large numbers; **menerjuni 1** to jump in(to); **2** to occupy yourself with; **menerjunkan** to cause something to dive downward; **penerjun** person who jumps; **penerjun payung** parachutist; **penerjunan** jumping; **penerjunan payung** parachuting.

terka, menerka to guess, to suspect; **Anda bisa menerka umur saya?** can you guess my age?; **terkaan** guess, supposition; **penerka** person who guesses; **penerkaan** guess, supposition.

terkam, menerkam to pounce on; **harimau menerkam turis itu** the tiger pounced on the tourist; **terkaman 1** a pounce; **2** grip of a predator.

terlanjur too late to do anything else.

terlantar neglected.

terminal terminal; **terminal dua** terminal two; **terminal komputer** computer terminal.

termometer thermometer.

termos thermos.

ternak livestock; **ternak potong** beef cattle; **beternak** breed; **peternak** breeder of livestock; **peternakan** animal husbandry; **peternakan adalah mata pencarian yang penting bagi bangsa Timor** raising livestock is an important way of making a living for the Timorese.

terobos, menerobos, menerobosi 1 to break through; **2** to cut into a queue; **penerobos 1** piercer; **2** person who cuts into a queue or breaks regulations; **penerobosan 1** a break-in; **2** a breakthrough; **terobosan** breakthrough, penetration.

terompet bugle, trumpet.

teropong 1 binoculars, telescope; **2** tube; **meneropong 1** to look through a telescope; **2** to examine, to observe carefully; **meneropongi** to focus closely on; **peneropongan 1** telescopic research; **2** study, close observation.

terowongan tunnel.

tertib 1 order; **tata tertib** law and order; **2** ceremony; **3** correct, orderly; **menertibkan 1** to put in order, to tidy up; **2** to control, to curb; **ketertiban**

1 law and order, orderliness; 2 correct conduct; **penertib** person who keeps order; **penertiban** control.

teruna 1 youth, youthful; 2 cadet.

terus 1 direct, straight; **terus saja!** straight ahead!, keep on!, continue!; **terus saja sampai di simpang empat** go straight on until you get to the crossroad; **terus terang** bluntly, frankly; **berterus terang** being straightforward; **keterusterangan** candour, straightforwardness; 2 immediately, straightaway; **setibanya di kantor dia terus menelepon majikannya** she telephoned her boss immediately she got to the office; 3 continue, keep on; **hujan terus** continuous rain; 4 next, then; **terus dia pukul anaknya** then she slapped her child; **seterusnya** from now on; **dan seterusnya mereka tidak bicara lagi** and they never spoke again; **terus-menerus** continuously, on and on; **hujan yang terus-menerus** non-stop rain; **meneruskan** 1 to continue; **akan diteruskan** to be continued; 2 to forward, to pass on; **kantor pos akan meneruskan semua surat ke alamat baru** the post office will forward all mail to the new address; **terusan** 1 continuation, sequel; 2 canal, channel; **Terusan Suez** Suez Canal; **penerus** person or thing that continues something; **penerusan** 1 continuation, sequel; 2 continuity.

tetamu guest.

tetangga neighbour; **rukun tetangga (RT)** neighbourhood association; **bertetangga** be neighbours; **bertetanggakan** have as a neighbour.

tetap constant, permanent; **rumah tetap** permanent residence; **penduduk tetap** permanent resident; **menetap** 1 to reside, to settle at; **dia menetap di Jayapura** he resides at Jayapura; 2 to stabilize; **menetapi** 1 to fulfil; **menetapi janji** to keep a promise; 2 to carry out; **menetapkan** 1 to decide, to determine; 2 to establish, to maintain; **ketetapan** 1 decision; **peraturan dan ketetapan sekolah** the school rules; 2 determination, firmness; 3 constancy, steadiness; **penetapan** 1 deciding, determining; 2 fulfilment.

tetapi, tapi but, yet; **kecil tetapi kuat** small but strong;

a b c d e f g h i j k l m n o p q r s t u v w x y z

saya akan berusaha, tetapi tidak akan mudah I'll try, but it won't be easy.

tewas killed, slain; **menewaskan** to kill, to slay; **kecelakaan itu menewaskan dua belas orang** twelve people were killed in the accident.

tiada no, not, not existing; **tiada orang** there's no-one; **dia telah tiada** she/he has died; **meniadakan, mempertiadakan 1** to abolish, to destroy; **2** to consider not to exist; **ketiadaan 1** lack, non-existence; **2** nothingness; **peniadaan 1** negation; **2** abolition.

tiang 1 mast, pillar, pole; **tiang bendera** flagpole; **2** something essential; **meniangi** to provide with poles or supports.

tiap 1 each, every; **2** each time; **setiap, tiap-tiap** each and every; **(tiap-)tiap kali** each and every time; **ada sesuatu untuk setiap anak** there's something for each and every child.

tiarap face downward; **bertiarap** lie prone; **meniarap** to lie face down; **meniarapkan** to put something face down; **tertiarap** fallen face down.

tiba arrive; **tiba di Jakarta** arrive at Jakarta; **kereta api itu tiba lima menit yang lalu** the train arrived five minutes ago; **pada saat itu polisi tiba** at that point the police arrived; **tiba-tiba** suddenly, unexpectedly; **secara tiba-tiba** all of a sudden; **Asrul tiba-tiba mulai tertawa** Asrul suddenly started to laugh; **tiba-tiba lampu-lampu padam** suddenly the lights went out; **tiba-tiba terbakar** to burst into flames; **setibanya** upon arrival.

tidak no, not, nothing *(with verbs, adjectives and adverbs)*; **tidak besar** not large; **tidak cocok** not suitable; **tidak sekarang** not now; **dia tidak beli apa-apa** she bought nothing; **saya tidak tahu** I don't know; **Supri tidak menelepon** Supri didn't phone; **tidak sendirian!** not all alone!; **sama sekali tidak** not at all; **saya harap tidak** I hope not; **kami pun tidak dapat pergi** we can't go either; **kalau tidak** if not, or else; **ayo cepatlah, kalau tidak kita akan ketinggalan kereta api itu** hurry up, or else we'll miss that train; **tidak ada yang baru** nothing's new; **tapi tidak ada apa-apa di situ** but there was nothing there; **saya tidak**

melihat apa-apa I saw nothing; **tidak ada apa-apa yang terjadi** there's nothing happening; **tidak adil** unjust, unfair; **ketidakadilan** injustice; **tidak cocok** not fitting, incompatible; **ketidakcocokan** incompatibility; **tidak jelas** not clear; **ketidakjelasan** obscurity; **tidak jujur** dishonest; **ketidakjujuran** dishonesty; **setidak(-tidak)nya 1** at the least; **2** in any case.

tidur sleep, go to sleep; **pergi tidur** go to bed; **tidur sebentar** have a nap; **tidur nyenyak** be fast asleep, sleep soundly; **tidur ayam**, doze, nap, sleep lightly; **Sutanto sedang tidur** Sutanto's sleeping; **(ber)tiduran** lie down; **menidurkan 1** to put to bed; **menidurkan anak-anak** to put the children to bed; **2** to lay something down; **tertidur** to fall asleep; **saya tertidur waktu mendengarkan pidato itu** I fell asleep while listening to the speech.

tiga three; **tiga belas** thirteen; **tiga puluh** thirty; **simpang tiga** three-way intersection; **membagi tiga** to divide into three; **bertiga** group of three, do in threes; **kami bertiga mau pergi nonton** the three of us are going to a movie; **bertiga-tiga** do something three at a time; **mereka masuk bertiga-tiga** they went in three at a time; **ketiga 1** third; **di lantai (ke)tiga** on the third floor; **Dunia Ketiga** the Third World; **2** all three; **ketiga anak itu membeli baju yang sama** the three boys bought the same shirt; **(ke)tiga-tiganya** all three; **sepertiga** a third; **dua pertiga** two-thirds.

tikai difference; **bertikai** have a difference of opinion, to quarrel; **mempertikaikan** to make something the subject of a quarrel; **pertikaian** controversy, disagreement.

tikam wound by stabbing; **bertikam-tikaman, tikam-menikam** stab each other; **menikam** to stab; **menikamkan** to stab with; **tikaman** a jab or stab; **penikam 1** person who stabs; **2** thing you stab with; **penikaman** a stab, a stabbing.

tikar a woven mat; **bertikarkan** to use something as a mat.

tiket ticket.

tikung, menikung to turn right or left; **tikungan** bend or curve.

tikus mouse, rat.

a b c d e f g h i j k l m n o p q r s t u v w x y z

a b c d e f g h i j k l m n o p q r s t u v w x y z

tilam mattress, something to sleep on, **bertilam** have something to sleep on; **bertilam pasir** sleep on the sand, to be homeless.

tilgram telegram; **menilgram** to send a telegram.

tilik visit; **menilik 1** to consider; **menilik permintaan Anda** considering your request; **2** to inspect, to supervise; **pekerjaannya menilik sekolah-sekolah swasta** her/his job is inspecting private schools; **tilikan 1** examination, observation; **2** control, supervision; **penilik** inspector, supervisor; **penilik sekolah** school inspector; **penilikan 1** control, supervision; **2** observation.

tim team.

timah tin; **timah hitam** lead; **timah daun** tin foil.

timba bucket, well dipper; **menimba** to draw water from a well.

timbal balancing; **bertimbal-balik** from both sides; mutual.

timbang weighing; **timbang terima** transfer; **menimbangterimakan** to hand over, to transfer; **setimbang 1** in balance; **2** in proportion; **kesetimbangan** balance, harmony; **bertimbang** to be of equal importance or weight; **timbang-menimbang** to consider each other's feelings; **menimbang 1** to weigh; **menimbang beras** to weigh rice; **2** to consider, to take into account; **mempertimbangkan** to consider; **mempertimbangkan segala sesuatu** all things considered; **timbangan** set of scales, weights; **penimbang** set of scales; **penimbangan** act of weighing; **pertimbangan 1** judgement, opinion; **2** consideration; **3** review *(of films etc.)*.

timbul 1 float to the surface; **2** appear, emerge; **menimbulkan 1** to make something come to the surface; **2** to cause a thing to happen, to give rise to; **air kotor itu menimbulkan berjangkitnya penyakit kolera** the contaminated water caused an outbreak of cholera; **menimbulkan rasa kecewa** give rise to disappointment.

timbun heap, pile; **bertimbun** in piles; **bertimbun-timbun** in heaps, piled up; **menimbuni** to bury, to fill up **menimbun(kan) 1** to heap things up, **2** to accumulate, to hoard; **timbunan** sizeable heap; **penimbun** hoarder; **penimbunan 1** accumulation, piling up; **2** hoarding; **3** reclaiming land (from the sea, for example) by piling up earth.

timpa, menimpa 1 to fall on; **waktu gunung api meledak batu-batu besar menimpa desa itu** when the volcano erupted large stones rained down on that village; **2** to descend upon, to strike down; **menimpakan 1** to cause things to fall on; **2** to blame; **tertimpa, ketimpa** struck down; **timpaan** burden, load, weight.

timpang unstable, unbalanced; **berjalan timpang** walk with a limp; **ketimpangan 1** imbalance; **2** lameness; **3** one-sidedness, partiality.

timun, ketimun, mentimun cucumber.

timur east; **Timur Jauh** the Far East;**Timur Tengah** Middle East; **timur laut** northeast; **di bagian timur laut Australia** in northeast Australia; **di sebelah timur** in the east; **Timor Timur** East Timor; **angin timur** an east wind; **ketimuran** eastern, Asian.

tindak act, action; **bertindak 1** take steps, measures; **2** act; **ia bertindak seketika** she acted at once; **menindak** to take action against; **Amerika Serikat suka menindak musuhnya** the United States tends to take action against its enemies; **tindakan 1** measure, step; **tindakan darurat** emergency measures; **2** action; **penindakan** taking measures.

tindas, menindas to oppress, to suppress; **penindas** oppressor; **penindasan** oppression.

tindih, bertindih-tindihan to lie on each other; **pemain sepak bola bertindih-tindihan di lapangan** the soccer players lay all over each other on the field; **anak-anak anjing itu tidur bertindih-tindihan** the puppies lie sleeping in a heap; **ketindihan** be crushed under; **ketika terjadi gempa bumi di Turki banyak orang tertindih bata** many people were crushed under bricks during the earthquake in Turkey.

tinggal 1 live, stay; **saya tinggal sendirian di rumah itu** I live by myself in that house; **Trihatmojo tinggal di Cirebon** Trihatmojo lives in

Cirebon; **2** remain, stay; **saya akan tinggal di sini** I'll stay here; **berapa lama Anda akan tinggal?** how long are you staying?; **3** be left, remaining; **nasinya tinggal sedikit** there's only a little rice left; **uang kita tinggal berapa?** how much money do we have left?; **4** all that is left, all that remains; **tinggal tulang** extremely thin; **tinggal landas** take off; **meninggal, meninggal dunia** to die; **meninggali 1** to live in, to stay at; **saya takut meninggali rumah berhantu itu** I'd be afraid to stay in that haunted house; **2** to bequeath, to leave in a will; **meninggalkan** to leave behind; **tertinggal** left behind; **ketertinggalan** fact of having fallen behind; **ketinggalan 1** be accidentally omitted, left out; **2** be unintentionally left behind; **kuncinya ketinggalan** he unintentionally left his keys behind; **peninggalan 1** estate, inheritance; **2** relic, remains.

tinggi high, tall; **pada kecepatan yang tinggi** at high speed; **tinggi saya 1,7 meter** I'm 1.7 metres tall; **tinggi hati** proud, snobbish; **tembok itu tinggi sekali** the wall is very high; **matahari sudah tinggi** it's already late in the morning; **pejabat tinggi** senior official; **tingginya** height; **tingginya hampir dua meter** he's almost two metres tall; **setinggi-tingginya** the highest possible; **meninggi 1** to rise higher and higher; **pesawat terbang makin meninggi** the plane flew higher and higher; **2** to boast; **meninggikan 1** to heighten, to raise; **2** to increase; **mereka sudah meninggikan harga** they've already increased the price; **mempertinggi 1** to make something higher; **mempertinggi semangat** to boost somebody's morale; **2** to enhance; **ketinggian 1** too high; **2** elevated place; **3** altitude, height; **4** boastful; **petinggi** persons in high position; **peninggian** enhancement, raising; **tertinggi** maximum, the highest; **kecepatan yang tertinggi** the maximum speed; **keuntungan yang tertinggi** maximum profits.

tingkah 1 action, behaviour; **2** whim; **tingkah laku** behaviour.

tingkat 1 floor, storey; **rumah dua tingkat, rumah bertingkat dua** a two-storey house; **2** rung, step;

3 degree, level; **tingkat tinggi** high level; **setingkat 1** one level; **2** of the same level; **bertingkat-tingkat 1** multi-storeyed; **gedung bertingkat-tingkat** a multi-storeyed building; **2** with many consecutive levels; **meningkat** to increase, to rise; **panasnya meningkat** the temperature rose; **meningkatkan 1** to increase, to step up; **2** to upgrade; **mutu pendidikan harus ditingkatkan** the quality of education must be improved; **tingkatan 1** floor, storey; **2** class, level; **3** phase, stage; **peningkatan 1** raising, upgrading; **2** increase, rise; **peningkatan perang di Bosnia** escalation of the conflict in Bosnia.

tinja human waste matter, sewage.

tinjau be on your guard; **tinjau-meninjau** observe each other; **meninjau 1** to observe, to watch; **2** to consider, to view; **3** to observe, to survey; **peninjau** observer; **peninjauan** observation; **tinjauan 1** observation; **2** contemplation, consideration.

tinju 1 fist; **dia memukulkan tinjunya di atas meja** he banged his fist on the table; **2** *(sport)* boxing; **pertandingan tinju** boxing match; **bertinju, meninju** to be engaged in a fist fight, to punch at; **bertinju-tinjuan, tinju-meninju 1** to punch each other; **2** to engage in a fist fight; **petinju** boxer; **pertinjuan** matters relating to boxing.

tinta ink.

Tionghoa Chinese; **bangsa Tionghoa** the Chinese people; **Tionghoa peranakan** Indonesian Chinese; **Tionghoa totok** China-born Chinese; **ketionghoaan** Chineseness *(note that for some time Cina replaced Tionghoa, but there is now a movement back to Tionghoa as Cina is felt to be less polite).*

Tiongkok China; **bangsa Tiongkok** the Chinese nation; **daratan Tiongkok** the Chinese mainland.

tipes typhoid.

tipex correction fluid.

tipis 1 thin; **2** slight, very small; **3** fine; **menipis 1** to become thin; **2** to become less; **menipiskan 1** to make thin; **2** to dilute; **3** to decrease, to reduce.

tipu deceit, fraud, trick; **menipu** to deceive; **tipuan** deceit; **penipu** deceiver,

a b c d e f g h i j k l m n o p q r s t u v w x y z

impostor; **penipuan** deception.

tirai 1 blinds, curtain; 2 partition, screen; **tirai bambu** the bamboo curtain; **tirai besi** the iron curtain; 3 backdrop.

tiram oyster.

tiri step-; **adik tiri, kakak tiri** stepbrother or stepsister; **anak tiri** stepchild; **Ayah tiri, Bapak tiri** stepfather; **Ibu tiri** stepmother.

tiru, meniru to imitate; **jangan coba meniru saya!** don't try to copy me!; **menirukan** to imitate; **dia pintar sekali menirukan suara aneka burung** she/he's very clever at imitating all kinds of bird calls; **tiruan 1** copy, imitation; **2** counterfeit, forgery; **peniru** imitator; **peniruan** imitation.

titel degree, title; **bertitel** to have a degree or title.

titi, titian wooden or bamboo footbridge; **meniti** to walk on something long and narrow and elevated.

titik 1 drop; **titik air mata** teardrop; **2** full-stop, full point; **titik dua** colon; **titik beku** freezing point; **titik cair** melting point; **titik berat** centre of gravity; **menitikberatkan 1** to emphasize, to stress; **2** to count heavily on; **penitikberatan** stressing; **bertitik 1** to drip; **2** to have a full-stop; **bertitik-titik** dotted; **menitikkan** to cause something to drip; **menitikkan air mata** to cry.

titip, menitipkan to temporarily entrust something to a person; **menitipi** to entrust to someone; **titipan 1** goods left; **2** deposit; **penitip (uang)** depositor; **penitipan 1** depositing; storage place.

tiup to blow; **bertiup** blow; **angin bertiup keras sekali** the wind is blowing really hard; **meniup 1** to blow; **2** to blow air into or through; **meniup balon** to blow up a balloon; **meniupi** to blow on a thing; **tiupan** blast of wind, blowing; **peniup** person who blows; **peniup suling** flute player.

tobat repentance; **bertobat** repent; **menobatkan** to get a person to repent, to bring a person to his/her senses.

todong, tukang todong a person who points a weapon at another person; **menodong, menodongkan** to threaten by pointing a weapon; **todongan** a threat with a weapon; **penodong** hold-up person; **penodongan** hold-up.

tok *(colloquial)* just, only; **Anda hanya bisa bicara tok!** you're all talk!

toke, tokek 1 large gecko lizard; **2** sound of the gecko.

toko shop, store; **pelayan toko** shop assistant; **pemilik toko** shopkeeper; **pertokoan 1** shop matters; **2** shopping plaza.

tokoh 1 figure, form, shape; **2** prominent person; **tokoh terkenal** a famous figure; **3** character in a story.

tolak, bertolak 1 depart, leave; **2** take as a starting point; **menolak 1** to repel; **2** to reject, to refuse; **saya menolak** I refused; **dia menolak untuk menolong** he refuses to help; **saya tidak dapat menolak** I can't resist; **tolakan** a reject; **barang tolakan** rejected goods; rejects; **penolak 1** rejecter; **2** repellent; **penolak bisa** antidote; **penolakan 1** refusal, rejection; **2** warding off.

toleh, menoleh to turn your head to look toward; **saya menoleh untuk melihat orang yang berteriak** I turned to see the person shouting.

tolol simple-minded, stupid; **dia agak tolol** he's a bit dumb; **ketololan** foolishness, stupidity; **si tolol** moron.

tolong 1 help; **minta tolong** to ask for help; **2** please; **tolong bukakan pintu itu** can you open the door please?; **bertolong-tolongan, tolong-menolong** give mutual assistance, help one another; **menolong** to aid, to assist, to help; **apakah saya dapat menolong Anda?** can I help you?, do you need a hand?; **dia tak dapat menolong** she couldn't help; **tolonglah bantu saya memindahkan meja ini** please give me a hand to move the table; **menolongi** repeatedly help with; **tertolong 1** helped; **2** can be helped; **penolong 1** helper; **2** rescuer; **pertolongan** aid, help; **pertolongan pertama** first-aid.

tomat tomato; **saus tomat** tomato sauce.

tombak 1 lance, spear; **2** measure of length, approximately 3.6 metres; **bertombak** armed with a spear; **menombak** to spear.

tombok *(colloquial)* additional amount of money, pay extra; **menomboki** to add extra money to, to pay extra.

tombol **1** knob; **2** button, switch.

tong barrel, cask; **tong sampah** rubbish bin; **setong bir** a barrel of beer.

tongkang a barge *(with a flat bottom)*.

tongkat walking stick; **tongkat hoki** a hockey stick; **memakai tongkat ketiak** to be on crutches; **bertongkat** use a cane; **bertongkatkan** to rest on; **menongkat** to raise high; **menongkatkan** **1** to hold up with something; **2** to raise.

tongkrong, menongkrong **1** to squat; **2** to sit around doing nothing, to hang out; **3** idle, not in use.

tonjol, bertonjol bulge; **sakunya bertonjol dengan uang** his pocket is bulging with money; **bertonjol-tonjol** bumpy; **jalan yang bertonjol-tonjol tidak baik untuk mobil Anda** the bumpy road is no good for your car; **menonjol** **1** to jut out, to stick out; **2** to be conspicuous; **kepintarannya menonjol sekali** his cleverness is very conspicuous; **kemenonjolan** conspicuousness; **menonjolkan** **1** to stick something out; **orang tidak boleh menonjolkan kepalanya dari jendela mobil** people must not stick out their heads from the car's window; **2** to show off; **orang itu suka sekali menonjolkan kekayaannya** that person likes very much to show off his/her wealth.

tonton, (me)nonton **1** to watch for entertainment; **saya pernah menonton film itu** I had seen the film before; **2** to go to the movies; **mereka pergi nonton** they've gone to the movies; **menontoni** to look at; **menontonkan, mempertontonkan** **1** to exhibit, to show; **2** to play, to perform; **tontonan** **1** performance, show; **2** spectacle; **tontonan kembang api** a fireworks display; **penonton** **1** spectator; **2** onlooker.

topan hurricane, typhoon.

topeng mask; **bertopeng** **1** wear a mask; **2** put on a front; **bertopengkan** use something as a cover-up; **mempertopeng** **1** to hide, to mask; **2** to use as a mask.

topi hat; **bertopi** to wear a hat.

toserba (toko serba ada) department store.

total **1** total; **2** completely; **habis total** completely finished; **men(t)otalkan** to add up, to total; **ketotalan** totality.

totok 1 full-blooded; **2** a full-blooded Chinese; **3** newcomer.

tradisi tradition; **tradisional** traditional.

traktir, mentraktir to treat; **ayo traktir saya kali ini** come on, you treat me this time; **traktiran** treating.

traktor tractor.

trampil skilful; **ketrampilan** skill.

transaksi transaction.

transfusi transfusion.

transisi transition.

transistor transistor.

transkrip transcript.

transmigran transmigrant, someone who has been settled in another region under the government program.

transportasi transportation.

trem tram.

trendi trendy.

tri tri *(three)*, prefix used in some compound words.

triwulan quarterly.

trompet trumpet.

tropis tropical.

truk truck.

tua 1 old; **kuda tua** an old horse; **kaum tua** old people, the elderly; **2** pure; **emas tua** pure gold; **setua** of the same age, as old as; **menua 1** to age, to become old; **2** to ripen; **menuakan 1** to let grow older, to ripen; **2** to make or consider a person the head; **ketua** chairman; **ketuaan** too old; **penuaan** ageing.

tuah 1 good luck, good fortune; **2** magic power, **3** honour, prestige, respect; **bertuah 1** lucky; **2** bring good luck; **3** have magic power; **ketuahan** be endowed with special luck or power; **petuah** advice from parents or older people to the young.

tuai, menuai to harvest rice with a small knife called *ani-ani*; **penuai** knife for harvesting rice; **penuaian** rice harvesting.

tuak fermented palm wine.

tuan, Tn Mr, sir *(mainly used for non-Indonesians)*; **Tuan Henderson** Mr Henderson; **apakah tuan sudah siap?** are you ready, sir?; **tuan besar** boss; **bertuan 1** to have a master; **2** to use the term of address '*tuan*'.

tuang, menuang to pour; **menuang kopi ke gelas** to

a b c d e f g h i j k l m n o p q r s t u v w x y z

pour coffee into a glass; **menuangi** to pour into; **menuangi teko dengan air panas** to pour hot water into a teapot; **menuangkan 1** to pour out; **saya menuangkan teh ke cangkirnya** I poured the tea into her/his cup; **2** to cause to pour out; **3** to cast, to mould; **tuangan 1** something poured out; **2** a mould used in casting; **penuangan** casting, moulding, pouring.

tubruk, bertubrukan collide; **hampir saja saya bertubrukan dengan orang itu** I very nearly collided with that person; **menubruk 1** to lunge at; **2** to collide, to run into; **mobil itu menubruk tiang lampu** the car ran into the lamp-post; **menubrukkan** to make something crash into; **ketubruk, tertubruk 1** slammed into; **2** struck; **tubrukan 1** collision, crash; **2** impact; **penubrukan** colliding, crashing.

tubuh body; **bertubuh** having a body; **bertubuh langsing** of slender build; **bersetubuh** have sexual intercourse.

tuduh, menuduh to accuse; **polisi menuduh mereka menghasut kerusuhan** the police accused them of starting the riot; **tertuduh** the accused; **tuduhan** accusation, charge; **penuduh 1** prosecutor; **2** accuser, plaintiff; **penuduhan** accusation.

tudung 1 cover, veil; **tudung lampu** lampshade; **2** sun hat; **bertudung 1** covered, **2** use a veil; **bertudungkan** covered with; **menudungi** to cover up carefully; **menudungkan** to use for a cover; **tertudung** covered; **penudung** cover; **penudungan** covering.

tugas 1 duty; **malam ini dia bebas tugas** he's off-duty tonight; **2** assignment, order; **3** job, task; **tugas ini tidak gampang** it's not an easy job; **dia melakukan tugasnya dengan baik** she made a good job of it; **bertugas** be on duty, have as a duty; **bertugas malam** on night duty; **menugasi** to give an assignment to; **menugaskan 1** to assign as a task; **2** to assign a person to a task; **petugas 1** official; **2** employee; **penugasan** giving an assignment.

tugu 1 column, pillar, post; **2** monument; **Tugu Nasional** the National Monument.

Tuhan God; **bertuhan 1** believe in God; **2** have a God; **bertuhankan** have as a God; **mempertuhankan** to

a b c d e f g h i j k l m n o p q r s t u v w x y z

consider as a God; **ketuhanan** deity, divinity; **berketuhanan** devout.

tuil a lever; **menuil** to lever up.

tuju, setuju 1 agree; **saya tidak setuju** I don't agree; **2** like; **bersetuju 1** having the same aim or purpose; **2** agree; **menyetujui** to agree to, to approve of; **bertujuan 1** have as a purpose; **2** head for, go in a particular direction; **bertujuan ke Menteng** heading for Menteng; **menuju 1** to go in the direction of; **dia menuju rumah pacarnya** he headed for his girlfriend's house; **2** to aim, to strive; **menujukan 1** to point with; **2** to aim; **tujuan 1** aim, objective, purpose; **mencapai tujuannya** to achieve an aim; **tujuan kita ialah mengontrol polusi** our aim is to control pollution; **2** destination, direction; **tujuan kita ialah Ujung Pandang** our destination is Ujung Pandang; **persetujuan 1** agreement, treaty; **2** approval.

tujuh seven, seventh; **di lantai tujuh** on the seventh floor; **tanggal tujuh Maret** the seventh of March; **tujuh belas** seventeen; **tujuh puluh** seventy; **bertujuh** be in a group of seven; **bertujuh-tujuh** seven at a time; **ketujuh 1** seventh; **anak ketujuh** the seventh child; **2** all seven; **ketujuh anak itu** the seven children.

tukang skilled labourer or crafts person; **tukang las** welder; **tukang sate** satay seller; **tukang sayur** vegetable vendor; **bertukang**, **menukang** be a skilled worker; **pertukangan** trade.

tukar exchange; **tukar cincin** engagement; **upacara tukar cincin** engagement ceremony; **bertukar** change; **bertukar pikiran** to swap ideas; **bertukar kereta** change trains; **bertukar pakaian** to change clothes; **bertukar-tukar 1** alternating; **2** continually changing; **bertukar-(tukar)an** mutually exchange; **tukar-menukar** to exchange with each other; **menukar 1** to change; **kalau ini tidak pas, boleh ditukar?** can I change this if it doesn't fit?; **mereka saling menukar tempatnya** they changed places; **2** to barter, to exchange; **dia menukar sepedanya dengan sebuah komputer** he's swapped his bike for a computer; **menukarkan** to give in exchange; **menukarkan cek**

a b c d e f g h i j k l m n o p q r s t u v w x y z

to cash a cheque; **bolehkah saya menukarkan kemeja ini dengan yang lebih kecil?** can I exchange this shirt for a smaller one?; **mempertukarkan 1** to barter; **2** to alternate; **penukar uang** money changer; **penukaran** exchange; **pertukaran 1** exchange; **2** change.

tulang bone; **tulang punggung** backbone, spinal column; **bertulang** having bones, bony.

tular, menular contagious, infectious; **menulari** to contaminate, to infect, to spread; **menularkan** to cause to spread; **ketularan** infected; **dia ketularan demam berdarah** he's caught dengue fever; **penular** infectious agent; **penularan** infecting, spreading.

tulen genuine, pure; **ketulenan** authenticity, genuineness.

tuli deaf; **bisu tuli** deaf-mute; **menulikan** to make deaf, to deafen.

tulis write; **tulislah sebuah kalimat dalam bahasa Indonesia** write a sentence in Indonesian; **bertulisan** written on with a notice; **papan itu bertulisan 'dilarang masuk'** the board said 'no entry'; **bertuliskan** inscribed with; **tulis-menulis** correspondence, writing; **menulis** to write; **saya menulis surat kepada Heather kemarin** I wrote to Heather yesterday; **menulisi 1** to write on; **2** to doodle on; **menuliskan 1** to write down; **2** to write with; **tulisan 1** something written; **tulisan tangan** handwriting; **2** an article, writing; **penulis** writer; **penulisan** process of writing.

tulus honest, sincere; **setulus-tulusnya** as sincerely as possible; **ketulusan** honesty, sincerity.

tumbang fall down with a crash; **banyak pohon yang tumbang karena topan** many trees fell down because of the typhoon; **bertumbangan** to fall *(in large numbers)*; **menumbangkan 1** to cause to come crashing down; **2** to overthrow; **penumbang rekor** record breaker *(sport)*; **penumbangan** causing something to crash down; **pertumbangan** collapse; **pertumbangan bursa** stockmarket crash.

tumbuh 1 grow; **pohon mangga tumbuh di Queensland** mango trees grow in Queensland; **tumbuh luas** grow extensively;

menumbuhluaskan 1 to make flourish; **2** to appear from below; **bertumbuhan** grow like mushrooms; **menumbuhi** to sprout up over; **menumbuhkan 1** to make grow; **2** to cause to emerge, to sprout; **tumbuh-tumbuhan** all kinds of plants, vegetation; **penumbuhan 1** the act of growing; **2** emergence; **pertumbuhan** development, growth.

tumbuk pound; **kopi tumbuk** ground coffee; **bertumbuk 1** fight; **2** slam against each other; **3** coincide; **bertumbukan** collide, slam against each other; **menumbuk 1** to crush, to pound; **2** to strike; **3** to crash into.

tumit heel; **sepatu bertumit tinggi** high-heeled shoes.

tumor tumour.

tumpah spilled; **susunya tumpah** he spilled the milk (unintentionally); **hati-hati supaya tidak tumpah** watch you don't spill it; **menumpahi** to spill on; **saya telah menumpahi karpet dengan anggur** I've spilled wine on the carpet; **menumpahkan 1** to cause to spill; **menumpahkan darah** to spill/shed blood; **2** to spill out; **ketumpahan** have something spilled on it; **tumpahan** something spilled.

tumpang join with others; **(me)numpang 1** to go by, to ride in/on; **Fahmi numpang kereta api pulang ke Bandung** Fahmi went home to Bandung by train; **2** to stay with; **sekarang saya numpang di rumah Suminah** at present I'm staying at Suminah's place; **numpang alamat** to use someone else's address; **3** may I, please; **numpang tanya?** may I ask a question?; **menumpangi** to be a passenger in, to ride in; **tumpangan 1** lodging; **2** fare, passenger; **3** inclusion; **penumpang 1** passenger; **2** boarder; **berpenumpang** having passengers; **penumpangan** place to stay.

tumpas annihilated, destroyed, exterminated; **menumpas** to annihilate, to destroy; **penumpasan** annihilation, destroying, extermination.

tumpu 1 foothold, footing, support; **2** springboard; **bertumpu 1** rest on; **2** have support; **menumpukan** to provide support for; **tumpuan 1** pillar, prop, support; **2** stepping stone; **penumpu** support.

a b c d e f g h i j k l m n o p q r s t u v w x y z

a b c d e f g h i j k l m n o p q r s t u v w x y z

tumpuk heap, pile, stack; **bertumpuk-(tumpuk) 1** be in piles, stacks; **2** in groups; **menumpuk** to accumulate, to pile up; **kalau Anda tidak rajin nanti pekerjaannya akan menumpuk** if you're not industrious the work will pile up; **menumpuki** to pile up on top of; **dia menumpuki nasinya dengan lauk-pauk** she piled side dishes on top of her rice; **menumpukkan 1** to pile up; **mereka menumpukkan mayat-mayat** they piled up the bodies; **2** to accumulate, to hoard; **tertumpuk 1** piled up; **2** hoarded; **tertumpuk** accidentally piled on; **tumpukan 1** heap, stack; **tumpukan yang terpisah** separate pile; **tumpukan piring** a stack of plates; **2** group; **penumpukan** accumulation, hoarding.

tumpul 1 blunt, dull; **2** dull, obtuse, stupid; **menumpulkan** to blunt; **kayu keras itu menumpulkan gergaji** the hard wood blunted the saw; **ketumpulan** bluntness, dullness.

tuna– prefix generally indicating a lack; **orang-orang tunawisma** the homeless; **tunabusana** naked, without clothing; **tunanetra** blind; **tunakarya** unemployed.

tunai, uang tunai cash; **membayar tunai** to pay cash; **menunaikan** to carry out, to fulfil; **penunaian 1** cash payment, settlement; **2** fulfilment, **penunaian** fulfilment, payment, settlement.

tunang, bertunangan be betrothed, engaged; **mereka bertunangan** they're engaged; **mempertunangkan, menunangkan** to arrange an engagement; **tunangan** fiance; **pertunangan** engagement *(to marry)*; **cincin pertunangan** engagement ring.

tunas bud, shoot; **bertunas** bud, sprout.

tunda, menunda 1 to delay, to postpone; **keputusan itu ditunda sampai besok** the decision has been delayed until tomorrow; **2** to adjourn; **tertunda-tunda** delayed repeatedly; **penundaan** adjournment, postponement.

tunduk 1 be bent down; **2** be bent in submission; **anak-anak harus tunduk pada perintah orang tua** children have to obey their parents' instructions; **menunduk** to bow the head; **menundukkan 1** to cause to bow; **menundukkan kepala** to bow the head; **2** to cause someone to submit; **tertunduk** bent, bowed; **ketundukan 1** submision; **2** loyalty, obedience; **penundukan 1** submission, subjection; **2** subjugation.

tunggal just one, one and only one, solo; **anak tunggal** an only child; **keluarga yang berorang tua tunggal** a single-parent family; **bermain tunggal** to play solo; **penyanyi tunggal, pemain tunggal** soloist; **pertandingan tunggal wanita** the women's singles *(in tennis)*; **tunggal ika** unity; **Bhineka Tunggal Ika** Unity in Diversity *(the Indonesian slogan)*; **ketunggalikaan** singleness, unity.

tunggang, menunggang to mount and ride; **dia menunggang kerbaunya** he's riding his buffalo; **menunggangi 1** to ride; **2** to get a free ride on, to be a freeloader; **tunggangan 1** animal for riding, mount; **2** carriage, vehicle; **penunggang** passenger, rider; **penunggang kuda** horse rider.

tunggu wait; **tunggu saya!** wait for me!; **tunggu tanda!** wait for the signal!; **kamar tunggu** waiting room; **harap tunggu sebentar** wait a moment, please; **menunggu 1** to wait for; **dia membiarkan saya menunggu** she kept me waiting; **2** to look forward to; **menunggu-nunggu** to look forward to quite anxiously; **menunggui 1** to guard, to watch over; **jangan coba pegang anjing yang menunggui tulangnya** don't try to pet that dog that's guarding its bone; **2** to nurse, to take care of; **menunggukan** to watch over for someone; **penunggu 1** guard, watchman; **2** attendant; **3** guardian spirit.

tunjang to receive support or subsidy; **menunjang 1** to support; **untuk menunjang beton ini, tiangnya kurang banyak** there aren't enough pillars to support this concrete slab; **2** to support financially; **tunjangan 1** support; **tunjangan anak** child support; **tunjangan hari tua** age pension; **2** subsidy; **3** alimony; **penunjang** person or thing that supports; **penunjangan** the act of supporting.

a b c d e f g h i j k l m n o p q r s t u v w x y z

a b c d e f g h i j k l m n o p q r s t u v w x y z

tunjuk show; **tunjuk muka** to show oneself; **tunjuk silang** cross-reference; **menunjuksilangkan** to cross-reference; **penunjuksilangan** cross-referencing; **menunjuk** **1** to indicate, to point toward; **2** to indicate, to show; **3** to appoint, to designate; **4** to raise your hand; **5** with reference to; **menunjuk surat Anda** with reference to your letter; **menunjuki** to show someone something; **menunjukkan** **1** to point out; **menunjukkan jalan pada** to show the way to somebody; **2** to indicate; **3** to refer; **mempertunjukkan** **1** to exhibit, to show; **pameran untuk mempertunjukkan barang-barang kerajinan tangan** an exhibition to display handicrafts; **2** to demonstrate; **petunjuk** **1** guideline, instruction; **bacalah petunjuk pemakaian itu dengan teliti** read the instructions carefully; **2** advice, guidance; **3** clue, hint; **mereka sudah mendapat beberapa petunjuk** they already have a few clues; **4** direction; **penunjuk 1** thing that indicates; **buku penunjuk telepon** telephone directory; **tanda penunjuk jalan** road sign; **2** person who indicates; **penunjukan** appointment *(to a position)*; **pertunjukan** **1** exhibition, show; **2** performance; **pertunjukan itu mulai jam delapan** the performance starts at eight.

tuntun guided by, **menuntun** **1** to lead someone by the hand; **2** to give guidance to; **tuntunan** guidance; **penuntun 1** guide; **2** guide, manual; **penuntunan** **1** leading with a line; **2** giving guidance.

tuntut, menuntut 1 to demand; **mereka menuntut hak-haknya** they demanded their rights; **2** to prosecute, to sue; **3** to strive for; **tuntutan 1** a demand; **2** striving; **3** charge, indictment; **penuntut** **1** person who demands something; **2** claimant; **3** person who strives; **penuntutan 1** demanding; **2** pursuit, study; **3** prosecution.

tupai squirrel.

tur tour; **turis** tourist.

turbin turbine.

Turki Turk, Turkish, Turkey.

turun 1 descend, go down; **turun dari kereta api** get off the train; **2** decrease; **semalam suhu udara turun**

sampai minus lima belas derajat the temperature fell to minus fifteen last night; **3** befall; **4** *(sun)* set; **5** take a break; **turun naik** fluctuate, go up and down; **turun temurun** from generation to generation, hereditary; **dituruntemurunkan** be passed on from generation to generation; **menurun 1** to descend, to go down; **2** to decrease, to decline, to sink; **3** to be hereditary; **menuruni 1** to go down along; **2** to descend, to go down; **berlari menuruni tangga** to run down the stairs; **menurunkan 1** to cause to go down or come down; **dia berhasil menurunkan kucing itu** he managed to get the cat down; **2** to discharge passengers or cargo; **3** to lower, to reduce; **menurunkan pangkat** to demote; **4** to send something down to your inferiors; **kepala sekolah menurunkan peringatan kepada semua murid** the school head issued a warning to all the pupils; **keturunan 1** decline; **2** descent, offspring; **3** generation; **4** inherit; **berketurunan 1** for generations; **2** of ethnic heritage; **berketurunan Aborijin** of Aboriginal descent; **turunan 1** descendant; **2** generation; **3** copy; **4** descent, slope; **penurunan 1** descent, slope; **2** discharge, unloading; **3** lowering, taking down; **4** decline, reduction.

turut join in; **turut campur** interfere; **turut serta** go along with, participate; **turut nonton** go along to the movies with; **berturut-turut** in a row, in succession; **empat kali berturut-turut** four times in a row; **menurut 1** to follow; **2** according to; **menurut Menteri** according to the Minister; **3** to follow, to obey; **menuruti 1** to follow; **2** to comply with; **menurutkan 1** to follow, to obey; **2** to copy, to imitate; **3** to get a person to follow or join in; **memperturutkan** to follow, to obey; **penurut 1** someone obedient; **2** a follower.

tusuk 1 a pin; **2** skewer, stick; **menusuk 1** to stab; **pencuri menusuk perut pembantu dengan pisau dari dapur** the thief stabbed the maid in the stomach with a knife from the kitchen; **2** to prick; **kegemaran menusuk tubuh** the craze for body piercing; **3** to skewer; **menusuk daging**

a b c d e f g h i j k l m n o p q r s t u v w x y z

untuk sate skewer the meat for satay; **4** to punch a ballot paper; **5** to penetrate; **menusuki 1** to perforate in many places; **2** to penetrate; **menusukkan** to stab or prick; **tertusuk** get stabbed; **tusukan** a stab, prick; **penusuk** thing to perforate or stab with; **penusukan 1** stabbing; **2** perforation.

tutup 1 closed, shut; **tutuplah mata Anda!** close your eyes!; **tutup mulut!** shut up!; **jangan tutup pintu itu dulu** don't close the door; **2** cover, lid; **tutup botol** bottle top; **3** complete, full; **bertutup** having a cover; **menutup 1** to close, to shut; **menutup mata** to die; **2** to cover; **menutup muka** to cover the face; **3** to conceal, to hide; **4** to cover over, to fill in; **menutupi 1** to provide a cover for; **menutupi luka** to cover the wound; **kami menutupi semua mebel sebelum berangkat** we covered all the furniture before we left; **2** to cover up; **dia mencoba menutupi kerugian itu** he tried to cover up the financial losses; **3** to cover or shut over and over; **menutupkan 1** to cover; **2** to close or cover; **tertutup 1** closed, shut; **2** locked, secured; **3** *(feelings)* closed off; **ketertutupan** reticence; **penutup** cover, lid; **sebagai penutup** in conclusion; **penutupan 1** covering; **2** closing, shutting.

tutur say, speech, talk; **tutur katanya lemah lembut** the way she/he speaks is polite and gentle; **bertutur** speak, talk; **bertutur-kata** speak; **menuturkan 1** to narrate, to tell about; **2** to pronounce; **3** to announce, to inform; **tuturan 1** narrative, story; **2** announcement, information; **penutur** announcer, narrator, speaker; **penuturan 1** speech, talk; **2** discussion, narrative; **3** announcement; **pertuturan 1** conversation; **2** word, phrase.

TV (televisi) television, TV; **berTV** have a television set; **perTVan** television business; **TVRI (Televisi Republik Indonesia)** the Indonesian National Television Service.

U u

uang 1 money; **uang kontan** cash; **uang muka** down payment; **uang palsu**

counterfeit money; **uang saku** pocket money; **mata uang asing** foreign currency; **uang kecil** small change; **apakah ada uang kecil? saya hanya ada Rp. 50.000** do you have small change? I've only got Rp. 50,000; **menjumlahkan uang** to count money; **2** coin; **uang emas** gold coin; **beruang** be well off, have money; **menguangkan 1** to cash; **menguangkan cek** to cash a cheque; **2** to sell something; **keuangan** finances; **uang-uangan** play money; **penguangan** cashing of cheques, money orders, etc.; **peruangan** monetary affairs.

uap fumes, steam, vapour; **uap air** water vapour; **beruap** be steamed, steaming; **menguap** to become steam, to evaporate; **menguapi** to steam something; **menguapkan 1** to steam; **2** to allow to evaporate; **penguapan 1** evaporation; **2** distillation.

ubah difference; **tidak ubahnya dengan** not different from, the same as; **berubah** become different, change; **berubah-ubah** be changeable; **mengubah** to alter, to change; variation; **pengubah** someone who changes, corrects things; **pengubahan** altering, changing; **perubahan** alteration, change.

uban grey hair; **beruban** have grey hair.

ubi edible tuber; **ubi kayu, kaspe** cassava; **ubi jalar** sweet potato; **ubi-ubian** various kinds of tubers.

ubin floor tile; **mengubini** to tile (a floor).

ubur-ubur jellyfish.

ucap, ucapan saying, word; **mengucap(kan)** to express; **saya mengucapkan selamat kepada Adrian atas hasil ujiannya** I congratulated Adrian on his exam results; **kami mengucapkan terima kasih kepada mereka** we thanked them; **ucapan 1** communication, expression, statement; **beberapa ucapan pendek** a few brief remarks; **2** pronunciation; **pengucapan** pronouncing.

udang prawn, shrimp; **udang galah** large prawn, lobster; **tentu ada udang di balik batu!** what's the catch?; **udang-udangan 1** various kinds of shrimp; **2** imitation shrimp.

udara 1 air; **udara segar** fresh air; **ke luar menghisap udara** to go out for a breath of air; **2** atmosphere; **udara**

a b c d e f g h i j k l m n o p q r s t u v w x y z

politik political atmosphere; **3** sky, space; **4** weather; **udara di Jakarta panas** the weather in Jakarta is hot; **mengudara 1** to broadcast; **2** to go up in the air; **mengudarakan 1** to broadcast; **2** to let something fly, to put something in the air; **anak itu mengudarakan burung merpatinya** the child let her/his pigeon fly into the air.

udik 1 upper reaches of a river; **2** inland, interior; **orang udik** country person, person from a village.

ujar statement, utterance; **berujar** to speak; **ujaran** statement, pronouncement.

uji experiment, test, trial; **uji coba** a try-out; **menguji-cobakan** to try a person or thing out; **menguji 1** to examine; **2** to put to the test, to try; **ujian 1** examination; **menempuh ujian** to sit an exam; **lulus ujian** to pass an exam; **gagal ujian** to fail an exam; **ujian mengendarai mobil** a driving test; **ujian lisan** oral exam; **2** experiment, test, trial; **penguji** examiner; **pengujian** testing, trial.

ujung 1 point, tip, top; **ujung jari** fingertip; **2** end; **ujung tahun** end of the year; **di ujung jalan** at the end of the street; **berujung 1** be pointed; **pensil berujung tumpul** a pencil with a blunt point; **2** end in; **terujung, paling ujung** the extreme end.

ukir, berukir be carved, engraved; **berukir-ukir** ornately carved; **berukiran** having a carving; **mengukiri** to carve; **mengukir** to carve, to engrave; **Ali mengukir motif naga pada kosen pintu** Ali carved a dragon motif on the doorframe; **mengukirkan** to carve into or on something; **Ali mengukir kosen pintu dengan motif naga** Ali carved the doorframe with a dragon motif; **terukir** carved; **ukiran** a carved object; **pengukir** carver, engraver; **pengukiran** act of carving.

ukur 1 measure; **2** measuring tape; **berukuran** to have a measurement of; **kamar ini berukuran empat kali lima meter** this room measures four by five metres; **mengukur** to measure, to survey; **mengukurkan** to measure against something; **ukuran 1** measurement; **ukuran dada** chest measurement; **2** dimension, size; **Anda pakai ukuran**

berapa what size do you take?; **ukuran ruang itu** the dimensions of the room; **3** format; **4** criterion, norm, standard; **5** measuring stick; **pengukur 1** gauge; **2** someone who measures; **pengukuran** gauging, measuring.

ulang often, repeatedly; **ulang alik** go back and forth; **pesawat ulang-alik** shuttle service; **ulang tahun** birthday; **berulang tahun** have a birthday; **berulang** happen again; **berulang-ulang** repeatedly; **mengulang 1** to repeat something; **2** to study over again; **mengulangi** to do something again; **ulangan 1** thing that is done again; **2** test; **ulangan umum** general test; **pengulang** person who repeats; **pengulangan** recurrence, repetition.

ular snake; **ular sendok** cobra; **ular-ularan** toy snake.

ulas, mengulas 1 to review, to comment on; **2** to analyse, to explain; **mengulaskan** to divide into sections; **ulasan 1** commentary, review; **2** analysis; **pengulas** commentator, reviewer; **pengulas olahraga** sports commentator.

ulat 1 caterpillar; **2** maggot; **berulat** worm-eaten.

uleg, ulek, ulek-ulek pestle; **mengulek** to grind; **ulekan 1** pestle; **2** something ground with a pestle.

ulung capable, excellent, skilled; **dokter gigi yang ulung** a brilliant dentist; **keulungan** excellence, experience, skill, superiority.

ulur, mengulur 1 to extend; **2** to make concessions; **uluran tangan** offer to help; **mengulur-ulur** repeatedly extend something; **mengulur-ulur cicilan** to stall on paying the instalments; **mengulur-ulur waktu** to buy time; **menguluri** to hand over to someone; **mengulurkan** to extend, to pay, to pass something out; **terulur 1** stretched out; **2** projecting, protruding.

umat the members of a community *(particularly a religious one)*; **umat Islam** the Moslems; **umat Kristen** the Christians; **umat manusia** humanity.

umbai fringe, tassle; **umbai cacing** appendix *(anatomy)*.

umpama 1 (for) example; **sebagai umpama** as an example; **2** as, like; **seumpama 1** equal, like;

a b c d e f g h i j k l m n o p q r s t u v w x y z

2 supposing; **(se)umpamanya** for example, supposing; **berumpama** talk hypothetically; **mengumpamakan** to use as an example; **perumpamaan** parable.

umpan bait, food; **umpan balik** feedback.

umpat curse, slander, scandal, swearword; **mengumpat** to curse, to slander, to swear; **mengumpati** to swear at someone; **umpatan** curse, slander, verbal abuse; **pengumpat** person who curses, slanderer.

umum 1 common, general; **secara umum** generally; **rapat umum** a general meeting, a mass meeting; **2** public; **telepon umum** public phone; **tidak dijual untuk umum** not for sale to the public; **umumnya, pada umumnya, seumumnya** generally, in general; **mengumumkan 1** to announce, to notify; **2** to publish; **pengumuman** announcement, notification.

umur age; **berapa umur Anda?** how old are you?; **seumur** of the same age; **dihukum seumur hidup, dijatuhi hukuman seumur hidup** to be sentenced for life; **berumur 1** reach the age of; **Yuli berumur sepuluh tahun** Yuli is ten years old; **anak laki-laki berumur belasan tahun** a teenage boy; **2** be old, be grown up; **dia sudah berumur** he/she's already advanced in age.

undang[1], mengundang to invite, to summon; **mereka mengundang kita ke perkawinannya** they've asked us to their wedding; **undangan 1** invitation; **undangan untuk makan malam** an invitation to dinner; **2** invited guest.

undang[2], undang-undang act, law, legislation; **undang-undang dasar** constitution *(for a state)*; **mengundangkan** to legislate; **perundang-undangan** legislation.

undi lot; **mengundi** to draw lots; **mengundi suara** to vote; **undian** lottery; **undian berhadiah** raffle; **menang undian** to win the lottery; **pengundi** person who draws the lots.

undur, mengundurkan 1 to go back, to withdraw; **mengundurkan diri** to resign, to retire; **2** to postpone; **mengundur-undurkan** to keep postponing; **pengunduran** postponement, retreat, withdrawal.

unggas bird, fowl; **perunggasan** poultry-keeping.

unggul excellent, superior; **mengungguli** to surpass; **mengunggulkan** to gain advantage by using your superior qualities; **diunggulkan 1** to be considered superior; **2** *(sport)* seeded; **mengunggul-unggulkan** to show off; **keunggulan** superiority; **unggulan** person or thing considered superior.

unggun woodpile; **api unggun** campfire.

ungkap, mengungkap 1 to express *(with looks, words, etc.)*; **2** to reveal; **mengungkapi** to dig up, to uncover; **mengungkapkan 1** to express yourself, to give expression to; **2** to pronounce, to utter; **3** to reveal, to uncover; **ungkapan 1** expression; **2** idiom.

ungkit, mengungkit (-ungkit) 1 to bring up a matter, to make an issue; **jangan mengungkit(-ungkit) masalah itu lagi** don't bring up that matter again; **2** to prise; **pengungkit** lever; **pengungkitan** leverage.

ungsi, mengungsi to evacuate, to flee; **mengungsikan** to evacuate people; **pengungsi** evacuee, refugee; **pengungsian 1** evacuation; **2** asylum, refuge.

ungu purple; **ungu muda** violet *(colour)*.

uni union; **Uni Afrika Selatan** Union of South Africa.

unifikasi unification.

universitas university; **keuniversitasan** matters relating to university, **universiter** concerning universities.

unjuk show something; **unjuk rasa** demonstration; **unjuk kekuatan** show of force; **pengunjuk rasa** protestor.

unsur element, substance; **berunsur** have an element.

unta camel; **burung unta** ostrich.

untuk 1 for, on behalf of; **saya yang akan membayar untuk Lola** I'm paying for Lola; **bensin untuk mobil** petrol for the car; **lalap untuk makan siang** salad for lunch; **ini untuk apa?** what's it for?; **apa bahasa Indonesianya untuk 'cat'?** what's the Indonesian for 'cat'?; **2** to, in order to; **saya datang untuk menolong** I came to help; **memperuntukkan** to

a b c d e f g h i j k l m n o p q r s t u v w x y z

a b c d e f g h i j k l m n o p q r s t u v w x y z

allocate, to assign; **teruntuk** intended for; **peruntukan** allocation, allotment.

untung **1** fortune, good luck; **2** have good luck; **untung dia datang** luckily she/he came; **katanya ini membawa untung** it's supposed to be lucky; **3** gain, profit; **untung bersih** net profit, **seuntung-untungnya** as profitable as possible; **beruntung 1** be lucky; **kalau beruntung** with a bit of luck; **2** be successful; **3** make a profit; **keberuntungan** luck; **menguntungkan** to enable someone to gain a profit or benefit; **keuntungan 1** profit; **keuntungan kotor** gross profit; **keuntungan yang tertinggi** maximum profits; **2** advantage; **ada beberapa keuntungan** there are several advantages; **mengambil keuntungan dari** to take advantage of something.

upacara **1** ceremony, ritual; **mengadakan upacara, menyelenggarakan upacara** to hold a ceremony; **upacara pelantikan Presiden** presidential inauguration ceremony; **2** regalia

upah pay, wages; **upah mingguan** weekly wage; **berupah** to be paid a wage; **mengupah(i)** to pay someone wages; **orang upahan** hired worker.

upaya **1** efforts; **2** means; **berupaya** make serious efforts; **mengupayakan** to strive for.

urai apart, asunder; **berurai 1** fall apart; **2** disperse, scatter; **mengurai** to become untangled; **menguraikan 1** to loosen, to untangle; **2** to scatter; **3** to explain; **uraian 1** analysis; **2** explanation; **uraian itu kurang bagus** it was a lousy explanation.

urap[1]**, mengurapi** to rub with ointment or salve.

urap[2] grated fresh coconut mixed with spices; **urap-urap** salad with grated coconut mixture; **urapan** vegetables for making this salad.

urat **1** tendon; **2** nerve; **gangguan urat syaraf** a nervous breakdown; **3** vein; **berurat** to be muscular.

urus, berurusan **1** contact, get in touch with; **2** have business with; **jangan pernah berurusan dengan dia** never have anything to do with him/her; **mengurus 1** to arrange matters; **Lex yang mengurus perjalanan** Lex looks after travelling (arrangements); **2** to manage, to take care of; **Anda pintar mengurus orang** you're good at handling people; **mengurusi** to take care of; **mengurusi anak-anak** to take care of, to organize the children; **menguruskan 1** to manage, to run; **2** to handle for someone; **terurus** organized, taken care of; **visa-visa sudah terurus** the visas have all been taken care of; **urusan 1** affair, matter; **itulah urusan saya!** that's my business!; **2** arrangement; **3** division of administration; **pengurus 1** board, management; **2** manager; **pengurusan 1** handling, management; **2** arrangement; **kepengurusan** leadership, management of an organization.

urut[1], diurut get massaged; **mengurut** to massage, to rub.

urut[2], berurut(an) chronological, be in a series; **kejadian berurutan** a sequence of events; **berurutan betul** in the correct order; **mengurut 1** to put in the correct order; **2** to trace something; **mengurutkan** to put something in the correct order; **mengurutkan menurut abjad, mengurutkan sesuai abjad** to put in alphabetical order; **urutan** order, sequence; **urut-urutan 1** consecutively, in sequence; **2** *(sport)* seeded.

usah, tak usah it is not necessary, there's no need to; **tak usah membantah** there's no point in arguing; **tidak usah membawa apa-apa** don't bother bringing anything; **usahkan 1** let alone, not counting; **2** instead of.

usaha 1 effort, exertion; **beberapa usaha** several attempts; **sebagai usaha terakhir** as a last resort; **2** trade, work; **berusaha 1** endeavour, try; **saya dapat berusaha** I can try; **berusaha sedapat mungkin, berusaha sedapat-dapatnya** to do your best; **saya berusaha sedapat mungkin** I tried as best I could, it's the best I can do; **2** be running a business; **mengusahakan 1** to carry on; **2** to manage, to organize; **dia mengusahakan tekstil** she's in the textile business, **pengusaha** entrepreneur, industrialist; **pengusahaan** effort, exertion; **perusahaan** business, enterprise;

perusahaan negara, perusahaan pemerintah state enterprise; **perusahaan-perusahaan kecil** small businesses; **dia mengelola suatu perusahaan perjalanan** she manages a travel agency.

usai finished, ready; **seusai** after.

usap, mengusap 1 to wipe something off; **mengusap air mata** to dry one's tears; **2** to caress, to stroke; **usapan** a caress.

usia age; **lanjut usia** elderly; **seusia** of the same age as; **berusia** attain the age of.

usik, mengusik 1 to annoy, to tease; **2** to touch on; **terusik** to be disturbed; **kuda itu terusik gonggongan anjing** the horse was disturbed by the dog's barking; **usikan 1** annoyance, disturbance; **2** criticism, meddling; **pengusik 1** disturber; **2** meddler.

usir, berusir-usiran, usir-mengusir to chase each other; **mengusir** to chase away, to expel; **orang usiran** an exile, a fugitive; **pengusir** person or thing that chases away; **pengusiran** eviction, expulsion.

uskup bishop; **uskup agung** archbishop; **keuskupan 1** diocese; **2** bishop's office.

usul motion, proposal, suggestion; **usulan** proposals; **mengusulkan** to make a suggestion, to propose; **usulan** proposal, suggestion; **pengusul** proposer.

usung, mengusung to carry on the shoulders *(with the help of others)*; **usungan** stretcher; **pengusung** person who carries on the shoulders; **pengusung peti jenazah** pallbearer; **pengusungan** carrying something on the shoulders.

usus intestines; **usus halus** small intestine; **penyakit usus buntu** appendicitis.

usut, mengusut 1 to feel all over; **2** to examine; **polisi belum juga mengusut pembunuhan itu** the police haven't yet investigated the murder; **pengusut** investigator; **pengusutan** examination, investigation.

utama 1 eminent, prominent; **2** principal, prime; **bagian utama** the main section; **peran utama** the main role; **mengutamakan** to give first place to; **terutama 1** best, superior; **2** especially, particularly; **ada banyak pariwisata, terutama di Bali**

there are lots of tourists, especially in Bali; **3** most important; **keutamaan 1** excellence, superiority; **2** decency, virtue; **pengutamaan** giving priority to.

utara north; **di sebelah utara** in the north; **bagian utara, sebelah utara** the north side; **angin utara** a north wind; **Kutub Utara** North Pole.

utas 1 cord, string; **2** classifier for long, thin, bendable things; **seutas tali** a length of rope or string.

utus, mengutus to delegate someone; **utusan 1** messenger; **2** delegate, envoy; **pengutusan** mission; **perutusan** delegation.

uzur weak *(because of old age or illness)*; **keuzuran 1** suffer from weakness; **2** aged.

V v

vakansi vacation.

vaksin vaccine.

vaksinasi vaccination; **memvaksinasi(kan)** to vaccinate.

vakum vacuum; **memvakumkan** to put in a vacuum; **kevakuman** when a vacuum exists.

validasi validation.

validitas validity.

valuta currency; **valuta asing** foreign currency.

vandalisme vandalism.

vandel souvenir pennant.

variasi variation; **bervariasi** be varied.

varietas kind, sort, variety.

vas vase.

vaselin vaseline.

vegetaris vegetarian.

ventilasi ventilation.

verifikasi verification; **memverifikasikan** to verify.

versi version.

versus versus.

veteran veteran, in particular of the Indonesian Revolution.

veto veto; **hak veto** right of veto; **memveto** to veto.

vetsin monosodium glutamate.

via via.

video 1 video cassette; **2** video performance.

vila villa, weekender.

violis violinist.

VIP (Very Important Person) something reserved for VIPs; **memvipkan** *(colloquial)* **1** to reserve something for VIPs; **2** to give someone VIP status.

Virgo Virgo.

virus virus.

visa visa.

visi perspective, point of view, vision.

visum any official written document stating that a matter has been officially and properly dealt with; **visum dokter** medical report; **visum et repertum** report of an autopsy.

vital vital; **kevitalan** vitality.

vitrage lace curtain.

vla kind of custard.

VOC (Verenigde Oost Indische Companie) Dutch East India Company.

vokalis vocalist.

voli volleyball.

volt volt.

voltase voltage.

volume **1** amount of liquid content, volume; **2** loudness, volume.

vonis verdict; **memvonis** to condemn, to sentence someone.

vulkano volcano.

vulkanis volcanic.

vulkanisir, memvulkanisir vulcanization.

vuring lining for clothing.

W w

wabah epidemic.

wadah **1** container; **wadah air** weir; **2** coordinating organization.

waduk reservoir.

wafat die, pass away; **wafatnya** death.

wah well! wow! *(exclamation of surprise or annoyance).*

wajah face; **wajahnya terkenal** his face is familiar; **saya melihat wajah saya di cermin** I looked at myself in the mirror; **berwajah** have a face of a certain kind; **berwajah bulat** round faced.

wajan wok.

wajar **1** natural, proper; **2** genuine; **sewajarnya** fittingly, properly; **kewajaran** **1** genuineness; **2** naturalness.

wajib **1** obligatory; **wajib daftar** compulsory

registration; **kita wajib membayar pajak** we're obliged to pay taxes; **2** must; **kita wajib menolong orang miskin** we must help the poor; **mewajibkan** to make something compulsory; **dia menegaskan bahwa hal itu tidak diwajibkan** he emphasized that it wasn't compulsory; **kewajiban** duty, obligation; **berkewajiban** to have a duty to do; **Anda berkewajiban memberitahu kami** you have a duty to inform us.

wakil **1** representative; **2** vice, deputy; **wakil presiden** vice-president; **3** agent (for a company); **mewakili** to represent; **duta besar bertugas mewakili negerinya** the ambassador has the duty to represent his country; **perwakilan 1** delegation; **2** agency; **3** representative; **Dewan Perwakilan Rakyat** parliament, people's representative body.

waktu **1** time; **waktu senggang** spare time; **waktu luang** free time; **sudah waktu** it's already time; **waktu sudah habis** time's up; **dia datang tepat pada waktunya** she arrived dead on time; **2** when; **waktu Wahyu tiba** when Wahyu arrives; **3** while, during; **pada waktu malam** during the night; **4** then, at that time; **kami tinggal di Kupang waktu itu** we were living in Kupang then; **5** time zone; **Waktu Indonesia Barat** Western Indonesian Time; **sewaktu, pada waktu** when, at the time that; **sewaktu-waktu 1** from time to time; **2** at any time.

walau, walaupun although; **walaupun dia sibuk, dia mau menolong kita** although she's busy, she's willing to help (us); **kami tetap pergi walaupun hujan** we went in spite of the rain; **walaupun demikian** nevertheless, in spite of that; **baju itu mahal sekali. Walaupun demikian dia tetap mau membelinya** the dress is very expensive. Nevertheless she still wants to buy it.

wali guardian; **wali kota** mayor; **mewalikan, memperwalikan** to appoint someone as a guardian; **perwalian 1** guardianship; **2** custody, trusteeship; **3** protectorate.

wangi fragrant, nice-smelling; **mewangikan** to give something perfume; **kewangian** fragrance; **wangi-wangian** perfumery, all kinds of scents; **pewangi** something to give fragrance; **pewangi mobil** car air freshener.

wanita woman; **kewanitaan** **1** feminity; **2** womanhood; **kewanita-wanitaan** effeminate.

waras having full possession of your senses, mentally healthy; **kurang waras** a bit crazy; not quite sane; **kewarasan** mental health.

warga **1** member; **2** citizen; **warga negara Indonesia** Indonesian citizen; **kewarganegaraan** **1** citizenship; **2** *(school subject)* civics; **berkewarganegaraan** holding citizenship; **pewarganegaraan** naturalization; **kewargaan** **1** membership; **2** citizenry.

waris heir; **mewarisi** to inherit something; **mewariskan** to bequeath something; **warisan** legacy, inheritance; **pewaris, ahli waris** heir; **pewarisan** **1** inheriting; **2** inheritance.

warna colour; **pola warna** colour scheme; **buta warna** colour blind; **warna-warni** various colours; **berwarna** coloured; **film berwarna** colour film; **berwarna-warna, berwarna-warni** multi-coloured; **baju berwarna-warna** a colourful outfit; **mewarnai** to colour, to apply a colour to; **mewarnai kertas itu biru** to colour the paper blue; **pewarna** dye.

warta **1** communication report; **2** news, **warta berita** news broadcast; **wartawan** male journalist, correspondent; **wartawati** woman journalist, correspondent; **mewartakan** to report, to inform; **kewartawanan** journalism; **pewartaan** reporting.

warung small shop, stall; **warung kopi** coffee kiosk.

wasit referee, umpire; **mewasiti** to be the referee in.

waspada be vigilant, on guard; **mewaspadai** keep on guard against; **kewaspadaan** vigilance.

wassalam Peace be with you *(at the end of a letter, in a greeting)*.

waswas anxious, becoming suspicious; **kewaswasan** anxiety, uneasiness.

watak disposition, nature; **perwatakan** characterization.

wawancara interview; **mengadakan wawancara** to hold an interview; **mewawancarai** to interview someone; **pewawancara** interviewer.

wayang puppet performance, usually of a Hindu epic, most commonly with leather shadow puppets; **wayang kulit** leather shadow puppet; **wayang golek** wooden puppet (Sunda); **wayang wong** traditional drama performance *(Java and Bali)*; **mewayangkan 1** to present in *wayang* form; **2** to act, to perform; **wayangan 1** a ***wayang*** performance; **2** attend a ***wayang*** performance.

WC *(water closet)* toilet; **apakah ada WC di sekitar sini?** is there a toilet around here?

wejang, mewejang(i) to advise, to instruct; **wejangan 1** advice; **2** speech containing advice.

wenang qualified; **berwenang** be competent to, have jurisdiction; **kewenangan** competence; **sewenang-wenang** arbitrarily; **kesewenang-wenangan 1** arbitrariness; **2** despotism.

wesel, poswesel money order.

wewenang authority; competence, right; **berwewenang** have the authority or competence.

wibawa authority, power; **berwibawa** have the authority or prestige; **kewibawaan** authority, prestige.

wilayah 1 district, region; **2** zone; **Menteng adalah sebagian dari wilayah Jakarta** Menteng is part of the Jakarta area; **di wilayah Sydney** in the Sydney area; **wilayah waktu** time zone; **berwilayah** to have an area; **perwilayahan** district matters.

wiraswasta entrepreneur; **berwiraswasta** to run a private enterprise; **kewiraswastaan** entrepreneurship.

wisata tour; **berwisata** make a tour; **wisatawan** tourist; **ada banyak wisatawan, terutama di Bali** there are lots of tourists, especially in Bali.

wiski whisky.

wisma mess, public building.

wisuda graduation ceremony; **wisudawan** graduate.

WNA (Warga Negara Asing) citizen of a foreign country.

WNI (Warga Negara Indonesia) **1** citizen of Indonesia; **2** naturalized citizen of Indonesia; **menjadi WNI** become a citizen of Indonesia; **meWNIkan** to cause someone to become an Indonesian citizen; **keWNIan** matters relating to Indonesian citizenship.

wong *(Javanese)* person.

wortel carrot.

wujud form, shape; **berwujud** **1** have the shape of; **2** concrete, tangible; **mewujudkan 1** to create, to give shape to; **2** to materialize; **terwujud** materialized; **keterwujudan** materialization; **perwujudan** **1** form, shape; **2** realization; **3** phenomenon.

Y y

ya 1 yes; **'Bapak Soesanto?' 'ya, betul'** 'Are you Mr Soesanto?' 'yes, I am'; **2** *(as a response to a call to attract your attention)* **ya, apa?** yes, what is it?; **3** OK?; **jangan lupa, ya?** don't forget, OK?; **4** *(question tag word, hesitation marker, etc.)* **Anda mau ikut juga, ya?** you want to come along too, don't you?; **lupa lagi, ya?** you forgot again, didn't you?

yad (yang akan datang), bulan yad next month; **majalah yad** the magazine to be issued next.

Yahudi Jew, Jewish.

yaitu that is, i.e., viz.

yakin convinced, sure; **Anda yakin?** are your sure?; **saya yakin dia akan lupa** I am sure he'll forget; **seyakin-yakinnya** absolutely convinced, as convinced as possible; **meyakini** to be convinced about something; **meyakinkan 1** to convince someone; **cobalah menyakinkan mereka** try to convince them; **2** to make convincing; **keyakinan** belief, conviction; **keyakinan politik** political conviction; **berkeyakinan** be convinced, have the conviction.

yakni that is, i.e., namely.

yang 1 the one who, the thing which, etc.; **saya mau yang merah** I want the red one; **'anak yang mana?' 'yang lari'** 'which boy?' 'the one who ran away'; **tolong beri saya yang lain** please give me the other one; **2** who, which, that *(in clauses)*; **beritahu saya apa yang Anda beli** tell me what you bought; **dia menceritakan kepada saya apa yang terjadi** she told me what had happened; **buku yang Anda pinjam dari saya** the book which you borrowed from me; **teman saya yang tinggal di Ujung Pandang** my friend who lives in Ujung Pandang; **teman-teman yang kita undang** the friends whom we invited; **3** this one, that one, which one, etc.; **saya suka sepeda itu, tetapi yang ini lebih murah** I like that bike but this one is cheaper; **apakah Anda ingin baju renang yang hijau atau yang kuning** do you want the green swimsuit or the yellow one?; **'anak anjing yang mana?' 'yang itu'** 'which pup?' 'that one'; **'dia pinjam rok dari saya' 'yang mana?'** 'she borrowed a skirt from me' 'which one?'; **yang akan datang** the next to come, etc.

yasmin, melati jasmine.

yatim fatherless child; **yatim piatu** orphan.

yayasan foundation, institute.

ybl (yang baru lalu) last.

yl (yang lain) the other.

yl (yang lalu) last, past.

yoga meditation, yoga.

yogia, yogya proper, fitting; **seyogyanya** as it should be, obviously, properly.

you you *(informal)*.

yth (yang terhormat) the honourable *(used in letters as a salutation)*.

yudo judo.

Yunani Greece, Greek.

yunior **1** *(sport)* junior; **bulu tangkis yunior** junior badminton competition; **2** son of; **keyunioran** being a junior.

Z z

zakat alms; **zakat fitrah** alms given by Muslims during the fasting month; **menzakatkan** to donate something.

zaman age, era, time; **zaman dahulu** previous time; **zaman Jepang** the Japanese era (of occupation); **ketinggalan zaman** old-fashioned, behind the times.

zamrud emerald.

zat essence, substance; **zat air** hydrogen; **zat asam** oxygen.

zebra zebra.

ziarah pilgrimage, visit to the grave; **berziarah ke** to visit a sacred place, to make a pilgrimage to; **berziarah ke kuburan** visit a grave; **peziarah** visitor to a sacred place.

SYSTEM OF AFFIXATION AND PRONUNCIATION GUIDE

This section of the dictionary gives you two kinds of information. First, it gives you a brief explanation of the system of affixation in Indonesian. Second, it gives you a guide to the pronunciation of Indonesian.

You have to know the system of affixation to look up many Indonesian words. The explanation given here is not an explanation of Indonesian grammar – you will have to study this grammar with your teacher or from a grammar book. The purpose of this section is only to show you how to find words in the dictionary. After a while you will find that you will quickly be able to recognise the appropriate base word to look up. In the section below, the first column gives you a word you might be trying to look up and the second column gives you the word you will need to look for in the dictionary.

ber-

The **ber-** prefix is always written **ber-** except with words beginning with **r**, when it is written as **be-**. It is also written as **be-** with some words where the first syllable ends with '**r**', like the word **bekerja**, **bepergian**, **beserta**. **Belajar** is an important exception to the general rule for the prefix **ber-**.

belajar	**ajar**
berangkat	**angkat**
berlumpur	**lumpur**
bernama	**nama**
berolahraga	**olahraga**
bersekolah	**sekolah**
bersepeda	**sepeda**
berceritera	**ceritera**
berubah	**ubah**

di-

There are no spelling changes with **di-**. The **di-** form is not given throughout this dictionary, because once you know the grammar you can easily work out the meaning from the base word.

dibangun	**bangun**
diiris	**iris**
ditangkap	**tangkap**

ke-an

When **ke** is prefixed to a base word **an** is also suffixed to the word.

keadaan	**ada**
kebersihan	**bersih**
kekayaan	**kaya**
kebanjiran	**banjir**
kehujanan	**hujan**
ketinggian	**tinggi**
kemahalan	**mahal**

me- and pe-

The spelling of the **me-** and **pe-** prefixes changes, depending on the first letter of the base word. The **pe-** form is generally not given throughout this dictionary, because once you know the grammar you can easily work out the meaning from the base word. In this section, the first two columns give you words you might be trying to look up and the third column gives you the word you will need to look for in the dictionary. You will find that there is not always a **me-** word or a **pe-** word for every base word.

1 words beginning with **l**, **m**, **n**, **r**, **w**, **y**, **ny**, **ng**

melamun	**pelamun**	**lamun**
melukis	**pelukis**	**lukis**
memalaskan	**pemalas**	**malas**
memudakan	**pemuda**	**muda**
memulai	**pemula**	**mula**
menasihati	**penasihat**	**nasihat**
menganga	**penganga**	**nganga**
menilai(kan)	**penilai**	**nilai**
menyanyi	**penyanyi**	**nyanyi**
merampok	**perampok**	**rampok**
mewangikan	**pewangi**	**wangi**
mewarisi	**pewaris**	**waris**
meyakinkan		**yakin**

2 **me-** becomes **meng-** and **pe-** becomes **peng-** with words beginning with a **vowel** or **g**, **h k**. Note that the **k** is dropped.

mengajar	**pengajar**	**ajar**
mengambil	**pengambil**	**ambil**
mengedar	**pengedar**	**edar**
mengiris	**pengiris**	**iris**
mengobati	**pengobat**	**obat**
mengomong	**pengomong**	**omong**
mengubah	**pengubah**	**ubah**
menggilas	**penggilas**	**gilas**
menghapus	**penghapus**	**hapus**
mengenal	**pengenal**	**kenal**

3 **me-** becomes **mem-** and **pe-** becomes **pem-** with words beginning with **b f p**. Note that the **p** is dropped

membantu	**pembantu**	**bantu**
membuat	**pembuat**	**buat**
memfatwakan	**pemfatwa**	**fatwa**
memfitnah	**pemfitnah**	**fitnah**
memakai	**pemakai**	**pakai**
memotong	**pemotong**	**potong**

Exceptions:

mempunyai	**punya**

and foreign derivations

memprotes	**pemerotes**	**protes**

4 **me-** becomes **men-** and **pe-** becomes **pen-** with words beginning with **c**, **d**, **j**, **t**, **z**. Note that the **t** is dropped.

mencuri	**pencuri**	**curi**
mendaftar	**pendaftar**	**daftar**
menduduki	**penduduk**	**duduk**
menjabat	**pe(n)jabat**	**jabat**
menjadi	**penjadi**	**jadi**
menakuti	**penakut**	**takut**
menolong	**penolong**	**tolong**
menziarahi	**pe(n)ziarah**	**ziarah**

Exceptions: foreign derivations

mentraktir	**pentraktir**	**traktir**

5 **me-** becomes **meny-** and **pe-** becomes **peny-** with words beginning with **s**. Note that the **s** is dropped.

menyakiti	**penyakit**	**sakit**
menyapu	**penyapu**	**sapu**
menyusul	**penyusul**	**susul**

Exceptions: foreign derivations

standar	**menstandarkan**

There are other exceptions to the above. The most predictable ones are with words of only one syllable. No matter what letter they begin with **me-** becomes **menge-** and **pe-** becomes **penge-**. Sometimes you will find an older form of these words where **me-** was written as **men-** This form is no longer used.

mengebom	**pengebom**	**bom**
mengecek	**pengecek**	**cek**
mengepak	**pengepak**	**pak**
mengetik	**pengetik**	**tik**

6 The prefix **pe-** is often combined with the suffix **-an**. Always check the meanings for these. For example:

pelajar	student	**ajar**
pelajaran	lesson, course, training	
pengedar	circulator, dealer	**edar**
pengedaran	circulating, circulation	
pe(n)jabat	official	**jabat**
pe(n)jabatan	office, service	

memper-

The only spelling change associated with this prefix is that the **r** is dropped when the base word begins with **r**.

mempercepat	**cepat**
memperasakan	**rasa**
mempertanggungkan	**tanggung**
mempertanggungjawabkan	**tanggungjawab**

per-

There are no spelling changes with **per-**.

perbuatan	**buat**
perlawanan	**lawan**
perlombaan	**lomba**
persatuan	**satu**
pertanyaan	**tanya**

ter-

There are only a few spelling changes with **ter-**. It becomes **te-** with words beginning with **r** or when the first syllable of the word ends in **r**. The **ter-** form is only given in this dictionary when the meaning is not obvious, or there is more than one meaning; for example, **ternyata 1** apparently; **2** it turns out.

tekerjakan	**kerja**
tepercaya	**percaya**
terasa	**rasa**
terawat	**rawat**
terajin	**rajin**
terencana	**rencana**

ter with all other words

terakhir	**akhir**
terbaik	**baik**
terbagi	**bagi**
terletak	**letak**
terpenting	**penting**
tersedia	**sedia**
tertidur	**tidur**
tertinggi	**tinggi**

Sample entry

This entry for **ajar** shows you the meanings of the words with the different affixes.

ajar, belajar to study, to learn; **kami sedang belajar Bahasa Indonesia** we're studying Indonesian; **mengajar** to teach, to train; **dia mengajar di SMU** he teaches in senior high school; **mengajarkan** to teach something; **ibunya mengajarkan ilmu pasti** her mum teaches maths; **mengajari** to teach something to someone; **dia mengajari saya** she's teaching me; **ajaran** teaching; **tahun ajaran** school year; **pelajar** student, learner; **pelajaran** lesson, course; **mata pelajaran** school subject; **pengajar** instructor, teacher; **pengajaran** instruction, teaching; **terpelajar** educated; **mempelajari** study carefully, in depth; **sebaiknya Anda mempelajari adat-istiadat negeri itu sebelum berangkat** it's better if you study the customs of the country before you leave.

The pronunciation of Indonesian is easy once you learn the sound for each letter. Except for the letter 'e', each letter of Indonesian has only one sound.

Vowels

The vowel sounds are:

a is pronounced like the 'a' sound in English words *Mama* or the 'ar' of *farmer*. Examples of words with this sound are: **apa**, **nama**, **kerja**, **tanpa**.

e is pronounced in two main ways. The first is like the 'e' sound in the English word *pet*. This sound generally occurs when both syllables of a two-syllable word have 'e'. Some words that have this sound are: **ekor**, **bebek**, **merah**, **sate**, **boleh**, **aneh**. The second pronunciation is like the 'er' sound on the end of English words like *teacher* or *farmer*. Examples of words with this sound are: **ke**, **enam**, **kerja**, **belajar**, **pelatih**.

i is pronounced like the 'i' sound in English words *bit* or *pin*. Examples of words with this sound are **bibit**, **ambil**, **ini**, **pagi**.

o is pronounced like the 'o' sound in English word *top*. Examples of words with this sound are: **tolong**, **oleh**, **besok**.

u is pronounced like the 'u' sound in English words *put* or *foot*. Examples of words with this pronunciation are: **bumi**, **Bandung**, **itu**, **tutup**. Be careful not to pronounce it like the sounds in the words *lung* or *duty*.

Diphthongs

There are also some vowel combinations, called diphthongs, in Indonesian. Diphthongs include the 'ai' sound, the 'au' sound and the 'oi' sound; 'ai' is pronounced like 'i' in the English words *fight* or *kite*. Examples of words with this sound are **pantai** and **pakai**. 'Au' is pronounced like 'ow' in *now*. Examples of words with this sound are **kalau** and **pulau**. 'Oi' is pronounced like 'oy' in *boy*. Words with this sound include **koboi** and **sepoi**.

Not all combinations of two vowels are pronounced as diphthongs. For example, in these words the vowel combinations are pronounced as two syllables.

air	**a:ir**
dua	**du:a**
haus	**ha:us**
siang	**si:ang**

Consonants

The consonants are pronounced like this.

'b' b as in English *bad.*

'c' ch as in English *chook.*

'd' d as in English *down.*

'f' f as in English *fill.*

'g' g as in English *good.*

'h' h as in English *here.* It is important in Indonesian to say the h sound when it comes at the end of a syllable or word. So you must let out a puff of breath at the ends of words like **boleh**. Be careful of words like **tahu**. If you say the h, the word means tofu. If you do not say the h, the word means know or understand.

'j' j as in English *jumper.*

'k' k as in English *skin.* Do not say this letter like the k in *kitten* or *kick.* However, at the ends of words the k can have two different pronuncitations, though most people who are not native speakers of Indonesians do not hear the difference. You say the k in the back of your throat, but quite softly. Examples of words like this are **tidak**, **kakak**.

'l' l as in English *list.*

'm' m as in English *meet.*

'n' n as in English *never.*

'p' p as in English *pink.*

'r' in Indonesian r is generally trilled. It is a bit like the r sound in the English word *trip*.

's' s as in English *sand*.

't' t as in English *talk*.

'v' f as in English *fast*. V is only found in introduced words in Indonesian.

'w' w as in English *walk*.

'y' y as in English *yellow*.

'z' z as in English *zip*. However, in Indonesian the sound j is now generally substituted for this sound; for example, **zaman** is more commonly **jaman**.

There are also two consonant combinations that are common in Indonesian and will be rather unusual for English speakers. These are 'ny' and 'ng'. 'Ny' is pronounced like the 'ny' in the word *banyan* or like 'ni' in *onion*. It can occur at the beginning of a word, as in **nyata**, or in the middle, as in **senyum**. 'Ng' is pronounced as one sound like the 'ng' in the English word *ring*. It can also occur at the beginning of a word as in **nganga**, in the middle as in **tangan** or at the end as in **senang**. It is important to remember that this combination does not represent the sequence of n and g that occurs in the English word *finger*. When this sequence of sounds is needed it is spelt 'ngg' as in **tanggal**.

Word stress

In Indonesian, the stress is placed on the second last syllable. This means that as prefixes and suffixes are added, the stress moves to remain in the second last syllable. For example, **nya´man**, **menyaman´kan**, **kenyaman´an**.

A a

a, an *indefinite article* **1** *(not usually translated into Indonesian)* **a cat is an animal** kucing adalah binatang; *(sometimes translated by the following: sebuah, seekor, seorang)* **there's a cat on the roof tiles** ada seekor kucing di genteng; **2** satu.

abandon *verb* meninggalkan.

abbreviation *noun* singkatan.

ability *noun* kemampuan; **the ability to drive a car** kemampuan mengendarai mobil.

able *adjective* **1** bisa, dapat; **he's not able to come** dia tidak bisa datang; **2** *(have sufficient funds)* mampu; **I'm not able to buy that house** saya tidak mampu membeli rumah itu.

abnormal *adjective* **1** abnormal; **abnormal behaviour** tingkah laku yang abnormal; **2** luar biasa; **an abnormal amount of rain** hujan yang luar biasa banyaknya.

about *preposition* **1** *(on the subject of)* mengenai, tentang; **what's it about?** mengenai apa?, tentang apa?; **a book about trains** buku tentang kereta api; **2** perihal; **a letter about her/his resignation** surat perihal pengunduran dirinya; **3** bagaimana; **what about my share?** bagaimana dengan bagian saya?
adverb **1** *(approximately)* kira-kira; **it's about five o'clock** sekarang kira-kira jam lima; **2 to be about to do** baru saja mau, baru saja akan; **I'm (just) about to leave** saya baru saja mau berangkat, saya baru saja akan berangkat.

above *preposition* **1** di atas; **above the clouds** di atas awan; **2 above all** yang terpenting.

abroad *adverb* luar negeri; **to go abroad** pergi ke luar negeri; **to live abroad** tinggal di luar negeri.

abscess *noun* abses.

abseiling *noun* abseiling.

absent *adjective* absen, tidak hadir; **she was absent yesterday** kemarin dia absen.

a
b
c
d
e
f
g
h
i
j
k
l
m
n
o
p
q
r
s
t
u
v
w
x
y
z

a
b
c
d
e
f
g
h
i
j
k
l
m
n
o
p
q
r
s
t
u
v
w
x
y
z

absent-minded *adjective* pelupa; *(because of old age)* pikun.

absolute *adjective* **1** penuh; **I have absolute confidence in you** saya menaruh kepercayaan penuh kepada Anda; **2** absolut, mutlak; **absolute power** kuasa mutlak; **3 an absolute disaster** bencana besar.

absolutely *adverb* betul-betul; **you're absolutely right** Anda betul-betul benar.

absorb *verb* menyerap.

abuse *noun*
1 penyalahgunaan; **alcohol abuse** penyalahgunaan alkohol; **2** *(violent treatment of a person)* siksaan; **3** *(insults)* makian.
verb memperlakukan dengan kejam, menyiksa.

academic *adjective* akademis; **the academic year** tahun akademis.

accelerate *verb* mempercepat; **the workers were able to accelerate production** para pekerja dapat mempercepat produksi.

accelerator *noun* pedal gas, akselerator.

accent *noun* aksen, logat; **he has an Australian accent** ia berbicara dengan logat Australia.

accept *verb* menerima; **the medical faculty only accepts students with high grades** fakultas kedokteran hanya menerima siswa-siswi yang mendapat angka tinggi.

acceptable *adjective* dapat diterima.

acceptance *noun* penerimaan.

access *noun* akses; **I don't have access to that information** saya tidak dapat mengakses informasi itu; **access road** jalan akses, jalan masuk.
verb mengakses; **how do you access that computer program?** bagaimana mengakses program komputer itu?

accessory *noun* aksesori, asesori, tambahan.

accident *noun* **1** kecelakaan; **to have an accident** mendapat kecelakaan; **a road accident** kecelakaan di jalan, kecelakaan lalu lintas; **a car accident** kecelakaan mobil; **2** *(by chance)* kebetulan; **I found it by accident** saya menemukannya secara kebetulan; **3** secara tidak sengaja; **I broke the plate by accident** dengan tidak sengaja saya memecahkan piring itu.

accidental *adjective* kebetulan; **an accidental discovery** suatu penemuan yang kebetulan.

accidentally *adverb* **1** *(without meaning to)* tidak sengaja; **I accidentally broke the plate** dengan tidak sengaja saya memecahkan piring itu; **2** *(by chance)* kebetulan; **I ran into him accidentally** kebetulan saya bertemu dengan dia.

accommodate *verb* memuat, menampung; **the sports centre can accommodate fifteen hundred people** gedung olahraga ini dapat menampung seribu lima ratus orang.

accommodating *adjective* suka membantu; **Yudhi is very accommodating** Yudhi adalah orang yang suka membantu.

accommodation *noun* akomodasi, penginapan; **we're looking for accommodation** kami sedang mencari penginapan.

accompany *verb* **1** menemani; **I accompanied her** saya menemaninya; **2** mendampingi; **Pak Soeharto and Ibu Tien were accompanied by their children** Pak Soeharto dan Ibu Tien didampingi oleh anak-anaknya.

according *in phrase* **according to** menurut; **according to the Minister** menurut Menteri.

accordion *noun* akordion.

account *noun* **1** *(in a bank or shop)* rekening; **to open a bank account** membuka rekening bank; **2 on account of** karena, sebab; **all the banks are closed on account of the riots** semua bank ditutup karena kerusuhan; **3 to take something into account** mempertimbangkan sesuatu; **we will take that problem into account** kami akan mempertimbangkan masalah itu.

accountant *noun* akuntan; **she's an accountant** dia seorang akuntan.

accuracy *noun* keakuratan, ketelitian.

accurate *adjective* akurat, cermat, teliti.

accurately *adverb* secara akurat, dengan teliti, dengan cermat.

accuse *verb* menuduh; **she was accused of theft** dia dituduh mencuri; **the police**

a b c d e f g h i j k l m n o p q r s t u v w x y z

accused them of starting the riot polisi menuduh mereka memulai kerusuhan.

ace *noun (in cards)* as; **the ace of spades** kartu as sekop. *adjective* yang hebat, jago *(colloquial)* **he's an ace player** dia pemain yang hebat.

ache *verb* sakit; **my head aches** kepala saya sakit.

achieve *verb* mencapai, meraih; **Tracy achieved a great deal** Tracy mencapai hasil yang baik; **to achieve an aim** mencapai tujuan; **to achieve success** mencapai sukses.

achievement *noun* prestasi; **a great achievement** prestasi besar, prestasi hebat.

acid *noun* asam.

acid rain *noun* hujan asam.

acne *noun* akne, jerawat.

acrobat *noun* akrobat.

across *preposition* **1** melintasi, menyeberangi; **we walked across the park** kami melintasi taman itu; **the cat ran across the road** kucing itu berlari menyeberangi jalan; **2** seberang; **the house across the street** rumah di seberang jalan; **across from** di seberang; **she usually sits across from me** biasanya dia duduk di seberang saya.

acrylic *noun* akrilik.

act *noun* **1** perbuatan; **2** *(of a play)* babak. *verb* **1** *(in a play)* memainkan; **to act the part of Hanuman** memainkan peran Hanuman; **2** *(to take action)* bertindak **she acted at once** ia bertindak seketika itu juga.

action *noun* perbuatan, tindakan.

active *adjective* aktif, bersemangat, giat.

activity *noun* aktivitas, kegiatan.

actor *noun* aktor, pemain.

actress *noun* aktris, pemain.

actual *adjective* aktual, sebenarnya; **his actual words** kata-katanya yang sebenarnya.

actually *adverb* **1** *(in fact, as it happens)* sebenarnya, sebetulnya; **actually I don't want to go** sebetulnya saya tidak mau pergi; **2** *(really and truly)* benar-benar, betul-betul; **did she actually say that?** apakah dia benar-benar berkata demikian?

acupuncture *noun* akupungtur, tusuk jarum.

acute *adjective* akut, gawat.

ad *noun (informal)* advertensi, iklan; **to put an ad in the paper** memasang iklan dalam surat kabar; **the classified ads** iklan baris, iklan mini.

AD [Anno Domini] *abbreviation* TM [Tarich Masehi], sesudah Masehi; **in 400 AD** pada 400 TM.

adapt *verb* **1** merubah, mengadaptasi; **they adapted their farming methods** mereka merubah cara pertaniannya; **2 to adapt to** membiasakan, menyesuaikan; **I can't adapt to the new system** saya tidak bisa menyesuaikan diri dengan sistem yang baru.

adaptor *noun* adaptor.

add *verb* tambah, menambahkan; **add thirty dollars** tambah tiga puluh dolar lagi.

- **to add something up** menjumlahkan.

addict *noun* pecandu; **a drug addict** pecandu narkotika; **she's a football addict** dia pecandu sepak bola.

addicted *adjective* kecanduan; **to become addicted to smoking** kecanduan merokok.

addition *noun* **1** *(adding up)* penjumlahan; **2 in addition** lagi pula, tambahan pula; **in addition we have to do maths homework** tambahan pula kami harus mengerjakan pr matematika; **3 in addition to** di samping, selain; **in addition to that we have to do a translation** di samping itu kami harus membuat terjemahan.

additional *adjective* ekstra, tambahan; **additional costs** ongkos tambahan.

additive *noun* aditif, bahan tambahan.

address *noun* alamat; **what's your address** di mana alamat Anda? **to change address** pindah alamat, pindah rumah.

address book *noun* buku alamat.

adequate *adjective* cukup.

adhesive *noun* bahan perekat.
adjective **adhesive tape 1** *(for the body)* plester; **2** pita perekat, selotep.

adjective *noun* kata sifat.

adjust *verb* **1 to adjust something** mengatur, menyetel; **adjust the height** mengatur tingginya; **2 to adjust to** membiasakan, menyesuaikan pada; **I can't adjust to this climate** saya tidak bisa menyesuaikan diri pada iklim ini.

adjustable *adjective* dapat disetel, dapat dicocokkan.

a b c d e f g h i j k l m n o p q r s t u v w x y z

administration *noun* administrasi, tata usaha.

admiral *noun* laksamana.

admiration *noun* kekaguman.

admire *verb* mengagumi; **we admire Susi as a badminton player** kami mengagumi Susi sebagai pemain bulu tangkis.

admission *noun* hak masuk, ijin masuk; **no admission** dilarang masuk; **admission free** masuk secara gratis.

admit *verb* **1** *(confess)* mengaku(i); **she admits she cheated** dia mengaku bahwa dia menipu; **2** *(concede)* mengakui; **I must admit you're right** saya harus mengakui bahwa Anda benar; **3** *(allow to enter)* memasukkan; **to be admitted to hospital** dimasukkan ke rumah sakit.

adolescence *noun* masa remaja.

adolescent *noun* anak remaja.

adopt *verb* **1** *(a child)* mengadopsi, mengangkat; **2** *(a method, for example)* menggunakan.

adopted *adjective* angkat; **adopted child** anak angkat.

adoption *noun* adopsi, pengangkatan.

adore *verb* **1** *(love)* mencintai; **2** *(admire)* mengagumi; **3** *(praise God)* memuji.

adult *noun* (orang) dewasa. *adjective* dewasa; **the adult population** penduduk dewasa.

Adult Education *noun* pendidikan orang dewasa.

advance *noun* kemajuan; **advances in technology** kemajuan-kemajuan di bidang teknologi. *verb* **1** *(make progress)* memajukan; **to advance technologically this century is urgent for Indonesia's economy** maju secara teknologi pada abad ini penting untuk ekonomi Indonesia; **2** *(bring forward)* memajukan; **to advance the date of departure** memajukan tanggal keberangkatan.

advanced *adjective* lanjutan, maju; **an advanced class** kelas lanjutan.

advantage *noun* **1** keuntungan; **there are several advantages to using this system** ada beberapa keuntungan memakai sistem ini; **2** memanfaatkan; **I took advantage of the cheap fare** saya memanfaatkan tarip yang murah; **Tati takes**

advantage of everybody Tati memanfaatkan semua orang.

adventure *noun* pertualangan.

adverb *noun* kata keterangan.

advert, advertisement *noun* advertensi, iklan; **I saw an advert for a bike in the paper** saya melihat advertensi mengenai sepeda di surat kabar.

advertise *verb* mengiklankan; **to advertise a job in the newspaper** mengiklankan lowongan kerja di surat kabar; **Wayan advertised his house in *Kompas*** Wayan mengiklankan rumahnya di surat kabar *Kompas*.

advertising *noun* periklanan.

advice *noun* nasihat; **to ask for advice about work** meminta nasihat tentang pekerjaan; **a piece of advice** sebuah nasihat.

advise *verb* **1** menasihati; **Nasution advised Suleiman to study harder** Nasution menasihati Suleiman supaya belajar lebih keras; **I advised him to stop smoking** saya menasihatinya supaya berhenti merokok; **2** menyarankan; **I advised her not to wait** saya menyarankan supaya dia jangan menunggu.

aerial *noun* antena.

aerobics *noun* senam erobik; **to do aerobics** bersenam erobik, melakukan erobik.

aeroplane *noun* kapal terbang, pesawat terbang.

aerosol *noun* erosol.

affair *noun* **1** urusan; **international affairs** urusan antar bangsa; **2** hubungan; **a love affair** hubungan cinta, hubungan asmara.

affect *verb* mempengaruhi.

affection *noun* kasih sayang.

affectionate *adjective* penuh kasih sayang; **affectionate love** cinta kasih.

afford *verb* **1** mampu; **we can't afford to go overseas** kami tidak mampu ke luar negeri; **2** mengambil; **I can't afford to take the risk** saya tidak bisa mengambil risiko tersebut.

afraid *adjective* **1** takut akan; **why are you afraid of dogs?** mengapa Anda takut akan anjing?; **2** *(colloquial)* kira, rasa; **I'm afraid there's no milk left** saya kira tidak ada susu lagi; **I'm afraid so** saya rasa begitu; **I'm afraid not** saya kira tidak; **3** jangan-jangan; **I'm afraid Anwar might have had an accident**

jangan-jangan Anwar terlibat dalam kecelakaan.

Africa *noun* Afrika.

African *noun* orang Afrika. *adjective* Afrika; **African languages** bahasa-bahasa Afrika.

after *adverb, conjunction, preposition* **1** sesudah; **after ten o'clock** sesudah jam sepuluh; **after lunch** sesudah makan siang; **2 the day after tomorrow** lusa; **soon after** tidak lama setelah; **to run after somebody** mengejar orang; **could you go after the dog please?** tolong cari anjing itu.

after all *adverb* bagaimana pun (juga), betapa pun; **after all, she's just a child!** bagaimana pun juga dia masih kecil!

afternoon *noun* siang hari *(until about 2 p.m.)*, sore hari *(from about 2 p.m. until sunset)*; **this afternoon** siang ini, sore ini; **tomorrow afternoon** besok siang, besok sore; **on Sunday afternoon** pada hari Minggu sore; **every afternoon** setiap siang, setiap sore.

afterwards *adverb* kemudian, lalu, sesudah itu; **shortly afterwards** tidak lama sesudah itu.

again *adverb* lagi, sekali lagi; **I saw her again yesterday** saya melihatnya lagi kemarin; **try again** coba sekali lagi; **never again!** tidak pernah lagi!

against *preposition* **1** pada; **against the wall** pada tembok; **2** melawan, menentang; **I'm against the idea** saya menentang ide itu.

age *noun* umur, usia; **at the age of five** pada umur lima tahun.

aged *adjective* berumur; **a child aged three** anak berumur tiga tahun; **middle-aged** setengah baya; **the aged** orang jompo, orang yang sudah tua.

agenda *noun* acara, agenda.

agent *noun* agen; **an estate agent** agen perumahan; **a travel agent** agen perjalanan.

ages, for ages sudah lama sekali; **I haven't seen them for ages** sudah lama sekali saya tidak bertemu dengan mereka.

aggression *noun* agresi.

aggressive *adjective* agresif.

ago *adverb* **1** yang lalu; **an hour ago** sejam yang lalu; **2** lama; **a long time ago** sudah lama sekali; **not long ago** belum lama ini; **how**

long ago was it? itu sudah berapa lama?

agree *verb* **1** setuju, menyetujui; **I agree with Feisal** saya setuju dengan Feisal; **Kathy's agreed to help us** Kathy setuju untuk membantu kita; **we agree to your proposal** kami menyetujui usul Anda; **2** mengakui; **I agree that it's too late now** saya mengakui bahwa sekarang sudah terlambat; **3** *(not agree with, refering to food)* tidak bisa; **pepper doesn't agree with me** saya tidak bisa makan merica.

agreement *noun* perjanjian, persetujuan.

agricultural *adjective* yang berhubungan dengan pertanian.

agriculture *noun* pertanian.

ahead *adverb* **1** di depan, di muka; **careful! there's something in the middle of the road ahead of you** awas! ada sesuatu di tengah jalan di depan Anda; **2** terus; **go ahead!** terus saja! **go straight ahead until you get to the crossroads** terus saja sampai di simpang empat; **3** menang; **our team is ten points ahead** regu kita menang sepuluh poin; **4 to be ahead of time, early** awal.

aid *noun* **1** bantuan, pertolongan; **aid to developing countries** bantuan kepada negara yang sedang berkembang; **2 in aid of** untuk membantu; **in aid of the flood victims** untuk membantu korban banjir.

AIDS *noun* AIDS; **to have AIDS** mengidap AIDS.

aim *noun* maksud, tujuan; **our aim is to control pollution** tujuan kita ialah mengontrol polusi.
verb **1 to aim to do** bermaksud, hendak; **we're aiming to finish the work today** kami bermaksud menyelesaikan pekerjaan ini pada hari ini; **2** mengarahkan; **a campaign aimed at older people** suatu kampanye yang diarahkan untuk manula; **3** *(a firearm)* membidik.

air *noun* **1** udara; **to go out for a breath of air** ke luar untuk menghirup udara; **2** angin; **to put some air in the tyres** memompa ban; **to travel by air** naik pesawat terbang.

air-conditioned *adjective* pakai AC; **the room is air-conditioned** ruangan ini telah dilengkapi dengan alat pendingin.

air conditioning *noun* AC.

air force *noun* angkatan udara.

airline *noun* perusahaan penerbangan.

airline attendant *noun* pramugari *(female)*, pramugara *(male)*.

airmail *noun* pos udara.

airport *noun* bandara (bandar udara), lapangan terbang, pelabuhan udara.

aisle *noun* gang.

alarm *noun* **1** sirene; **a fire alarm** sirene kebakaran; **2** alat tanda bahaya; **a burglar alarm** alat tanda bahaya (dipasang pada pintu atau jendela); **a false alarm** tanda bahaya palsu.

alarm clock *noun* weker.

album *noun* album.

alcohol *noun* alkohol, minuman keras.

alcoholic *noun* pecandu minuman keras.
adjective **alcoholic drinks** minuman beralkohol, minuman keras.

Algeria *noun* Aljazair.

alike *adjective* **1** sama; **they're all alike** semuanya sama; **2 to look alike** mirip, serupa; **the two sisters look alike** kedua kakak beradik perempuan itu kelihatan serupa, kedua adik berkakak perempuan itu sangat mirip.

alive *adjective* hidup.

all *adjective* **1** semua; **all the knives** semua pisau; **they've eaten it all** mereka sudah makan semuanya; **they're all here** semuanya ada di sini; **2 after all** bagaimanapun (juga), betapapun; **3 all alone** sendirian, seorang diri saja; **I'm all alone at the moment** saya sendirian saja sekarang; **4 all day** sehari suntuk, sepanjang hari; **5 not at all** sama sekali tidak; **he's not sick at all** dia sama sekali tidak sakit; **6 not at all** sama-sama; **'thank you very much' – 'not at all'** 'terima kasih banyak' – 'sama-sama'; **7 it's all I have** itu semua yang saya punyai; *(I don't have any more)* saya sudah tidak punya apa-apa lagi; *(I don't own anything else)* hanya ini yang saya miliki; **8 three all** tiga sama; **9 all the time** tak henti-hentinya, terus-menerus.

all along *adverb* selamanya; **I knew it all along** saya sudah lama tahu.

allergic *adjective* alergik, alergis; **to be allergic to cats** alergis terhadap kucing.

allow *verb*
1 memperbolehkan,

mengizinkan; **the teacher allowed them to go home** guru mengizinkan mereka pulang; **I'm not allowed to go** saya tidak diizinkan pergi; **2 to allow time** menyediakan waktu; **don't forget to allow enough time to eat first** jangan lupa menyediakan cukup waktu untuk makan dulu.

all right *adverb* **1** baik(lah) **'come over tonight' – 'all right'** 'datanglah nanti malam'– 'baiklah'; **the meal was all right** makanannya cukup baik; **2** sudah sembuh; **she's all right now** dia sudah sembuh sekarang; **3** baik-baik saja; **are you all right?** apakah Anda baik-baik saja? **is everything all right?** apakah semua baik-baik saja?; **4 is it all right to...?** apakah boleh…? **is it all right to borrow the car?** apakah bisa pinjam mobilnya?; **5 it's all right by me** saya tidak keberatan.

almond *noun* buah almond.

almost *adverb* hampir; **almost every day** hampir setiap hari; **almost everybody** hampir semua orang; **almost never** hampir tidak pernah.

alone *adjective* **1** sendirian, seorang diri; **he lives alone** dia tinggal sendirian; **2 leave me alone!** jangan ganggu saya! **3 leave those papers alone!** surat-surat itu jangan diapa-apakan! *(colloquial).*

along *preposition* **1** sepanjang; **there are trees all along the road** ada banyak pohon di sepanjang jalan itu; **to go for a walk along the beach** berjalan di sepanjang pantai; **2 she lives along the road from me** dia tinggal sejalan dengan saya.

aloud *adverb* keras; **to read aloud** membaca keras.

alphabet *noun* abjad, alfabet.

already *adverb* sudah, telah; **the train's already left** kereta api itu sudah berangkat; **it's six o'clock already** sudah jam enam; **I've already been to the dentist** saya telah ke dokter gigi.

also *adverb* juga, pula, pun; **she's also invited me** dia juga mengundang saya; **he's also going to Jayapura** dia akan pergi ke Jayapura juga.

alter *verb* mengubah.

alternate *adjective* berganti, berselang; **on alternate days** berselang hari; **we usually meet on alternate weeks** kami bertemu tiap dua minggu sekali.

a b c d e f g h i j k l m n o p q r s t u v w x y z

alternative *noun*
1 cadangan; **there are several alternatives** ada beberapa cadangan;
2 alternatif, jalan lain, pilihan; **there is no alternative** tak ada pilihan lain, tak ada jalan lain.
adjective **to take an alternative route** mengambil jalan lain.

alternatively *adverb* sebagai kemungkinan lain; **alternatively, we could go to Taman Mini** sebagai kemungkinan lain kita bisa ke Taman Mini.

alternative medicine *noun* pengobatan alternatif, pengobatan tradisionil.

although *conjunction* meskipun, walaupun; **although busy she's willing to help** walaupun sibuk dia bersedia menolong.

altogether *adverb*
1 semuanya; **the trip cost a thousand dollars altogether** ongkos perjalanan itu seribu dolar semuanya;
2 sepenuhnya; **I'm not altogether convinced** saya tidak yakin sepenuhnya.

aluminium *noun* aluminium.

always *adverb* selalu, senantiasa; **he always comes at seven** dia selalu datang pada jam tujuh.

am *verb* SEE **be**.

a.m. *abbreviation* pagi *(up to 10 a.m.)*, siang *(from 10 a.m. to 2 p.m.)*; **at 6 a.m.** jam enam pagi.

amateur *noun* amatir; **an amateur production** produksi amatiran.

amaze *verb* mengagumkan, mengherankan; **what amazes me is...** yang mengherankan saya adalah...

amazed *adjective* **1** heran *(surprised)*; **I was amazed to see her there** saya heran melihatnya di sana; **2** kagum *(in awe)* **the tourists were amazed at the beauty of Borobudur** para turis kagum melihat keindahan candi Borobudur.

amazing *adjective* **1** *(as a compliment)* hebat; **your outfit is amazing!** pakaian Anda hebat! **they've got an amazing house** rumahnya hebat sekali;
2 mengagumkan; **an amazing story** cerita yang mengagumkan.

ambassador *noun* duta besar (dubes).

ambition *noun* ambisi, cita-cita, hasrat.

ambitious *adjective* ambisius, berambisi.

ambulance *noun* ambulans.

amenities *plural noun* fasilitas.

America *noun* Amerika.

American *noun* orang Amerika.
adjective Amerika.

amnesty *noun* amnesti.

among, amongst *preposition* di antara; **I found it amongst my books** saya menemukannya di antara buku-buku saya; **you can decide among yourselves** silahkan putuskan hal itu antara kalian sendiri.

amount *noun* **1** banyak; **an enormous amount of food** banyak sekali makanan; **he has a huge amount of work** banyak sekali pekerjaannya; **2** jumlah; **an amount of money** sejumlah uang.

amp *noun* **1** *(electricity)* amper; **2** *(amplifier)* pengeras suara.

amplifier *noun* pengeras suara.

amuse *verb* menghibur, menggelikan.

amusement arcade *noun* tempat hiburan.

amusing *adjective* lucu, menggelikan.

an *article* SEE **a**.

anaesthetic *noun* anestesi, obat bius.

analyse *verb* menganalisa, menganalisis.

analysis *noun* analisa, analisis.

ancestor *noun* leluhur, nenek moyang.

ancient *adjective* **1** kuno; **an ancient monument** monumen kuno, tugu kuno; **2** purbakala; **ancient history** sejarah purbakala; **3** tua sekali; **an ancient pair of jeans** jeans yang tua sekali.

and *conjunction* **1** dan **Wiwik and Fermi** Wiwik dan Fermi; **shoes and socks** sepatu dan kaos kaki; **2** *(often not translated)* **louder and louder** makin lama makin keras; **there and back again** pulang pergi.

angel *noun* malaikat.

anger *noun* kemarahan, murka.

angle *noun* sudut.

angrily *adverb* dengan marah.

angry *adjective* marah; **she's angry with me** dia marah dengan saya; **to get angry** menjadi marah.

animal *noun* binatang hewan.

ankle *noun* pergelangan kaki; **I've twisted my ankle** pergelangan kaki saya keseleo.

a b c d e f g h i j k l m n o p q r s t u v w x y z

anniversary *noun* hari ulang tahun; **a wedding anniversary** hari ulang tahun perkawinan.

announce *verb* memberitahukan, mengumumkan.

announcement *noun* pemberitahuan, pengumuman.

annoy *verb* menjengkelkan; **he always annoys me** dia selalu menjengkelkan saya; **to be annoyed** merasa jengkel; **to get annoyed** menjadi jengkel.

annoying *adjective* menjengkelkan.

annual *adjective* tahunan.

anorexia *noun* penyakit anoreksia, penyakit anorexia.

another *adjective* **1** *(different)* yang lain; **would you like another one?** apakah Anda mau yang lain?; **2** lagi; **another two years** dua tahun lagi.

answer *noun* **1** *(to a question)* jawaban; **the right answer** jawaban yang benar; **2 the answer to a problem** penyelesaian masalah; **3** *(reply)* balasan.
verb **1** *(to a question)* menjawab; **he hasn't answered my question** dia belum menjawab pertanyaan saya; **2 to answer the door** membuka pintu; **please answer the door** coba buka pintu, coba lihat siapa di pintu; **3 to answer the telephone** mengangkat telepon.

answering machine *noun* alat penjawab telepon.

ant *noun* semut.

Antarctica *noun* Antartika.

anthem *noun* lagu, nyanyian; **the national anthem** lagu kebangsaan.

antibiotic *noun* antibiotika.

antique *noun* barang antik.
adjective antik; **an antique table** meja antik; **antique shop** toko barang-barang antik.

antiseptic *noun* antiseptik, penangkal infeksi.

anxious *adjective* cemas, gelisah, resah.

anxiously *adverb* dengan cemas, dengan gelisah; **we waited anxiously for the news** kita menunggu kabar itu dengan gelisah.

any *adjective* **1** *(not translated in Indonesian)* **is there any oil?** apakah ada minyak? **is there any money?** apakah ada uang? **are there any eggs?** apakah ada telur? **there isn't any flour** tak ada tepung; **there aren't any bananas** tak ada pisang; **2** *(meaning a little)* sedikit; **is there any butter?** apakah ada sedikit mentega? **I don't want any** saya tidak mau sedikit pun; **3 not...any more** tidak...lagi; **there isn't any more rice** tak ada beras lagi; **I don't want to go there any more** saya tidak mau ke sana lagi.

anybody, anyone *pronoun* **1** *(not translated in Indonesian)* **is anyone in?** apakah ada orang? **does anybody want to eat now?** adakah yang mau makan sekarang?; **2** siapa (saja), siapa pun; **anybody who wants some beer just help yourselves** siapa (saja) yang mau minum bir silahkan ambil sendiri; **there isn't anybody at home** tak ada siapa pun di rumah; **anybody can go** siapa pun boleh pergi.

anyhow *adverb* SEE **anyway**.

anyone *pronoun* SEE **anybody**.

anything *pronoun* **1** sesuatu; **is there anything I can do to help?** apakah ada sesuatu yang dapat saya tolong?; **2 not anything** tidak...apa-apa; **there isn't anything on the table** tidak ada apa-apa di meja; **3** apa saja; **anything could happen** apa saja dapat terjadi.

anyway, anyhow *adverb* bagaimana pun juga, namun demikian, toh *(colloquial)*; **anyway, I'll ring you before I leave** bagaimana pun juga, saya akan menelepon sebelum berangkat; **Nunung took those things anyway** bagaimana pun Nunung mengambil barang-barang itu.

anywhere *adverb* **1** *(not translated in Indonesian)* **have you seen my keys anywhere?** apakah Anda melihat kunci saya?; **2** di mana-mana, ke mana-mana; **I can't find the car keys anywhere** saya tidak bisa menemukan kunci mobil di mana-mana; **are you going anywhere tonight?** apakah Anda pergi ke mana-mana nanti malam?; **3** di mana saja; **put the shopping down anywhere** taruh belanjaan di mana saja.

apart *adjective, adverb* **1** jauhnya; **to be two metres apart** terpisah dua meter jauhnya; **2** berjauhan; **we don't like being apart** kami tidak suka berjauhan; **3** pecah; **the toy boat came apart** perahu-perahuan itu pecah; **4** berantakan; **his project fell apart** proyeknya berantakan; **5 apart from** selain dari; **apart from Adrie everyone was there** selain dari Adrie semua ada di situ.

apartheid *noun* apartheid.

apartment *noun* apartemen.

apologize *verb* minta maaf; **he apologizes for his behaviour** dia minta maaf atas kelakuannya; **he apologized to Tanya** dia minta maaf kepada Tanya.

apology *noun* permintaan maaf.

apostrophe *noun* tanda apostrofi.

apparatus *noun* alat, perlengkapan.

apparent *adjective* jelas kelihatan, nyata.

apparently *adverb* rupanya, tampaknya.

appeal *noun* permohonan, seruan.
verb **1** memohon; **to appeal for help** memohon bantuan; **2** menarik; **violent films don't appeal to me** film keras tidak menarik buat saya.

appear *verb* **1** tampil; **Mick appeared in yellow trousers** Mick tampil dengan celana kuning; **2** muncul; **to appear on television** muncul di televisi; **3** *(seem)* kelihatannya, tampaknya; **it appears that somebody has wiped the program off the computer** kelihatannya program itu telah dihapus dari komputer.

appearance *noun*
1 penampilan; **he's so interested in his own appearance** dia begitu tertarik pada penampilannya sendiri; **2** keadaan; **the appearance of the building is appalling** keadaan gedung itu mengerikan.

appendicitis *noun* radang usus buntu.

appetite *noun* nafsu makan; **the smell from the kitchen spoiled my appetite** bau dari dapur melenyapkan nafsu makan saya.

applaud *verb* bertepuk-tangan.

applause *noun* tepuk tangan.

apple *noun* buah apel.

apple tree *noun* pohon apel.

applicant *noun* pelamar.

application *noun* **1** lamaran; **a job application** lamaran kerja; **job application form** formulir lamaran pekerjaan; **2** permintaan; **credit application** permintaan kredit; **credit application**

form formulir permintaan kredit.

apply *verb* **1** melamar; **to apply for a job** melamar pekerjaan; **2 to apply to** berlaku; **that doesn't apply to students** itu tidak berlaku untuk murid.

appointment *noun* janji; **to make a dental appointment** membuat janji dengan dokter gigi; **to break an appointment** membatalkan janji; **to keep an appointment** menepati janji.

appreciate *verb* **1** menghargai; **I appreciate your advice** saya menghargai nasihat Anda; **2** berterima kasih; **I'd appreciate if you could put the videos back afterwards** saya akan berterima kasih kalau video-video tersebut dikembalikan ke tempatnya nanti.

apprentice *noun* magang.

apprenticeship *noun* pekerjaan sebagai magang.

approach *verb* **1** *(come near to)* mendekati; **we're approaching Jakarta now** kita sedang mendekati Jakarta; **2** *(tackle a task or problem)* menangani; **how did you approach the problem?** bagaimana Anda menangani persoalan itu?; **3** menjelang; **approaching Christmas** menjelang hari Natal.

appropriate *adjective* cocok, sesuai, tepat.

approval *noun* pengesahan.

approve *verb* **to approve of** menyukai, suka dengan; **they don't approve of her behaviour** mereka tidak menyukai kelakuannya.

approximate *adjective* kira-kira, kurang lebih, lebih kurang.

approximately *adverb* kira-kira; **approximately 200 people** kira-kira dua ratus orang.

April *noun* April.

April Fool's Day *noun* tanggal satu April (hari untuk berolok-olok).

Aquarius *noun* Aquarius.

Arab *noun* orang Arab. *adjective* Arab; **the Arab countries** negara-negara Arab.

arch *noun* lengkungan.

archaeologist *noun* ahli ilmu purbakala, arkeolog.

archaeology *noun* arkeologi, ilmu purbakala

archbishop *noun* uskup agung.

architect *noun* arsitek, ahli bangunan.

a b c d e f g h i j k l m n o p q r s t u v w x y z

architecture *noun* arsitektur, ilmu bangunan.

Arctic *noun* Arktik.

are *verb* SEE **be**.

area *noun* **1** daerah; **an expensive area** daerah mewah; **a rough area** daerah kasar; **in the Wonosobo area** di daerah Wonosobo; **a built-up area** daerah yang banyak gedung dan rumahnya; **2** luas **what's the area of this triangle?** berapa luas segitiga ini?

argue *verb* bertengkar, membantah; **they're arguing about the procedure** mereka bertengkar tentang tatacaranya; **there's no point in arguing** tak usah membantah.

argument *noun* argumen, percekcokan; **to have an argument** membantah, menentang.

Aries *noun* Aries.

arm *noun* lengan, tangan; **to break your arm** patah lengan; **to fold your arms** melipat tangan; **arm in arm** bergandengan tangan; **with open arms** dengan tangan terbuka.

armchair *noun* kursi tangan.

armed *adjective* bersenjata.

army *noun* angkatan darat, tentara; **to join the army** masuk tentara.

around *adverb* **1** *(with time, ages or amounts)* kira-kira, sekitar; **we'll be there around three** kami akan tiba sekitar jam tiga; **we need around half a dozen** kita perlu kira-kira setengah lusin; **2** *(surrounding)* keliling, sekitar; **the countryside around Bandung** daerah (pedalaman) sekitar Bandung; **3** *(wrapped around)* sekeliling; **the goat had a rope around its leg** ada tali di sekeliling kaki kambing itu; **4** *(near)* dekat; **is there a toilet around here?** apakah ada WC dekat tempat ini?

arrange *verb* **1** mengatur; **we've arranged to go to a concert on Saturday** kami telah mengatur untuk pergi ke konser pada hari Sabtu; **2** menata, menyusun; **please arrange these files** tolong susun map-map ini.

arrest *verb* menahan, menangkap, mengamankan; **the police arrested the students** polisi mengamankan mahasiswa-mahasiswi; **to be under arrest** ditahan, ditangkap.

arrival *noun* kedatangan, waktu tiba; **dead on arrival**

dia meninggal sebelum tiba.

arrive *verb* datang, tiba; **the train arrived five minutes ago** kereta api itu tiba lima menit yang lalu.

arrow *noun* (anak) panah, tanda panah.

art *noun* kesenian, seni; **modern art** seni modern; **art school** sekolah kesenian.

artery *noun* urat nadi.

art gallery *noun* balai budaya, galeri seni, musium kesenian.

article *noun* **1** *(in a newspaper)* karangan, tulisan; **2** barang, perabot **household articles** perabot rumah tangga.

artificial *adjective* bikinan, buatan, sintetis.

artist *noun* artis, seniman *(male)*, seniwati *(female)*.

artistic *adjective* artistik.

as *adverb, conjunction* **1** sebagai; **he works as a taxi driver in the evenings** dia bekerja sebagai sopir taksi pada malam hari; **2** seperti; **as you know** seperti sudah Anda ketahui; **as usual** seperti biasa; **as I told you** seperti telah saya katakan kepada Anda; **3** oleh karena; **as there were no trains, we took the bus** oleh karena tidak ada kereta api, kami naik bis; **4 as...as** sama, se...; **he's as tall as his brother** dia setinggi kakaknya, dia sama tingginya dengan kakaknya; **you must be as tired as I am** Anda pasti secapai saya; **5 as much...as, as many...as** se...; **I don't have as much time as you do** saya tidak ada waktu sebanyak Anda; **we have as many problems as they do** masalah kita sebanyak masalah mereka; **6 as long as** asal; **we'll go tomorrow as long as it's not raining** kita akan pergi besok asal tidak hujan; **7 for as long as** selama; **you can stay for as long as you like** Anda boleh tinggal di sini selama Anda mau; **8 as soon as** secepat; **as soon as possible** secepat mungkin.

asbestos *noun* asbes.

ASEAN *acronym* **Association of South East Asian Nations** Perhimpunan Bangsa-Bangsa Asia Tenggara.

ash *noun* abu.

ashamed *adjective* **to be ashamed** malu; **you should be ashamed of yourself!** tidak tahu malu! *(literally: you know no shame).*

ashtray *noun* asbak, tempat abu.

Asia *noun* Asia.

a b c d e f g h i j k l m n o p q r s t u v w x y z

Asian *noun* orang Asia. *adjective* Asia; **Asian flu** flu Asia; **Asian food** makanan Asia.

ask *verb* **1** *(to request something)* minta; **I asked for three coffees** saya minta kopi tiga gelas, **ask Fauzi to give you a hand** mintalah tolong pada Fauzi; **she's asked me to go with her** dia minta saya ikut dengan dia; **2** *(a question)* bertanya, menanyakan, menanyai; **you can ask at reception** silakan bertanya di bagian resepsionis; **Ruli asked the teacher about that problem** Ruli menanyakan soal itu kepada guru; **3** *(invitation)* mengundang; **they've asked us to their wedding** mereka mengundang kita ke perkawinannya; **4** *(an order)* menyuruh; **the teacher asked me to read** guru menyuruh saya membaca.

asleep *adjective* tidur; **to be asleep** (sedang) tidur; **the baby's asleep** bayi sedang tidur; **to fall asleep** tertidur.

asparagus *noun* asparagus, asperses.

aspirin *noun* aspirin.

assembly *noun* sidang; **general assembly** sidang umum.

assess *verb* **1** *(estimate)* menaksir; **2** *(evaluate)* menilai.

assignment *noun* tugas.

assist *verb* membantu, menolong.

assistance *noun* bantuan, pertolongan.

assistant *noun* pelayan, pembantu; **shop assistant** pelayan toko, pramuniaga.

association *noun* asosiasi, perkumpulan, persatuan.

assorted *adjective* beraneka macam, beraneka ragam, bermacam-macam, rupa-rupa.

assortment *noun* bermacam-macam, campuran.

assume *verb* menduga, mengasumsikan, mengira.

assumption *noun* asumsi.

assure *verb* **1** *(guarantee)* menjamin, menanggung; **2** meyakinkan; **Mina assured her mother she would be home by 10 o'clock** Mina meyakinkan ibunya bahwa dia akan pulang selambat-lambatnya jam sepuluh.

asthma *noun* asma, sakit bengek.

astrology *noun* astrologi, ilmu perbintangan.

astronaut *noun* astronot, antariksawan *(male)*, antariksawati *(female)*, kosmonot.

astronomy *noun* astronomi, ilmu falak, ilmu bintang(-bintang).

at *preposition* **1** di; **at home** di rumah; **at school** di sekolah; **at the beach** di pantai; **2** *(talking about the time)* pada; **at six o'clock** pada jam enam; **at the weekend** pada akhir pekan; **at night** pada malam hari; **3** kepada **Dewi looked at Marzuki and laughed** Dewi melihat ke Marzuki dan tertawa; **4 at last** akhirnya; **I've found a job at last** akhirnya saya mendapat pekerjaan.

athlete *noun* atlet.

athletic *adjective* atletik.

athletics *noun* atletik.

Atlantic *noun* Atlantik.

atlas *noun* atlas, buku peta.

atmosphere *noun* **1** atmosfir; **2** suasana; **the atmosphere before the election was really tense** suasana sebelum pemilihan umum tegang sekali.

atom *noun* atom.

atomic *adjective* atom.

attach *verb* melampirkan, mengikatkan.

attached *adjective* **1** dempet; **to be attached to** dempet; **attached house** rumah dempet; **2** terlampir; **the attached document** dokumen terlampir, surat terlampir.

attack *noun* **1** serangan; **the criminal's attack** serangan narapidana; **2** serbuan; **Japan's attack on Australia wasn't successful** serbuan Jepang terhadap Australia tidak berhasil.
verb **1** *(a thing)* menyerang; **2** *(a problem)* memecahkan.

attempt *noun* percobaan; **at the first attempt** pada percobaan pertama; **several attempts** beberapa percobaan.
verb **to attempt to do** berusaha, mencoba.

attend *verb* menghadiri; **to attend a class** menghadiri kelas.

attention *noun* perhatian; **the painting caught my attention** lukisan itu menarik perhatian saya; **to pay attention** memperhatikan; **please pay attention!** harap perhatikan! **you weren't paying attention** Anda tak memperhatikan.

attic *noun* loteng.

attitude *noun* sikap.

a b c d e f g h i j k l m n o p q r s t u v w x y z

attract *verb* menarik; **try to attract their attention** coba menarik perhatian mereka.

attraction *noun* atraksi, daya tarik; **have no attraction for me** tidak mempunyai daya tarik bagi saya.

attractive *adjective* menarik.

aubergine *noun* terung.

auction *noun* lelang.

audience *noun* hadirin, penonton.

August *noun* (bulan) Agustus.

aunt, auntie *noun* bibi, tante.

Australia *noun* Australia; **in Australia** di Australia; **to Australia** ke Australia.

Australian *noun* orang Australia.
adjective Australia.

Austria *noun* Austria.

Austrian *noun* orang Austria.
adjective Austria.

author *noun* pengarang, penulis.

autobiography *noun* autobiografi, otobiografi.

autograph *noun* autograf.

automatic *adjective* otomatis.

automatically *adverb* secara otomatis.

autumn *noun* musim gugur, musim rontok.

availability *noun* tersedianya.

available *adjective* tersedia, yang ada.

avenue *noun* jalan.

average *noun* rata-rata; **on average** rata-rata; **above average** luar biasa.
adjective biasa, rata-rata, sedang; **the average temperature** suhu rata-rata.

avocado *noun* avokad.

avoid *verb* menghindari, menghindarkan; **she avoided Komang** dia menghindari Komang; **avoid speaking to him if you can** kalau bisa, lebih baik menghindari berbicara dengan dia.

awake *adjective* **to be awake** bangun; **is Nina awake?** Apakah Nina sudah bangun? **Are you still awake?** apakah Anda masih belum tidur?

award *noun* penghargaan; **to win an award** mendapat penghargaan.

aware *adjective* sadar, tahu, mengetahui; **to be aware of a noise** mengetahui bahwa ada bunyi, sadar bahwa ada bunyi; **I'm not aware of any problem** saya tidak tahu kalau ada masalah; **as far as I'm aware** setahu saya.

away *adverb* **1** pergi; **I'll be away next weekend** saya

a b c d e f g h i j k l m n o p q r s t u v w x y z

akan pergi (keluar kota) pada akhir pekan; **they've gone away for a month** mereka pergi selama satu bulan; **go away!** pergilah! **2 to run away** lari *(people)*; **all the children ran away** semua anak lari; hilang *(animals)*; **Mat's dog has run away** anjing Mat hilang; **3** jauh **the shopping centre is only two kilometres away** pusat perbelanjaan hanya dua kilometer jauhnya; **how far away is it?** berapa jauhnya? **not far away** tidak begitu jauh; **4 to put something away** menyimpan; **I'll just put my books away** saya menyimpan buku-buku dulu; **5 to give away** memberikan; **she's given away all her tapes** dia memberikan semua kasetnya (kepada orang lain).

away match *noun* pertandingan di kota lain.

awful *adjective* **1** buruk, jelek sekali; **the play was awful!** sandiwara itu buruk sekali; **2** sakit; **I feel awful** *(ill)* saya merasa sakit; **3** amat menyesal; **I feel awful about it** saya amat menyesal tentang itu; **4 an awful lot of** banyak sekali.

awkward *adjective* **1** risih, tegang, menegangkan; **it's an awkward situation** ini keadaan yang menegangkan; **it's a bit awkward** itu agak menegangkan; **2** canggung; **an awkward child** anak yang canggung; **3** sukar dijawab; **an awkward question** pertanyaan yang sukar dijawab.

axe *noun* kampak, kapak. *verb* **to be axed from a position** dipecat dari jabatan.

B b

baby *noun* bayi.

babysit *verb* mengasuh anak, menjaga anak.

babysitter *noun* pengasuh anak, penjaga anak.

babysitting *noun* pekerjaan mengasuh anak, pekerjaan menjaga anak.

back *noun* **1** *(of a person or animal)* punggung; **I have a sore back** punggung saya sakit; **2** *(of a piece of paper, your hand)* sebelah belakang; **on the back of** di sebelah belakang; **a garden at the back of the house** kebun di belakang rumah; **3** *(in football or hockey)* pemain

belakang; **4 to do something behind someone's back** melakukan sesuatu di luar pengetahuan seseorang, melakukan sesuatu secara diam-diam.
adjective belakang; **the back seat of the car** tempat duduk mobil di bagian belakang; **the back door** pintu belakang; **the back yard** halaman belakang; **back door** pintu belakang.
adverb **1 to go back** kembali; **to go back to school** kembali ke sekolah; **Lucy's gone back to Denpasar** Lucy sudah kembali ke Denpasar; **2 to come back** kembali, pulang; **they've come back from Jayapura** mereka sudah pulang dari Jayapura; **Chelsea's still not back at work** Chelsea belum kembali ke kantor; **we went by bus and walked back** kami pergi naik bis dan kembali jalan kaki; **3 to phone back** telepon kembali; **I'll ring back later** nanti saya akan telepon kembali; **4 to give back** mengembalikan; **5 to go there and back again** pulang pergi.
verb **1** *(to support)* mendukung *(a candidate, for example)*; **almost all the Indonesian uni students backed Megawati for president** hampir seluruh mahasiswa Indonesia mendukung Megawati untuk menjadi presiden; **2** *(to bet on)* bertaruh **don't back that horse** jangan bertaruh pada kuda itu.

- **to back up** *(computing)* membackup; **to back up a file** membackup file.
- **to back somebody up** mendukung.

backache *noun* sakit punggung.

backbone *noun* tulang punggung.

backfire *verb (go wrong)* **his plan backfired** rencananya gagal.

background *noun* latar belakang; **the temple in the background** candi di latar belakang; **background music** iringan musik, musik latar belakang.

backhand *noun* backhand.

backing *noun* **1** *(on sticky-back plastic, for example)* lapisan belakang; **2** *(moral support)* dukungan moril; **3** *(in music)* iringan; **backing group** iringan musik.

backpack *noun* ransel.

backside *noun* pantat.

backstage *adverb* belakang panggung.

backstroke *noun* gaya punggung.

back to front *adverb* terbalik; **your jumper's on back to front** baju jamper Anda terbalik.

backup *noun* **1** *(support)* sokongan; **2** *(in computing)* backup; **a backup disk** disket backup.

backwards *adverb (to lean or fall)* ke belakang.

bacon *noun* lemak babi *(literally pork fat)*; **bacon and eggs** telur mata sapi dan lemak babi.

bad *adjective* **1** *(not good)* buruk, jelek; **bad work** pekerjaan yang jelek; **her new film's not bad** filmnya yang baru tidak jelek; **bad weather** cuaca buruk; **his handwriting is bad** tulisannya jelek; **2** *(serious)* serius, parah; **a bad accident** kecelakaan yang serius; **a bad illness** penyakit yang parah; **3** *(rotten)* busuk; **bad meat** daging busuk; **to go bad** membusuk; **4** *(rude)* **bad language** bahasa kasar; **5** *(naughty)* jahat; **bad dog!** anjing jahat! **a bad person** orang jahat; **6 too bad!** sayang! **bad luck!** sial!

badge *noun* lencana.

badly *adverb* **1** *(appearance, sound, communication, etc.)* buruk, jelek; **he writes badly** dia menulis dengan buruk; **2** *(seriously)* parah; **badly hurt** luka parah; **3 the car was badly damaged** mobil rusak sekali; **I slept badly** tidur saya tidak nyenyak; **the exam went badly** saya gagal dalam ujian.

bad-mannered *adjective* tidak tahu adat.

badminton *noun* bulu tangkis; **to play badminton** main bulu tangkis; **badminton player** pebulu tangkis, pemain bulu tangkis.

bad-tempered *adjective* pemarah, pemberang; **he's very bad-tempered** dia bersifat pemarah.

bag *noun* **1** *(handbag or plastic bag)* tas; **2** *(suitcase)* kopor.

bags *plural noun* **1** bagasi, barang-barang, kopor-kopor; **to pack your bags** mengepak kopor **2 to have bags under your eyes** bagian bawah matanya hitam.

baggage *noun* bagasi, barang-barang, kopor-kopor.

baggage allowance *noun* berat bagasi yang diizinkan.

baggage reclaim *noun* tempat mengambil bagasi,

a b c d e f g h i j k l m n o p q r s t u v w x y z

a b c d e f g h i j k l m n o p q r s t u v w x y z

tempat mengambil kopor-kopor.

bake *verb* memanggang; **to bake a cake** memanggang kue.

baked *adjective* panggang.

baker *noun* pembuat roti.

bakery *noun* toko roti (dan kue).

balance *noun* **1** keseimbangan; **to lose your balance** kehilangan keseimbangan; **2** *(money in your bank account)* saldo.

balanced *adjective* **1** stabil; **2** berimbang; **a balanced diet** diet yang berimbang.

balcony *noun* balkon.

bald *adjective* botak.

Bali *noun (the island)* pulau Bali.

Balinese *noun (a person)* orang Bali; *(the language)* bahasa Bali.
adjective Bali; **Balinese cuisine** masakan Bali.

ball *noun* bola.

ballet *noun* balet, sendratari.

balloon *noun* balon.

ballot *noun* pemilihan; **ballot paper** kartu pemilihan.

ballpoint (pen) *noun* (pena) bolpoin.

ban *noun* larangan; **a ban on political activity** larangan kegiatan politik.

banana *noun* pisang.

band *noun* **1** *(playing music)* band, grup; **a rock band** grup rok; **2** sinar; **a band of light** sinar cahaya; **a rubber band** gelang karet.

bandage *noun* pembalut, perban.

bang *noun (noise)* bunyi keras, letusan, suara keras.
verb **1** *(to hit)* memukulkan; **he banged his fist on the table** dia memukulkan tinjunya di atas meja; **2** *(to knock)* mengetukkan; **Fahmi banged the plate on the table** Fahmi mengetukkan piring ke meja; **3** terbentur; **I banged into the table** saya terbentur pada meja itu; **I banged my head on the cupboard** kepala saya terbentur pada lemari itu; **4** menggedor; **to bang on the door** menggedor pintu.

banisters, bannisters *plural noun* pegangan pada tangga, sandaran tangan.

bank *noun* **1** *(for money)* bank; **2** *(of a river or lake)* pinggir, tebing, tepi.
verb menabung uang.

bank account *noun* tabungan, rekening bank.

bank balance *noun* saldo.

bank card *noun* kartu bank.

banknote *noun* uang kertas.

bank statement *noun* pernyataan bank.

bar *noun* **1** *(selling drinks)* bar; **Ted works in a bar** Ted bekerja di bar; **2** batang; **a bar of soap** sebatang sabun. *verb* **1** *(to block physically)* menghalangi; **to bar someone's way** menghalangi jalan orang; **2** *(to ban from an activity)* melarang.

barbecue *noun* barbecue. *verb* memanggang; **to barbecue a chicken** memanggang ayam; **barbecued chicken** ayam panggang.

barbed wire *noun* kawat (ber)duri.

bare *adjective* gundul, kosong.

barefoot *adjective* tidak beralas kaki; **to walk barefoot** berjalan tanpa alas kaki.

bargain *noun* *(a good buy)* harga yang murah sekali; **he got a bargain** dia dapat membeli barang dengan harga yang murah sekali; **it's a bargain** itu murah sekali. *verb* menawar.

bark *noun* **1** *(of a tree)* kulit kayu; **2** *(of a dog)* gonggongan, salak anjing. *verb* menggonggong, menyalak.

barmaid *noun* perempuan yang bekerja di bar.

barman *noun* lelaki yang bekerja di bar.

barn *noun* gudang.

barrel *noun* tong.

barrier *noun* rintangan.

base *noun* dasar, kaki.

baseball *noun* baseball.

based *adjective* **1 to be based on** berdasarkan; **the film is based on an Indian legend** film itu berdasarkan dongeng India; **2 to be based in** bertugas; **she's based in Ubud** dia bertugas di Ubud.

basement *noun* basement.

bash *noun* **1** peot; **that car's got a bash on the door** mobil itu peot di pintunya; **2 let's have a bash!** marilah berpesta! *verb* **I bashed my head** kepala saya terbentur.

basic *adjective* **1** pokok; **basic salary** gaji pokok; **2** dasar; **basic knowledge** pengetahuan dasar; **the basic facts** fakta-fakta dasar; **3** *(not luxurious)* sederhana; **the accommodation's a bit basic** penginapan itu agak sederhana.

basically *adverb* **1** pada dasarnya; **you're basically correct** pada dasarnya, Anda benar; **2** sebenarnya; **basically, I don't want to go** sebenarnya, saya tak mau pergi.

basics *noun* hal-hal yang dasar.

basin *noun (washbasin)* baskom.

basis *noun* dasar; **on the basis of** berdasarkan pada; **on a regular basis** secara tetap.

basket *noun* keranjang; **a waste-paper basket** keranjang sampah.

basketball *noun* bola basket, bola keranjang; **to play basketball** main bola basket.

bass *noun* bas; **to sing bass** menyanyi dengan suara bas.

bass drum *noun* genderang bas.

bass guitar *noun* gitar bas.

bat *noun* **1** alat pemukul; **2** *(animal)* kalong, kampret, kelelawar.

bath *noun* **1 to have a bath** mandi; **she's in the bath** dia sedang mandi; **2** *(bathtub to hold water, not for bathing in)* bak mandi; **the bath's empty again** bak mandinya kosong lagi.

bathe *verb* **1** *(a person, animal)* memandikan; **2** *(a wound)* membersihkan; **3** *(go swimming)* berenang.

bathroom *noun* kamar mandi.

baths *plural noun* kolam renang.

bath towel *noun* handuk.

batter *noun (for frying)* adonan; **bananas in batter** pisang goreng; **pancake batter** adonan panekuk.

battery *noun* **1** *(for a torch or radio, for example)* baterai; **2** *(for a car)* aki.

battle *noun* peperangan, pertempuran.

bay *noun* teluk.

BC [Before Christ] *abbreviation* sebelum Masehi.

be *verb* **1** *(does not translate into Indonesian in these expressions)* **don't be late** jangan terlambat; **I am sick** saya sakit; **he's my student** dia siswa saya; **it was fine yesterday** cuacanya bagus kemarin; **it's five o'clock** sekarang jam lima; **what time is it?** jam berapa (sekarang)?; **2** *(indicating existence in time, be present)* (ber)ada; **he's here** dia (ada) di sini; **I am in Jakarta** saya (ber)ada di Jakarta; **3** sedang; **she's typing the report now** dia sedang mengetik laporan itu; **4** *(future marker)* akan; **they'll leave next month** bulan depan mereka akan berangkat.

beach *noun* pantai; **on the beach** di pantai.

bead *noun* manik-manik.

beak *noun* paruh.

beam *noun* **1** *(of light)* sinar; **2** *(for a roof)* balok, tiang.

bean *noun* kacang; **snake beans** kacang panjang; **bean sprouts** tauge; **string beans** buncis.

bear *noun* beruang.
verb **1** tidak suka; **I can't bear him** saya tidak suka padanya; **she can't bear the idea** dia tidak suka ide itu; **2** ingat; **to bear in mind** mengingat.

- **to bear up** tahan; **although the wound was painful she bore up** walaupun lukanya sakit sekali dia bisa tahan.

beard *noun* jenggot.

bearded *adjective* berjenggot.

bearings *plural noun* **to get one's bearings** menentukan tempat.

beast *noun* **1** *(animal)* binatang; **2** bangsat, jahanam; **you beast!** bangsat kamu! *(very rude)*.

beat *noun* **1** *(musical)* gerakan, irama; **2** debar, denyut(an); **heart beat** debar jantung.
verb **1** *(defeat)* mengalahkan; **Tuti beat him** Tuti mengalahkan dia; **2** *(hit)* memukul; **3** mengaduk, mengocok; **beat the eggs** mengocok telur; **4** tidak ada lainnya yang lebih baik; **you can't beat a good meal** tidak ada apa-apa yang lebih memuaskan daripada makanan yang enak.

- **to beat up** memukuli; **Frank beat Tony up** Frank memukuli Tony.

beautiful *adjective* bagus, cantik, elok, indah; **a beautiful day** hari bagus; **a beautiful woman** perempuan cantik, perempuan elok; **a beautiful picture** gambar indah; **a beautiful place** tempat bagus.

beautifully *adverb (depending on the context)* **she sings beautifully** dia menyanyi dengan merdu; **he dresses beautifully** dia berpakaian bagus; **she dances beautifully** dia menari dengan indah, dia menari dengan gemulai.

beauty *noun* kecantikan, keelokan, keindahan.

beauty spot *noun* **1** *(for tourists)* lokasi indah, tempat indah; **2** *(on the face)* tahi lalat.

a b c d e f g h i j k l m n o p q r s t u v w x y z

a
b
c
d
e
f
g
h
i
j
k
l
m
n
o
p
q
r
s
t
u
v
w
x
y
z

because *conjunction*
1 karena, sebab; **because it's you** karena Anda; **because it's cold** karena dingin; **2 because of** disebabkan oleh, oleh karena, oleh sebab; **because of the accident** disebabkan oleh kecelakaan itu.

become *verb* menjadi.

bed *noun* **1** tempat tidur; **in bed** di tempat tidur; **to go to bed** pergi tidur; **2** *(flower bed)* tempat menanam bunga.

bedclothes *plural noun* pakaian tidur.

bedding *noun* seprei *(sheet)*, selimut *(blanket)*.

bedroom *noun* kamar tidur; **bedroom furniture** mebel kamar tidur, perabot kamar tidur.

bedside *noun* sisi tempat tidur; **a bedside table** meja di sisi tempat tidur.

bedspread *noun* penutup tempat tidur.

bedtime *noun* waktu tidur.

bee *noun* lebah, tawon.

beef *noun* daging sapi; **beef curry** kari daging (sapi).

beefburger *noun* hamburger.

beer *noun* bir; **two beers please** bisa minta dua gelas bir.

beetle *noun* kumbang.

beetroot *noun* sayur bit.

before *preposition* **1** sebelum; **before Monday** sebelum hari Senin; **the day before** sehari sebelumnya; **the week before** seminggu sebelumnya; **she left before us** dia berangkat sebelum kita; **2** dulu, dahulu; **the day before yesterday** kemarin dulu; **I've seen her before somewhere** saya pernah melihatnya dulu; **I had seen the film before** saya pernah menonton film itu dahulu. *conjunction* sebelum; **I locked the windows before leaving** saya mengunci jendela sebelum berangkat; **phone me before you leave** harap telepon saya sebelum berangkat; **oh, before I forget** ah, sebelum saya lupa.

beforehand *adverb (ahead of time)* sebelumnya; **please phone beforehand** harap menelepon sebelumnya.

beg *verb* **1** *(ask for money)* mengemis; **2** *(ask)* meminta, memohon; **he begged Mei not to leave** dia meminta supaya Mei tidak pergi; **I beg your pardon** maafkan saya.

begin *verb* mulai, **the film begins at eight** film itu mulai (pada) jam delapan; **all the words beginning with 'S'** semua kata yang mulai dengan huruf 'S'; **to begin to do** mulai melakukan; **at last he's beginning to understand** akhirnya dia mulai mengerti.

beginner *noun* pemula; **she's a beginner at tennis** dia pemula dalam olahraga tenis.

beginning *noun* awal, permulaan; **at the beginning of this week** pada awal minggu ini; **at the beginning of the play** pada permulaan sandiwara itu.

behalf *noun* **on behalf of** atas nama.

behave *verb* **1** berkelakuan; **Kim behaved badly** Kim berkelakuan jelek; **2 behave yourselves!** jangan nakal!

behaviour *noun* kelakuan.

behind *noun* pantat.
preposition, *adverb* **1** di belakang **behind the car** di belakang mobil; **the car behind** mobil yang di belakang; **2** *(not making progress)* terbelakang; **he's behind in class** dia terbelakang di kelas; **3 to leave something behind** *(unintentionally)* ketinggalan; **he left his keys behind** kuncinya ketinggalan; *(intentionally)* meninggalkan; **they left the children behind** mereka meninggalkan anak-anak.

beige *adjective* krem.

belief *noun* kepercayaan, keyakinan; **political beliefs** keyakinan politik.

believe *verb* **1** percaya; **I believe her** saya percaya dia; **I don't believe you!** saya tak percaya Anda!; **2 to believe in** percaya akan; **to believe in ghosts** percaya akan hantu.

bell *noun* **1** *(in a church)* bel, genta, lonceng; **ring the bell** membunyikan bel, mengebel; **2 that name rings a bell** saya kenal nama itu.

belong *verb* **1 to belong to** kepunyaan; **that jacket belongs to Robbie** jaket itu kepunyaan Robbie; **2** anggota; **I belong to a club** saya menjadi anggota klub itu, saya menjadi anggota perkumpulan itu; **3** *(go)* seharusnya, semestinya; **that lamp belongs on the desk** lampu itu semestinya di atas meja tulis itu.

belongings *plural noun* harta milik; **personal belongings** barang-barang pribadi.

below *preposition* di bawah; **below the window** di bawah jendela.
adverb bawah; **that scream came from below** jeritan itu dari bawah; **she went below** dia pergi ke bawah; **the one below** yang di bawah.

a b c d e f g h i j k l m n o p q r s t u v w x y z

belt *noun* ikat pinggang, sabuk.

bench *noun* bangku.

bend *noun* belokan, tikungan. *verb* **1** *(to make a bend in)* menekuk *(your arm or leg)*; **2** *(to curve)* membengkokkan *(a wire)*; **3 to bend down or forwards** membongkok, membungkuk; **I bent down to look** saya membungkuk untuk melihat; **4** *(a path, trail)* membelok, menikung.

beneath *preposition* di bawah.

benefit *noun* **1** kebaikan, keuntungan, manfaat; **of great benefit** bermanfaat besar; **2 unemployment benefits** tunjangan pengangguran.

bent *adjective* bungkuk.

beret *noun* baret.

berth *noun* **1** *(in a harbour)* tempat berlabuh; **2** tempat tidur di kapal atau kereta api.

beside *preposition* *(next to)* di samping, di sebelah; **beside the video** di samping video; **that's beside the point** tidak penting, tidak mengenai pokoknya.

besides *adverb* **1** *(anyway)* lagi pula, tambahan pula; **besides, it's too late** lagi pula, sudah terlambat; **2** *(as well)* selain; **besides them, there are foreign tourists** selain mereka ada wisatawan mancanegara.

best *adjective, adverb* **1** paling baik, terbaik; **that's the best film** itu film yang paling baik, itu film yang terbaik; **she's the best at swimming** dia yang terbaik dalam olahraga renang; **he plays best** dia adalah pemain terbaik; **best of all** terbaik; **2** sebaik-baiknya, sedapat-dapatnya; **the best thing to do is to tell her everything** sebaiknya kita memberitahukan semuanya kepadanya; **3 to do one's best** berusaha sebaik-baiknya, berusaha sedapat-dapatnya; **he did his best to help me** dia berusaha sedapat-dapatnya untuk menolong saya; **4 she's my best friend** dia teman saya yang paling akrab; **to the best of my knowledge** sepanjang pengetahuan saya; **all the best!** selamat!

best man *noun* saksi laki-laki (pada perkawinan).

bet *verb* **1** bertaruh; **I bet our school will win** saya bertaruh sekolah kami akan menang; **2** yakin; **I bet you he'll forget** saya yakin dia akan lupa.

better *adjective, adverb* **1** *(appearance)* lebih bagus;

this hat's better than that topi ini lebih bagus daripada yang itu; **2** *(content)* lebih baik; **this book's better than that** isi buku ini lebih baik daripada yang itu; **I want to find a better job** saya ingin mencari pekerjaan yang lebih baik; **this pen writes better** pena ini lebih baik; **3 even better** lebih baik lagi; **4** *(health)* lebih baik; **she's better now** dia lebih baik sekarang; **to feel better** merasa lebih baik; **5** *(improve)* **to get better** (se)makin baik; **my Indonesian is getting better** Bahasa Indonesia saya makin baik; **the sooner the better** makin cepat makin baik. *adverb* lebih baik, sebaiknya; **you'd better phone her** lebih baik Anda meneleponnya; **I'd better not go** lebih baik saya tidak pergi; **I'd better go to the doctor** sebaiknya saya ke dokter.

better off *adjective* **1** *(richer)* lebih kaya; **they're better off than we are** mereka lebih kaya daripada kita; **2** *(more comfortable)* **you'd be better off in hospital** Anda tentu lebih baik di rumah sakit.

between *preposition* di antara; **between Jakarta and Bandung** di antara Jakarta dan Bandung; **between six and seven** antara jam enam dan jam tujuh; **between the two (of them)** antara mereka berdua.

beyond *preposition* **1** *(in space and time)* di seberang; **beyond the border** di seberang perbatasan itu; **2** di luar; **beyond my ability** di luar kemampuan saya; **3 it's beyond me!** terlalu sukar untuk saya!

Bible *noun* **the Bible** Alkitab, Kitab Suci.

bicycle *noun* sepeda; **by bicycle** naik sepeda.

bicycle lane *noun* jalur sepeda.

big *adjective* **1** besar; **a big event** peristiwa besar; **it's too big for me** terlalu besar untuk saya; **2 big brother** kakak.

bigheaded *adjective* berkepala besar, congkak, sombong; **he's so bigheaded** dia begitu sombong.

big screen *noun* layar besar, layar lebar.

big toe *noun* ibu jari kaki.

bike *noun* sepeda.

bikini *noun* bikini.

bilingual *adjective* berbicara dua bahasa, bilingual.

bill *noun* **1** *(in a restaurant)* bon; **may I have the bill**

please? bisa minta bonnya?; **2** *(for gas, electricity, etc.)* rekening.

billiards *noun* bilyar.

billion *noun* milyar.

bin *noun* tong; **rubbish bin** tong sampah.

binoculars *noun* teropong.

biochemistry *noun* biokimia.

biography *noun* biografi, riwayat hidup.

biology *noun* biologi, ilmu hayat.

bird *noun* burung.

bird sanctuary *noun* suaka unggas.

birdwatching *noun* **to go birdwatching** mengamati unggas.

biro *noun* bolpoin.

birth *noun* kelahiran; **to give birth** bersalin, melahirkan.

birth certificate *noun* akte kelahiran.

birth control *noun* pembatasan kelahiran.

birthday *noun* hari lahir, hari ulang tahun; **happy birthday** selamat ulang tahun; **a birthday present** hadiah ulang tahun.

biscuit *noun* biskuit.

bishop *noun* **1** uskup; **2** *(chess)* benteng, gajah, menteri.

bit *noun (of bread, cake, wood)* sedikit, sepotong; **a bit of chocolate** sepotong coklat.

bite *noun* **1** makan sedikit; **I like a bite before bedtime** saya suka makan sedikit sebelum tidur; **2** gigitan; **a mosquito bite** gigitan nyamuk.
verb menggigit; **to bite one's nails** menggigit kuku.

bitter *adjective* pahit.

black *adjective* hitam; **Yon's got black hair** rambut Yon hitam; **to turn black** menghitam, menjadi hitam; **black coffee** kopi tanpa susu, kopi hitam.

blackboard *noun* papan tulis.

blade *noun* mata pisau.

blame *noun* kesalahan; **to take the blame** menerima kesalahan.
verb bersalah, menyalahkan, salah; **she blamed Kris for the accident** dia menyalahkan Kris untuk kecelakaan itu; **she's to blame for it** dia yang bersalah; **you can't blame them** mereka tidak dapat disalahkan; **who's to blame?** siapa yang salah? **I don't blame you** saya tidak menyalahkan Anda.

blank *noun* kekosongan.
adjective **1** *(a page or a piece of paper, or a cheque)* kosong; **2 my mind went blank** pikiran saya kosong, saya tidak dapat berpikir.

blanket *noun* selimut.

blast *noun* **1** *(an explosion)* ledakan, letusan; **2** *(of air)* hembusan; **a blast of wind** hembusan angin; **3 to play music at full blast** main musik dengan keras sekali.

blaze *noun* lautan api, nyala api.
verb menyala dengan berkobar-kobar, **after the fire brigade left the scene the fire blazed fiercely up again** sesudah branwir meninggalkan tempat kebakaran itu api berkobar-kobar kembali dengan dahsyat.

blazer *noun* blazer, jas.

bleach *noun* obat pemutih.

bleed *verb* berdarah, mimisan; **my nose is bleeding** hidung saya mimisan.

blend *noun* campuran; **a blend of butter and sugar** campuran mentega dan gula.

blender *noun* blender.

bless *verb* memberkati, merestui.

blessing *noun* berkat, restu.

blind *noun* *(in a window)* gorden.
adjective buta, tunanetra; **to go blind** menjadi buta, menjadi tunanetra.

blink *verb* *(your eyes)* mengedipkan mata.

blister *noun* lepuh; **this shoe has given me a blister** sepatu ini menyebabkan kaki saya melepuh.
verb **this shoe has blistered my foot** sepatu ini menyebabkan kaki saya melepuh.

blob *noun* gumpal.

block *noun* **1** *(a square group of buildings)* blok, kompleks; **to go around the block** jalan sekeliling blok; **2 a block of flats** flat bertingkat, rumah bertingkat; **3 an office block** gedung kantor.
verb **1** *(an exit or a road)* merintangi; **2** *(a drain or a hole)* menyumbat; **the drain's blocked** selokan itu tersumbat.

blond(e) *adjective* berambut pirang.

blood *noun* darah.

blood test *noun* pemeriksaan darah, tes darah.

blotchy *adjective* berjerawat.

blouse *noun* blus.

a b c d e f g h i j k l m n o p q r s t u v w x y z

blow *noun* **1** *(physical)* pukulan; **2** *(emotional)* tamparan; **Teresa's refusal to dance with him was a blow to Sutanto's pride** penolakan Teresa untuk berdansa dengan Sutanto merupakan tamparan terhadap harga diri Sutanto.
verb **1** *(a person)* meniup; **the children competed to blow up balloons** anak-anak itu berlomba meniup balon; **2** *(the wind)* bertiup; **the wind blew strongly** angin bertiup dengan kencang; **3** *(in an explosion)* meledak; **the bomb blew up** bom meledak; **the bomb blew a hole in the wall** bom menyebabkan lobang di dinding; **4 to blow your nose** membersihkan hidung.
- **to blow something out** *(a candle, flames)* meniup.
- **to blow up** *(explode)* meledakkan.
- **to blow something up** *(a balloon or tire)* meniup; *(a building)* meledakkan; **they blew up the armory** mereka meledakkan gudang senjata itu.

blow-dry *noun* mengeringkan rambut dengan alat pengering rambut.

blue *adjective* biru; **to turn blue** membiru.

blues *noun* perasaan sedih.

bluish *adjective* kebiru-biruan

blunder *noun* kesalahan besar.

blunt *adjective* **1** *(knife or scissors)* tumpul; **2** *(person)* berterus terang, blak-blakan.

blurred *adjective* kabur.

blurry *adjective* kabur.

blush *verb* menjadi merah muka.

board *noun* **1** *(plank)* papan; **2** *(blackboard, whiteboard)* papan tulis; **3** *(notice board)* papan pengumuman; **4** *(for a board game)* papan mainan; **a chess board** papan catur; **5** *(accommodation)* indekos; **Natalie is looking for a place to board in Solo** Natalie sedang mencari tempat indekos di Solo; **6 on board** di kapal, di kapal terbang; **he drove on board the car ferry** dia mengendarai mobilnya naik ke feri.

boarder *noun* anak kos; **while in Yogya Louisa lived as a boarder** waktu di Yogya Louisa indekos.

board game *noun* permainan yang menggunakan papan.

boarding *noun* naik.

boarding pass *noun* pas naik (ke kapal, pesawat).

boarding school *noun* sekolah dengan asrama.

boast *verb* menyombongkan diri.

boat *noun* kapal, perahu, sampan.

body *noun* **1** *(living)* badan, tubuh; **2** *(dead)* bangkai *(animals)*; jenazah *(people, shows respect)*; **President Soekarno's body** jenazah Presiden Soekarno; mayat *(people, less respectful)*; **a body by the roadside** mayat di pinggir jalan.

bodybuilding *noun* binaraga.

bodyguard *noun* pengawal.

boil *noun (swelling)* bisul.
verb **1** mendidih; **the water's boiling** air sudah mendidih; **we must boil the water** kita harus mendidihkan airnya; **2** merebus; **to boil an egg** merebus telur; **this water hasn't been boiled** air ini belum dimasak.
• **to boil over** meluap.

boiled egg *noun* telur rebus; **soft-boiled egg** telur setengah matang.

boiler *noun* ketel.

boiling *adjective* **1** *(water)* mendidih; **2** panas sekali; **it's boiling hot today** panas sekali hari ini.

bolt *noun (on a door)* kunci grendel.
verb (to lock) memasang kunci grendel *(a door)*.

bomb *noun* bom.
verb mengebom.

bombing *noun (in a war)* pengeboman.

bone *noun* tulang.

bonfire *noun* api unggun.

book *noun* buku; **a book about society** buku tentang masyarakat; **a biology book** buku biologi; **a reference book** buku pintar, buku referensi.
verb memesan; **you'll have to book a table there** Anda harus memesan tempat di sana; **fully booked** sudah tidak ada tempat.

booking *noun* pemesanan.

booking office *noun* biro pemesanan, kantor pemesanan.

booklet *noun* **1** *(brochure)* brosur, buklet, buku kecil; **2** *(pamphlet)* pamflet.

boot *noun* **1** sepatu bot; **2** *(of a car)* (bagian) bagasi.

border *noun* perbatasan.

bore *noun* **1** orang yang membosankan; **2 what a bore!** sialan! **3** *(a well)* sumur.

bored *adjective* **to be bored** bosan; **I'm bored** saya bosan;

...t **bored** menjadi ...n.

boring *adjective* membosankan; **it was a boring film** film itu membosankan.

born *adjective* lahir; **to be born** lahir; **the baby was born last night** bayi itu lahir tadi malam.

Borneo *noun* Kalimantan.

borrow *verb* **1** meminjam; **can I borrow your pen?** bolehkah saya meminjam pena Anda?; **I'll borrow the car from Leanne** saya akan meminjam mobil dari Leanne.

boss *noun* atasan, bos, kepala, majikan.

bossy *adjective* suka memerintah orang.

both *pronoun* **1** berdua; **they both went** mereka berdua pergi; **2** kedua; **both my aunts were there** kedua tante saya ada di situ.
adverb baik...maupun; **both at home and at school** baik di rumah maupun di sekolah; **both in the dry and wet seasons** baik pada musim kemarau maupun pada musim hujan.

bother *noun* kesusahan; **Lasem's had a lot of bother with her son** anak lakilakinya sangat menyusahkan Lasem; **it's too much bother** terlalu menyusahkan; **it's no bother** tidak apa-apa.
verb **1** *(to disturb)* mengganggu; **I'm sorry to bother you** maaf, saya mengganggu Anda; **2** *(to worry)* mencemaskan; **that never bothers me** itu tidak pernah mencemaskan saya; **3** *(make an effort)* tidak usah; **don't bother about bringing anything** tidak usah membawa apa-apa; **don't bother!** tidak usah! **4 she didn't even bother to reply** dia sama sekali tidak menjawab.

bottle *noun* botol.

bottle opener *noun* pembuka botol.

bottom *noun* **1** dasar; **at the bottom of the sea** di dasar laut; **the bottom of the lake** dasar danau; **2** *(buttocks)* pantat.
adjective yang paling bawah, yang terbawah; **the bottom shelf** rak yang terbawah.

bounce *verb* melambung.

bouncer *noun* penjaga keamanan.

bound *adjective (certain)* pasti, tentu; **Eva's bound to be late** Eva tentu akan terlambat; **that was bound to happen** itu pasti terjadi.

boundary *noun* perbatasan.

bow *noun* **1** ikatan simpul; *(in a shoelace or ribbon)* **2 bow and arrow** busur dan anak panah.
verb menunduk.

bowels *plural noun* usus besar.

bowl *noun* **1** *(for noodles, for example)* mangkuk; **2** *(for washing or washing up)* baskom.
verb main boling.

bowler *noun* pemain boling.

bowling *noun (tenpin)* **to go bowling** main boling.

bow tie *noun* dasi kupu-kupu.

box *noun* **1** dos, kotak; **a box of chocolates** sekotak coklat; **2** peti; **(coffin)** peti jenazah; **3** *(on a form)* kotak.

boxer *noun (fighter)* petinju.

boxer shorts *plural noun* celana pendek petinju.

boxing *noun* tinju; **a boxing match** adu tinju, pertandingan tinju.

Boxing Day *noun* Hari Natal kedua.

box office *noun* loket karcis.

boy *noun* anak laki-laki.

boyfriend *noun* pacar (laki-laki).

bra *noun* beha, B.H.

brace *noun (for teeth)* bingkai penunjang gigi, penahan gigi.

bracelet *noun* gelang.

bracket *noun* tanda kurung; **in brackets** dalam tanda kurung.

brain *noun* otak.

brainwave *noun* ilham.

brake *noun* rem.
verb mengerem.

branch *noun* **1** *(of a tree)* cabang, dahan, ranting; **2** *(of a business, shop, bank)* kantor cabang; **our Bandung branch** cabang kita di Bandung.

brand *noun* merek, cap.

brand new *adjective* baru sekali.

brandy *noun* brendi, minuman keras.

brass *noun* **1** *(the metal)* kuningan; **2** *(in an orchestra)* **the brass** alat musik yang ditiup.

brass band *noun* orkes tiup.

brave *adjective* berani, gagah.

bread *noun* roti; **a slice of bread** sepotong roti.

breadfruit *noun* sukun.

break *noun* **1** *(a short rest)* istirahat; **ten minutes' break** istirahat sepuluh menit; **to take a break** istirahat; *(in school)* jam istirahat; **2** libur; **the Lebaran break** libur

a b c d e f g h i j k l m n o p q r s t u v w x y z

waktu Lebaran;
3 pemutusan, perpecahan; **a break in diplomatic relations** pemutusan hubungan diplomatik.
verb **1** memecahkan; **to break a record** memecahkan rekor; **I broke the eggs** saya yang memecahkan telur *(intentional)*; **I broke the glass** dengan tidak sengaja saya memecahkan gelas itu *(unintentional)*;
2 mematahkan, patah; **we broke the sticks for the fire** kami mematahkan kayu itu untuk membuat api *(intentional)*; **Bambang broke his tooth** gigi Bambang patah *(unintentional)*;
3 melanggar; **he broke the rules** dia melanggar peraturan; **4** merusakkan; **she's broken all her little sister's toys** dia merusakkan semua mainan adiknya;
5 menyampaikan; **to break the news** menyampaikan kabar; **6** mengingkari; **to break a promise** mengingkari janji.

- **to break down 1** mogok; **the car broke down** mobilnya mogok; **2** menangis; **she broke down when she heard the news** dia menangis ketika mendengar berita itu.
- **to break in** *(a thief)* memasuki, mendobrak.
- **to break out 1** *(a fire)* berkobar; **2** *(a fight or storm)* mulai; **3** *(a prisoner)* melarikan diri; **4** *(an epidemic)* berjangkit, timbul.
- **to break up 1** *(a family or couple)* bercerai, berpisah; **2** *(a crowd or clouds)* bubar; **we break up tomorrow** besok kita bubar.

breakdown *noun* **1** *(of a vehicle)* mogok; **we had a breakdown on Jalan Thamrin** tadi mobil kami mogok di Jalan Thamrin; **2** *(in talks or negotiations)* macet; **3** *(a nervous collapse)* gangguan; **to have a (nervous) breakdown** kena gangguan urat syaraf.

breakdown truck *noun* mobil derek.

breakfast *noun* makan pagi, sarapan; **Indonesians usually have rice for breakfast** orang Indonesia biasanya makan nasi waktu sarapan.

break-in *noun* pendobrakan (rumah)

breast *noun* **1** dada; **chicken breast** dada ayam; **2** buah dada, payudara *(women)*.

breaststroke *noun* gaya dada.

breath *noun* nafas; **out of breath** kehabisan nafas; **to take a deep breath** mengambil nafas panjang; **to have bad breath** mulut bau; **to get one's breath** istirahat sebentar.

breathe *verb* **1** bernafas; **Vera breathed deeply** Vera bernafas panjang; **2** menghirup; **they breathed in the smoke** mereka menghirup asap itu.

breathing *noun* pernafasan.

breed *noun (of dog, for example)* jenis, keturunan. *verb* **1** *(animals)* memelihara, mengembang biakkan; **2** *(to have young)* berbiak, berkembang biak, membiak; **rabbits breed fast** kelinci berkembang biak dengan cepat.

breeze *noun* angin sepoi-sepoi.

brew *verb (tea, beer)* membuat.

brick *noun* batu bata.

bride *noun* pengantin wanita; **the bride and groom** sepasang pengantin.

bridegroom *noun* pengantin laki-laki.

bridesmaid *noun* gadis pengiring pengantin.

bridge *noun* **1** *(over a river)* jembatan; **a bridge over the canal** jembatan lintas kanal; **2** *(card game)* bridge; **to play bridge** main bridge.

bridle *noun* kekang, kendali.

brief *adjective* pendek, singkat.

briefcase *noun* tas (kantor).

briefly *adverb* dengan singkat.

briefs *plural noun* celana dalam.

bright *adjective* **1** *(colour, light)* cemerlang; **a bright yellow shirt** kemeja kuning cemerlang; **2** terang; **bright sunshine** sinar matahari yang terang; **3** *(clever)* cerdas; **he's not very bright** dia tidak begitu cerdas; **4 to look on the bright side** optimis.

brighten up *verb* menjadi cerah; **the weather's brightening up** cuaca mulai cerah.

brilliant *adjective* **1** *(very clever)* brilian, jenius, pandai, ulung; **a brilliant dentist** dokter gigi yang ulung; **she's brilliant at maths** dia pandai dalam ilmu pasti; **2** *(wonderful)* brilian, hebat, **the game was brilliant!** pertandingan itu hebat!

bring *verb* **1** membawa; **they brought a gift** mereka

a b c d e f g h i j k l m n o p q r s t u v w x y z

membawa hadiah; **it brings good luck** membawa untung; **2** mengambil; **bring some water!** tolong ambilkan air!; **3** *(to return)* **to bring something back** mengembalikan.
- **to bring up** *(children)* membesarkan; **he was brought up by his grandmother** dia dibesarkan oleh neneknya.

bristle *noun* bulu.

Britain, Great Britain *noun* Britania Raya, negeri Inggris, Inggris Raya; **Britain is sending aid** negeri Inggris mengirim bantuan.

British *noun* orang Inggris; **the British** bangsa Inggris. *adjective* Inggris; **the British navy** angkatan laut Inggris; **the British Isles** Kepulauan Inggris.

broad *adjective* *(wide)* lebar.

broadcast *noun* siaran.

broccoli *noun* brokoli.

brochure *noun* brosur.

broke *adjective* kantong kering; **to be broke** *(no money)* tidak mempunyai uang.

broken *adjective* **1** pecah; **a broken window** jendela pecah; **2** patah; **his leg is broken** kakinya patah; **3** rusak; **this clock is broken** jam ini rusak.

bronchitis *noun* penyakit bronk(h)itis; **to have bronchitis** sakit bronk(h)itis.

brooch *noun* bros.

broom *noun* sapu.

brother *noun* saudara laki-laki; **little brother** adik laki-laki; **big brother** kakak laki-laki.

brother-in-law *noun* ipar laki-laki.

brown *adjective* coklat.

brown sugar *noun* gula aren, gula jawa.

bruise *noun* (luka) memar.

brush *noun* **1** *(for hair, clothes, shoes, etc.)* sikat; **toothbrush** sikat gigi; **2** *(paintbrush)* kuas. *verb* menyikat; **I've brushed the horse** saya sudah menyikat kuda itu.

bubble *noun* gelembung.

bucket *noun* ember.

buckle *noun* gesper.

Buddhism *noun* agama Buddha, Buddhisme.

Buddhist *noun* penganut Buddha, Buddhis.

budget *noun* anggaran belanja.

budgie *noun* burung parkit.

buffet *noun* bufet, bupet.

bug *noun* **1** *(insect)* kutu; **2** *(germ)* kuman penyakit; **a stomach bug** penyakit perut; **3** *(in a computer)* kerusakan.

build *verb* membangun, mendirikan; **they're building another office block** mereka sedang membangun gedung kantor lagi.

builder *noun* pembangun rumah.

building *noun* bangunan, gedung.

building site *noun* tempat pembangunan gedung atau rumah.

built-up *adjective* **a built-up area** daerah yang sudah dibangun.

bulb *noun* **1** *(light)* bohlam, bola lampu; **2** *(plant)* ubi-ubian.

bull *noun* sapi jantan.

bulldozer *noun* buldoser.

bullet *noun* peluru.

bulletin *noun* buletin, siaran singkat.

bully *verb* menggertak, memukuli, menakut-menakuti.

bum *noun* **1** *(bottom)* pantat; **2** *(person)* orang gelandangan; **3** yang tidak baik; **a bum deal** transaksi yang tidak baik.
verb **1 bum a ride** menumpang; **2 to bum around all day** luntang lantung saja sehari-hari.

bump *noun* **1** *(that sticks up)* benjol, jendul; **a bump on the head** benjol pada kepala; **2** *(jolt)* sentakan; **the plane landed with a bump** kapal terbang mendarat dengan sentakan; **3** *(noise)* bunyi keras.
verb **1** *(to bang)* menabrak, menubruk; **the car bumped into the pole** mobil menabrak tiang; **2 he bumped his head** kepalanya terbentur; **3 to bump into** *(meet by chance)* bertemu secara kebetulan; **I bumped into Helen at the supermarket** secara kebetulan saya bertemu dengan Helen di pasar swalayan.

bumper *noun* bemper.

bumpy *adjective* **1** *(road)* lekak-lekuk, tidak rata; **2** *(plane landing)* tidak mulus.

bun *noun* **1** *(bread)* roti dengan kismis; **2** *(in the hair)* konde, sanggul.

bunch *noun* ikat; **a bunch of flowers** seikat bunga.

bundle *noun* ikat.

bungalow *noun* bungalo.

a b c d e f g h i j k l m n o p q r s t u v w x y z

bunk *noun* tempat tidur; **bunk beds** tempat tidur bertingkat.

bureau *noun* biro, kantor.

burger *noun* hamburger.

burglar *noun* maling, pencuri.

burglar alarm *noun* alarm.

burn *noun* luka (kena) bakar. *verb* **1** membakar, terbakar; *(through sunburn)* **I burn easily** kulit saya mudah terbakar (oleh karena sinar matahari); **don't burn the rubbish there** jangan bakar sampah di situ; **I've burned myself with oil** saya kena luka bakar minyak panas; **careful! you'll burn your finger!** hati-hati! nanti jari Anda terbakar!
2 menyala; **this fire won't burn** api ini tidak mau menyala;
3 *(something you're cooking)* hangus; **you've burnt the rice again!** nasinya hangus lagi!

burnt *adjective* hangus, terbakar.

burst *verb* **1** *(a balloon or tyre, for example)* pecah; **a burst tyre** ban pecah; **2** tiba-tiba; **to burst out laughing** tiba-tiba tertawa; **to burst into tears** tiba-tiba menangis; **to burst into flames** tiba-tiba terbakar.

bury *verb* mengebumikan, mengubur.

bus *noun* bis, bus; **to go by bus** naik bis.

bus stop *noun* halte bis, perhentian bis.

bush *noun* semak belukar.

business *noun* **1** *(commercial dealings)* bisnis, dagang; **to be in business** berdagang; **she's in Dubbo on business** dia sedang ada urusan bisnis di Dubbo; **a business letter** surat bisnis; **she's in the textile business** dia berbisnis tekstil; **2** *(firm or company)* perusahaan; **small businesses** perusahaan-perusahaan kecil;
3 mind your own business! jangan ikut campur! **that's my business!** itu urusan saya!

business class *noun* kelas bisnis.

businessman *noun* pedagang, pengusaha, usahawan.

business trip *noun* bepergian untuk urusan dagang, kunjungan bisnis.

businesswoman *noun* wanita pengusaha.

bust *noun* buah dada, payudara.

busy *adjective* **1** sibuk *(a person, a day or a week)*; **don't**

disturb me, I'm busy jangan ganggu saya, saya sedang sibuk; **a busy day** hari sibuk; **2** ramai *(full of cars or people) (a road)*; **the shops were busy** toko-toko ramai; **the roads are busy** lalu lintas ramai; **3** sedang bicara *(phone)*; **the line's busy** (nomor itu) sedang bicara.

but *conjunction* tetapi; **small but strong** kecil (te)tapi kuat; **not Monday but Tuesday** bukan hari Senin tapi hari Selasa; **I'll try, but it's difficult** saya akan berusaha, tetapi tidak mudah.
preposition kecuali; **anything but that** apa saja kecuali itu; **everyone but Toni** semua orang kecuali Toni; **the last but one** satu sebelum yang terakhir.

butcher *noun* jagal, tukang daging.

butter *noun* mentega.

butterfly *noun* kupu-kupu.

button *noun* **1** *(on clothing)* kancing; **2** *(elevator)* kenop, tombol.

buttonhole *noun* lubang kancing.

buy *noun* pembelian.
verb membeli; **I couldn't buy the tickets** saya tidak dapat membeli karcis; **Jane bought Jenny a bracelet** Jane membeli gelang untuk Jenny, Jane membelikan Jenny gelang; **I bought this book from Louise** saya membeli buku ini dari Louise.

buzz *verb (a fly or bee)* dengung.

buzzer *noun* bel, lonceng listrik.

by *preposition* **1** oleh; **eaten by a rat** dimakan (oleh) tikus; **2** dengan; **by telephone** dengan telepon, lewat telepon; **by mistake** tidak dengan sengaja, dengan tak sengaja; **to come by bus** datang dengan bis; **by car** dengan mobil, naik mobil; **to go by plane** naik pesawat terbang; **3** dekat; **by the sea** dekat laut; **close by** dekat; **4** selambat-lambatnya; **ready by Monday** siap selambat-lambatnya hari Senin; **5 by oneself** sendirian; **I live by myself in the house** saya tinggal sendirian di rumah itu; **she did it by herself** dia melakukannya sendiri; **6 to take by the hand** memegang tangan; **the house was destroyed by fire** rumah itu musnah terbakar; **by the way** omong-omong.

bye *exclamation* **bye for now** sampai jumpa lagi, sampai

a b c d e f g h i j k l m n o p q r s t u v w x y z

lain kali, sampai nanti, selamat jalan, selamat tinggal.

bypass *noun* jalan bypass.

C c

cab *noun* **1** taksi; **cab stand** pangkalan taksi; **to call a cab** memanggil taksi; **2** *(on a truck)* tempat duduk.

cabbage *noun* kol, kubis.

cable *noun* kabel, kawat.

cable television *noun* televisi kabel.

cactus *noun* kaktus.

cafe *noun* kafe, warung kopi.

cage *noun* kandang, sangkar.

cake *noun* kue.

calculate *verb* menghitung, mengkalkulasi.

calculation *noun* kalkulasi, perhitungan.

calculator *noun* kalkulator.

calendar *noun* kalender, penanggalan.

calf *noun* **1** *(animal)* anak sapi; **2** *(of your leg)* betis.

call *noun* panggilan; **thank you for your call** terima kasih atas panggilan telepon Anda.
verb **1** memanggil; **to call the doctor** memanggil dokter; **they called the police** mereka memanggil polisi; **2** menelepon; **call this number** harap menelepon nomor ini; **3** menamakan; **we'll call her Susan** kami akan menamakannya Susan; **what's he called?** siapa namanya?

calm *adjective* tenang.
verb menenangkan.
- **to calm down** menenangkan; **the sea's calmed down a bit** laut sudah tenang lagi; **try to calm her down** cobalah menenangkannya.

calmly *adverb* dengan tenang.

calorie *noun* kalori.

camel *noun* unta.

camera *noun* kamera, fototustel.

cameraman *noun* juru kamera.

camp *noun* kemah.
verb berkemah.

campaign *noun* kampanye.

campervan *noun* karavan.

camping *noun* perkemahan; **to go camping** berkemah.

campsite *noun* lokasi perkemahan.

can *noun* **1** kaleng; **a can of tomatoes** sekaleng tomat; **2** *(for petrol or oil)* jerigen.

can *verb* **1** *(know how, possibility)* bisa, dapat; **can I help you?** apakah saya dapat menolong Anda? **I can't be there until six** saya tidak bisa berada di situ sebelum jam enam; **she can't help** dia tak dapat menolong; **she can play the guitar** dia bisa main gitar; **2** *(permission)* boleh; **you can leave your bike here** Anda boleh meninggalkan sepeda Anda di sini; **3** *(requesting help)* tolong; **can you open the door please?** tolong bukakan pintu itu; **could you answer the phone please?** tolong angkat telepon itu.

Canada *noun* (negeri) Kanada.

Canadian *noun* orang Kanada.
adjective Kanada.

canal *noun* kanal, terusan.

cancel *verb* membatalkan.

cancer[1] *noun* kanker.

Cancer[2] *noun* Sartan.

candidate *noun* calon.

candle *noun* lilin.

candlestick *noun* tempat lilin.

candy *noun* bonbon, gula-gula, kembang gula, permen.

canned *adjective* kalengan; **canned lychee** leci kalengan.

cannot, can't *verb* SEE **can**.

canoe *noun* kano.

canoeing *noun* berkano, mendayung kano.

can-opener *noun* pembuka kaleng.

canteen *noun* kantin.

canvas *noun* kanvas.

cap *noun* **1** *(hat)* topi; **a baseball cap** topi baseball; **2** *(on a bottle or tube)* tutup, sumbat.

capable *adjective* mampu, sanggup.

capacity *noun* **1** *(volume)* kapasitas; **2** *(power)* daya muat.

capital *noun* **1** *(city)* ibu kota; **2** *(letter)* huruf besar; **3** *(business)* kapital, modal.

Capricorn *noun* Makara.

capsize *verb* terbalik.

captain *noun* kapten.

capture *verb* **1** *(general)* menangkap; **2** *(in battle)* **capture an enemy** menawan musuh.

car *noun* mobil.

caramel *noun* gula bakar, karamel.

a b c d e f g h i j k l m n o p q r s t u v w x y z

a b c d e f g h i j k l m n o p q r s t u v w x y z

caravan *noun* kafilah, karavan.

card *noun* kartu.

cardboard *noun* kardus, kertas karton.

cardigan *noun* baju panas (yang ditutup dengan kancing di depannya).

cardphone *noun* telepon kartu.

care *noun* **1** ketelitian, perhatian; **Ludi wrote the address with great care** Ludi menulis alamat itu dengan hati-hati sekali; **2** perawatan; **in intensive care** di bawah perawatan intensif; **3** *(be careful)* hati-hati! **take care!** berhati-hati *(when saying goodbye)*.
verb **1 to care about** memperhatikan; **to care about the environment** memperhatikan lingkungan hidup; **2** peduli; **she doesn't care** dia tidak peduli; **I couldn't care less** saya tidak peduli sama sekali.

career *noun* karier.

careful *adjective* **1** berhati-hati, cermat; **a careful driver** sopir yang cermat; **2 be careful!** awas!, hati-hati!

carefully *adverb* **1** dengan teliti; **read the instructions carefully** baca instruksinya dengan teliti; **2** *(handle)* dengan cermat, dengan hati-hati; **she carried the kitten carefully** dia membawa anak kucing itu dengan hati-hati; **to drive carefully** menyetir mobil dengan cermat.

careless *adjective* **1** lengah; **he's very careless** dia lengah sekali; **2** sembrono, **such careless work!** pekerjaan yang sembrono!; **careless driving** mengemudikan mobil dengan sembrono.

caretaker *noun* pengurus, penjaga.

car ferry *noun* feri mobil, kapal tambang untuk mobil.

car hire *noun* sewa mobil.

carnation *noun* bunga anyelir.

carnival *noun* karnaval, pesta.

carpark *noun* tempat parkir.

carpenter *noun* tukang kayu.

carpet *noun* karpet, permadani.

car radio *noun* radio mobil.

carriage *noun* *(of a train)* gerbong.

carrier bag *noun* tas.

carrot *noun* wortel.

carry *verb* **1** membawa; **let me carry those parcels** biar saya bawa barang-barang itu; **2** *(transport)* membawa, mengangkut; **the truck was**

carrying sheep truk itu mengangkut domba.

- **to carry on** meneruskan; **she just carried on talking** dia terus berbicara.

carsick *adjective* mabuk darat.

carton *noun* **1** slof; **a carton of cigarettes** satu slof rokok; **2** karton, dos.

cartoon *noun* **1** *(a film, drawing)* kartun; **2** *(a comic strip)* komik.

cartridge *noun* patrun.

carve *verb* **1** *(wood)* mengukir; **2** *(meat)* memotong-motong.

case[1] *noun* **1** *(suitcase)* koper; **to pack a case** mengisi koper; **2** *(a wooden box for wine, for example)* kotak, peti; **pencil case** kotak pensil; **3** *(for spectacles or small things)* tempat.

case[2] *noun* **1** begitu; **in that case** kalau begitu; **that's not the case** tidak begitu; **2** penyakit; **a case of flu** penyakit flu; **3 in case** jika, jikalau, kalau, seandainya; **in case I'm late** seandainya saya terlambat; **check first, in case** periksa dulu, kalau-kalau diperlukan; **4** walaupun begitu; **in any case we have to be there** walaupun begitu kita harus ke sana; **5 court case** perkara.

cash *noun (money in general)* uang, uang kontan, uang tunai; **he never has any cash** dia tak pernah membawa uang tunai; **to pay cash** membayar kontan.

cash desk *noun* kasa.

cash dispenser *noun* ATM.

cashew *noun* kacang mede, kacang mete; **cashew fruit** jambu monyet.

cashier *noun* kasir.

cassava *noun* singkong, ubi kayu.

cassette *noun* kaset.

cassette recorder *noun* kaset.

cast *noun* para pemain sandiwara; **the whole cast is on stage** para pemain sandiwara ada di panggung.

castle *noun* **1** istana; **2** *(in chess)* benteng.

casual *adjective* **1** informal; **2** *(temporary)* sementara; **casual work** pekerjaan sementara.

casualty *noun* **1** *(in an accident)* korban; **2** *(a hospital department)* bagian (gawat) darurat.

cat *noun* kucing; **a tabby cat** kucing berloreng; **it's raining**

a b c d e f g h i j k l m n o p q r s t u v w x y z

cats and dogs hujan lebat; **to let the cat out of the bag** membuka rahasia.

catalogue *noun* daftar, katalog.

catastrophe *noun* bencana, malapetaka.

catch *noun* **1** *(on a door)* jepitan; **2** *(a drawback)* udang di balik batu *(literally, a shrimp behind the rock)*; **what's the catch?** tentu ada udang di balik batu!
verb **1** menangkap; **Lisa caught the ball** Lisa menangkap bola itu; **he was caught taking bribes** dia tertangkap basah menerima sogokan; **2** *(transport)* naik; **we're catching the next plane** kami akan naik pesawat terbang yang berikut; **3** *(an illness)* ketularan; **he's caught dengue fever** dia ketularan demam berdarah; **4** *(what somebody says)* mendengar; **I didn't catch your name** saya tidak mendengar nama Anda.
- **to catch up with** bertemu kembali; **Cheryl caught up with some old school friends** Cheryl bertemu kembali teman lama dari sekolah.

category *noun* kategori.

catering *noun* jasa boga, katering.

caterpillar *noun* ulat.

cathedral *noun* katedral.

Catholic *noun* Katolik.

cattle *noun* lembu, sapi, ternak.

cauliflower *noun* blumkol, kembang kol.

cause *noun* **1** penyebab, sebab; **the cause of the accident** penyebab kecelakaan itu; **2** alasan; **you had no cause to hit her** Anda tak punya alasan untuk memukulnya; **3** tujuan; **for a good cause** untuk tujuan yang baik.
verb menimbulkan, menyebabkan; **to cause problems** menyebabkan masalah; **the contaminated water caused an outbreak of cholera** air kotor itu menimbulkan berjangkitnya penyakit kolera.

caution *noun* berhati-hati, perhatian.

cautious *adjective* berhati-hati.

cave *noun* gua.

CD *noun* CD.

CD player *noun* alat CD.

CD-ROM *noun* CD-ROM.

ceiling *noun* langit-langit.

celebrate *verb* merayakan; **they're celebrating Idul Fitri** mereka merayakan Hari Idul Fitri.

celebrity *noun* selebriti.

celery *noun* seledri.

cell *noun* **1** *(biological)* sel; **2** *(prison)* bui.

cellar *noun* gudang di bawah tanah.

cello *noun* celo, selo.

cement *noun* semen.

cemetery *noun* kuburan, pekuburan, makam.

centenary *noun* abad, seratus tahun.

centigrade *adjective* Celsius.

centimetre *noun* senti (meter).

central *adjective* pusat, sentral; **central Jakarta** Jakarta pusat; **the office is very central** kantornya di pusat kota.

centre *noun* pusat, tengah; **in the centre of** di pusat, di tengah; **in the town centre** di pusat kota; **a shopping centre** pusat perbelanjaan.

century *noun* abad; **in the twenty-first century** pada abad kedua puluh satu.

cereal *noun* biji-bijian; **breakfast cereal** makanan untuk sarapan yang dibuat dari biji-bijian dan dicampur dengan susu (*definition only, Indonesians do not eat breakfast cereal*).

ceremony *noun* upacara.

certain *adjective* pasti, (ter)tentu; **a certain number** jumlah tertentu; **are you certain of that?** apakah Anda tahu pasti mengenai itu? **he's certain to be late** dia pasti terlambat.

certainly *adverb* pasti, tentu (saja) **certainly not** tentu tidak, sudah terang tidak; **certainly not!** tentu saja tidak!

certificate *noun* **1** sertifikat, surat; **2** akte, surat; **a birth certificate** akte kelahiran.

chain *noun* rantai.

chair *noun* kursi.

chalk *noun* kapur.

challenge *noun* tantangan; **the challenge of new ideas** tantangan ide baru.
verb menantang.

champion *noun* jago, juara, kampiun; **world champion** juara dunia.

chance *noun* **1** *(an opportunity)* kesempatan; **if you have the chance, go to Bromo** kalau ada kesempatan, berkunjunglah ke Bromo; **I've never had the chance to telephone** saya belum sempat menelepon;

a b c d e f g h i j k l m n o p q r s t u v w x y z

a b c d e f g h i j k l m n o p q r s t u v w x y z

2 *(likelihood)* ada kemungkinan **there's no chance of winning now** tak ada kemungkinan menang sekarang; **do you know her name, by any chance?** apakah mungkin Anda tahu namanya?; **3** *(luck)* kebetulan; **I ran into her by chance** kebetulan, saya bertemu dengannya.

change *noun* **1** perubahan; **a change of plan** perubahan rencana; **there have been many changes in Jakarta** ada banyak perubahan di Jakarta; **2** pengganti; **rice makes a change from potatoes** nasi dapat dimakan sebagai pengganti kentang; **3 let's go to a play for a change** mari kita nonton sandiwara saja; **4** *(money)* uang kecil, uang kembali; **I haven't any (small) change** saya tidak mempunyai uang kecil; **do you have change from fifty thousand Rupiah?** apakah ada uang kembali untuk lima puluh ribu rupiah?
verb **1** *(transform completely)* mengubah; **it's changed my life** mengubah hidup saya; **to change your mind** mengubah pikiran; **2** *(to switch from one thing to another)* (ber)ganti, pindah; **I'll just change (clothes) first** saya mau berganti pakaian dulu; **we have to change trains at Strathfield** kita harus pindah kereta api di Strathfield; **3** *(to exchange in a shop)* tukar; **can I change this if it doesn't fit?** kalau ini tidak pas, boleh ditukar?; **they changed places** mereka tukar tempat.

changing room *noun (for sport or swimming)* ruang ganti baju.

channel *noun* **1** *(on TV)* saluran; **to change channels** mengganti saluran; **2** terusan; **the English Channel** Terusan Inggris.

chaos *noun (informal)* kekacau-balauan; **it was total chaos** kacau-balau sekali.

chapel *noun* kapel.

chapter *noun* **1** *(in books)* bab; **2** *(in the Bible)* fatsal, pasal.

character *noun* **1** *(personality)* karakter, watak; **2** *(somebody in a book, play or film)* peran; **the main character** peran utama.

characteristic *noun* ciri-ciri.

charcoal *noun* arang.

charge *noun* **1** *(what you pay)* bayaran, harga, ongkos; **a booking charge** ongkos pesan; **an extra or additional charge** harga tambahan;

there's no charge gratis, tanpa biaya, tanpa ongkos; **2** kuasa, pimpinan, urusan; **Tom took charge of the little children** Tom mengurus anak-anak kecil; **who's in charge here?** siapa yang bertanggung jawab di sini?; **3** tuduhan, tuntutan; **to be on a charge of theft** dituduh mencuri.
verb **1** mengenakan bayaran; **how much do you charge for a day?** Anda mengenakan bayaran berapa seharinya?; **they charge twelve dollars a go** biayanya dua belas dolar sekali jalan; **2** *(a battery)* mengisi; **3 to charge with** *(a crime, for example)* menuduh; **the police charged Edi with stealing** polisi menuduh Edi mencuri.

charity *noun* amal, derma.

charm *noun* daya tarik, pesona.
verb memesonakan.

charming *adjective* mempesona, sangat menarik.

chart *noun* **1** *(table)* grafik; **the weather chart** grafik cuaca; **2 the charts** daftar lagu yang top; **number one on the charts** lagu yang terpopuler.

charter flight *noun* penerbangan carteran.

chase *noun* pengejaran; **a car chase** pengejaran mobil.
verb (a person or animal) memburu, mengejar.

chat *noun* obrolan; **to have a chat with** ngobrol dengan.

chatter *verb (gossip)* mengobrol.

cheap *adjective* murah; **cheap trousers** celana yang murah; **cheap rate** harga murah; **that's very cheap!** murah sekali!

cheaper *adjective* lebih murah.

cheaply *adverb* (dengan) murah.

cheat *noun* penipu.
verb menipu.

check *noun* **1** pemeriksaan; **passport check** pemeriksaan paspor; **2** pengecekan; **car check** pengecekan mobil; **3** *(in chess)* **check!** cek!
verb **1** memeriksa, mengecek; **she checked their names** dia memeriksa nama-namanya; **check they're all here** periksalah bahwa semuanya ada di sini; **2** mencocokkan; **Lance checked his answers with the key** Lance mencocokkan jawabannya dengan kunci.
• **to check in** cek-in.

check-in *noun* cek-in.

check-out *noun* cek-out.

a b c d e f g h i j k l m n o p q r s t u v w x y z

check-up *noun* pemeriksaan.

cheek *noun* **1** *(part of face)* pipi; **2** *(nerve)* kurang ajar; **what cheek!** kurang ajar! *(informal).*

cheeky *adjective* **1** kurang ajar; **2** *(rude)* muka tebal.

cheer *noun* **1** sorak (-sorai); **three cheers for Ken** bersoraklah tiga kali untuk Ken; **2** *(when you have a drink)* **cheers!** silahkan minum! horas!

- **to cheer up** bergembira; **cheer up!** bergembiralah!
- **to cheer somebody up** menggembirakan; **your news has cheered me up** kabar Anda menggembirakan saya.

cheerful *adjective* gembira, riang.

cheese *noun* keju; **a cheese sandwich** roti dengan keju; **cheese cake** kue keju *(actually a plain cake with grated cheese on top).*

chef *noun* juru masak, koki.

chemical *noun* bahan kimia.

chemist *noun* **1** apoteker; **2 chemist's** apotek; **3** *(scientist)* ahli kimia.

chemistry *noun* ilmu kimia

cheque *noun* cek; **to pay by cheque** membayar dengan cek; **to write a cheque** menulis cek.

chequebook *noun* buku cek.

chess *noun* catur; **to play chess** main catur.

chessboard *noun* papan catur.

chest *noun* **1** *(part of the body)* dada; **2** *(box)* peti; **3 a chest of drawers** lemari berlaci.

chew *verb* mengunyah.

chewing gum *noun* permen karet.

chick *noun* *(of a hen)* anak ayam.

chicken *noun* ayam; **barbecue chicken** ayam panggang; **chicken thighs** paha ayam.

chickenpox *noun* cacar air.

child *noun* anak.

childish *adjective* kekanak-kanakan.

child-minder *noun* pengasuh anak, penjaga anak.

chill *noun* **1** *(weather)* dingin; **2** *(illness)* masuk angin, pilek. *verb* mendinginkan.

chilled *adjective* *(wine, for example)* dingin.

chilli *noun* cabai, cabe.

chilly *adjective* dingin, sejuk; **it's chilly today** dingin hari ini.

chimney *noun* cerobong asap.

chimpanzee *noun* simpanse.

chin *noun* dagu.

china *noun* barang pecah-belah, porselin.

China *noun* Cina, Tiongkok.

Chinese *noun* **1** orang Cina, orang Tionghoa; **the Chinese** bangsa Tiongkok *(people)*; **2** *(language)* bahasa Cina.
adjective Cina, Tiongkok; **a Chinese person** orang Cina, orang Tionghoa; **a Chinese meal** makanan Cina.

chip *noun* **1** *(fried potato)* kentang goreng; **2** *(microchip)* mikrocip; **3** *(in glass or china)* pecahan kaca.

chipped *adjective* gumpil, pecah (sedikit).

chives *noun* lokio.

chocolate *noun* coklat.

choice *noun* pilihan; **you have a choice of two flights** Anda bisa memilih antara dua penerbangan.

choir *noun* koor, paduan suara.

choke *noun* *(on a car)* cok.
verb **1** *(by yourself)* tercekik; **she was choking on a fishbone** dia tercekik karena tulang ikan; **2** *(by someone else)* mencekik.

choose *verb* memilih; **you chose well** saudara memilih dengan baik; **it's hard to choose between the two** sulit memilih antara keduanya.

chop *noun* potongan daging; **a lamb chop** potongan daging domba.
verb membelah, memotong, mencincang.
- **to chop down** menebang *(a tree)*.

chopstick *noun* sumpit.

chord *noun* paduan nada.

chorus *noun* **1** *(when all join in the song)* refrein; **2** *(a group of singers)* paduan suara.

Christ *noun* Isa al-Masih, Kristus, Nabi Isa.

christening *noun* pembaptisan.

Christian *adjective* Kristen, Nasrani.

Christian name *noun* nama baptis, nama kecil.

Christmas *noun* Natal; **Happy Christmas!** Selamat Hari Natal!

Christmas card *noun* kartu Natal.

Christmas carol *noun* lagu Natal.

Christmas Day *noun* hari Natal.

Christmas dinner *noun* makanan Natal.

a b c d e f g h i j k l m n o p q r s t u v w x y z

a b c d e f g h i j k l m n o p q r s t u v w x y z

Christmas Eve *noun* malam Natal, tanggal 24 Desember.

Christmas present *noun* hadiah Natal.

Christmas tree *noun* pohon Natal.

chunk *noun* gumpal, potong.

church *noun* gereja.

churchyard *noun* halaman gereja.

chute *noun (in a swimming pool or playground)* peluncuran.

cigar *noun* cerutu.

cigarette *noun* rokok, sigaret.

cinema *noun* (gedung) bioskop; **to go to the cinema** menonton (di bioskop), pergi ke bioskop.

circle *noun* **1** bulatan, lingkaran; **to sit in a circle** duduk membuat lingkaran; **2** lingkungan **my circle of friends** lingkungan kawan-kawan saya; **3 to go round in circles** berputar-putar di situ saja.

circuit *noun* **1** *(for athletes)* tempat perlombaan olahraga, **2** *(for cars)* sirkuit.

circumcise *verb* mengkhitan, menyunat.

circumcision *noun* khitanan, sunatan.

circumstances *plural noun* keadaan; **under the circumstances** dalam keadaan itu; **under no circumstances** bagaimana pun juga tidak.

circus *noun* sirkus.

citizen *noun* **1** *(of a country)* warganegara; **2** *(of a city)* warga.

citizenship *noun* kewarganegaraan.

city *noun* kota; **the city of Melbourne** kota Melbourne.

city centre *noun* pusat kota.

civil *adjective* sipil; **civil engineer** insinyur sipil.

civilization *noun* peradaban.

civil servant *noun* pegawai negeri; **he's a civil servant** dia pegawai negeri.

civil war *noun* perang saudara.

claim *verb* **1** mengatakan; **I don't claim to know it all** saya tak mengatakan bahwa saya tahu semuanya; **2** mengklaim; **the Philippines no longer claims Sabah as its territory** Pilipina tidak lagi mengklaim Sabah sebagai wilayahnya.

clap *verb* bertepuk tangan; **everyone clapped** semuanya bertepuk tangan.

clapping *noun* tepuk tangan.

clarinet *noun* klarinet.

clash *noun (between police and demonstrators, for example)* bentrokan; perselisihan, pertengkaran.
verb **1** *(rival groups)* berbentrok dengan, bertentangan dengan; **2** *(colours)* tidak cocok; **the furniture clashes with the curtains** mebel itu tidak cocok dengan gorden.

clasp *noun* gesper, jepitan.

class *noun* **1** *(a group of students or pupils)* kelas; **I think you're in the same class as me** saya kira bahwa kita sekelas, saya rasa bahwa kita sekelas; **2** *(a lesson)* kelas, pelajaran; **a biology class** pelajaran biologi; **3** *(division)* golongan; **a social class** golongan sosial.

classic *adjective* klasik.

classical *adjective* klasik; **classical music** musik klasik.

classroom *noun* ruangan kelas.

claw *noun* cakar, kuku.

clay *noun* **1** *(for modelling)* tanah lempung, tanah liat; **2 a clay court** lapangan tenis dari tanah liat.

clean *adjective* bersih; **a clean shirt** kemeja yang bersih.
verb **1** membersihkan; **we've cleaned the car** kami sudah membersihkan mobil itu; **2 to clean your teeth** menyikat gigi.

cleaner *noun* **1** pembersih; **2 a dry cleaner's** binatu, penatu.

cleaning *noun* pembersihan; **to do the cleaning** membersihkan.

cleanser *noun* obat pembersih.

cleansing milk *noun* susu pembersih.

clear *adjective* **1** *(that you can see through)* bening; **clear glass** kaca bening; **2** *(cloudless)* cerah; **3** *(easy to understand)* jelas; **clear instructions** perintah yang jelas; **is that clear?** apakah itu jelas? sudah jelas?; **it's clear that** jelas bahwa.
verb **1** *(papers, rubbish, clothes, etc.)* merapikan; **have you cleared your room?** apakah Anda sudah merapikan kamar Anda?; **2** *(a table or a room)* mengangkat, merapikan; **please clear the table** tolong angkat barang-barang dari meja; **3** *(a road or a path)* membersihkan; **4** *(fog, snow, etc.)* **the weather's cleared** cuaca sudah cerah kembali; **the rain's cleared up** hujan

a b c d e f g h i j k l m n o p q r s t u v w x y z

sudah berhenti; **the fog's cleared away** kabut sudah lenyap; **5 to clear your throat** mendehem.

- **to clear something up** 1 mengangkat; **please clear up your mess** tolong angkat barang-barang Anda;
  2 membereskan; **I just want to clear this up with you** saya hanya mau membereskan hal ini dengan Anda.
- **to clear something out** mengosongkan; **can you help me clear out the storeroom?** apakah Anda bisa menolong saya mengosongkan gudang?

clearly *adverb* **1** dengan jelas; **2** nyata; **he's clearly frightened** jelas bahwa dia takut.

clever *noun* **1** berbakat, cerdik, pandai, pintar; **a talented child** anak berbakat; **she's very clever** dia pandai sekali; **2** *(ingenious)* baik; **a clever plan** rencana yang baik.

client *noun* **1** *(of a lawyer)* klien; **2** *(of a bank)* nasabah; **3** *(customer)* langganan, pelanggan.

cliff *noun* tebing curam.

climate *noun* iklim.

climb *verb* **1** *(a hill)* naik, menaiki; **2** *(a mountain)* memanjat, mendaki.

climber *noun* pendaki.

climbing *noun* pendakian, mendaki; **they like mountain climbing in New Zealand** mereka suka mendaki gunung di Selandia Baru.

clinic *noun* balai pengobatan, klinik.

clip *noun* **1** *(from a film)* potongan; **2** *(for your hair)* jepitan.

cloakroom *noun* tempat penggantungan jas.

clock *noun* **1** jam; **to put the clocks forward two hours** jam dimajukan dua jam; **to put the clocks back** jam dimundurkan; **2 an alarm clock** weker.

clock radio *noun* radio dengan jam.

close *adjective, adverb* **1** *(result)* dekat, sempit; **2** *(friend or relation)* akrab, karib; **3** *(near)* dekat; **the bus stop is very close** halte bis dekat dari sini; **not very close** tidak begitu dekat.

close *noun* akhir; **at the close** pada akhir(nya).
verb menutup; **don't close the door** jangan tutup pintu itu; **the bank closes at five** bank tutup jam lima.

closed *adjective* tutup; **the banks are closed on Sundays** bank-bank tutup pada hari Minggu.

closely *adverb* dengan teliti; **to examine closely** memeriksa dengan teliti.

closing date *noun* tanggal penutupan, tanggal terakhir; **the closing date for registration** tanggal terakhir untuk mendaftar.

closing-down sale *noun* obral tutup toko.

closing time *noun* jam tutup.

cloth *noun* **1** *(fabric by the metre)* kain; *(for the floor)* kain pel, lap; **2** *(for drying dishes)* serbet; **3** taplak; **tablecloth** taplak meja.

clothes *plural noun* baju, pakaian; **to put your clothes on** mengenakan pakaian; **to take your clothes off** menanggalkan pakaian; **to change your clothes** mengganti pakaian.

clothes hanger *noun* gantungan baju, gantungan pakaian.

clothes line *noun* tali jemuran, gantungan cucian.

clothes peg *noun* jepitan pakaian.

clothing *noun* pakaian, sandang.

cloud *noun* awan, mega.

cloudy *adjective* berawan, mendung.

clove *noun* **1** cengkih; **clove cigarettes** rokok kretek; **2 a clove of garlic** sebutir bawang putih.

clown *noun* badut, pelawak.

club *noun* **1** *(association)* klub, perkumpulan; **he's in the tennis club** dia anggota perkumpulan tenis; **2** *(in cards)* klaver; **the Queen of clubs** ratu klaver; **3** *(golfing iron)* pemukul golf.

clue *noun* **1** petunjuk; **2 I haven't a clue** saya sama sekali tidak tahu.

clumsy *adjective* canggung, kagok *(colloquial)*.

clutch *noun* *(in a car)* kopling.
verb menggenggam; **Ali clutched his mother's hand tightly** Ali menggenggam tangan ibunya dengan erat.

coach *noun* **1** *(bus)* bis; **by coach** dengan bis; **2** *(sports trainer)* pelatih; **3** *(railway wagon)* gerbong kereta.

coach station *noun* stasiun bis, terminal.

coach trip *noun* **to go on a coach trip** bepergian dengan bis.

coal *noun* batu bara.

a b c d e f g h i j k l m n o p q r s t u v w x y z

coal mine *noun* tambang batu bara.

coal miner *noun* buruh tambang batu bara.

coarse *adjective* kasar.

coast *noun* pantai, pesisir; **on the west coast** di pesisir barat.

coat *noun* **1** jas; **2** lapisan; **a coat of paint** selapis cat.

coat hanger *noun* gantungan baju.

cobweb *noun* jaringan laba-laba.

cockerel *noun* ayam jantan.

Coca Cola™ *noun* Coca Cola™, koka-kola.

cocoa *noun* **1** *(drink)* coklat, kakao; **2** *(powder)* bubuk coklat.

coconut *noun* kelapa.

coconut cream *noun* santan.

coconut milk *noun* air kelapa.

code *noun* kode; **the highway code** kode lalu lintas.

coffee *noun* kopi; **a cup of coffee** secangkir kopi; **a black coffee, please** minta kopi pahit *(without sugar, usually also black)*, minta kopi tanpa susu; **a white coffee** kopi susu; **strong coffee** kopi kental; **ground coffee** kopi bubuk.

coffee break *noun* istirahat untuk minum kopi, waktu minum kopi.

coffee cup *noun* cangkir kopi.

coffee table *noun* meja tamu.

coffin *noun* peti jenazah.

coin *noun* (mata) uang logam; **a dollar coin** satu dolar (mata uang logam).

coincidence *noun* kejadian yang kebetulan.

Coke™ *noun* koka kola; **two Cokes™ please** minta dua botol koka-kola.

cold *noun* **1** *(the weather)* dingin; **to be out in the cold** di luar di hawa dingin; **2** *(illness)* pilek; **to have a cold** kena flu, kena pilek, kena selesma; **to catch cold** kena pilek, masuk angin. *adjective* dingin; **your hands are cold** tangan Anda dingin; **cold milk** susu dingin.

collaborate *verb* bekerjasama, berkolaborasi.

collapse *verb* **1** *(a roof or a wall)* roboh, runtuh; **2** *(a person)* (jatuh) pingsan; **she collapsed at school** dia jatuh pingsan di sekolah.

collar *noun* **1** *(on clothing)* kerah; **2** *(for a dog)* ban leher.

collarbone *noun* tulang selangka.

colleague *noun* kolega, rekan, teman sekerja.

collect *noun* 1 mengumpulkan; **to collect the homework** mengumpulkan pekerjaan rumah; *(as a hobby)* **she collects coins** dia mengumpulkan uang logam; **2** *(a person)* mengambil, menjemput; **to collect the children from school** menjemput anak-anak dari sekolah; **3** *(a thing)* mengambil; **collect a book from the library** mengambil buku dari perpustakaan.

collection *noun* koleksi, kumpulan.

college *noun* **1** *(for higher education)* perguruan tinggi, akademi; **to go to college** masuk akademi; **2** *(a school)* sekolah menengah.

collide *verb* menabrak, menubruk.

collie *noun* anjing collie.

collision *noun* bentrokan, tabrakan, tubrukan.

colonialism *noun* kolonialisme, penjajahan.

colonize *verb* mendiami suatu daerah baru, menjajah.

colonizer *noun* penjajah.

colour *noun* **1** warna; **what colour is his bike?** sepedanya warna apa? *verb (with paints or crayon)* memberi warna pada, mewarnai; **to colour something blue** mewarnainya biru, memberi warna biru pada sesuatu.

colour blind *noun* buta warna.

colour film *noun* film berwarna.

colourful *noun* **1** berwarna-warni; **a colourful outfit** baju berwarna-warni; **2** berani dan aktif; **a colourful figure** seseorang yang berani dan aktif.

colouring book *noun* buku warna.

colour scheme *noun* pola warna.

colour supplement *noun* bagian yang diberi warna.

column *noun* **1** *(newspaper)* kolom; **2** *(structure)* tiang.

comb *noun* sisir. *verb* menyisir; **to comb your hair** menyisir rambut.

combine *verb (two separate things)* menggabungkan; **to combine work and play** menggabungkan pekerjaan dengan kesenangan.

come *verb* **1** ayo; **come along!** ayo!; **come quickly!**

a b c d e f g h i j k l m n o p q r s t u v w x y z

a b c d e f g h i j k l m n o p q r s t u v w x y z

ayo cepat ke sini!; **2** datang; **Nick came by bike** Nick datang naik sepeda; **3** berasal; **Wayan comes from Bali** Wayan berasal dari Bali; **4 to come down** *(the stairs or the street)* menuruni; **5 to come up** *(the stairs or the street)* naik; **6 to come in** masuk; **come in!** silahkan masuk!; **7 to come for** *(a person)* menjemput; **my father's coming for me** ayah akan menjemput saya; **8 to come over** datang, mampir; **can you come over for a swim?** apakah Anda bisa mampir untuk berenang?

- **to come back** kembali; **she's coming back to fetch it** dia akan kembali untuk mengambilnya.
- **to come off** *(a button or handle, for example)* copot, terlepas.
- **to come out** keluar; **she came out at once** dia langsung keluar.
- **to come up to** datang pada; **Lyn came up to me in the yard** Lyn datang pada saya di halaman.

comedian *noun* pelawak, pemain komedi.

comedy *noun* komedi.

comfortable *adjective* **1** enak; **this chair's really comfortable** kursi ini enak; **2 to feel comfortable** *(a person)* merasa betah, merasa nyaman; **are you comfortable there?** apakah Anda merasa nyaman di situ?

comfortably *adverb* dengan senang.

comic *noun* **1** *(person)* pelawak; **2** *(that you read)* komik.

comic strip *noun* cerita bergambar, komik.

comma *noun* koma.

command *noun* **1** perintah; **obey her commands** taat kepada perintahnya; **2 to be in command** berkuasa.

commence *verb* memulai.

comment *noun (in a conversation)* komentar; **he made a rude comment about my shirt** dia memberi komentar yang kasar tentang kemeja saya.

commentary *noun* komentar, uraian; **it was a lousy commentary** komentar yang buruk.

commentator *noun* juru ulas, komentator; **a sports commentator** juru ulas olahraga.

commercial *noun* iklan. *adjective* periklanan, perniagaan.

commit *verb* berjanji untuk melakukan.

commitment *noun* komitmen.

committee *noun* komite, panitia.

common *adjective* **1** biasa; **it's a common problem** masalah yang biasa; **2** bersama, persamaan, yang sama; **they have a love of sport in common** mereka punya minat yang sama dalam olahraga; **we have nothing in common** tak ada persamaan antara kita.

common sense *noun* pikiran sehat.

communicate *verb* berkomunikasi.

communication *noun* komunikasi, perhubungan.

communion *noun* kerukunan, hubungan erat.

communism *noun* komunisme.

communist *noun* komunis.

community *noun* masyarakat; **the European community** masyarakat Eropa.

commute *verb* pulang pergi ke tempat kerja; **to commute between Bogor and Jakarta** pulang pergi dari Bogor ke Jakarta setiap hari untuk bekerja.

commuter *noun* orang yang pulang pergi setiap hari untuk bekerja.

compact disc *noun* compact disk, CD.

compact disc player *noun* CD.

company *noun* **1** *(business)* perusahaan; **an insurance company** perusahaan asuransi; **she's set up a company** dia sudah membentuk perusahaan; **2** menemani; **to keep company** menemani; **the dog keeps me company** anjing itu menemani saya.

comparative *adjective* komparatif.

comparatively *adverb* secara relatif; **it's still a comparatively young horse** kuda itu relatif masih muda.

compare *verb* membandingkan; **if you compare the Indonesian word with the English word** kalau kata Indonesia dibandingkan dengan kata Inggris; **our pool's small compared to yours** kolam kami agak kecil kalau dibandingkan dengan kolam Anda.

comparison *noun* (per)bandingan; **in**

a b c d e f g h i j k l m n o p q r s t u v w x y z

a b c d e f g h i j k l m n o p q r s t u v w x y z

comparison with kalau dibandingkan dengan.

compartment *noun* bagian ruangan, kompartemen.

compass *noun* kompas, pedoman.

compatible *adjective* cocok, rukun, selaras.

compete *verb* **1** berlomba, bertanding; *(race, event)* **to compete in a race** ikut bertanding dalam balapan; **2** berkompetisi; **twenty people competing for the job** dua puluh orang berkompetisi untuk mendapat pekerjaan; **3** bersaing; **it's a pity they always have to compete with each other** sayang mereka selalu bersaing satu sama lain.

competent *adjective* kompeten, mampu.

competition *noun* **1** kompetisi, pertandingan; **a basketball competition** pertandingan bola basket; **2** persaingan.

competitor *noun* saingan.

complain *verb* **1** mengadu; **I'm going to file a complaint with the police** saya akan mengadu kepada polisi; **2** mengeluh; **we complained about the meals** kami mengeluh mengenai makanannya.

complete *adjective* komplit, lengkap, sempurna; **the complete collection** koleksi yang lengkap.
verb (to finish) menyelesaikan.

completely *adverb* betul-betul, sama sekali; **the tank's completely empty** tanki itu kosong sama sekali.

complexion *noun* corak kulit, warna muka.

complicated *adjective* **1** rumit; **a complicated machine** pesawat yang rumit; **2** sulit; **a complicated process** cara yang sulit.

compliment *noun* pujian; **to pay a compliment** memberi pujian kepada.

compose *verb* **1** *(music)* menggubah; **2 composed of** terdiri dari, terdiri atas.

composer *noun* pengarang, penggubah.

comprehend *verb* mengerti, paham.

compromise *noun* kompromi perjanjian.

compulsory *adjective* wajib, diwajibkan.

computer *noun* komputer.

computer engineer *noun* insinyur komputer.

computer game *noun* permainan komputer.

computer programmer *noun* pemrogram komputer.

computer science *noun* ilmu komputer.

conceited *adjective* congkak, sombong.

concentrate *verb* berkonsentrasi, memusatkan; **I can't concentrate** saya tak bisa memusatkan pikiran saya; **I was concentrating on the match** saya sedang memusatkan perhatian saya kepada pertandingan itu.

concentration *noun* konsentrasi, pemusatan, perhatian.

concern *noun (worry)* keprihatinan, perhatian, prihatin; **there's no cause for concern** tak ada alasan untuk berprihatin.
verb **1** *(to affect)* **this doesn't concern you** ini bukan urusan Anda; **2 as far as he's concerned** mengenai dia.

concert *noun* konser.

conclude *verb* **1** menyimpulkan; **2** menutup.

conclusion *noun* kesimpulan; **in conclusion** sebagai kesimpulan, sebagai penutup.

concrete *adjective (not abstract)* konkrit.

concrete *noun* beton.

condemn *verb* mengutuk.

condemnation *noun* kutukan.

condition *noun* **1** keadaan, kondisi; **in good condition** dalam keadaan yang baik; **weather conditions** keadaan cuaca; **2** kondisi, situasi **conditions in Indonesia are getting better** situasi di Indonesia semakin baik; **3** *(something you agree to)* syarat; **the conditions of sale** syarat penjualan; **on condition that you let me pay** dengan syarat Anda membolehkan saya membayar.

conditional *noun* bersyarat.

conditioner *noun (for your hair)* conditioner, obat perawat rambut.

condom *noun* kondom.

conduct *noun* kelakuan, tingkah laku.
verb (an orchestra or a piece of music) memimpin.

conductor *noun* **1** *(of an orchestra)* dirigen, pemimpin; **2** *(on a bus)* kondektur.

cone *noun* **1** *(for ice-cream)* eskrim horen; **2** *(for traffic)* alat berbentuk kerucut.

a b c d e f g h i j k l m n o p q r s t u v w x y z

conference *noun* konferensi, pertemuan, perundingan.

confess *verb* mengakui.

confession *noun* pengakuan.

confidence *noun* kepercayaan; **to be lacking in confidence** tak mempunyai kepercayaan kepada diri sendiri; **our class does not have confidence in that teacher** pelajar kelas kami tidak menaruh kepercayaan pada guru itu.

confident *adjective* **1** *(sure of yourself)* percaya diri; **2** *(sure that something will happen)* yakin, pasti.

confirm *verb* membenarkan, menegaskan; **we'll confirm the date** kami akan menegaskan tanggalnya.

confuse *verb* **1** *(a person)* membingungkan; **2** salah kira; **I confuse Nick with his brother** saya sering mengira bahwa Nick adalah kakaknya.

confused *adjective* bingung; **I'm confused about the exam dates** saya bingung tentang tanggal ujian.

confusing *adjective* membingungkan; **the instructions are confusing** perintah-perintah itu membingungkan.

confusion *noun* kebingungan.

congratulate *verb* mengucapkan selamat; **we congratulated them on winning** kami mengucapkan selamat kepada mereka atas kemenangannya.

congratulations *noun* selamat; **congratulations on the baby!** selamat atas kelahiran bayi Anda!

conjurer *noun* tukang sulap.

connect *verb (to plug in to the mains)* bersambung, menyambung *(a refrigerator or TV, for example)*; **I can't connect this hairdryer because the plug is different** saya tidak bisa menyolok pengering rambut ini karena colokannya tidak cocok.

connection *noun* **1** *(between two ideas or events)* koneksi, pertalian; **there's no connection between that story and my decision** tak ada pertalian antara cerita itu dan keputusan saya; **2** *(between trains or planes)* hubungan, sambungan; **Anton missed his connection** Anton terlambat untuk sambungannya; **3** *(electrical)* sambungan; **a faulty connection** sambungan yang salah; **4** *(social)* koneksi; **most people get their jobs through connections** kebanyakan orang mendapat pekerjaan karena koneksi.

conscience *noun* hati nurani, suara hati; **to have a guilty conscience** merasa salah.

conscious *adjective* sadar, siuman.

consequence *noun* akibat.

consequently *adverb* sebagai akibatnya.

conservation *noun (of nature)* konservasi, perlindungan cagar alam.

conservative *noun, adjective* konservatif.

conservatory *noun* **1** konservatorium, sekolah musik; **2** rumah kaca.

consider *verb* **1** *(to give thought to)* mempertimbangkan *(a suggestion or an idea)*; **all things considered** setelah mempertimbangkan segala sesuatu; **2** *(other people)* memikirkan, mengingat; **we should consider the people first** kami harus memikirkan rakyat dulu.

considerate *adjective (a person)* memikirkan kepentingan orang lain.

consideration *noun* perhatian, pertimbangan.

considering *preposition* mengingat; **considering her health** mengingat kesehatannya.

consist *verb* **to consist of** terdiri atas, terdiri dari.

consonant *noun* huruf mati, konsonan.

constant *adjective* konstan, tetap.

constipated *adjective* sembelit.

construct *verb* membangun, mendirikan.

construction *noun* bangunan, konstruksi.

consult *verb* berkonsultasi.

consultation *noun* konsultasi.

consumer *noun* konsumen, pemakai.

contact *noun* **1** *(touch)* hubungan; **to be in contact with old school friends** berhubungan dengan teman-teman lama dari sekolah; **we've lost contact** kami sudah tidak ada hubungan lagi; **2** *(people you know)* kenalan; **Sheng-yi has several contacts in the advertising business** Sheng-yi mempunyai beberapa koneksi di bidang periklanan.

a b c d e f g h i j k l m n o p q r s t u v w x y z

verb kontak, menghubungi; **he hasn't contacted me yet** dia belum menghubungi saya, dia belum mengadakan kontak dengan saya.

contact lens *noun* lensa kontak.

contain *verb* berisi, mengandung.

container *noun* **1** *(for shipping)* peti kemas; **2** *(in Indonesian you will have to use the name of the type of container)* botol, kotak, kaleng, tempat.

contemporary *adjective* kontemporer.

contents *plural noun* isi; **the contents of this box** isi kotak ini.

contest *noun* kontes, pertandingan.

contestant *noun* kontestan, peserta pertandingan.

continent *noun* benua; **the Continent** Benua Eropa.

continental *noun* yang bertalian dengan benua; **a continental holiday** berlibur di Eropa.

continue *verb* melanjutkan, meneruskan; **they continued (with) their journey** mereka melanjutkan perjalanannya; **to be continued** akan disambung, akan diteruskan, akan dilanjutkan.

continuous *adjective* terus-menerus; **continuous assessment** penilaian yang terus-menerus.

contraceptive *noun* alat pencegah kehamilan, obat pencegah kehamilan.

contract *noun* kontrak, perjanjian.
verb mengontrak.

contradict *verb* menyangkal.

contradiction *noun* kontradiksi, sesuatu yang berlawanan.

contrary *noun* kebalikan; **on the contrary** sebaliknya.

contrast *noun* kontras, perbedaan.
verb **1** membandingkan, membedakan; **they contrasted the boys' results with the girls'** mereka membandingkan hasil anak laki-laki dengan hasil anak perempuan; **2** berkontras, merupakan kontras; **the colours of these two fabrics contrast well** warna kedua kain ini merupakan kontras yang bagus.

contribute *verb (money)* menyumbang(kan).

contribution *noun* kontribusi, sumbangan.

control *noun* kontrol, penguasaan, **the police have lost control of the crowd**

polisi tak sanggup menguasai orang banyak itu; **the fire was out of control** kebakaran itu tak dapat dikuasai.
verb **1** *(a crowd or animals or a fire, for example)* mengontrol, menguasai; **2 to control oneself** mengendalikan diri.

convenient *adjective* **1** praktis, tidak menyusahkan; **frozen food is very convenient** makanan yang beku sangat praktis; **if that's convenient for you** kalau tidak menyusahkan Anda; **2** dekat; **the house is convenient for shops and schools** rumah itu dekat dengan toko dan sekolah.

conventional *adjective* **1** konvensional, yang biasa; **2** *(a person)* biasa, menurut adat, menurut kebiasaan.

conversation *noun* percakapan.

convert *verb* mengubah; **we're going to convert this bedroom into a study** kami akan mengubah kamar tidur ini menjadi kamar belajar.

convince *verb* meyakinkan; **try to convince them** cobalah menyakinkan mereka; **I'm convinced he's wrong** saya yakin bahwa dia salah.

convincing *adjective* meyakinkan.

cook *noun* koki, juru masak, tukang masak.
verb **1** memasak; **who's cooking tonight?** siapa yang akan masak nanti malam?; **2** *(a meal)* **David's busy cooking dinner** David sedang sibuk menyediakan makanan malam; **3** *(cooked completely)* **the chicken's cooking** ayam itu sedang dimasak; **is the roast cooked?** apakah daging panggang itu sudah masak?

cooker *noun* kompor.

cookery *noun* cara masak.

cookery book *noun* buku resep masakan.

cooking *noun* masakan; **to do the cooking** memasak; **Indonesian cooking** masakan khas Indonesia.

cool *noun* **1** *(coldness)* kesejukan; **the cool of the morning** kesejukan pagi; **stay in the cool** diam di tempat sejuk; **2** *(calm)* ketenangan; **to lose one's cool** menjadi marah; **he kept his cool** dia tetap tenang
adjective **1** *(cold)* adem, sejuk; **it's cool inside** di dalam sejuk; **a cool drink** minuman dingin; **2** *(laid-back)* yang tenang;

a b c d e f g h i j k l m n o p q r s t u v w x y z

a b c d e f g h i j k l m n o p q r s t u v w x y z

3 *(sophisticated)* baik sekali *(informal)*.
verb mendingin, menjadi dingin; **while the engine was cooling down** sementara mesin menjadi dingin.

cop *noun* **1** *(police, informal)* polisi; **2 a fair cop** mendapat ganjaran.
verb mendapat; **Jackie copped a lot of flack from the teacher** Jackie mendapat kecaman dari guru; **to cop it** menjadi sasaran.

cope *verb* **1** mengatur, mengurus *(manage)*; **she copes well** dia dapat mengatur dengan baik; **2 to cope with** *(children or work)* menguasai; **I'll cope with this assignment** saya akan menguasai tugas ini; **3** *(problems)* menanggulangi; **she's had a lot to cope with** ada banyak masalah yang harus ditanggulanginya; **4** tahan; **she can't cope with the humidity** dia tak tahan kelembaban.

copy *noun* **1** salinan; **please make a copy of this** tolong buat salinannya; **2** *(of a book)* kopi; **there are two copies of this book in the library** ada dua kopi buku ini di perpustakaan; **photocopy** fotokopi.
verb **1** menyalin; **I copied down all the details** saya menyalin semua perincian; **2** meniru **don't try to copy me!** jangan coba meniru saya!

cord *noun* kabel, tali.

cordless telephone *noun* telepon seluler (ponsel).

core *noun* *(of an apple or pineapple)* biji, bagian tengah.

cork *noun* *(in a bottle)* sumbat.

corkscrew *noun* pembuka sumbat botol.

corn *noun* jagung *(sweetcorn)*.

corner *noun* **1** pojok; **in a corner of the room** di pojok kamar; **2** simpang, sudut; **at the corner of the street** di sudut jalan; **it's just round the corner** dekat sekali dari simpang jalan; **3 out of the corner of your eye** melirik kepada.

cornflakes™ *noun* cornflakes.

corpse *noun* **1** *(animals)* bangkai; **2** *(people)* jenazah, mayat.

correct *adjective* **1** benar, betul; **yes, that's correct** ya itu betul; **the correct answer** jawaban yang benar; **2** tepat; **the correct amount** jumlah yang tepat.

verb **1** *(errors)* membenarkan, membetulkan; **2** *(an essay, for example)* memeriksa, mengoreksi.

correction *noun* koreksi, pembetulan.

correspond *verb* surat-menyurat.

corridor *noun* gang.

cosmetics *noun* bahan kecantikan, kosmetik.

cost *noun* **1** *(for things)* harga; **the cost of a new camera** harga kamera baru; **2** *(for services)* biaya, ongkos; **the cost of the repairs** ongkos reparasi; **the cost of living** biaya hidup.
verb **1** harga; **how much do the mangoes cost?** berapa harga mangga itu?; **the book costs thirty dollars** harga buku itu tiga puluh dolar; **2** ongkos; **it cost two-hundred dollars to repair the car** ongkos perbaikan mobil dua ratus dolar.

costume *noun* baju, kostum, pakaian.

cosy *adjective* hangat dan menyenangkan.

cot *noun* tempat tidur bayi.

cottage *noun* pondok.

cotton *noun* **1** *(fabric)* katun; **a cotton skirt** rok dari kain katun; **2** *(thread)* benang.

cotton wool *noun* kapas.

couch *noun* dipan.

cough *noun* batuk; **a nasty cough** batuk keras; **to have a cough** batuk.
verb batuk.

could *verb* **1** bisa, dapat; **if I could, I'd pay** kalau bisa, tentu saya bayar; **2** *(know how to)* bisa, dapat; **he couldn't drive** dia tidak bisa mengemudikan mobil; **she couldn't swim** dia tidak dapat berenang; **3** *(with seeing, hearing or smelling)* **I could hear the sirens** saya dapat mendengar sirene; **4** *(might)* **could I help you?** apakah saya dapat menolong Anda? **she couldn't help** dia tak dapat menolong; **you could ask Ray** coba tanya Ray; **you could have let me know** Anda seharusnya dapat memberitahu saya.

council *noun* dewan; **security council** dewan keamanan.

count *verb* **1** *(reckon up)* menghitung, menjumlahkan; **he's just counting the money** dia sedang menjumlahkan uang itu; **2** dianggap; **children over twelve count as adults** anak-anak yang berumur di atas dua belas tahun dianggap dewasa; **it seems**

a b c d e f g h i j k l m n o p q r s t u v w x y z

my ideas count for nothing tampaknya ide saya tidak dianggap penting; 3 termasuk; **fifteen not counting the children** jumlahnya lima belas tidak termasuk anak-anak.

counter *noun* **1** *(in a shop or cafe)* meja pajangan; **2** *(for board games)* keping.

country *noun* **1** *(physical)* negeri; **a foreign country** negeri asing; **2** *(political)* negara; **an independent country** negara merdeka; **3** *(not town)* daerah pedalaman, pedesaan; **to live in the country** tinggal di daerah pedalaman; **a country road** jalan di desa.

countryside *noun* daerah luar kota, daerah pedalaman.

couple *noun* **1** pasangan, suami-istri; **2 a couple of** beberapa; **a couple of times** beberapa kali.

courage *noun* keberanian.

courier *noun* **1** *(on a package holiday)* pesuruh; **2** *(delivery service)* kurir, titipan khusus; **by courier** dengan kurir, dengan titipan khusus.

course *noun* **1** *(lessons)* kursus; **an advanced course** kursus lanjutan; **a design course** kursus pola, kursus desain; **to go on a course** mengikuti kursus; **2** *(part of a meal)* **the main course** makanan utama; **3 a golf course** lapangan golf; **4 of course** tentu (saja); **yes, of course!** ya, tentu saja!

court *noun* **1** *(for sports)* lapangan; **2** *(for law suits)* mahkamah, pengadilan.

courtyard *noun* halaman gedung.

cousin *noun* (saudara) sepupu.

cover *noun* **1** *(for a book)* sampul; **2** *(for a duvet or cushion)* sarung; **a pillow cover** sarung bantal; **3** *(for a box, saucepan, etc.)* penutup, tutup.
verb **1** *(a book)* menyampul; **2** *(to protect or cover up)* menutupi; **to cover the wound** menutupi lukanya.

cow *noun* lembu, sapi; **mad cow disease** penyakit sapi gila.

coward *noun* penakut, pengecut.

cowboy *noun* koboi.

crab *noun* kepiting.

crack *noun* **1** *(in a wall or cup)* retak; **2** *(a cracking noise)* letusan.
verb **1** *(to make a crack in)* meretakkan *(a cup, chair or bone)*; **2** *(to break)*

memecahkan *(a nut or an egg)*; **3** *(to split by itself: ice, for example)* pecah, retak.

cracker *noun (biscuit)* biskuit kering, kue.

crackle *verb* suara api.

craft *noun (at school)* kerajinan tangan, ketrampilan.

cramp *noun* kejang, kram; **to have cramp in your leg** menderita kejang di kaki.

crane *noun* derek.

crash *noun* **1** *(an accident)* tabrakan, tubrukan; **a car crash** tabrakan mobil; **2** *(smashing noise)* suara; **a crash of broken glass** suara kaca pecah.
verb **1** bertubrukan, bertabrakan; **the two planes crashed into each other** kedua pesawat itu bertabrakan; **2** *(involving a fall)* jatuh; **the plane crashed** pesawat terbang itu jatuh.

crash course *noun* kursus singkat.

crash helmet *noun* helm.

crate *noun* peti kayu.

crawl *verb* **1** *(a person, a baby)* merangkak; **2** *(cars in a jam)* maju dengan pelan-pelan; **we were crawling along** kami maju dengan pelan-pelan.

crayon *noun* krayon, pensil lilin yang berwarna.

craze *noun* kegemaran; **the craze for body piercing** kegemaran menusuk tubuh.

crazy *adjective* gila.

creak *verb* berbunyi keriat-keriut.

cream *noun* krim; **strawberries and cream** (buah) arbei dengan krim.

crease *noun* lipatan.

creased *adjective* berlipat.

create *verb* **1** menciptakan; **2** *(a problem)* menimbulkan.

creative *adjective* berdaya cipta, kreatif *(a person)*.

creature *noun* makhluk.

creche *noun* tempat penitipan balita.

credit *noun* kredit.

credit card *noun* kartu kredit.

cress *noun* kangkung.

crew *noun* **1** *(on a ship or plane)* awak, kru; **2** *(rowing)* regu dayung; **3** *(filming or work)* pekerja, pegawai.

cricket *noun* **1** *(game)* kriket; **2** *(insect)* jengkerik.

cricket bat *noun* alat pemukul kriket.

crime *noun* kejahatan; **murder is a crime** pembunuhan adalah suatu

a b c d e f g h i j k l m n o p q r s t u v w x y z

kejahatan; **the fight against crime** usaha memberantas kejahatan.

criminal *adjective* kriminal. *noun* narapidana, penjahat.

crimson *adjective* merah tua.

crisis *noun* krisis.

crisp *noun* **1** keripik; **a packet of (potato) crisps** sebungkus keripik (kentang); **2** *(biscuit, apple)* garing, renyah.

critical *adjective* **1** *(somebody's condition, a moment)* genting, kritis; **2** *(a person)* bersifat kritis.

criticism *noun* kecaman.

criticize *verb* mencela, mengecam, mengkritik.

Croatia *noun* Kroasia.

crockery *noun* barang pecah-belah, barang tembikar.

crocodile *noun* buaya.

crook *noun* *(criminal)* bajingan *(informal)*.

crop *noun* hasil bumi, panen.

cross *noun* **1** *(religious)* kayu salib; **2** palang; **The Red Cross** Palang Merah.
adjective jengkel, marah; **he's always cross** dia selalu marah.
verb **1** *(to cross over)* melintasi, menyeberang; **to cross the road** menyeberang jalan; **2** bersilang; **to sit cross-legged** duduk bersilang kaki; **3** *(to cross each other)* **the two roads cross here** kedua jalan itu melintang di sini.

- **to cross out** *(a mistake, for example)* mencoret.

cross-country *noun* lintas alam; **a cross-country (motor) race** balapan (motor) lintas alam.

crossing *noun* lintasan, penyeberangan; **a pedestrian crossing** penyeberangan pejalan kaki; **a level crossing** lintasan jalan kereta api.

cross-legged *adjective* bersilang; **to sit cross-legged** duduk bersilang kaki.

crossroads *noun* perempatan, persimpangan (jalan), simpang empat.

crossword *noun* teka-teki silang.

crouch *verb* meringkuk.

crow *noun* burung gagak; **ten kilometres as the crow flies** sepuluh kilometer jalan lurus.
verb *(a cockerel)* berkokok.

crowd *noun* orang banyak, khalayak ramai; **in the crowd** di antara orang banyak; **a crowd of three thousand** orang sebanyak tiga ribu.

verb **to crowd into** berdesak-desakan *(a room or bus, for example)*; **they all crowded into the room** mereka semua berdesak-desakan masuk ke dalam ruang itu.

crowded *adjective* penuh, ramai, sesak.

crown *noun* mahkota.

crude *adjective* **1** *(rough and ready)* sederhana; **2** *(vulgar)* kasar.

cruel *adjective* kejam.

cruise *noun* pesiar; **to go on a cruise** naik kapal pesiar.

crumb *noun* remah-remah.

crumple *verb* meremas-remas.

crunch *verb (an apple)* mengunyah; **we could hear Budi crunching banana crisps** kami dapat mendengar Budi mengunyah kripik pisang.

crunchy *adjective* garing, renyah.

crush *noun* orang-orang yang berdesak-desak.

crust *noun* kulit (yang garing).

crusty *adjective (bread)* berkulit garing.

crutch *noun* tongkat ketiak; **to be on crutches** jalan dengan tongkat ketiak.

cry *noun* jeritan, teriakan. *verb* **1** *(weep)* menangis; **2** *(call out)* berteriak.

crystal *noun* kristal.

cub *noun* **1** *(animal)* anak; **2** *(scout)* kurcaci.

cube *noun* kubus; **an ice cube** es batu.

cubic *adjective (for measurements)* kubik; **five cubic metres** lima meter kubik.

cubicle *noun* ruangan kecil.

cucumber *noun* ketimun, mentimun.

cuddle *noun* pelukan. *verb* memeluk.

cue *noun (billiards, pool, snooker)* tongkat bilyar.

cuff *noun (on a shirt)* manset.

cul-de-sac *noun* jalan buntu.

culture *noun* kebudayaan, kultur.

cunning *adjective* cerdik, pintar (*positive meaning*), licik (*negative meaning*).

cup *noun* **1** *(for drinking)* cangkir; **a cup of coffee** secangkir kopi; **2** *(a trophy)* piala.

cupboard *noun* lemari.

cure *noun* **1** obat; **2** penyembuhan. *verb* menyembuhkan.

a b c d e f g h i j k l m n o p q r s t u v w x y z

curiosity *noun* keingin-tahuan.

curious *adjective* **1** *(wanting to know)* ingin tahu; **Cindy was curious to know who phoned** Cindy ingin tahu siapa yang menelepon; **2** *(unusual)* aneh **that's a curious-looking creature** itu makhluk yang aneh.

curl *noun* keriting.
verb melengkung, menggulung.

curly *adjective* keriting.

currant *noun* kismis.

currency *noun* mata uang; **foreign currency** mata uang asing, valuta asing.

current *noun (of electricity or water)* arus.
adjective (a situation, for example) (zaman) sekarang.

current affairs *noun* kejadian-kejadian yang hangat.

curriculum *noun* kurikulum.

curry *noun* kari; **chicken curry** kari ayam; **goat curry** gulai kambing.

curtain *noun* gorden.

cushion *noun* bantal.

custard *noun* vla.

custom *noun* adat, adat istiadat.

customer *noun* langganan, pelanggan.

customs *plural noun* bea dan cukai; **to go through customs** melewati pabean.

customs hall *noun* ruang pabean.

customs officer *noun* pegawai pabean.

cut *noun* **1** *(injury)* luka; **2** *(haircut)* potongan.
verb **1** memotong; **to cut the grass** memotong rumput; **2** menggunting *(with scissors)*; **3** memangkas; **to get your hair cut** memangkas rambut; **Tony cut Frank's hair** Tony memangkas rambut Frank; **4 I've cut myself!** tangan saya kena pisau! *(depending on the body part that has been cut).*

- **to cut down** *(a tree)* menebang.
- **to cut down on** *(reduce)* mengurangi.
- **to cut out 1** *(a shape, a newspaper article)* menggunting; **2** *(sugar, fatty food, etc.)* menghentikan makan.
- **to cut up** *(food)* memotong-motong.

cutlery *noun* garpu, pisau dan sendok *(forks, knives and spoons).*

CV [Curriculum Vitae] *noun* riwayat hidup.

cycle *noun* sepeda.
verb bersepeda, naik sepeda; **do you like cycling?** apakah

Anda suka naik sepeda?; **we cycle to school** kami bersepeda ke sekolah.

cycle lane *noun* jalur sepeda.

cycle race *noun* balapan sepeda.

cycling *noun* olahraga naik sepeda.

cycling holiday *noun* berlibur naik sepeda.

cyclist *noun* pengendara sepeda.

D d

dad *noun* **1** ayah, bapak; **Nicole's dad** ayah Nicole; **2** ayah, papa, papi; **Dad's in the garden** papa berada di kebun.

daily *adjective* harian; **daily paper** koran harian.
adverb (se)tiap hari.

dairy products *plural noun* makanan yang mengandung susu.

daisy *noun* semacam bunga aster *(definition only).*

dam *noun* bendungan.

damage *noun* kerusakan; **to cause damage** menyebabkan kerusakan.

damn *noun* **he doesn't give a damn** ia tak peduli sama sekali *(informal).*
exclamation **damn!** sialan *(informal).*

damp *adjective* basah, lembab.
noun kelembaban, uap; **because of the damp** oleh karena kelembaban.

dance *noun* dansa, tari(an); **a folk dance** tarian rakyat.
verb berdansa, menari; **I don't dance very well** saya kurang pintar berdansa.

dancer *noun* penari.

dancing *noun* berdansa, menari.

dancing class *noun* kelas berdansa, kelas menari.

dandruff *noun* ketombe.

Dane *noun* orang Denmark.

danger *noun* bahaya; **there's no danger any more** tak ada bahaya lagi.

dangerous *adjective* berbahaya; **it's dangerous to drive too fast** mengendarai (mobil) terlalu cepat berbahaya.

Danish *adjective* berasal dari Denmark.

dare *noun* tantangan.
verb **1** berani; **to dare to do** berani melakukan; **I don't dare suggest it** saya tidak berani menyarankan begitu;

a b c d e f g h i j k l m n o p q r s t u v w x y z

I dare you! kalau berani, silahkan! *(informal)*; **2 don't you dare tell them** jangan ceritakan kepada mereka.

daring *adjective* berani; **that was a bit daring** berani benar!

dark *noun* gelap; **in the dark** dalam gelap; **after dark** waktu malam.
adjective **1** *(colour)* tua; **a dark green blouse** blus warna hijau tua; **2** gelap; **it's dark already** sudah gelap; **it's dark in here** di sini gelap; **we're still in the dark about the result** kami masih belum mengetahui hasilnya.

darkness *noun* kegelapan; **in darkness** dalam kegelapan.

darling *noun* sayang, kekasih, tercinta.

dart *noun* anak panah; **to play darts** main anak panah.

data *noun* data, fakta.

database *noun* database, kumpulan data.

date *noun* tanggal; **1 the date of departure** tanggal berangkat; **to fix a date** menentukan tanggal; **2 what's the date today?** tanggal berapa hari ini?; **3 out of date** *(passport, driving licence, etc.)* berakhir, daluarsa; **my passport's out of date** paspor saya telah daluarsa; *(technology, method, information, etc.)* model kuno, sudah ketinggalan zaman; **4 use-by date** tanggal kedaluarsaan; **5** *(fruit)* buah korma.

date of birth *noun* tanggal lahir.

daughter *noun* anak perempuan, putri; **Linda's daughter** putri Linda.

daughter-in-law *noun* menantu (perempuan).

dawn *noun* fajar, subuh.

day *noun* **1** hari; **four days later** empat hari kemudian; **it rained all day yesterday** kemarin hujan sepanjang hari; **we spent the day in Semarang** kami mampir sehari di Semarang; **the day after** sehari sesudah; **the day before** sehari sebelum; **it looks like a nice day** kelihatannya hari ini bagus; **2 the day after tomorrow** lusa; **my uncle's arriving the day after tomorrow** paman saya akan tiba lusa; **3 the day before yesterday** kemarin dulu; **4 the other day** baru-baru ini; **5 these days** masa sekarang, zaman sekarang; **6 one of these days** kapan-kapan.

daylight *noun* siang (hari), waktu siang.

dead *adjective*, *adverb* **1** mati; **the tiger's dead** harimau itu mati; **the motor's dead** mesinnya mati; **2** meninggal; **the man's dead** orang itu telah meninggal; **3** *(really)* betul-betul, sama sekali *(informal)*; **he's dead nice** dia betul-betul menarik; **it was dead good** bagus sekali; **you're dead right** Anda benar sekali; **she arrived dead on time** dia datang tepat pada waktunya.

dead end *noun* jalan buntu.

deadline *noun* batas waktu, garis batas.

deaf *adjective* tuli.

deafening *adjective* menulikan.

deal *noun* **1** *(involving money)* transaksi; **it's a good deal** itu transaksi yang baik; **2** perjanjian; **I'll make a deal with you** saya siap membuat perjanjian dengan Anda; **3 a great deal of** banyak (sekali); **he doesn't have a great deal of money** dia tak punya banyak uang. *verb* **1** *(in cards)* membagi; **come on, deal!** ayo, bagi dong! *(colloquial)*; **2** *(trade)* berdagang.
- **to deal with something** menangani, mengurus; **Lex deals with travel arrangements** Lex mengurus (urusan) perjalanan; **he says he'll deal with it tomorrow** katanya dia mau mengurus itu besok.

dear *adjective* **1** kekasih, sayang; **my dear** kekasihku; **2** *(in salutations)* **Dear Sir** Saudara (+ name) yang terhormat, Bapak (+ name) yang terhormat; **Dear Henry** saudara Henry yang terhormat; **3** *(expensive)* mahal.

death *noun* **1** kematian, maut; **after her mother's death** sesudah kematian ibunya; **2 you'll frighten the monkey to death** Anda sangat menakut-nakuti monyet itu; **I'm bored to death** saya sangat bosan; **I'm sick to death of hearing about it** *(informal)* saya sudah bosan mendengar tentang itu.

death penalty *noun* hukuman mati.

debate *noun* perdebatan. *verb* memperdebatkan.

debt *noun* utang, hutang; **to get into debt** berutang, berhutang.

decade *noun* dasawarsa, dekade.

decaffeinated *adjective* kopi dekaf.

a b c d e f g h i j k l m n o p q r s t u v w x y z

a b c d e f g h i j k l m n o p q r s t u v w x y z

deceive *verb* mencurangi, menipu.

December *noun* (bulan) Desember.

decent *adjective* **1** baik, layak, lumayan; **a decent wage** gaji yang layak; **a decent meal** makanan yang lumayan; **2** *(informal)* **he's a decent enough guy** dia seorang yang baik hati.

decide *verb* **1** bermaksud; **they've decided to buy the house** mereka sudah bermaksud membeli rumah itu; **2** memutuskan, mengambil keputusan; **she's decided not to buy that car** dia mengambil keputusan untuk tidak membeli mobil itu.

decimal *adjective* desimal.

decimal point *noun* tanda desimal.

decision *noun* keputusan; **the right decision** keputusan yang benar; **to make a decision** membuat keputusan.

deck *noun* **1** *(on a ship)* geladak; **2** *(of cards)* kartu main lengkap.

deckchair *noun* kursi lipat dengan tempat duduk dari kanvas (*definition only*).

declare *verb* **1** *(to Customs, for example)* melaporkan, menerangkan; **2** *(publicly)* mengumumkan.

decorate *verb* mendekorasi, menghiasi; **to decorate the Christmas tree with stars** menghiasi pohon Natal dengan bintang-bintang; **we're decorating the house** kami sedang menghias rumah.

decoration *noun* dekorasi, hiasan.

decrease *noun* pengurangan, potongan; **a decrease in the number of** pengurangan dalam jumlah. *verb* mengurangi.

deduct *verb* memotong, mengurangi.

deep *adjective* **1** dalam; **the river is very deep here** sungai ini dalam sekali di sini; **how deep is the swimming pool?** berapa dalam kolam renang ini?; **2** mendalam; **a deep feeling of sorrow** rasa dukacita yang mendalam.

deep end *noun* bagian yang dalam.

deep freeze *noun* tempat yang dingin sekali.

deeply *adverb* (men)dalam.

deer *noun* kijang, rusa.

defeat *noun* kekalahan. *verb* mengalahkan, menggagalkan.

defect *noun* cacat, kerusakan.

defence *noun* **1** pertahanan; **Department of Defence** Departemen Pertahanan; **2** pembelaan; **3** penjagaan; **nothing got past their defence** tidak ada yang lewat penjagaan mereka.

defend *verb* membela; **that's the lawyer who defended Netti** itulah pengacara yang membela Netti; **to defend the country** membela tanah air.

defender *noun* pembela.

define *verb* memberi definisi, mendefinisikan.

definite *adjective* **1** nyata; **a definite change** perubahan yang nyata; **a definite improvement** kemajuan yang nyata; **2** *(certain)* tertentu; **it's not definite yet** belum tentu; **3** *(exact)* pasti; **a definite answer** jawaban yang pasti; **I don't have a definite idea of what I want** saya belum tahu pasti apa yang saya inginkan.

definitely *adverb* pasti, tentu; **'do you really like this one better?' – 'definitely'** 'apakah Anda benar-benar lebih suka yang ini?' – 'tentu'; **she's definitely going to be there** dia sudah pasti akan ada di situ; **I'm definitely not going** saya pasti tak akan pergi; **your Indonesian is definitely better than mine** bahasa Indonesia Anda pasti lebih baik dari bahasa Indonesia saya; **the blue one is definitely the best** yang biru itulah yang terbaik.

definition *noun* definisi, ketentuan.

degree *noun* **1** derajat; **thirty degrees** tiga puluh derajat; **2** gelar; **a master's degree** gelar S2.

delay *noun* keterlambatan; **a two-hour delay** keterlambatan dua jam. *verb* **1** *(make late)* terlambat; **the flight was delayed by bad weather** penerbangan itu terlambat oleh karena cuaca buruk; **2** *(postpone)* menunda; **the decision has been delayed until tomorrow** keputusan itu ditunda sampai besok.

delete *verb* mencoret, menghapuskan.

deliberate *adjective* (dengan) sengaja, yang disengaja.

deliberately *adverb* dengan sengaja; **he did it deliberately** dia melakukan itu dengan sengaja; **it's been left there deliberately** barang itu ditinggalkan di situ dengan sengaja.

a b c d e f g h i j k l m n o p q r s t u v w x y z

a b c d e f g h i j k l m n o p q r s t u v w x y z

delicate *adjective* **1** lembut; **a delicate colour** warna yang lembut; **2** lemah; **a delicate child** anak yang lemah; **3** mudah pecah; **delicate chinaware** barang pecah belah yang mudah pecah.

delicious *adjective* enak, lezat.

delighted *adjective* sangat gembira, sangat senang; **we're delighted to hear your news** kami merasa sangat gembira mendengar kabar Anda.

deliver *verb* **1** mengantarkan; **they're delivering the new computer tomorrow** mereka akan mengantarkan komputer baru itu besok; **2** menyampaikan *(message)*.

delivery *noun* pengantaran, pengiriman.

demand *noun* permintaan, tuntutan.
verb **1** meminta; **I demand your help** saya meminta bantuanmu; **2** menuntut; **they demanded their rights** mereka menuntut hak mereka.

demo *noun (informal, protest)* demonstrasi.

democracy *noun* demokrasi.

democratic *adjective* demokratis.

demolish *verb* membongkar, menghancurkan.

demonstrate *verb* **1** *(a machine, product or technique)* menunjukkan; **2** *(protest)* berdemonstrasi; **to demonstrate against tax increases** berdemonstrasi menentang kenaikan pajak.

demonstration *noun* **1** *(of machine, product or technique)* percobaan; **2** *(protest)* demonstrasi.

demonstrator *noun* demonstran, pengunjuk rasa *(in protest)*.

denim *noun* bahan jin, denim.

Denmark *noun* Denmark.

dense *adjective* **1** tebal; **dense fog** kabut tebal; **2** lebat; **dense forest** hutan lebat; **3** padat; **dense population** penduduk padat.

density *noun* kepadatan; **population density** kepadatan penduduk.

dent *noun* lekukan, peok *(colloquial)*, peot *(colloquial)*, penyok.
verb melekukkan.

dental *adjective* **1** yang berhubungan dengan gigi *(definition only)*; **dental care** pemeliharaan gigi; **dental floss** benang untuk perawatan gigi; **dental**

hygiene kebersihan gigi; **2 a dental appointment** janji dengan dokter gigi.

dental surgeon *noun* ahli bedah gigi.

dentist *noun* dokter gigi.

deny *verb* mengingkari, menyangkal.

deodorant *noun* deodoran.

depart *verb* berangkat.

department *noun* **1** *(in government, school, university)* departemen; **the language department** departemen bahasa; **Department of Religion** Departemen Agama; **2** *(in a shop)* bagian; **the men's department** bagian perlengkapan pria.

department store *noun* toko serba ada (toserba).

departure *noun* keberangkatan.

departure lounge *noun* ruang keberangkatan.

depend *verb* **to depend on** bergantung pada, tergantung pada; **it depends on the weather** tergantung pada cuaca; **whether I go depends on how I feel** apakah saya pergi atau tidak bergantung pada perasaan saya.

deposit *noun* **1** *(when renting or hiring or booking something)* uang panjar, uang tanggungan; **to pay a deposit** membayar uang tanggungan; **2** deposito, setoran; **bank deposit** deposito bank.

depressed *adjective* depresi, muram, sedih.

depressing *adjective* yang menyedihkan.

depth *noun* dalam, kedalaman.

deputy *noun* wakil.

deputy head *noun* wakil kepala (sekolah).

descend *verb* turun.

describe *verb* melukiskan, menggambarkan.

description *noun* deskripsi, gambaran.

desert *noun* gurun pasir, padang pasir.

desert island *noun* pulau yang tidak ada penduduknya.

deserve *verb* berhak mendapat.

design *noun* **1** desain, model; **the design of the car** model mobil itu; **2** *(artistic design)* pola; **fashion design** pola mode; **3** *(pattern)* motif; **a floral design** motif berbunga.
verb menggambar, merencanakan.

a b c d e f g h i j k l m n o p q r s t u v w x y z

designer *noun* **1** *(graphic designer)* desainer; **2** *(fashion designer)* ahli mode, perancang.

desire *noun* keinginan. *verb* menginginkan.

desk *noun* **1** meja tulis; **2** bagian; **the reception desk** bagian resepsionis.

despair *noun* kehilangan harapan, keputus-asaan.

desperate *adjective* **1** nekat; **a desperate attempt** usaha nekat; **2 to be desperate to** sangat ingin; **Matt's desperate to meet Anita** Matt sangat ingin bertemu dengan Anita.

despise *verb* memandang rendah, menghina.

dessert *noun* kue-kue, makanan pencuci mulut; **what's for dessert?** makanan pencuci mulutnya apa?

destination *noun* (tempat) tujuan.

destroy *verb* memusnahkan, menghancurkan, merusakkan.

destruction *noun* kehancuran, pembongkaran *(of a building)*

detached house *noun* rumah terpisah.

detail *noun* perincian.

detailed *adjective* rinci, terperinci.

detective *noun* **1** *(police)* reserse; **2** detektip; **private detective** detektip swasta.

detective story *noun* cerita detektip.

detention *noun* penahanan, tahanan.

detergent *noun* deterjen.

determined *adjective* bertekad, tekun; **I'm determined to go** saya bertekad akan pergi.

detour *noun* jalan belokan, jalan memutar.

develop *verb* **1** mencuci; **to get a film developed** mencuci film; **2** berkembang menjadi; **the way children develop** bagaimana anak-anak berkembang menjadi besar; **3** memperkembangkan, mengembangkan; **to develop an industry** memperkembangkan industri.

developing country *noun* negara berkembang.

development *noun* perkembangan.

devil *noun* iblis, roh jahat, setan, syaitan.

devote *verb* mempersembahkan,

mencurahkan; **to devote one's attention to** mencurahkan perhatian kepada.

devoted *adjective* sayang pada; **she's devoted to her little sister** dia sayang pada adik perempuannya.

diabetes *noun* diabetes, penyakit gula, penyakit kencing manis.

diabetic *noun* penderita penyakit kencing manis; **to be (a) diabetic** penderita penyakit gula.

diagonal *adjective* diagonal, sudut-menyudut.

diagram *noun* diagram, sketsa.

dial *verb* memutar angka, menekan angka; **lift the receiver and dial 0011** angkat tilpon dan tekan angka 0011.

dialling tone *noun* nada pilih.

dialogue *noun* dialog.

diamond *noun* **1** berlian, intan; **2** *(in cards)* ret; **the queen of diamonds** ratu wajit; **3** *(shape)* suatu bentuk segi empat.

diarrhoea *noun* diare, mencret; **to have diarrhoea** sakit mencret.

diary *noun* buku harian.

dice *noun* dadu; **to throw the dice** bermain dadu.

dictation *noun* dikte, pendiktean.

dictionary *noun* kamus.

did *verb* SEE **do**.

die *verb* **1** mati; **the horse died** kuda itu mati; **2** meninggal dunia; **my grandmother died in March** nenek saya meninggal dunia pada bulan Maret; **3 to be dying to do** ingin sekali; **we're dying to go** kami ingin sekali pergi.

diesel *noun* disel; **diesel oil** minyak disel, minyak solar.

diet *noun* **1** makanan; **a healthy diet** makanan yang sehat; **2** *(slimming or special)* diet; **to be on a diet** mengikuti diet, berdiet; **a salt-free diet** diet bebas garam.

difference *noun* **1** perbedaan; **what's the difference between rambutans and lychees?** apa perbedaan antara rambutan dan leci?; **2** berbeda; **another thousand dollars will make a difference** seribu dolar lagi akan menyebabkan perbedaan; **3 it makes no difference to me** sama saja untuk saya.

a b c d e f g h i j k l m n o p q r s t u v w x y z

different *adjective* berbeda, tidak sama; **the children are all very different** masing-masing anak itu berbeda; **she's very different from her mother** dia sangat berbeda dari ibunya.

difficult *adjective* sukar, sulit; **it's difficult to decide** sukar sekali memutuskannya.

difficulty *noun* kesukaran, kesulitan; **I had difficulty getting your phone number** saya mengalami kesukaran mendapatkan nomor telepon Anda.

dig *verb* menggali; **to dig a hole** menggali lobang.

digest *verb (food)* mencernakan.

digestion *noun* pencernaan.

digital *adjective* dijital; **digital recording** rekaman dijital.

diligent *adjective* rajin.

dim *adjective* **1** suram; **a dim light** lampu yang suram; **2** tolol; **he's a bit dim** *(informal)* dia agak tolol.

dimension *noun* dimensi, ukuran.

din *noun* keriuhan, hiruk-pikuk, riuh; **those dogs make a dreadful din** anjing-anjing itu riuh sekali; **stop making such a din!** jangan hiruk-pikuk!

dinghy *noun* sampan kecil; **a sailing dinghy** sampan kecil untuk berlayar (*description only*).

dining room *noun* kamar makan, ruang makan.

dinner *noun* **1** *(evening)* makan malam, **to invite to dinner** mengundang makan malam; **2** *(midday)* makan siang; **to have school dinner** makan siang di sekolah.

dinner party *noun* pesta makan malam.

dinner time *noun* waktu makan malam.

dinosaur *noun* dinosaurus.

diploma *noun* diploma, ijazah.

direct *adjective* langsung. *verb* **1** *(program, film)* menyutradarai; **2** *(traffic)* mengatur.

direction *noun* **1** arah; **in the other direction** ke arah yang lain; **2** petunjuk; **to ask for directions** meminta petunjuk; **3 directions for use** aturan pakai.

directly *adverb* **1** (dengan) langsung; **2 directly afterwards** segera sesudahnya.

director *noun* **1** *(of a company)* direktur; **2** *(of a program)* pemimpin; **3** *(film or play)* sutradara.

directory *noun* petunjuk; **telephone directory** buku petunjuk telepon.

dirt *noun* **1** *(filth)* kotoran; **2** *(earth)* tanah.

dirty *adjective* kotor; **to get dirty** menjadi kotor; **to get something dirty** mengotorkan; **don't get your dress dirty** jangan kotorkan bajunya; **you'll get your dress dirty** nanti baju Anda kotor.

disabled *adjective* cacat; **disabled people** orang-orang cacat.

disadvantage *noun* **1** keadaan yang merugikan; **2 to be at a disadvantage** berada dalam keadaan yang tidak menguntungkan.

disagree *verb* **1** tidak sependapat, tidak setuju; **I disagree** saya tidak setuju; **I disagree with her** saya tidak sependapat dengan dia; **2** berselisih; **they always disagree on that topic** mereka selalu berselisih pendapat tentang hal itu.

disappear *verb* hilang, lenyap; **the cat's disappeared** kucing itu hilang; **the water slowly disappeared** pelan-pelan air itu menghilang.

disappearance *noun* kehilangan, hilangnya, lenyapnya.

disappoint *verb* mengecewakan.

disappointed *adjective* kecewa; **he was disappointed with his marks** dia kecewa dengan angkanya.

disappointment *noun* kekecewaan.

disaster *noun* **1** bencana; **a natural disaster** bencana alam; **2** kemalangan, malapetaka; **it was a complete disaster** itu betul-betul suatu malapetaka.

disastrous *adjective* yang membawa malapetaka.

discipline *noun* disiplin.

disc *noun* disk, piringan; **a compact disc** compact disk; **a slipped disc** piringan sendi yang tergelincir.

disc-jockey *noun* penyiar radio.

disco *noun* **1** pesta disko; **2** *(club)* diskotik, disko.

discount *noun* diskon, korting, potongan.

discourage *verb* mengecilkan hati.

discover *verb* menemukan.

discovery *noun* penemuan.

discreet *adjective* berhati-hati, bijaksana.

a b c d e f g h i j k l m n o p q r s t u v w x y z

discrimination *noun* diskriminasi; **racial discrimination** diskriminasi rasial.

discuss *verb* membicarakan, merundingkan; **we'll discuss the problem tomorrow** besok kita akan membicarakan masalah itu; **I'm going to discuss it with Richard** saya akan membicarakannya dengan Richard.

discussion *noun* diskusi, pembicaraan, perundingan.

disease *noun* penyakit.

disgraceful *adjective* memalukan.

disguise *noun* penyamaran; **to be in disguise** menyamar.
verb **1** menyembunyikan; **to disguise your feelings** menyembunyikan perasaan; **2** menyamar; **Fran's disguising herself** Fran sedang menyamarkan diri; **disguised as a bear** menyamar sebagai beruang.

disgust *noun* rasa jijik, rasa muak.
verb memuakkan, menjijikkan.

disgusted *adjective* jijik.

disgusting *adjective* **1** *(book, movie)* cabul; **2** menjijikkan.

dish *noun* **1** piring; **to do the dishes** mencuci piring; **2** hidangan, makanan, masakan; **he prepared my favourite dish** dia memasak makanan favorit saya.

dishcloth *noun (for drying up)* lap piring, serbet.

dishonest *adjective* tidak jujur.

dishonesty *noun* ketidakjujuran.

dish towel *noun* lap piring, serbet.

dishwasher *noun* mesin pencuci piring.

disinfect *verb* membasmi hama atau kuman, mendesinfeksi.

disinfectant *noun* obat pembasmi kuman.

disk *noun* disk; **a floppy disk** disket; **store on a disk** menyimpan dalam disket.

diskette *noun* disket.

dislike *noun* benci, perasaan tidak suka.
verb membenci, tidak suka; **she dislikes pop music** dia tidak suka musik pop.

dismay *noun* kecemasan, kekhawatiran.

dismiss *verb (an employee)* memecat.

disobedient *adjective* bandel *(colloquial)*, tidak patuh, tidak taat, tidak tunduk.

display *noun* **1** pameran; **a handicraft display** pameran kerajinan tangan; **to be on display** dipamerkan; **2 a window display** etalase; **3** tontonan; **a fireworks display** tontonan kembang api.

disposable *adjective* yang dapat dibuang.

dispose *verb* membuang.

disqualify *verb* mendiskualifikasi.

disrupt *verb* mengacau, mengganggu.

dissolve *verb* **1** melarutkan; **to dissolve a cup of sugar** melarutkan satu cangkir gula; **2** membubarkan; **to dissolve a partnership** membubarkan perseroan.

distance *noun* jarak; **it's within walking distance** jaraknya dapat ditempuh dengan jalan kaki; **from a distance** dari jauh.

distant *adjective* jauh; **distant star** bintang yang jauh.

distinct *adjective* jelas, nyata, terang.

distinctly *adverb* **1** *(clearly)* dengan jelas; **2 it's distinctly odd** itu aneh benar.

distract *verb* mengalihkan.

distribute *verb* **1** membagikan, menyebarkan *(leaflets, for example)*; **2** mendistribusikan *(food)*.

district *noun* **1** *(administrative area)* distrik, wilayah; **2** daerah; **a poor district of Jakarta** daerah miskin di Jakarta.

disturb *verb* mengganggu; **sorry to disturb you** maaf saya mengganggu Anda.

disturbance *noun* gangguan.

ditch *noun* got, selokan. *verb (informal)* membuang, menyingkirkan; **they ditched the old car behind the shoe factory** mereka membuang mobil tua itu di belakang pabrik sepatu.

dive *noun* penyelaman. *verb* menyelam.

diver *noun* penyelam.

diversion *noun (traffic)* pengalihan.

divert *verb* mengalihkan.

divide *verb* membagi, memisahkan.
- **to divide up** membagi-bagikan.

diving *noun* penyelaman, *(sport)* loncat indah.

diving board *noun* papan loncat.

division *noun* divisi, pembagian.

divorce *noun* perceraian, talak *(Islam)*.

a b c d e f g h i j k l m n o p q r s t u v w x y z

verb **1** bercerai; **Desi has divorced her husband** Desi sudah bercerai dari suaminya; **2** menceraikan, menjatuhkan talak; **Ronald divorced Faith** Ronald menceraikan Faith.

divorced *adjective* bercerai.

DIY [do-it-yourself] *abbreviation, noun* kerjakan sendiri.

dizzy *adjective* pusing; **she felt dizzy** dia merasa pusing.

DJ [disc jockey] *noun* penyiar radio.

do *verb* **1** mengerjakan, melakukan; **what are you doing?** Apa yang sedang Anda kerjakan?; **he's doing his homework** dia mengerjakan pekerjaan rumahnya; **2** menyelesaikan; **I have to do this work before we leave** saya harus menyelesaikan pekerjaan ini sebelum kita berangkat; **3** *(questions in Indonesian are formed by using question words or 'apakah' at the beginning, or in speech often just with intonation)* **do you want some mango?** (apakah) Anda mau makan mangga?; **when does it start?** jam berapa mulainya?; **how did you get it open?** bagaimana Anda dapat membukanya?; **what have you done with the newspaper?** koran ditaruh di mana?; **4** *(negatives are formed with 'tidak' for* verbs*)* **they don't like jazz** mereka tidak suka musik jaz; **Ruth doesn't play sport** Ruth tidak berolahraga; **he didn't shut the door** dia tidak menutup pintu itu; **it doesn't matter** tidak apa-apa; **didn't they go?** tidakkah mereka pergi?; **5** *(when it refers back to another* verb, *'do' is not translated)* **'do you live here?' – 'yes, I do'** 'apakah Anda tinggal di sini?' – 'betul'; **Fay has more time than I do** Fay lebih banyak waktu dari saya'; **'I live in Perth' – 'so do I'** 'saya tinggal di Perth' – 'saya juga'; **'Peter didn't phone Lesley' – 'neither did I'** 'Peter tidak menelepon Lesley' – 'saya juga tidak'; **6 don't you?, doesn't he?** bukan, kan?; **you know Megan, don't you?** Anda kenal akan Megan, (bu)kan?; **she dropped by yesterday, didn't she?** kemarin dia mampir di sini, kan?; **7 that'll do** cukup; **it'll do like that** begitu saja cukup.

- **to do something up** **1** *(shoes, clothing)* menutup; **Eric did the**

buttons of his shirt up Eric menutup kancing bajunya; **2** *(a house)* memperbarui; **the young couple bought an old house and did it up** pasangan muda itu membeli rumah tua dan memperbaruinya.

- **do without** tidak perlu; **we can do without knives** kami tidak perlu pisau.

dock *noun* dermaga.

doctor *noun* dokter.

document *noun* **1** surat; **2** *(legal document)* akte, dokumen.

documentary *noun* film dokumenter.

dog *noun* anjing.

dole *noun* tunjangan pengangguran; **be on the dole** menerima tunjangan pengangguran.

doll *noun* boneka.

dollar *noun* dolar.

dolphin *noun* ikan lumba-lumba.

domino *noun* gaplek, kartu domino; **to play dominoes** bermain gaplek, bermain domino.

donkey *noun* keledai.

don't *verb* SEE **do**.

door *noun* **1** pintu; **the front door** pintu depan; **2** rumah; **he lives three doors down** dia tinggal tiga rumah dari (sini).

doorbell *noun* bel pintu; **to ring the doorbell** membunyikan bel pintu.

doorstep *noun* ambang pintu.

dope *noun* dungu; **he's a real dope** dia sugguh-sungguh dungu.

dot *noun* **1** *(written)* titik; **2** *(on fabric)* bintik; **3** tepat; **at five on the dot** jam lima tepat.

double *adjective*, *adverb* **1** dobel, dua; **a double helping** dua porsi; **2** dua kali (lipat) **double the time** dua kali waktunya; **3 a double room** kamar untuk dua orang; **4** ganda; **a double role** peran ganda.

double bass *noun* bas viol.

double-breasted *adjective* berkancing dua baris.

double-decker bus *noun* bis bertingkat.

doubles *noun (in sport)* ganda; **to play a game of doubles** bermain ganda.

doubt *noun* kesangsian, keragu-raguan; **there's no doubt about it** tak sangsi lagi; **to be in doubt about** sangsi akan; **I have my doubts** saya ragu-ragu; **no doubt** sudah pasti.

a b c d e f g h i j k l m n o p q r s t u v w x y z

verb **to doubt something** menyangsikan, ragu; **I doubt it** saya menyangsikan itu; **to doubt that** ragu bahwa; **I doubt he'll come** saya rasa dia tak akan datang.

doubtful *adjective* **1** ragu-ragu, sangsi; **to be doubtful about doing** sangsi akan; **I'm doubtful about inviting them together** saya sangsi apakah saya akan mengundang mereka bersama-sama atau tidak; **2 it's doubtful** belum tentu.

dough *noun* **1** adonan; **2** *(slang for money)* duit, uang.

doughnut *noun* donat.

down *adverb, preposition* **1** di bawah, ke bawah; **he's down in the lobby** dia di bawah di lobi; **2** *(nearby)* dekat; **down the road** dekat sini; **there's a video rental just down the road** ada toko sewa video dekat dari sini; **3 to go down, to come down** turun (ke bawah); **he went down to the study** dia turun (ke bawah) ke ruang belajar; **4 she came down from her bedroom** dia turun dari kamar tidurnya; **to walk down the street** berjalan sepanjang jalan; **to run down the stairs** menuruni tangga sambil berlari; **5 to sit down** duduk; **everybody sit down!** semua harap duduk!

downstairs *adverb, noun* **1** ruang bawah; **she's downstairs in the sitting-room** dia di ruang duduk di bawah; **2** di lantai bawah; **the flat downstairs** apartemen di lantai bawah; **the people downstairs** orang-orang yang tinggal di lantai bawah.

doze *verb* tidur-tiduran; **to doze off** tertidur.

dozen *noun* dosin, lusin; **a dozen eggs** selusin telur.

drag *noun (informal)* **1** membosankan; **what a drag!** sangat membosankan!; **he's a bit of a drag** dia orang yang membosankan; **2** *(on a cigarette)* mengisap rokok.
verb **1** tarik; **can you help me drag this log?** tolong saya menarik batang kayu ini; **2** berlarut-larut; **the match dragged on** pertandingan itu berlarut-larut.

dragon *noun* naga.

dragonfly *noun* capung.

drain *noun* saluran.
verb **1** *(vegetables)* mengeringkan; **2** mengalirkan; **to drain the rice fields** mengalirkan air dari sawah.

drama *noun* 1 sandiwara, seni drama; **2 he made a big drama out of it** *(informal)* dia membesar-besarkan hal itu.

dramatic *adjective* dramatis, beraksi.

draught *noun* aliran angin.

draw *noun* 1 *(in a match)* **it was a draw** berakhir seri; 2 *(lottery)* tarikan.
verb 1 menggambar; **to draw a picture** menggambar; **she can draw really well** dia pintar sekali menggambar; **2 to draw the curtains** menutup gorden; **3 to draw a crowd** menarik orang banyak; **4 to draw lots** mengundi; **5 to draw money** *(from the bank)* mengambil uang.

drawback *noun* kekurangan.

drawer *noun* laci.

drawing *noun* gambar.

drawing pin *noun* paku payung.

dreadful *adjective* menakutkan, mengerikan.

dreadfully *adverb* sangat; **I'm dreadfully wet** saya sangat basah; **I'm dreadfully sorry** saya sangat menyesal.

dream *noun* impian, mimpi; **to have a dream** bermimpi; **I had a wonderful dream last night** semalam impian saya sangat indah.
verb **to dream about** memimpikan.

drenched *adjective* basah kuyup; **I got drenched on the way here** saya basah kuyup waktu datang ke sini.

dress *noun* baju, pakaian.
verb **to dress a child** mengenakan baju pada anak.
- **to dress up** berdandan, berpakaian; **Sari dressed up as an angel** Sari berpakaian bagaikan malaikat.

dressed *adjective* berpakaian; **is Mike dressed yet?** apakah Mike sudah berpakaian? **she was dressed all in black** dia berpakaian serba hitam; **to get dressed** berpakaian, memakai baju.

dresser *noun* lemari rias.

dressing gown *noun* baju rumah.

dressing table *noun* meja rias.

dressmaker *noun* penjahit, modiste.

drier *noun* pengering; **a hair drier** pengering rambut.

drift *noun* aliran, arus.

drill *noun* bor.
verb 1 *(hole, tooth)* mengebor; 2 melatih; **to drill recruits** melatih calon-calon prajurit.

a b c d e f g h i j k l m n o p q r s t u v w x y z

drink *noun* **1** minuman; **a hot drink** minuman panas; **2 would you like a drink?** Anda mau minum?; **3 to go out for a drink** *(informal)* jalan-jalan ke bar.
verb minum; **the kitten drank a bowl of milk** anak kucing itu minum susu semangkuk.

drive *noun* **1** perjalanan; **to go for a drive** pergi naik mobil; **2** *(up to a house)* jalan mobil.
verb **1** mengemudikan, mengendarai, menyetir; **she drives very fast** dia mengendarai (mobil) cepat sekali; **to drive a car** menyetir mobil; **I must learn to drive** saya harus belajar mengemudi; **can you drive?** Anda bisa menyetir (mobil)?; **2** naik mobil; **we drove to Melbourne** kami naik mobil ke Melbourne; **3 to drive somebody (to a place)** mengantarkan dengan mobil; **Paul drove me to the airport** Paul mengantarkan saya (dengan mobil) ke lapangan udara; **she drives me mad!** dia membuat saya marah!

driver *noun* pengemudi, supir.

driving instructor *noun* guru mengemudikan mobil.

driving lesson *noun* pelajaran mengemudikan mobil.

driving licence *noun* surat ijin mengemudi (SIM).

driving test *noun* ujian mengemudi; **take your driving test** ujian mengemudi; **Jake's passed his driving test** Jake sudah dapat SIMnya.

drop *verb* **1** menjatuhkan; **he dropped the bowl** dia menjatuhkan mangkuk itu; **2** keluar, melepaskan; **Fred dropped history** Fred melepaskan sejarah; **3 drop it!** lupakan saja!; **4** *(a person)* mengantarkan; **could you drop me at the video store?** apakah bisa mengantarkan saya ke toko video?

drown *verb* tenggelam; **he drowned in the lake** dia tenggelam di danau.

drug *noun* **1** *(medicine)* obat; **2** *(illegal)* obat bius; **drugs** obat-obat bius.

drug abuse *noun* penyalahgunaan obat bius.

drug addict *noun* pecandu obat bius.

drug addiction *noun* kecanduan obat bius.

drum *noun* **1** drum, tong *(for oil, for example)*; **drum of oil** drum minyak; **2** gendang, genderang, tambur; **to play drums** main tambur.

drummer *noun* pemain tambur.

drunk *noun* pemabuk. *adjective* mabuk.

dry *adjective* kering. *verb* **1** mengeringkan; **to dry your hair** mengeringkan rambut; **to dry the dishes** mengeringkan piring; **to let dry** membiarkan menjadi kering; **2** mengusap; **to dry your tears** mengusap air mata.

dry-clean *verb* dry clean.

dry cleaner's *noun* binatu.

dryer *noun* SEE **drier**.

dubbed *adjective* isi suara; **a dubbed film** film yang digantijadi bahasa lain.

duck *noun* bebek, itik.

due *adjective, adverb* **1 to be due to** seharusnya akan; **we're due to leave tomorrow** kita seharusnya akan berangkat besok; **Pete's due back next week** Pete seharusnya akan kembali minggu depan; **2 due to** (oleh) karena, sebab; **the flight's been cancelled due to bad weather** penerbangan dibatalkan karena cuaca buruk.

duke *noun* adipati.

dull *adjective* **1** berawan; **dull weather** cuaca berawan; **2** *(boring)* membosankan; **3** bodoh.

dumb *adjective* **1** bisu, kelu; **to be deaf and dumb** tuli dan bisu; **2** bodoh; **Mick always asks some dumb questions** Mick selalu mengajukkan pertanyaan yang bodoh.

dummy *noun (for a baby)* dot.

dump *verb* **1** *(rubbish)* membuang; **2** *(a person, informal)* meninggalkan, putus hubungan; **she's dumped another boyfriend** dia meninggalkan pacarnya lagi.

dungarees *noun* celana jengki, jins *(jeans)*.

dungeon *noun* tempat tahanan *(definition only)*.

during *preposition* pada waktu; **during the night** pada waktu malam; **they met during the holidays** mereka bertemu pada waktu liburan.

dusk *noun* petang.

dust *noun* debu. *verb* membersihkan, menyapu debu.

dustbin *noun* tong sampah.

dustman *noun* tukang sampah.

dustpan *noun* kaleng sampah.

a b c d e f g h i j k l m n o p q r s t u v w x y z

dusty *adjective* berdebu.

Dutch *noun* **1** *(language)* bahasa Belanda; **2 the Dutch** bangsa Belanda, orang Belanda *(people)*.
adjective Belanda.

duty *noun* **1** kewajiban; **to have a duty to do** berkewajiban; **you have a duty to inform us** Anda berkewajiban memberitahu kami; **2** tugas; **to be on duty** bertugas; **to be on night duty** bertugas malam; **he's off duty tonight** malam ini dia bebas tugas.

duty-free *adjective* bebas bea; **duty-free purchases** pembelian bebas bea.

dwarf *noun* orang katai, orang kerdil.

Dyak *noun* orang Dayak.

dye *noun* **1** *(for fabric)* bahan celup; **2** *(for hair)* cat rambut.
verb **to dye your hair** mengecat rambut; **I'm going to dye my hair pink** saya mau mengecat rambut dengan warna merah muda.

dynamic *adjective* bersemangat, dinamis.

dynamite *noun* dinamit.

dysentery *noun* berak darah, disentri; **to have dysentery** sakit disentri.

dyslexia *noun* disleksia.

dyslexic *adjective* penderita disleksia.

E e

each *adjective, pronoun* **1** masing-masing; **my sisters each have a pet** adik saya masing-masing mempunyai binatang peliharaan; **each of you** Anda masing-masing; **we each got a prize** kami masing-masing mendapat hadiah; **the books cost forty dollars each** harga buku itu masing-masing empat puluh dolar; **2** setiap, tiap(-tiap); **each time** tiap kali; **there's a toy for each child** ada mainan untuk setiap anak.

each other *pronoun* **1** saling; **they love each other** mereka saling mencintai; **2** satu sama lain; **we know each other** kami kenal satu sama lain; **do you often see each other?** apakah Anda sering ketemu satu sama lain?

eagle *noun* burung elang, burung garuda, burung rajawali.

ear *noun* telinga.

earache *noun* sakit telinga; **to have earache** sakit telinga.

earlier *adverb* **1** *(a while ago)* tadi; **your boss phoned earlier** atasan Anda menelepon tadi; **2** *(not as late)* lebih awal; **we should have left earlier** kita seharusnya berangkat lebih awal.

early *adverb* **1** *(in the morning)* pagi-pagi; **to get up early** bangun pagi-pagi; **it's too early** masih terlalu pagi; **2** *(for an appointment)* awal, cepat; **we're early, the film doesn't start until eight** kami terlalu awal, film ini baru mulai jam delapan; **Randy likes to be early** Randy suka datang awal.
adjective **1** *(one of the first)* awal; **in the early days** dahulu, pada awalnya; **2** awal, cepat; **to have an early lunch** makan siang lebih awal, makan siang lebih cepat; **we should make an early start** lebih baik kita berangkat awal; **3 school finishes in the early afternoon** sekolah bubar siang hari; **in the early hours** pagi-pagi (sekali); **let's get the early train** mari kita naik kereta api pagi.

earn *verb (money)* mendapat bayaran, mendapat gaji; **Geoff earns thirty-five dollars an hour** Geoff mendapat bayaran tiga puluh lima dolar sejam.

earnings *plural noun* pendapatan.

earring *noun* anting-anting.

earth *noun* bumi; **life on earth** kehidupan di bumi; **what on earth were you thinking of?** apa yang Anda pikirkan?

earthquake *noun* gempa bumi.

easily *adverb* **1** *(to do something)* dengan mudah; **2** *(by far)* **she's easily the best** dia yang paling baik.

east *noun* timur; **in the east** di sebelah Timur; **East Timor** Timor Timur.
adjective, adverb **the east side** bagian timur, sebelah timur; **an east wind** angin timur; **east of Katoomba** sebelah timur Katoomba.

Easter *noun* Paskah; **Happy Easter!** Selamat Paskah!

Easter Day *noun* Hari (Minggu) Paskah.

Easter egg *noun* telur Paskah.

Eastern Europe *noun* Eropa Timur.

easy *adjective* gampang, mudah; **it's easy** gampang, mudah; **it was easy to**

a b c d e f g h i j k l m n o p q r s t u v w x y z

decide mudah memutuskannya.

eat *verb* makan; **they usually eat rice** biasanya mereka makan nasi; **to eat out** makan di restoran, makan di luar.

EC [European Community] *noun* Masyarakat Eropa.

echo *noun* gema, pantulan suara.

ecological *adjective* ekologis.

ecology *noun* ekologi.

economical *adjective* hemat, irit; **it's more economical to buy ten at once** lebih hemat membeli sepuluh sekaligus.

economics *noun* ilmu ekonomi.

economy *noun* ekonomi.

eczema *noun* eksema.

edge *noun* **1** tebing; **the edge of the cliff** tebing jurang; **2** pinggir; **at the edge of town** di pinggir kota; **3** tepi; **at the edge of the lake** di tepi danau; **4 to be on edge** tegang dan lekas marah.

edible *adjective* dapat dimakan.

edit *verb* mempersiapkan (naskah) untuk diterbitkan, mengedit.

editor *noun (of a newspaper)* editor.

editorial *noun* editorial, tajuk rencana; **editorial staff** redaksi.

educate *verb (teach)* melatih, mendidik.

education *noun* edukasi, pendidikan.

educational *adjective* yang berhubungan dengan pendidikan; **educational institute** institut pendidikan.

effect *noun* **1** akibat; **the effect of the drugs** akibat obat; **2** efek; **special effects** efek yang luar biasa, **side-effect** efek sampingan.

effective *adjective* berhasil guna, efektif.

efficient *adjective* berdayaguna, efisien.

effort *noun* upaya, usaha; **to make an effort** berusaha; **Gareth made an effort to study** Gareth berusaha belajar.

e.g. [for example] *abbreviation* misalnya, umpamanya.

egg *noun* telur; **a dozen eggs** selusin telur; **a fried egg** telur mata sapi; **soft-boiled egg** telur setengah matang; **scrambled egg** telur aduk goreng; **salted egg** telur asin, **egg white** putih telur, **egg yolk** merah telur, **eggshell** kulit telur; **egg cup** cangkir tempat telur.

eggplant *noun* terong.

eight *number* delapan; **eight o'clock** jam delapan.

eighteen *number* delapan belas; **Sarah's eighteen** Sarah berumur delapan belas tahun.

eighth *number* **1** delapan; **the eighth of June** tanggal delapan Juni; **2** (yang) kedelapan; **on the eighth floor** di lantai kedelapan.

eighty *number* delapan puluh; **eighty-five** delapan puluh lima.

Eire *noun* Irlandia.

either *pronoun* **1** *(one or the other)* salah satu (dari dua); **take either (of them)** silahkan ambil salah satu (dari kedua benda); **either is possible** salah satu mungkin terjadi; **2** *(both)* **he doesn't want either (of them)** dia tidak mau keduanya. *conjunction* **1** **either...or** atau; **either today or tomorrow** hari ini atau besok; **either Ross or Jason** Ross atau Jason; **I'll either phone or e-mail** saya akan menelepon atau mengirim e-mail; **3** *(with a negative)* juga, pun; **we can't go either** kami pun tidak dapat pergi; **she doesn't know them either** dia pun tidak kenal mereka, dia tidak kenal mereka juga.

elastic *noun, adjective* elastis.

elastic band *noun* gelang karet.

elbow *noun* siku.

elder *adjective* lebih tua, senior; **elder sister, elder brother** kakak; **elder brother** abang, kakak laki-laki.

elderly *adjective* lanjut usia, tua; **the elderly** kaum tua, manula (manusia usia lanjut), yang sudah lanjut usia.

eldest *adjective* sulung, tertua; **her eldest brother** kakak sulungnya.

elect *verb* memilih; **she has been elected** dia telah terpilih.

election *noun* pemilihan; **general election** pemilihan umum.

electric *adjective* yang berhubungan dengan listrik; **an electric cooker** kompor listrik.

electrical *adjective* yang berhubungan dengan listrik; **an electrical engineer** insinyur listrik.

electrician *noun* tukang listrik.

electricity *noun* listrik; **to turn off the electricity** mematikan listrik.

a b c d e f g h i j k l m n o p q r s t u v w x y z

electronic *adjective* elektronik.

electronics *noun* ilmu elektronika.

elegant *adjective* anggun, elok.

elephant *noun* gajah.

eleven *number* sebelas; **Boy is eleven** Boy berumur sebelas tahun; **at eleven o'clock** pada jam sebelas; **a football eleven** kesebelasan sepak bola.

eleventh *number* **1** sebelas; **the eleventh of March** tanggal sebelas Maret; **2** (yang) kesebelas **on the eleventh floor** pada lantai kesebelas.

eliminate *verb* **1** menghapuskan; **2** menyisihkan **our team has already been eliminated** regu kita sudah disisihkan.

else *adverb* **1** (yang) lain; **somebody else** orang lain; **did you see anyone else?** apakah Anda melihat orang lain?; **I don't want anything else** saya tidak perlu apa-apa lagi; **something else** yang lain; **would you like something else?** mau yang lain?; **somewhere else** di tempat yang lain; **2 or else** kalau tidak; **hurry up, or else we'll miss the train** ayo cepatlah, kalau tidak kita akan ketinggalan kereta api.

e-mail *noun* e-mail.

embankment *noun* tambak, tanggul.

embarrassed *adjective* malu; **I was terribly embarrassed** saya malu sekali.

embarrassing *adjective* memalukan.

embarrassment *noun* keadaan yang memalukan.

embassy *noun* kedutaan besar; **the Australian Embassy** Kedutaan Besar Australia.

embroider *verb* menyulam.

embroidery *noun* sulaman.

emergency *noun* darurat; **in an emergency, break the glass** dalam keadaan darurat, pecahkan kaca; **it's an emergency** keadaan darurat.

emergency exit *noun* pintu darurat.

emergency landing *noun* pendaratan darurat.

emergency room *noun* unit gawat darurat (UGD).

emotion *noun* emosi.

emotional *adjective* **1** *(a person)* emosional; **he was quite emotional** dia sangat emosional; **2** *(a speech or an* *occasion)* yang emosional, yang penuh perasaan.

emperor *noun* kaisar.

emphasize *verb* menegaskan, menekankan, menggarisbawahi; **he emphasized that it wasn't compulsory** dia menegaskan bahwa hal itu tidak diwajibkan.

empire *noun* kekaisaran, kerajaan; **the Roman Empire** Kekaisaran Romawi.

employ *verb* mempekerjakan.

employee *noun* karyawan, pegawai, pekerja.

employer *noun* atasan, majikan, pemekerja.

employment *noun* jabatan, pekerjaan.

empty *adjective* kosong; **an empty bottle** botol kosong; **the room was empty** ruang itu kosong.
verb mengosongkan; **please empty the garbage bin** tolong kosongkan tempat sampah itu.

enchanting *adjective* mempesona.

enclose *verb (in a letter)* melampirkan; **please find enclosed a cheque** terlampir adalah cek.

encore *noun* permintaan dari penonton untuk memberikan lagu atau pertunjukan tambahan pada akhir suatu pertunjukan (*definition only*).

encourage *verb* memberi semangat, membesarkan hati, mendorong, menganjurkan; **Mum encouraged me to try again** Ibu menganjurkan supaya saya mencoba lagi.

encouragement *noun* desakan, dorongan, semangat.

encouraging *adjective* memberi semangat, membesarkan hati, mendorong.

encyclopaedia *noun* ensiklopedi.

end *noun* **1** *(last part)* akhir, bagian akhir; **'The End'** 'Tamat'; **at the end of the film** pada bagian akhir film itu; **by the end of the day** pada akhir hari; **he resigned at the end of May** dia mengundurkan diri pada akhir bulan Mei; **in the end I went home** akhirnya saya pulang; **2** ujung *(of a table, garden, stick or road, for example)*; **hold the other end** tolong pegang ujung itu; **at the end of the street** di ujung jalan.
verb **1** *(to put an end to)* mengakhiri, menghentikan;

they've ended the strike mereka sudah mengakhiri pemogokan itu; **2** *(to come to an end)* berakhir, berhenti; **the event ended with fireworks** peristiwa itu berakhir dengan pertunjukan kembang api.
- **to end up** akhirnya; **we ended up taking a taxi** akhirnya kami naik taksi; **to end up doing** mengakhiri.

ending *noun* akhir, bagian terakhir.

endless *adjective (a day or journey, for example)* tak henti-hentinya, tanpa henti, terus-menerus.

enemy *noun* lawan, musuh; **to make enemies** membuat musuh.

energetic *adjective* penuh semangat.

energy *noun* energi, tenaga, daya; **atomic energy** tenaga atom.

engaged *adjective* **1** *(to be married)* bertunangan; **they're engaged** mereka bertunangan; **2** *(a phone or toilet)* sedang dipakai, sibuk; **it's engaged. I'll ring later** sedang sibuk. saya akan menelepon lagi nanti.

engagement *noun (to marry)* pertunangan.

engagement ring *noun* cincin pertunangan.

engine *noun* **1** *(in a car)* mesin; **2** *(pulling a train)* lokomotip.

engineer *noun* **1** *(who comes for repairs)* tukang; **2** *(university-trained)* insinyur. *verb* merekayasa.

engineering *noun* ilmu teknik.

England *noun* negeri Inggris.

English *noun* **1** *(the language)* bahasa Inggris; **do you speak English?** apakah Anda berbahasa Inggris?; **please speak English** harap bicara bahasa Inggris; **2** *(the people)* orang Inggris; **the English** bangsa Inggris. *adjective* Inggris; **the English team** regu Inggris.

English Channel *noun* Terusan Inggris.

Englishman *noun* orang laki-laki Inggris.

Englishwoman *noun* orang perempuan Inggris.

enjoy *verb* **1** menikmati; **did you enjoy the party?** apakah Anda menikmati pesta itu?; **2 to enjoy doing** senang, suka; **I enjoy horse-riding** saya suka naik kuda; **do you enjoy living in Medan?** apakah Anda senang bertempat tinggal di

a b c d e f g h i j k l m n o p q r s t u v w x y z

Medan?; **we really enjoyed ourselves there** kami betul-betul bersenang-senang di sana; **enjoy yourselves!** harap bersenang-senang!; **are you enjoying yourself?** apakah Anda senang di sana?

enjoyable *adjective* yang menyenangkan, nikmat; **an enjoyable meal** makanan yang nikmat.

enlarge *verb (a photo, for example)* membesarkan, memperbesar.

enlargement *noun (of a photo)* pembesaran.

enormous *adjective* raksasa, sangat besar; **enormous project** proyek raksasa.

enough *adjective, adverb* cukup; **there's enough for everyone** ada cukup untuk semua orang; **big enough** cukup besar; **slowly enough** cukup lambat; **that's enough!** cukuplah!

enquire *verb* bertanya, menanyakan; **I'm going to enquire about the trains** saya mau bertanya tentang kereta api.

enquiry *noun* penyelidikan; **to make enquiries about payment methods** mengadakan penyelidikan tentang cara membayar, menanyakan keterangan tentang cara membayar.

enrol *verb* mendaftarkan, mengikuti; **I want to enrol in the course** saya ingin mengikuti kursus itu; **have you already enrolled?** apakah Anda sudah mendaftarkan diri?

enter *verb* **1** *(to go inside)* masuk, memasuki *(a room or building)*; **we all entered the mosque** kami semua memasuki mesjid itu; **2** *(an exam)* menempuh; **3** *(a competition)* mengikuti.

entertain *verb* **1** *(to keep amused)* menghibur; **games to entertain the children** permainan untuk menghibur anak-anak; **2** *(to have people around)* menjamu; **they don't like to entertain much** mereka tidak begitu suka menjamu tamu.

entertaining *noun* perjamuan; **they do a lot of entertaining** mereka sering mengadakan perjamuan. *adjective* yang menghibur, yang menyenangkan orang.

entertainment *noun (fun)* hiburan; **there isn't much entertainment in the evenings** tak ada banyak hiburan pada waktu malam.

enthusiasm *noun* antusiasme, semangat besar.

enthusiast *noun* penggemar; **he's a boxing enthusiast** dia penggemar tinju.

enthusiastic *adjective* antusias, bergairah, bersemangat.

entire *adjective* seluruh; **the entire school** seluruh sekolah.

entirely *adverb* sama sekali; **father and son are entirely different** bapak dan anak itu berbeda sama sekali.

entrance *noun* jalan masuk, pintu masuk.

entry *noun (the way in)* masuk; **'no entry'** 'dilarang masuk'.

envelope *noun* amplop, sampul.

environment *noun* lingkungan hidup.

environmental *adjective* yang berhubungan dengan lingkungan hidup.

environmentally friendly *adjective* tidak merusak lingkungan.

envy *noun* cemburu, iri hati, sirik.

epidemic *noun* epidemi.

epileptic *noun* orang ayan, orang penderita epilepsi.

episode *noun* babak, episode.

equal *noun* sederajat, sama; **equal quantities** sama banyaknya; **equal rights** hak-hak yang sederajat, hak-hak yang sama.
verb sama dengan.

equally *adverb (to share)* sama rata; **we divided it equally** kami membaginya sama rata.

equality *noun* persamaan.

equator *noun* ekuator, khatulistiwa.

equip *verb* melengkapi; **to equip an expedition** melengkapi ekspedisi; **well equipped for the climb** cukup perlengkapan untuk pendakian itu.

equipment *noun* perlengkapan; **laboratory equipment** perlengkapan laboratorium.

equivalent *adjective* ekuivalen, sama dengan, sepadan; **one dollar is equivalent to five thousand Rupiah** satu dolar sama dengan lima ribu Rupiah.

erase *verb* menghapus.

eraser *noun* penghapus.

error *noun* kesalahan; **a spelling error** kesalahan ejaan.

erupt *verb* meletus; **the volcano erupted again** gunung berapi itu meletus lagi.

eruption *noun* erupsi, letusan.

escalator *noun* eskalator, tangga berjalan.

escape *noun (from prison)* pelarian.
verb lepas dari, melarikan diri; **Edi escaped from prison** Edi melarikan diri dari penjara.

escort *noun* kawalan, pengantar; **a police escort** kawalan polisi.

especially *adverb* **1** *(above all)* khususnya, terutama; **there are lots of tourists, especially in Bali** ada banyak wisatawan, terutama di Bali; **2** *(unusually)* begitu; **'is he rich?' – 'not especially'** 'apakah dia orang kaya?' – 'tidak begitu'.

essay *noun* esei, karangan; **an essay on pollution** sebuah karangan tentang polusi.

essential *adjective* esensial, perlu; **it's essential that we reply quickly** kita perlu menjawab secepatnya.

establishment *noun (an organization)* perusahaan, yayasan.

estate *noun* **1** *(a housing estate)* estat, perumahan; **2** *(a big house and grounds)* perkebunan.

estate agent *noun* agen perumahan.

estimate *verb* mengestimasi, menaksir; **I estimate it will cost about sixty thousand Rupiah** saya taksir harganya kira-kira enam puluh ribu rupiah.

etc. *abbreviation* dan lain-lain, dan sebagainya.

ethnic *adjective* etnis, kesukuan; **an ethnic minority** suku minoritas.

EU [European Union] *abbreviation, noun* Uni Eropa.

Europe *noun* Eropa

European *noun* orang Eropa. *adjective* Eropa.

European Union *noun* Uni Eropa.

eve *noun* malam; **Christmas Eve** malam Natal; **New Year's Eve** malam Tahun Baru.

even[1] *adverb* **1** pun; **even Bambang didn't like it** Bambang pun tidak menyukainya; **without even asking** tanpa bertanya apa pun; **2 even if** sekali pun, sungguh pun; **even if they come** sungguh pun mereka datang; **3 not even** pun tidak; **I don't like seafood, not even fish** saya tidak suka makanan laut, ikan pun tidak; **4** lagi; **even bigger** lebih besar lagi; **even more**

a b c d e f g h i j k l m n o p q r s t u v w x y z

embarrassing lebih memalukan lagi; **even faster** lebih cepat lagi; **5 even more than** lebih lagi; **6 even so** meskipun demikian; **even so, we had a good time** meskipun demikian, kami senang.

even² *adjective* **1** *(a surface or layer)* datar, rata; **2** *(a number)* genap; **six is an even number** enam adalah bilangan genap; **3** *(with the same score)* seri; *(competitors)* **Heryanto and Fahmi are even** Heryanto dan Fahmi bermain seri.

evening *noun* malam; **this evening** nanti malam, malam ini; **at six o'clock in the evening** jam enam malam; **tomorrow evening** besok malam; **on Saturday evening** pada malam Minggu; **the evening before** malam sebelumnya; **the evening meal** makan malam.

evening class *noun* kelas malam.

event *noun* **1** kejadian, peristiwa; **2 track events** perlombaan, pertandingan; **3 in any event, at all events** bagaimana pun juga.

eventual *adjective* akhirnya.

eventually *adverb* akhirnya.

ever *adverb* **1** *(at any time)* pernah; **have you ever noticed that...?** apakah Anda pernah perhatikan bahwa...?; **2 hardly ever** hampir tidak; **3** *(always)* (seperti) biasa; **the same as ever** sama seperti biasa; **hotter than ever** lebih panas daripada biasa; **more slowly than ever** lebih pelan daripada biasa; **4 ever since** sejak; **it's been raining ever since yesterday** hujan turun sejak kemarin; **5 no-one ever came** tidak pernah ada yang datang.

every *adjective* **1** (se)tiap, tiap-tiap; **every house has a garage** (se)tiap rumah punya garasi; **every day** setiap hari; **every Monday** setiap hari Senin; **every ten kilometres** tiap sepuluh kilometer; **2 every other** setiap dua...sekali; **every other day** setiap dua hari sekali, berselang hari; **3 every now and then** sekali-sekali.

everybody, everyone *pronoun* semuanya, semua orang, setiap orang; **everybody knows that...** semua orang tahu bahwa...; **everyone else** orang lainnya.

everything *pronoun* **1** segala-galanya, segala sesuatu, semua; **everything is ready** segala sesuatu sudah siap, semua sudah siap;

everything's fine semuanya baik-baik saja; **everything you said** segala sesuatu yang Anda katakan; **2 everything else** semua yang lain.

everywhere *adverb* **1** di mana-mana, ke mana-mana; **there was mud everywhere** di mana-mana ada lumpur; **everywhere she went** ke mana-mana dia pergi; **2 everywhere else** di tempat-tempat lain.

evidently *adverb* jelaslah, kenyataannya.

evil *noun* kejahatan. *adjective* jahat.

exact *adjective* persis, tepat; **the exact opposite** persis sebaliknya; **the exact amount** jumlah yang tepat.

exactly *adverb* **1** betul-betul, persis; **I can't tell the twins apart. they look exactly the same** saya tidak bisa membedakan kedua anak kembar itu. mereka betul-betul sama; **they're exactly the same age** mereka persis seumur; **2** tepat; **Jason's answer is not exactly right** jawaban Jason kurang tepat; **yes, exactly** ya, tepat sekali; **3** justru *(for emphasis)*; **Laura came just not at the right moment** Laura datang justru pada saat yang kurang tepat.

exaggerate *verb* melebih-lebihkan, membesar-besarkan.

exaggeration *noun* pernyataan yang dibesar-besarkan, pernyataan yang dilebih-lebihkan.

exam *noun* ujian; **a history exam** ujian sejarah; **to sit an exam** menempuh ujian; **to pass an exam** lulus ujian; **to fail an exam** gagal ujian.

examination *noun* **1** *(school, university)* ujian; **2** *(medical, customs, etc.)* pemeriksaan.

examine *verb* **1** *(students)* menguji; **2** *(a patient, witness, etc.)* memeriksa.

examiner *noun* **1** penguji; **2** *(customs)* pemeriksa.

example *noun* contoh, misal; **for example** misalnya; **to set a good example** memberikan contoh yang baik.

excellent *adjective* baik sekali, hebat.

except *preposition* kecuali; **except in October** kecuali pada bulan Oktober; **every day except Friday** tiap hari kecuali hari Jumat; **except when it rains** kecuali pada waktu hujan.

exception *noun* perkecualian, pengecualian; **without exception** tanpa

a b c d e f g h i j k l m n o p q r s t u v w x y z

pengecualian; **with the exception of** dengan perkecualian, kecuali.

exchange *noun* ganti, pertukaran; **in exchange for our help** sebagai ganti bantuan kita; **an exchange visit** kunjungan pertukaran; **exchange student** mahasiswa pertukaran, siswa pertukaran.
verb menukarkan; **can I exchange this shirt for a smaller one?** bolehkah saya menukarkan kemeja ini dengan yang lebih kecil?

exchange rate *noun* kurs valuta asing.

excite *verb* membangkitkan gairah.

excited *adjective* **1** *(a person or animal)* bergairah; **the children are excited** anak-anak itu bergairah; **2 to get excited** menjadi gelisah; **cats usually get excited when it's windy** kucing-kucing biasanya menjadi gelisah waktu ada banyak angin.

exciting *adjective* menggairahkan; **a really exciting concert** konser yang betul-betul menggairahkan.

exclamation mark *noun* tanda seru.

excursion *noun* darmawisata, ekskursi.

excuse *noun* alasan; **Mehmet has a good excuse** Mehmet punya alasan yang tepat; **that's no excuse** itu bukan alasan.
verb (apologizing) memaafkan; **excuse me!** Maafkan saya!

exercise *noun* latihan; **a maths exercise** latihan ilmu pasti, latihan matematika; **physical exercise** gerak badan.

exercise bicycle *noun* sepeda yang tetap di tempat dan dipakai untuk gerak badan *(definition only)*.

exercise book *noun* buku tulis.

exhausted *adjective* kehabisan tenaga, sangat letih.

exhaust fumes *noun* asap mobil.

exhaust (pipe) *noun* knalpot.

exhibition *noun* ekshibisi, pameran; **the art exhibition** pameran seni rupa.

exist *verb* ada, berada.

exit *noun* jalan keluar, pintu keluar.

expect *verb* **1** *(guests or a baby)* mengharapkan; **we're expecting about five hundred people** kami mengharapkan kedatangan kira-kira lima ratus orang; **2** *(something to happen)* menyangka; **I didn't expect that** saya tidak menyangka itu; **I didn't expect it at all** saya sama sekali tidak menyangka; **3** *(as a supposition)* kira; **I expect you're tired** saya kira Anda letih; **yes, I expect so** ya, saya kira begitu.

expedition *noun* ekspedisi.

expel *verb* mengeluarkan; mengusir; **to be expelled** *(from school)* dikeluarkan.

expenses *plural noun* biaya, ongkos-ongkos, pengeluaran.

expensive *adjective* mahal; **those shoes are too expensive for me** sepatu itu terlalu mahal untuk saya; **the most expensive car** mobil yang paling mahal.

experience *noun* pengalaman.
verb mengalami.

experienced *adjective* berpengalaman.

experiment *noun* eksperimen, percobaan; **to do an experiment** melakukan percobaan.

expert *noun* ahli; **she's a computer expert** dia ahli komputer.

expire *verb* berakhir, daluarsa, habis waktunya.

expiry date *noun* tanggal kadaluarsa.

explain *verb* menerangkan, menjelaskan.

explanation *noun* keterangan, penjelasan.

explode *verb* meledak.

explore *verb* menjelajahi.

explosion *noun* ledakan.

exposure *noun* *(of a film)* pencahayaan; **a 24-exposure film** film yang isinya dua puluh empat.

express *noun* *(a train)* kereta api kilat.
verb **1** mengirimkan dengan ekspres; **2 to express yourself** menyatakan, mengungkapkan.
adjective kilat; **express post** pos kilat.

expression *noun* ucapan, ungkapan.

extend *verb* **1** *(a building)* memperluas; **2** *(a visa, vacation, etc.)* memperpanjang.

extension *noun* **1** *(to a building)* perluasan; **2** *(of a visa etc.)* perpanjangan; **3** *(telephone)* pesawat; **can I have extension 2456 please?** minta pesawat dua empat lima enam; **3** *(electrical)* kawat sambungan.

extension lead *noun* kabel sambungan.

a b c d e f g h i j k l m n o p q r s t u v w x y z

a b c d e f g h i j k l m n o p q r s t u v w x y z

extension number *noun* nomor pesawat.

exterior *noun* bagian luar.

extinguish *verb* memadamkan.

extinguisher *noun* alat pemadam; **fire extinguisher** alat pemadam api, alat pemadam kebakaran.

extra *adjective* ekstra, tambahan; **extra homework** pekerjaan rumah tambahan; **tax and service are extra** ada tambahan untuk pajak dan servis; **you have to pay extra** Anda harus membayar ekstra; **at no extra charge** tidak ada biaya ekstra. *adverb* istimewa; **extra-hot chillies** cabe yang istimewa pedasnya; **extra large** istimewa besarnya.

extraordinary *adjective* luar biasa.

extra-special *adjective* istimewa.

extra time *noun (in football)* waktu tambahan; **to go into extra time** masuk waktu tambahan.

extravagant *adjective (a person)* boros, royal.

extreme *noun* bukan main, ekstrim; **to go to extremes** berbuat keterlaluan. *adjective* ekstrim.

extremely *adverb* luar biasa; **extremely fast** kecepatan yang luar biasa.

eye *noun* **1** mata; **my left eye** mata kiri saya; **Andy is making eyes at Hikmah** Andy sedang bermain mata dengan Hikmah; **2 to keep an eye on** mengawasi, menjaga; **3 to catch someone's eye** menarik perhatian seseorang.

eyebrow *noun* alis.

eyelash *noun* bulu mata.

eyelid *noun* kelopak mata.

eyeliner *noun* pensil mata.

eye make-up *noun* hiasan mata.

eyesight *noun* penglihatan.

F f

fabric *noun (cloth)* bahan kain, barang tenunan.

fabulous *adjective* hebat; seperti dalam dongeng.

face *noun* **1** *(of a person)* muka, paras, rupa, wajah; **2 to pull a face** bikin muka; **3** *(of a clock or watch)* bagian depan.

verb **1** *(a person)* menghadapi; **2** berhadapan dengan; **the school faces the beach** sekolah itu berhadapan dengan pantai; **3** *(to stand the idea of)* tahan **I can't face working there again** saya tak tahan bekerja di situ lagi; **4 to face up to something** menghadapi dengan penuh keberanian.

facilities *plural noun* **1** fasilitas; **the hotel has good facilities** hotel itu fasilitasnya baik.

fact *noun* fakta, kenyataan; **the fact is that...** kenyataannya ialah...; **2 in fact** sebenarnya, sebetulnya; **is that a fact?** apakah itu betul?

factory *noun* pabrik.

fade *verb* **1** *(fabric)* luntur, menjadi pudar; **faded jeans** jeans yang warnanya pudar; **2 the colours have faded** warna-warna itu sudah luntur.

fail *verb* **1** *(a test or an exam)* gagal; **he failed his driving test** dia gagal ujian SIMnya; **2** *(not to do)* **to fail to do** lalai, lupa; **don't fail to call!** jangan lupa menelepon!; **without fail** jangan lupa; **ring her without fail** jangan lupa meneleponnya.

failure *noun* **1** kegagalan; **I feel such a failure** saya merasa saya gagal; **2** *(a breakdown in a machine)* gangguan, kerusakan; **a power failure** gangguan listrik.

faint *adjective* **1** lemah; **to feel faint** merasa lemah; **2** *(slight)* sedikit; **a faint smell of gas** bau gas sedikit; **3** *(low in volume)* kecil; **4 I haven't the faintest idea** saya sama sekali tidak dapat membayangkan, saya tidak tahu sama sekali.
verb jatuh pingsan; **Kent fainted** Kent jatuh pingsan.

fair *noun* pasar malam, pekan raya.
adjective **1** adil; **that's not fair** tak adil; **2** *(hair)* pirang; **he's fair-haired** dia berambut pirang; **3** *(skin)* kuning langsat; **people with fair skin** orang-orang yang berkulit kuning langsat; **4** *(fairly good)* lumayan, sedang; *(a chance, condition or performance)* **her Indonesian is fair** bahasa Indonesianya lumayan; **5** *(weather)* cerah, terang; **it should be fair tomorrow** mudah-mudahan besok cuacanya cerah.

fairground *noun* lapangan pasar malam.

fairly *adverb* *(quite)* agak; **I'm fairly happy here** saya agak senang di sini.

fairy *noun* bidadari, peri.

a b c d e f g h i j k l m n o p q r s t u v w x y z

fairy-tale *noun* cerita dongeng.

faith *noun* **1** *(trust)* kepercayaan; **to have faith in somebody** menaruh kepercayaan kepada seseorang; **2** *(religious belief)* agama, iman, keyakinan.

faithful *adjective* **1** setia; **faithful friend** kawan yang setia; **2** sesuai; **faithful to reality** sesuai dengan kenyataan.

faithfully *adverb* **1** dengan setia; **Ruth followed Naomi faithfully** Ruth mengikuti Naomi dengan setia; **2** dengan tepat; **the event was faithfully described** peristiwa itu digambarkan dengan tepat; **3** (*in correspondence*) **yours faithfully** hormat kami, hormat saya.

fake *noun* palsu, tiruan; **the watch is a fake** jam ini tiruan.
adjective palsu; **fake diamonds** intan palsu; **fake watches** jam-jam palsu; **a fake passport** paspor yang palsu.

fall *noun* jatuh; **to have a fall** jatuh.
verb **1** jatuh; **Ralph fell off the swing** Ralph jatuh dari ayunan itu; **2** *(the temperature)* turun; **it fell to minus fifteen last night** semalam suhu turun sampai minus lima belas derajat.

false *adjective* palsu; **a false alarm** tanda bahaya yang palsu.

false teeth *plural noun* gigi palsu.

fame *noun* kemasyhuran, nama harum, ketenaran.

familiar *adjective* biasa, dikenal, tak asing lagi; **his face is familiar** wajahnya tak asing lagi.

family *noun* keluarga; **Shanty's like one of the family** Shanty seperti anggota keluarga.

famous *adjective* kenamaan, tenar, terkenal, termasyhur, tersohor.

fan *noun* **1** penggemar *(informal)*; **Kevin's a Spice Girls fan** Kevin penggemar Spice Girls; **2** *(for cooling)* kipas (angin).

fanatic *noun* orang yang fanatik.

fancy *noun* kegemaran; keinginan, kesukaan; **to take someone's fancy** menjadi kesukaan seseorang; **the painting took his fancy** lukisan itu menarik hatinya.
adjective (equipment) yang rumit.

verb **1** *(to want)* **do you fancy going to the beach?** apakah Anda ingin ke pantai?; **2 I really fancy him** saya betul-betul naksir padanya; **3 (just) fancy that!** bayangkan itu!; **fancy you being here!** siapa sangka Anda ada di sini!

fancy dress *noun* pakaian aneh yang dipakai di pesta; **a fancy-dress party** pesta dengan aneka macam pakaian yang aneh.

fantastic *adjective* fantastis, luar biasa, menakjubkan, sangat bagus *(informal)*; **really? that's fantastic!** benar? fantastis!; **a fantastic holiday** liburan yang luar biasa.

far *adjective, adverb* **1** jauh; **how far is it?** berapa jauhnya?; **we got a lift as far as Newcastle** kami diantar sampai Newcastle; **2 by far** paling; **the oldest by far** yang paling tua; **3** *(much)* jauh lebih; **far better** jauh lebih baik; **far faster** jauh lebih cepat; **4 so far** hingga sekarang, sampai kini; **so far everything's going well** hingga sekarang semuanya berjalan baik; **as far as I know** sepanjang pengetahuan saya, setahu saya.

fare *noun* biaya perjalanan, ongkos perjalanan, harga karcis; **half fare** separoh harga (karcis); **full fare** harga karcis penuh; **the return fare** harga karcis pulang-pergi.

Far East *noun* Timur Jauh.

farm *noun* kebun, tanah pertanian.

farmer *noun* orang tani, petani.

farmhouse *noun* rumah petani.

farming *noun* pertanian.

fascinating *adjective* mempesona, sangat menarik.

fashion *noun* mode, populer; **in fashion** sedang mode, sedang populer; **out of fashion** ketinggalan zaman.

fashionable *adjective* modern, sesuai dengan mode terakhir.

fashion model *noun* peragawati.

fashion show *noun* pameran mode.

fast¹ *noun* puasa; **to break the fast** buka puasa. *verb* berpuasa.

fast² *adjective* cepat; **a fast car** mobil cepat; **you're ten minutes fast** Anda sepuluh menit terlalu cepat.

a b c d e f g h i j k l m n o p q r s t u v w x y z

adverb **1** dengan cepat; **he runs fast** dia berlari dengan cepat; **2 to be fast asleep** tidur nyenyak.

fast forward *noun* memutar cepat.

fat *noun* lemak.
adjective gemuk; **a fat man** orang (lelaki yang) gemuk; **to get fat** menjadi gemuk.

fatal *adjective* fatal, yang membawa maut, yang menyebabkan kematian.

father *noun* ayah, bapak; **my father's car** mobil ayah saya.

Father Christmas *noun* Sinterklas.

father-in-law *noun* ayah mertua, mertua laki-laki.

fault *noun* **1** *(when you are responsible)* kesalahan, salah; **it's not our fault** bukan salah kita; **2** *(defect)* kekurangan; **there's a fault in this sweater** sweater ini cacat; **3** *(in tennis)* fol(t).

favour *noun* **1** *(a kindness)* bantuan, pertolongan; **to do somebody a favour** membantu seseorang; **can you do me a favour?** dapatkah Anda menolong saya?; **to ask a favour of somebody** meminta bantuan seseorang; **2 to be in favour of** setuju untuk; **I'm in favour of hiring a car** saya setuju kalau kita meyewa mobil.

favourite *adjective* favorit, kesayangan; **my favourite group** grup favorit saya.

fear *noun* ketakutan, rasa takut.
verb kuatir akan, takut akan; **he fears snakes** dia takut akan ular; **to fear the worst** kuatir akan kejadian yang terburuk.

feather *noun* bulu.

feature *noun* **1** *(of your face)* roman muka; **to have delicate features** beroman muka halus; **2** *(of a car or machine)* keistimewaan.

February *noun* Februari.

fed up *adjective* **I'm fed up** bosan, muak; *(informal)*; **I'm fed up with working here** saya sudah muak bekerja di sini.

feed *verb* memberi makan; **the dog's been fed already** anjing itu sudah diberi makan.

feel *verb* **1** merasa; **she doesn't feel well** dia merasa tidak enak badan; **you won't feel a thing** Anda tidak akan merasa apa-apa; **to feel afraid** merasa takut; **to feel cold** merasa dingin; **to feel thirsty** merasa haus; **2 to feel like** ingin; **I feel like going to**

the beach saya ingin ke pantai; **3 to feel that** kira, pikir; **I feel that** saya pikir (bahwa); **4** *(touch)* meraba.

feeling *noun* **1** *(in your mind or body)* perasaan; **a feeling of embarrassment** perasaan malu; **to show your feelings** memperlihatkan perasaan; **a dizzy feeling** perasaan pusing; **2** *(an impression or intuition)* merasa; **I have the feeling Stephen doesn't like me** saya merasa bahwa Stephen tidak suka kepada saya.

felt-tip *noun* *(pen)* spidol.

female *noun* **1** *(person)* perempuan, wanita; **2** *(animal)* betina.

feminine *adjective* berhubungan dengan perempuan, feminin.

feminist *noun* feminis, pejuang hak-hak wanita. *adjective* feminis.

fence *noun* pagar.

fern *noun* pakis.

ferry *noun* feri, perahu tambang, kapal tambang.

fertilizer *noun* pupuk, rabuk.

festival *noun* *(for films, art or music)* festival, perayaan, pesta.

fetch *verb* **1** mengambil (kan); **Gary's fetching the Esky™** Gary sedang mengambil Esky™; **2** menjemput; **Sri usually fetches the children** biasanya Sri menjemput anak-anak.

fever *noun* demam, panas.

few *adjective, pronoun* **1** sedikit, tidak banyak; **few people think that...** tidak banyak orang yang berpikir bahwa...; **2 a few** beberapa; **a few days later** beberapa hari kemudian; **in a few minutes** beberapa menit lagi; **3 quite a few** banyak juga, cukup banyak; **there were quite a few mistakes** ada cukup banyak kesalahan.

fewer *adjective* lebih sedikit; **there'll be fewer tourists next year** tahun depan wisatawan akan menjadi lebih sedikit.

fiction *noun* fiksi.

field *noun* **1** *(with grass or crops)* ladang, padang; **a field of wheat** ladang gandum; **a field of rice** sawah; **2** *(for sport)* lapangan; **3** *(the kind of work you do)* bidang.

fierce *adjective* **1** galak; **a fierce dog** anjing galak; **2** sengit; **a fierce battle** pertempuran sengit.

fifteen *number* lima belas; **Barry's fifteen** Barry berumur lima belas tahun.

a b c d e f g h i j k l m n o p q r s t u v w x y z

fifth *number* lima, yang kelima; **the fifth of December** tanggal lima Desember; **on the fifth floor** pada lantai yang kelima, pada lantai lima.

fifty *number* lima puluh.

fight *noun* **1** *(a scuffle)* perkelahian, pertengkaran; **2** *(in boxing)* pertandingan tinju; **3** *(against illness)* pemberantasan.
verb **1** *(to have a fight)* berkelahi; **they were fighting** mereka berkelahi; **2** *(to quarrel)* bertengkar; **they're always fighting** mereka selalu bertengkar; **3** *(in war)* bertempur; **4** *(eradicate)* memberantas *(poverty or disease)*.

fighting *noun* **1** *(in the streets or a pub, for example)* perkelahian; **2** *(in war)* pertempuran.

figure *noun* **1** *(number)* angka, bilangan; **a five-figure number** bilangan berangka lima; **2** *(body shape)* bentuk badan; **bad for your figure** tidak baik untuk bentuk badan; **3** *(person)* tokoh; **a familiar figure** tokoh terkenal; **4** *(diagram)* gambar.

file *noun* **1** *(for records of a person or case)* arsip, catatan; **2** *(cardboard folder)* map; **3** *(on a computer)* file, simpanan; **4** kikir; **a nail file** kikir kuku.
verb **1** *(documents)* menyimpan; **2** mengikir; **to file your nails** mengikir kuku.

fill *verb* **1** mengisi; **I filled his glass** saya mengisi gelasnya; **2** memenuhi; **the crowd filled the stadium** orang banyak itu memenuhi stadion itu.
- **to fill in, to fill out** mengisi.
- **to fill in for (someone)** mengganti (orang).

film *noun* film (*current usage*), filem, pilem (*old spellings*).

film star *noun* bintang film.

filter *noun* filter, saringan.

filthy *adjective* kotor.

fin *noun* sirip.

final *noun* final, yang terakhir.
adjective terakhir; **the final instalment** cicilan yang terakhir.

finally *adverb* akhirnya.

find *verb* menemukan; **did you find your ring?** apakah Anda menemukan cincin Anda?
- **to find out 1** *(to enquire)* mencaritahu, mencari keterangan; **I don't know, but I'll find out** saya tidak tahu, tetapi akan mencari keterangan; **2 to find something out** *(the facts or*

an answer) mengetahui; **I've found out where he went** saya sudah mengetahui ke mana dia pergi.

fine noun *(for infringement)* denda.
adjective 1 *(in good health)* baik, sehat; **'how are you?' – 'fine thanks'** 'apa kabar?' – 'baik-baik saja'; **2** *(very good)* bagus, baik, pintar; **she's a fine singer** dia penyanyi yang baik, dia pintar menyanyi; **3** *(convenient)* baiklah; **'ten o'clock?' – 'yes, that's fine'** 'jam sepuluh?' – 'ya, baiklah'; **4** *(sunny)*, cuaca cerah; **if it's fine** kalau cuaca cerah; **5** *(not coarse or thick)* halus; **fine silk** sutera halus.

finely adverb *(chopped or grated)* halus.

finger noun jari.

fingernail noun kuku.

finish noun **1** *(end)* akhir, tamat; **2** *(in a race)* akhir.
verb **1** selesai; **wait, I haven't finished** tunggulah, saya belum selesai; **2** *(to finish off)* menyelesaikan *(work on a project)*; **have you finished the essay?** apakah Anda sudah menyelesaikan karangan itu?; **3 is the beer finished?** apakah bir sudah habis?; **4 to finish school** menamatkan sekolah; **Ali finished school last year and is already working** Ali menamatkan sekolah tahun lalu dan sekarang sudah bekerja; **when does school finish?** kapan sekolah bubar? kapan sekolah selesai?
- **to finish with** menyelesaikan; **have you finished with the computer?** apakah Anda sudah selesai dengan komputer ini?

Finland noun Finlandia.

Finn noun *(the people)* orang Finlandia.

Finnish noun *(the language)* bahasa Finlandia.
adjective Finlandia.

fir tree noun pohon cemara.

fire noun **1** *(in a grate)* api; **to light a fire** menyalakan api; **sitting by the fire** duduk di dekat api; **2 to catch fire** menyala, terbakar; **3** *(accidental)* **to be on fire** kebakaran; **a fire in a bank** kebakaran di bank; **4 to set on fire** membakar.
verb **1** *(to shoot)* menembak; **the terrorists were firing** gerombolan teroris sedang menembak; **to fire at somebody** menembak seseorang; **to fire a gun** menembakkan pistol; **2** *(to sack)* memberhentikan, memecat.

a b c d e f g h i j k l m n o p q r s t u v w x y z

fire alarm *noun* tanda bahaya kebakaran.

fire brigade *noun* pasukan pemadam kebakaran.

fire engine *noun* mobil pemadam kebakaran.

fire escape *noun* tangga kebakaran.

fire extinguisher *noun* alat pemadam api.

fire fighter *noun* branwir, pemadam api, pemadam kebakaran.

firefly *noun* kunang-kunang.

fireplace *noun* perapian, tungku.

fire station *noun* pos barisan pemadam kebakaran.

firework *noun* kembang api, mercon; **what a great firework display!** pertontonan kembang api yang hebat!

firm *noun* firma, perusahaan. *adjective* **1** tetap, **a firm price** harga tetap; **2** tegas; **a firm attitude** sikap yang tegas; **3 this fence is not very firm** pagar ini kurang kuat.

first *adjective, adverb* **1** (yang) pertama; **Sarah's the first** Sarah (adalah) yang pertama; **for the first time** untuk pertama kali; **2** *(to begin with)* pertama; **first, I'm going to have a coffee** pertama, saya mau minum kopi; **3 at first** mula-mula; **at first he was shy** mula-mula dia agak malu; **4** satu; **the first of September** tanggal satu September; **I came first in the hundred metres** saya pemenang nomor satu dalam perlombaan lari seratus meter.

first-aid *noun* pertolongan pertama pada kecelakaan (P3K).

first-class *adjective* **1** kelas satu; **a first-class ticket** tiket kelas satu.

first floor *noun* lantai pertama, lantai satu; **on the first floor** di lantai satu.

firstly *adverb* pertama-tama.

first name *noun* nama kecil.

fish *noun* ikan; **do you eat fish?** apakah Anda suka makan ikan?

fish and chips *noun* ikan goreng dengan kentang goreng.

fisherman *noun* nelayan, penangkap ikan.

fishing *noun* memancing, pemancingan; **I hate fishing** saya tidak suka memancing; **to go fishing** pergi memancing.

fishing rod *noun* tangkai pancing.

fishing tackle *noun* alat pancingan, alat penangkap ikan.

fist *noun* tinju.

fit *noun* **1** *(of rage)* **to have a fit** marah sekali, naik pitam; **your dad'll have a fit when he sees that ring in your nose!** ayah Anda akan marah sekali bila melihat cincin di hidung Anda!; **2 an epileptic fit** serangan penyakit ayan.
adjective *(healthy)* bugar; **I feel really fit** saya merasa betul-betul bugar; **to keep fit** memelihara kebugaran.
verb **1** *(to be the right size for)* pas; **these shoes don't fit me** sepatu ini tidak pas; **2** *(be able to put into)* masuk; **will these cases all fit in the boot?** apakah semua tas ini dapat masuk ke dalam bagasi?; **the key doesn't fit the lock** kunci ini tidak masuk ke lubang kunci; **3** *(install)* memasang; **they've fitted an alarm** mereka sudah memasang alat tanda bahaya.

fitting room *noun* ruang pas.

five *number* lima.

fix *verb* **1** *(repair)* membetulkan, memperbaiki; **Mum's fixed the computer** Ibu sudah memperbaiki komputer itu; **2** *(to decide on)* menentukan; **to fix a date** menentukan tanggal; **at a fixed price** harga mati, harga pas; **3** *(a meal)* menyediakan; **can you fix dinner?** tolong sediakan makan malam.

fizzy *adjective* yang mengandung gas; **fizzy drinks** minuman yang mengandung gas.

flag *noun* bendera.

flame *noun* lidah api.

flamingo *noun* burung flaminggo.

flap *verb* mengepak-ngepak; **birds flap their wings** burung mengepak-ngepakkan sayapnya.

flash *noun* **1** cahaya; **a flash of lightning** cahaya kilat; **2 to do in a flash** mengerjakan secepat kilat; **3** *(on a camera)* blits.
verb **1** *(a light)* mengedipkan; **to flash your headlights** mengedipkan lampu besar (mobil); **2 to flash by or past** meluncur dengan cepat.

flashback *noun* kilas balik.

flashlight *noun* lampu senter.

flat *noun* flat; **a basement flat** flat di basemen.
adjective **1** datar; **a flat landscape** tanah datar; **2** kempes; **a flat tyre** ban

a b c d e f g h i j k l m n o p q r s t u v w x y z

kempes; **3** rata; **flat shoes** sepatu bertumit rata, sepatu tidak bertumit.

flatmate *noun* teman satu flat, teman serumah.

flatter *verb* bermulut manis, memuji, merayu.

flattering *adjective* memuji-muji, merayu-rayu.

flavour *noun (taste)* aroma, rasa, selera; **this sauce has no flavour** saus ini tiada rasa. *verb* **1** membumbui; **2 chocolate-flavoured** rasa coklat.

flea *noun* kutu (anjing).

flea market *noun* pasar loak.

flesh *noun* daging.

flex *noun* kawat, tali; **electric flex** kawat listrik.

flexible *adjective* fleksibel, mudah dibengkokkan.

flight *noun* **1** penerbangan; **a charter flight** penerbangan carteran; **2 a flight of stairs** tingkat tangga.

fling *verb* melemparkan.

flipper *noun* sirip.

flirt *verb* bercumbu-cumbuan, main cinta, main suka-sukaan.

float *verb* terapung, mengapung.

flood *noun* **1** banjir; **the floods during the wet season** banjir waktu musim hujan; **2** *(of letters, complaints, etc.)* kebanjiran. *verb* **1** meluap, membanjir; **2** *(deliberately)* mengairi; **to flood the rice fields** mengairi sawah.

floodlight *noun* lampu sorot.

floor *noun* **1** lantai; **2** *(a storey)* lantai, tingkat; **on the fifth floor** di tingkat kelima.

floppy disk *noun* disket.

florist *noun* ahli bunga, pedagang bunga, pemiara bunga.

flour *noun* tepung.

flow *verb* mengalir.

flower *noun* bunga, kembang; **a bunch of flowers** seikat bunga; **a hibiscus flower** kembang sepatu.

flu *noun* flu, influenza; **to have flu** sakit flu.

fluent *adjective* lancar; **she speaks fluent Indonesian** dia lancar berbahasa Indonesia.

fluently *adverb* dengan lancar.

flush *verb* **1** *(to go red)* menjadi merah; **2** menyiram; **to flush the lavatory** menyiram kakus.

flute *noun* suling.

fly *noun* lalat. *verb* **1** terbang; **most birds can fly** sebagian besar burung dapat terbang; **we**

flew to Adelaide kami terbang ke Adelaide; **2** *(a kite)* main layang-layang; **3** *(to pass quickly)* berlalu dengan cepat *(time)*.

fly spray *noun* obat pembasmi lalat.

foam *noun* busa; **a foam mattress** kasur dari karet busa.

focus *noun* fokus; **to be in focus** jelas, terang; **to be out of focus** kabur, tidak jelas. *verb (a camera)* menyetel.

fog *noun* halimun, kabut.

foggy *adjective* berkabut; **it's foggy out** di luar berkabut.

foil *noun (kitchen foil)* kertas timah.

fold *noun* lipatan. *verb* **1** melipat; **to fold a letter** melipat surat; **2 to fold your arms** melipat tangan.

folder *noun* berkas, map.

folding *adjective* yang dapat dilipat; **a folding table** meja yang dapat dilipat.

follow *verb* **1** mengikuti, menyusul; **follow me!** ikutilah saya!; **2 do you follow me?** apakah Anda mengerti pembicaraan saya?

following *adjective* yang berikutnya, selanjutnya; **the following day** hari berikutnya.

fond *adjective* sayang; **we're very fond of the dog** kami sayang pada anjing itu.

food *noun* **1** makanan; **2** masakan; **I like Chinese food** saya suka masakan Tionghoa.

fool *noun* orang goblok, orang tolol.

foot *noun* **1** kaki; **Carmen came on foot** Carmen datang berjalan kaki; **2** *(the bottom)* bawah, kaki; **at the foot of the hill** di kaki bukit.

football *noun* **1** *(the game)* sepak bola *(soccer)*; futbal *(for example, Aussie rules)* **to play football** bermain futbal, bermain sepak bola; **2** *(the ball)* bola.

footballer *noun* pemain futbal, pemain sepak bola.

footpath *noun* jalan setapak (untuk berjalan kaki), trotoar.

footprint *noun* jejak kaki, tapak kaki.

footstep *noun* langkah (kaki).

for *preposition* **1** untuk; **a present for Bambang** hadiah untuk Bambang; **2** *(time expressions)* selama; **I studied Javanese for three years** saya belajar bahasa Jawa selama tiga tahun; **3** atas; **thank you for helping** terima

a b c d e f g h i j k l m n o p q r s t u v w x y z

kasih atas pertolongan Anda; **4** supaya; **please arrange for him to come** tolong urus supaya dia datang.

forbid *verb* melarang; **he forbade me to go out** dia melarang saya keluar.

forbidden *adjective* dilarang; **forbidden to smoke** dilarang merokok.

force *noun* **1** kekuatan; **wind force** kekuatan angin; **2** tenaga; **labour force** tenaga kerja; **3** gaya; **force of gravity** gaya berat; **4** kekerasan, paksaan; **by force** dengan kekerasan, dengan paksa.
verb **to force somebody to do** memaksa.

forecast *noun* prakiraan, ramalan.

forefinger *noun* (jari) telunjuk.

foreground *noun* bagian (ter)depan; **in the foreground** di bagian depan.

forehead *noun* dahi, jidat.

foreign *adjective* asing; **in a foreign country** di negara asing.

foreigner *noun* orang asing.

foresee *verb* meramalkan.

forest *noun* hutan.

forever *adverb* **1** selamalamanya; **you can't stay here forever** Anda tidak bisa tinggal di sini selamalamanya; **2** *(non-stop)* selalu; **they're forever asking questions** mereka selalu bertanya.

forget *verb* lupa; **I always forget his name** saya selalu lupa namanya.

forgive *verb* mengampuni, memaafkan; **to forgive somebody** memaafkan seseorang.

fork *noun* garpu.

form *noun* **1** formulir; **to fill in a form** mengisi formulir; **2** *(shape or kind)* bentuk; **in the form of** berbentuk; **3** kondisi; **to be on form** dalam kondisi; **4** *(in school)* kelas.

formal *adjective* formal, resmi *(invitation, event, complaint, etc.)*.

format *noun* bentuk, format, pola.

former *adjective* bekas, mantan, yang terlebih dahulu; **a former pupil** bekas murid; **former President Bush** mantan Presiden Bush.

fortnight *noun* dua minggu.

fortunately *adverb* untung.

forty *number* empat puluh.

forward *noun* *(in sport)* pemain depan.
adverb depan, muka; **to move forward** maju ke depan.

foster child *noun* anak angkat.

foul *noun (in sport)* main curang.
adjective buruk sekali; **the weather's foul** cuaca buruk sekali.

fountain *noun* air mancur.

fountain pen *noun* pulpen, vulpen.

four *number* empat; **it's four o'clock** sekarang jam empat; **on all fours** merangkak.

fourteen *number* empat belas; **Lucie's fourteen** Lucie berumur empat belas tahun.

fourth *number* keempat; **on the fourth floor** di tingkat keempat; **the fourth of July** pada tanggal empat Juli.

fox *noun* rubah.

fragile *adjective* **1** *(for things)* gampang pecah, mudah pecah; **2** *(for people)* lemah.

frame *noun* bingkai.

France *noun* Perancis.

frantic *adjective* **1** dalam keadaan takut, dalam keadaan bingung; **they were frantic with worry** mereka tadi dalam keadaan takut; **2** gila; **Lana's voice drives me frantic** suara Lana membuat saya gila.

freckle *noun* bintik-bintik (pada kulit).

free *adjective* **1** *(when you don't pay)* gratis; **the meal is free** makanan itu gratis; **a free ticket** karcis gratis; **2** *(not occupied)* kosong, punya waktu, prei (*colloquial*); **is this seat free?** apakah tempat duduk ini kosong? **are you free tomorrow?** apakah Anda punya waktu besok? apakah Anda prei besok?; **3** tidak mengandung; **sugar-free** bebas gula, tidak mengandung gula; **4** bebas, merdeka; **a free country** negara merdeka.
verb membebaskan.

freedom *noun* kebebasan, kemerdekaan.

free gift *noun* hadiah gratis.

freeze *verb* **1** membekukan; **frozen vegetables** sayuran yang dibekukan; **2 it's freezing outside** di luar sangat dingin.

freezer *noun* lemari es, lemari pendingin.

freezing *noun* beku; **two degrees below freezing** dua derajat di bawah titik beku.
adjective **I'm freezing** *(informal)* saya merasa sangat dingin; **it's freezing out** di luar dingin sekali.

French *noun* **1** *(the language)* bahasa Perancis; **2** *(the people)* **the French** orang Perancis.

a b c d e f g h i j k l m n o p q r s t u v w x y z

a b c d e f g h i j k l m n o p q r s t u v w x y z

adjective Perancis; **Jean-Paul is French** Jean-Paul adalah orang Perancis.

French bean *noun* buncis.

French dressing *noun* semacam bumbu selada.

French fries *noun* cips, kentang goreng yang diiris panjang-panjang.

frequent *adjective* berkali-kali, berulang-ulang, sering.

fresh *adjective* **1** baru; **fresh eggs** telur baru; **2** segar; **I need some fresh air** saya perlu udara segar.

Friday *noun* (hari) Jumat; **next Friday** hari Jumat depan; **last Friday** hari Jumat yang lalu; **Friday evening** Jumat malam; **on Fridays** pada setiap hari Jumat; **Good Friday** Jumat Suci.

fridge *noun (informal)* kulkas *(colloquial)*, lemari es.

friend *noun* kawan, sahabat, teman; **a friend of mine** teman saya; **close friends** kawan akrab; **to be friends** bersahabat; **to make friends** berteman *(in a general way)*.

friendly *noun* ramah tamah.

friendship *noun* persahabatan.

fries *noun* SEE **French fries.**

fright *noun* rasa takut; **get a fright** takut; **you gave me a fright** Anda membuat saya takut.

frighten *verb* menakuti, menakut-nakuti; **don't frighten the children** jangan menakut-nakuti anak-anak itu.

frightened *adjective* takut akan; **Luke's frightened of spiders** Luke takut akan laba-laba.

frightening *adjective* menakutkan; **it was a frightening experience** pengalaman itu menakutkan.

fringe *noun* pinggir.

frog *noun* katak, kodok.

from *preposition* **1** dari; **a message from Jordan** kabar dari Jordan; **five years from now** lima tahun dari sekarang; **2** mulai; **from now on** mulai sekarang; **3** sejak; **from the time I was born** sejak saya lahir.

front *noun* **1** *(of a building)* muka; **the address is on the front** alamatnya ada di bagian muka; **2** depan; **standing in the front** berdiri di (bagian) depan; **in front of** di depan, di muka; **in front of the TV** di muka

televisi; **in front of me** di depan saya.
adjective depan, muka; **in the front row** di jajaran depan; **the front page** halaman muka, halaman depan; **front door** pintu depan.

frontier *noun* batas, perbatasan, tapal batas.

frost *noun* embun beku.

frosty *adjective* sangat dingin; **it's frosty this morning** cuaca sangat dingin pagi ini.

frown *verb* **1** mengerutkan dahi; **he frowns a lot** dia sering mengerutkan dahi; **2** bermuka masam.

frozen *adjective (in a freezer)* beku, yang dibekukan; **a frozen pizza** pizza yang dibekukan.

fruit *noun* buah (-buahan); **we bought fruit and vegetables** kami membeli buah-buahan dan sayur-mayur; **fruit juice** air buah, sari buah.

fruit salad *noun* campuran buah-buahan, salad buah-buahan.

frustrated *adjective* frustrasi.

fry *verb* menggoreng; **fried fish** ikan goreng; **a fried egg** telor mata sapi (goreng).

frying pan *noun* kuali, penggorengan, wajan.

fuel *noun* bahan bakar.

full *adjective* **1** penuh; **this bottle is full** botol ini penuh; **at full speed** kecepatan maksimum; **2** lengkap; **to write out in full** menulis secara lengkap; **3** kenyang; **I'm full** saya sudah kenyang; **4 full moon** bulan purnama; **at full volume** suara keras.

full stop *noun* **1** *(cease moving)* berhenti samasekali; **2** *(in writing)* tanda titik.

full-time *adjective* purna waktu; **a full-time job** pekerjaan purna waktu.

fully *adverb* secara lengkap, sepenuhnya.

fun *noun* **1** kegembiraan, kesenangan; **to have fun** bergembira, bersenang-senang; **we had fun building sandcastles** kami bersenang-senang membangun istana-istana dari pasir; **I do it for fun** saya melakukannya hanya untuk bersenang-senang, saya melakukannya hanya untuk iseng-iseng; **motor racing is fun** balapan mobil menyenangkan; **2 have fun!** bersenanglah!, semoga senang!; **to make fun of somebody** menertawakan seseorang.

funds *plural noun* dana.

funeral *noun* pemakaman, penguburan.

funfair *noun* pekan raya.

funny *adjective* **1** *(when you laugh)* lucu; **you are funny** Anda lucu; **a funny story** cerita lucu; **2** *(strange)* aneh; **that's funny, I'm sure I packed it** aneh, saya yakin saya mengepaknya; **a funny noise** bunyi yang aneh.

fur *noun* bulu.

furious *adjective* sangat marah; **she's furious with Marny** dia sangat marah pada Marny.

furniture *noun* mebel, perabot rumah; **to buy some furniture** membeli mebel; **a piece of furniture** sebuah mebel.

further *adverb* lebih jauh; **further than the post office** lebih jauh dari kantor pos; **five kilometres further** lima kilometer lebih jauh; **further forward** lebih (jauh) ke depan; **further back in time** lebih jauh ke masa yang lampau.

fuse *noun* sekering.

fuss *noun* cerewet, ribut-ribut; **to make a fuss** ribut-ribut tentang, repot tentang; **to make a fuss about the bill** ribut-ribut tentang bonnya.

fussy *adjective* **to be fussy about something** cerewet, rewel *(food, for example)*.

future *noun* **1** masa depan; **in the future** pada masa depan; **in future** lain kali, seterusnya; **2** *(in grammar)* **a verb in the future tense** kata kerja masa mendatang.

G g

gadget *noun* alat, perkakas.

gain¹ *noun* keuntungan, laba.

gain² *verb* **1** memperoleh; **to gain strength** memperoleh kekuatan; **2** menambah; **to gain speed** menambah kecepatan; **I'm gaining weight** berat badan saya bertambah, saya menjadi lebih gemuk.

gale *noun* angin kencang, angin ribut, taufan.

gallery *noun* balai, galeri; **art gallery** balai kesenian, galeri seni.

gamble *verb* **1** berjudi; **2** mengadu untung; **to gamble on the Stock Exchange** mengadu untung di Bursa.

game *noun* **1** permainan; **children's games** permainan anak-anak; **to play a game of**

tennis main tenis; **2** pertandingan; **a game of football** pertandingan sepak bola; **Olympic Games** Olimpiade.

gang *noun* **1** gerombolan; **gang warfare** perkelahian antar-gerombolan; **2** teman-teman; **all the gang were there** teman-teman semua ada di situ.

gangster *noun* bandit, penjahat.

gap *noun* **1** *(between boards)* celah; **2** *(hole, space)* jurang pemisah; **to reduce the gap** memperkecil jurang pemisah; **3** kekosongan; **her departure leaves a gap** kepergiannya menyebabkan kekosongan.

garage *noun* **1** *(at home)* garasi; **2** *(for repairs)* bengkel.

garden *noun* kebun, taman; **botanical garden** kebun raya.

gardener *noun* tukang kebun.

gardening *noun* berkebun.

garlic *noun* bawang putih.

garment *noun* pakaian.

gas *noun* **1** gas; **natural gas** gas alam; **2** *(petrol)* bensin.

gas cooker *noun* kompor gas.

gate *noun* **1** pintu gerbang; **there's always a guard at the gate** selalu ada penjaga di pintu gerbang; **2** pintu masuk; **gate four** pintu masuk nomor empat.

gather *verb* **1** *(people)* kumpul; **a crowd gathered** banyak orang berkumpul; **2** *(fruit, vegetables, flowers, etc.)* mengumpulkan; **they gathered up their belongings** mereka mengumpulkan barang-barangnya; **3 as far as I can gather** setahu saya.

gay *adjective* **1** homoseksual; **2** gembira, riang.

gaze *verb* memandang, menatap; **to gaze at something** memandang sesuatu, menatap sesuatu.

gear *noun* **1** *(in a car)* persneling, (roda) gigi; **to change gear** menukar persneling, (meng)ganti gigi; **to shift into third gear** masuk ke persneling tiga; **2** *(equipment, things)* alat, perlengkapan; **camping gear** perlengkapan kemah.

gear lever *noun* tangkai persneling.

gel *noun* jel.

Gemini *noun* Gemini.

gender *noun* gender, jenis kelamin.

general *noun* *(military rank)* jend(e)ral; *adjective* umum; **in general** pada umumnya.

a b c d e f g h i j k l m n o p q r s t u v w x y z

general election *noun* pemilihan umum.

general knowledge *noun* pengetahuan umum.

generally *adverb* biasanya, umumnya.

generation *noun* **1** angkatan, generasi; **the generation gap** jurang perbedaan antara generasi; **the young generation** angkatan muda; **2** keturunan; **from generation to generation** turun-temurun.

generator *noun* dinamo, generator, pembangkit listrik.

generous *adjective* **1** *(of people)* murah hati; **2** banyak sekali; **a generous serving of chicken** sajian ayam yang banyak sekali.

genetics *noun* (ilmu) genetika, ilmu keturunan.

Geneva *noun* Jeneva.

genius *noun* cerdas, jenius; **she's an absolute genius** dia cerdas sekali.

gentle *adjective* **1** lemah-lembut; **a gentle touch** sentuhan yang lemah-lembut; **2** jinak; **a gentle horse** kuda jinak.

gentleman *noun* **1** pria yang sopan santun; **2** bapak, tuan; **ladies and gentlemen!** Bapak-bapak dan Ibu-ibu yang terhormat!

gently *adverb* **1** dengan hati-hati; **Alice carried the puppy gently** Alice menggendong anak anjing dengan hati-hati; **2** dengan lemah-lembut; **to speak gently** berbicara dengan lemah-lembut.

gents *noun* kamar kecil untuk pria, kloset, WC, *(marked on the door)* pria.

genuine *adjective* **1** *(real)* asli, murni, sejati, tulen; **a genuine diamond** berlian asli; **2** *(sincere, without expecting anything in return)* sungguh-sungguh, ikhlas; **they gave genuine assistance** mereka memberikan bantuan yang sungguh-sungguh.

geography *noun* geografi, ilmu bumi.

germ *noun* kuman.

German *noun* **1** *(person)* seorang Jerman; **2** *(language)* bahasa Jerman.
adjective Jerman.

Germany *noun* negeri Jerman; **Federal Republic of Germany** Republik Federal Jerman.

get *verb* **1** *(obtain, receive)* mendapat, memperoleh, menerima; **I got your letter yesterday** saya menerima surat Anda kemarin; **she got a gold bracelet for her birthday** Dia mendapat gelang mas untuk ulang tahunnya; **I got a-hundred-and-twenty dollars for my bike** saya memperoleh seratus dua puluh dolar untuk sepeda saya; **2** *(fetch)* mengambil; **I'll get my book first** saya akan mengambil buku saya dulu; **could you get me that pen?** tolong ambilkan saya pena itu; **3 to have got to do** harus; **I've got to phone the bank** saya harus menelepon bank; **4 to get to somewhere** sampai, tiba; **we'll get to Bandung at 11 o'clock** kita akan tiba di Bandung jam sebelas; **we'll get there soon** tidak lama lagi kita sampai di sana; **5** *(become)* mulai; **I'm getting tired** saya mulai lelah; **6 to get something done** menyelesaikan; **I got my homework done** saya menyelesaikan pekerjaan rumah; **7 I got a haircut yesterday** saya gunting rambut kemarin; **8** *(have)* **he's got brown eyes** matanya berwarna coklat.

- **to get back** kembali; **they got back from Garut yesterday** mereka kembali dari Garut kemarin.
- **to get something back** mendapat kembali; **I got my essay back this morning** tadi pagi saya mendapat kembali esei saya.
- **to get into 1** *(a vehicle)* naik; **he got into the car** dia naik ke mobil; **2** *(an institution)* masuk; **she got into medicine** dia masuk fakultas kedokteran, dia diterima di fakultas kedokteran.
- **to get off** turun; **they got off the train** mereka turun dari kereta api.
- **to get on** *(in general)*; **how's Desi getting on?** bagaimana dengan Desi?
- **to get on** naik; **where did Haris get on the train?** di mana Haris naik kereta api?
- **to get on with something** maju; **how's Desi getting on with her study?** bagaimana kemajuan Desi dalam pelajarannya?
- **to get on with somebody** cocok, dapat bergaul; **they don't seem to be getting on well** kelihatannya mereka tidak dapat bergaul dengan baik; **I don't get on with her at all** saya sama sekali tidak cocok dengan dia.

a b c d e f g h i j k l m n o p q r s t u v w x y z

a b c d e f g h i j k l m n o p q r s t u v w x y z

- **to get out of something** turun; **Budi got out of the taxi at the railway station** Budi turun dari taksi di setasiun kereta api.
- **to get something out** mengeluarkan; **Hetty got her guitar out** Hetty mengeluarkan gitarnya.
- **to get together** berkumpul; **let's get together again tomorrow** ayo kita berkumpul lagi besok.
- **to get up** bangun; **Ros usually gets up at 6 o'clock** biasanya Ros bangun jam enam.

ghost *noun* hantu.

giant *noun* raksasa; **a giant of a man** orang laki-laki yang besar sekali.
adjective besar sekali; **a giant truck** truk yang besar sekali.

gift *noun* **1** hadiah, kado, pemberian; **2 to have a gift for something** berbakat; **Feri has a real gift for languages** Feri betul-betul berbakat dalam bahasa.

gifted *adjective* berbakat.

gigantic *adjective* dahsyat, raksasa, sangat besar.

ginger *noun* jahe.

giraffe *noun* jerapah.

girl *noun* **1** anak perempuan; **2** gadis; **3** pemudi, puteri; **girls' high school** sekolah menengah puteri.

girlfriend *noun* **1** pacar; **Budi's gone to a film with his girlfriend** Budi pergi menonton film bersama pacarnya; **2** teman; **Susi's gone to the beach with her girlfriends** Susi pergi ke pantai dengan teman-temannya.

give *verb* memberi; **what did he give you for your birthday?** dia memberi apa untuk hari ulang tahun Anda?; **to give something to somebody** memberikan; **she gave the ticket to me** dia memberikan karcis kepada saya; **to give a test** menguji.

- **to give away**
  1 menyumbang; **she gave a donation to the Red Cross** dia menyumbang uang kepada Palang Merah; **2** memberikan; **she's given away all her books** dia memberikan (kepada orang lain) semua bukunya.
- **to give something back** mengembalikan; **Tuti's already given the book back** Tuti sudah mengembalikan buku itu.
- **to give in** mengalah; **in the end she had to give in** akhirnya dia terpaksa

mengalah; **they gave in to family pressures** mereka mengalah kepada tekanan-tekanan keluarganya.

- **to give up** menyerah(kan); **I give up** saya menyerah; **he gave himself up to the police** ia menyerahkan diri kepada polisi.
- **to give up doing** berhenti; **he gave up smoking** ia berhenti merokok.

glad *adjective* senang; **I'm glad you're better** saya senang Anda sudah lebih baik.

glance *noun* sekejap mata, pandangan sekilas.
verb **1** melihat sekilas; **Damian glanced at her** Damian melihat sekilas padanya; **2 Vera only glanced at the newspaper** Vera hanya membaca surat kabar sepintas-lalu.

glass *noun* **1** kaca beling; **not all bottles are made of glass** tidak semua botol dibuat dari kaca; **2** gelas; **a glass of milk** segelas susu.

glasses *noun* kacamata.

glider *noun* pesawat luncur.

global *adjective* global, sedunia.

global warming *noun* pemanasan global.

globe *noun* **1** *(geographical)* bola bumi; **2** *(electrical)* bohlam, bola lampu.

glove *noun* sarung tangan; **a pair of gloves** sepasang sarung tangan.

glove compartment *noun* laci kecil di dekat setir mobil.

glue *noun* lem, perekat.

go *noun* **1** *(in a game)* giliran; **whose go is it?** giliran siapa?; **2 to have a go at doing** kesempatan; **give Henky a go at fixing it** berilah Henky kesempatan untuk memperbaikinya.
verb **1** pergi; **Tri's gone to the dentist's** Tri sudah pergi ke dokter gigi; **2** *(with another verb)* **she's gone fishing** dia pergi memancing ikan; **3** *(leave)* berangkat; **they're going on Sunday** mereka akan berangkat hari Minggu; **4** *(an event)* berjalan, berlalu; **the party went well** pesta itu berjalan baik.

- **to go away 1** pergi; **go away!** pergilah!; **2** *(of pain)* hilang; **her headache's gone** sakit kepalanya sudah hilang.
- **to go back 1** kembali; **I'm going back for my passport** saya akan kembali untuk

mengambil paspor saya; **2** *(home)* pulang; **Franz is going back home to Germany** Franz mau pulang ke Jerman; **I'm going (back) home now** saya mau pulang (sekarang).

- **to go down 1** turun; **to go downstairs** turun tangga; **he's gone down to the first floor** dia turun ke lantai satu; *(price, temperature)* **the price of rice has gone down** harga beras sudah turun; **2** berkurang; **the population of this town is going down** jumlah penduduk di kota ini berkurang; **3** terbenam; **the sun goes down at 6.30** matahari terbenam pada jam enam tiga puluh; **4** *(tyre, balloon, airbed)* kempes; **the tyre's gone down** bannya kempes.
- **to go in** masuk; **Jo went in and shut the door** Jo masuk dan menutup pintu.
- **to go into** masuk; **Sri went into the bank** Sri masuk ke bank.
- **to go off 1** *(bomb)* meledak; **2** *(alarm)* bunyi; **my alarm clock went off at five o'clock** weker saya berbunyi pada jam lima; **3** *(food)* basi, busuk; **this rice has gone off** nasi ini sudah basi.
- **to go on 1 what's going on?** ada apa?; **2** terus; **go straight on!** terus saja!; **how can they go on like that?** bagaimana mereka bisa terus-menerus begitu?; **to go on talking** berbicara terus; **3** melanjutkan; **let's go on to another topic** mari kita lanjutkan dengan topik lain.
- **to go out 1** (pergi) keluar; **I'm going out for dinner tonight** nanti malam saya akan keluar untuk makan; **out you go!** ayo, keluar!; **2** *(light, lamp, fire)* mati; **the light went out** lampu mati; **3 to go out with somebody** berteman dengan; **Taufik's going out with my sister** Taufik berteman dengan adik perempuan saya.
- **to go past** lewat; **we went past your house** kami lewat rumah Anda; **we've already gone past** kami sudah lewat.
- **to go round to (somebody's house)** mampir; **last night Koes went round to Rose's place** semalam Koes

mampir di rumah Rose.

- **to go around** mengelilingi; **they went right around the temple** mereka mengelilingi candi itu.
- **to go through 1** lewat; **this train doesn't go through Tasikmalaya** kereta ini tidak lewat Tasikmalaya; **2** mengalami; **Hans has been through so much lately** baru-baru ini Hans mengalami begitu banyak masalah.
- **to go up 1** *(person, prices, temperature)* naik; **she's gone upstairs** dia sudah naik ke atas; **prices are going up** harga-harga naik; **2** *(rates)* meningkat; **the death rate has gone up** angka kematian sudah meningkat; **3** *(buildings)* dibangun; **many new buildings have gone up on Jl Gatot Subroto** banyak gedung baru sudah dibangun di Jl Gatot Subroto.

goal *noun* **1** cita-cita; **to have high goals** mempunyai cita-cita yang tinggi; **2** gol; **to score a goal** membuat gol, mencetak gol; **3** tujuan; **life goal** tujuan hidup.

goalkeeper *noun* kiper, penjaga gawang.

goat *noun* kambing.

god[1] *noun* dewa.

God[2] *noun* Tuhan (yang Maha Esa), Allah.

goddess *noun* dewi.

godparent *noun* seorang laki-laki atau perempuan yang menjadi wali atas seorang bayi *(definition only)*.

goggles *noun* kacamata yang dipakai untuk berenang atau untuk menahan debu *(definition only)*.

gold *noun* emas; **solid, pure gold** emas murni.

goldfish *noun* ikan mas.

golf *noun* golf; **to play golf** main golf.

golfer *noun* pegolf, pemain golf.

golf course *noun* lapangan golf.

good *adjective* **1** bagus, baik; **he'll be a good vet** dia akan menjadi dokter hewan yang baik; **2** baik, budiman; **a good man** seorang yang baik, budiman; **3** enak; **the mangoes are good** mangga-mangga ini enak; **4** senang, menyenangkan; **it was a good party** pesta itu menyenangkan; **5 to be good at** pandai; **good at**

a b c d e f g h i j k l m n o p q r s t u v w x y z

painting pandai melukis; **6 to be good for** berguna; **this tool is no good for the job** alat ini tidak berguna untuk pekerjaan ini; **7 to be good to** baik; **they've been good to him** mereka baik terhadap dia; **8 for good** untuk selama-lamanya; **I've stopped smoking for good** saya sudah berhenti merokok untuk selama-lamanya.

good afternoon *exclamation (from about 10 a.m. to 2 p.m.)* selamat siang; *(from about 2 p.m. to sunset)* selamat sore.

good-looking *adjective* cantik, ganteng, tampan; **Heny's boyfriend is really good-looking** pacar Heny betul-betul ganteng.

good morning *exclamation (up to about 10 a.m.)* selamat pagi; *(from about 10 a.m. to 2 p.m.)* selamat siang.

goodness **1** kebaikan; **2** *(exclamation)* waduh! Masya Allah!

goodnight *exclamation (greeting, farewell)* selamat malam; *(to person going to bed)* selamat tidur.

goods *noun* barang-barang, harta benda.

goods train *noun* kereta barang.

goose *noun* angsa.

goose pimples *noun (because of fear, not cold)* berdiri bulu roma.

gorgeous *adjective* indah, permai, sangat bagus.

gorilla *noun* gorela.

gosh *exclamation* wah!

gossip *noun* **1** *(person)* penggunjing, tukang gosip; **2** *(news)* cakap angin.

government *noun*
1 pemerintah; **government regulation** peraturan pemerintah;
2 pemerintahan; **democratic government** pemerintahan demokratis.

grab *verb* **1** merebut; **don't grab (for) the lollies** jangan merebut gula-gula itu; **2** memegang erat-erat; **Meiti grabbed my arm** Meiti memegang lengan saya erat-erat.

graceful *adjective* anggun, lemah-gemulai.

grade *noun (mark)* angka; **to get high grades** mendapat angka yang tinggi.

gradual *adjective* berangsur-angsur, lambat-laun, sedikit demi sedikit.

gradually *adverb* berangsur-angsur, lambat-laun; **my health is gradually improving**

kesehatan saya berangsur-angsur pulih.

graffiti *noun* grafiti.

grain *noun* biji, butir; **a grain of rice** sebutir padi (beras).

grammar *noun* tatabahasa.

grammar school *noun* *(from ages eleven to fifteen)* Sekolah Menengah Pertama (SMP); *(from ages fifteen to eighteen)* Sekolah Menengah Atas (SMA).

grammatical *adjective* berhubungan dengan tatabahasa.

gram, gramme *noun* gram.

gran, grandma, granny *noun* nenek.

grandchild *noun* cucu; *(female)* cucu perempuan; *(male)* cucu lelaki.

grandad, grandpa *noun* kakek.

granddaughter *noun* cucu perempuan.

grandfather *noun* kakek.

grandmother *noun* nenek.

grandparents *plural noun* kakek nenek.

grandson *noun* cucu lelaki.

grape *noun* buah anggur.

grapefruit *noun* semacam jeruk yang besar.

graph *noun* grafik.

grasp *verb* **1** memegang; **the child grasped the rail tightly** anak itu memegang sandaran tangga erat-erat; **2** menangkap, mengerti, memahami; **I can't grasp your meaning** saya tidak menangkap maksud Anda.

grass *noun* rumput.

grasshopper *noun* belalang.

grate *verb* memarut; **grated coconut** kelapa parut.

grateful *adjective* berterima kasih.

grater *noun* parutan.

grave *noun* kubur(an).

gravel *noun* (batu) kerikil.

graveyard *noun* makam, pekuburan.

gravy *noun* kuah (daging), saus.

grease *noun* lemak.

greasy *adjective* berlemak, berminyak.

great *adjective* **1** jago, juara; **a great badminton player** (seorang) jago bulu tangkis; **2** terkenal, termashyur; **a great poet** penyair yang terkenal; **3** *(terrific)* hebat; **that's great!** sungguh hebat!; **4 a great deal of** banyak; **a great many** banyak; **there are a great many things still to be done** masih banyak yang harus dilakukan.

a b c d e f g h i j k l m n o p q r s t u v w x y z

Great Britain *noun* Britannia, Inggris Raya.

Greece *noun* Negeri Yunani.

greedy *adjective* rakus, tamak.

Greek *noun* **1** *(person)* orang Yunani; **2** *(language)* bahasa Yunani.

green *noun* **1** *(colour)* hijau; **2 greens** *(vegetables)* sayur-sayuran; **3 the Greens** *(ecologists)* kelompok hijau. *adjective* **1** *(colour)* hijau; **2 the Green Party** Partai Hijau, Partai Lingkungan Hidup.

greengrocer *noun* tukang sayur.

greenhouse *noun* rumah kaca, ruang kaca.

greenhouse effect *noun* efek rumah kaca.

greeting card *noun* kartu ucapan selamat; **Christmas card** kartu natal; **Lebaran card** kartu Lebaran.

greetings *plural noun* salam, sambutan.

grey *adjective* abu-abu, kelabu.

greyhound *noun* anjing (yang dipakai untuk) pacuan.

grid *noun* **1** *(grating)* alat pemanggangan, kisi-kisi; **2** *(network)* jaringan.

grief *noun* dukacita, kesedihan.

grill *noun* alat pemanggang, tempat pembakar. *verb* memanggang; **I grilled the sausages** saya memanggang sosis itu.

grim *adjective* cemberut, seram, suram.

grin *noun* menyengir, seringai. *verb* menyeringai, menyengir.

grip *noun* pegangan. *verb* memegang erat-erat.

grit *noun* pasir.

groan *noun* rintihan. *verb* merintih; **to groan in pain** merintih kesakitan.

grocer *noun* penjual bahan makanan dan minuman.

groceries *plural noun* bahan makanan.

grocer's *noun* toko yang menjual bahan makanan, toko pangan.

groom *noun* *(bridegroom)* pengantin laki-laki.

gross *adjective* **1** yang menyolok; **a gross injustice** ketidakadilan yang menyolok; **2** besar; **a gross error** kesalahan besar; **3** *(disgusting)* memuakkan, menjijikkan; **gross food** makanan yang memuakkan; **a gross sight** pandangan menjijikkan.

ground *noun* **1** tanah; **2** *(for sport)* lapangan.

adjective giling; **ground coffee** kopi giling.

ground floor *noun* lantai dasar.

group *noun* kelompok, rombongan.

grow *verb* **1** *(plant, hair)* tumbuh; **vegetables grow well in our garden** sayuran tumbuh baik di taman kami; **2** (*number, size)* bertambah; **the number of students has grown** jumlah mahasiswa sudah bertambah; **my little brother has grown a lot this year** adik laki-laki saya makin bertambah besar tahun ini; **3** *(fruit, vegetables)* tanam; **I like growing flowers** saya senang menanam bunga-bunga; **4** memelihara *(a beard)* **he's growing a beard** dia memelihara jenggot.

- **to grow up 1** (menjadi) dewasa; **2** dibesarkan; **Flora grew up in Canada** Flora dibesarkan di Kanada; **we grew up together** kami dibesarkan bersama-sama.

growl *verb* menggeram.

grown-up *noun* (orang) dewasa.

growth *noun* perkembangan, pertumbuhan.

grudge *noun* dendam; **to bear a grudge against** dendam, sakit hati kepada; **she bears me a grudge** ia sakit hati kepada saya.

gruesome *adjective* yang mengerikan, yang menjijikkan.

grumble *verb* mengeluh, menggerutu.

guarantee *noun* garansi, jaminan.
verb menjamin.

guard *noun* pengawal, penjaga.
verb menjaga.

guard dog *noun* anjing jaga.

guess *noun* **1** perkiraan, taksiran; **one guess is as good as another** kita sama-sama tidak tahu; **2** terkaan; **have a guess!** coba terka!; **3** dugaan; **it's anybody's guess** itu dugaan orang.
verb **1** menerka; **guess how much!** coba terka berapa harganya!; **2** *(estimate)* menaksir; **I guess she's about forty-five** saya taksir umurnya kira-kira empat puluh lima tahun; **3** menduga; **to guess right** menduga tepat.

guest *noun* tamu.

guide *noun* **1** *(person)* pandu, pemandu; **tourist guide** pemandu pariwisata, pramuwisata; **2** *(book)* buku panduan; buku pedoman, buku petunjuk; **3** *(girl guide)* pramuka puteri.

guidebook *noun* buku panduan; buku pedoman, buku petunjuk.

guide dog *noun* anjing penuntun.

guideline *noun* pedoman.

guilty *adjective* bersalah; **to feel guilty, to have a guilty conscience** merasa bersalah.

guinea pig *noun* **1** *(pet)* marmot; **2** *(in an experiment)* kelinci percobaan; **they're using her as a guinea pig** mereka menggunakan dia sebagai kelinci percobaan.

guitar *noun* gitar.

gum *noun* **1** *(in mouth)* gusi; **2** *(chewing gum)* permen karet.

gun *noun* **1** *(revolver)* pistol; **2** *(rifle)* senapan.

gust *noun* hembusan; **a gust of wind** hembusan angin.

gutter *noun* *(in the street)* got, parit, selokan.

guy *noun* orang (laki-laki); **he's a nice guy** dia orang yang baik.

gym *noun* **1** *(the activity)* senam; **2** *(the place)* gimnasium, gedung olahraga, ruang olahraga.

gymnasium *noun* gimnasium, gedung olahraga, ruang olahraga.

gymnast *noun* pesenam.

gymnastics *noun* gimnastik, olahraga senam.

gym shoe *noun* sepatu olahraga.

H h

habit *noun* kebiasaan; **to have a habit of going to bed late** kebiasaan tidur malam; **it's a bad habit** kebiasaan yang buruk.

habitat *noun* habitat, pemukiman, tempat kediaman, tempat tinggal.

hail *noun, verb* hujan es.

hailstone *noun* gumpalan es.

hailstorm *noun* hujan es disertai angin ribut.

hair *noun* **1** *(on the head)* rambut; **2** *(on the body or an animal)* bulu.

hairbrush *noun* sikat rambut.

haircut *noun* **1** pangkas rambut, potong rambut; **2 to have a haircut** pangkas rambut, potong rambut.

a b c d e f g h i j k l m n o p q r s t u v w x y z

hairdresser *noun* penata rambut.

hair drier *noun* alat pengering rambut.

hair gel *noun* jel rambut.

hairgrip *noun* jepit rambut.

hair remover *noun* obat untuk menghapuskan bulu.

hairslide *noun* tusuk konde.

hairspray *noun* semprot rambut.

hairstyle *noun* rias rambut, tata rambut.

hairy *adjective* berbulu.

half *noun* **1** separuh; **half of** separuh dari; **2 to cut in half** membagi dua; membelah; **3** setengah; **three and a half** tiga setengah; **half an hour** setengah jam; **every half hour** setiap setengah jam; **it's half past four** sekarang jam setengah lima; **half a litre** setengah liter; **half a cup** setengah cangkir; **half-yearly** setengah tahunan.

half-price *adjective*, *adverb* separuh harga, setengah harga.

half-time *noun* waktu istirahat.

halfway *adverb* setengah jalan.

hall *noun* **1** *(in a house)* gang; **2** *(public)* aula, ruang.

ham *noun* ham; **a ham sandwich** roti berlapiskan ham.

hamburger *noun* hamburger.

hammer *noun* martil, palu, tukul.

hamster *noun* tikus besar.

hand *noun* **1** tangan; **Marjolein held Mira's hand** Marjolein memegang tangan Mira; **2 to give a hand** membantu, menolong; **do you need a hand?** dapatkah saya membantu Anda?; **3 on the other hand** di pihak lain; **4 the hour hand** jarum pendek.
verb memberikan, menyerahkan; **I handed him the keys** saya menyerahkan kunci tersebut kepadanya.

- **to hand something in** menyerahkan; **I've handed in my homework** saya sudah menyerahkan pekerjaan rumah saya.
- **to hand something out** membagi-bagikan; **Endang handed out the tests** Endang membagi-bagikan kertas ujian itu.

handbag *noun* tas (tangan).

handcuffs *plural noun* belenggu, borgol.

handful *noun* segenggam; **a handful of rice** segenggam beras.

a b c d e f g h i j k l m n o p q r s t u v w x y z

handkerchief *noun* saputangan.

handicapped *adjective* cacat jasmaniah.

handle *noun* **1** *(of a broom, spoon)* tangkai; **2** *(of a drawer, bag)* pegangan; **3** *(of a knife, tennis racket)* gagang.
verb **1** melakukan, menangani; **Itje handles the accounts** Itje menangani rekening; **2** mengurus, menangani; **you're good at handling people** Anda pintar mengurus orang.

handlebars *plural noun* gagang sepeda.

hand luggage *noun* bagasi yang dibawa sendiri ke dalam pesawat.

handsome *adjective* gagah, ganteng, tampan; **he's a handsome guy** dia seorang laki-laki yang ganteng.

handwriting *noun* tulisan tangan.

handy *adjective* **1** berguna; **this little knife is really handy** pisau kecil ini betul-betul berguna; **2** dekat; **the supermarket is very handy** pasar swalayan itu dekat sekali.

hang *verb* **1** menggantungi dengan, menggantung(kan); **Damian hung a painting on his bedroom wall** Damian menggantungkan lukisan pada dinding kamar tidurnya; **can you hang out the washing please?** tolong gantungkan cucian; **2** *(a person)* menggantung; **he was hanged yesterday** dia digantung kemarin, dia dihukum gantung kemarin.

- **to hang around** nganggur; **they always hang around that disco** mereka selalu nganggur di disko itu.
- **to hang down** menggantung, tergantung.
- **to hang on** bertahan, menunggu; **hang on a second!** tunggu sebentar!
- **to hang up** *(on the phone)* memutuskan pembicaraan; **don't hang up on me!** jangan putuskan pembicaraan! jangan tutup telponnya!
- **to hang something up** menggantungkan; **you can hang up your clothes in this cupboard** Anda boleh menggantungkan pakaian Anda di dalam lemari ini.

hang-gliding *noun* meluncur dengan pesawat terbang layang; **to go hang-gliding** meluncur dengan pesawat terbang layang.

hangover *noun* akibat mabuk; **to have a hangover** perasaan sakit pada waktu bangun karena terlalu banyak minum minuman keras *(definition only)*.

happen *verb* **1** terjadi; **what's happening?** ada apa?; **it happened last night** peristiwa itu terjadi semalam; **2** di mana; **what's happened to the can opener?** di mana pembuka kaleng?; **3** kebetulan saja; **if you happen to see Jill** kalau kebetulan saja Anda bertemu dengan Jill.

happily *adverb* **1** dengan gembira; **she smiled happily** dia tersenyum gembira; **2** *(willingly)* mau, senang; **I'll happily do it for you** saya akan melakukannya untuk Anda dengan senang hati.

happiness *noun* kebahagiaan, kesenangan.

happy *adjective* bahagia, gembira, senang; **Happy Birthday!** Selamat Hari Ulang Tahun!

harbour *noun* pelabuhan.

hard *adjective* **1** keras; **to become hard, to go hard** menjadi keras; **2** *(difficult)* sukar, sulit, susah; **a difficult question** pertanyaan yang sulit; **it's hard to know** sukar menduga, sukar mengetahui. *adverb* **1** keras; **to work hard** bekerja keras; **to try hard** berusaha keras; **2** lebat; **it's raining hard** hujan lebat.

hard disk *noun* hard disk.

hardly *adverb* **1** hampir tidak; **I can hardly hear you** saya hampir tidak dapat mendengar Anda; **there's hardly any rice left** hampir tidak ada beras sama sekali, berasnya hanya tinggal sedikit; **2 hardly ever** jarang; **I hardly ever go to the movies** saya jarang pergi menonton film.

hard up *adjective* kekurangan uang.

hare *noun* kelinci.

harm *noun* rugi; **it won't do you any harm** tak ada ruginya bagi Anda, itu tidak akan membahayakan Anda. *verb* **1** merugikan; **they did not harm him** mereka tidak merugikannya; **2** membahayakan; **a cup of coffee won't harm you** secangkir kopi tak akan membahayakan Anda.

harmful *adjective* berbahaya.

harmless *adjective* tidak berbahaya.

harvest *noun* hasil panen. *verb* memanen, memetik hasil panen.

hat *noun* topi.

a b c d e f g h i j k l m n o p q r s t u v w x y z

a b c d e f g h i j k l m n o p q r s t u v w x y z

hate *verb* (mem)benci; **I hate housework** saya benci pekerjaan rumah tangga.

hatred *noun* kebencian, rasa benci.

have *verb* **1** mempunyai; **Ami has three children** Ami mempunyai tiga anak; **we've got two dogs** kami mempunyai dua ekor anjing; **2** memegang; **what have you got in your hand?** Anda memegang apa di tangan?; **3** telah, pernah, sudah *(to form past tenses in positive statements and questions)*; **I've finished** saya sudah selesai; **4** belum (pernah) *(with negatives)*; **Shanti hasn't arrived yet** Shanti belum datang; **5 to have to do** harus; **I have to phone home** saya harus menelepon ke rumah; **6** ingin; **what will you have?** Anda ingin apa?; **7** makan; **to have dinner** makan malam; **to have lunch** makan siang; **8 to have something done** akan (mengerjakan sesuatu); **I'm going to have my hair cut** saya akan gunting rambut; **9** ber–; **to have a dream** bermimpi; **to have the flu** kena flu, sakit flu; **10** ada, punya; **what have you got there?** Anda punya apa di situ?

hay *noun* rumput kering, jerami.

hay fever *noun* penyakit bersin yang disebabkan kepekaan terhadap rumput kering *(definition only)*.

hazelnut *noun* semacam buah kemiri *(definition only)*.

he *pronoun* beliau, dia, ia.

head *noun* **1** kepala; **2** bagian depan; **at the head of the queue** di bagian depan antrean; **3** *(of a school)* kepala sekolah; **4** *(when tossing a coin)* **'heads or tails?' – 'heads'** 'atas atau bawah?' – 'atas'.

- **to head for** mengarah, menuju; **Azril headed for the door** Azril menuju pintu.

headache *noun* sakit kepala; **I've got a headache** saya sakit kepala.

headlight *noun* lampu depan; **put on the headlights now** nyalakan lampu depan sekarang.

headmaster *noun* kepala sekolah (pria).

headmistress *noun* kepala sekolah (wanita).

headphones *noun* hedfon.

headteacher *noun* guru kepala.

health *noun* kesehatan.

health centre *noun* pusat kesehatan.

healthy *adjective* **to be healthy** sehat; **a healthy lifestyle** gaya hidup yang sehat.

heap *noun* banyak sekali; **I've got heaps of things to do** ada banyak sekali yang harus saya lakukan.

hear *verb* **1** mendengar; **I can't hear you** saya tidak bisa mendengar Anda; **I can't hear anything** saya tak bisa mendengar apa-apa; **2** *(news)* mendengar kabar, mendapat kabar.
- **to hear about** mendengar tentang; **have you heard about the concert?** apakah Anda sudah mendengar tentang konser itu?
- **to hear from** mendapat kabar dari; **have you heard from Yanti?** apakah Anda sudah mendapat kabar dari Yanti?

heart *noun* **1** *(the physical organ)* jantung; **2** *(figurative)* hati; **broken-hearted** patah hati; **heart to heart** dari hati ke hati; **3 to learn by heart** menghafalkan; **4** *(in cards)* **the jack of hearts** jack heart.

heart attack *noun* serangan jantung.

heat *noun* kepanasan, panas. *verb* memanaskan; **the soup's heating** sop itu sedang dipanaskan; **I'll go and heat the water** saya akan memanaskan air.
- **to heat** memanaskan.

heater *noun* alat pemanas.

heating *noun* pemanasan.

heatwave *noun* gelombang panas terik.

heaven *noun* **1** surga; **2** *(Hindu)* kayangan; kahyangan.

heavy *adjective* **1** berat; **a heavy bag** tas yang berat; **2** ramai; **heavy traffic** lalu lintas ramai; **3 heavy rain** hujan deras, hujan lebat.

heavy metal *noun* logam berat.

hectic *adjective* repot sekali, sibuk sekali; **a hectic day** hari yang repot sekali.

hedge *noun* pagar hidup.

heel *noun* tumit.

height *noun* ketinggian, tingginya.

helicopter *noun* helikopter.

hell *noun* neraka; **it's hell here!** disini rasanya seperti di neraka!

hello **1** halo; **hello! how are you?** halo! apa kabar?; **2** salam; **say hello to the**

family sampaikan salam saya kepada keluarga.

helmet *noun* helm, topi baja.

help *noun* bantuan, pertolongan; **do you need any help?** apakah Anda perlu bantuan?
verb **1** membantu, menolong; **can you help me move the bed?** tolong saya untuk memindahkan tempat tidur ini, tolong pindahkan tempat tidur ini; **2 to help yourself** ambil sendiri; **help yourself to the sambal** silahkan ambil sambal sendiri; **help yourself!** silahkan ambil sendiri!
3 help! tolong!

helpful *adjective* berguna, suka menolong.

hem *noun* kelim, sisi, tepi.

hen *noun* ayam betina, induk ayam.

her *pronoun* dia, ia, –nya; **I met her yesterday** saya berjumpa dengan dia kemarin; **please give this to her** tolong berikan ini kepadanya; **this is not her book** ini bukan bukunya.

herb *noun* **1** *(medicinal)* herba, jamu; **2** *(culinary)* bumbu (tanaman yang daunnya dipakai untuk memasak).

here *adverb* **1** di sini; **not far from here** tidak jauh dari sini; **2** kemari, ke sini; **come here!** kemari!; **3 here is, here are** ini; **here's my phone number** ini nomor telepon saya; **here are the photos** ini foto-fotonya; **and here they are!** inilah mereka!; **4** begini; **here's how to do it** begini cara melakukannya.

hero *noun* pahlawan.

heroin *noun* heroin.

heroine *noun* pahlawan wanita, pahlawati.

herring *noun* ikan haring.

hers *pronoun* kepunyaannya; **that car is not hers** mobil itu bukan kepunyaannya.

herself *pronoun* dia, dirinya, sendiri(an); **she said it herself** dia mengatakannya sendiri; **she did it by herself** dia mengerjakannya sendirian; **she's hurt herself** dia terluka.

hesitate *verb* ragu-ragu; **don't hesitate to ask** jangan ragu-ragu bertanya; **they hesitated before coming in** mereka ragu-ragu sebelum masuk.

heterosexual *adjective* heteroseks.

hi *exclamation* hai, halo.

hiccups *plural noun* sedakan; **to have the hiccups** tersedak.

hidden *adjective* terpendam, tersembunyi.

hide *verb* **1** bersembunyi; **she hid behind the door** dia bersembunyi di belakang pintu; **2** menyembunyikan; **who's hidden the chocolate?** siapa yang menyembunyikan coklat itu?

hide-and-seek *noun* permainan bercari-carian; **to play hide-and-seek** main sembunyi-sembunyian.

high *adjective* **1** tinggi; **the wall is very high** tembok itu tinggi sekali; **it's two metres high** tingginya dua meter; **at high speed** pada kecepatan yang tinggi; **2** mahal, tinggi; **food prices are very high** harga makanan mahal; **3** nyaring, tinggi; **a high voice** suara nyaring; **4 high winds** angin kencang; **high tide** pasang naik; **high spot** puncak.

high-heeled *adjective* bertumit tinggi; **high-heeled shoes** sepatu bertumit tinggi.

high jump *noun* loncat tinggi.

highly *adverb* sangat.

highway *noun* jalan raya.

hijack *verb* membajak; **to hijack a plane** membajak pesawat terbang.

hijacker *noun* pembajak.

hike *verb* berjalan kaki.

hilarious *adjective* lucu sekali.

hill *noun* bukit; **you can see the hills from here** And dapat melihat bukit-bukit itu dari sini.

him *pronoun* dia, ia, –nya; **I met him yesterday** saya berjumpa dengan dia kemarin; **I don't want to go with him** saya tidak mau pergi dengan dia; **please give this to him** tolong berikan ini kepadanya; **I'll send him a cheque** saya akan mengiriminya cek.

himself *pronoun* dia, dirinya, sendiri(an); *(pria)* **he said it himself** dia mengatakannya sendiri; **he did it by himself** dia mengerjakannya sendirian; **he's hurt himself** dia terluka.

Hindu *adjective* Hindu.

hip *noun* pinggul.

hippie *noun* hippi.

hippopotamus *noun* badak sungai, kuda nil.

hire *noun* sewa; **hire car** mobil sewaan; **for hire** untuk disewakan; **car hire** penyewaan mobil.
verb menyewa; **let's just hire a car** mari kita menyewa mobil saja.

a b c d e f g h i j k l m n o p q r s t u v w x y z

his *pronoun* kepunyaannya, –nya; **this is his room** ini kamarnya; **that's not his motorbike** motor itu bukan kepunyaannya; **this is my tape, not his** ini kaset saya, bukan kasetnya.

history *noun* sejarah.

hit *noun* sukses; **their latest hit** lagu terbarunya yang sukses; **the film is a huge hit** film itu betul-betul sukses.
verb **1** memukul; **to hit the ball** memukul bola;
2 terbentur; **she hit her head on the cupboard door** kepalanya terbentur pintu lemari; **3** membentur, menabrak; **the car hit a tree** mobil itu menabrak pohon; **4** ditabrak; **to be hit by a car** ditabrak mobil.

hitch *noun* halangan, rintangan; **there's been a slight hitch** telah ada rintangan kecil.
verb menumpang; **to hitch a lift** menumpang.

hitchhike *verb* menumpang naik mobil; **we hitchhiked to Madiun** kami menumpang naik mobil ke Madiun.

hitchhiker *noun* orang yang menumpang kendaraan.

HIV-negative *adjective* HIV negatif.

HIV-positive *adjective* HIV positif.

hobby *noun* hobi, kegemaran, kesukaan.

hockey *noun* (olahraga) hoki; **to play hockey** main hoki.

hockey stick *noun* pemukul hoki.

hold *verb* **1** memegang; **Kate held the child's hand** Kate memegang tangan anak itu; **2** *(contain)* memuat; **this room can hold three hundred people** ruangan ini dapat menampung tiga ratus orang; **3** berisi; **a jug that holds a litre of water** kendi yang berisi satu liter air; **4 to hold a meeting** mengadakan rapat; **5** *(wait)* menunggu; **hold on!** tunggu! *(on telephone)*; **can you hold the line please** harap tunggu sebentar.

- **to hold somebody up** *(delay)* menahan; **Pak Ali held me up so I couldn't get home** saya tertahan oleh Pak Ali sehingga tidak bisa pulang; **I was held up at the office** saya tertahan di kantor.
- **to hold something up** *(raise)* mengangkat; **hold up your hand!** angkat tangan!

hold-up *noun* **1** *(delay)* penundaan; **2** *(traffic jam)* macet; **3** *(robbery)* perampokan.

hole *noun* lubang.

holiday *noun* **1** liburan; **have a good holiday!** selamat berlibur!; **the school holidays** liburan sekolah; **to be away on holiday** berlibur; **to go on holiday** berlibur; **2** *(from work)* cuti; **I'm taking two days' holiday next week** saya akan cuti dua hari minggu depan; **3 a public holiday** hari besar, hari libur; **Monday's a holiday** hari Senin adalah hari libur.

Holland *noun* negeri Belanda.

hollow *adjective* berlubang, kosong.

holy *adjective* kudus, suci.

home *noun* **1** rumah; **to stay at home** tinggal di rumah; **make yourself at home** anggaplah seperti di rumah sendiri; **2** panti asuhan, perumahan; **an old people's home** panti asuhan, perumahan orang lanjut usia.
adverb pulang; **Kepi's gone home** Kepi sudah pulang; **to get home** tiba di rumah.

homeless *adjective* tunawisma; **the homeless** orang-orang tunawisma.

homemade *adjective* buatan sendiri; **homemade cakes** kue-kue buatan sendiri.

home match *noun* pertandingan di kota sendiri.

homesick *adjective* rindu; **to be homesick** rindu.

homework *noun* pekerjaan rumah.

homosexual *adjective*, *noun* homoseks, homoseksual.

honest *adjective* jujur, lurus hati.

honestly *adverb* secara jujur.

honesty *noun* kejujuran.

honey *noun* madu.

honeymoon *noun* bulan madu.

honour *noun* kehormatan.

hood *noun* kerudung (kepala), tudung.

hook *noun* **1** dudukan; **Patrick took the phone off the hook** Patrick mengangkat gagang telepon dari tempatnya; **2** kaitan; **just hang your umbrella on that hook** gantunglah payung Anda pada kaitan itu saja.

hooligan *noun* buaya darat, penjahat.

hooray *exclamation* hore, hure.

hope *noun* harapan; **to give up hope** hilang harapan. *verb* **1** berharap, mengharap; **we hope that you'll be able to come** kami berharap Anda akan dapat datang; **2** mudah-mudahan; **here's hoping!** mudah-mudahan!; **I hope so** mudah-mudahan begitu; **I hope not** mudah-mudahan tidak; **hoping to see you next week** mudah-mudahan kita ketemu lagi minggu depan.

hopefully *adverb* mudah-mudahan; **hopefully the film won't have started** mudah-mudahan film itu belum mulai.

hopeless *adjective* bodoh sekali; *(informal)* **I'm completely hopeless at history** saya bodoh sekali mengenai sejarah.

horizontal *adjective* horizontal, mendatar.

horn *noun* **1** *(of an animal)* tanduk; **2** *(of a car)* klakson; **to sound your horn** membunyikan klakson; **3** *(musical instrument)* terompet; **to play the horn** main terompet.

hornbill *noun* burung enggang.

horoscope *noun* horoskop.

horrible *adjective* **1** buruk sekali; **the weather was horrible** cuacanya buruk sekali; **2** *(person)* jahat, jelek; **he's really horrible** dia seorang yang mempunyai sifat yang jelek; **she was really horrible to me** dia betul-betul jahat terhadap saya.

horror *noun* kengerian, perasaan ngeri.

horror film *noun* film horor, film yang mengerikan.

horse *noun* kuda.

horseshoe *noun* besi tapak kuda, ladam.

hose *noun* selang karet.

hospitable *adjective* keramah-tamahan, suka memberi tumpangan, suka menjamu.

hospital *noun* rumah sakit; **to be in hospital** dirawat di rumah sakit, opname; **to be taken to hospital** dibawa ke rumah sakit; **to go to hospital** masuk rumah sakit.

hospitality *noun* kesanggrahan, keramah-tamahan; **hospitality industry** industri perhotelan dan pariwisata.

hostage *noun* sandera.

hostel *noun* asrama, hostel, losmen, pondok; **youth hostel** asrama pemuda.

hostess *noun* nyonya rumah; **an air hostess** pramugari.

hot *adjective* **1** *(temperature)* panas; **a hot drink** minuman panas; **to be hot** merasa panas; **2** *(food: spicy)* pedas; **the sambal's too hot for me** sambal ini terlalu pedas bagi saya.

hot dog *noun* hotdog

hotel *noun* hotel.

hour *noun* jam; **two hours later** dua jam kemudian; **I waited for an hour** saya menunggu sejam; **three hours ago** tiga jam yang lalu; **to be paid by the hour** digaji menurut jumlah jam kerjanya; **every hour** setiap jam; **half an hour** setengah jam; **a quarter of an hour** seperempat jam; **an hour and a half** satu jam setengah.

house *noun* rumah.

housemaid *noun* pembantu rumah tangga.

housewife *noun* ibu rumah tangga.

housework *noun* pekerjaan rumah tangga; **to do the housework** melakukan pekerjaan rumah tangga.

hovercraft *noun* hovercraft.

how *adverb* **1** bagaimana; **how did you do it?** bagaimana Anda melakukannya?; **2** berapa; **how much?** berapa?; **how much money do you have?** berapa jumlah uang Anda?; **how much is it?** *(price)* berapa harganya?; **how many?** berapa?; **how many brothers and sisters do you have?** Anda punya berapa saudara?; **how old are you?** berapa umur Anda?; **how far is it?** berapa jauhnya?; **how long will it take?** makan waktu berapa lama?; **3** apa; **how are you?** apa kabar?; **how come you're late?** apa sebabnya Anda terlambat? kenapa Anda terlambat?

however *adverb* bagaimana pun, betapa pun, biar pun. *conjunction* namun, (akan) tetapi.

hug *noun* pelukan, rangkulan; **she gave me a hug** ia memeluk saya.
verb memeluk, merangkul.

huge *adjective* dahsyat, raksasa, sangat besar.

hum *verb* bersenandung.

human *adjective* bersifat manusia.

human being *noun* manusia.

humour *noun* humor, kelucuan; **to have a sense of humour** mempunyai selera humor.

hundred *number* ratus; **two hundred** dua ratus; **one**

a b c d e f g h i j k l m n o p q r s t u v w x y z

a b c d e f g h i j k l m n o p q r s t u v w x y z

hundred seratus; **a hundred people** seratus orang; **about a hundred** sekitar seratus, kira-kira seratus; **hundreds of insects** ratusan serangga.

Hungary *noun* Honggaria.

hunger *noun* kelaparan, rasa lapar.

hungry *adjective* lapar; **I'm hungry** saya lapar.

hunt *verb* **1** *(an animal)* berburu, memburu; **2** *(a person)* mengejar.

hunting *noun* pemburuan; **to go pig hunting** berburu babi.

hurry *noun* terburu-buru, tergesa-gesa; **to be in a hurry** tergesa-gesa; **he's always in a hurry** dia selalu tergesa-gesa. *verb* bergegas; **I must hurry** saya harus bergegas; **let's hurry home** mari kita bergegas pulang; **hurry up!** cepatlah!; **don't hurry** janganlah tergesa-gesa.

hurt *verb* **1** menyakiti; **you're hurting me!** Anda menyakiti saya!; **2** sakit; **that hurts!** aduh sakit!; **my back hurts** punggung saya sakit; **3** terluka; **did you hurt yourself?** apakah Anda terluka? *adjective* **1** *(in an accident)* terluka, mendapat luka, melukai; **fifty people were hurt** lima puluh orang terluka; **2** *(feelings)* merasa tersinggung; **s/he felt hurt** dia merasa tersinggung.

husband *noun* suami.

hutch *noun* kandang (kelinci).

hymn *noun* kidung (gereja), nyanyian pujian.

hyphen *noun* tanda penghubung.

I i

I *pronoun* **1** *(formal)* saya; **I am Australian** saya orang Australi(a); **2** *(informal)* aku; **3** *(Jakarta dialect)* gue.

ice¹ *noun* es; **ice bag** kantong es.

ice² *adjective* dingin; **ice-cold** dingin sekali.

ice-cream *noun* es krim.

ice-cube *noun* es batu.

idea *noun* **1** ide, gagasan, pikiran; **what a good idea!** gagasan yang baik; **2** maksud; **the idea is to...** maksudnya...; **3 to have an idea about something** kira; **I had no idea you were coming** saya kira Anda tidak akan datang; **4 I've no idea**

at all saya sama sekali tidak tahu.

ideal *adjective* bagus sekali, baik, ideal, teladan; **ideal student** mahasiswa teladan. *noun* idaman, teladan.

identical *adjective* identik, sama, serupa; **identical twins** anak kembar identik.

identification *noun* identifikasi, pengenalan.

identify *verb* mengidentifikasikan, mengenal.

identity card *noun* kartu pengenal.

idiom *noun* idiom, ungkapan.

idiot *noun* idiot, orang bodoh, orang dungu, orang tolol.

idiotic *adjective* bodoh, idiot, tolol, dungu.

idyllic *adjective* sempurna.

i.e. [that is] *abbreviation* yaitu, yakni.

if *conjunction* **1** jika, kalau, jikalau; **if Garin's there** kalau Garin ada di situ; **if I won the lottery** jika saya menang lotere; **if I were you I'd forget it** kalau saya Anda, saya akan melupakannya; **2 if only** kalau saja; **if only you'd told me** kalau saja Anda memberitahu saya; **3 even if** sekali pun, sungguh pun; **even if it rains** sungguh pun hujan.

ignore *verb* mengabaikan; tak menghiraukan.

ill *adjective* sakit, tidak enak badan; **to fall ill** jatuh sakit; **to be taken ill** jatuh sakit; **I feel ill** saya merasa sakit.

illegal *adjective* gelap, tidak sah, tak legal.

illegible *adjective* tidak terbaca.

illness *noun* penyakit.

illusion *noun* ilusi, khayal(an).

illustrated *adjective* bergambar, berilustrasi; **an illustrated book** buku bergambar.

illustration *noun* gambar, ilustrasi.

image *noun* **1** *(impression)* citra, kesan; **2** *(shadow)* bayang-bayang; **3** *(drawing)* gambar; **4 he's the spitting image of his father** dia sangat mirip bapaknya.

imagination *noun* daya khayal, imajinasi; **to show imagination** memperlihatkan daya khayal.

imaginative *adjective* imajinatif.

imagine *verb* membayangkan, mengkhayalkan; **you can't imagine how horrible the**

a b c d e f g h i j k l m n o p q r s t u v w x y z

accident was Anda tak dapat membayangkan betapa mengerikannya kecelakaan itu.

imitate *verb* meniru.

imitation *noun* imitasi, tiruan.

immediate *adjective* segera.

immediately *adverb* dengan segera; **I rang them immediately** saya menelepon mereka dengan segera; **immediately before** segera sebelum; **immediately after** segera sesudah.

immigrant *noun* imigran, pendatang.

immigration *noun* imigrasi.

impatience *noun* ketidaksabaran.

impatient *adjective* tidak sabar; **Frank got impatient with Nani** Frank menjadi tidak sabar terhadap Nani.

impatiently *adverb* dengan tidak sabar.

imperfect *noun (of a verb)* imperfek; **in the imperfect** dalam bentuk imperfek.

import *verb* impor.

importance *noun* pentingnya.

impossible *adjective* mustahil, tidak mungkin; **it's impossible to find a telephone here** tidak mungkin ada telepon di sini.

impress *verb* mengesankan.

impressed *adjective* terkesan; **I'm not impressed** saya tidak terkesan; **I'm not at all impressed by that idea** saya sama sekali tidak terkesan oleh gagasan itu.

impression *noun* **1** impresi, kesan; **Josie made a good impression on her teacher** Josie menimbulkan kesan yang baik pada gurunya; **2 I got the impression he was feeling poorly** saya merasa bahwa dia tidak enak badan.

impressive *adjective* impresif, mengesankan.

improve *verb* **1** memperbaiki; **to improve the living standard** memperbaiki tingkat kehidupan masyarakat; **to improve your grades** memperbaiki angka; **2** *(get better)* bertambah baik, membaik; **the weather is improving** cuaca membaik; **3** *(in health)* mulai sembuh; **she's beginning to improve** dia mulai sembuh; **4** memperlancar; **to improve traffic flow** memperlancar arus lalu lintas.

improvement *noun* kemajuan, perbaikan.

in *preposition, adverb* **1** di; **in Jayapura** di Jayapura; **2** dalam; **in Indonesian**

dalam bahasa Indonesia; **3** di dalam; **in my pocket** di dalam saku saya; **4** pada; **in 1994** pada tahun 1994; **in winter** pada musim dingin; **in time** pada waktunya; **in the morning** pada pagi hari; **at eleven in the morning** pada jam sebelas siang; **5** lagi; **I'll phone you in ten minutes** sepuluh menit lagi saya akan menelepon Anda; **6** menurut, pada; **in my opinion** menurut pendapat saya, pada pendapat saya; **7 dressed in white** berbaju putih; **the girl in the yellow dress** gadis yang berbaju kuning; **8 to come in, to go in** masuk; **we went into the cinema** kami masuk ke bioskop; **9 to be in** ada; **Firdaus is not in at the moment** Firdaus tidak ada sekarang.

incident *noun* insiden, kejadian, peristiwa.

include *verb* memasukkan; **please include these items** tolong masukkan barang-barang ini; **dinner is included in the price** tarip itu termasuk makan malam; [illegible] termasuk pelayanan.

including *preposition* termasuk; **Rp. 300,000 including tax** tiga ratus ribu rupiah termasuk pajak; **everyone including children** semua orang termasuk anak-anak; **including Sundays** termasuk hari Minggu.

income *noun* pendapatan, penghasilan.

income tax *noun* pajak penghasilan.

inconvenient *adjective* tidak menyenangkan, menyusahkan.

increase *noun (in price, for example)* kenaikan, pertambahan.
verb **1** menambah; **to increase speed** menambah kecepatan; **2** menaikkan; **to increase the salary** menaikkan gaji; **to increase the price** menaikkan harga.

incredible *adjective* luar biasa, tak dapat dipercaya, tak masuk akal.

incredibly *adverb (very)* betul-betul; **the film's incredibly boring** film itu betul-betul membosankan.

indeed *adverb* **1** *(to emphasize)* memang, sungguh; **she's very pleased indeed** dia memang senang; **I'm very tired indeed** saya sungguh-sungguh lelah; **2** *(certainly)* **'can you hear his radio?' – 'indeed I can!'** 'apakah Anda dapat mendengar radionya?' – 'tentu saja'.

a b c d e f g h i j k l m n o p q r s t u v w x y z

indefinite adjective *adjective* tak tentu.

indefinite article *noun (in grammar)* kata sandang tak tentu.

independence *noun* kebebasan, kemerdekaan.

independent *adjective* 1 mandiri; **an independent person** orang yang mandiri; 2 merdeka; **an independent state** negeri yang merdeka.

index *noun* daftar kata, indeks.

India *noun* India.

Indian *noun* Indian *(American)*; orang India *(from India)*. *adjective* India.

indicate *verb* menunjukkan.

indication *noun* indikasi, petunjuk, tanda.

indigestion *noun* sakit pencernaan; **to have indigestion** sakit maag, sakit pencernaan.

individual *noun* individu, perseorangan. *adjective (a serving or a contribution, for example)* perseorangan; **individual tuition fee** biaya kuliah perorangan.

indoor *adjective* di dalam rumah atau gedung; **an indoor swimming pool** kolam renang tertutup.

indoors *adverb* di dalam; **it's cooler indoors** lebih sejuk di dalam (rumah).

industrial *adjective* berhubungan dengan industri.

industrial estate *noun* daerah industri.

industry *noun* industri, kerajinan; **the advertising industry** industri periklanan.

inefficient *adjective* tidak berdayaguna, tidak efisien.

inevitable *adjective* mau tak mau, tidak dapat dielakkan, tidak dapat dihindarkan.

inevitably *adverb* yang tidak terelakkan.

inexperienced *adjective* kurang berpengalaman.

infant *noun* bayi.

infant school *noun* taman kanak-kanak.

infected *adjective* kejangkitan, ketularan.

infection *noun* infeksi; **an eye infection** infeksi mata; **a throat infection** infeksi tenggorokan.

infectious *adjective* menular; **an infectious disease** penyakit menular.

infinitive *noun* infinitif; **in the infinitive** dalam bentuk infinitif.

(in)flammable *adjective* mudah terbakar.

inflatable *adjective (a mattress or a boat)* yang dapat ditiup; **inflatable life jacket** jaket pengaman yang dapat ditiup.

inflate *verb (a mattress or a boat)* memompa, meniup.

inflation *noun* inflasi.

influence *noun* pengaruh; **Terri is a good influence on the other girls** Terri berpengaruh yang baik atas anak perempuan lain. *verb* mempengaruhi.

inform *verb* **1** memberitahu; **they informed us that there was a problem** mereka memberitahu kami bahwa ada masalah; **2 to inform on** melaporkan.

informal *adjective* informal, tak resmi *(a meal or event, for example)*, **an informal expression** ungkapan informal.

information *noun* informasi, keterangan; **I need some information about flights to Manado** saya perlu keterangan tentang penerbangan ke Manado; **a piece of information** sedikit informasi.

information desk, information office *noun* bagian penerangan, kantor penerangan.

information technology, IT *noun* teknologi informasi.

infuriating *adjective* membuat marah, menggusarkan.

ingredient *noun* bahan, bumbu.

inhabitant *noun* penduduk.

initials *plural noun* paraf; **put your initials here** silakan memaraf di sini.

initiative *noun* inisiatif, prakarsa.

injection *noun* injeksi, suntikan; **to give a patient an injection** menyuntik pasien.

injure *verb* melukai.

injured *adjective* mendapat luka, terluka.

injury *noun* luka; **injuries** luka-luka.

ink *noun* tinta.

in-laws *plural noun* anggota kerabat suami atau isteri.

inner *adjective* bagian dalam, sebelah dalam.

innocent *adjective* suci, tak berdosa, tidak bersalah.

insane *adjective* gila, sakit ingatan.

inscription *noun* inskripsi, prasasti.

a b c d e f g h i j k l m n o p q r s t u v w x y z

insect *noun* serangga; **an insect bite** gigitan serangga.

insect repellent *noun* obat pengusir serangga.

inside *noun* bagian dalam; **the inside of the oven** bagian dalam oven.
preposition di dalam; **inside the classroom** di dalam ruang kelas.
adverb di dalam, ke dalam; **Mum's inside, I think** saya kira Ibu ada di dalam; **to go inside** masuk ke dalam.

inside out *adjective* terbalik.

insincere *adjective* bermuka dua, tidak jujur, tidak tulus.

insist *verb* **1 to insist on** bersikeras, mendesak; **he insisted on paying** dia bersikeras untuk membayar; **2 to insist that** tetap berkata bahwa, tetap berpendapat bahwa; **Didin insisted that I was wrong** Didin tetap berpendapat bahwa saya yang salah.

insomnia *noun* insomnia, tak bisa tidur.

inspector *noun* inspektur, pemeriksa, penyelidik.

install *verb* memasang.

installation *noun* pemasangan.

instalment *noun* cicilan, angsuran.

instance *noun* misal, contoh; **for instance** misalnya, umpamanya.

instant *noun* **1** segera; **come here this instant** datanglah segera ke sini; **2** seketika *(immediate)* **an instant success** sukses seketika; **3 instant coffee** kopi instan.

instantly *adverb* dengan segera.

instead *adverb* **1** sebagai pengganti; **Dadang couldn't go, so he sent his sister instead** Dadang tidak bisa pergi, jadi dia menyuruh kakaknya pergi sebagai pengganti; **2 instead of** bukan, daripada; **instead of pudding we had cheese** kami makan keju, bukan puding; **instead of playing tennis we went to the beach** kami ke pantai, tidak main tenis; **let's go for a walk instead** mari kita jalan-jalan saja.

instinct *noun* naluri.

institute, institution *noun* institut, lembaga.

instruct *verb* **1** melatih, mengajar; **Henry instructed Fermi how to play golf** Henry melatih Fermi bermain golf; **Ratna instructed Miranda in playing piano** Ratna mengajar Miranda bermain piano; **2** memberi perintah, menginstruksikan; **the teacher instructed the children to stay together** guru itu memerintahkan murid-muridnya supaya tidak berpencar.

instructions *plural noun* **1** instruksi, perintah; **2** petunjuk; **read the instructions carefully** bacalah petunjuk itu dengan teliti; **'instructions for use'** 'petunjuk pemakaian.

instructor *noun* instruktur, pelatih; **the archery instructor** pelatih panahan.

instrument *noun* alat, instrumen; **to play an instrument** main alat musik.

insulin *noun* insulin.

insult *noun* penghinaan. *verb* menghina.

insurance *noun* asuransi; **travel insurance** asuransi perjalanan.

intelligence *noun* inteligensi, kecerdasan.

intelligent *adjective* cerdas, pandai.

intend *verb* berkehendak, bermaksud; **as I intended** seperti yang saya maksudkan; **to intend to do** bermaksud untuk; **we intend to spend the night in Cirebon** kami bermaksud menginap di Cirebon.

intensive *noun* intensif; **in intensive care** di bagian perawatan intensif; **intensive care unit** unit perawatan intensif.

intention *noun* maksud; **I have no intention of paying** saya tidak ada maksud untuk membayar.

interest *noun* **1** menarik perhatian; **Sports don't interest them** olahraga tidak menarik perhatian mereka; **2** *(hobby)* kegemaran*;* **what are your interests?** apa kegemaran Anda?; **3 to have an interest in** berminat dalam, berminat pada; **he has an interest in jazz** dia berminat pada jazz; **4** *(finance)* bunga*;* **15 per cent interest** bunga lima belas persen. *verb* menarik perhatian; **that doesn't interest me** itu tidak menarik perhatian saya.

interested *adjective* **to be interested in** tertarik; **Nugroho's very interested in all kinds of insects** Nugroho tertarik pada segala macam serangga.

interesting *adjective* menarik.

a b c d e f g h i j k l m n o p q r s t u v w x y z

a b c d e f g h i j k l m n o p q r s t u v w x y z

interfere *verb* **1 to interfere with** *(to fiddle with it)* utak-atik; **don't interfere with the computer** jangan utak-atik komputer itu; **2 to interfere in** *(someone else's affairs)* campur tangan, turut campur.

interior design *noun* seni interior.

international *adjective* antarbangsa, internasional.

internet *noun* internet.

interpret *verb* **1** *(act as an interpreter)* menerjemahkan; **2** *(a sign or remark)* menafsirkan; menginterpretasikan.

interpreter *noun* juru bahasa, penafsir.

interrupt *verb* menginterupsi, mengganggu, menyelang, merintangi.

interruption *noun* interupsi, gangguan.

intersection *noun (of a road or street)* persimpangan.

interval *noun (in a play or concert)* selingan.

interview *noun* wawancara; **a job interview** wawancara pekerjaan.
verb (on TV, radio) menginterpiu, mengadakan wawancara dengan, mewawancarai.

interviewer *noun* penginterpiu, pewawancara.

into *preposition* **1** ke dalam **he's gone into the bank** dia masuk ke dalam bank; **2** ke; **to go into town** ke kota; **Irwan's gone into the office** Irwan pergi ke kantornya; **to get into bed** naik ke tempat tidur; **3** menjadi **to grow into a man** tumbuh menjadi seorang (lelaki) dewasa; **4 to be into football** *(informal)* menggemari sepak bola; **to change dollars into Rupiah** menukar dolar dengan rupiah.

introduce *verb* memperkenalkan; **she introduced me to her father** dia memperkenalkan saya kepada bapaknya; **can I introduce you to my fiancée?** bolehkah saya memperkenalkan Anda kepada tunangan saya?

introduction *noun (in a book)* kata pendahuluan, kata pengantar, prakata.

intruder *noun (in affairs)* pengganggu.

intuition *noun* bisikan kalbu, kata hati, intuisi.

invade *verb* menyerbu.

invalid[1] *noun* penderita cacad.

invalid[2] *adjective* tidak berlaku, tidak sah.

invent *verb* menciptakan, menemukan.

invention *noun* ciptaan, penemuan.

inventor *noun* pencipta, penemu.

inverted commas *plural noun* tanda kutip, tanda petik; **in inverted commas** di antara tanda kutip.

invest *verb* *(money, capital)* menanam modal, menginvestasikan.

investigation *noun* investigasi, pemeriksaan; **an investigation into the incident** pemeriksaan terhadap insiden tersebut.

investment *noun* investasi, penanaman modal.

invisible *adjective* gaib, tak kelihatan.

invitation *noun* undangan; **an invitation to dinner** undangan untuk makan malam.

invite *verb* mengundang; **Mahdi's invited me to his wedding** Mahdi mengundang saya ke pesta perkawinannya.

inviting *adjective* yang menarik.

involve *verb* **1** membutuhkan, memerlukan; **that project will involve a lot of work** proyek itu akan memerlukan banyak pekerjaan; **2** melibatkan; **the play will involve everybody** sandiwara itu akan melibatkan semua orang; **two cars were involved in the accident** dua mobil terlibat dalam kecelakaan itu.

involvement *noun* keterlibatan.

Iran *noun* Iran.

Iraq *noun* Irak.

irate *adjective* sangat marah.

Ireland *noun* Irlandia.

iron *noun* **1** *(for clothes)* setrika; **2** *(the metal)* besi. *verb* menyetrika.

ironing *noun* setrikaan; **to do the ironing** menyetrika.

ironing board *noun* papan setrika.

irregular *adjective* tidak beres, tidak teratur; **irregular verb** kata kerja tak beraturan.

irrelevant *adjective* tidak berhubungan, tidak bertalian, tidak relevan.

irritable *adjective* kesal, (suka) lekas marah.

irritate *verb* **1** mengganggu, menjengkelkan; **2** *(eyes, skin)* memedihkan.

a b c d e f g h i j k l m n o p q r s t u v w x y z

irritating *adjective* memedihkan, mengganggu, menyengkelkan; **irritating to the eyes** memedihkan mata; **his behaviour is very irritating** kelakuannya sangat menjengkelkan.

Islam *noun* Islam.

Islamic *adjective* yang berhubungan dengan Islam.

island *noun* pulau.

Israel *noun* Israel.

Israeli *noun* orang Israel.
adjective Israel.

issue *noun* **1** *(something you discuss)* isu, persoalan; **a political issue** isu politik, persoalan politik; **2** *(of a magazine)* nomor, terbitan.
verb **1** *(hand out)* membagikan, memberikan; **2** *(magazines, stamps, etc.)* mengeluarkan.

it *pronoun* **1** itu, –nya; **it's my dog** itu anjing saya; **'who is it?' 'it's me'** 'siapa (itu)?' – 'saya'; **I can't find it** saya tidak dapat menemukannya; **2** *(not translated)* **'where is my book? – 'it's under the bed'** 'di mana buku saya?' – 'di bawah tempat tidur'; **yes, it's true** ya, benar; **it doesn't matter** tidak apa-apa; **what is it?** ada apa?; **it's raining** sedang hujan; **it's a nice day** hari cerah sekali; **it's two o'clock** jam dua.

IT [information technology] *abbreviation, noun* teknologi informasi.

Italian *noun* **1** *(the language)* bahasa Italia; **2** *(person)* orang Italia.
adjective Italia.

italic *noun* huruf miring.

Italy *noun* Italia.

itch *verb* gatal; **my foot is itching** kaki saya gatal; **this wool sweater itches** baju wol ini menggatalkan badan.

item *noun* **1** artikel, barang, pokok; **2** *(news)* berita.

its *determiner* itu, –nya, kepunyaan; **the dog has lost its collar** ban leher anjing itu hilang.

itself *pronoun* **1** sendiri(an), dirinya **the government itself denies the rumours** pemerintah sendiri menyangkal desas-desus itu; **2 he left the dog by itself** anjing itu ditinggalkan sendirian; **the cat's licking itself** kucing itu menjilati badannya sendiri.

ivory *noun* gading; **ivory tusk** taring gading.

J j

jack *noun* **1** *(in cards)* jack; **2** *(for a car)* dongkerak.

jacket *noun* jaket, jas.

jacket potato *noun* kentang bakar yang tidak dikupas.

jackfruit *noun* (buah) nangka.

jackpot *noun* jackpot.

jail *noun* bui, kurungan (*colloquial*), penjara.
verb membui (*colloquial*), memenjarakan, mengurung dalam penjara.

jam *noun* **1** *(that you eat)* sele; **2** kemacetan; **a traffic jam** kemacetan (lalu lintas).

jammed *adjective* macet.

January *noun* bulan Januari.

Japan *noun* Jepang, negeri Sakura.

Japanese *noun* **1** *(the language)* bahasa Jepang; **2** *(the people)* orang Jepang; **the Japanese** bangsa Jepang.
adjective Jepang.

jar *noun* **1** *(small)* botol; **a jar of jam** sebotol sele; **2** *(larger)* kendi, guci.

jasmine *noun* bunga melati, jasmin.

Java *noun* (pulau) Jawa.

Javanese *noun* **1** *(language)* bahasa Jawa; **2** *(person)* orang Jawa.
adjective Jawa.

javelin *noun* lembing, tombak.

jaw *noun* rahang.

jazz *noun* jazz.

jealous *adjective* cemburu, iri hati.

jeans *noun* jeans, jins; **a pair of jeans** celana jeans.

jelly *noun* agar-agar *(jelly made with gelatin is not normally eaten in Indonesia)*

jellyfish *noun* ubur-ubur.

jersey *noun* **1** *(a pullover)* baju kaos; **2** *(for football)* baju kaos pemain sepak bola.

Jesus *noun* **Jesus Christ** Nabi Isa *(Islam)*, Tuhan Yesus, Yesus Kristus *(Christianity)*.

jet *noun* pesawat jet.

jet lag *noun* senjang jet.

jetty *noun* dermaga.

Jew *noun* orang Yahudi.

jewel *noun* (batu) permata

jeweller *noun* tukang emas.

jeweller's *noun* toko emas.

jewellery *noun* barang-barang perhiasan.

a b c d e f g h i j k l m n o p q r s t u v w x y z

a b c d e f g h i j k l m n o p q r s t u v w x y z

Jewish *adjective* Yahudi.

jigsaw *noun* teka-teki menyusun potongan-potongan gambar.

job *noun* **1** *(paid work)* pekerjaan; **what's your job?** apa pekerjaan Anda?; **a job offer** tawaran pekerjaan; **out of a job** tunakarya; **2** *(a task)* tugas; **it's not an easy job** tugas ini tidak gampang.

jobless *adjective* menganggur, tunakarya.

jockey *noun* joki.

jog *verb* joging.

join *verb* **1** *(become a member of)* menjadi anggota; **I've joined the judo club** saya menjadi anggota pekumpulan judo; **2** *(to meet up with)* ikut, menyusul; **I'll join you later** nanti saya menyusul; **won't you join the game?** ayo ikut main, mari ikut main; **3** *(things together)* menyambung.

- **to join in** ikut serta; **Herman never joins in** Herman tidak pernah ikut serta.

joiner *noun* pembuat mebel.

joint *noun* **1** *(of meat)* potongan daging; **2** *(in your body)* tulang sendi.

joke *noun* *(a funny story)* gurauan, kelakar, lelucon; **to tell a joke** menceritakan lelucon.

joking *noun* bergurau, berkelakar; **you must be joking!** Anda hanya berkelakar saja!; **I was only joking** saya hanya bergurau saja.

Jordan *noun* Yordania.

journalism *noun* jurnalisme, kewartawanan.

journalist *noun* jurnalis, wartawan *(male)*, wartawati *(female)*.

journey *noun* perjalanan; **our journey to Timika** perjalanan kita ke Timika.

joy *noun* kegembiraan.

joystick *noun* *(for computer games)* joystick.

judge *noun* hakim.
verb **1** *(a time or distance)* menduga, menaksir; **2** *(legal)* menghakimi.

judgement *noun* **1** *(estimation)* penaksiran; **2** *(opinion)* pendapat.

judgment *noun* *(legal)* keputusan, penghakiman.

judo *noun* yudo; **do judo** bermain yudo.

jug *noun* kendi.

juice *noun* air buah, jus, sari buah.

juicy *adjective* yang mengandung banyak air.

July *noun* (bulan) Juli.

jumble sale *noun* obral bermacam-macam barang bekas.

jumbo jet *noun* jet jumbo.

jump *noun* **1** lompatan, loncatan; **high jump** loncat tinggi; **broad jump** lompat jauh; **2 a parachute jump** terjun payung.
verb melompat, meloncat.

jumper *noun* **1** *(clothing)* baju hangat, sweater; **2** *(person)* pelompat.

June *noun* (bulan) Juni.

jungle *noun* hutan rimba.

junior *adjective* muda, yunior; **the juniors** yang muda, kaum muda; **a junior tennis match** pertandingan tenis yunior; **a junior school** sekolah dasar.

junk *noun* barang-barang loakan, barang-barang rombengan.

junk food *noun* makanan yang kurang sehat.

junk shop *noun* toko loak.

jury *noun* (dewan) juri.

just[1] *adjective* **1** hanya; **just after evening prayer** hanya beberapa saat sesudah magrib; **just for fun** hanya berkelakar saja; **2** baru saja; **to have just done** baru saja mengerjakan; **Subagio has just called** Subagio baru saja menelepon; **3** sedang **to be just doing** sedang melakukan; **Wibowo's just finishing the inspection** Wibowo sedang menyelesaikan pemeriksaan itu; **4** *(only)* masih; **he's just a child** dia masih kecil; **5** tepat; **just in time** tepat pada waktunya; **6 just coming!** saya datang!; **just sit down!** silakan duduk!; **just be quiet** diam saja!

just[2] *adjective* *(fair)* adil.

justice *noun* **1** *(fairness)* keadilan; **2** *(system)* kehakiman.

justify *verb* membenarkan.

K k

kangaroo *noun* kangguru.

karaoke *noun* karaoke.

karate *noun* karate.

kebab *noun* kebab, sate.

keen *adjective* **1** *(enthusiastic)* antusias, tertarik; **he doesn't look too keen** kelihatannya dia tidak begitu antusias; **she's not keen on camping** dia kurang tertarik untuk

a b c d e f g h i j k l m n o p q r s t u v w x y z

berkemah; **2** *(committed)* andal, tekun; **she's a keen photographer** dia juru potret yang andal; **Herman is a keen worker** Herman pekerja yang tekun; **3** suka; **I'm not keen on fish** saya kurang suka ikan

keep *verb* **1** menyimpan; **you kept the letter** Anda simpan surat itu; **to keep a secret** menyimpan rahasia; **where do you keep the coffee mugs?** di mana cangkir kopi disimpan?; **2 to keep somebody waiting** membuat orang menunggu; **3 will you keep my seat?** tolong jaga tempat duduk saya; **they kept her in hospital overnight** dia diharuskan bermalam di rumah sakit; **they kept him in jail overnight** dia dipenjara semalam; **4 to keep on doing** terus-menerus melakukan; **don't keep on talking** jangan mengobrol terus-menerus; **keep straight on** terus (saja); **5 keep calm!** tenang saja!; **6 to keep a promise** menepati janji.

kennel *noun* **1** *(for one dog)* kandang (anjing); **2** *(for boarding)* **kennels** tempat penitipan untuk anjing atau kucing.

kerb *noun* pinggir jalan.

kettle *noun* ceret, ketel; **to put the kettle on** masak air untuk teh atau kopi.

key *noun* **1** *(for a lock)* kunci; **a bunch of keys** seikat kunci; **answer key** kunci jawaban; **2** *(on a keyboard or typewriter)* tombol jari; **3** *(on a piano)* tuts piano.

keyboard *noun* keyboard.

key-ring *noun* gantungan kunci.

kick *noun* **1** *(from a person or horse)* tendangan; **Jerry gave the dog a kick** Jerry menendang anjing itu; **2** *(in football)* sepakan; **3 to get a kick out of doing** untuk iseng-iseng saja.
verb menendang, menyepak; **Peter kicked the pickpocket** Peter menyepak tukang copet itu; **to kick the ball** menendang bola.
- **to kick off** memulai.

kick-off *noun* pembukaan, permulaan.

kid *noun* **1** *(human)* anak; **2** *(goat)* anak kambing.

kidnap *verb* menculik.

kidnapper *noun* penculik.

kidney *noun* ginjal.

kidney bean *noun* kacang merah.

kill *verb* **1** *(accidentally)* mati, tewas; **she was killed in an**

accident dia tewas dalam kecelakaan; **2** *(deliberately)* membunuh.

killer *noun* *(murderer)* pembunuh.

kilo *noun* kilo, kilogram; **a kilo of rice** satu kilo beras.

kilogram *noun* kilo, kilogram.

kilometre *noun* kilo, kilometer.

kilt *noun* pakaian nasional berupa rok pendek yang dipakai laki-laki Scotlandia.

kind *noun* macam; **all kinds of people** segala macam orang. *adjective* baik, baik hati; **Wiranto was very kind to me** Wiranto baik kepada saya.

kindness *noun* kebaikan (hati).

king *noun* raja; **King George** Raja George; **the king of spades** raja sekop.

kingdom *noun* **1** kerajaan; **2** dunia; **the animal kingdom** dunia hewan.

kiosk *noun* **1** *(for newspapers or snacks)* kios; **2** *(for a phone)* wartel (warung telepon).

kiss *noun* ciuman; **to give a person a kiss** mencium orang. *verb* mencium; **kiss me!** ciumlah saya!; **we kissed each other** kami berciuman.

kit *noun* **1** *(of tools)* kotak; **a tool kit** kotak alat-alat; **2** *(clothes)* pakaian; **where's my football kit?** di mana pakaian sepak bola saya?; **3** *(for making a model, piece of furniture)* perlengkapan untuk membuat sesuatu.

kitchen *noun* dapur.

kitchen foil *noun* kertas aluminium.

kitchen garden *noun* apotik hidup, kebun sayuran.

kite *noun* layang-layang; **to fly a kite** bermain layang-layang.

kitten *noun* anak kucing.

kiwi fruit *noun* buah kiwi.

knee *noun* dengkul, lutut; **on (your) hands and knees** dalam posisi merangkak.

kneel *verb* berlutut.

knickers *plural noun* celana dalam.

knife *noun* pisau.

knight *noun* *(in chess)* kuda.

knit *verb* merajut.

knob *noun* kenop, tombol.

knock *noun* **1** pukulan; **a knock on the head** pukulan di kepala; **2** ketukan; **a knock at the door** ketukan di pintu. *verb* **1** *(to bang)* menabrak; **I knocked my elbow on the doorframe** siku saya tertabrak kosen pintu; **2** mengetuk; **to knock on the door** mengetuk pintu.

- **to knock down 1** *(in a traffic accident)* menabrak *(a person)*; **2** *(to demolish)* membongkar, meruntuhkan *(a building)*.
- **to knock out 1** *(to make unconscious)* mengK-O, merobohkan; **2** *(in sport, to eliminate)* mengalahkan.

knot *noun* simpul; **to tie a knot in a rope** membuat simpul pada tali.

know *verb* **1** tahu; **I know they've left the country** saya tahu mereka sudah keluar negeri; **yes, I know** ya, saya tahu; **you never know!** siapa tahu!; **2** *(be personally acquainted with)* kenal; *(a person)* **do you know Tasem?** apakah Anda kenal Tasem?; **I don't know his sister** saya tidak kenal adiknya; **3 to know how to, to know about** bisa, dapat, mengerti, tahu bagaimana *(machines, cooking, etc.)*; **Yati knows how to make gado-gado** Yati tahu bagaimana membuat gado-gado; **I know how to mend it** saya dapat memperbaikinya; **Syafrie knows about computers** Syafrie mengerti tentang komputer; **4 to know by heart** hafal.

knowledge *noun* pengetahuan.

Koran *noun* Kuran, Kur'an, Qur'an.

kosher *adjective* halal.

kris *noun* keris.

L l

lab *noun* laboratorium.

label *noun* label.

laboratory *noun* laboratorium.

labour *noun* buruh; **to vote for the Labour Party** memilih Partai Buruh.

lace *noun* **1** *(for a shoe)* tali sepatu; **2** *(for curtains, for example)* renda.

lad *noun* anak laki-laki.

ladder *noun* *(for climbing)* tangga.

ladies *noun* *(lavatory)* WC, Wanita; **'Ladies'** *(on a sign)* 'Wanita'.

lady *noun* nyonya, perempuan, wanita; **ladies and gentlemen** Ibu-ibu dan Bapak-bapak (yang terhormat).

lager *noun* bir ringan.

laid-back *adjective* tenang.

lake *noun* danau, tasik, telaga; **Lake Toba** Danau Toba.

lamb *noun* anak domba; **a leg of lamb** paha anak domba.

lame *adjective* pincang; **he is lame** dia pincang.

lamp *noun* lampu.

lamppost *noun* tiang listrik.

lampshade *noun* kap lampu.

land *noun* **1** daratan; **I can see land** saya bisa melihat daratan; **2** *(property)* tanah; **a piece of land** sebidang tanah.
verb **1** *(plane, passenger)* mendarat, mendaratkan; **2** *(leave a ship)* mendarat.

landing *noun* **1** *(on the stairs)* landasan; **2** *(of a plane)* pendaratan; **3** *(from a boat)* tempat penyeberangan kapal.

landlady *noun* induk semang, nyonya rumah.

landlord *noun* tuan tanah.

landscape *noun* pemandangan alam.

lane *noun* **1** *(a passage or path)* gang, lorong; **2** *(of a motorway)* jalur, lajur.

language *noun* bahasa; **a foreign language** bahasa asing; **bad language** bahasa pasar *(grammatically incorrect)*, bahasa kasar *(socially inappropriate)*.

language lab *noun* laboratorium bahasa.

lap *noun* **1** *(your knees)* pangkuan; **on my lap** di pangkuan saya; **2** *(in races)* putaran.

laptop *noun* komputer laptop.

larder *noun* lemari makanan, ruang penyimpan makanan.

large *adjective* **1** besar; **a large house** rumah besar; **2** luas; **a large lake** danau yang luas; **3** banyak; **a large number** banyak.

laser *noun* laser.

last *adjective* **1** yang terakhir; **the last time** saat yang terakhir; **2** (yang) lalu; **last week** minggu lalu; **3 last night** kemarin malam, semalam, tadi malam.
adverb terakhir; **Rob arrived last** Rob yang terakhir tiba; **at last!** akhirnya!; **I last saw them in May** saya terakhir bertemu dengan mereka bulan Mei.
verb berlangsung; **the play lasted two hours** sandiwara itu berlangsung selama dua jam.

late *adjective, adverb* **1** terlambat; **we're late** kita terlambat; **they arrived late**

mereka tiba terlambat; **we were late for the film** kami terlambat menonton film; **the flight was an hour late** penerbangan itu terlambat satu jam; **too late!** terlambat!; **2** *(late in the day)* **we got up late** kami kesiangan bangun; **the chemist is open late** apotik buka sampai jauh malam.

lately *adverb* akhir-akhir ini, belakangan ini.

later *adverb* **1** nanti; **I'll explain later** nanti saya akan menerangkannya; **2** lagi *(literally again)* **see you later** sampai bertemu lagi, sampai jumpa, sampai ketemu lagi.

latest *adjective* **1** yang terakhir; **the latest news** kabar yang terakhir; **2 at the latest** paling lambat; **3** mutakhir, terbaru; **the latest fashion** mode yang mutakhir, mode yang terbaru.

Latin *noun* bahasa Latin.

laugh *noun* gelak, tertawa; **to do something for a laugh** ***(informal)*** berbuat untuk lucu-lucuan saja.
verb **1** tertawa; **everybody laughed** semua orang tertawa; **2 to laugh at** menertawakan; **I tried to explain but they laughed at me** saya mencoba menerangkan tetapi mereka menertawakan saya.

lavatory *noun* kamar kecil, WC.

law *noun* **1** *(as a concept)* hukum; **it's against the law** melanggar hukum; **2** *(subject of study)* ilmu hukum; **3** *(regulations)* undang-undang, peraturan; **it's better to obey the law** lebih baik mematuhi peraturan; **court of law** pengadilan.

lawn *noun* halaman rumput.

lawnmower *noun* mesin pemotong rumput.

lawyer *noun* advokad, ahli hukum, pengacara.

lay *verb* **1** *(put)* meletakkan; **she lay the card on the table** dia meletakkan kartu itu di atas meja; **2** *(spread out)* memasang; **we're having a new carpet laid** kami akan memasang karpet baru; **3** menutupi; **we laid newspaper on the garden so the weeds wouldn't grow** kami menutupi kebun dengan kertas koran supaya rumput liar tidak tumbuh.

lay-by *noun* barang yang dibayar secara mencicil dan tidak diambil sampai cicilannya lunas *(definition)*.

layer *noun* lapisan.

lazy *adjective* malas.

lead[1] *noun* **1** *(when you are ahead)* **to be in the lead** di depan; **we have a lead of three points** kami tiga angka di depan; **2** *(electric)* kabel; **3** *(for a dog)* rantai, tali pengikat; **walk the dog on a lead** menuntun anjing dengan tali pengikat.
adjective *(a role or a singer)* peranan penting.
verb **1** menuju; **this track leads to the sea** jalan ini menuju ke laut; **2** memimpin; **to lead the way** memimpin; **to lead the group** memimpin kelompok itu; **3 to lead to something** *(an accident or problems, for example)* menyebabkan akibat.

lead[2] *noun* **1** *(the metal)* timah; **2 lead pencil** pensil, potlot.

leader *noun* **1** *(of a group)* pemimpin; **2** *(as a hero)* tokoh; **3** *(in a race)* olahragawan yang terdepan.

lead-free petrol *noun* bensin bebas timah.

lead singer *noun* penyanyi utama.

leaf *noun* daun.

leaflet *noun* surat selebaran.

league *noun* liga, persatuan, persekutuan.

leak *noun* kebocoran; **a gas leak** kebocoran gas.

lean *verb* **1** bersandar; **to lean on your friend** bersandar pada kawan; **2** menyandarkan; **lean the ladder against the wall** menyandarkan tangga pada tembok; **3** keluar; **to lean out the window** mengeluarkan bagian badan dari jendela.

leap *verb* melompat.

leap year *noun* tahun kabisat.

learn *verb* belajar; **to learn Indonesian** belajar bahasa Indonesia; **to learn (how) to drive** belajar mengemudikan mobil, belajar menyetir mobil.

learner *noun* pelajar; **to be a fast learner** pelajar cerdas.

learner driver *noun* pelajar mengemudi.

least *adjective* **1** paling tidak; **I like strawberry flavour least** saya paling tidak suka rasa arbei; **2** paling sedikit; **Putri has the least money** uang Putri paling sedikit; **at least eighty people** delapan puluh orang paling sedikit; **3 at least** setidak-tidaknya; **at least you could have let me know** setidak-tidaknya Anda dapat memberitahu saya; **4 I haven't the least idea** saya sama sekali tidak tahu; **the least expensive** yang paling murah.

a b c d e f g h i j k l m n o p q r s t u v w x y z

leather *noun* kulit; **a leather jacket** jas kulit.

leave *noun* cuti; **three days' leave** cuti tiga hari.
verb **1** berangkat, pergi; **they're leaving next month** mereka akan berangkat bulan depan; **we left early** kami berangkat awal;
2 keluar, meninggalkan; **I left the office at five** saya meninggalkan kantor jam lima; **she left the cinema before the end of the film** dia keluar dari bioskop sebelum filmnya selesai;
3 meninggalkan; **let's just leave them behind** mari kita tinggalkan mereka;
4 membiarkan; **leave them!** biarkan mereka!; **leave them alone!** jangan ganggu mereka!; **5** *(by accident)* tertinggal, ketinggalan; **he left his briefcase on the train** tasnya tertinggal di kereta api; **6 be left** lagi, sisa, tersisa; **there's nothing left** tak ada lagi yang tersisa; **there isn't much rice left** tidak banyak nasi yang tersisa; **we have ten minutes left** sisa waktu sepuluh menit; **I don't have any money left** saya tidak punya uang lagi.

lecture *noun* **1** *(at university)* kuliah; **2** *(public)* ceramah.

lecturer *noun* dosen, penceramah.

leek *noun* bawang bakung.

left *noun* sebelah kiri; **on my left** di sebelah kiri saya; **turn left at the mosque** belok kiri di mesjid itu.
adjective kiri; **don't give or take anything with your left hand** jangan memberikan atau menerima apa pun dengan tangan kiri.

left-hand *adjective* kiri; **the left-hand side** sebelah kiri.

left-handed *adjective* kidal.

left luggage office *noun* kantor barang-barang yang tertinggal.

leftovers *plural noun* sisa makanan.

leg *noun* **1** kaki; **the left leg** kaki sebelah kiri; **to break your leg** patah kaki; **2** *(in cooking)* paha; **a chicken leg** paha ayam; **a leg of lamb** paha anak domba; **to pull somebody's leg** mempermainkan orang; **quit pulling my leg!** jangan mempermainkan saya!

legal *adjective* legal, menurut undang-undang, sah.

legend *noun* dongeng.

leggings *plural noun* leggings.

leisure *noun* waktu luang; **in my leisure time** pada waktu luang saya.

lemon *noun* jeruk lemon, sitrun.

lemonade *noun* limun.

lemongrass *noun* (daun) serai.

lemon juice *noun* air jeruk lemon.

lend *verb* meminjamkan; **I lent Sugianto my bike** saya meminjamkan sepeda saya kepada Sugianto; **will you lend it to me?** apakah Anda mau meminjamkan itu kepada saya?; **to lend a hand** membantu, menolong.

length *noun* panjang(nya).

lens *noun* lensa; **contact lenses** lensa kontak.

Lent *noun* waktu puasa umat Kristen.

lentil *noun* miju-miju.

Leo *noun* Leo; **are you Leo?** apakah bintang Anda Leo?

lesbian *noun* homoseks wanita, lesbi, lesbian.

less *pronoun, adjective, adverb* **1** lebih sedikit; **Rukmana eats less** Rukmana makan lebih sedikit; **2** kurang; **less interesting** kurang menarik; **3 less than** kurang dari; **less than three hours** kurang dari tiga jam; **less than a kilo** kurang dari sekilo.

lesson *noun (class)* pelajaran; **a history lesson** pelajaran sejarah; **that accident is a lesson for Helen** kecelakaan itu adalah suatu pelajaran bagi Helen.

let[1] *verb* **1** *(allow)* membiarkan; **the police let us through** polisi membiarkan kami lewat; **2** *(as a suggestion or a command)* mari; **let's go** mari kita pergi; **let's eat out** mari makan di luar; **let me see** *(show me)* mari saya lihat; **3** *(negative)* **don't let** jangan sampai; **don't let the fire go out** jangan sampai api itu mati; **4** *(better not)* sebaiknya; **let's not talk about it** sebaiknya kita tidak membicarakannya.

- **to let off 1** *(fireworks, a bomb)* meletuskan, meledakkan; **2** *(to excuse from)* membebaskan *(homework, for example)*.

let[2] *verb (to rent out)* dikontrakkan, menyewakan; **'house to let'** 'rumah untuk disewakan', 'rumah untuk dikontrakkan'.

letter *noun* **1** surat; **a letter for you from Mr Gontha** ada surat untuk Anda dari Pak Gontha; **2** huruf; **G is the letter after F** G adalah huruf sesudah F.

letter box *noun* kotak surat.

lettuce *noun* (daun) selada.

a b c d e f g h i j k **l** m n o p q r s t u v w x y z

leukaemia *noun* leukemia.

level *noun* tingkat; **at street level** lantai dasar.
adjective **1** *(a shelf or floor)* rata; **2** *(ground)* datar.

level crossing *noun* penyeberangan jalan kereta api.

lever *noun* tuas, ungkit.

liar *noun* pembohong, pendusta.

liberal *adjective* liberal; **the Liberal Democrats** kaum Liberal Demokrat.

Libra *noun* Libra.

librarian *noun* pustakawan *(male)*, pustakawati *(female)*.

library *noun* perpustakaan; **the public library** perpustakaan umum.

licence *noun* surat ijin; *(for driving or fishing)* **a driving licence** SIM (Surat Ijin Mengemudi).

lick *verb* menjilat.

lid *noun* penutup, tutup; **she took the lid off** dia membuka penutupnya.

lie *noun* bohong, dusta; **to tell a lie (or lies)** berbohong, berdusta.
verb **1** *(to be stretched out)* berbaring; **Sigit was lying on the bed** Sigit sedang berbaring di tempat tidur; **2** berada, terletak; **his sarong lay on the floor** sarungnya terletak di lantai; **let's go and lie down in the sun** mari kita berjemur; **3** *(not to tell the truth)* berbohong, berdusta.

lie-in *noun* **to have a lie-in** kesiangan.

life *noun* hidup, kehidupan; **all her life** seluruh hidupnya; **that's life!** begitulah kehidupan!

lifebelt *noun* baju pelampung, rompi pelampung.

lifeboat *noun* sekoci penyelamat.

life jacket *noun* baju penyelamat, rompi penyelamat.

lifestyle *noun* gaya hidup.

lift *noun* **1** lift, pengangkat; **don't take the lift if there's a fire** jangan gunakan lift waktu kebakaran; **2** *(a ride)* mengantar, menumpang; **Judy gave Nurul a lift to the airport** Nurul menumpang dengan Judy ke bandara.
verb mengangkat; **he lifted the box** dia mengangkat dos itu.

light *noun* **1** lampu; **will you turn your light on?** tolong nyalakan lampu Anda; **to turn off the light** mematikan lampu; **streetlights** lampu

jalan; **headlights** lampu depan mobil; **are your lights on?** apakah lampunya sudah menyala?; **indicator** *(on a machine)* lampu penunjuk; **traffic lights** lampu lalu lintas; **the lights are green now** lampunya sudah hijau; **2 have you got a light?** ada korek api?
adjective **1** *(in colour)* muda; **light blue** biru muda; **2** *(not night)* terang; **it gets light at about five-thirty** hari sudah terang sekitar jam setengah enam; **3** *(not heavy or strong)* ringan; **a light breeze** angin sepoi-sepoi.
verb menyalakan; **we lit a fire** kami menyalakan api; **it won't light** tidak mau menyala.

lighter *noun* geretan, pemantik api.

lighthouse *noun* mercu suar.

lightning *noun* halilintar, kilat; **a flash of lightning** sinar kilat; **to be struck by lightning** disambar kilat, disambar geledek.

light switch *noun* tombol lampu.

like[1] *preposition, conjunction* seperti; **like a duck** seperti itik; **like I said** seperti saya katakan; **Bambang looks like his father** Bambang mirip ayahnya; **what's the weather like?** bagaimana keadaan cuaca?; **like this** begini.

like[2] *verb* **1** suka; **I don't like fish** saya tidak suka ikan; **Harjo likes eating** Harjo suka makan; **2** ingin, mau; **I would like to become an engineer** saya ingin menjadi insinyur; **would you like a coffee?** maukah Anda minum kopi?; **what would you like to eat?** mau makan apa?; **yes, if you like** ya, kalau Anda mau.

likely *adjective* mungkin; **it's not very likely** mungkin tidak; **she's likely to phone soon** mungkin dia akan menelepon sebentar lagi.

lily *noun* bunga bakung, teratai.

lime *noun* jeruk nipis, jeruk limau.

limit *noun* batas; **the speed limit** batas kecepatan.

limp *noun* pincang; **to have a limp** (berjalan) pincang.

line *noun* **1** garis; **a straight line** garis lurus; **to draw a line** membuat garis; **2 a railway line** jalan kereta api; **3** *(a queue of people or cars)* barisan; **to stand in line** antri, berbaris; **six lines of poetry** enam baris puisi; **4** *(telephone)* saluran; **the line's bad** salurannya buruk;

a b c d e f g h i j k l m n o p q r s t u v w x y z

hold the line, please harap tunggu sebentar; **5** tali; **a fishing line** tali pancing.
verb (a coat) melapisi.

linen *noun* kain lena, linen; **a linen skirt** rok linen.

lining *noun* lapisan.

link *noun* hubungan, kaitan; **what's the link between the two?** apa kaitan antara mereka berdua?
verb (two places) menghubungkan; **the towns are linked by a railway line** kota-kota itu dihubungkan dengan jalan kereta api.

lion *noun* singa.

lip *noun* bibir.

lip-read *verb* memahami kata-kata hanya dengan memandang bibir.

lipstick *noun* cat pemerah bibir, gincu, lipstik.

liquid *adjective, noun* cairan.

list *noun* daftar.

listen *verb* **1 to listen to** mendengarkan; **to listen to music** mendengarkan musik; **listen to him!** dengarkan dia!; **2 you're not listening to me** Anda tidak memperhatikan saya; **I wasn't listening** tadi saya tidak memperhatikan.

listener *noun (to the radio)* pemiarsah, pendengar.

literally *adverb* (secara) harfiah.

literature *noun* kesusasteraan.

litre *noun* liter; **a litre of oil** seliter minyak.

litter *noun (rubbish)* sampah.

litter bin *noun* tempat sampah.

little *adjective, pronoun* **1** *(small)* kecil; **a little child** anak kecil; **2** *(not much)* sedikit; **they have little money** mereka miskin; **a little** sedikit; **we have a little money** kami mempunyai sedikit uang; **just a little, please** minta sedikit saja; **it's a little late** sedikit terlambat; **a little more** sedikit lagi; **a little less** kurang sedikit; **little by little** sedikit demi sedikit.

little finger *noun* kelingking.

live[1] *verb* **1** *(in a house or town)* menetap, tinggal; **Trihatmojo lives in Cirebon** Trihatmojo tinggal di Cirebon; **2** *(be or stay alive, spend one's life)* hidup; **civet cats live in several parts of Indonesia** musang terdapat di beberapa tempat di Indonesia; **those bats live on fruit** kelelawar itu hidup dengan makan buah-buahan.

live^2 *adjective* **1** *(a broadcast)* langsung; **a live broadcast from Surabaya** siaran langsung dari Surabaya; **2** *(alive)* yang hidup.

lively *adjective* *(a party or restaurant, for example)* meriah, ramai.

liver *noun* hati, lever, limpa.

living *noun* mata pencarian; **raising livestock is an important way of making a living for the Timorese** peternakan adalah mata pencarian yang penting untuk orang Timor; **to earn a living** mencari nafkah.

living room *noun* kamar tamu.

lizard *noun* cicak, kadal.

load *noun* **1** *(on a lorry)* muatan; **a (lorry-)load of bricks** muatan batu bata; **a bus-load of school children** sebuah bis penuh dengan anak-anak sekolah; **2** *(informal)* **loads of** banyak sekali; **loads of time** banyak sekali waktunya; **they've got loads of money** mereka banyak sekali uangnya.
verb memuati; **to load a lorry with sand** memuati truk dengan pasir; **a truck loaded with sand** sebuah truk yang dimuati pasir.

loaf *noun* **a loaf of bread** sebatang roti.

loan *noun* pinjaman.
verb meminjamkan. SEE **lend**.

loathe *verb* benci akan; **I loathe getting up early** saya benci bangun pagi-pagi.

lobster *noun* udang karang, udang laut.

local *noun* lokal, setempat; **the locals** penduduk setempat.
adjective **1** setempat; **the local library** perpustakaan setempat; **the local newspaper** koran setempat; **2** daerah; **local government** pemerintahan daerah, pemerintahan setempat; **3** *(telephone call)* telepon lokal.

lock *noun* **1** *(with a key)* kunci; **2** *(on a canal)* pintu air.
verb mengunci; **to lock the door** mengunci pintu; **the cupboard was locked** lemari itu dikunci.

locker *noun* lemari, locker.

locker room *noun* ruangan dengan lemari-lemari untuk menyimpan sesuatu *(definition)*.

lodger *noun* orang yang indekos, orang yang mondok *(colloquial)*, penyewa kamar.

loft *noun* loteng.

a b c d e f g h i j k l m n o p q r s t u v w x y z

log *noun* batang kayu; **a log fire** api yang dibuat dengan batang-batang kayu.

logical *adjective* logis.

London *noun* London.

lonely *adjective* sepi, sunyi; **to feel lonely** merasa kesepian.

long *adjective, adverb* **1** panjang; **a long lesson** pelajaran yang panjang; **a long day** hari yang panjang; **all night long** sepanjang malam; **fifty metres long** lima puluh meter panjangnya; **2** lama; **he stayed for a long time** dia lama di sini; **I haven't seen her for a long time** sudah lama saya tidak ketemu dengan dia; **it's an hour long** sejam lamanya; **this won't take long** ini tidak makan waktu lama; **how long?** berapa lama?; **how long have you been here?** sudah berapa lama Anda berada di sini?; **3** jauh; **it's a long way to the nearest swimming pool** jauh sekali ke kolam renang yang terdekat; **4 long ago** zaman dulu; **a long time ago** dahulu, waktu yang lampau; **5 as long as** selama; **stay as long as you like** silahkan menetap di sini selama Anda menghendakinya; **6** asalkan, asal saja, jikalau; **as long as you don't lose it** asalkan tidak hilang.
verb **1** ingin; **to long to start** ingin mulai; **2** rindu; **I'm longing for you all** saya rindu akan kalian semua.

long-distance call *noun* telepon interlokal.

longer *adverb* **1** lebih lama, lebih panjang; **2 no longer** tidak lagi; **I no longer have it** saya tidak lagi mempunyainya; **they no longer live here** mereka tidak bertempat tinggal di sini lagi; **that building isn't there any longer** gedung itu tidak ada di situ lagi.

long jump *noun* lompat jauh.

long-life milk *noun* susu tahan lama.

loo *noun* kakus, WC.

look *noun* **1** *(a glance)* **to have a look at something** melihat, menengok; **2** *(a tour)* melihat-lihat; **to have a look around the shops** melihat-lihat di toko-toko; **3 to have a look for** *(something lost)* mencari.
verb **1** melihat; **I wasn't looking** (tadi) saya tidak melihat; **Heri was looking at the photos** Heri sedang melihat foto-foto itu; **2** kelihatan; **Melanie looks pleased** Melanie kelihatan

senang; **the sate looks delicious** sate itu kelihatannya enak sekali; **3 to look like** menyerupai; **Purwanto looks like his father** Purwanto menyerupai bapaknya; **4** seperti; **what does the house look like?** rumahnya seperti apa?

- **to look after**
  1 memelihara; **they really look after their dog** mereka betul-betul memelihara anjingnya;
  2 menjaga; **the maid's looking after the baby** pembantu itu sedang menjaga bayi;
  3 *(arrangements or things)* mengurus.
- **to look for** mencari; **I'm looking for the keys** saya sedang mencari kuncinya.
- **to look forward to** *(a party or a trip, for example)* sangat mengharapkan.
- **to look out** *(to be careful)* berhati-hati; **look out, it's hot** awas, panas.
- **to look up** *(in a dictionary or directory)* mencari; **look up the word 'menyapu' in the dictionary** carilah kata 'menyapu' di kamus.

loose *adjective* **1** *(a screw or knot, a garment)* longgar; **2** *(a tooth)* goyah; **3 loose change** uang kecil, uang receh; **I'm at a loose end** tak ada pekerjaan tertentu yang harus saya kerjakan sekarang.

lorry *noun* truk.

lose *verb* **1** kalah; **we lost the match** regu kita kalah (dalam pertandingan); **2** kehilangan; **Sari's lost her bracelet** Sari kehilangan gelangnya; **3 to get lost** tersesat; **we got lost in the tea plantation** kami tersesat di perkebunan teh.

loss *noun* **1** *(financial)* kerugian **2** *(objects, power, etc.)* kehilangan.

lost *adjective* hilang.

lost property *noun* barang-barang hilang.

lot *noun* **1 a lot** banyak; **goats eat a lot** kambing makan banyak; **I spent a lot** saya membelanjakan banyak uang; **a lot of** banyak; **a lot of coffee** banyak kopi; **lots of people** banyak orang; **'what are you doing tonight?' – 'not a lot'** 'nanti malam Anda melakukan apa?' – 'tidak banyak'; **2 he's a lot better** dia jauh lebih baik.

lottery *noun* lotere, undian; **to win the lottery** menang lotere.

a b c d e f g h i j k l m n o p q r s t u v w x y z

a b c d e f g h i j k l m n o p q r s t u v w x y z

loud *adjective* **1** keras, riuh; **in a loud voice** dengan suara keras; **2 to say something out loud** mengatakan apa yang sedang dipikirkan.

loudly *adverb* dengan keras.

loudspeaker *noun* pengeras suara.

lounge *noun* **1** *(in a house or hotel)* kamar duduk, kamar tamu; **2** *(in an airport)* ruang; **the departure lounge** ruang keberangkatan.

love *noun* **1** asmara, cinta; **she's fallen in love with Sugianto** dia jatuh cinta dengan Sugianto; **they're in love with each other** mereka saling mencintai; **with love from Sadikin** salam manis dari Sadikin, salam mesra dari Sadikin; **2** *(in tennis)* nol, kosong.
verb **1** *(a person)* cinta; **I love you** aku cinta padamu; **2** *(food, sport, music, hobby)* gemar (akan); suka sekali; **she loves Cirebon** dia suka sekali Cirebon; **Ali loves seafood** Ali gemar akan makanan laut; **3** ingin sekali, senang sekali, suka akan; **I love staying at the Chedi** saya senang sekali menginap di Chedi; **I'd love to come with you** saya ingin sekali ikut Anda.

lovely *adjective* **1** *(to look at)* baik, menarik; **lovely earings** anting-anting yang indah; **their garden is lovely** kebun mereka bagus sekali; **a lovely hotel** hotel yang baik; **2** menyenangkan; **all the guests thought it was a lovely party** pesta itu menyenangkan semua tamu; **3** *(gift)* bagus, elok, indah; **all her gifts were lovely** semua hadiahnya indah.

low *adjective* **1** rendah; **a low table** meja yang rendah; **2** *(price)* murah; **at a low price** dengan harga murah; **3** *(voice)* rendah; **in a low voice** dengan suara kecil; **4** sedikit; **we're running low on cooking oil** minyak goreng kita tinggal sedikit.

lower *adjective* **1** *(not as high)* lebih rendah; **2 Lower House** Majelis Rendah.
verb menurunkan.

low-fat milk *noun* susu yang mengandung sedikit lemak.

luck *noun* keberuntungan, nasib, rezeki; **with a bit of luck** kalau beruntung; **good luck!** semoga sukses!; **bad luck!** sayang! sialan!

luckily *adverb* untung; **luckily for them** untunglah buat mereka.

lucky *adjective* mujur, untung; **to be lucky**

beruntung; **we were lucky** kami mujur; **it's supposed to be lucky** katanya ini membawa untung; **my lucky number** nomor keberuntungan saya, nomor mujur saya.

luggage *noun* bagasi, barang-barang, kopor-kopor; **my luggage is in the boot** kopor-kopor saya di bagasi.

lump *noun* bengkak, gumpal.

lunch *noun* makan siang; **to have lunch** makan siang; **we had lunch at Pondok Indah Mall** kami makan siang di Mal Pondok Indah.

lunch break *noun* istirahat makan siang.

lunch hour, lunch time *noun* waktu makan siang.

lung *noun* paru-paru.

luxurious *adjective* mewah.

luxury *noun* kemewahan.

lyrics *plural noun* lirik.

M m

macaroni *noun* makaroni; **we had macaroni cheese** kami makan makaroni dengan keju.

machine *noun* mesin, pesawat.

machinery *noun* mesin-mesin.

mackerel *noun* ikan bawal.

mad *adjective* **1** *(insane)* gila; **he's completely mad** dia betul-betul gila; **2** *(angry)* marah; **my mum will be mad!** ibu saya pasti akan marah!; **3** *(infatuated)* **to be mad about** gemar sekali akan; **she's mad about basketball** dia gemar sekali akan bola basket.

madam *noun* nyonya.

madman, madwoman *noun* orang gila.

madness *noun* kegilaan, penyakit gila.

magazine *noun* **1** gudang senjata; **2** *(for reading)* majalah.

maggot *noun* belatung, tempayak.

magic *noun* sihir, sulap. *adjective* **1 a magic spell** mantera; **2** *(great)* hebat sekali.

magician *noun* **1** *(wizard)* tukang sihir; **2** *(conjurer)* tukang sulap.

magnificent *adjective* bagus sekali, baik sekali, luar biasa.

a b c d e f g h i j k l m n o p q r s t u v w x y z

magnifying glass *noun* kaca pembesar, lensa pembesar, suryakanta.

mahogany *noun* (kayu) mahoni.

maiden name *noun* nama keluarga seorang wanita sebelum menikah *(definition only)*.

mail *noun* pos; **by mail** melalui pos; **e-mail** *(electronic mail)* e-mail.

mail order *noun* pesanan melalui pos; **a mail-order catalogue** daftar barang yang dapat dipesan melalui pos.

main *adjective* **1** pokok; **the main topic** topik pokok; **2** utama; **the main entrance** pintu masuk utama.

mainly *adverb* pokoknya, sebagian besar, terutama.

main road *noun* jalan raya, jalan utama.

maize *noun* jagung.

major *adjective* besar, utama.

majority *noun* golongan terbesar, kebanyakan, mayoritas, sebagian besar.

make *noun* mer(e)k; **what make is your bike?** apa merek sepeda Anda?
verb **1** membikin, membuat; **she makes me laugh** dia membuat saya tertawa; **he made me wait for him** dia membuat saya menunggunya; **the smell of onions frying makes me hungry** bau bawang goreng membuat saya lapar; **'made in Indonesia'** 'buatan Indonesia', 'dibuat di Indonesia'; **2** menjadi; **two and three make five** dua tambah tiga adalah lima, dua tambah tiga menjadi lima; **3 to make happy** menyenangkan; **4** *(money)* **he makes $40,000 a year** penghasilannya empat puluh ribu dolar setahun; **to make a living** mencari nafkah; **5** *(force)* menyuruh; **she made him take the dog back** dia menyuruhnya mengembalikan anjing itu; **6 to make a meal** memasak; **I've just made an omelette** saya baru saja memasak telur dadar; **7 to make a phone call** menelepon; **I have to make a few phone calls** saya harus menelepon beberapa orang; **8 I can't make it on Saturday** saya tidak dapat datang hari Sabtu; **9 to make a bed** merapikan tempat tidur.

- **to make up 1** mencari-cari; **he made up an excuse** dia mencari-cari alasan; **2** *(after a quarrel)* menjadi baik kembali, menjadi teman lagi; **they've made up after their quarrel** mereka berbaik kembali setelah pertengkaran mereka.

make-up *noun* rias.

male *adjective* **1** *(animal)* jantan; **a male rat** tikus jantan; **2** pria, laki-laki; **a male role** peran pria; **a male voice** suara laki-laki; **a male student** murid laki-laki.

male chauvinist *noun* seorang pria yang beranggapan bahwa pria lebih penting dari wanita *(definition only)*.

man *noun* orang laki-laki (lelaki).

manage verb **1** *(business, team)* melaksanakan, mengelola; **she manages a travel agency** dia mengelola suatu biro perjalanan; **2** *(cope)* mampu menangani; **I can manage** saya mampu menangani; **3 to manage to do** berhasil; **he managed to get the cat down** dia berhasil menurunkan kucing itu; **we didn't manage to get in touch with Handoko** kami tidak berhasil menghubungi Handoko.

management *noun* **1** manajemen, pengelolaan; **a management course** kursus manajemen; **2** direksi, pimpinan; **a meeting with management** rapat dengan direksi.

manager *noun* manajer, pengurus.

mandarin (orange) *noun* jeruk manis.

mango *noun* mangga.

mania *noun* kegemaran yang berlebihan, kegilaan, keranjingan, maniak.

maniac *noun* orang gila, maniak; **she drives like a maniac** dia mengendarai mobil seperti orang gila.

mankind *noun* umat manusia.

man-made *adjective* buatan manusia.

manner *noun* **1** cara; **manner of doing** cara melakukan; **2** kelakuan, sikap; **to have good manners** berkelakuan baik, tahu adat; **it's bad manners to talk like that** tak tahu adat berbicara begitu; **3 in a manner of speaking** boleh dikatakan.

manpower *noun* tenaga kerja.

mantelpiece *noun* rak di atas tungku.

manual *noun* buku pedoman.

manufacture *verb* membuat, manufaktur.

manure *noun* pupuk, rabuk.

a b c d e f g h i j k l **m** n o p q r s t u v w x y z

many *adjective, pronoun* banyak; **does she have many friends?** apakah dia mempunyai banyak teman?; **so many** banyak sekali, begitu banyak; **I have so many things to do!** banyak sekali yang harus saya kerjakan!; **I've never eaten so many mangos** belum pernah saya makan begitu banyak mangga; **take as many as you can** ambil sebanyak mungkin; **take as many as you like** ambil sebanyak Anda mau; **too many** terlalu banyak; **I've got too many things to do** terlalu banyak yang harus saya kerjakan; **there were too many people** ada terlalu banyak orang; **that's far too many!** itu terlalu banyak!; **how many?** berapa (banyak)?; **how many are there?** ada berapa?

map *noun* peta; **a road map** peta jalan.

marathon *noun* maraton.

marble *noun* **1** batu pualam, marmer; **a marble floor** lantai marmer; **2** gundu, kelereng; **to play marbles** main kelereng.

March¹ *noun* Maret; **the eleventh of March** tanggal sebelas Maret.

march² *noun* mars. *verb* **1** berjalan berbaris; **2** *(as a protest)* berunjuk rasa.

mare *noun* kuda betina.

margarine *noun* margarin.

margin *noun* garis tepi, marjin, pinggiran.

marijuana *noun* ganja.

mark *noun* **1** *(at school)* angka, nilai; **what mark did you get for biology?** Anda mendapat nilai berapa untuk biologi?; **2** *(stain, scar)* bekas, tanda. *verb* menilai; **the teacher marks our work** guru menilai pekerjaan kami.

market *noun* pasar.

marketing *noun* pemasaran.

marmalade *noun* marmelade, selai kulit jeruk.

maroon *adjective* merah tua, warna sawo matang; **a maroon sarong** sarung berwarna sawo matang.

marriage *noun* perkawinan, pernikahan.

married *adjective* kawin, menikah; **a married woman** wanita yang telah menikah, seorang isteri; **a married couple** sepasang suami-istri *(husband and wife)*; **they've been married for twenty years** mereka sudah menikah selama dua puluh tahun.

marry *verb* **1 marry off** mengawinkan, menikahkan; **Pak Budi married off his youngest daughter yesterday** Pak Budi mengawinkan putri bungsunya kemarin, Pak Budi menikahkan putri bungsunya kemarin; **2 to marry, to get married** kawin, nikah *(subject can be male or female)*; **they got married last year** mereka kawin tahun yang lalu, mereka menikah tahun yang lalu; **Susi married Rudi** Susi kawin dengan Rudi; **Rudi married Susi** Rudi menikah dengan Susi; **3** mengawini, menikahi *(subject must be male)*.

marvellous *adjective* bagus sekali; **the weather's marvellous** cuacanya bagus sekali.

mascara *noun* maskara.

masculine *noun* bersifat laki-laki, jantan, maskulin.

mash *verb* melumatkan, menumbuk.

mashed potatoes *plural noun* kentang pure.

mask *noun* kedok, topeng.

mass *noun* **1** massa, umum; **mass media** media massa; **a mass meeting** rapat raksasa, rapat umum; **2 masses of** banyak sekali, sejumlah besar; **they've got masses of money** mereka mempunyai banyak sekali uang; **there's masses left over** ada banyak sisanya; **3** *(religious)* misa; **to go to mass** mengikuti misa, pergi ke kebaktian (gereja).

massage *noun* pijat, urut.

massive *adjective* besar sekali, raksasa.

master *noun* ahli, pemilik, tuan, tuan rumah.

masterpiece *noun* karya agung.

mat *noun* **1** keset; **2** tikar; **3 a table mat** tatakan meja.

match *noun* **1** geretan, korek api; **a box of matches** satu dos korek api;
2 pertandingan; **a soccer match** pertandingan sepak bola.
verb sepadan dengan; **the jacket matches the skirt** warna jaket itu sepadan dengan roknya.

matching *adjective* cocok, selaras, sesuai; **the curtains and cushions do not match** gorden dan bantal kursinya tidak selaras.

mate *noun* kawan, teman; **I'm going out with my mates tonight** nanti malam saya akan keluar bersama teman-teman.

material *noun* **1** *(fabric)* kain; **2** *(substance)* bahan, materi;

a b c d e f g h i j k l m n o p q r s t u v w x y z

a b c d e f g h i j k l m n o p q r s t u v w x y z

raw materials bahan mentah.

mathematics *noun* ilmu pasti, matematika.

maths *noun* ilmu pasti, matematika; **Mahdi's good at maths** Mahdi pandai dalam matematika.

matter *noun* **1** hal, perkara, persoalan, soal; **look into the matter** memeriksa persoalan; **to be a matter of opinion** soal pendapat; **2 what's the matter?** ada apa (dengan Anda)?
verb **1** berarti; **it matters a lot to me** itu sangat berarti untuk saya; **2** penting; **the things that matter** segala sesuatu yang penting; **3 it doesn't matter** tidak apa-apa, tidak ada masalah; **you can write it in English or Indonesian, it doesn't matter** tidak ada masalah kalau ditulis dalam bahasa Inggris atau dalam bahasa Indonesia.

mattress *noun* kasur.

mature *adjective* **1** *(people)* dewasa; **2** *(fruit, vegetables)* masak, matang.

maximum *noun* maksimum.
adjective **1** maksimum, tertinggi; **the maximum speed** kecepatan tertinggi; **maximum profits** keuntungan maksimum; **2 the maximum penalty** hukuman seberat-beratnya.

May[1] *noun* bulan Mei.

may[2] *verb* **1** mungkin; **she may be ill** mungkin dia sakit; **we may go to Timika** kami mungkin akan ke Timika; **2** *(asking permission)* boleh; **may I close this door?** bolehkah saya menutup pintu ini?

maybe *adverb* barangkali, boleh jadi, mungkin; **maybe not** barangkali tidak, mungkin tidak; **maybe he's forgotten** barangkali dia lupa; **maybe they've got lost** boleh jadi mereka tersesat.

May Day *noun* Hari Buruh (dirayakan di beberapa negara).

mayonnaise *noun* mayones.

mayor *noun* walikota.

me *pronoun* **1** saya; **she knows me** dia kenal saya; **can you help me please?** dapatkah Anda membantu saya?; **she's older than me** dia lebih tua dari saya; *(often not translated)* **I took her with me** saya mengajaknya pergi; **can you let me have the car?** bolehkah saya meminjam mobil?; **can you give me your address?** bolehkah saya minta alamat Anda?; **excuse me!** maaf, permisi!; **2** *(used* *with intimate friends)* aku; **3** gue *(slang)*.

meal *noun* makanan.

mean *verb* **1** maksud; **what do you mean?** apa maksud Anda?; **that's not what I meant** itu bukan maksud saya; **2 to mean to do** bermaksud untuk; **I meant to phone my mother** saya bermaksud untuk menelepon ibu saya; **3** berarti; **what does that mean?** apa artinya?; **4 to be meant to do** seharusnya melakukan; **she was meant to be here at six** dia seharusnya tiba jam enam. *adjective* **1** *(with money)* kikir, pelit *(informal)*; **2** *(unkind)* jahat, nakal; **she's really mean to her little sister** dia memang jahat terhadap adik perempuannya; **what a mean thing to do!** (perbuatan) jahat sekali!

meaning *noun* arti, makna.

means *noun* alat, cara, jenis; **a means of transport** alat transportasi; **a means of doing** cara melakukan; **we have no means of contacting them** kami tidak tahu bagaimana caranya menghubungi mereka; **by means of** dengan memakai; **by all means** tentu saja.

meantime *adverb* sementara; **for the meantime** untuk sementara; **in the meantime** sementara itu.

measles *noun* cacar, penyakit campak.

measure *verb* mengukur.

measurements *plural noun* ukuran; **the measurements of the room** ukuran ruang(an); **my chest measurement** ukuran dada saya.

meat *noun* daging.

Mecca *noun* Mekah; **the whole village went to Mecca** seluruh penduduk desa itu pergi ke Mekah.

mechanic *noun* ahli mesin, montir; **he's a mechanic** dia seorang montir.

mechanical *adjective* dikerjakan dengan mesin; **mechanical engineering** teknik mesin.

medal *noun* bintang jasa, medali; **the gold medal** medali mas.

media *noun* media; **the mass media** media massa.

medical *noun* pemeriksaan badan, pemeriksaan medis. *adjective* yang berhubungan dengan pengobatan medis, kedokteran.

medicine *noun* **1** obat; **I'd like some cough medicine**

a b c d e f g h i j k l m n o p q r s t u v w x y z

saya minta obat batuk; **2** *(subject of study)* ilmu kedokteran; **she's studying medicine** dia sedang belajar ilmu kedokteran; **3** pengobatan; **alternative medicine** pengobatan alternatif.

Mediterranean *noun* **the Mediterranean** Lautan Tengah.

medium *adjective* medium, sedang.

medium-sized *adjective* medium, ukuran sedang.

meet *verb* **1** berjumpa dengan, bertemu dengan; **I met Suci outside the library** saya berjumpa dengan Suci di depan perpustakaan; **2** kenal; **Oscar, have you met Mira?** Oscar, apakah Anda sudah kenal Mira?; **3** *(from train, bus, etc.)* jemput; **will you meet me at the station?** tolong jemput saya di stasiun (kereta api).

meeting *noun* rapat; **there's a meeting at ten o'clock** ada rapat pada pukul sepuluh; **she's in a meeting** dia sedang rapat.

megabyte *noun* megabyte.

melody *noun* lagu, melodi.

melon *noun* melon, (buah) semangka.

melt *verb* **1** meleleh, mencair; **the ice-cream melted** es krim mencair; **2** mencairkan; **melt the butter in a saucepan** mencairkan mentega di dalam panci.

member *noun* anggota; **she's a member of the Labour Party** dia anggota Partai Buruh.

Member of Parliament *noun* anggota parlemen.

membership *noun* keanggotaan.

membership card *noun* kartu keanggotaan.

membership fee *noun* uang iuran.

memorial *noun* tanda peringatan; **a war memorial** tugu peringatan perang.

memorial service *noun* upacara peringatan.

memorize *verb* menghafalkan; **to memorize a poem** menghafalkan sebuah syair.

memory *noun* **1** *(of a person or information)* daya ingatan, ingatan; **you have a good memory** ingatan Anda baik sekali; **2** *(of the past)* kenangan; **I have good memories of my visit to Lombok** saya punya kenangan yang indah tentang kunjungan saya ke Lombok.

men *noun* orang lelaki; *(on a sign)* **'Men'** 'Pria'.

mend *verb* memperbaiki.

meningitis *noun* meningitis.

mental *adjective* **1** batin dan watak; **2** mental; **a mental illness** penyakit jiwa; **3 mental arithmetic** berhitung di kepala, mencongak.

mention *verb* berkata, menyebutkan.

menu *noun* daftar makanan, menu; **on the menu** dalam daftar makanan.

mercy *noun* ampun, belas kasihan.

meringue *noun* semacam kue yang manis (*definition only*).

merit *noun* faedah, jasa, kebaikan.

mermaid *noun* putri duyung, putri laut.

merry *adjective* **1** selamat; **Merry Christmas** selamat Natal; **2** *(from drinking)* mabuk; **Nathan got a bit merry at the Christmas party** Nathan agak mabuk di pesta Natal; **3** ceria; **today she looks merry** hari ini dia kelihatan ceria.

merry-go-round *noun* komedi putar.

mess *noun* berantakan, kekacauan; **to make a mess** membuat sesuatu menjadi berantakan; **what a mess!** berantakan sekali! *(informal)*; **my documents are in a mess** surat-surat saya berantakan.

- **to mess about** bermain-main, memboroskan waktu; **stop messing about!** jangan bermain-main!
- **to mess about with** bermain-main dengan; **it's dangerous to mess about with matches** berbahaya jika bermain-main dengan korek api.
- **to mess up** *(informal)* membuat sesuatu menjadi berantakan; **you've really messed up on that exam, haven't you?** ujiannya betul-betul berantakan, bukan?, Anda kacau sekali dalam ujian, bukan?

message *noun* pesan; **a telephone message** pesan telepon.

messenger *noun* kurir, pengantar, pesuruh.

messy *adjective* **1** kacau; **it's such a messy job!** pekerjaan yang kacau sekali!; **2** berantakan; **he's a messy eater** cara makannya berantakan sekali; **her**

writing's really messy tulisannya seperti cakar ayam.

metal *noun* logam, metal.

meter *noun* **1** *(electricity, gas, taxi)* meteran; **to read the meter** membaca meteran; **2** meter.

method *noun* cara, metode.

metre *noun* meter.

metric *adjective* metrik.

Mexico *noun* Meksiko.

microchip *noun* mikrocip.

microphone *noun* corong pengeras suara, mikropon.

microscope *noun* kaca pembesar, mikroskop.

microwave *noun* microwave.

microwave oven *noun* microwave.

midday *noun* tengah hari; **at midday** pada tengah hari, pada jam dua belas siang.

middle *noun* **1** tengah, pertengahan; **in the middle of the room** di tengah kamar, di tengah ruang; **in the middle of the night** di tengah malam; **2 to be in the middle of doing** sedang melakukan; **when she phoned I was in the middle of washing my hair** ketika dia menelepon saya sedang mencuci rambut.

middle-aged *adjective* setengah baya, setengah umur; **a middle-aged man** pria setengah baya.

middle-class *adjective* kelas menengah; **a middle-class family** keluarga kelas menengah.

Middle East *noun* Timur Tengah.

midnight *noun* tengah malam; **at midnight** tengah malam.

midsummer day *noun* pertengahan musim panas.

might *verb* barangkali, mungkin; **'are you going to phone him?' – 'I might'** 'apakah Anda akan menelepon dia?' – 'mungkin'; **I might invite Ridwan** barangkali saya akan mengundang Ridwan; **he might have forgotten** mungkin dia lupa.

migraine *noun* migrain, sakit kepala.

migrant *noun* migran.

migrate *verb* bermigrasi.

migration *noun* migrasi.

mike *noun* corong pengeras suara, mikropon.

mild *adjective* **1** sejuk; **the weather's quite mild today** hawanya agak sejuk hari ini; **2** sedikit; **it's only a mild curry** karinya hanya sedikit

a b c d e f g h i j k l m n o p q r s t u v w x y z

pedas; **a mild headache** sakit kepala sedikit; **3** ringan; **mild beer** bir ringan.

mile *noun* **1** mil; **2** *(informal)* jauh; **that's miles better** jauh lebih baik.

military *adjective* ketentaraan, militer.

milk *noun* susu; **long-life milk** susu tahan lama, susu Ultra; **fresh milk** susu segar; **chocolate milk** susu coklat.

milk chocolate *noun* coklat susu.

milk jug *noun* tempat susu.

milkman *noun* tukang susu.

milkshake *noun* susu kocok.

millimetre *noun* milimeter.

million *noun* juta; **a million people** sejuta orang; **five million Rupiah** lima juta rupiah.

millionaire *noun* jutawan.

mimic[1] *noun* mimik.

mimic[2] *verb* meniru-niru, menirukan.

mince *noun* daging cincang. *verb* mencincang

mind *noun* **1** pikiran; **it crossed my mind that...** terlintas dalam pikiran saya bahwa...; **to change your mind** berubah pikiran; **I've changed my mind** saya sudah berubah pikiran; **2 to make up your mind** mengambil keputusan; **he can never make up his mind** dia tak pernah bisa mengambil keputusan. *verb* **1** menjaga; **can you mind my bag for me?** bisakah Anda menjaga tas saya sebentar?; **could you mind the baby for a moment?** bisakah Anda menjaga bayi ini sebentar?; **2** keberatan; **do you mind if I...?** apakah Anda keberatan jika saya...; **do you mind if I ask her out?** apakah Anda keberatan jika saya mengajaknya keluar?; **I don't mind** saya tak keberatan; **3** awas, hati-hati; **mind the step!** hati-hati tangga!; **4 never mind!** tidak apa!

mine[1] *noun* tambang; **a gold mine** tambang mas.

mine[2] *pronoun* **1** kepunyaan saya, milik saya; **she took her car and I took mine** dia membawa mobilnya sendiri dan saya membawa mobil saya; **the green one's mine** yang hijau itu kepunyaan saya; **it's not mine** bukan milik saya; **2** ranjau.

miner *noun* pekerja tambang, penambang.

mineral water *noun* air mineral.

miniature *adjective* kecil sekali, miniatur.

a b c d e f g h i j k l m n o p q r s t u v w x y z

a b c d e f g h i j k l m n o p q r s t u v w x y z

minibus *noun* bis mini.

minimum *noun* minimum; **a minimum of** minimum dari, paling rendah, paling sedikit.
adjective terkecil, minimum; **the minimum age** umur termuda; **the minimum safety standards** standar keselamatan minimum; **the minimum amount** jumlah mininum.

miniskirt *noun* rok mini.

minister *noun* **1** *(in government)* menteri; **2** *(of a church)* domine, pendeta.

ministry *noun* kementerian.

minor *adjective* kecil, kurang penting, minor.

minority *noun* golongan kecil, golongan minoritas.

mint *noun* **1** *(herb)* daun mint; **2** *(sweet)* permen; **3** tempat mencetak uang.

minus *preposition* **1** kurang; **seven minus four is three** tujuh kurang empat sama dengan tiga; **2** minus; **it was minus ten degrees this morning** tadi pagi suhunya minus sepuluh derajat.

minute[1] *noun* **1** menit; **it's five minutes' walk from here** hanya lima menit berjalan dari sini; **2** sebentar; **just a minute** (tunggu) sebentar; **I'll be ready in a minute** saya akan siap sebentar lagi.

minute[2] *adjective* kecil sekali; **the bedrooms are minute** kamar tidurnya kecil sekali.

miracle *noun* keajaiban, mujizat.

mirror *noun* **1** cermin; **I looked at myself in the mirror** saya melihat diri sendiri di cermin; **2** *(rearview mirror in a car)* kaca spion.

misbehave *verb* berbuat jahat, berbuat nakal, berlaku tak pantas.

mischief *noun* kenakalan; **to get up to mischief** berbuat nakal.

mischievous *adjective* jahat, nakal.

miserable *adjective* **1** sangat sedih; **Grant was miserable without Fiona** Grant merasa sangat sedih tanpa Fiona; **2** *(various translations, depending on context)* **she gets paid a miserable wage** upahnya kecil dan tidak mencukupi; **it's miserable weather** cuacanya tidak menyenangkan.

misfire *verb* **1** gagal, meleset; **our plans misfired** rencana kami meleset; **2** *(of a gun)* tidak meletus.

misfortune *noun* kemalangan, nasib sial.

misjudge *verb* **1** keliru mempertimbangkan; **2** salah menilai; *(a person)* **everybody had misjudged her** semua orang salah menilai tentang dia.

mislay *verb* lupa meletakkan di mana sehingga tak dapat menemukan kembali *(definition only)*; **I've mislaid my keys again** saya tidak ingat di mana saya meletakkan kunci-kunci saya.

misleading *adjective* menyesatkan; **it's a misleading advertisement** iklan yang menyesatkan.

miss *verb* **1** ketinggalan, tidak dapat; **we've missed the train** kami ketinggalan kereta api; **2** tidak masuk; **the ball missed the goal** bola itu tidak masuk gawang; **3** tidak menangkap; **Fauzi missed the ball** bola tidak tertangkap oleh Fauzi; **4** absen; **he's missed several classes** dia absen dari beberapa kelas; **5** kehilangan; **to miss an opportunity** kehilangan kesempatan; **6** rindu; **she's missing her little sister** dia rindu akan adik perempuannya; **I miss Australia** saya rindu akan Australia.

Miss *noun* nona; **Miss Marshall** Nona Marshall.

missing *adjective* **1** yang hilang; **she's found the missing pieces** dia menemukan bagian-bagian yang hilang; **there's a missing link in that case** ada mata rantai yang hilang dalam kasus itu; **three people are still missing** tiga orang masih hilang; **2 to go missing** lenyap,menghilang; **several things have gone missing** beberapa barang lenyap.

missionary *noun* penyebar Injil, misionaris.

mist *noun* halimun, kabut.

mistake *noun* **1** kekeliruan, kesalahan; **2 to make a mistake** *(be mistaken)* keliru, membuat kesalahan; **he made a big mistake** dia membuat kesalahan besar; **sorry I made a mistake** maaf, saya salah; **3 by mistake** dengan tak sengaja. *verb* salah mengira; **I mistook you for your older brother** saya kira Anda adalah kakak laki-laki Anda.

mistaken *adjective* **to be mistaken** keliru, salah mengira; **you're mistaken** Anda keliru; Anda salah mengira.

a b c d e f g h i j k l m n o p q r s t u v w x y z

misty *adjective* berkabut; **a misty morning** pagi yang berkabut; **it's often misty in the mountains** di gunung sering berkabut.

misunderstand *verb* keliru menangkap, salah mengerti; **I misunderstood** saya salah mengerti; saya keliru menangkap.

misunderstanding *noun* salah paham, salah pengertian; **there's been a misunderstanding** ada kesalahpahaman.

mix *noun* **1** pergaulan; **a good mix of people** pergaulan yang bagus; **2** adonan; **a cake mix** adonan kue.
verb **1** aduk, membuat adonan, mencampurkan; **mix all the ingredients together** aduk semua bahan; **2 to mix with** bergaul dengan; **she mixes with a rough crowd** dia bergaul dengan orang-orang yang kasar.

- **to mix up 1** mengacaukan; **you've mixed up all the papers** Anda mengacaukan semua surat; **2** *(confuse)* bingung, (salah) mengira; **I get Michael mixed up with his brother** saya selalu bingung membedakan Michael dengan kakaknya; **Doreen got the days mixed up; she thought it was Tuesday** Doreen mengira hari itu adalah hari Selasa.

mixed *adjective* bermacam-macam, campuran; **a mixed program** acara campuran.

mixed salad *noun* salad campur.

mixed school *noun* sekolah untuk anak laki-laki dan perempuan *(definition only)*.

mixture *noun* campuran; **it's a mixture of jazz and rock** musik itu adalah campuran jazz dan rok.

moan *verb* mengeluh, mengerang, merintih; **stop moaning!** berhentilah mengeluh!

mobile home *noun* karavan, rumah berjalan.

mobile phone *noun* telepon genggam, telepon HP (handphone), telepon selular (ponsel).

mock *verb* mengejek, menertawakan; **stop mocking me!** jangan mengejek saya!

model *noun* **1** model; **the latest model** model mutakhir; **he makes models** dia membuat contoh-contoh model; **a model of Borobudur** model dari

Borobudur; **2** *(fashion model)* peragawati *(female)*; peragawan *(male)*.

model aeroplane *noun* model pesawat terbang.

model railway *noun* model rel kereta api.

model village *noun* desa teladan.

modem *noun* modem.

moderate *adjective* moderat, sedang.

modern *adjective* modern.

modern languages *plural noun* bahasa-bahasa modern.

modernize *verb* memodernisasi.

modest *adjective* rendah hati, sederhana, sopan.

modify *verb* memodifikasi, mengubah.

moisture *noun* embun, uap air di udara atau permukaan.

moisturizer *noun* **1** *(lotion)* pelembab; **2** *(cream)* krem pelembab.

mole *noun* *(on skin)* tahi lalat.

molecule *noun* molekul.

molehill *noun* timbunan tanah yang dibuat oleh binatang *(definition only)*.

moment *noun* **1** sebentar; **just a moment** (tunggu) sebentar; **2** saat, waktu; **at the moment** pada saat ini, pada waktu ini; **at the right moment** pada saat yang tepat; **he'll be here in a moment** dia akan tiba beberapa saat lagi.

monarchy *noun* kerajaan, monarki.

monastery *noun* biara, kuil.

Monday *noun* **on Monday** pada hari Senin; **every Monday** setiap hari Senin; **last Monday** hari Senin yang lalu; **next Monday** hari Senin depan.

money *noun* uang; **I don't have enough money** saya tidak punya cukup uang; **to make money** mencari rezeki, mencari uang; **they gave me my money back** mereka mengembalikan uang saya *(in a shop)*; **money order** poswesel.

money box *noun* celengan, tabungan.

mongrel *noun* anjing blasteran, anjing kampung.

monitor *noun* *(on computer)* monitor.
verb memantau, memonitor.

monk *noun* biarawan, rahib.

monkey *noun* **1** monyet, kera; **2** *(informal)* **you little monkey!** monyet!

monotonous *adjective* membosankan, monoton.

a b c d e f g h i j k l m n o p q r s t u v w x y z

monster *noun* monster, raksasa.

month *noun* bulan; **in the month of May** pada bulan Mei; **this month** bulan ini; **next month** bulan depan; **last month** bulan lalu; **every month** setiap bulan; **in two months' time** dua bulan lagi; **at the end of the month** pada akhir bulan.

monthly *adjective* bulanan; **a monthly payment** bayaran bulanan; **paid monthly** dibayar tiap bulan.

monument *noun* monumen, tugu; **the National Monument** tugu nasional, monumen nasional (monas).

mood *noun* keadaan jiwa, suasana hati; **to be in a good mood** suasana hati yang menyenangkan; **to be in a bad mood** suasana hati yang tidak menyenangkan.

moody *adjective* murung, tidak bersemangat.

moon *noun* bulan; **full moon** bulan purnama; **to be over the moon** gembira sekali.

moonlight *noun* sinar bulan; **by moonlight** pada waktu terang bulan.

moor *noun* padang, rawah. *verb (a boat)* menambatkan.

mope *verb* bermuram, durja.

moral *noun* akhlak, moral; **the moral of the story** inti moral cerita.

morals *plural noun* akhlak susila.

morale *noun* semangat; **he's been trying to boost the team's morale** dia berusaha meningkatkan semangat regu itu.

more *adverb, adjective, pronoun* **1** lebih; **more interesting** lebih menarik; **more difficult** lebih sulit; **more slowly** lebih pelahan; **they have more money than we do** mereka mempunyai lebih banyak uang daripada kita; **he eats more than me** dia makan lebih banyak daripada saya; **2 more...than** lebih...daripada; **this is more expensive than that** yang ini lebih mahal daripada yang itu; **3** *(of something you have already)* lagi; **we need a few more glasses** kami perlu beberapa gelas lagi; **I'd like a little more sambal** saya ingin sedikit sambal lagi; **we need three more** kami perlu tiga lagi; **would you like some more soup?** apakah Anda ingin tambah sop?; **I'll have a little more** saya mau tambah sedikit lagi; **I don't want any more** saya tidak mau lagi; **4 more and more**

semakin, kian lama; **rice is getting more and more expensive** beras semakin lama semakin mahal; **it takes more and more time** membutuhkan makin banyak waktu; **5 more or less** kurang lebih; **it's more or less finished** kurang lebih sudah selesai.

morning *noun* **1** *(up to 11 a.m.)* pagi; **this morning** pagi ini, tadi pagi; **tomorrow morning** besok pagi; **on Sunday morning** pada hari Minggu pagi; **on Sunday mornings** pada setiap hari Minggu pagi; **at five o'clock in the morning** pukul lima pagi; **every morning** setiap pagi; **2** *(from 11 a.m. to 2 p.m.)* siang.

Moslem *noun* orang Islam, Muslim.

mosque *noun* mesjid.

mosquito *noun* nyamuk.

most *adjective, adverb, pronoun* **1** kebanyakan; **most children like chocolate** kebanyakan anak suka coklat; **most of my friends** kebanyakan teman saya; **2** sebagian besar; **they've eaten most of the meat** sebagian besar dagingnya sudah mereka makan; **3** paling, sangat; **the most interesting film** film yang paling menarik; **the most dreadful accident** kecelakaan yang sangat mengerikan; **the most boring person** orang yang paling membosankan; **what I hate most is the noise** yang sangat saya benci adalah kegaduhan itu.

moth *noun* ngengat.

mother *noun* ibu; **my mother** ibu saya.

mother-in-law *noun* ibu mertua, mertua perempuan.

Mother's Day *noun* Hari Ibu.

motion *noun* gerakan, mosi.

motivated *adjective* bermotivasi.

motivation *noun* motivasi.

motor *noun* mesin, motor.

motorbike *noun* sepeda motor.

motorcyclist *noun* pengendara sepeda motor.

motorist *noun* pengemudi mobil, pengendara mobil.

motor racing *noun* balapan mobil.

motor vehicle *noun* kendaraan bermotor.

motorway *noun* jalan raya (untuk mobil).

mouldy *adjective* **1** apek; **it smells mouldy** bau apek; **2** berjamur.

a b c d e f g h i j k l m n o p q r s t u v w x y z

mountain *noun* gunung.

mountain bike *noun* sepeda untuk naik gunung.

mountaineer *noun* pendaki gunung.

mountainous *noun* bergunung-gunung.

mouse *noun* **1** *(animal)* tikus; **2** *(for a computer)* mouse.

mousse *noun* mousse.

moustache *noun* kumis.

mouth *noun* mulut.

mouthful *noun* sesuap.

mouth organ *noun* harmonika; **to play the mouth organ** main harmonika.

move *noun* **1** *(to a different house)* pindah (rumah); **2** *(in a game)* giliran; **your move** giliran Anda.
verb **1** bergerak; **she didn't move** dia tidak bergerak; **the traffic was hardly moving** lalu lintas macet (hampir tidak bergerak); **2** *(house)* pindah; **we're moving on Friday** kami akan pindah rumah hari Jumat; **they've moved to Sulawesi** mereka sudah pindah ke Sulawesi; **3 to move forward** bergerak maju; **he moved forward two steps** dia bergerak maju dua langkah; **4** *(an object)* **can you move your bag, please?** tolong geser tasnya, tolong pindahkan tasnya.
- **move up** bergeser, merapat; **move up a bit** bergeser sedikit.

movement *noun* gerakan, pergerakan.

movie *noun* film, filem, pilem; **to go to the movies** menonton film, pergi ke bioskop.

moving *adjective* **1** bergerak; **a moving vehicle** kendaraan yang bergerak; **2** *(emotionally)* mengharukan; **it's a very moving play** sandiwara itu sangat mengharukan.

mow *verb* memotong; **to mow the grass** memotong rumput.

mower *noun* alat pemotong rumput.

MP *noun* [member of parliament] anggota DPR; **she is an MP** dia adalah anggota DPR.

Mr *noun* Tuan; **Mr Howard** Bapak Howard, Tuan Howard.

Mrs *noun* Nyonya, Ibu; **Mrs Palmer** Ibu Palmer.

Ms *noun* Nyonya atau Nona.

much *adjective, adverb, pronoun* **1** banyak; **she doesn't eat much** dia tidak makan banyak; **we don't have much time** kami tidak punya banyak waktu; **very much** banyak sekali; **thank you very much** terima kasih banyak; **there isn't much left** tidak banyak yang tersisa; **2** jauh lebih; **much more** jauh lebih banyak; **much shorter** jauh lebih pendek; **3 not much** tidak banyak; *(depending on the context, there are several ways of saying this in Indonesian)* **'do you have much homework?' – 'no, not much'** 'apakah Anda ada banyak pekerjaan rumah?' – 'tidak, tidak begitu banyak'; **there isn't much rice left** berasnya tinggal sedikit; **we don't entertain much** kami tidak begitu sering menjamu; **I don't watch television very much** saya jarang nonton televisi; **4 so much** banyak sekali, begitu banyak, sangat; **we like it so much** kami sangat menyukainya; **I have so much to do** banyak sekali yang harus saya kerjakan; **5 so much** sekian banyak; **'how much?' – 'about so much'** 'berapa banyak?' – 'sekian banyak'; **6 as much as** sebanyak; **you can take as much as you like** silahkan ambil sebanyak Anda mau; **7 too much** terlalu banyak; **her parents give her too much money** orang tuanya memberikan terlalu banyak uang kepadanya; **that's far too much** jauh terlalu banyak; **8 how much** berapa (banyak); **how much is it?** berapa harganya?; **how much do you want?** Anda mau berapa banyak?; **how much sugar do you want?** berapa banyak gula yang Anda inginkan?

mud *noun* lumpur.

muddle *noun* dalam keadaan kacau-balau; **to be in a muddle** bingung, kacau-balau.

muddy *noun* **1** *(path, road)* becek, berlumpur; **your boots are muddy** sepatu Anda berlumpur; **the alley is really muddy** gang itu betul-betul becek; **2** *(water)* keruh.

mug *noun* semacam cangkir. *verb* menodong, merampok dengan kekerasan; **to be mugged** ditodong, dirampok dengan kekerasan; **my brother was mugged in the park** adik lelaki saya ditodong di taman, kakak lelaki saya ditodong di taman.

mugging *noun* penodongan, perampokan dengan kekerasan.

multiplication *noun* ganda, penggandaan, perkalian;

a b c d e f g h i j k l m n o p q r s t u v w x y z

multiplication sign tanda kali.

multiply *verb* mengalikan, memperbanyak.

mum, mummy *noun* ibu *(often shortened to 'bu)*; **I'll ask your mum** saya akan bertanya kepada ibu Anda.

mumps *noun* penyakit gondok.

murder *noun* pembunuhan. *verb* membunuh.

murderer *noun* pembunuh.

muscle *noun* otot, urat.

muscular *adjective* berotot, kuat (tegap).

museum *noun* museum.

mushroom *noun* jamur; **mushroom soup** sop jamur.

music *noun* musik.

musical *noun* film dengan musik, sandiwara dengan musik.
adjective **1** musik; **a musical instrument** alat musik; **2** berbakat musik; **they're very musical** mereka berbakat musik..

musician *noun* pemain musik.

Muslim *noun* Muslimin (*male*), Muslimat (*female*), penganut agama Islam.

mussel *noun* remis, semacam kerang.

must *verb* **1** *(to express obligation)* harus, mesti; **we must leave now** kami harus berangkat sekarang; **I must tell you what happened** saya harus memberitahu Anda apa yang terjadi; **you must be here by eight** Anda harus sudah berada di sini selambat-lambatnya pukul delapan; **you must learn the vocabulary** Anda harus menghafalkan kosa-kata itu; **2** *(to express probability)* pasti, tentu; **you must be tired** pasti Anda lelah; **it must be six o'clock** tentu sudah jam enam; **he must have forgotten** pasti dia lupa.

mustard *noun* mostar.

mutter *verb* bersungut-sungut, memberengut.

my *adjective* kepunyaan saya, saya; **my brother** adik laki-laki saya, kakak laki-laki saya; **my dog** anjing saya; **my address** alamat saya; **I had a glass in my hand** saya memegang gelas di tangan.

myself *pronoun* **1** diri, sendiri; **I said it myself** saya mengatakannya sendiri; **2 by myself** saya sendiri(an); **I spend a lot of time by myself** saya sering sendirian; **3 I've hurt myself** kaki saya luka *(literally 'my leg is* *wounded' – you specify where you are hurt in Indonesian).*

mysterious *adjective* aneh, misterius.

mystery *noun* misteri; *(book)* cerita misteri.

myth *noun* dongeng, mitos.

mythology *noun* mitologi.

N n

nail *noun* **1** *(on finger or toe)* kuku; **2** *(metal)* paku.

nailbrush *noun* sikat kuku.

nail file *noun* kikir kuku.

nail scissors *plural noun* gunting kuku.

nail varnish *noun* cat kuku.

nail varnish remover *noun* pembersih cat kuku.

naked *adjective* telanjang.

name *noun* **1** nama; **I've forgotten her name** saya lupa namanya; **what's your name?** siapa nama Anda?; **my name's...** (nama) saya...; **2** *(reputation)* nama, reputasi.

nap *noun* **to have a nap** tidur sebentar, tidur siang.

napkin *noun* serbet.

nappy *noun* popok.

narrow *adjective* sempit.

nasty *adjective* **1** *(disgusting)* keji; **that was a nasty thing to do** itu kelakuan yang keji; **2** *(unpleasant)* sangat tidak menyenangkan; **that's a nasty job** pekerjaan itu tidak menyenangkan; **3** *(bad)* busuk; **a nasty smell** bau busuk; **4** *(mean)* jahat; **Damien is very nasty to me** Damien jahat terhadap saya.

nation *noun* bangsa.

national *adjective* **1** nasional; **national debt** hutang nasional; **2** kebangsaan; **national anthem** lagu kebangsaan.

nationality *noun* kebangsaan.

national park *noun* taman nasional.

natural *adjective* **1** alam; **natural resources** sumber-sumber alam, sumber daya alam; **2 natural gas** gas bumi; **3** wajar; **to die a natural death** meninggal dengan wajar.

naturally *adverb* tentu saja.

nature *noun* alam; **by nature** pada dasarnya.

nature reserve *noun* cagar alam.

naughty *adjective* nakal.

navy *noun* angkatan laut.

navy-blue *adjective* biru laut.

near *adjective* dekat.
adverb, preposition dekat; **they live quite near** mereka tinggal agak dekat; **to come nearer** mendekati.

nearby *adverb* dekat.

nearly *adverb* hampir; **nearly empty** hampir kosong; **we're nearly there** kita hampir sampai.

neat *adjective* necis, rapi; **a neat room** kamar yang rapi.

neatly *adverb* dengan rapi; **to be neatly dressed** berpakaian rapi.

necessarily *adverb* **1** perlu; **not necessarily** *(not needed)* tidak perlu; **2** *(not certain)* kurang pasti.

necessary *adjective* penting, perlu; **if necessary** kalau perlu.

neck *noun* leher.

necklace *noun* kalung.

need *noun* kebutuhan, keperluan; **I have few needs** kebutuhan saya sedikit; **there's no need to wait** tak perlu menunggu, tak usah menunggu.
verb **1** *(requirement)* membutuhkan, memerlukan; **we need bread** kami memerlukan roti; **they need help** mereka perlu bantuan; **everything you need** semua keperluan Anda; **2** *(to have to)* harus; **I need to drop in at the bank** saya harus mampir di bank; **3** *(not have to)* perlu, usah; **you needn't decide right away** Anda tidak usah memutuskan sekarang juga; **you needn't wait** Anda tak perlu menunggu.

needle *noun* jarum.

negative *noun* **1** negatif; **2** *(of a photo)* klise.

neglect *verb* menterlantarkan

neglected *adjective* terlantar, diterlantarkan.

neighbour *noun* tetangga.

neighbourhood *noun* lingkungan; **a nice neighbourhood** lingkungan yang baik; **neighbourhood association** rukun tetangga.

neither *conjunction* **1 neither...nor** baik...maupun; **neither she nor I can go** baik dia mau pun saya tidak bisa pergi; **I have neither the time nor the money** saya tidak punya waktu mau pun uang; **2 neither do I** saya juga tidak; **'I don't eat meat' – 'neither do I'** 'saya tidak makan daging' – 'saya juga tidak'; **'he wasn't invited' – 'neither**

was I' 'dia tidak diundang' – 'saya juga tidak'; **3** keduanya tidak; **'which do you like?' – 'neither'** 'Anda suka yang mana?' – 'saya tidak suka keduanya'; **'which of the two will come?' – 'neither'** 'yang mana dari kedua orang itu akan datang?' – 'keduanya tidak akan datang'.

nephew *noun* kemenakan laki-laki, keponakan laki-laki.

nerve *noun* **1** *(in the body)* syaraf; **2** keberanian; **you've got a nerve!** berani betul Anda!; **3 to lose one's nerve** menjadi takut; **it gets on my nerves** *(informal)* menjengkelkan saya.

nervous *adjective* gugup, senewen (*colloquial*); **a nervous breakdown** gangguan urat syaraf.

nest *noun* sarang.

net *noun* **1** *(for fishing)* jala; **2** *(in football or tennis)* jaring.

Netherlands *noun* negeri Belanda.

nettle *noun* semacam tanaman liar (*definition only*).

network *noun* jaringan.

neutral *noun* kenetralan; **to be in neutral** pakai gigi netral.
adjective netral.

never *adjective* **1** tidak pernah; **Jusuf never smokes** Jusuf tidak pernah merokok; **never again** tidak sekali lagi; **2** belum pernah; **'have you ever been to Kupang?' – 'no, never'** 'apakah Anda pernah ke Kupang?' – 'belum pernah'; **I've never seen the film** saya belum pernah nonton film itu; **3 never mind** tidak apa-apa.

new *adjective* baru; **new house** rumah baru; **new friend** teman baru.

newcomer *noun* pendatang baru.

news *noun* berita, kabar; **a piece of good news** kabar baik; **any news?** apakah ada kabar?; **the news** warta berita.

newsagent *noun* agen surat kabar.

newspaper *noun* koran, surat kabar.

newsreader *noun* pembaca berita radio/TV, penyiar berita.

New Year *noun* Tahun Baru; **Happy New Year!** Selamat Tahun Baru!

New Year's Day *noun* tanggal satu Januari.

New Year's Eve *noun* Malam Tahun Baru.

New Zealand *noun* Selandia Baru.

a b c d e f g h i j k l m n o p q r s t u v w x y z

next *adjective* **1** yang berikut, yang selanjutnya; **the next train is at ten** kereta api yang berikut berangkat jam sepuluh; **on the next page** di halaman berikut; **2** depan, yang akan datang; **next week** minggu depan, minggu yang akan datang; **the next day** keesokan harinya; **3** *(next door)* sebelah; **in the next room** di kamar sebelah. *adverb* **1** *(afterwards, now)* selanjutnya, sesudah itu; **what did he say next?** apa katanya sesudah itu?; **what do you want to do next?** Anda ingin melakukan apa selanjutnya?; **2** sebelah, samping; **next to the building** di samping gedung itu; **sit next to me!** duduklah di sebelah saya!

next door *adverb* di sebelah; **they live next door** mereka tinggal di sebelah.

nice *adjective* **1** *(pleasant)* menyenangkan; **a nice evening** malam yang menyenangkan; **have a nice time!** semoga senang!; **2** *(attractive to look at)* menarik; **that's a nice outfit** baju itu menarik; **3** *(kind, friendly)* baik; **she's really nice** dia betul-betul baik; **4** *(tasting good)* enak; **that looks like a nice meal** makanan itu kelihatannya enak; **5** *(weather)* bagus; **it's a nice day** cuaca hari ini bagus.

nick *verb (informal)* mencuri.

nickname *noun* nama julukan, nama panggilan.

niece *noun* kemenakan perempuan, keponakan perempuan.

night *noun* malam; **what did you do last night?** Anda melakukan apa semalam?; **good night** *(parting company)* selamat malam; *(retiring for the night)* selamat tidur.

nightclub *noun* klub malam.

nightie *noun* baju tidur.

nightmare *noun* mimpi buruk.

nil *noun* nol, kosong; **they won four–nil** mereka menang empat–kosong.

nine *number* sembilan.

nineteen *number* sembilan belas.

ninety *number* sembilan puluh.

ninth *number* **1** sembilan; **the ninth of July** tanggal sembilan Juli; **2** kesembilan; **on the ninth floor** di lantai kesembilan.

no *adverb* **1** tidak, nggak *(informal)*; **I said no** saya berkata tidak; **2 no, thank**

you terima kasih *('terima kasih' as a refusal must be accompanied by the appropriate hand gesture, otherwise it signifies acceptance).*
adjective **1** tidak *(with verbs, adjectives and adverbs)*; **we've got no onions** kami tidak punya bawang; **no problem** tidak ada masalah; **2** bukan *(with nouns and pronouns)*; **no problem** bukan masalah; **no friend of mine** bukan teman saya; **3** dilarang; **'no smoking'** 'dilarang merokok'; **'no parking'** 'dilarang parkir'.

nobody *pronoun* tidak seorang pun; **there's nobody home** tidak ada seorang pun di rumah; **nobody answered** tidak ada orang yang menjawab; **'who's there?' – 'nobody'** 'siapa di situ?' – 'tak ada orang', 'tak ada siapa-siapa'.

nod *verb* menganggukkan kepala; **he nodded** dia mengangguk tanda setuju, dia menganggukkan kepala.

noise *noun* **1** berisik, ribut, riuh; **don't make a noise** jangan berisik; **2** bunyi; **what's that noise?** bunyi apa itu?

noisy *adjective* gaduh, ribut; **those kids are so noisy** anak-anak itu ribut sekali.

none *pronoun* **1** *(not one)* tidak seorang pun, tidak satu pun; **'how many students failed the exam?' – 'none'** 'berapa murid yang gagal ujian itu?' – 'tidak seorang pun'; **none of the mangoes is ripe** semua mangga ini belum masak; **2 there is/are none left** tidak ada sisanya.

nonsense *noun* omong kosong; **to talk nonsense** omong kosong; **nonsense! she's at least thirty** omong-kosong! paling sedikit umurnya sudah tiga puluh tahun.

non-smoker *noun* bukan perokok, orang yang tidak merokok.

non-stop *adjective (a train or flight)* nonstop, tanpa berhenti.
adverb terus-menerus; **she talks non-stop** dia bicara terus-menerus.

noodles *plural noun* mie.

noon *noun* tengah hari.

no-one *pronoun* tidak seorang pun; **there's no-one home** tidak ada seorang pun di rumah; **no-one knows me** tiada seorang pun yang kenal saya; **'who's there?' – 'no-one'** 'siapa di situ?' – 'tak ada orang', 'tak ada siapa-siapa'.

nor *conjunction* **neither...nor** baik...maupun; **neither she nor I can go** baik dia maupun saya tidak bisa pergi; **I have neither the time nor the money** saya tidak punya waktu maupun uang.

normal *adjective* **1** normal; **2** *(usual)* biasa.

normally *adverb* biasanya.

north *noun* utara; **northeast** timurlaut; **northwest** baratlaut.
adjective **the north side** bagian utara, sebelah utara; **a north wind** angin utara.

North America *noun* Amerika Utara.

northeast *noun* timurlaut.
adjective timurlaut; **in northeast Australia** di bagian timurlaut Australia.

Northern Ireland *noun* Irlandia Utara.

North Pole *noun* Kutub Utara.

North Sea *noun* Laut Utara.

northwest *noun* baratlaut.
adjective baratlaut; **in northwest Australia** di bagian baratlaut Australia.

Norway *noun* Norwegia.

Norwegian *noun* bahasa Norwegia *(language)*, orang Norwegia *(person)*.

nose *noun* hidung; **to blow your nose** membuang ingus.

nosebleed *noun* mimisan.

not *adverb* **1** tidak; **not on Fridays** tidak pada hari Jumat; **not all alone!** tidak sendirian!; **not at all** sama sekali tidak; **I don't know** saya tidak tahu; **I hope not** saya harap tidak; **2** bukan; **it's not my car** itu bukan mobil saya; **3 not yet** belum.

note *noun* **1** *(a short letter)* surat; **she left me a note** dia meninggalkan surat untuk saya; **2** catatan; **to take notes** mencatat; **3** *(a banknote)* uang kertas; **a fifty-thousand-rupiah note** (uang kertas) lima puluh ribu rupiah; **4** *(in music)* not.

notebook *noun* buku catatan.

notepad *noun* kertas tulis.

nothing *pronoun* tidak ada apa-apa; **'what did you say?' – 'nothing'** 'apa yang Anda katakan?' – 'tidak apa-apa'; **I saw nothing** saya tidak melihat apa-apa; **there's nothing happening** tidak ada apa-apa yang terjadi; **there's nothing new** tidak ada yang baru.

notice *noun* **1** *(a sign)* pemberitahuan, pengumuman; **2** *(an*

advertisement) pengumuman; **3 don't take any notice of her!** jangan perhatikan dia! jangan ladeni dia!; **4 to do the work at short notice** segera melakukan pekerjaan setelah menerima perintah.
verb meladeni, melihat, memperhatikan; **I didn't notice anything** saya tidak melihat apa-apa.

noticeable *adjective* kelihatan, tampak.

noticeboard *noun* papan pengumuman.

noun *noun* kata benda.

novel *noun* (cerita) novel, roman.

novelist *noun* pengarang cerita roman, penulis.

November *noun* bulan November; **in November** pada bulan November.

now *adverb* **1** sekarang; **where are they now?** mereka di mana sekarang?; **they've got three children now** sekarang mereka sudah punya tiga anak; **2** baru saja; **I saw her just now in the corridor** baru saja saya melihatnya di gang itu; **3** saat ini; **do it right now!** lakukan sekarang juga!; **he's busy just now** dia sibuk pada saat ini; **4 now and then** kadang-kadang.

nowhere *adjective* **1** tidak...di mana pun juga; **nowhere in Indonesia** tidak ada di mana pun juga di Indonesia; **2 there's nowhere to park** tidak ada tempat parkir.

nuclear *adjective* nuklir; **a nuclear power station** reaktor nuklir.

nude *noun* telanjang; **in the nude** dalam keadaan telanjang.
adjective telanjang.

nuisance *noun* gangguan, kerepotan; **it's such a nuisance your living so far away from here** repot sekali karena Anda tinggal jauh dari sini.

numb *adjective* mati rasa.

number *noun* **1** *(of a house, telephone, account, etc.)* nomor; **she lives at number five** dia tinggal di rumah nomor lima; **my new phone number** nomor telepon saya yang baru; **2** *(a written figure)* angka, bilangan; **the third number is a seven** angka yang ketiga adalah tujuh; **3** *(an amount)* jumlah; **a number of bats** sejumlah kelelawar; banyak **a large number of bats** banyak kelelawar.

a b c d e f g h i j k l m n o p q r s t u v w x y z

a b c d e f g h i j k l m n o p q r s t u v w x y z

number plate *noun* plat nomor mobil.

nun *noun* biarawati, suster.

nurse *noun* jururawat, perawat; **Josie's a nurse** Josie adalah jururawat.
verb **1** *(back to health)* merawat; **2** *(a baby)* menyusui.

nursery *noun* **1** *(for children)* kamar anak-anak; **2** *(for plants)* taman bibit.

nursery school *noun* taman kanak-kanak.

nut *noun* **1** *(that you eat)* kacang-kacangan; **2** *(slang for crazy)* orang aneh, orang gila; **you're nuts!** gila kamu!; **3** *(slang for liking a lot)* tergila-gila pada, suka benar kepada; **Ichsan's nuts about Fitri** Ichsan suka benar kepada Fitri, Ichsan tergila-gila pada Fitri; **4** *(for a bolt)* mur.

nutmeg *noun* pala.

nylon *noun* nilon.

O o

oar *noun* dayung, kayuh.

oats *noun* havermot; **porridge oats** havermot; **oatmeal porridge** bubur havermot.

obedient *adjective* patuh, taat.

obey *verb* mematuhi, menaati, menurut; **to obey the rules** menaati peraturan.

object *noun* barang, benda, obyek.
verb berkeberatan, menolak; **if you don't object** kalau Anda tidak berkeberatan.

objection *noun* keberatan.

oblong *adjective* berbentuk panjang; empat persegi panjang.

oboe *noun* alat musik dari kayu.

obscene *adjective* cabul.

observe *verb* melihat, memperhatikan.

obsessed *adjective* terobsesi; **she's obsessed with her diet** pikirannya terobsesi pada dietnya.

obstacle *noun* halangan, rintangan.

obstinate *adjective* keras kepala.

obstruct *verb* *(people or the traffic)* menghalangi, merintangi.

obtain *verb* mendapat(kan), memperoleh.

obvious *adjective* jelas, kentara, nyata, terang.

obviously *adverb* **1** *(of course)* jelaslah, nyatanya; **'do you want to come too?' – 'obviously, but it's a bit difficult'** 'apakah Anda juga mau datang?' – 'jelaslah, tetapi agak sulit'; **2** *(looking at something)* jelas, pasti, tentu; **the house is obviously empty** jelas rumah itu kosong.

occasion *noun* kesempatan, peristiwa, waktu; **a special occasion** peristiwa yang khusus.

occasionally *adverb* kadang-kadang, sekali-sekali.

occupation *noun* jabatan, pekerjaan, kedudukan.

occupied *adjective* **1** *(with work)* sibuk; **I'm occupied with my homework now** saya sedang sibuk mengerjakan pekerjaan rumah saya; **2** *(of space)* sedang dipakai, sedang terisi; **this chair is occupied** kursi ini diduduki orang.

occupy *verb* dijajah, menduduki; **Indonesia was occupied by the Dutch for three-and-a-half centuries** Indonesia dijajah Belanda selama tiga setengah abad.

occur *verb* **1** terpikir oleh, terlintas di pikiran; **it occurs to me that we've forgotten to make a booking** terlintas di pikiran saya bahwa kami lupa memesan tempat; **it never occurred to me** tak pernah terpikir oleh saya; **2** *(happen)* terjadi; **the accident occurred on Monday** kecelakaan itu terjadi hari Senin.

ocean *noun* lautan, samudra.

o'clock *noun* jam, pukul; **at ten o'clock** pada pukul sepuluh; **it's five o'clock** sekarang jam lima.

October *noun* bulan Oktober.

octopus *noun* ikan gurita.

odd *adjective* **1** *(strange)* aneh; **that's odd, I'm sure I heard the phone** aneh, saya yakin tadi saya mendengar bunyi telepon; **2** *(number)* ganjil, gasal; **three is an odd number** tiga adalah bilangan ganjil; **3** berbeda; **to be the odd one out** orang yang berbeda.

odds and ends *plural noun* rupa-rupa barang kecil.

of *preposition* **1** *(not translated in Indonesian)* **a kilo of rice** sekilo beras; **the sixth of June** tanggal enam Juni; **the beginning of the concert**

a b c d e f g h i j k l m n **o** p q r s t u v w x y z

permulaan konser; **the name of the flower** nama bunga itu; **2** dari; **made of** dibuat dari; **a bracelet made of silver** gelang yang dibuat dari perak; **3** karena **to die of an illness** meninggal karena penyakit; **4 to be fond of** suka akan; **two of us** kita berdua.

off *adverb, adjective, preposition* **1** *(switched, turned off)* mati; **is the telly off?** apakah Teve itu sudah mati?; **to turn off the tap** mematikan keran; **2** *(turned off at the meter or a supply cut)* mati, putus; **the electricity is off** listrik mati; **3** *(to leave)* **to be off** berangkat; **I'm off** saya mau berangkat; **4** cuti, libur; **a day off** cuti sehari; **Aslena took three days off work** Aslena mengambil cuti tiga hari; **to be off sick** istirahat karena sakit; **5** lepas; **the knob has come off** tombolnya lepas; **6** *(cancelled)* batal; **the match is off** pertandingannya dibatalkan; **7** didiskon, dipotong; **20 per cent off shoes** harga sepatu yang dipotong dua puluh persen.

offence *noun* **1** *(crime)* kejahatan, pelanggaran; **2 to take offence** merasa tersinggung; **Lies takes offence easily** Lies mudah tersinggung.

offer *noun* **1** tawaran; **a job offer** tawaran pekerjaan; **2 'on offer'** 'diperdagangkan'.
verb **1** *(a present, a reward or a job)* menawari, menawarkan; **Sumadi offered Sita the job** Sumadi menawari Sita pekerjaan itu; **to offer to do** menawarkan melakukan; **I offered to help** saya menawarkan bantuan; **2** memberikan; **don't offer her a bribe** jangan berikan uang suap kepadanya.

office *noun* kantor; **we work in the same office** kami bekerja sekantor.

office block, office building *noun* gedung kantor.

official *noun* **1** pegawai negeri, pejabat; **2** *(sport)* ofisial.
adjective (secara) resmi.

often *adverb* sering (kali), kerapkali; **he's often late** dia sering terlambat; **how often do you see Setiadi?** berapa sering Anda bertemu dengan Setiadi?; **I'd like to see Sadikin more often** saya ingin bertemu lebih sering dengan Sadikin.

oil *noun* **1** minyak; **olive oil** minyak zaitun; **cooking oil**

minyak goreng; **crude oil** minyak mentah; **2** *(engine oil)* oli.

oil painting *noun* lukisan cat minyak.

oil rig *noun* alat pembor minyak.

ointment *noun* salep.

okay *adjective* **1** baiklah, jadi, oke; **okay, tomorrow at ten** baiklah, besok jam sepuluh; **'is it okay with you if I don't do it until Friday?' – 'OK'** 'apakah Anda keberatan kalau saya tidak melakukan itu sampai hari Jumat?' – 'baiklah, oke'; **2** *(person)* baik; *(thing)* bagus; **Desi's okay** Desi adalah orang baik; **the book is okay** buku itu bagus; **3** *(nothing special)* lumayan; **the film was okay** film itu lumayan; **4** *(not ill)* sembuh, tidak sakit; **are you okay?** apakah Anda tidak sakit?; **I've been ill but I'm okay now** tadi saya sakit tetapi sekarang sudah sembuh.

old *adjective* **1** *(not young, not new)* tua; **an old tree** pohon tua; **old people** kaum tua; **2** *(previous)* lama; **our old car was a Datsun** mobil kami yang lama adalah Datsun; **bring some old clothes** bawa pakaian lama; **I've only got the old phone number** saya hanya punya nomor telepon yang lama; **3** *(talking about age)* umur; **Yuli is ten years old** Yuli berumur sepuluh tahun; **4 she's older than I am** dia lebih tua dari saya; **he's a year older than Nat** dia setahun lebih tua dari Nat; **5 older sibling** kakak; **my older sister** kakak perempuan saya; **older brother** kakak laki-laki.

old age *noun* lanjut usia.

old-age pensioner *noun* orang pensiunan.

old-fashioned *adjective* **1** *(objects)* ketinggalan mode, kuno; **2** *(a person)* kolot, orang yang ketinggalan jaman.

olive *noun* zaitun.

olive oil *noun* minyak zaitun.

Olympic Games, Olympics *plural noun* Olimpiade.

omelette *noun* telur dadar; **a cheese and tomato omelette** telur dadar dengan keju dan tomat.

on *preposition* **1** di atas; **on the desk** di atas meja tulis; **2** di; **on the beach** di pantai; **I met Mona on the train** saya bertemu dengan Mona di kereta; **on TV** di televisi; **on the radio** di radio; **3** *(in expressions of time)* pada; **on**

a b c d e f g h i j k l m n o p q r s t u v w x y z

a b c d e f g h i j k l m n o p q r s t u v w x y z

11 March pada tanggal sebelas Maret; **he's arriving on Tuesday** dia akan tiba pada hari Selasa; **on page ten** pada halaman sepuluh; **on the ceiling** pada langit-langit; **4** naik; **let's go on our bikes** mari kita pergi naik sepeda; **she arrived on the bus** dia datang naik bis; **5** (pada) waktu; **on holiday** pada waktu berlibur; **6 on strike** sedang mogok; **on average** rata-rata.
adjective **1** *(switched on)* menyala; **all the lights were on** semua lampu menyala; **2** *(happening)* ada apa; **what's on on TV?** ada acara apa di televisi?; **what's on this weekend?** ada apa pada akhir minggu ini?

once *adverb* **1** sekali; **I've tried once already** saya sudah mencoba sekali; **try once more** cobalah sekali lagi; **once a day** sehari sekali; **more than once** lebih dari sekali; **2** *(immediately)* **at once** segera; **the doctor came at once** dokter segera datang; **3** *(at the same time)* **at once** sekaligus; **I can't do two things at once** saya tidak bisa melakukan dua hal sekaligus.

one *number* satu, se; **one son** seorang anak laki-laki; **one mango** sebuah mangga; **if you want a pen I've got one** kalau Anda mau pena saya ada satu; **at one o'clock** pada pukul satu.
pronoun yang; **one never knows** tidak ada yang tahu; **this one** yang ini; **I like that bike but this one is cheaper** saya suka sepeda itu, tetapi yang ini lebih murah; **that one** yang itu; **'which pup?'– 'that one'** 'anak anjing yang mana?' – 'yang itu'; **which one?** yang mana?; **'my finger's hurting' – 'which one?'** 'jari saya sakit' – 'yang mana?'

one's *determiner* orang, nya; **one can only do one's best** orang hanya bisa berusaha sedapat-dapatnya; **to pay for one's mistakes** menjalani hukuman untuk perbuatannya sendiri; **to love one's children** mencintai anak-anaknya; **to wash one's hands** mencuci tangannya.

oneself *noun* **1** diri sendiri; **to wash oneself** mandi sendiri; **to do everything oneself** melakukan segala sesuatu sendiri; **2 (all) by oneself** sendirian.

one-way street *noun* jalan satu arah.

onion *noun* bawang.

only *adjective* **1** satu-satunya; **the only free seat** satu-satunya tempat duduk kosong; **the only thing to do** satu-satunya hal yang dapat dilakukan; **2** tunggal; **an only child** anak tunggal.
adverb, conjunction **1** hanya; **the house has only got one bathroom** di rumah itu hanya ada sebuah kamar mandi saja; **Harmin's only free on Fridays** Harmin hanya bebas pada hari Jumat; **there are only three left** hanya tinggal tiga; **'how long did they stay?' – 'only a week'** 'berapa lama mereka tinggal?' – 'hanya seminggu'; **2** cuma; **I'd walk, only it's raining** saya ingin jalan, cuma sekarang hujan.

onto *preposition* di (atas), ke; **to get onto a horse** menaiki kuda, naik (ke) kuda.

open *noun* luar; **in the open** di luar.
adverb **1** *(not shut)* terbuka; **the door's open** pintu itu terbuka; **the chemist is not open yet** apotik belum buka; **2 in the open air** di alam terbuka, di luar; **an open-air swimming pool** kolam renang di alam terbuka.
verb buka, membuka; **the bank opens at nine** bank buka pada pukul sembilan; **can you open the door for me?** tolong buka pintu itu untuk saya; **the cat opened its eyes** kucing itu membuka matanya; **the door opened slowly** pintu itu terbuka perlahan-lahan.

opera *noun* opera.

operate *verb* **1** *(a machine, piece of equipment)* menjalankan; **2** *(surgery)* membedah, mengoperasi; **he was operated on** dia dibedah; **3** *(a business)* mengusahakan.

operation *noun* operasi, pembedahan; **I've never had an operation** saya belum pernah menjalani pembedahan.

opinion *noun* **in my opinion** pada pendapat saya; **public opinion** pendapat umum; **to have the same opinion** sependapat.

opinion poll *noun* jajak pendapat.

opponent *noun* lawan.

opportunity *noun* kesempatan; **to have the opportunity of doing** berkesempatan melakukan; **I took the opportunity to visit the puppet museum** saya mengambil kesempatan untuk mengunjungi museum wayang.

a b c d e f g h i j k l m n **o** p q r s t u v w x y z

opposite *noun* kebalikan, lawan, sebaliknya; **quite the opposite** persis kebalikannya.
adjective **1** *(a direction, side or view, for example)* berlawanan, bertentangan; **she went off in the opposite direction** dia pergi menuju arah yang berlawanan; **2** *(facing)* berhadapan dengan, di hadapan, di seberang; **in the house opposite** di rumah di seberang; **they live opposite the mosque** rumah mereka berhadapan dengan mesjid.

optician *noun* ahli kaca mata.

optimistic *adjective* penuh harapan, optimistis.

option *noun* opsi, pilihan; **we have no option** kami tidak ada pilihan lain.

optional *adjective* pilihan; **optional subjects** mata pelajaran pilihan.

or *conjunction* **1** atau; **Indonesian or English** bahasa Indonesia atau bahasa Inggris; **today or tomorrow** hari ini atau besok; **2** *(or else)* kalau tidak, nanti; **phone Mum, or she'll worry** harap telepon Ibu, nanti dia khawatir.

oral *noun (an exam)* (ujian) lisan; **the Indonesian oral** ujian lisan bahasa Indonesia.

orange *noun* jeruk; **orange juice** air jeruk.
adjective jingga tua, oranye; **an orange dress** baju berwarna jingga tua.

orchestra *noun* orkes.

order *noun* **1** *(arrangement)* urutan; **in the right order** urutan yang benar; **in alphabetical order** menurut abjad; **2** *(in a restaurant)* pesanan; **can I take your orders now?** pesan apa?; **3 'out of order'** 'rusak'; **4 in order to do** agar, supaya; **we hurried in order to be on time** kami bergegas supaya tiba tepat pada waktunya.
verb **1** *(in a restaurant or hotel)* memesan; **we ordered goat curry and steamed rice** kami pesan gulai kambing dengan nasi putih;
2 memerintah, menyuruh; **I just hate it when he orders me around** saya benci kalau dia menyuruh-nyuruh saya.

ordinary *adjective* biasa.

organ *noun* **1** *(anatomy)* alat tubuh, bagian badan; **2** *(music)* organ, orgel.

organic *adjective (food)* organik.

organization *noun* organisasi.

organize *verb* mengadakan, mengatur, mengorganisir.

original *adjective* **1** asli; **the original version was better** versi yang asli lebih baik; **2** orisinal; **it's a really original novel** itu cerita yang benar-benar orisinal.

originally *adverb* tadinya, sebetulnya; **originally we wanted to get a Suzuki** tadinya kami ingin mendapatkan mobil Suzuki.

ornament *noun* ornamen, perhiasan.

orphan *noun* anak yatim-piatu.

ostrich *noun* burung unta.

other *adjective* **1** yang lain; **we took the other road** kami mengambil jalan lain; **where are the others?** di mana yang lain?; **the other two possibilities** dua kemungkinan yang lain; **2 every other week** tiap minggu kedua; **3 the other day** baru-baru ini.

otherwise *adverb (in other ways)* tetapi; **the house is a bit small, but otherwise it's lovely** rumahnya agak kecil, tetapi selain itu menarik. *conjunction (or else)* kalau tidak; **I'll phone home first, otherwise they'll worry** saya akan menelepon keluarga dulu, kalau tidak mereka akan khawatir.

ought *verb* **1** *(be better)* sebaiknya; **we ought to go now** sebaiknya kita berangkat sekarang; **2** *(probability)* seharusnya; **they ought to know the address** seharusnya mereka sudah tahu alamatnya; **you oughtn't to have any problems** seharusnya Anda tidak mendapat masalah.

our *adjective* **1** *(including the listener)* **our government** pemerintah kita; **our parents** orang tua kita; **2** *(not including the listener)* **this is our house** ini rumah kami; **we'll go and get our coats** kami akan mengambil jas kami.

ours *pronoun* **1** kepunyaan kami, kepunyaan kita, milik kami, milik kita; **their garden's bigger than ours** kebun mereka lebih besar daripada kebun kita; **his house is smaller than ours** rumahnya lebih kecil daripada rumah kami; **the green one's ours** yang hijau itu milik kami; **a friend of ours** teman kita, teman kami.

ourselves *pronoun* diri, sendiri; **we introduced ourselves to her** kami memperkenalkan diri kami kepadanya; **in the end we**

a b c d e f g h i j k l m n o p q r s t u v w x y z

did it ourselves akhirnya kami melakukannya sendiri.

out *adverb* **1** *(outside)* di luar; **it's cold out there** di luar dingin; **the children like playing out in the rain** anak-anak suka bermain di luar di hujan; **they're out in the garden** mereka ada di taman; **2 to go out** pergi ke luar; **he went out of the room** dia (pergi) ke luar kamar; **are you going out this evening?** apakah Anda akan ke luar nanti malam?; **they threw it out of the window** mereka melemparnya ke luar jendela; **3 to take out** mengeluarkan; **she took the photo out of her bag** dia mengeluarkan foto dari tasnya; **4** *(light, fire)* mati, padam; **are all the lights out?** apakah semua lampu sudah padam?; **the fire has gone out** api itu telah mati; **5 to drink out of a glass** minum dari gelas; **6 Pak Rustam is out** Pak Rustam tidak ada di rumah; **Allison's going out with Rudi at the moment** Allison berpacaran dengan Rudi sekarang; **she's asked me out** dia mengajak saya keluar.

outdoor *adjective (an activity or sport)* alam terbuka, di luar; **an outdoor restaurant** rumah makan di alam terbuka.

outdoors *adverb* di alam terbuka, di luar rumah.

outing *noun* pesiar, tamasya; **to go on an outing** berpesiar, bertamasya.

outline *noun* garis besar, sketsa.

out-of-date *noun* **1** *(no longer valid)* tidak berlaku lagi, tidak terpakai lagi; **my passport's out-of-date** paspor saya sudah tidak berlaku lagi; **2** *(old-fashioned)* ketinggalan mode, ketinggalan zaman; **they played out-of-date music** mereka memainkan musik yang ketinggalan zaman.

outside *adjective, noun* bagian luar, sebelah luar; **it's blue (on the) outside** bagian luarnya berwarna biru.
adverb, preposition di luar, ke luar; **it's cold outside** di luar dingin; **I'll meet you outside the cinema** saya akan bertemu dengan Anda di luar bioskop.

outskirts *noun* daerah pinggiran, pinggir; **on the outskirts of Jakarta** di daerah pinggiran Jakarta.

oval *adjective* bulat lonjong, lonjong.

oven *noun* kompor; **it's a gas oven** itu adalah kompor gas.

over *preposition* **1** *(above)* di atas; **there's a mirror over the stairs** ada kaca di atas tangga itu; **2** *(involving movement)* melewati, melalui; **it jumped over the fence** dia loncat melewati pagar; **over the phone** melalui telepon; **3 over here** di sini; **the drinks are over here** minuman ada di sini; **4 over there** di sana; **she's over there talking to Julian** dia ada di sana, bercakap-cakap dengan Julian; **5** *(more than)* lebih dari; **it will cost over a hundred dollars** harganya lebih dari seratus dolar; **6** *(during)* selama; **over the weekend** selama akhir minggu; **over Lebaran** selama hari Lebaran; **7** *(finished)* berakhir, selesai; **when the meeting's over** kalau rapat sudah berakhir; **it's all over now** semua sudah berakhir sekarang; **8 all over the place** di mana-mana, di seluruh tempat; **all over the house** di seluruh rumah; **9 to ask over** mengundang.

overseas *adverb* di luar negeri; **Detty works overseas** Detty bekerja di luar negeri.

oversleep *verb* kesiangan, tidur terlalu lama.

overtake *verb (another vehicle)* mendahului, mengejar, menyusul.

overtime *noun* lembur; **to work overtime** bekerja lembur.

overweight *adjective* kegemukan, terlalu gemuk.

owe *verb* berhutang; **I owe Rizal fifty thousand Rupiah** saya berhutang lima puluh ribu rupiah pada Rizal.

owing *adjective* **1** *(to pay)* belum dibayar, berhutang; **there's five dollars owing** masih ada lima dolar yang belum dibayar; **2 owing to** oleh karena; **we couldn't get there owing to the floods** kami tidak bisa sampai di sana oleh karena banjir.

owl *noun* burung hantu.

own *adjective* sendiri; **my own computer** komputer saya sendiri; **I've got my own room** saya mempunyai kamar sendiri; **Syaiful did it on his own** Syaiful melakukannya sendiri.
verb memiliki, mempunyai; **Dave owns a Honda** Dave mempunyai mobil Honda.

owner *noun* pemilik, yang mempunyai.

a b c d e f g h i j k l m n o p q r s t u v w x y z

oxygen *noun* oksigen, zat asam.

oyster *noun* tiram.

ozone layer *noun* lapisan ozon.

P p

pace *noun* gaya jalan, kecepatan, langkah; **at a brisk pace** dengan (langkah) cepat.

pacific *adjective* **1** suka damai; **2 the Pacific Ocean** Lautan Pasifik, Lautan Teduh.

pack *noun* **1** bungkusan; **2** pak; **a pack of cards** satu bungkus kartu.
verb **1** membungkus, mengemas, mengepak; **I haven't packed yet** saya belum mengepak; **I'll pack my case tonight** saya akan mengemas koper saya nanti malam; **2** memasukkan; **have you packed your toothbrush?** apakah Anda sudah memasukkan sikat giginya?

package *noun* bingkisan, bungkus(an).

package holiday, package tour *noun* paket wisata.

packed lunch *noun* bekal makan siang.

packet *noun* bungkus; **a packet of biscuits** sebungkus biskuit.

packing *noun* pengepakan; **to do your packing** mengemas, mengepak.

pad *noun (of paper)* bloknot.

paddle *noun (for a canoe)* dayung, kayuh.
verb (at the seaside) **to go paddling** berdayung.

padlock *noun* gembok, kunci gantung.

page *noun* halaman; **on page fifteen** pada halaman lima belas.

pain *noun* rasa sakit; **I've got a pain in my leg** kaki saya sakit; **to be in pain** kesakitan, menderita sakit; **Putri's a real pain** Putri adalah orang yang sangat menjengkelkan.

painful *adjective* sakit.

paint *noun* cat; **'wet paint'** 'cat basah'.
verb mengecat; **to paint the rubbish bins yellow** mengecat tong sampah dengan warna kuning.

paintbrush *noun* kuas.

painter *noun* **1** *(art)* pelukis; **2** *(of a building)* tukang cat.

painting *noun (a picture)* lukisan; **a painting by Dede** lukisan oleh Dede.

pair *noun* pasang; **two pairs of socks** dua pasang kaus kaki; **a pair of scissors** (sebuah) gunting; **a pair of jeans** sebuah celana jeans; **to work in pairs** bekerja berpasangan.

Pakistan *noun* Pakistan.

Pakistani *noun* orang Pakistan.

palace *noun* istana; **Freedom Palace** Istana Merdeka; **the sultan's palace** keraton.

pale *adjective* **1** *(colour)* muda; **pale green** hijau muda; **2** *(a person)* pucat; **to turn pale** menjadi pucat.

palm *noun* **1** *(of your hand)* telapak tangan; **2** *(a palm tree)* pohon palem.

pan *noun* **1** *(saucepan)* panci; **a pan of water** sepanci air; **2** *(frying pan)* penggorengan, wajan *(wok)*.

pancake *noun* kue pankuk, panekuk

panel *noun* **1** *(on radio or TV, for a discussion)* juri, panel; *(for a quiz show)* regu; **2** *(for a wall, for example)* papan.

panel game *noun* permainan beregu.

panic *noun* kecemasan, kepanikan.
verb menjadi gugup, menjadi panik.

panther *noun* macan tutul.

pannier *noun (definition only)* tas atau keranjang besar yang dipasang pada sisi sepeda atau kuda.

pantomime *noun* pantomim, sandiwara bisu.

pants *noun* celana panjang.

paper *noun* **1** kertas; **a sheet of paper** sehelai kertas; **2 a paper cup** cangkir kertas; **3** *(newspaper)* koran, surat kabar.

paperback *noun* buku bersampul tipis.

paperclip *noun* jepitan kertas, penjepit kertas.

paper shop *noun* toko agen surat kabar.

paper towel *noun* handuk kertas, lap kertas.

parachute *noun* parasut.

parachuting *noun* terjun payung; **to go parachuting** terjun payung.

parade *noun* berjalan berbaris, parade, pawai.

paradise *noun* firdaus, surga.

paraffin *noun* **1** *(wax)* lilin; **2** *(kerosene)* parafin.

a b c d e f g h i j k l m n o p q r s t u v w x y z

paragraph *noun* paragraf.

parallel *adjective* berjajar, sejajar.

paralyzed *adjective* lumpuh.

parcel *noun* bungkusan, paket.

pardon *noun* maaf; **I beg your pardon** maafkan saya; **pardon, what did you say?** maaf, apa yang Anda katakan?

parent *noun* orang tua; **my parents are Acehnese** orang tua saya orang Aceh.

Paris *noun* Paris.

park *noun* **1** kebun raya, taman; **a theme park** taman impian; **2 a carpark** lapangan parkir mobil, pelataran parkir mobil. *verb* parkir; **to park a car** memarkir mobil; **where did you park the car?** mobilnya diparkir di mana?

parking *noun* parkir; **'no parking'** 'dilarang parkir'.

parking meter *noun* meter parkir.

parking space *noun* tempat parkir.

parking ticket *noun* **1** karcis parkir; **2** *(fine)* denda parkir.

parliament *noun* parlemen.

parrot *noun* burung nuri, burung kakatua.

parsley *noun* daun sop, peterseli.

part *noun* **1** bagian; **the last part of the film** bagian terakhir film itu; **that's part of his job** itu bagian dari pekerjaannya; **2 to take part in something** berpartisipasi, ikut serta, turut serta; **3** *(a role in a play)* peranan; **4 spare parts** onderdil, suku cadang.

particular *adjective* teliti; **he's not so particular** dia tidak begitu teliti; **nothing in particular** tidak ada yang istimewa.

particularly *adverb* **1** begitu; **not particularly difficult** tidak begitu sulit; **2** *(in particular)* terutama sekali; **particularly since you're leaving tomorrow** terutama karena Anda akan berangkat besok.

parting *noun* *(in your hair)* belahan rambut.

partly *adverb* sebagian.

partner *noun* **1** *(in a game)* mitra, pasangan; **2** *(the person you live with)* pasangan, jodoh; **3** *(in business)* mitra; **business partner** mitra bisnis.

part-time *adjective, adverb* paruh waktu; **part-time work** pekerjaan paruh waktu; **to**

work part-time bekerja paruh waktu.

party *noun* **1** pesta; **a Christmas party** pesta Natal; **to have a birthday party** mengadakan pesta hari ulang tahun; **2** *(group)* kelompok, kumpulan orang; **a party of school children** sekelompok anak sekolah; **3** *(in politics)* partai; **the Labour party** Partai Buruh.

party game *noun* permainan di pesta.

pass *noun* **1** *(to let you in)* kartu tanda masuk, pas jalan; **boarding pass** pas naik; **2** *(a mountain pass)* pas jalan; **3** *(in an exam)* lulus; **to get a good pass in history** lulus dengan baik dalam pelajaran sejarah.
verb **1** *(go past, a place or building)* melalui, melewati, melintasi; **we passed your house** kami melewati rumah Anda; **2** *(to overtake)* mendahului; **3** *(give)* menyampaikan, memberikan; **could you pass me that book please?** tolong sampaikan buku itu kepada saya; **4** *(time)* lalu, lewat; **the time passed quickly** waktu berlalu dengan cepat; **5** *(in an exam)* lulus; **did you pass?** apakah Anda lulus?

passage *noun* **1** *(a corridor)* gang; **2** *(a piece of text)* bagian.

passenger *noun* penumpang.

passerby *noun* orang yang lalu, orang yang lewat.

passion *noun* keinginan yang besar, nafsu.

passionate *adjective* bernafsu, penuh gairah.

passive *noun* pasif.
adjective pasif, tidak giat.

Passover *noun (definition only)* Pesta Paskah.

passport *noun* paspor.

past *noun* masa lalu, masa lampau; **in the past** dahulukala, dulu, pada masa lampau.
adjective **1** lalu; **in the past few days** beberapa hari yang lalu; **2** lewat; **the dry season is past** musim kemarau sudah lewat.
preposition, adverb lewat; **Hetty went past in her new car** Hetty lewat naik mobil barunya; **it's just past the mosque** langsung melewati masjid; **ten past six** jam enam lewat sepuluh menit; **half-past two** jam setengah tiga.

pasta *noun* makaroni, pasta.

a b c d e f g h i j k l m n o p q r s t u v w x y z

pasteurize verb *(definition only)* memanaskan sesuatu hingga 70°C untuk memberantas kuman-kuman penyakit, pasteurisasi.

pastry noun kue kering.

patch noun *(fabric, for mending)* tambalan.

path noun jalan kecil, lorong.

pathetic adjective **1** menyedihkan, kasihan, patetis; **it's pathetic the way they treat their animals** kasihan binatang peliharaan mereka; **2** *(useless, hopeless)* tak berguna; **what a pathetic thing to say** komentar yang tak berguna.

patience noun **1** kesabaran; **2** *(card game)* permainan kartu (untuk seorang saja).

patient noun pasien, si sakit. *adjective* sabar.

patiently adverb dengan sabar.

patio noun emper terbuka, patio.

patrol car noun mobil patroli.

pattern noun **1** *(on fabric, wallpaper)* motif; **2** *(dressmaking)* pola; **3** *(of behaviour)* contoh, teladan.

pause noun istirahat, jeda, pause.

pavement noun jalan aspal, kaki lima, trotoar.

paw noun cakar, kaki.

pawn noun bidak, pion.

pay noun bayaran, gaji, upah. *verb* **1** membayar; **I'm going to pay cash** saya mau membayar tunai; **it's all paid for** semuanya sudah dibayar; **to pay by credit card** membayar dengan kartu kredit; **to pay back** *(money)* membayar kembali; **2 paid** lunas; **3** guna; **I don't think it will pay me to do it** saya rasa tidak berguna bagi saya untuk melakukannya; **4** *(revenge)* membalas dendam; **5 to pay attention** memperhatikan; **6 to pay a visit** berkunjung ke, mengunjungi.

pay desk noun kas(s)a.

payment noun *(of a bill)* pembayaran.

pay phone noun telepon umum.

PC noun *(computer)* PC.

pea noun ercis, kacang polong.

peace noun damai, perdamaian.

peaceful adjective *(day, scene)* damai, tenang.

peacock noun burung merak.

peahen noun burung merak.

peak *noun (of a mountain)* puncak.

peak period *noun (for holidays)* musim liburan, musim ramai.

peak rate *noun (for phoning)* tarip tertinggi.

peak time *noun (for traffic)* jam sibuk, waktu sibuk.

peanut *noun* kacang tanah.

peanut butter *noun* pindakas, selei kacang tanah.

pear *noun* buah per.

pearl *noun* mutiara.

pebble *noun* batu kerikil.

peculiar *adjective* aneh, ganjil.

pedal *noun* pedal.

pedestrian *noun* pejalan kaki.

pedestrian crossing *noun* tempat menyeberang pejalan kaki.

pedestrian precinct *noun* tempat atau jalan khusus untuk pejalan kaki.

peel *noun* kulit.
verb mengupas.

peep *verb* mengintip.

peer *verb* memandang dengan tajam; **to peer at** memandang dengan tajam.

peg *noun* **1** *(hook)* cantelan, sangkutan; **2 clothespeg** jepitan pakaian; **3 a tent peg** pancang tenda.

pen *noun* pena; **a felt pen** spidol.

penalty *noun* **1** *(a fine)* hukuman (denda); **2** *(in football)* penalti.

pencil *noun* pensil, potlot; **to write in pencil** menulis dengan pensil.

pencil case *noun* kotak pensil; **eyebrow pencil** penghitam alis.

pencil sharpener *noun* peraut pensil.

pendant *noun* liontin, perhiasan yang bergantung pada kalung.

penfriend *noun* sahabat pena, teman pena; **my Indonesian penfriend is called Indra** teman pena Indonesia saya bernama Indra.

penguin *noun* penguin.

penis *noun* kemaluan laki-laki, penis.

penknife *noun* pisau lipat.

pension *noun* pensiun.

pensioner *noun* orang pensiunan, purnakaryawan.

people *plural noun* **1** rakyat; **people around here** rakyat di daerah ini; **2** *(when you're counting them)* orang-orang; **ten people** sepuluh orang;

a b c d e f g h i j k l m n o p q r s t u v w x y z

a b c d e f g h i j k l m n o p q r s t u v w x y z

several people beberapa orang; **people say he's really mean** kata orang, dia pelit sekali; **nice people** orang-orang baik; **3** bangsa; **the Indonesian people** bangsa Indonesia.

pepper *noun* **1** lada; **black pepper** lada hitam; **2** merica; **white pepper** merica; **3** lombok; **a green pepper** lombok hijau besar.

peppermint *noun* permen pedas.

per *preposition* per, setiap, tiap(-tiap); **5000 Rupiah per person** lima ribu rupiah tiap orang.

per cent *adverb* persen; **sixty per cent of government employees** enam puluh persen dari pegawai negeri.

percentage *noun* persentase.

percussion *noun* alat musik yang dipukul, misalnya drum atau tamborin (*definition only*).

perfect *adjective* **1** sempurna; **she speaks perfect Indonesian** dia berbahasa Indonesia dengan sempurna; **2** *(ideal)* idaman, ideal; **the perfect place for a picnic** tempat yang ideal untuk bertamasya.

perfectly *adverb* **1** dengan sempurna; **2** benar-benar; **that's perfectly understandable** itu benar-benar dapat dimengerti.

perform *verb* **1** *(a piece of music or a play)* memainkan; **2** *(a song)* menyanyi.

performance *noun* **1** *(playing or acting)* pagelaran; **a wonderful performance of the Ramayana** pagelaran Ramayana yang hebat sekali; **2** *(play)* sandiwara; **the performance starts at eight** sandiwara itu mulai jam delapan; **3** *(the results of a team or company)* kinerja.

performer *noun* pelaku, pemain sandiwara.

perfume *noun* minyak wangi, parfum.

perhaps *adverb* barangkali, boleh jadi, mungkin; **perhaps it's in the drawer** mungkin ada di laci; **perhaps he's missed the train** boleh jadi dia ketinggalan kereta api.

period *noun* **1** jangka waktu; **a two-year period** jangka waktu dua tahun; **2** *(in school)* jam pelajaran; **a forty-five-minute period** jam pelajaran yang lamanya empat puluh lima menit;

3 *(menstruation)* datang bulan, haid; **during your period** waktu datang bulan, pada waktu haid.

perm *noun* pengeritingan rambut.

permanent *adjective* permanen, tetap.

permanently *adverb* secara tetap.

permission *noun* izin, permisi; **to get permission to do** mendapat izin untuk melakukan.

permit *noun* surat izin. *verb* **1** mengizinkan, memperbolehkan; **our teacher permitted Grant to go outside** guru kami mengizinkan Grant ke luar; **smoking is not permitted** merokok tidak diizinkan; **2** memungkinkan; **weather permitting** kalau cuaca memungkinkan.

person *noun* **1** orang; **there's room for one more person** ada tempat untuk satu orang lagi; **2 in person** secara pribadi, sendiri; **I talked to him in person** saya berbicara dengannya sendiri.

personal *adjective* pribadi.

personality *noun* kepribadian.

personally *adverb* pribadi, sendiri; **personally, I'm against it** saya pribadi tidak setuju, saya sendiri tidak setuju.

perspiration *noun* keringat, peluh.

persuade *verb* membujuk, mengajak; **we persuaded him to leave** kami membujuk dia supaya pergi.

pessimistic *adjective* pesimistis.

pest *noun* **1** *(fruit fly, for example)* hama; **2** *(annoying person)* (orang) pengganggu.

pet *noun* kesayangan; **do you have a pet?** apakah Anda mempunyai binatang kesayangan?; **a pet dog** anjing kesayangan; **Lena is teacher's pet** Lena adalah kesayangan guru.

petal *noun* kelopak bunga, daun bunga.

pet name *noun* nama panggilan.

petrol *noun* bensin; **to fill up with petrol** mengisi bensin; **to run out of petrol** kehabisan bensin.

petrol station *noun* pom bensin, pompa.

pharmacy *noun* apotek, farmasi.

pheasant *noun* burung pegar.

philosophy *noun* filsafat.

a b c d e f g h i j k l m n o p q r s t u v w x y z

phone *noun* telepon, telpon; **she's on the phone** dia sedang berbicara di telepon; **you can book by phone** Anda dapat memesan melalui telepon.
verb menelepon; **while I was phoning** waktu saya menelepon; **I'll phone you tonight** saya akan menelepon Anda nanti malam.

phone book *noun* buku petunjuk telepon.

phone box *noun* gardu telepon.

phone call *noun* panggilan telepon; **phone calls are expensive here** menelepon mahal di sini; **to make a phone call** menelepon.

phone card *noun* kartu telepon.

phone number *noun* nomor telepon.

photo *noun* foto, potret; **to take a photo** memotret; **I took a photo of the temple** saya memotret candi itu.

photocopier *noun* mesin fotokopi.

photocopy *verb* memfotokopi.

photograph *noun* foto, potret; **to take a photograph** mengambil potret.

photographer *noun* juru potret.

photography *noun* fotografi, pemotretan.

phrase *noun* kelompok kata, frase.

phrase-book *noun* buku ungkapan, buku frase.

physical *adjective* jasmani(ah); **physical exercise** latihan jasmani.

physicist *noun* ahli ilmu fisika.

physics *noun* ilmu fisika.

physiotherapist *noun* ahli pijat, fisioterapis.

physiotherapy *noun* fisioterapi.

pianist *noun* pemain piano.

piano *noun* piano; **to play the piano** main piano.

pick *noun* pilih; **take your pick!** pilih saja!
verb **1** *(to choose)* memilih; **pick a card** silahkan pilih kartu; **I've been picked for Saturday** saya dipilih untuk main olahraga hari Sabtu; **2** *(fruit or flowers)* memetik.

- **to pick up 1** *(lift)* mengangkat; **he picked up the box and went out** dia mengangkat dos itu dan keluar; **2** *(small things)* memungut; **Sandra picked up the beads** Sandra memungut manik-manik; **3** *(collect)* menjemput; **I'll pick you**

up at six saya akan menjemput Anda jam enam; **4** mengambil; **I'll pick up the keys tomorrow** saya akan mengambil kunci itu besok; **5** *(learn)* belajar, mendapat, mengerti; **you'll soon pick it up** Anda pasti cepat mengerti.

pickpocket *noun* pencopet, tukang copet.

picnic *noun* piknik, tamasya; **to have a picnic** bertamasya.

picture *noun* **1** *(a painting)* gambar, lukisan; **a picture by Afandi** lukisan Afandi; **he painted a picture of fighting cocks** dia melukis ayam aduan; **2** *(a drawing)* gambar; **draw me a picture of your little sister** gambarkan adik perempuan Anda; **a book with lots of pictures** buku dengan banyak gambar; **3** *(the cinema)* film; **the pictures** film; **to go to the pictures** menonton film.

pie *noun* pastel; **an apple pie** pastel apel.

piece *noun* **1** potong(an); **a big piece of cake** sepotong kue besar; **the pieces of a jigsaw** potongan-potongan teka-teki gambar; **2 to take to pieces** membongkar-bongkar; **3** buah; **four pieces of luggage** empat buah kopor; **4** sedikit; **a piece of information** sedikit keterangan; **that's a piece of luck!** itu keuntungan!; **5** *(a coin)* satuan; **a ten-cent piece** satuan bernilai sepuluh sen.

pier *noun* dermaga.

pierce *verb* menusuk.

pierced *adjective* tertusuk; **to have pierced ears** telinganya ditindik.

pig *noun* babi.

pigeon *noun* burung dara, burung merpati.

piggy bank *noun* celengan, tabungan.

pigtail *noun* rambut kucir, taucang.

pile *noun* tumpukan; **a pile of plates** tumpukan piring.
- **to pile up** menumpuk.

pill *noun* pil; **the pill** *(contraceptive)* pil pencegah kehamilan.

pillar *noun* pilar, tiang.

pillow *noun* bantal.

pilot *noun* penerbang, pilot.

pimple *noun* jerawat.

pin *noun* *(for sewing)* jarum pentol, jarum penyemat.
- **to pin up 1** *(a hem)* menyematkan; **2** *(a poster)* menggantungkan.

a b c d e f g h i j k l m n o p q r s t u v w x y z

PIN [Personal Identification Number] *noun* nomor identifikasi pribadi.

pinball *noun* jakpot; **to play pinball** main jakpot; **a pinball machine** alat main jakpot.

pinch *noun (of salt, for example)* sejumput.
verb **1** *(steal)* mencuri; **somebody's pinched my lunch** ada orang yang mencuri makanan siang saya; **2** mencubit; **to pinch the baby** mencubit bayi.

pine *noun* cemara; **a pine table** meja (yang dibuat dari) kayu cemara.

pineapple *noun* nanas.

pine cone *noun* kerucut pohon cemara.

ping-pong *noun* pingpong, tenis meja; **to play ping-pong** main tenis meja.

pink *adjective* merah muda.

pip *noun (in a fruit)* biji buah.

pipe *noun* **1** *(for gas or water)* pipa; **2** *(to smoke)* pipa; **he smokes a pipe** dia mengisap pipa.

pirate *noun* bajak laut, perompak.

pirated *adjective* dibajak; **a pirated video** video (yang) dibajak.

Pisces *noun* Pisces.

pit *noun* lubang.

pitch *noun* lapangan; **a football pitch** lapangan sepak bola.
verb memancangkan, memasang; **to pitch a tent** memasang tenda.

pity *noun* **1** kasihan, sayang; **what a pity!** alangkah sayangnya!; **2** *(feeling sorry for somebody)* kasihan.
verb mengasihani.

pizza *noun* pizza.

place *noun* **1** tempat; **in a cool place** di tempat yang sejuk; **Ubud is a wonderful place** Ubud adalah tempat yang bagus sekali; **2** rumah, tempat tinggal; **at your place** di tempat tinggal Anda; **let's go round to Zafir's place** mari kita ke rumah Zafir; **3 to take place** berlangsung; **the competition will take place at four** pertandingan itu akan berlangsung jam empat.
verb menaruh, menempatkan; **he placed his cup on the table** dia menempatkan cangkirnya di meja.

plain *noun* padang, tanah datar.
adjective **1** sederhana; **plain cooking** masakan sederhana; **2** biasa; **3** *(not patterned)* polos; **plain fabric** kain polos; **4 plain rice** nasi putih.

plait *noun* jalin rambut, kepang.

plan *noun* **1** rencana; **what are your plans for the holiday?** apa rencana Anda untuk liburan?; **to go according to plan** berjalan menurut rencana; **2** *(a map)* gambar, peta.
verb **1** bermaksud, membuat rencana; **to plan to tour at Kakadu** membuat rencana untuk berwisata di Kakadu; **we're planning to buy a new house** kami bermaksud membeli rumah baru; **2** *(to make plans for)* merencanakan; **Boy's planning a party** Boy merencanakan pesta; **I'm planning my day** saya sedang merencanakan kegiatan saya hari ini; **3** *(to design, a house or garden)* merencanakan, menggambar.

plane *noun* pesawat terbang; **we went by plane** kami naik pesawat terbang.

planet *noun* planet.

plank *noun* papan.

plant *noun* tanam-tanaman, tumbuh-tumbuhan.

plaster *noun* **1** *(sticking plaster)* plester; **2** *(for walls)* plester; **3** *(for a cast)* gips.

plastic *noun* plastik; **a plastic bag** tas plastik.

plate *noun* piring.

platform *noun* **1** *(in a station)* peron; **the train leaves from platform four** kereta api akan berangkat dari peron empat; **2** *(for lecturing or performing)* panggung, podium.

play *noun* lakon, sandiwara; **a play by Rendra** sandiwara Rendra; **our school is putting on a play** sekolah kami akan menggelar sandiwara.
verb bermain, bermain-main, main; **the dog loves playing with a ball** anjing itu suka bermain-main dengan bola; **they play all kinds of music** mereka bermain aneka macam musik; **to play tennis** main tenis; **they were playing cards** mereka bermain kartu; **play me your new CD** tolong mainkan CD baru itu.

player *noun* pemain; **a football player** pemain sepak bola.

playground *noun* lapangan bermain, tempat bermain.

playgroup *noun* kelompok anak-anak kecil untuk bermain bersama-sama.

playing field *noun* gelanggang olahraga, lapangan olahraga.

a b c d e f g h i j k l m n o p q r s t u v w x y z

playroom *noun* kamar bermain.

plaza *noun* mal, plaza; **a shopping plaza** mal perbelanjaan, plaza perbelanjaan.

pleasant *adjective* enak, menyenangkan, nyaman, sedap.

please *adverb* **1** *(in offers)* silahkan; **please come in** silahkan masuk; **please take one** silahkan ambil satu; **2** *(in requests)* tolong, minta, –lah; **two coffees please** minta kopi dua cangkir; **could you turn the sound down please?** tolong kecilkan suaranya; **please help me** tolonglah saya; **3** harap; **please contact us** harap hubungi kami.

pleased *adjective* puas, senang; **I was really pleased** saya senang sekali; **pleased to meet you!** senang bertemu dengan Anda!; **she was pleased with the result** dia puas dengan hasilnya.

pleasure *noun* kesenangan.

plenty *pronoun* **1** *(lots)* banyak; **there's plenty of rice** ada banyak nasi; **she's got plenty of money** dia mempunyai banyak uang; **2** *(quite enough)* cukup; **we've got plenty of time for a coffee** kita ada banyak waktu untuk minum kopi; **thank you, that's plenty!** sudah cukup, terima kasih!

plot *noun (of a film or novel)* jalan cerita.

plough *verb* membajak (tanah).

plug *noun* **1** *(electrical)* steker; **2** *(in a bath or sink)* sumbat; **to pull out the plug** mencabut sumbat.

plum *noun* buah zahib, prem, semacam buah.

plumber *noun* tukang ledeng, tukang pipa; **your wife's not a plumber** istri Anda bukan tukang ledeng.

plump *adjective* gemuk (bayi), montok, sintal.

plunge *verb (into a pool)* terjun.

plural *noun* bentuk jamak; **in the plural** dalam bentuk jamak.

plus *preposition* tambah; **three plus six equals nine** tiga tambah enam sama dengan sembilan.

p.m. [post meridiem] *adverb* **1** *(from 11 a.m up to 2 p.m.)* siang; **at 2 p.m.** pada jam dua siang; **2** *(from 2 p.m. to nightfall)* sore; **4 p.m.** jam empat sore; **3** *(after dark)* malam; **9 p.m.** jam sembilan malam.

poached egg *noun* *(definition only)* telur tanpa kulit yang direbus di air yang mendidih.

pocket *noun* kantung, saku.

pocket money *noun* uang saku.

poem *noun* sajak, syair.

poet *noun* penyair.

poetry *noun* puisi.

point *noun* **1** *(tip)* ujung; **the point of the pencil** ujung pensil; **2** *(in time)* saat, titik; **at that point the police arrived** pada saat itu polisi tiba; **freezing point** titik beku; **3** maksud, pendapat; **to get the point** menangkap maksudnya; **that's not the point** itu bukan maksudnya; **that's a good point** itu pendapat yang baik; **4** gunanya, perlunya; **what's the point of waiting** apa perlunya menunggu; **there's no point phoning, he's out** tak ada gunanya menelepon, dia tidak ada di tempat; **5** pendapat; **from my point of view** menurut pendapat saya; **6** bakat; **her strong point** bakat dia; **7** *(in scoring)* angka, biji; **to win by five points** menang lima angka; **8** *(in decimals)* koma; **six point four** enam koma empat.

verb **1** menunjuk(kan); **a sign pointing to the museum** sebuah tanda yang menunjuk ke arah museum; **Nita pointed out the cathedral** Nina menunjukkan katedral itu; **2** *(with finger, considered rude by Indonesians, unless done with the thumb)*; **he pointed at one of the children** dia menunjuk pada salah satu anak; **3** menunjukkan, menjelaskan; **I'd like to point out that he's too young** saya ingin menunjukkan bahwa dia terlalu muda.

pointless *adjective* tidak ada gunanya, tidak berarti; **it's pointless to keep on asking** tidak ada gunanya meminta terus-menerus.

poison *noun* **1** *(from animals, such as snakes)* bisa; **2** *(chemical)* racun.

poisonous *adjective* berbisa, beracun.

Poland *noun* Polandia.

polar bear *noun* beruang es.

pole[1] *noun* **1** *(for a tent, for example)* galah, tiang, **2** kutub; **the North Pole** Kutub Utara.

Pole[2] *noun* *(a Polish person)* orang Polandia.

a b c d e f g h i j k l m n o p q r s t u v w x y z

police *noun* polisi; **the police are coming** polisi akan datang.

police car *noun* mobil polisi.

policeman *noun* polisi.

police station *noun* kantor polisi, pos polisi.

policewoman *noun* polisi wanita (polwan).

polish[1] *noun* poles, semir; **shoe polish** semir sepatu. *verb* **1** *(furniture, car)* memoles, menggosok, mengkilapkan; **2** *(shoes)* menyemir.

Polish[2] *adjective* dari Polandia, bahasa Polandia.

polite *adjective* sopan (santun); **to be polite to anybody** sopan santun kepada siapa saja.

political *adjective* politik.

politician *noun* politikus, politisi.

politics *noun* politik.

polluted *adjective* kotor, tercemar.

pollution *noun* pencemaran, pengotoran, polusi.

polythene bag *noun* tas plastik.

pond *noun* kolam.

pony *noun* kuda kecil, kuda kerdil.

ponytail *noun* **1** *(on the animal)* ekor kuda; **2** *(on hair)* kucir, taocang.

poodle *noun* anjing pudel.

pool *noun* **1** *(swimming pool)* kolam renang; **2** *(of labour)* gabungan, kelompok, pool; **3** *(puddle)* genangan; **4** *(game)* kantung bilyar; **to have a game of pool** main bilyar; **5** *(for a lottery)* arisan tebak-tebakan.

poor *adjective* **1** miskin; **a poor district** daerah miskin; **2** *(unlucky)* malang; **the poor kid!** anak yang malang!; **3** kasihan; **poor Eko's failed his exams** kasihan, Eko gagal dalam ujiannya; **4** *(bad)* jelek; **this is poor work** ini pekerjaan yang jelek; **5** buruk; **the weather was pretty poor** cuacanya buruk.

pop *noun* **1** pop; **a pop star** bintang pop; **2** *(sound)* letusan.

- **to pop into** masuk untuk sementara; **just pop into the bank** masuk ke bank untuk sementara.
- **to pop up** naik.

popcorn *noun* jagung kembang.

pope *noun* Sri Paus.

poppy *noun* bunga madat.

popular *adjective* populer.

population *noun* penduduk, populasi.

porch *noun* beranda, serambi.

pork *noun* daging babi.

porridge *noun* **1** *(rice cooked into a porridge form)* bubur; **2** *(rolled oat porridge)* havermot.

port *noun* pelabuhan; **the ship is in port** kapal itu ada di pelabuhan.

porter *noun* **1** *(at a station)* kuli pengangkut barang; **2** *(in a hotel)* penjaga pintu, portir.

portion *noun* *(of food)* porsi.

portrait *noun* gambar orang, lukisan orang, potret orang.

Portugal *noun* Portugal.

Portuguese *noun* **1** *(language)* bahasa Portugis; **2** *(person)* orang Portugis. *adjective* Portugal, Portugis.

posh *adjective* mewah; **a posh house** rumah mewah.

position *noun* kedudukan, posisi.

positive *adjective* **1** *(sure)* pasti; **I'm positive** saya pasti; **2** *(enthusiastic)* positif, tegas; **her reaction was very positive** reaksinya positif sekali; **try to be more positive** cobalah lebih positif.

possess *verb* memiliki, mempunyai.

possessions *noun* milik; **all my possessions are in this bag** semua barang (milik) saya ada di dalam tas ini.

possibility *noun* kemungkinan.

possible *adjective* mungkin; **it's possible** mungkin; **if possible** kalau mungkin; **as quickly as possible** secepat mungkin.

possibly *adverb* **1** *(maybe)* barangkali, mungkin; **'will you be here next week?' – 'possibly'** 'apakah Anda akan datang ke sini minggu depan?' – 'mungkin'; **2** *(for emphasis)* mungkin; **I can't possibly eat dog meat!** saya tidak mungkin bisa makan daging anjing!; **3 how can you possibly believe her?** bagaimana Anda dapat mempercayai dia?

post *noun* **1** pos; **to send something by post** mengirim dengan pos; **2** *(letters)* surat; **is there any post for me?** apakah ada surat untuk saya?; **3** *(a pole)* tonggak; **4** *(a job)* jabatan, tempat tugas. *verb* mengeposkan; **to post a letter** mengeposkan surat, mengirim surat lewat pos.

postbox *noun* bis surat.

postcard *noun* kartu pos.

postcode *noun* kode pos.

poster *noun* **1** *(for decoration)* poster; **I've bought a Midnight Oil poster** saya membeli poster Midnight Oil; **2** *(advertising)* plakat, poster; **I saw a poster for the concert** saya melihat plakat untuk konser itu.

postman *noun* pengantar pos, tukang pos; **has the postman been here?** apakah pengantar pos sudah ke sini?

post office *noun* kantor pos; **the post office is opposite the mosque** kantor pos di seberang mesjid.

postpone menangguhkan, menunda; **to postpone a test** menunda ujian.

pot *noun* **1** *(jar)* botol, kendi; **a pot of honey** sebotol madu; **2** *(teapot)* teko teh; **I'll make a pot of tea** saya akan membuat teh; **3** panci; **the pots and pans** panci-panci; **to take pot luck** makan seadanya.

potato *noun* kentang; **fried potatoes** kentang goreng; **mashed potatoes** kentang pure.

potato crisps *noun* keripik kentang.

pottery *noun* barang pecah belah, tembikar.

pour *verb* **1** *(liquid)* menuangkan; **he poured the milk into the pan** dia menuangkan susu ke dalam panci; **2** mengalir; **letters poured in** surat-surat mengalir masuk; **3** *(with rain)* turun; **it's pouring** hujan turun dengan lebat sekali.

poverty *noun* kemiskinan.

powder *noun* **1** *(for the body or face)* bedak; **2** *(medicine, soap, etc.)* bubuk.

power *noun* **1** daya, tenaga; *(electricity)* tenaga listrik; **a power cut** listrik mati; **nuclear power** tenaga nuklir; **2** *(over other people)* kekuasaan; **to be in power** berkuasa.

powerful *adjective* berkuasa, sangat kuat.

power point *noun* stopkontak.

power station *noun* pembangkit tenaga listrik.

practical *adjective* mudah dilaksanakan, praktis.

practically *adverb* **1** *(almost)* hampir; **2** *(in a practical way)* secara praktis.

practice *noun* **1** latihan; **football practice** latihan sepak bola; **to do your piano practice** berlatih (main) piano; **to be out of practice**

telah lama tidak melakukan; **2 in practice** biasanya.

practise *verb* berlatih; **a week in Yogya to practise my Indonesian** seminggu di Yogya untuk mempraktekkan bahasa Indonesia; **the team practises on Wednesdays** regu itu berlatih tiap hari Rabu.

praise *verb* memuji.

pram *noun* kereta bayi.

prawn *noun* udang.

pray *verb* bersembahyang, berdoa.

prayer *noun* doa, sembahyang.

precaution *noun* tindakan pencegah; **to take precautions** mencegah.

precinct *noun* daerah; **a shopping precinct** daerah perbelanjaan; **a pedestrian precinct** jalan khusus untuk pejalan kaki.

precious *adjective* berharga, bernilai.

precisely *adverb* persis, tepat; **at precisely eleven o'clock** tepat pada pukul sebelas.

preface *noun* kata pengantar, pendahuluan.

prefer *verb* lebih suka; **I prefer water to sweet drinks** saya lebih suka air daripada minuman manis.

pregnant *adjective* **1** *(people)* berbadan dua, hamil, mengandung; **2** *(animals)* bunting.

prejudice *noun* prasangka; **to oppose racial prejudice** menentang prasangka rasial; **to have a prejudice against** berprasangka terhadap.

prejudiced *adjective* berprasangka; **to be prejudiced against** berprasangka terhadap.

preliminary *adjective* pendahuluan; **preliminary examination** ujian persiapan.

preparation *noun* persiapan; **the preparations for Idul Fitri** persiapan untuk Idul Fitri.

prepare *verb* mempersiapkan, menyiapkan; **to prepare somebody for** menyiapkan seseorang untuk *(a surprise or shock)*; **to be prepared for the worst** bersiap-siap menghadapi yang paling buruk.

prepared *adjective* bersedia, bersiap; **I'm prepared to pay half** saya bersedia membayar separoh.

preposition *noun* kata depan, kata perangkai, preposisi.

prescription *noun* resep (dokter); **on prescription** harus ada resep.

presence *noun* keberadaan, kehadiran; **my presence** kehadiran saya; **presence of mind** kesadaran.

present *noun* **1** *(a gift)* hadiah; **to give the bride a present** memberi pengantin hadiah; **2** *(the time now)* sekarang ini; **that's all for the present** sudah cukup untuk sekarang ini; **in the present (tense)** kata kerja masa kini, (bentuk waktu ini).
adjective **1** *(attendance)* hadir; **is Mira present?** apakah Mira hadir?; **to be present at** hadir pada; **two thousand people were present at the funeral** dua ribu orang hadir pada pemakaman; **2** *(existing now)* sekarang; **the present situation** keadaan sekarang; **3 at the present time** pada masa kini.
verb **1** *(a prize)* memberikan, menyampaikan; **2** *(introduce)* memperkenalkan.

presenter *noun* pengantar acara.

presently *adverb* **1** *(soon)* segera; **2** *(at present)* kini, sekarang.

president *noun* **1** *(of a country)* presiden; **2** *(of a club)* ketua; **3** *(of a business)* direktur.

press *noun* **the press** pers.
verb menekan; **press here to open** tekan di sini untuk membuka; **he pressed the button** dia menekan tombol itu.

press conference *noun* konperensi pers.

pressure *noun* tekanan.

pressure group *noun* kelompok penekan.

pretend *verb* berpura-pura; **to pretend to do** berpura-pura melakukan; **he's pretending not to hear** dia berpura-pura tidak mendengar.

pretty *adjective* **1** cantik, manis, molek; **a pretty bird** burung yang cantik; **2** *(fairly)* agak; **it was pretty silly** agak bodoh.

prevent *verb* mencegah; **there's nothing to prevent you from leaving** tak ada yang mencegah Anda pergi.

previous *adjective* yang lebih dahulu, sebelum(nya).

previously *adverb* sebelum itu, sebelum(nya).

price *noun* harga; **the price per kilo** harga satu kilo; **CDs have gone up in price** harga CD telah naik.

price list *noun* daftar harga.

price ticket *noun* label harga.

prick verb menusuk; **Cinderella pricked her finger** Cinderella tertusuk jarinya.

pride *noun* kebanggaan.

priest *noun* **1** *(Islamic)* imam, kiyai; **2** *(Christian)* pastor, pendeta.

primary school *noun* sekolah dasar.

primary (school) teacher *noun* guru sekolah dasar.

Prime Minister *noun* Perdana Menteri.

prince *noun* pangeran; **Prince Bernard** Pangeran Bernard.

princess *noun* putri; **Princess Anne** Putri Anne.

principal *noun* *(of a college)* kepala sekolah. *adjective* *(main)* pokok, utama, yang terpenting.

principle *noun* **1** asas, dasar; **that's true in principle** pada dasarnya itu benar; **2** pendirian, prinsip; **on principle** pada prinsipnya, pada pokoknya; **to have high principles** berpendirian tinggi, berprinsip tinggi.

print *noun* **1** *(letters)* huruf, cetakan; **read the small print** baca huruf kecil; **2** *(a photo)* foto, potret; **a colour print** foto berwarna.

printer *noun* **1** pencetak; **2** *(computer)* printer.

print-out *noun* cetakan.

prison *noun* penjara; **in prison** meringkuk di penjara.

prisoner *noun* orang hukuman, orang tahanan; **prisoner of war** tawanan perang.

private *adjective* **1** pribadi; **'private property'** 'milik pribadi'; **2** *(lesson)* privat; **to have private lessons** mengambil les privat; **3 a private school** sekolah swasta.

prize *noun* hadiah; **to win a prize** memenangkan hadiah.

prize-giving *noun* upacara pemberian hadiah.

prizewinner *noun* pemenang hadiah.

probable *adjective* mungkin; **her probable reason** alasannya yang mungkin.

probably *adverb* mungkin.

problem *noun* masalah, problim, soal; **it's a serious problem** masalah yang serius; **no problem!** tak ada masalah!

process *noun* **1** proses; **2 to be in the process of doing** tengah melakukan, dalam proses melakukan.

a b c d e f g h i j k l m n o **p** q r s t u v w x y z

produce *noun (food)* hasil bumi.
verb **1** mengeluarkan; **I produced my passport** saya mengeluarkan paspor saya; **2** mengeluarkan, menghasilkan; **it produces a lot of heat** menghasilkan banyak panas; **3** menimbulkan, menyebabkan; **it produced an itchy feeling** menimbulkan rasa gatal.

producer *noun (of a film or program)* produser.

product *noun* hasil, produk.

production *noun* **1** *(of a film, opera or play)* pagelaran; **a new production of Opera Kecoa** pagelaran Opera Kecoa; **2** *(of a factory)* penghasilan, produksi.

profession *noun* pekerjaan, profesi.

professional *noun* profesional; **he's a professional** dia seorang profesional.
adjective profesional; **he's a professional boxer** dia petinju profesional.

professor *noun* profesor.

profile *noun* profil.

profit *noun* keuntungan, laba, untung.

profitable *adjective* menguntungkan.

program *noun* **1** *(for a play, event)* acara, program; **2** program; **a computer program** program komputer.

progress *noun* **1** kemajuan; **to make progress** memperoleh kemajuan; **2 to be in progress** sedang berlangsung.

project *noun* **1** *(at school)* proyek; **2** *(a plan)* rencana; **a project to build a bridge** rencana untuk membangun jembatan.

projector *noun* proyektor.

promise *noun* janji; **to make a promise** berjanji, menjanjikan; **to break a promise** mengingkari janji; **it's a promise!** janji!
verb berjanji, menjanjikan; **I've promised to bring the salads** saya berjanji akan membawa salad.

promote *verb* menaikkan pangkat; **to be promoted** dinaikkan pangkat.

promotion *noun* kenaikan kedudukan, kenaikan pangkat, promosi.

promptly *adverb* **1** *(at once)* cepat; **he promptly fell off again** dia cepat jatuh lagi; **2** *(quickly)* secepat mungkin; **please reply promptly** harap jawab secepat mungkinnya; **3** *(on time)* tepat; **promptly at**

five o'clock tepat pada jam lima.

pronoun *noun* kata ganti.

pronounce *verb* mengucapkan; **it's hard to pronounce** sulit diucapkan.

pronunciation *noun* pengucapan, ucapan.

proof *noun* bukti; **there's no proof that** tak ada bukti bahwa.

propaganda *noun* propaganda.

propeller *noun* baling-baling.

proper *adjective* **1** *(real, genuine)* yang sebenarnya; **a proper doctor** dokter yang sebenarnya; **2** *(correct)* tepat; **the proper answer** jawaban tepat; **3 I need a proper meal** saya perlu makanan yang baik.

properly *adverb* sebagaimana mestinya; **hold it properly** peganglah sebagaimana mestinya; **is it properly wrapped?** apakah itu dibungkus sebagaimana mestinya?

property *noun* **1** *(your belongings)* barang milik; **'private property'** 'milik pribadi'; **2** *(real estate)* properti.

proposal *noun* **1** proposal, tawaran, usul; **2** *(marriage)* lamaran.

propose *verb* **1** *(suggest)* mengusulkan; **2** *(marriage)* melamar; **he proposed marriage** dia melamar.

protect *verb* melindungi, menjaga, memproteksi; **to protect the environment** melindungi lingkungan hidup.

protection *noun* penjagaan, perlindungan, proteksi.

protein *noun* protein.

protest *noun* protes, sanggahan.
verb **1** *(grumble)* memprotes; **2** *(demonstrate)* memprotes, menyanggah.

Protestant *noun* Protestan.

protester *noun* pemrotes, penyanggah.

protest march *noun* unjuk rasa.

proud *adjective* bangga.

prove *verb* membuktikan.

proverb *noun* pepatah, peribahasa.

provide *verb* memberikan, menyediakan.

provided *conjunction* asal; **provided you do it now** asal Anda melakukannya sekarang.

prune *verb* memangkas, memotong.

a b c d e f g h i j k l m n o p q r s t u v w x y z

psychiatrist *noun* dokter penyakit jiwa, psikiater; **she's a psychiatrist** dia psikiater.

psychological *adjective* psikologis, bersifat kejiwaan.

psychologist *noun* psikolog.

psychology *noun* ilmu jiwa, psikologi.

PTO [Please Turn Over] *abbreviation* lihat halaman sebaliknya.

pub *noun* bar, pub, tempat minum minuman keras.

public *noun* umum; **the public** rakyat umum, masyarakat; **in public** di muka umum.
adjective umum; **the public library** perpustakaan umum.

public address system *noun* corong pengeras suara *(definition only)*.

public holiday *noun* hari libur (nasional); **17 August is a public holiday** 17 Agustus adalah hari libur nasional.

publicity *noun* publisitas, reklame.

public school *noun* sekolah negeri.

public transport *noun* pengangkutan umum, transportasi umum.

publish *verb* menerbitkan.

publisher *noun* penerbit.

pudding *noun* poding.

puddle *noun* genangan, kubang.

puff *noun (of smoke)* hembusan, tiupan.

pull *verb* menarik; **pull hard!** tarik keras-keras!; **to pull a rope** menarik tali; **he pulled a rabbit out of the hat** dia menarik kelinci dari topi; **you're pulling my leg!** Anda bercanda saja!

- **to pull down** *(a blind, for example)* menurunkan.
- **to pull in** *(at the roadside)* berhenti.

pullover *noun* baju hangat, pulover, sweater.

pump *noun* pompa; **a bicycle pump** pompa sepeda; **a water pump** pompa air.
verb memompa; **they were pumping the water out of the canal** mereka memompa air dari terusan.

- **to pump up** *(a tyre)* memompa, menambah angin.

pumpkin *noun* labu kuning.

punch *noun* **1** *(with the fist)* pukulan; **2** *(drink)* minuman campuran.
verb **1** menghantam, meninju; **she punched the policeman** dia menghantam polisi; **2** *(a ticket)* melubangi, memotong, menggunting.

punctual *adjective* tepat pada waktunya.

punctuation *noun* tanda baca.

punctuation mark *noun* tanda baca.

puncture *noun* kebocoran (ban); **we had a puncture on the way here** ban kami bocor dalam perjalanan ke sini, ban kami kempes dalam perjalanan ke sini.

punish *verb* menghukum.

punishment *noun* hukuman.

pupil *noun* murid.

puppet *noun* golek, wayang; **a puppet show** pertunjukan wayang kulit, pertunjukan wayang golek.

puppy *noun* anak anjing.

pure *adjective* **1** *(of water, air)* bersih; **2** *(of gold, alcohol, etc.)* murni.

purple *noun* warna ungu.

purpose *noun* **1** maksud; **what was the purpose of her call?** apa maksud dia menelepon?; **2 on purpose** dengan sengaja; **he closed the door on purpose** dia menutup pintu dengan sengaja; **she didn't do it on purpose** dia melakukannya dengan tidak sengaja.

purr *verb* berdengkur.

purse *noun* dompet.

push *noun* dorongan; **a gentle push** dorongan yang lembut; **to give the car a push** mendorong mobil. *verb* **1** mendorong; **he pushed me** dia mendorong saya; **2** mendesak; **his teacher is pushing him to take another subject** gurunya mendesaknya supaya mengambil satu mata kuliah lagi.

- **to push something away** menepikan, mengesampingkan; **she pushed her plate away** dia mengesampingkan piringnya.

pushchair *noun* kursi dorong.

put *verb* **1** menaruh; **where did you put my passport?** di mana Anda menaruh paspor saya?; **who put your suitcase here?** siapa yang menaruh koper Anda di sini?; **2** memasukkan; **you can put the milk in the fridge** susu itu dapat dimasukkan ke dalam lemari es; **3** beri; **don't put sugar in my tea** teh saya jangan diberi gula; **4** *(write)* menulis; **put your address here** tulis alamat Anda di sini.

- **to put away** menyimpan; **I'll put the shopping away**

a b c d e f g h i j k l m n o p q r s t u v w x y z

saya akan menyimpan belanjaan.

- **to put back 1** menaruh kembali, mengembalikan; **I put it back in the drawer** saya mengembalikannya ke laci; **2** *(postpone)* mengundurkan, menunda; **the exam has been put back until Thursday** ujian itu ditunda sampai hari Kamis.
- **to put down** menaruh; **she put the cups down on the table** dia menaruh cangkir-cangkir itu di atas meja.
- **to put off 1** *(postpone)* mengundurkan, menunda; **they've put off the trip until next week** mereka menangguhkan lawatannya sampai minggu depan; **2** *(turn off, a light or TV, for example)* mematikan; **don't forget to put off the modem** jangan lupa mematikan modem itu; **3** menurunkan selera; **it's really put me off Menadonese food!** betul-betul menurunkan selera saya terhadap makanan khas Manado.
- **to put on 1** *(clothing, make-up)* memakai, mengenakan; **I'll just put on my shoes** saya hanya akan mengenakan sepatu; **2** *(switch on, a light or air-conditioning, for example)* memasang; **could you put the lamp on?** tolong pasang lampu itu; **he's put on AC/DC** dia telah memasang AC/DC; **3** *(a play)* mengadakan; **we're putting on a shadow play** kami akan mengadakan suatu pertunjukan wayang kulit.
- **to put out 1** *(put outside)* mengeluarkan; **have you put the rubbish out?** apakah Anda sudah mengeluarkan sampah?; **2** *(a fire, light or cigarette)* memadamkan; **they've put the fire out** mereka sudah memadamkan api itu; **3 to put out your hand** merentangkan tangan.
- **to put up 1** *(your hand)* mengangkat; **I put up my hand** saya mengangkat tangan; **2** *(to hang up)* menggantung; **I've put up some weavings in my room** saya telah menggantung kain tenun di kamar saya; **3** *(a notice)* memasang; **4** *(the price)* menaikkan; **they've put up the price of the**

tickets mereka telah menaikkan harga karcis; **5** *(for the night)* menampung, menginap; **can you put me up for the weekend?** dapatkah Anda menampung saya selama akhir minggu?

- **to put up with** bersabar, tahan; **I don't know how she puts up with all those children** saya tak mengerti bagaimana dia bersabar dengan anak-anak itu.

puzzle *noun (jigsaw)* teka teki.

puzzled *adjective* bingung.

pyjamas *noun* piyama; **a pair of pyjamas** sesetel piyama; **where are my pyjamas?** di mana piyama saya?

pyramid *noun* limas, piramid.

python *noun* ular sanca, ular sawah.

Q q

qualification *noun* **1** *(certificate, exam, degree)* ijasah, ijazah; **2 qualifications** kualifikasi; **vocational qualifications** kualifikasi keahlian.

qualified *adjective* berijazah, berkualifikasi, bermutu; **she's a qualified tennis instructor** dia pelatih tenis yang berkualifikasi; **a qualified architect** arsitek yang berkualifikasi.

qualify *verb (to be eligible)* memenuhi syarat; **we don't qualify for assistance** kami tidak memenuhi syarat untuk mendapat pertolongan; **he qualified for the team** dia telah memenuhi syarat untuk bermain dalam regu itu.

quality *noun* mutu, kwalitas; **good-quality vegetables** sayur-mayur bermutu baik.

quantity *noun* jumlah, kwantitas.

quarantine *noun* karantina.

quarrel *noun* perselisihan, pertengkaran; **we have no quarrel with them** kami tidak berselisih dengan mereka; **to have a quarrel** bertengkar. *verb* berselisih, bertengkar; **they're always quarrelling** mereka selalu bertengkar.

quarter *noun* (se)perempat; **a quarter** seperempat; **three-quarters of the students** tigaperempat dari murid-murid itu; **to divide into quarters** membagi menjadi empat bagian; **a quarter past**

a b c d e f g h i j k l m n o p q r s t u v w x y z

ten jam sepuluh lewat seperempat; **a quarter of an hour** seperempat jam; **an hour and three quarters** satu tigaperempat jam.

quartet *noun* kwartet; **a jazz quartet** kwartet jazz.

quay *noun* dermaga, pangkalan pelabuhan.

queen *noun* ratu; **Queen Elizabeth** Ratu Elizabeth; **queen consort** permaisuri; **queen bee** induk lebah.

query *noun* pertanyaan; **are there any queries?** apakah ada pertanyaan?

question *noun* **1** pertanyaan; **to ask a question** bertanya; **to raise a question** mengajukan pertanyaan; **2** soal; **it's a question of time** ini soal waktu; **it's out of the question** bukan persoalannya, tidak mungkin.

question mark *noun* tanda tanya.

questionnaire *noun* daftar pertanyaan, kuesioner; **to fill in a questionnaire** mengisi kuesioner.

queue *noun* antre, antri; **to stand in a queue** mengantri. *verb* antri; **we were queuing for check-in** kami (meng)antri untuk check-in.

quick *adjective* **1** cepat; **a quick lunch** makan siang dengan cepat; **it's quicker on the toll road** lebih cepat lewat jalan tol; **2** cepat, lekas; **quick! there's the bus!** lekaslah! bis datang!; **be quick!** cepatlah!

quickly *adverb* dengan cepat; **I'll just quickly phone home** saya ingin cepat-cepat menelepon keluarga.

quiet *adjective* **1** *(silent)* diam; **the children are very quiet** anak-anak sangat diam; **to keep quiet** diam; **'quiet please'** 'harap diam'; **2** *(gentle)* jinak; **a quiet horse** kuda jinak; **3** *(volume)* kecil; **some quiet music** musik dengan suara kecil; **in a quiet voice** dengan suara kecil; **4** *(peaceful)* sepi, tenang; **a quiet street** jalan sepi.

quietly *adverb* dengan diam-diam.

quilt *noun* selimut tebal.

quite *adverb* **1** sangat, sungguh; **it's quite cold outside** sangat dingin di luar; **that's quite a good idea** itu ide yang sungguh bagus; **he sings quite well** dia menyanyi dengan merdu; **quite often** sungguh sering; **2 not quite** belum betul-betul; **the meat's not quite**

cooked daging itu belum betul-betul masak; **3** agak, juga; **quite a lot of** agak banyak; **we've got quite a lot of friends here** banyak juga teman kami di sini.

quiz *noun* kuis; **quiz show** acara kuis.

quotation *noun (from a book)* kutipan.

quotation marks *noun* tanda kutip; **in quotation marks** dalam tanda kutip.

quote *noun* **1** *(from a book)* kutipan, petikan; **in quotes** dalam tanda kutip; **2** *(estimate)* penentuan, penetapan.
verb **1** mengutip; **2** memberikan harga.

R r

rabbi *noun* pendeta Yahudi.

rabbit *noun* kelinci.

rabbit hutch *noun* kandang kelinci.

rabies *noun* penyakit anjing gila.

race *noun* **1** *(a sports event)* balapan, pacuan, perlombaan; **a cycle race** balapan sepeda; **a horse race** pacuan kuda; **to have a race** mengadakan perlombaan; **2** *(an ethnic group)* bangsa, ras.

racer *noun (car, bike, horse)* kuda pacuan, mobil balap, pelari, pembalap (sepeda, kuda).

racetrack *noun* **1** *(for horses)* tempat pacuan kuda; **2** *(for cars, cycles)* lapangan balapan (mobil, sepeda).

racial *adjective* rasial; **racial discrimination** diskriminasi rasial.

racing *noun* balapan.

racing car *noun* mobil balap.

racing driver *noun* pengemudi mobil balap.

racism *noun* rasialisme.

racist *noun* rasialis

rack *noun (for luggage)* rak, rak tempat barang.

racket *noun* **1** *(for tennis)* raket; **here's your tennis racket** ini raket Anda; **2** *(noise)* kegaduhan, keributan, kerusuhan.

radiation *noun* penyinaran, radiasi.

radiator *noun* radiator.

radio *noun* radio; **to listen to the radio** mendengarkan radio; **to hear a song on the**

radio mendengar lagu di radio.

radioactive *adjective* radioaktip.

radio-controlled *adjective* dikendalikan oleh sinar radio.

radio station *noun* stasiun pemancar radio.

radish *noun* lobak.

rag *noun* kain-kain tua, topo.

rage *noun* kegusaran, kemarahan; **she's in a rage** dia marah sekali; **it's all the rage** itu digemari umum.

raid *noun* penggerebekan, razzia.

rail *noun* **1** *(the railway)* kereta api; **to go by rail** naik kereta api; **2** *(on a balcony or bridge)* jeruji; **3** *(for a train)* rel jalan kereta api.

rail strike *noun* pemogokan pegawai perusahaan kereta api.

railing(s) *noun* kisi-kisi, susur tangga.

railway *noun* **1** *(the system)* **the railways** perkereta-apian; **2 a railway line** *(from one place to another)* jalan kereta api; **3** *(the rails)* rel kereta api.

railway carriage *noun* gerbong kereta api.

railway station *noun* stasiun kereta api.

rain *noun* hujan; **playing in the rain** bermain di hujan; **to be caught in the rain** kehujanan.
verb hujan; **it's raining** hujan; **it's going to rain** akan hujan.

rainbow *noun* bianglala, pelangi.

raincoat *noun* jas hujan.

raindrop *noun* tetesan air hujan.

rainy *adjective* banyak hujan; **rainy season** musim hujan.

raise *verb* **1** *(lift up)* mengangkat; **she raised her head** dia mengangkat kepalanya; **2** *(increase) (a price or salary, rank, flag)* menaikkan; **3** mengumpulkan; **to raise money for victims of the floods** mengumpulkan uang untuk korban banjir; **4 to raise the alarm** memberitahukan ada bahaya; **5** *(to raise standards, somebody's spirits)* meningkatkan; **6** *(a child)* membesarkan.

raisin *noun* kismis.

rake *noun* penggaruk.

rally *noun* **1** *(a meeting)* rapat umum; **2** *(in tennis)* permainan dengan pukulan yang bertubi-tubi.

a b c d e f g h i j k l m n o p q r s t u v w x y z

Ramadan *noun* Ramadan, bulan Puasa.

rambler *noun* kelana, pengembara.

rambling *noun* bertele-tele; **a rambling speech** pidato yang bertele-tele.

ramp *noun (for a wheelchair, for example)* jalur, tempat landai.

ranch *noun* peternakan.

range *noun* **1** *(a choice)* banyak sekali, berbagai; **we offer a range of activities** kami menawarkan berbagai kegiatan; **in a wide range of colours** dalam banyak warna; **2** *(of mountains)* barisan, jajaran; **top-of-the-range computer** komputer yang paling unggul.

rank *noun* pangkat.

rape *noun* perkosaan.
verb memperkosa.

rare *adjective* **1** jarang, langka; **a rare animal** binatang langka; **2** *(a steak)* setengah masak.

rarely *adverb* jarang.

rash *noun* kudis, ruam; **heat rash** ruam karena terlalu panas.
adjective terburu-buru, tergesa-gesa; **a rash decision** keputusan yang terburu-buru diambil.

raspberry *noun* buah frambus; **raspberry jam** selai frambus.

rat *noun* tikus besar.

rate *noun* **1** *(a charge)* tarip, suku, upah; **what are the rates for adults?** berapa tarip untuk orang dewasa?; **reduced rates** tarip yang dipotong; **interest rates** suku bunga; **2** *(a level)* angka; **a high cancellation rate** angka pembatalan yang tinggi; **3** *(foreign exchange)* kurs; **4** kecepatan; **at the rate of 80 kilometres per hour** dengan kecepatan delapan puluh kilometer per jam; **5 at any rate** bagaimanapun juga, pendeknya.

rather *adverb* **1** agak; **I'm rather busy** saya agak sibuk; **rather a lot** agak banyak; **I've got rather a lot of homework** pekerjaan rumah saya agak banyak; **2 rather than** daripada; **in the dry season rather than the wet** pada musim kemarau daripada musim hujan; **3** lebih suka; **I'd rather wait** saya lebih suka menunggu; **they'd rather come next month** mereka lebih suka datang bulan depan.

rave *noun* kegila-gilaan kepada; **Phil raves about the group Killing Heidi** Phil kegila-gilaan kepada grup Killing Heidi.

raw *adjective* mentah.

razor *noun* pisau cukur.

razor blade *noun* silet.

RE [religious education] *noun* pendidikan agama.

reach *noun (of your hand)* jangkauan; **out of reach** di luar jangkauan, tidak terjangkau; **within reach** dekat, terjangkau; **within easy reach of the sea** dekat sekali dengan laut.
verb **1** sampai; **when you reach the mosque** bila sampai di mesjid;
2 mencapai; **to reach a decision** mencapai keputusan; **to reach the top** mencapai puncak.

react *verb* bereaksi.

reaction *noun* reaksi.

read *verb* membaca; **what are you reading at the moment?** Anda sedang membaca apa pada saat ini?; **he read out the list** dia membacakan daftar itu.

reading *noun* **1** bacaan, membaca; **I don't much like reading** saya kurang suka membaca; **2** bacaan; **some easy reading for the holiday** bacaan yang ringan untuk liburan.

ready *adjective* sedia, siap; **dinner's not ready yet** makan malam belum siap; **are you ready to go?** apakah Anda sudah siap untuk pergi?; **to get ready** mempersiapkan; **I'm getting ready to go out** saya sedang mempersiapkan diri untuk jalan-jalan; **she's getting ready for university** dia sedang bersiap-siap untuk masuk universitas; **I'll get breakfast ready** saya akan menyediakan makan pagi.

real *adjective* **1** asli, sejati, tulen; **it's a real pearl** itu mutiara asli; **2** benar, betul-betul; **he's a real bore** dia betul-betul membosankan; **is that his real name?** apakah itu namanya yang benar?; **her real father is dead** ayah kandungnya sudah meninggal dunia.

realistic *adjective* realistis.

reality *noun* kenyataan, realitas.

realize *verb* insyaf akan, menyadari; **he is not aware of his mistakes** dia belum insyaf akan kesalahannya; **I hadn't realized** saya belum menyadari; **I didn't realize he was a Batak** saya tidak sadar bahwa dia adalah orang Batak; **do you realize what**

a b c d e f g h i j k l m n o p q r s t u v w x y z

time it is? apakah Anda sadar jam berapa sekarang?

really *adverb* benar-benar, sungguh-sungguh; **is it really midnight?** sungguh-sungguh sudah tengah malam?; **the film was really good** film itu benar-benar hebat; **really?** benar?, sungguh?; **not really** tidak juga.

rear *noun* **1** *(buttocks)* pantat; **2** *(of a room, place)* bagian belakang.
adjective belakang; **the rear door** pintu belakang.

reason *noun* alasan, sebab; **the reason for the delay** alasan keterlambatan; **the reason why I phoned** alasan saya menelepon.

reasonable *adjective* **1** *(price, person)* layak, pantas; **2** *(assumption, conclusion)* masuk akal.

reassure *verb* menenteramkan, menenangkan hati, menjamin kembali.

reassuring *adjective* menenangkan, menenteramkan.

rebuild *verb* membangun kembali.

receipt *noun* kwitansi, surat tanda terima, resi.

receive *verb* menerima.

receiver *noun* alat penerima, tangkai telepon; **to pick up the receiver** mengangkat telepon.

recent *adjective* akhir-akhir ini, baru-baru ini.

recently *adverb* akhir-akhir ini, baru-baru ini.

reception *noun*
1 resepsionis; **he's waiting at reception** dia sedang menunggu di resepsionis;
2 pesta, sambutan, resepsi; **a big wedding reception** pesta perkawinan yang besar; **to get a good reception** mendapat sambutan yang hangat.

receptionist *noun* resepsionis.

recipe *noun* resep (makanan); **can I have the recipe for your goat curry?** boleh saya minta resep untuk gulai kambing itu?

reckon *verb* berpendapat, kira; **I reckon it's a good idea** saya berpendapat bahwa itu adalah ide yang bagus.

recognize *verb* mengenali.

recommend *verb* merekomendasi; **can you recommend a good dentist?** apakah Anda dapat merekomendasi dokter gigi yang baik?; **I recommend the**

a b c d e f g h i j k l m n o p q r s t u v w x y z

a b c d e f g h i j k l m n o p q r s t u v w x y z

fish soup saya merekomendasi sop ikan itu.

record *noun* **1** rekor; **it's a world record** itu rekor dunia; **record sales for the CD** rekor penjualan CD; **2** catatan resmi; **to keep a record of** menyimpan catatan; **the hottest day on record** hari terpanas yang pernah tercatat; **3** *(music)* piringan hitam; **4** *(office files)* dokumen; **I'll just check your records** saya akan memeriksa dokumen Anda. *verb (on tape or CD)* merekam; **they're recording a new album** mereka sedang merekam album baru.

recorder *noun* **1** (semacam) suling; **to play the recorder** main suling; **2 a cassette recorder** kaset; **a video recorder** VCR, mesin video.

recording *noun* rekaman.

record player *noun* gramofon.

recover *verb* sembuh; **she's recovered now** dia sudah sembuh.

recovery *noun (from an illness)* kesembuhan, penyembuhan.

recovery vehicle *noun* pesawat pulihan.

rectangle *noun* bujur sangkar.

rectangular *adjective* berbentuk bujur sangkar, persegi empat panjang.

recycle *verb* mendaur-ulang

red *adjective* merah; **a bright red bird** burung berwarna merah terang; **to go red** memerah, menjadi merah; **to have red hair** berambut merah.

Red Cross *noun* Palang Merah.

redecorate *adjective* menghiasi lagi; **they've redecorated the dormitory** asrama itu dihiasi lagi.

redo *verb* mengerjakan lagi, mengulangi.

reduce *verb* mengurangi, menurunkan; **they've reduced the price** harganya diturunkan; **to reduce speed** mengurangi kecepatan.

reduction *noun* diskon, korting, penurunan, potongan.

redundant *adjective* berlebih-lebihan; **to be made redundant** diberhentikan karena jasanya tidak diperlukan lagi.

reel *noun (of cotton)* gulung, rol.

referee *noun (in sport)* penengah, wasit.

reference *noun (for a job)* referensi, sumber acuan.

reference book *noun* buku referensi.

refill *noun* pengisian kembali. *verb* mengisi kembali.

reflect *verb* membayangkan, mencerminkan, menggambarkan.

reflection *noun* **1** bayangan, refleksi; **2** pemikiran; **on reflection** setelah memikirkan secukupnya.

refreshing *adjective* menyegarkan.

refrigerator *noun* kulkas, lemari es.

refugee *noun* pelarian, pengungsi.

refund *noun* pembayaran kembali.
verb mengembalikan uang.

refusal *noun* penolakan.

refuse *noun* sampah.
verb menolak; **I refused** saya menolak; **he refuses to help** dia menolak untuk menolong.

regards *plural noun* salam hormat, salam; **'regards to your parents'** salam hormat kepada orang tua Anda; **Subekti sends his regards** Subekti mengirim salamnya.

region *noun* daerah, kawasan, wilayah.

regional *adjective* kedaerahan, regional.

register *noun (in school)* (buku) daftar, register.
verb mendaftarkan.

registered letter *noun* surat tercatat.

registration number *noun* nomor registrasi.

regret *verb* menyesal, menyesali, menyesalkan; **he regretted what he had done** dia menyesal akan perbuatannya; **he regretted his action** dia menyesali perbuatannya; **he regretted his decision** dia menyesalkan keputusannya.

regrets *plural noun* penyesalan; **Fred sends his regrets** Fred menyampaikan penyesalannya.

regular *adjective* biasa, reguler, tetap; **regular hospital visits** kunjungan tetap.

regularly *adverb* secara teratur, secara tetap.

regulation *noun* peraturan, regulasi.

rehearsal *noun* gladi resik, latihan.

rehearse *verb* melatih (lagi), mengulang.

reheat *verb* memanaskan kembali.

rein *noun* tali kekang.

reject *verb* menolak.

related *adjective* berhubungan; **we're not related** kami tidak ada hubungan keluarga.

relation *noun* keluarga, famili; **my relations** famili saya; **there were just relations and close friends** hanya ada sanak-saudara dan teman-teman akrab.

relationship *noun* hubungan; **we have a good relationship** kita mempunyai hubungan baik.

relative *noun* famili, sanak keluarga; **there were a few relatives at the wedding** ada beberapa sanak keluarga di pesta perkawinan itu; **all my relatives** seluruh famili saya.

relatively *adverb* secara relatif.

relax *verb* beristirahat, bersantai-santai, bersenang-senang, rileks; **I'm going to relax and watch telly tonight** saya akan rileks dan menonton televisi malam ini.

relaxed *adjective* santai, rileks.

relaxing *adjective* yang bersantai, yang bersenang senang.

relay race *noun* perlombaan beranting, perlombaan estafet.

release *noun* **1** penerbitan, pengeluaran; **this week's new releases** pengeluaran baru minggu ini; **2** *(of a prisoner or hostage)* pembebasan, pelepasan. *verb* **1** *(a record or film)* menerbitkan; **2** *(a person)* membebaskan, mengeluarkan.

relevant *adjective* relevan.

reliable *adjective* dapat diandalkan, dapat dipercaya.

relief *noun* perasaan lega; **what a relief!** alangkah leganya!

relieve *verb (pain)* mengurangi.

relieved *adjective* merasa lega; **I was relieved to hear you weren't injured** saya merasa lega waktu saya mendengar bahwa Anda tidak cedera.

religion *noun* agama.

religious *adjective* **1** *(a person)* beragama, beriman, religius, saleh, taat pada agama; **Janet's not religious** Janet kurang beriman; **Hamid is very religious** Hamid adalah seorang yang amat saleh; **2** *(of art or music, for example)* religius.

rely *verb* **1** mengandalkan; **I'm relying on you for Sunday** saya mengandalkan Anda untuk (menolong) hari Minggu; **2** tergantung; **he relies on me for everything** dia tergantung pada saya.

remain *verb* **1** tinggal; **they remained there after school** mereka tinggal di situ sesudah sekolah; **2** tetap; **please remain seated** harap tetap duduk.

remains *noun* bekas, sisa; **the remains of the chicken** sisa daging ayam; **the remains of a temple** bekas-bekas candi itu.

remark *noun* kata-kata, ucapan; **a few brief remarks** beberapa ucapan pendek. *verb* berkata; **Rudi remarked that it was late** Rudi berkata bahwa sudah malam.

remarkable *adjective* hebat, luar biasa.

remarkably *adverb* (dengan, secara) luar biasa.

remember *verb* ingat, mengingat; **I don't remember** saya tidak ingat; **I can't remember the date** saya tidak ingat tanggalnya; **to remember to do** ingat melakukan; **I remembered to bring the CDs** saya ingat membawa CDnya; **remember to shut the door** jangan lupa tutup pintu.

remind *verb* **1** mengingatkan; **remind your mother to pick me up** tolong ingatkan ibu Anda untuk menjemput saya; **2 he reminds me of Taufiq** dia mengingatkan saya akan Taufiq; **oh, that reminds me** oh, saya teringat sekarang.

remote *adjective* jauh sekali, terasing, terpencil.

remote control *noun* remote control.

remove *verb* **1** melepaskan; **he removed his wet shoes** dia melepaskan sepatunya yang basah; **2** memindahkan, mengangkat; **the books have all been removed** semua buku sudah diangkat, semua buku sudah dipindahkan.

renew *verb (a passport or licence)* memperbarui, memperpanjang.

rent *verb* menyewa; **Ismail's rented a new house** Ismail menyewa rumah baru.

rental *noun* uang sewa.

reorganize *verb* mengatur kembali, mereorganisir.

repair *verb* membetulkan, memperbaiki; **we've had the television repaired** televisi kami sudah diperbaiki.

repay *verb* membayar kembali; **he repaid all the money he owed me** dia

a b c d e f g h i j k l m n o p q r s t u v w x y z

membayar kembali semua utangnya kepada saya.

repeat *noun* *(of a program)* ulangan.
verb mengulangi.

repeatedly *adverb* berulang-ulang, berkali-kali.

repertoire *noun* repertoar, persediaan lagu dan sebagainya yang siap untuk dimainkan *(definition only).*

repetitive *adjective* berulang-ulang.

replace *verb* menaruh kembali, menempatkan lagi, mengganti.

reply *noun* jawaban, sahutan; **I didn't get a reply to my application** saya tidak mendapat jawaban atas lamaran saya; **there's no reply** tidak ada sahutan; *(on the telephone)* tak ada yang angkat.
verb menjawab *(to a letter or a question)*, menyahut *(to a question)*; **I still haven't replied to that letter** saya masih belum menjawab surat itu.

report *noun* **1** *(of your activities)* laporan; **2** *(from the school)* rapor.
verb melaporkan; **we've reported the theft** kami sudah melaporkan pencurian itu.

reporter *noun* jurnalis, wartawati *(female)*, wartawan *(male)*.

represent *verb* mewakili.

representative *noun* wakil.

reproach *verb* mengkritik, memarahi seseorang dengan cara yang halus *(definition only)*.

reproduction *noun* barang tiruan, salinan, pertunjukan, reproduksi.

reptile *noun* binatang melata, binatang merayap, reptil.

republic *noun* republik.

reputation *noun* nama, reputasi; **a good reputation** nama baik; **she has a reputation for honesty** dia mempunyai reputasi sebagai orang jujur.

request *noun* permintaan, permohonan; **on request** atas permintaan.

rescue *noun* pertolongan, penyelamatan; **Carl came to Jordan's rescue** Carl menyelamatkan Jordan.
verb menolong, menyelamatkan; **they've rescued the landslide victims** mereka sudah menyelamatkan korban tanah longsor itu.

rescue party *noun* rombongan penolong.

rescue work *noun* pekerjaan penyelamatan.

research *noun* penelitian, riset; **for research into AIDS** untuk riset penyakit AIDS; **to do research** meneliti; **research worker** peneliti, penyelidik.
verb **to research into** meneliti, mengadakan riset, menyelidiki; **a well-researched program** program yang diteliti dengan baik.

resemblance *noun* kemiripan, keserupaan, persamaan.

reservation *noun (a booking)* pemesanan tempat; **to make a reservation** memesan tempat.

reserve *noun* cadangan; **we have some in reserve** kami punya beberapa sebagai cadangan; *(for a match)* **reserve player** pemain cadangan; **a nature reserve** cagar alam.
verb memesan; **this table is reserved** meja ini sudah dipesan.

reservoir *noun* waduk air.

residence *noun* tempat kediaman.

resident *noun* penduduk, penghuni.

residential *adjective* pemukiman; **a residential area** daerah pemukiman.

resign *verb* berhenti, meletakkan jabatan, mengundurkan diri.

resignation *noun (from a post)* pengunduran diri, permintaan berhenti.

resist *verb (an offer or temptation)* menolak; **I can't resist** saya tidak dapat menolak.

resit *verb (an exam)* menempuh ujian lagi, mengulangi ujian.

resort *noun* **1** *(for holidays)* tempat beristirahat; **a holiday resort** tempat berlibur; **a ski resort** tempat bermain ski; **a seaside resort** daerah pantai; **2** usaha; **as a last resort** sebagai usaha terakhir.

respect *noun* **1** kehormatan, rasa hormat; **with respect** dengan hormat; **2 with respect to** mengenai.
verb **1** menghormati; **to respect the employer** menghormati majikan; **2** mematuhi, menaati; **to respect the law** menaati hukum.

respectable *adjective* pantas dihormati, terpandang.

a b c d e f g h i j k l m n o p q r s t u v w x y z

respectful *adjective* hormat; **to be respectful towards** hormat kepada, menghormati.

responsibility *noun* pertanggung-jawaban.

responsible *adjective* bertanggung jawab; **he's responsible for the delay** dia yang harus bertanggung jawab atas keterlambatan itu; **I'm responsible for the catering** saya bertanggung jawab atas jasa boga; **he's not very responsible** dia tidak begitu bertanggung jawab.

rest *noun* **1** sisa; **the rest** sisanya; **the rest of the day** sisa hari; **the rest of the meat** sisa daging; **2** *(the others)* yang lainnya; **the rest have gone home** yang lainnya sudah pulang; **3** istirahat; **ten days' complete rest** sepuluh hari beristirahat total; **to have a rest** beristirahat; **4** tidur; **a good night's rest** tidur nyenyak sepanjang malam. *verb (have a rest)* beristirahat; **to rest for a while** beristirahat sebentar.

restaurant *noun* restoran, rumah makan.

restful *adjective* **1** penuh istirahat; **a restful holiday** libur yang penuh istirahat; **2** tenang, tenteram; **a restful place** tempat tenang.

restless *adjective* gelisah, resah, risau.

restrain *verb* mengendalikan, mengekang, menahan (nafsu, kemarahan, diri).

restrict *verb* membatasi.

restriction *noun* pembatasan.

result *noun* **1** hasil; **the exam results** hasil ujian; **2** akibat; **as a result** sebagai akibat; **as a result we missed our connection** akibatnya, kami tidak mendapat sambungan penerbangan.

retire *verb (from work)* berhenti kerja, mengundurkan diri, pensiun; **she retires in June** dia akan mengundurkan diri pada bulan Juni; **for retired people** untuk orang pensiunan.

retirement *noun* pensiun, pengunduran diri.

return *noun* **1** datangnya kembali, kembalinya, perjalanan kembali, pulangnya; **the return journey** perjalanan kembali; **by return post** kirim dengan pos yang berikut; **2 in return** sebagai gantinya, sebagai balasan; **in return for your help** sebagai balasan atas

pertolongan Anda; **many happy returns!** selamat ulang tahun!
verb **1** *(come back)* kembali; **they returned ten minutes later** mereka kembali sepuluh menit kemudian; **2** *(get home)* pulang; **to return from abroad** kembali, pulang dari luar negeri; **I'll ask her to phone as soon as she returns** saya akan minta supaya dia menelepon sekembalinya di rumah/kantor; **3** *(give back)* mengembalikan; **Gemma's never returned my notebook** Gemma tidak pernah mengembalikan notes (buku catatan) saya.

return fare *noun* ongkos, tarip pulang-pergi.

return ticket *noun* karcis pulang-pergi.

reveal *verb* mengungkapkan.

reverse *verb* **1** *(in a car)* mundur; **2** memutar-balikkan; **to reverse the charges** *(collect call)* biaya ditanggung si penerima.

review *noun* *(of a book, play or film)* resensi; **to write a review of a film** menulis resensi film.
verb *(a play or concert)* meresensi; **the film was well reviewed** film itu diresensi dengan baik.

revise *verb* merevisi; **Leila's busy revising for the exams** Leila sedang sibuk merevisi pelajarannya untuk ujian.

revision *noun* perbaikan, revisi.

revive *verb* menyadarkan, menghidupkan kembali.

revolting *adjective* memuakkan; **the sausages are revolting** sosis itu memuakkan.

revolution *noun* revolusi.

revolving door *noun* pintu putar.

reward *noun* hadiah, penghargaan; **a $1000 reward** hadiah seribu dolar.

rewarding *adjective* memuaskan.

rewind *verb* *(a cassette or video)* memutar kembali.

rhinoceros *noun* badak.

rhubarb *noun* rabarber, semacam tanaman.

rhyme *noun* sajak.

rhythm *noun* irama.

rib *noun* iga, tulang rusuk.

ribbon *noun* pita.

rice *noun* **1** *(cooked)* nasi; **boiled rice** nasi putih; **fried rice** nasi goreng; **2** *(uncooked)* beras; **a kilo of rice** sekilo beras; **3** *(growing in the field)* padi; **4** *(unhulled)* gabah; **5 sticky rice** ketan.

a b c d e f g h i j k l m n o p q r s t u v w x y z

a b c d e f g h i j k l m n o p q r s t u v w x y z

rice field *noun* sawah.

rich *adjective* berada, kaya; **we're not very rich** kami tidak begitu kaya; **the rich and the poor** yang kaya dan yang miskin.

rid *adjective* membuang, menjual; **please get rid of this rubbish** tolong buang sampah ini; **we got rid of that old car** kami menjual mobil tua itu.

riddle *noun* teka-teki, tebakan.

ride *noun* perjalanan; **to go for a ride (on a bike)** naik sepeda; **to go for a ride (on a horse)** naik kuda.
verb **1** naik; **to learn to ride a bike** belajar naik sepeda; **can you ride a bike?** apakah Anda dapat naik sepeda?; **2 to learn to ride (a horse)** belajar naik kuda; **I've never ridden a horse** saya belum pernah naik kuda.

rider *noun (on a horse, bike)* penunggang.

ridiculous *adjective* edan, gila-gilaan, menggelikan; **a ridiculous outfit** pakaian yang menggelikan, pakaian yang gila-gilaan.

riding *noun* **to go riding** naik kuda.

riding school *noun* sekolah belajar naik kuda.

rifle *noun* senapan.

right *noun* **1** *(not left)* kanan; **on the right** di sebelah kanan; **on my right** di sebelah kanan saya; **2** *(to do something)* hak; **the right to strike** hak mogok; **you have no right to say that** Anda tidak berhak berkata begitu.
adjective, adverb **1** *(not left)* kanan; **my right hand** tangan kanan saya; **turn right at the lights** belok kanan di lampu lalu lintas; **2** *(correct)* (dengan) benar, betul, tepat; **the right answer** jawaban yang benar; **the right telephone number** nomor telepon yang benar; **the right amount of money** jumlah uang yang tepat; **the right time** jam yang tepat, waktu yang tepat; **is this the right address?** apakah ini alamat yang benar?; **you're not doing it right** Anda tidak melakukannya dengan benar; **3** *(completely)* persis; **right at the bottom** persis di bawah; **right at the beginning** persis pada permulaan; **right in the middle** persis di tengah; **4** *(moral)* baik; **it's not right to talk like that** tidak baik berkata begitu; **5** *(okay)* baiklah; **right, let's go** baiklah, mari kita berangkat; **6 right now** sekarang juga, segera; **we**

have to go right now kami harus berangkat sekarang juga; sekarang ini; **he's busy right now** dia sibuk sekarang ini.

right-hand *adjective* sebelah kanan; **on the right-hand side** di sebelah kanan.

right-handed *adjective* tangan kanan, tidak kidal.

rind *noun* kulit.

ring *noun* **1** *(on the phone)* bel, menelepon; **2** *(for your finger)* cincin; **3** *(circle)* lingkaran; **4 there was a ring at the door** ada bel.
verb **1** *(a bell or phone)* berdering-dering; **the phone rang** telepon berdering-dering; **2** *(a bell)* membunyikan; *(phone)* menelepon; **I'll ring you tomorrow** saya akan menelepon Anda besok; **could you ring for a taxi?** tolong telepon taksi.
- **to ring back** menelepon kembali; **I'll ring you back later** nanti saya akan menelepon Anda kembali.
- **to ring off** tutup telepon.

ring road *noun* jalan bebas hambatan.

rinse *verb* **1** *(clothes)* membilas; **2** *(mouth)* berkumur.

riot *noun* huru-hara, keributan, kerusuhan.

rioting *noun* kerusuhan.

rip *verb* merobek.

ripe *adjective* masak, matang; **are the mangoes ripe?** apakah mangga itu sudah masak?

rip-off *noun* pencurian, penipuan; **it's a rip-off!** itu penipuan!, itu pencurian!

rise *noun* **1** kenaikan; **a rise in price** kenaikan harga; **a pay rise** kenaikan gaji; **2** terbit; **sunrise** matahari terbit.
verb **1** *(the sun)* terbit; **when the sun rose** saat matahari terbit; **2** *(prices)* naik.

risk *noun* risiko; **to take risks** mengambil risiko.
verb mengambil risiko; **he risks losing everything** dia mengambil risiko akan kehilangan semuanya.

river *noun* kali, sungai; **we picnicked on the edge of the river** kami bertamasya di pinggir sungai; **the rivers of Java** sungai-sungai di Jawa.

road *noun* jalan; **the road to Sidoardjo** jalan ke Sidoardjo; **the mosque is on the other side of the road** mesjid itu terletak di seberang jalan; **they live across the road**

a b c d e f g h i j k l m n o p q r s t u v w x y z

a b c d e f g h i j k l m n o p q r s t u v w x y z

from us mereka tinggal di seberang jalan rumah kami.

road accident *noun* kecelakaan di jalan, kecelakaan lalu lintas.

road map *noun* peta jalan.

roadside *noun* pinggir jalan; **by the roadside** di pinggir jalan.

road sign *noun* tanda penunjuk jalan.

roadworks *noun* pembuatan jalan, perbaikan jalan.

roast *noun* daging panggang. *adjective* panggang; **roast meat** daging panggang.

rob *verb* menyamun, merampas, merampok.

robber *noun* penyamun, perampok.

robbery *noun* perampokan; **a bank robbery** perampokan bank.

robot *noun* robot.

rock *noun* **1** *(big stone)* batu, karang; **she was sitting on a rock** dia duduk di atas batu; **2** *(the material)* batu, karang; **3** *(music)* musik rok.

rock climbing *noun* mendaki tebing; **to go rock climbing** mendaki tebing.

rock star *noun* bintang musik rok.

rocket *noun* roket.

rocking horse *noun* kuda goyang (mainan).

rocky *adjective* berbatu-batu.

rod *noun* batang, tangkai; **a fishing rod** tangkai pancing.

role *noun* peran; **to play the role of** berperan sebagai.

roll *noun* **1** gulung, rol; **a roll of fabric** segulung kain cita, segulung kain; **a roll of Sellotape™** serol selotep; **a toilet roll** segulung kertas tisu WC; **2 a bread roll** roti kecil.

roller *noun* alat penggulung.

rollerblades *noun* sepatu roda.

roller skates *noun* sepatu roda.

Roman Catholic *noun, adjective* Roma Katolik.

romantic *adjective* romantis.

roof *noun* atap.

roof rack *noun (definition only)* rak yang dipasang di atas mobil supaya barang-barang dapat diangkut.

room *noun* **1** kamar, ruang; **bedroom** kamar tidur; **Ning's in her room** Ning ada di kamar tidurnya; **dining room** ruang makan; **family room** ruang keluarga; **sitting room** ruang tamu; **2** tempat; **enough room for two** tempatnya cukup untuk dua orang; **very little room** tempatnya sempit, sedikit ruang.

roommate *noun* teman sekamar.

root *noun* akar.

rope *noun* tali.

rose *noun* bunga mawar.

rosebush *noun* pohon bunga mawar.

rot *verb* membusuk.

rota *noun* daftar giliran kerja.

rotten *adjective* **1** *(food, air)* busuk; **2** *(person)* jahat; **3** *(weather)* buruk.

rough *adjective* **1** *(scratchy)* kasar; **2** *(vague)* secara kasar; **a rough idea** perkiraan secara kasar; **3** *(stormy)* buruk; **a rough sea** laut dengan gelombang ombak yang besar; **in rough weather** dalam cuaca buruk; **4** *(difficult)* sukar; **to have a rough time** dalam keadaan yang sukar.

roughly *adverb* **1** secara kasar(nya); **2** *(approximately)* kira-kira; **roughly ten per cent** kira-kira sepuluh persen; **it takes roughly three hours** makan waktu kira-kira tiga jam.

round *noun* **1** *(in a tournament)* babak; **2** *(of cards)* ronde; **3** giliran, serentetan; **a round of events** serentetan kejadian; **it's my round** ini giliran saya. *adjective* bulat, bundar; **a round table** meja bundar. *adverb* **1 to go round to somebody's house** mengunjungi rumah orang; **we invited Pak Lurah round to lunch** kami mengundang Pak Lurah untuk makan siang; **2 all the year round** sepanjang tahun. *preposition* **1** keliling, sekitar; **round the city** keliling kota, sekitar kota; **round my arm** di sekeliling lengan saya; **2** mengelilingi; **to go round a museum** mengelilingi museum; **they were sitting round the table** mereka duduk di sekitar meja; **3 to go round the shops** berjalan-jalan ke toko; **it's just round the corner** letaknya di sebelah tikungan.

roundabout *noun* **1** *(for traffic)* bundaran; **2** *(in a fairground)* komidi putar.

route *noun* **1** *(that you plan)* jalan; **the best route is via Magelang** jalan yang paling baik melalui Magelang; **2** rute; **a bus route** rute bis.

routine *noun* kebiasaan sehari-hari, rutin.

row[1] *noun* **1** baris, jajaran; **in the front row** di jajaran depan; **in the back row** di jajaran belakang; **2** deretan; **a row of books** sederetan buku; **3** berturut-turut; **four times in a row** empat kali berturut-turut.

row² *verb (in a boat)* mendayung, mengayuh; **it's your turn to row** giliran Anda untuk mendayung; **we rowed across the lake** kami mengayuh ke seberang danau.

row³ *noun* **1** *(a quarrel)* percekcokan; **a row about nothing** percekcokan mengenai hal kecil; **to have a row** bertengkar; **they've had a row** mereka telah bertengkar; **I had a row with my boyfriend** saya bertengkar dengan pacar saya; **2** *(noise)* kegaduhan, keributan; **they were making a terrible row** mereka tadi ribut sekali.

rowing *noun* mendayung; **to go rowing** mendayung.

rowing boat *noun* perahu dayung.

royal *adjective* berhubungan dengan raja atau ratu; **the royal family** keluarga raja/ratu.

rub *verb* menggosok; **to rub your eyes** menggosok mata.
• **to rub out** menghapus.

rubber *noun* **1** *(an eraser)* penghapus; **2** *(material)* karet; **rubber band** gelang karet.

rubbish *noun* **1** *(for the bin)* kotoran, sampah; **2** *(nonsense)* omong-kosong; **you're talking rubbish** Anda bercakap omong-kosong; **3** jelek, tidak bagus; **the film was rubbish** film itu tidak bagus; **they're a rubbish band** band itu jelek.

rubbish bin *noun* keranjang sampah, tempat sampah.

rucksack *noun* ransel.

rude *adjective* kasar, kotor, tidak sopan; **that's rude** itu tidak sopan; **a rude joke** lelucon yang kasar; **a rude word** kata yang kasar.

rug *noun* **1** babut, permadani; **2** *(a blanket)* selimut kaki.

rugby *noun* semacam sepak bola *(definition only)*; **a rugby match** pertandingan rugby.

ruin *noun* kehancuran, keruntuhan; **in ruins** hancur lebur, menjadi puing.
verb merusak; **you'll ruin your jacket** Anda akan merusak jas Anda; **it ruined my evening** hal itu merusak citra malam saya.

rule *noun* **1** peraturan; **the rules of the game** peraturan permainan; **the school rules**

peraturan sekolah; **2 as a rule** biasanya, lazimnya.

ruler *noun* penggaris.

rum *noun* semacam minuman keras, rum.

rumour *noun* desas-desus, kabar angin.

run *noun* **1** lari; **to go for a run** berlari; **2 in the long run** dalam jangka panjang.
verb **1** lari; **I ran ten kilometres** saya lari sepuluh kilometer; **he ran across the park** dia lari melintasi taman itu; **Dipo ran for the bus** Dipo lari untuk naik bis; **2** *(organise)* memimpin, menjalankan; **who's running this conference?** siapa yang memimpin konperensi ini?; **3** *(a business)* menjalankan; **he ran the firm for forty years** dia menjalankan perusahaan itu selama empat puluh tahun; **4** *(a train or bus)* jalan; **the buses don't run on Sundays** bis-bis tidak jalan pada hari Minggu; **5 to run a bath** mengisi bak mandi.

- **to run away** melarikan diri.
- **to run into 1** menubruk; **the car ran into the lamp-post** mobil itu menubruk tiang lampu itu; **2** bertemu; **I ran into her at the market** saya bertemu dengan dia di pasar.
- **to run out of** kehabisan; **we've run out of cooking oil** kami kehabisan minyak goreng.
- **to run over** melindas, menggilas; **watch out! you'll get run over!** hati-hati! nanti terlindas mobil!

runner *noun* pelari.

runner-up *noun* nomor dua.

running *noun (for exercise)* lari.
adjective **1** mengalir; **running water** air mengalir, air ledeng; **2** berturut-turut; **three days running** tiga hari berturut-turut; **six times running** enam kali berturut-turut.

runway *noun* landasan terbang.

rush *noun (a hurry)* kerepotan, kesibukan; **the Christmas rush** kesibukan menjelang Hari Natal; **to be in a rush** sedang sibuk, tergesa-gesa; **sorry, I'm in a rush** maaf, saya sangat tergesa-gesa.
verb **1** *(hurry)* buru-buru; **I must rush!** saya harus buru-buru; **2** *(run)* lari; **she rushed into the street** dia lari ke jalan; **3** membawa cepat-cepat; **Pandu was**

a b c d e f g h i j k l m n o p q r s t u v w x y z

rushed to hospital Pandu cepat-cepat dibawa ke rumah sakit.

rush hour *noun* jam sibuk, waktu sibuk; **in the rush hour** pada jam sibuk, pada waktu sibuk.

Russia *noun* Rusia.

Russian *noun* **1** *(a person)* orang Rusia; **2** *(the language)* bahasa Rusia.
adjective Rusia.

rust *noun* karat.

rusty *adjective* berkarat.

rye *noun* semacam biji-bijian.

S s

Sabbath *noun* hari Sabat.

sack *noun* **1** karung; **2 to get the sack** dipecat.
verb **to sack an employee** memecat pegawai.

sad *adjective* sedih, susah.

saddle *noun* pelana, sadel.

sadly *adverb* **1** dengan sedih; **she looked at them sadly** dia melihatnya dengan sedih; **2** *(unfortunately)* sayang.

safe *adjective* aman, selamat; **to feel safe** merasa aman, merasa selamat; **it's not safe** tidak aman, tidak selamat; **the journey was safe** perjalanan itu selamat; **the path is safe** jalan itu aman.

safety *noun* keselamatan.

safety belt *noun* sabuk pengaman, tali pengaman.

safety pin *noun* peniti.

Sagittarius *noun* Sagitarius.

sail *noun* layar.

sailing *noun* berlayar; **Hugh went sailing yesterday** Hugh pergi berlayar kemarin.

sailing boat *noun* perahu layar.

sailor *noun* pelaut.

saint *noun* orang suci, santa *(female)*, santo *(male)*.

sake *noun* demi; **for your own sake** demi diri Anda sendiri, demi kebaikan Anda sendiri.

salad *noun* salad; **a tomato salad** salad tomat.

salad dressing *noun* saus salad.

salary *noun* gaji.

sale *noun* **1** *(selling)* penjualan; **the sale of the house** penjualan rumah; **'for sale'** 'untuk dijual'; **2 the sales** waktu obral; **I bought it in a sale** saya membelinya pada waktu obral.

sales assistant *noun* pelayan toko, pramuniaga.

salesman *noun* penjual.
saleswoman *noun* penjual.
salmon *noun* ikan salem, salmon.
salt *noun* garam.
salty *adjective* asin.
same *adjective* sama; **she said the same thing** dia mengatakan hal yang sama; **at the same time** pada waktu bersamaan, pada saat yang sama, pada waktu yang sama.
sample *noun* contoh, sampel.
sand *noun* pasir.
sandal *noun* sandal; **a pair of sandals** sepasang sandal.
sandpaper *noun* (kertas) amplas.
sandwich *noun* sandwich.
sanitary napkin *noun* pembalut wanita.
Santa Claus *noun* Sinterklas.
sarcastic *adjective* sarkastis.
sardine *noun* sarden, sardencis.
satchel *noun* tas.
satellite *noun* satelit.
satellite dish *noun* parabola, piring satelit.
satellite television *noun* televisi satelit.
satisfactory *adjective* memuaskan.
satisfied *adjective* puas.
satisfy *verb* memuaskan; **nothing satisfies her** tak ada yang memuaskannya.
satisfying *adjective* memuaskan; **a satisfying meal** makanan yang memuaskan.
Saturday *noun* hari Sabtu; **last Saturday** Sabtu lalu; **next Saturday** Sabtu depan.
sauce *noun* kuah, saus.
saucepan *noun* panci.
saucer *noun* piring kecil.
sausage *noun* sosis.
save *verb* **1** *(rescue)* menyelamatkan; **to save a life** menyelamatkan jiwa; **2** *(money)* menabung; **I've saved six million Rupiah** saya telah menabung enam juta rupiah; **3** *(avoid spending)* menghemat; **I walk to school to save money** saya berjalan ke sekolah untuk menghemat biaya; **we'll take a taxi to save time** kita naik taksi untuk menghemat waktu; **4** *(on a computer)* menyimpan, save.
- **to save up** menabung; **I'm saving up to go to Brazil** saya sedang menabung agar dapat pergi ke Brasilia.

savings *plural noun* tabungan.
savoury *adjective* yang berbumbu, lezat.

a b c d e f g h i j k l m n o p q r s t u v w x y z

saw *noun* gergaji.

sawdust *noun* ampas gergaji.

sax *noun (informal)* saksofon.

saxophone *noun* saksofon.

say *verb* **1** berkata, bilang; **she says she's bored** dia bilang bahwa dia bosan; **he said for us to wait here** dia berkata supaya kita menunggu di sini; **what did you say?** apa kata Anda?; **as they say** seperti mereka katakan; **that goes without saying** tak perlu dikatakan; **2** mengucapkan; **to say thank you** mengucapkan terima kasih.

saying *noun* pepatah, peribahasa; **as the saying goes** pepatah mengatakan.

scale *noun* **1** *(of a map or a model)* skala; **2** *(extent)* besar; **the scale of the damage** besarnya kerusakan; **3** *(in music)* not musik; **4** *(of a fish)* sisik.

scales *plural noun* timbangan.

scallop *noun* remis.

scandal *noun* skandal.

scar *noun* bekas luka.

scarce *adjective* jarang, langka.

scare *noun* ketakutan; **it caused a scare** menimbulkan ketakutan; **a bomb scare** ketakutan akan bom.

verb menakuti; **you scared me!** Anda menakuti saya!

scarecrow *noun* orang-orangan.

scared *adjective* takut; **I'm scared!** saya takut!; **she's scared of heights** dia takut akan ketinggian; **I'm scared of falling** saya takut terjatuh.

scarf *noun (long)* selendang.

scary *adjective* menakutkan.

scene *noun* **1** *(of an incident or a crime)* lokasi, tempat; **to be on the scene** berada di lokasi kejadian; **the scene of the crime** lokasi kejahatan; **2** *(view)* pemandangan; **3 to make a scene** membuat keonaran.

scenery *noun* **1** *(landscape)* pemandangan; **2** *(theatrical)* dekor.

scent *noun* bau, wangi-wangian.

scented *adjective* wangi.

schedule *noun* daftar, jadwal.

scheduled flight *noun* penerbangan yang dijadwalkan.

scheme *noun* pola, rencana, siasat, skema.

scholarship *noun* beasiswa.

school *noun* sekolah; **to go to school** pergi ke sekolah.

schoolbook *noun* buku sekolah.
schoolboy *noun* anak sekolah (laki-laki).
schoolchildren *plural noun* anak-anak sekolah.
school friend *noun* teman sekolah.
schoolgirl *noun* anak sekolah (perempuan).
science *noun* ilmu pengetahuan, sains.
science fiction *noun* fiksi ilmiah.
scientific *adjective* ilmiah.
scientist *noun* ilmiawan, ilmuwan.
scissors *noun* gunting; **a pair of scissors** sebuah gunting.
scoff[1] *verb* mencemoohkan.
scoff[2] *verb* *(eat) (informal)* makan cepat-cepat, rakus.
scooter *noun* **1** *(motor scooter)* skuter; **2** *(for a child)* sepeda dorong.
score *noun* angka, skor. *verb* **1** mencetak gol; **Goenawan scored a goal** Goenawan mencetak gol; **2** *(keep score)* menghitung angka.
Scorpio *noun* Skorpio.
Scot *noun* **the Scots** orang Skotlandia.
Scotland *noun* Skotlandia.
Scottish *adjective* Skotlandia; **a Scottish accent** aksen Skotlandia.
scout *noun* pandu, pramuka.
scrambled eggs *plural noun* telur adukan, telur orak-arik.
scrap *noun* carik, potongan-potongan; **a scrap of paper** secarik kertas; **scrap metal** besi tua.
scrapbook *noun* buku kliping.
scrape *verb* menggaruk, menggores, menggosok-gosok.
scratch *noun* **1** *(on your skin)* luka garutan; **2** *(on a surface)* goresan; **to start from scratch** mulai dari awal, mulai dari permulaan. *verb* *(scratch yourself)* menggaruk; **don't scratch a mosquito bite** jangan menggaruk gigitan nyamuk.
scream *noun* jeritan, teriakan. *verb* berteriak, menjerit.
screen *noun* layar.
screw *noun* sekrup. *verb* menyekerup.
screwdriver *noun* obeng.
scribble *verb* mencoret, menulisi.

scrub *verb* menggosok, menyikat.

sculpture *noun* patung.

sculptor *noun* pematung.

sea *noun* laut.

seafood *noun* makanan laut.

seagull *noun* burung laut.

seal *noun (animal)* anjing laut.
verb (envelope) menutup.

seaman *noun* pelaut.

search (for) *verb* mencari; **I've searched my desk but I can't find your essay** saya sudah mencarinya di atas meja saya tetapi saya tidak menemukan karangan Anda.

seashell *noun* kerang.

seasick *adjective* mabuk laut.

season *noun* musim; **the football season** musim sepak bola; **rambutan are not in season** belum musim rambutan.

season ticket *noun* karcis abonemen.

seat *noun* tempat duduk; **the front seat** tempat duduk di bagian depan; **take a seat** silahkan duduk; **to book a seat** memesan tempat duduk.

seatbelt *noun* sabuk pengaman.

seaweed *noun* rumput laut.

second *noun* **1** detik; **ten seconds** sepuluh detik; **2 can you wait a second?** bisakah Anda menunggu sebentar?
adjective **1** kedua; **for the second time** untuk kedua kalinya; **2** dua; **the second of June** tanggal dua Juni.

secondary school *noun* sekolah menengah.

secondhand *adjective* bekas; **a secondhand watch** jam bekas.

secondly *adverb* kedua.

secret *noun* rahasia; **in secret** secara rahasia.
adjective rahasia; **a secret plan** rencana rahasia.

secretarial college *noun* akademi sekretaris.

secretary *noun* sekretaris.

secretly *adverb* secara rahasia.

sect *noun* mazhab, sekte.

section *noun* bagian, seksi.

security *noun* keamanan.

security guard *noun* penjaga keamanan, satpam.

see *verb* **1** melihat; **I haven't seen Mr Hidayat for ages** saya sudah lama tidak melihat Pak Hidayat; **I can't see anything** saya tidak bisa melihat apa-apa;
2 *(understand)* mengerti;

I see what you mean saya mengerti apa maksud Anda; **3** bertemu, jumpa; **see you! see you soon!** sampai bertemu! sampai jumpa!; **I saw the Lurah** saya bertemu dengan Pak Lurah; **4** *(check, find out)* lihat; **I'll see what can be done** coba saya lihat apa yang dapat dilakukan; **5** menonton; **have you seen the film?** apakah Anda sudah menonton filmnya?
- **to see to** menyiapkan; **Jo's seeing to the drinks** Jo sedang meyiapkan minuman.

seed *noun* bibit, biji; **to plant seeds** menanam biji.

seem *verb* **1** rasanya, (rupa-) rupanya; **it seems that...** rupanya...; **2** *(look, appear to be)* kelihatannya, nampak, tampak; **he seems a bit shy** tampaknya dia pemalu; **it seems odd to me** bagi saya tampaknya aneh; **it seems he's left** kelihatannya dia sudah pergi, tampaknya dia sudah pergi.

seesaw *noun* papan jungkat-jungkit, wip-plank.

select *verb* memilih.

self-confidence *noun* percaya diri.

self-contained *adjective* serba lengkap; **a self-contained flat** apartemen yang serba lengkap.

self-employed *noun* wiraswasta, wirausahawan. *adjective* wiraswasta.

selfish *adjective* egoistis, mementingkan diri sendiri.

self-service *adjective* swalayan; **a self-service restaurant** rumah makan swalayan.

sell *verb* menjual; **I sold him my bike** saya menjual sepeda saya kepadanya; **the game's sold out** karcis untuk pertandingan itu telah terjual habis.

Sellotape™ *noun* pita perekat, Sellotape™. *verb* **to Sellotape™ something** *(informal)* memakai Sellotape™.

semi *noun* sebagian, setengah.

semicircle *noun* setengah lingkaran.

semicolon *noun* titik koma.

semi-detached house *noun* rumah petak.

semi-final *noun* semifinal.

semi-trailer *noun* truk bergandeng.

send *verb* mengirim; **I sent her a present for her birthday** saya mengirimkan hadiah untuk ulang tahunnya.
- **to send back** mengirimkan kembali.

a b c d e f g h i j k l m n o p q r s t u v w x y z

a b c d e f g h i j k l m n o p q r s t u v w x y z

sender *noun* pengirim.

senior citizen *noun* manula (manusia lanjut usia), orang jompo.

sensational *adjective* menggemparkan, sensasional.

sense *noun* **1** akal; **common-sense** akal sehat; **it doesn't make sense** tidak masuk akal; **2** rasa; **to have a sense of humour** mempunyai rasa humor; **a sense of responsibility** rasa tanggung jawab; **3 the sense of smell** indera penciuman; **the sense of touch** indera peraba; **the five senses** panca indera.

sensible *adjective* bijaksana, logis; **she's very sensible** dia sangat logis; **it's a sensible decision** keputusan yang sangat bijaksana.

sensitive *adjective* sensitif.

sentence *noun* **1** *(grammatical)* kalimat; **2** hukuman; **the death sentence** hukuman mati. *verb* menjatuhi, menjatuhkan hukuman; **to be sentenced to life** dijatuhi hukuman seumur hidup.

sentimental *adjective* sentimental.

separate *adjective* **1** terpisah; **we want separate rooms** kami ingin kamar yang terpisah; **2** *(different)* tersendiri; **that's a separate problem** itu masalah tersendiri. *verb* **1** memisahkan; **2** membuat jarak.

separately *adverb* terpisah.

separation *noun* pemisahan.

September *noun* bulan September.

sequel *noun* lanjutan, sambungan.

sequence *noun* **1** urutan; **a sequence of events** kejadian berurutan; **2 in sequence** bersambung.

sergeant *noun* sersan.

serious *adjective* **1** serius; **a serious decision** keputusan yang serius; **2** *(illness, injury, mistake, problem)* berat, parah; **a serious problem** masalah yang sangat berat; **a serious injury** luka berat, luka parah; **3** yang menyusahkan; **a serious traffic jam** lalu lintas yang sangat macet.

seriously *adverb* **1** betul-betul, sungguh-sungguh; **seriously, I must go now** saya betul-betul harus pergi sekarang; **seriously?** sungguh?; **2** serius; **to take seriously** menganggap secara serius; **3** *(ill, injured)* berat, keras; **she is seriously ill** dia sakit keras.

servant *noun* **1** *(domestic)* babu *(derogatory)*, bujang, pembantu rumah; **2 public servant** pegawai negeri.

serve *noun (in tennis)* giliran. *verb* **1** *(in tennis)* (memulai) memukul; **2** menghidangkan, menyajikan; **can you serve the soup, please?** dapatkah Anda menyajikan sopnya?; **it serves him right!** biar kapok!; **3** melayani; **Lindy served her guests** Lindy melayani tamunya.

service *noun* **1** *(in a restaurant, from a company)* pelayanan; **the service here is very slow** pelayanan di sini sangat lambat; **2** servis; **service is another ten per cent** tambahan servis sebesar sepuluh persen; **3** pertolongan; **the emergency services** pertolongan darurat; **4** *(church service)* kebaktian. *verb (a car or a machine)* menservis.

service area *noun* ruang serpis.

service charge *noun* ongkos pelayanan; **what is the service charge?** berapa ongkos pelayanannya?

service station *noun* bengkel.

serviette *noun* serbet.

session *noun* sidang.

set *noun* **1** *(for playing a game)* perlengkapan; **a chess set** perlengkapan catur; **a train set** perlengkapan mainan kereta api; **2** *(in tennis)* set. *adjective* yang ditentukan; **at a set time** waktu yang ditentukan. *verb* **1** *(date, time, price, record)* menetapkan; **2 to set the table** menyiapkan meja; **3** memasang; **to set an alarm clock** memasang weker; **4** *(sun)* matahari terbenam.

- **to set off** *(depart)* berangkat; **they set off yesterday** mereka berangkat kemarin.
- **to set something off** **1** *(firework, bomb)* meledakkan; **2** *(alarm)* membunyikan.
- **to set out for** berangkat; **they set out for Gidgid yesterday** mereka berangkat ke Gidgid kemarin.

settee *noun* dipan, sofa.

settle *verb* **1** *(a bill)* melunasi; **2** *(a problem)* menyelesaikan; **3** *(in a place)* menetap.

seven *number* tujuh.

a b c d e f g h i j k l m n o p q r s t u v w x y z

a b c d e f g h i j k l m n o p q r **s** t u v w x y z

seventeen *number* tujuh belas.

seventh *adjective* **1** tujuh; **the seventh of March** tanggal tujuh Maret; **2** ketujuh; **the seventh floor** lantai ketujuh.

seventies *noun* **the seventies** tahun tujuhpuluhan.

seventy *number* tujuh puluh.

several *adjective* beberapa; **I've read several of Pramoedya's novels** saya telah membaca beberapa novel karya Pramoedya; **they took several** mereka mengambil beberapa.

sew *verb* menjahit.

sewing *noun* jahitan; **poor-quality sewing** jahitan yang kurang baik; **I like sewing** saya suka menjahit.

sewing machine *noun* mesin jahit.

sex *noun* seks, jenis kelamin.

sex education *noun* pendidikan seks.

sexism *noun* seksisme.

sexist *adjective* seksis; **sexist insinuations** sindiran yang seksis.

sexual *adjective* seksual.

sexual equality *noun* persamaan hak bagi pria dan wanita, persamaan seks.

sexual harassment *noun* pelecehan seksual.

sexual organs *noun* alat kelamin, alat kemaluan.

sexuality *noun* seksualitas.

sexy *adjective* seksi.

shabby *adjective* buruk, tua.

shade *noun* **1** nuansa; **a pretty shade of blue** nuansa biru yang manis; **2** tempat teduh; **in the shade** di tempat teduh.

shadow *noun* bayangan; **shadow play** wayang kulit.

shake *verb* **1** *(tremble)* bergetar; **my hands are shaking** tangan saya bergetar; **2 to shake** menggoyangkan; **3 to shake hands** bersalaman tangan; **Supri shook hands with Eri** Supri bersalaman dengan Eri; **4 to shake your head** *(meaning no)* menggelengkan kepala.

shaken *adjective* terkejut; **I was shaken by the news** saya terkejut mendengar berita itu.

shall *verb* apakah, dapatkah; **shall I come with you?** apakah saya perlu ikut Anda?; **shall we stop now?** dapatkah kita berhenti sekarang?

shallow *adjective* dangkal; **shallow water** air dangkal.

shambles *noun (informal)* keadaan kacau; **it was a total shambles** kacau benar.

shame *noun* **1** rasa malu; **to shame** memalukan; **shame on you!** tak tahu malu!; **2** kasihan, sayang; **what a shame!** kasihan!; **it's a shame you can't join us** sayang, Anda tidak bisa ikut kami.

shameful *adjective* memalukan.

shampoo *noun* pencuci rambut, shampo.

shape *noun* bentuk.

share *noun* **1** bagian; **your share of the money** uang bagian Anda; **2** *(in a company)* saham, andil. *verb* **1** se–; **I'm sharing a room with Wati** saya sekamar dengan Wati; **2** membagi, memberikan; **she shared out the cakes** dia membagi kue-kue itu.

shareholder *noun* pemegang saham.

shark *noun* ikan hiu.

sharp *adjective* **1** tajam; **a sharp bend** sudut tajam; **2** *(for pointed things)* lancip; **a sharp pencil** pensil lancip; **3** *(clever)* cerdik, pintar; **she's sharp** dia pintar.

shave *noun, verb* bercukur, mencukur; **he's just having a shave** dia sedang bercukur; **to shave your legs** mencukur bulu kaki.

shaver *noun* silet; **an electric shaver** alat cukur listrik.

shaving cream *noun* krim cukur.

shaving foam *noun* sabun cukur.

she *pronoun* dia, ia; **she's a student** dia seorang pelajar.

shed *noun* gubuk.

sheep *noun* biri-biri, domba.

sheepdog *noun* anjing penggembala domba.

sheer **1** belaka; **it's sheer stupidity** kebodohan belaka; **2** *(fabric)* tembus pandang, tipis.

sheet *noun* **1** *(for a bed)* seprei; **2** helai, lembar; **a sheet of paper** sehelai kertas.

shelf *noun* rak; **a set of shelves** rak-rak.

shell *noun* **1** *(of an egg or a nut)* kulit; **egg shell** kulit telur; **2** *(seashell)* rumah kerang; **3** *(explosive)* bom, granat.

shellfish *noun* binatang laut seperti udang, kepiting dan lain lain *(definition only)*.

shelter *noun* **1** perlindungan, tempat bernaung; **to take shelter from the rain**

berlindung dari hujan; **2 a bus shelter** halte bis, perhentian bis.

shepherd *noun* gembala.

sheriff *noun* syerif *(in America)*.

sherry *noun* semacam minuman beralkohol.

shield *noun* perisai, tameng.

shift *noun* regu kerja; **the night shift** regu kerja malam; **to be on night shift** mendapat giliran kerja pada malam hari.
verb memindahkan, menggeserkan; **shift a table** menggeserkan meja.

shifty *adjective* licik; **he looks shifty** dia kelihatan licik.

shin *noun* garas, kaki sebelah muka dari lutut ke bawah.

shine *noun* kilau.

shiny *adjective* berkilau.

ship *noun* kapal; **a passenger ship** kapal penumpang.

shipbuilding *noun* pembuatan kapal.

shipyard *noun* galangan kapal.

shirt *noun* **1** *(woman's)* blus; **2** *(man's)* kemeja.

shiver *noun* menggigil.

shock *noun* **1** kejutan, syok; **it gave me a shock** itu membuat saya terkejut; **2 an electric shock** setrum; **to get an electric shock** tersetrum listrik.
verb mengejutkan.

shocked *adjective* kaget, terkejut.

shocking *adjective* mengejutkan.

shoe *noun* sepatu; **a pair of shoes** sepasang sepatu.

shoelace *noun* tali sepatu.

shoe polish *noun* semir sepatu.

shoe shop *noun* toko sepatu.

shoot *verb* **1** *(fire)* menembak *(intentional)*, tertembak *(unintentional)*; **to shoot at** menembak; **she shot him in the leg** dia menembaknya di kaki; **he was shot by terrorists** dia tertembak teroris; **2** *(execute)* menembak mati; **3** *(a goal)* tembak; **4 to shoot a film** membuat film.

shop *noun* toko; **to go round the shops** melihat-lihat di toko.

shop assistant *noun* pelayan toko, pramuniaga.

shopkeeper *noun* pemilik toko.

shoplifter *noun* pencuri di toko.

shoplifting *noun* pencurian di toko.

shopping *noun* belanjaan; **can you put the shopping**

away? apakah Anda bisa menyingkirkan barang belanjaan itu?; **to go shopping** pergi berbelanja.

shopping bag *noun* tas belanja.

shopping trolley *noun* kereta belanja.

shop window *noun* etalase, jendela pajangan.

short *adjective* **1** pendek; **a short dress** baju pendek; **2** sejenak; **to go for a short walk** jalan-jalan sejenak; **3** kekurangan; **we're a bit short of money at the moment** kami agak kekurangan uang saat ini.

shortage *noun* kekurangan.

shortbread *noun* roti biskuit.

shortcrust pastry *noun* adonan kue kering.

short cut *noun* jalan pintas.

shortly *adverb* tidak lama lagi.

shorts *noun* celana pendek.

short-sighted *adjective* rabun jauh.

short story *noun* cerita pendek, cerpen.

shot *noun* **1** *(from a gun)* tembakan; **2** *(a photo)* foto, potret.

shotgun *noun* senapan.

should *verb* **1** sebaiknya; **you should visit them** sebaiknya Anda mengunjungi mereka; **2** seharusnya; **you should pay before the end of the month** Anda seharusnya membayar sebelum akhir bulan.

shoulder *noun* bahu, pundak.

shoulder bag *noun* tas pundak.

shout *noun* teriakan.
verb berteriak; **stop shouting!** berhenti berteriak!; **they shouted at us to come back** mereka berteriak agar kita kembali.

shovel *noun* sekop.

show *noun* **1** *(on stage)* tontonan; **we went to see a show** kami pergi menonton; **2** *(on TV)* acara; **3** *(exhibition)* pameran; **the motor show** pameran mobil dan motor.
verb **1** memperlihatkan, menunjukkan; **I'll show you my photos** saya akan menunjukkan foto-foto saya kepada Anda; **he showed me how to make pancakes** dia memperlihatkan saya bagaimana membuat panekuk; **it shows!** kelihatan!; **2 to show off** *(formal)* menyombongkan diri, *(informal)* berlagak, sok aksi.

shower *noun* **1** *(bathe)* mandi dus; **2** *(rain)* hujan.

a b c d e f g h i j k l m n o p q r s t u v w x y z

show-jumping *noun* lompat kuda.

show-off *noun (informal)* orang yang sok aksi.

shriek *noun* jeritan, pekikan.

shrimp *noun* udang.

shrink *verb* menciut, mengecil, menyusut.

shrug *verb* mengangkat bahu.

shuffle *verb* mengocok; **to shuffle the cards** mengocok kartu.

shut *adjective* tutup.
verb menutup, tutup; **the banks shut at two** bank-bank tutup jam dua; **Rosa shut the door** Rosa menutup pintu.
- **to shut up** *(be quiet)* diam! tutup mulut.

shutter *noun* kerai.

shuttle *noun* bolak-balik, ulang-alik; **there's a shuttle service from the airport** ada transportasi ulang-alik dari bandar udara.

shuttlecock *noun* bola bulu tangkis, kok.

shy *adjective* pemalu, malu.

shyness *noun* perasaan malu.

sick *adjective* **1** *(ill)* sakit, **2** *(vomit)* mual, muntah; **to be sick** mual, muntah; **a sick joke** lelucon yang memuakkan; **3 sick of** bosan; **I'm sick of staying at home every night** saya bosan tinggal di rumah setiap malam.

sickness *noun* penyakit.

side *noun* **1** sebelah; **on this side of the street** di sebelah sini jalan; **2** pinggir; **on the side of the road** di pinggir jalan; **3** pihak; **I'm on your side** *(I agree with you)* saya berpihak pada Anda, saya setuju dengan Anda; **to take sides** memihak; **4** *(team)* regu; **she plays on our side** dia bermain untuk regu kita; **5 side by side** berdampingan, bersebelahan; **6 on the other side of the street** di seberang jalan; **on the wrong side** di lajur yang salah.

sideboard *noun* bupet.

sideburns *noun* cambang.

side-effect *noun* efek samping.

side street *noun* jalan kecil, jalan samping.

sieve *noun* saringan.

sigh *noun* keluhan, keluh-kesah.

sight *noun* **1** pemandangan; **to see the sights** melihat pemandangan; **2 at the sight of** ketika melihat; **Frank fainted at the sight of the blood** Frank pingsan ketika melihat darah; **to know somebody by sight** mengenal orang ketika melihatnya; **3** *(eyesight)* penglihatan; **poor sight** penglihatan lemah.

sightseeing *noun* melihat pemandangan, tamasya.

sign *noun* **1** *(notice)* tanda; **there's a sign on the door** ada sebuah tanda di pintu; **2** *(trace, indication)* jejak; **3** *(of the zodiac)* bintang; **what sign are you?** bintang Anda apa?
verb menandatangani; **to sign a cheque** menandatangani sebuah cek.
- **to sign on** *(as unemployed, for example)* mendaftar.

signal *noun* sinyal, tanda.

signature *noun* tanda tangan.

significance *noun* arti.

significant *adjective* berarti.

sign language *noun* bahasa isyarat.

signpost *noun* papan penunjuk jalan.

silence *noun* kesunyian.

silent *adjective* diam, sunyi.

silicon chip *noun* silikon chip.

silk *adjective, noun* sutra.

silky *adjective* lembut seperti sutra.

silly *adjective* bodoh.

silver *adjective, noun* perak.

similar *adjective* mirip, serupa.

simmer *verb* mendidih perlahan-lahan.

simple *adjective* biasa, mudah, sederhana.

simply *adverb* **1** dengan sederhana; **arranged simply** diatur dengan sederhana; **2** benar-benar, sungguh-sungguh; **a simply fantastic trip** kunjungan yang benar-benar hebat; **3** *(only)* hanya; **he simply did it to annoy you** dia berbuat itu hanya untuk menjengkelkan Anda.

sin *noun* dosa.

since *preposition, adverb, conjunction* **1** sejak; **I've been learning Indonesian since last year** saya belajar bahasa Indonesia sejak tahun lalu; **since I've been learning Indonesian** sejak saya mulai belajar bahasa Indonesia; **I haven't seen her since** saya belum bertemu dengannya sejak itu; **2** *(because)* (oleh) karena; **since it was raining, the match was cancelled** karena hujan, pertandingannya dibatalkan; **3 it's a long time since we met** sudah lama kita tidak bertemu.

a b c d e f g h i j k l m n o p q r s t u v w x y z

sincere *adjective* tulus hati.

sincerely *adverb* **1** dengan tulus hati; **Ahmad spoke sincerely** Ahmad berbicara dengan tulus hati; **2 Yours sincerely** *(in a business letter) (in Indonesian there are very formal formulae for signing letters)* hormat kami.

sing *verb* menyanyi.

singer *noun* penyanyi.

singing *noun* **1** nyanyian; **a singing lesson** pelajaran menyanyi; **2 I like singing** saya suka bernyanyi.

single *noun* sekali jalan; **a single to Madiun, please** karcis sekali jalan menuju Madiun.
adjective **1** *(not married)* bujang, tak beristri, tak bersuami; **2** tunggal; **a single bed** tempat tidur tunggal; **a single room** kamar dengan satu tempat tidur; **3** satu; **not a single** tidak satu pun; **I haven't had a single reply** saya belum mendapat jawaban sama sekali.

single parent *noun* orang tua tunggal.

singles *plural noun (in tennis)* pertandingan tunggal.

singular *noun* bentuk tunggal.

sink *noun* bak cuci.
verb tenggelam; **the enemy sank our ship** musuh menenggelamkan kapal kita; **the *Titanic* sank** kapal *Titanic* tenggelam.

sir *noun* bapak, pak, tuan.

siren *noun* sirene.

sister *noun* adik perempuan, kakak perempuan; **my little sister** adik perempuan saya; **my older sister** kakak perempuan saya.

sister-in-law *noun* ipar perempuan.

sit *verb* **1** duduk; **you can sit on that bench** Anda boleh duduk di bangku itu; **I can sit on the floor** saya bisa duduk di lantai; **Fitri was sitting cross-legged** Fitri duduk bersila; **2 to sit (for) an exam** menempuh ujian.
• **to sit down** duduk.

sitcom *noun* sinetron, sitkom.

site *noun* lokasi, tempat; **a building site** tempat pembangunan gedung.

sitting room *noun* ruang duduk.

situated *adjective* berlokasi, terletak; **the temple is situated on a hill** candi itu terletak di atas bukit.

situation *noun* keadaan, situasi.

six *number* enam.

a b c d e f g h i j k l m n o p q r s t u v w x y z

sixteen *number* enam belas.

sixth *adjective* 1 enam; **the sixth of July** tanggal enam Juli; 2 keenam; **on the sixth floor** di lantai keenam.

sixty *number* enam puluh.

size *noun* 1 *(precise measurements)* ukuran; **what size do you take?** Anda pakai ukuran berapa?; **I take a size thirty-eight** saya memakai ukuran tiga puluh delapan; 2 besarnya; **it depends on the size of the house** tergantung pada besarnya rumah.

skate *noun* 1 sepatu luncur; **an ice skate** sepatu luncur es; 2 **a roller skate** sepatu roda.
verb 1 *(ice-skate)* bermain sepatu es; 2 *(roller-skate)* bermain sepatu roda.

skateboard *noun* papan selancar beroda, skateboard.

skateboarding *noun* bermain skateboard.

skating *noun* 1 *(ice)* berskating; 2 *(roller-skating)* bersepatu roda.

skating rink *noun* arena skating, arena sepatu roda

skeleton *noun* kerangka.

sketch *noun* 1 *(drawing)* sketsa; 2 *(comedy routine)* sandiwara komedi.

ski *verb* bermain ski.

skid *verb* tergelincir, selip; **the car skidded** mobilnya selip.

skiing *noun* bermain ski.

skimmed milk *noun* susu skim.

skin *noun* kulit.

skinhead *noun* orang gundul.

skinny *adjective* kurus.

skip *noun* *(for rubbish)* tong sampah besar.
verb 1 *(a meal, part of a book)* melewati; 2 *(with a rope)* bermain tali lompat.

skirt *noun* rok; **a mini-skirt** rok mini.

skull *noun* tengkorak.

sky *noun* langit.

slam *verb* membanting; **Umi slammed the door** Umi membanting pintu.

slang *noun* bahasa informal, bahasa kasar.

slap *verb* menampar.

slate *noun* sabak, semacam batu.

sleep *noun* tidur; **I had a good sleep** saya tidur nyenyak.
verb **Sutanto's sleeping** Sutanto sedang tidur.

sleeping bag *noun* karung tidur.

a b c d e f g h i j k l m n o p q r s t u v w x y z

a b c d e f g h i j k l m n o p q r s t u v w x y z

sleeping pill *noun* obat tidur.

sleepy *adjective* mengantuk; **I'm getting sleepy** saya mulai mengantuk.

sleeve *noun* lengan; **long-sleeved** berlengan panjang; **to roll up your sleeves** menggulung lengan baju.

slice *noun* potong.
verb memotong.

slide *noun* **1** *(photo)* slide; **2** *(for sliding down)* tempat meluncur.
verb meluncur.

slight *adjective* sedikit; **there's a slight problem** ada sedikit masalah.

slightly *adverb* agak, sedikit.

slim *adjective* langsing.
verb melangsingkan.

sling *noun* gendongan; **to carry the baby in a sling** membawa bayi dalam gendongan.

slip *noun* **1** *(mistake)* kesalahan; **2** *(petticoat)* pakaian (rok) dalam.
verb **1** *(slide)* tergelincir, terpeleset; **2** kelupaan *(colloquial)*; **it had slipped my mind** saya kelupaan.

slipper *noun* sandal.

slippery *adjective* licin.

slope *noun* lereng.

slot *noun* celah, lobang, petak.

slot machine *noun* mesin jackpot, mesin judi.

slow *adjective* lambat.
- **to slow down** memperlambat.

slowly *adverb* dengan lambat, perlahan-lahan.

slug *noun* keong, siput (tanpa rumah).

slum *noun* perkampungan kumuh.

sly *adjective* *(person)* licik; **on the sly** secara diam-diam, secara rahasia.

smack *verb* memukul.

small *adjective* kecil.

smart *adjective* **1** *(well-dressed, posh)* berpakaian baik; **2** elite; **a smart restaurant** rumah makan elite; **3** *(clever)* pintar.

smash *noun* kecelakaan, tabrakan.
verb menghancurkan; **they smashed a window** mereka menghancurkan sebuah jendela.

smashing *adjective* hebat.

smell *noun* bau; **a nasty smell** bau menyengat; **a pleasant smell** bau wangi.
verb **1** mencium, **I can't smell anything** saya tidak dapat mencium apa-apa; **2** *(smell bad)* berbau; **the drains smell** selokannya bau.

smelly *adjective* bau; **that smelly cat** kucing yang bau itu.

smile *noun* senyuman. *verb* tersenyum.

smoke *noun* asap. *verb* merokok; **she doesn't smoke** dia tidak merokok.

smoker *noun* perokok.

smoking *noun* merokok, **'no smoking'** 'dilarang merokok'.

smooth *adjective* **1** licin; **a smooth surface** permukaan licin; **2** *(person)* pembujuk.

smug *adjective* puas dengan diri sendiri, sombong.

smuggle *verb* menyelundupkan.

smuggler *noun* penyelundup.

smuggling *noun* penyelundupan.

snack *noun* makanan kecil.

snail *noun* keong, siput.

snake *noun* ular.

snap *noun* *(card game)* snap. *verb* **1** *(break)* patah, putus; **the branch snapped** dahannya patah; **the rope snapped** tali itu putus; **2 to snap your fingers** menjentikan jari.

snapshot *noun* foto.

snarl *verb* menggertak.

snatch *verb* **1** *(steal)* menjambret, merampas, merebut; **the thief snatched her bag** pencuri menjambret tasnya; **2** *(take quickly)* merenggut; **he snatched my book** dia merenggut buku saya.

sneak *verb* menyelinap, menyusup; **he sneaked up on me** dia menyelinap ke arah saya.

sneeze *noun, verb* berbangkis, bersin.

sniff *noun* dengusan. *verb* mendengus.

snob *noun* orang congkak, orang sombong.

snobbery *noun* kecongkakan, kesombongan.

snooker *noun* snooker.

snooze *noun* beristirahat, tidur sebentar.

snore *verb* mendengkur, mengorok.

snow *noun* salju. *verb* bersalju.

so *conjunction, adverb* **1** sangat, sekali; **he's so lazy** dia sangat malas; **the coffee's so hot I can't drink it** kopinya sangat panas sehingga saya tidak bisa meminumnya; **I hate it so much!** saya sangat membencinya!; **2 not so** tidak begitu; **our house is a**

bit like yours, but not so big rumah kami agak mirip dengan rumah Anda tapi tidak begitu besar; **3 so much, so many** banyak sekali, begitu banyak, sangat banyak; **I've got so many essays to write** banyak sekali esai yang harus saya tulis; **4** *(therefore)* sehingga; **he got up late so he missed the train** dia terlambat bangun sehingga ketinggalan kereta api; **5** *(starting a sentence)* jadi; **so what's your name?** jadi nama Anda siapa?; **so what shall we do?** jadi apa yang akan kita kerjakan?; **so what?** jadi bagaimana?; **6** juga; **'I live in Kebayoran' – 'so do I'** 'saya tinggal di Kebayoran' – 'saya juga'; **'I hated that film' – 'so did we'** 'saya tidak suka film itu' – 'kami juga'; **so am I** saya juga; **7** begitu, demikian; **I hope so** saya harap begitu; **so it seems** kelihatannya demikian; **8 so and so** si anu.

soak *verb* merendam.

soaked, soaking *adjective* basah kuyup.

soap *noun* **1** sabun; **2** *(soap opera on TV)* sinetron.

soap powder *noun* sabun bubuk.

sober *adjective* tidak mabuk; **he's sober** dia tidak mabuk.

soccer *noun* sepak bola.

social *adjective* sosial.

socialism *noun* sosialisme.

socialist *noun* sosialis.

social security *noun* jaminan sosial; **to be on social security** menerima tunjangan.

social worker *noun* pekerja sosial.

society *noun* masyarakat.

sociology *noun* ilmu kemasyarakatan, sosiologi.

sock *noun* kaos kaki.

socket *noun* *(power point)* colokan.

sofa *noun* sofa.

soft *adjective* **1** *(food, voice)* lembek; **2** *(skin)* halus; **3** *(chair, bed)* empuk; **to have a soft spot for** merasa sayang kepada.

soft drink *noun* minuman lunak, sofdring, minuman tak beralkohol.

software *noun* *(for a computer)* perangkat lunak.

soft toy *noun* mainan lembut.

soil *noun* tanah.

solar energy *noun* energi matahari, tenaga matahari, tenaga surya.

soldier *noun* prajurit, tentara.

solicitor *noun* pengacara.

solid *adjective* **1** keras, padat; **solid food** makanan keras, makanan padat; **2** *(not flimsy)* kuat; **a solid structure** bangunan kuat; **a table made of solid teak** meja yang terbuat dari jati yang kuat; **3** murni; **solid gold** emas murni.

solo *noun* tunggal; *(flight)* penerbangan tunggal. *adjective, adverb* solo, tunggal; **a solo album** album tunggal; **to play solo** bermain tunggal.

soloist *noun* pemain tunggal, penyanyi tunggal.

solution *noun* **1** *(to a problem)* cara pemecahan, jalan keluar, penyelesaian, solusi; **2** *(chemical)* larutan.

solve *verb* melarutkan, memecahkan, menyelesaikan.

some *adjective, adverb* **1** beberapa; **some books** beberapa buku; **2** sedikit; **we need some more time** kami perlu sedikit waktu lagi; **would you like some butter?** mau mentega sedikit?; **3** *(often not translated)* **may I have some chilli sauce?** boleh minta sambal?; **can I borrow some money?** boleh saya pinjam uang?; **'would you like soup?' – 'thanks, I've got some'** 'mau sop?' – 'terima kasih saya masih ada'; **4** satu, suatu; **some day** suatu hari; **5** ada yang; **some are easy, some are difficult** ada yang mudah, ada yang sulit.

somebody, someone *pronoun* seseorang; **there's somebody in the garden** ada seseorang di taman.

somehow *adverb* **1** bagaimana pun juga; **I've got to finish this essay somehow** bagaimana pun juga saya harus menyelesaikan karangan ini; **2** entah bagaimana; **I somehow think they won't come** entah bagaimana, saya kira mereka tidak jadi datang.

something *pronoun* **1** sesuatu; **I've got something to tell you** ada sesuatu yang perlu saya katakan kepada Anda; **2 a guy called Colin something or other** seseorang bernama Colin yang saya lupa nama keluarganya; **their house is really something** rumahnya bukan main (besarnya, mewahnya, etc.).

sometime *adverb* kapan-kapan; **give me a ring sometime** kapan-kapan telepon saya.

a b c d e f g h i j k l m n o p q r s t u v w x y z

a b c d e f g h i j k l m n o p q r s t u v w x y z

sometimes *adverb* kadang-kadang; **I sometimes take the train** kadang-kadang saya naik kereta.

somewhere *adverb* *(usually translated using the* verb *'lupa' – forget)*; **I've put my bag down somewhere** saya lupa di mana saya meletakkan tas saya; **I've met you somewhere before** saya lupa di mana kita pernah bertemu dulu.

son *noun* anak laki-laki, putera.

song *noun* lagu, nyanyian.

son-in-law *noun* menantu (pria).

soon *adverb* **1** tidak lama lagi; **it will soon be the holidays** tidak lama lagi liburan; **2** segera; **we'll soon meet again** kita segera akan bertemu lagi; **3 as soon as** secepat, segera setelah, sesegera; **as soon as possible** secepat mungkin; **as soon as she arrives** segera setelah dia tiba; **4 it's too soon** terlalu cepat; **5 see you soon!** sampai jumpa!

sooner *adverb* **1** lebih cepat; **we should have started sooner** kita mestinya mulai lebih cepat; **2 I'd sooner wait** saya lebih suka menunggu; **3 sooner or later** cepat atau lambat.

soprano *noun* soprano.

sore *adjective* **1** sakit; **to have a sore leg** sakit kaki; **2 it's a sore point** hal yang menjengkelkan.

sorry *adjective* **1** *(apology)* maaf; **sorry!** maaf!; **I'm really sorry** saya sungguh-sungguh minta maaf; **sorry to disturb you** maaf mengganggu; **2** *(regret)* menyesal; **I'm really sorry I didn't go** menyesal saya tidak pergi; **3** *(pardon?)* **sorry?** apa katanya?; **4** kasihan; **to feel sorry for the lost generation** merasa kasihan terhadap generasi yang hilang.

sort *noun* **1** jenis; **what sort of music do you like?** musik jenis apa yang Anda suka?; **2** macam; **all sorts of** bermacam-macam; **that sort of person** orang macam itu. *verb* **1** *(things)* menyortir; **I must sort out these papers** saya harus menyortir surat-surat ini; **2** *(problem, arrangement)* menanggulangi, menyelesaikan; **Iskandar is sorting out the problem** Iskandar sedang menyelesaikan masalah tersebut.

so-so *adjective* lumayan; **'how was the film?' – 'so-so'** 'bagaimana dengan filmnya?' – 'ya, lumayan'.

soul *noun* **1** jiwa; **2** *(music)* musik soul.

sound *noun* **1** *(noise)* bunyi; **the sound of voices** bunyi suara; **2** *(volume)* suara; **to turn down the sound** mengecilkan suara.
verb **1** berbunyi; **the bells sounded out loudly** lonceng berbunyi keras; **sounds like** bunyinya seperti; **that sounds like Japanese** bunyinya seperti bahasa Jepang; **2** kedengaran; **it sounds easy** kedengarannya mudah; **3 it sounds as if she's happy** tampaknya dia bahagia.

sound asleep *adjective* tidur nyenyak.

sound effect *noun* efek suara.

soundtrack *noun* jalur suara.

soup *noun* sop.

soup plate *noun* mangkuk sop

soup spoon *noun* sendok sop.

sour *adjective* asam, basi; **the milk has gone sour** susunya basi, susunya sudah asam.

south *noun* selatan; **in the south** di selatan; **southeast** tenggara; **southwest** barat daya.
adjective, adverb selatan; **the south side** bagian selatan.

South Africa *noun* Afrika Selatan.

South America *noun* Amerika Selatan.

southeast *noun* tenggara.
adjective **in southeast Kalimantan** di Kalimantan Tenggara.

South Pole *noun* Kutub Selatan.

southwest *noun* barat daya.
adjective barat daya; **in southwest Kalimantan** di Kalimantan barat daya.

souvenir *noun* cenderamata, oleh-oleh, suvenir.

soya *noun* kedelai.

soy bean *noun* kacang kedelai.

soy sauce *noun* kecap.

space *noun* **1** *(room)* ruang; **is there enough space?** ada cukup ruang?; **2** *(gap)* tempat; **leave a space** sisakan tempat; **there's enough space for two more** ada cukup tempat untuk dua lagi; **3** *(outer space)* antariksa.

spacecraft *noun* pesawat antariksa.

spade *noun* sekop; **the queen of spades** ratu sekop.

Spain *noun* Spanyol.

Spaniard *noun* orang Spanyol.

a b c d e f g h i j k l m n o p q r s t u v w x y z

Spanish *noun (language)* bahasa Spanyol; **the Spanish** orang Spanyol.
adjective Spanyol; **Pedro is Spanish** Pedro adalah orang Spanyol.

spank *verb* memukul, menampar (bagian pantat).

spanner *noun* kunci Inggris.

spare *adjective* **1** *(part, battery)* lebih; **we have a spare ticket** kami mempunyai karcis lebih; **2** *(time)* waktu luang.
verb **1** *(with time)* meluangkan; **I can't spare the time** saya tidak dapat meluangkan waktu; **2** *(lend)* meminjamkan; **can you spare some rice?** bisa meminjamkan sedikit beras?

spare part *noun* onderdil, suku cadang.

spare room *noun* kamar kosong.

spare time *noun* waktu luang.

spare wheel *noun* roda serep.

sparkling *adjective* **1** bercahaya, berkilauan; **sparkling fairy lights** hiasan lampu yang berkilauan; **2** mengkilat; **sparkling clean** bersih mengkilat.

sparrow *noun* burung gereja.

speak *verb* **1** berbicara; **Wayan is speaking to Suwardi** Wayan sedang berbicara dengan Suwardi; **do you speak English?** apakah Anda berbahasa Inggris?; **who's speaking** *(on the phone)* siapa yang bicara?; **2 'could I speak to Tuladi please' – 'speaking'** 'bolehkah saya bicara dengan Tuladi' – 'saya sendiri'; **spoken Indonesian** bahasa Indonesia lisan.

speaker *noun* **1** *(on a music system)* pengeras suara; **2** *(at a public lecture)* pembicara, penceramah; **3** penutur; *(of a language)* **a Balinese speaker** penutur bahasa Bali; **native speaker** penutur asli.

special *adjective* istimewa, khusus, spesial.

specialist *noun* ahli, spesialis.

specialize *verb* **1** *(in a profession)* berspesialisasi; **2** mengkhususkan; **we specialize in Japanese decor** kami mengkhususkan dekorasi Jepang.

specially *adverb* **1** khusus; **not specially** tidak secara khusus; **2** *(specifically)* khususnya; **I came specially in order to see you** saya datang khusus untuk bertemu dengan Anda.

species *noun* jenis.

specific *adjective* spesifik.

spectacles *noun* kacamata.

spectacular *adjective* spektakuler.

spectator *noun* penonton.

speech *noun* **1** *(way of speaking)* cara bicara; **2** *(to an audience)* pidato; **to make a speech** berpidato, berceramah.

speechless *adjective* terdiam, kelu; **to be speechless with rage** terdiam karena marah benar; **I was speechless** lidah saya kelu, saya tidak bisa berkata apa-apa.

speed *noun* kecepatan; **top speed** kecepatan tertinggi; **what speed was he doing?** dia mengendarai dengan kecepatan berapa?
- **to speed up** mempercepat.

speeding *noun* melampaui batas kecepatan, mengebut; **he was fined for speeding** dia ditilang karena mengebut.

speed limit *noun* batas kecepatan.

spell *noun (of time)* masa; **a cold spell** masa dingin; **sunny spells** masa cerah. *verb* mengeja; **how do you spell it?** bagaimana mengejanya?

spelling *noun* ejaan; **a spelling mistake** kesalahan ejaan.

spend *verb* **1** *(money)* membelanjakan, mengeluarkan; **to spend money on a holiday trip** mengeluarkan uang untuk bepergian selama liburan; **2** tinggal; **we spent three days in Lombok** kami tinggal tiga hari di Lombok; **3** menghabiskan; **she spends all her time making sketches** dia menghabiskan seluruh waktunya untuk membuat gambar; **4** *(waste time)* memboroskan waktu, membuang-buang waktu; **5** *(until finished)* menghabiskan; **I've spent all my money** saya telah menghabiskan seluruh uang saya.

spice *noun* bumbu, rempah-rempah.

spicy *adjective* pedas; **spicy food** makanan pedas.

spider *noun* laba-laba.

spill *verb* tumpah; **I've spilled wine on the carpet** saya menumpahkan anggurnya di karpet dengan tidak sengaja.

spinach *noun* bayam.

spine *noun* tulang belakang, tulang punggung.

spiral *noun* spiral.

a b c d e f g h i j k l m n o p q r s t u v w x y z

spiral staircase *noun* tangga spiral.

spire *noun* puncak menara.

spirit *noun* **1** *(energy)* semangat; **2 to get into the spirit** ikut dalam suasana; **everybody got into the spirit of the Olympics** semua orang ikut dalam suasana kegembiraan Olimpiade.

spirits *noun* **1** *(alcohol)* minuman keras; **2** semangat; **to be in good spirits** bersemangat gembira; **3** roh; **evil spirits** roh jahat; **benevolent spirits** roh baik.

spit *verb* meludah.

spite *noun* **1 in spite of** betapa pun, biar pun, meski pun, walau pun; **we went in spite of the rain** kami pergi walau pun hujan; **2** *(nastiness)* dendam, dengki, irihati; **Jason hid Margy's books out of spite** Jason menyembunyikan buku-buku Margy karena merasa irihati.

spiteful *adjective* dengki, irihati.

splash *noun* **1** *(sound)* cipratan; **2 a splash of colour** sentuhan warna yang menyolok.

splendid *adjective* baik sekali, sungguh bagus.

splinter *noun* serpihan.

split *verb* **1** *(with an axe or a knife)* membelah; **to split a piece of wood** membelah kayu; **2** *(come apart)* robek; **the lining has split** lapisannya robek; **3** *(divide up)* membagi; **they split the money between them** mereka membagi uangnya (di antara mereka).

- **to split up 1** *(a couple or group)* berpisah; **she's split up with her boyfriend** dia berpisah dengan pacarnya; **2** *(a married couple)* bercerai *(divorce)*, berpisah *(separate)*.

spoil *verb* **1** mengganggu, merusak; **it completely spoiled the evening** merusak suasana malam (pesta); **his presence spoiled the fun at the party** kehadirannya mengganggu suasana gembira di pesta itu; **2** *(a child)* memanjakan.

spoiled *adjective* manja; **a spoiled child** anak yang manja.

spoilsport *noun* pengganggu kegiatan.

spoke *noun (of a wheel)* jari-jari.

spokesman *noun* juru bicara.

sponge *noun* sepon, lap serap.

sponge bag *noun* tas lap.

sponge cake *noun* kue bolu.

sponsor *noun* sponsor.

spontaneous *adjective* spontan.

spooky *adjective* seram; **a spooky story** cerita seram, cerita yang menyeramkan.

spoon *noun* sendok; **a soup spoon** sendok sop; **a dessertspoon** sendok makan.

spoonful *noun* sesendok, **a spoonful of sugar** sesendok gula.

sport *noun* olahraga; **to be good at sport** pandai berolahraga.

sports bag *noun* tas peralatan olahraga.

sports car *noun* mobil yang atasnya dapat dibuka, mobil sport.

sports centre *noun* pusat olahraga.

sports club *noun* perkumpulan olahraga.

sportsman *noun* olahragawan.

sportswoman *noun* olahragawati.

sporty *adjective* sportif; **she's very sporty** dia sangat sportif.

spot *noun* **1** *(in fabric)* bintik; **2** *(on your skin)* bintik, jerawat; **3** *(a stain)* noda; **you've got a spot on your shirt** ada noda di kemeja Anda; **4** *(spotlight)* lampu sorot; **5** *(immediately)* **on the spot** langsung; **we'll do it for you on the spot** kami akan langsung melakukannya untuk Anda; **6** *(at hand)* yang selalu bersedia; **they have experts on the spot** ada ahli yang selalu tersedia.
verb melihat; **I spotted her in the crowd** saya melihatnya di antara orang banyak.

spotless *adjective* bersih sekali, sempurna, tidak bernoda.

spotlight *noun* **1** lampu sorot; **2 to be in the spotlight** menjadi pusat perhatian umum.

spotty *adjective* *(pimply)* berjerawat.

spouse *noun* pasangan.

sprain *noun* keseleo, terkilir.
verb keseleo, terkilir; **to sprain your ankle** pergelangan kaki keseleo, pergelangan kaki terkilir.

spray *noun* *(spray can)* (alat) semprotan.
verb *(liquid)* menyemprot.

spread *noun* olesan.
verb **1** *(news or a disease)* menyebarkan, menyiarkan; **2** *(butter, jam, cement)*

a b c d e f g h i j k l m n o p q r s t u v w x y z

mengolesi, mengoleskan; **Judy spread some margarine on the bread** Judy mengoleskan mentega diatas roti, Judy mengolesi roti dengan mentega.

spreadsheet *noun* *(on a computer)* spreadsheet.

spring *noun* **1** *(the season)* musim semi; **2** *(made of metal)* per; **3** *(providing water)* mata air.

spring-cleaning *noun* pembersihan seluruh rumah.

springtime *noun* waktu musim semi.

spring water *noun* air dari mata air.

sprint *noun* lari cepat.

sprinter *noun* pelari cepat.

sprout *noun* pucuk, tunas; **bean sprouts** taoge.
verb bertunas.

spy *noun* mata-mata.
verb memata-matai.

spying *noun* spionase.

squabble *noun* bercekcok, bertengkar.

square *noun* **1** *(shape)* (empat) persegi; **2** alun-alun; **the village square** alun-alun desa; **to go back to square one** kembali lagi ke bagian permulaan.
adjective persegi; **a square box** kotak persegi.

squash *noun* **1** *(drink)* jus; **orange squash** jus jeruk; **2** *(sport)* **to play squash** bermain squash.

squeak *verb* **1** *(door hinge)* berderik; **2** *(animal)* mencicit.

squeeze *verb* **1** *(with tips of fingers)* memencet; **2** *(with whole hand)* memeras.

squid *noun* cumi-cumi.

squirrel *noun* bajing, tupai.

stab *verb* menikam, menusuk.

stable *noun* kandang kuda.

stack *noun* **1** tumpukan; **2 stacks of** banyak sekali; **she's got stacks of CDs** dia punya banyak sekali CD.

stadium *noun* gelanggang, stadion.

staff *noun* para pegawai, staf.

stage *noun* **1** *(for a performance)* panggung; **on stage** di atas panggung; **2** *(phase)* status, tahap, taraf; **at this stage of the project** bagian proyek pada taraf ini; **at this stage** pada tahap ini.

staggered *adjective* *(amazed)* terkejut.

stain *noun* noda.
verb mengotori, mengotorkan, menodai.

stainless steel *noun* baja tahan karat.

stair *noun* **1** *(step)* tangga; **2 stairs** tangga.

stale *adjective* basi.

stalemate *noun* jalan buntu.

stall *noun* **1** *(at a market or fair)* kedai, kios; **2** *(in a theatre)* **the stalls** tempat duduk yang murah.

stammer *noun* gagap; **to have a stammer** cara bicara yang gagap.
verb berbicara gagap.

stamp *noun* perangko.
verb **1** *(a letter)* mengecap; **2** menggertakkan; **to stamp your foot** menggertakkan kaki.

stamp album *noun* album perangko.

stamp collection *noun* koleksi perangko.

stand *verb* **1** berdiri; **we were standing outside the cinema** kami sedang berdiri di luar bioskop; **2 I've been standing here waiting for you for half an hour** saya berdiri menunggu Anda di sini selama setengah jam *(when you say somebody is standing somewhere, 'standing' is often not translated)*; **3** *(bear)* tidak tahan; **I can't stand him** saya muak dengan dia; **I can't stand waiting** saya tidak tahan menunggu.

- **to stand for** *(be short for)* singkatan; **'UN' stands for 'United Nations'** 'PBB' adalah singkatan dari 'Perserikatan Bangsa-bangsa'.
- **to stand up** berdiri; **everybody stood up** semua orang berdiri.

standard *noun* **1** standar, taraf; **the standard of living** standar kehidupan, taraf kehidupan; **2** bermutu; **her work is of a high standard** pekerjaannya bermutu tinggi.
adjective biasa, standar; **the standard price** harga biasa.

staple *noun* **1** kawat jepret, staples; **2** makanan utama.
verb menstapel.

star *noun* bintang; **film star** bintang film.
verb membintangi; **to star in a film** membintangi film.

stare *verb* menatap, melihat; **he was staring at her** dia menatapnya; **what are you staring at?** apa yang Anda lihat?

start *noun* **1** permulaan; **at the start of the book** pada bagian permulaan buku; **2 we knew from the start** kita tahu dari awal; **2 to make a start on** memulai; **I've made a start on my homework** saya sudah

a b c d e f g h i j k l m n o p q r s t u v w x y z

memulai pekerjaan rumah saya.
verb **1** memulai; **she started her career as a photo model** dia memulai karirnya sebagai model foto; **I've started the essay** saya sudah mulai menulis esei; **2** mulai; **the film starts at eight** filmnya mulai pukul delapan; **3** menyalakan; **to start a fire** menyalakan api; **4** menghidupkan; **to start a car** menghidupkan mobil.

starter *noun* **1** makanan pembuka *(food)*; **2** *(car)* stater.

starve *verb* **1** lapar sekali; **I'm starving** saya lapar sekali; **2** kelaparan; **people there are starving** masyarakat di sana kelaparan.

state *noun* **1** keadaan, kondisi; **the house is in a very bad state** rumahnya dalam kondisi buruk; **2** *(administrative district)* negara bagian; **3** *(country)* negara; **4 the States** Amerika Serikat (AS).
verb menyatakan.

statement *noun* pernyataan.

station *noun* **1** stasiun; **the railway station** stasiun kereta api; **the bus station** stasiun bis; **2** kantor, pos; **the police station** kantor polisi, pos polisi.

stationer's *noun* toko alat tulis.

statistics *plural noun* statistik; *(the subject)* ilmu statistik.

statue *noun* patung.

stay *noun* kunjungan, persinggahan; **our stay in Bali** persinggahan kami di Bali; **enjoy your stay!** selamat menikmati kunjungan Anda!
verb **1** tinggal; **I'll stay here** saya akan tinggal di sini; **2** menginap; **we're going to stay at Bromo overnight** kita akan menginap di Bromo; **to stay with** menginap di rumah.
- **to stay in** tinggal; **I'm staying in tonight** malam ini saya akan tinggal di rumah.

steady *adjective* **1** tetap; **a steady job** pekerjaan tetap; **2** terus-menerus; **a steady increase** penambahan terus-menerus; **3** erat, kuat; **please hold the ladder steady** tolong pegang tangga ini dengan erat.

steak *noun* bistek, bistik; **steak and salad** bistik dan salad.

steal *verb* mencuri.

steam *noun* uap.

steam engine *noun* mesin uap.

steam iron *noun* setrika uap.

steep *adjective* curam, terjal; **a steep slope** tanjakan terjal.

steeple *noun* puncak menara.

steering wheel *noun* roda kemudi, roda setir.

step *noun* **1** langkah; **to take a step forward** maju selangkah; **to take a step backward** mundur selangkah; **2 'mind the step'** 'hati-hati ada tangga', 'awas ada tangga'.
- **to step back** mundur.
- **to step forward** maju.
- **to step into** *(a lift)* masuk.

stepbrother *noun* adik tiri laki-laki, kakak tiri laki-laki.

stepdaughter *noun* anak tiri perempuan.

stepfather *noun* ayah tiri, bapak tiri.

stepladder *noun* tangga.

stepmother *noun* ibu tiri.

stepsister *noun* adik tiri perempuan, kakak tiri perempuan.

stepson *noun* anak tiri laki-laki.

stereo *noun* stereo.

sterling *noun* uang sterling; **pound sterling** mata uang pound.

stew *noun* daging dan sayur-sayuran yang direbus dengan api kecil.

steward *noun* pramugara.

stewardess *noun* pramugari.

stick *noun* **1** batang (kayu); **2 a walking stick** tongkat; **3 a hockey stick** tongkat hoki.
verb **1** *(with glue)* merekat; **2** *(put, colloquial)* menaruh; **stick them on my desk** taruhlah di atas meja saya.

sticker *noun* kertas tempel, stiker.

sticky *adjective* lengket; **my hands are sticky** tangan saya lengket.

sticky tape *noun* perekat, selotep.

stiff *adjective* **1** kaku; **to feel stiff** merasa kaku; **2 to be bored stiff** bosan sekali; **to be scared stiff** sangat ketakutan.

still *adjective* diam, tidak bergerak; **sit still!** diam!; **keep still!** jangan bergerak!
adverb **1** masih; **do you still live in Sukabumi?** Anda masih tinggal di Sukabumi?; **Try's still working** Try masih bekerja; **2 better still** lebih baik lagi.

sting *noun* sengatan; **a wasp sting** sengatan tawon.
verb menyengat; **I was stung by a bee** saya tersengat tawon.

stink *noun* bau busuk; **what a stink!** bau sekali!
verb bau; **it stinks of cigarette smoke in here** bau rokok di sini.

stir *verb* **1** *(mixture)* mengaduk, mengocok; **2** *(people)* menghasut.

stitch *noun* setik jahitan.

stock *noun* **1** *(in a shop)* persediaan; **to have something in stock** mempunyai persediaan; **2** *(supply)* cadangan barang, persediaan barang; **I always have a stock of pencils** saya selalu punya cadangan pensil; **3** *(for cooking)* kaldu; **chicken stock** kaldu ayam.
verb **1** *(in a shop)* mempunyai, menyediakan, menyimpan; **they don't stock dictionaries** mereka tidak menyimpan kamus.
- **to stock up on** menyimpan.

stock cube *noun* bumbu kaldu.

stocking *noun* kaus kaki, stocking.

stomach *noun* perut.

stomachache *noun* sakit perut.

stone *noun* **1** batu; **2** *(pebble)* kerikil; **3** *(in fruit)* biji.

stool *noun* bangku.

stop *noun* perhentian, setopan *(colloquial)*; **the bus stop** perhentian bis.
verb **1** berhenti; **he stopped in front of the shop** dia berhenti di depan toko; **Sumarjono's stopped smoking** Sumarjono berhenti merokok; **2** mencegah, menghentikan, menyetop; **she stopped me in the street** dia menghentikan saya di jalan; **there's nothing to stop you doing what you want** tidak ada yang dapat mencegah melakukan apa yang Anda inginkan.

stopwatch *noun* stopwatch.

store *noun* *(shop)* toko, warung.
verb **1** menyimpan; **2** *(on a computer)* menyimpan, save.

storey *noun* lantai, tingkat; **a three-storey house** rumah berlantai tiga, rumah bertingkat tiga.

storm *noun* *(wind)* angin topan, badai; **a rainstorm** hujan badai; **a thunderstorm** hujan angin ribut disertai petir dan guntur.

stormy *adjective* banyak badai.

story *noun* cerita, ceritera; **to tell a story** bercerita.

stove *noun* *(cooker)* kompor.

straight *adjective* lurus; **a straight line** garis lurus.
adverb **1** *(in direction)* terus; **go straight** jalan terus; **2** *(in time)* langsung; **he went straight to the doctor's** dia langsung ke dokter; **straightaway** langsung.

straightforward *adjective* terus terang.

strain *noun* beban, tekanan; **the strain of the last few weeks** beban selama beberapa minggu yang lalu.
verb (part of the body) tertarik; **Siagian's strained his back** urat tulang belakang Siagian tertarik.

strange *adjective* aneh; **a strange situation** keadaan yang aneh.

stranger *noun* orang asing, orang yang tak dikenal.

strangle *verb* mencekik.

strap *noun* tali.

strapless *adjective* strapless, tanpa lengan dan tak bertali bahu.

straw *noun* **1** jerami; **a straw hat** topi jerami, topi anyaman; **2** *(for drinking with)* sedotan.

strawberry *noun* arbei.

stray *adjective* tersesat; **a stray dog** anjing tersesat.

stream *noun* aliran, sungai kecil.

street *noun* jalan.

streetlamp *noun* lampu jalan.

street map *noun* peta jalan.

strength *noun* kekuatan.

stress *noun* ketegangan, stres, tekanan.
verb (emphasize) menegaskan, menekankan, menggarisbawahi; **to stress the importance of the report** menggarisbawahi pentingnya laporan tersebut.

stretch *verb* **1** *(garment)* melar; **this jumper has stretched** baju hangat ini melar **2** *(shoes)* melebarkan, melonggarkan; **3** *(your body)* menggeliat.

stretcher *noun* usungan.

stretchy *adjective* elastis, melar.

strict *adjective* ketat; **they were strict with the children** mereka sangat ketat terhadap anak-anak; **strict regulations** peraturan yang ketat.

strike *noun* pemogokan; **to go on strike** mogok.
verb **1** *(hit)* memukul; **2** *(clock)* berbunyi, berdentang; **the clock struck six** jam berdentang pukul enam; **3** *(with a vehicle)* menabrak; **4** *(workers)* mogok.

striker *noun* pemogok.

striking *adjective* menyolok; **a striking resemblance** kemiripan yang menyolok.

string *noun* tali.

strip *noun* carik, kepingan, potongan.
verb **1** *(undress)* membuka baju, menelanjangi; **2** *(the forest)* menebang; **3** *(a person of property, honour, etc.)* merampas.

strip cartoon *noun* kartun baris.

stripe *noun* belang, garis.

striped *adjective* bergaris, berjalur.

stroke *noun* **1** *(style of swimming)* gaya; **2** *(medical)* serangan otak, stroke; **a stroke of luck** keberuntungan, kemujuran.
verb menenangkan, mengusap-usap.

stroll *noun* jalan-jalan; **to go for a stroll** berjalan-jalan, pergi makan angin.
verb berjalan-jalan, pergi makan angin.

strong *adjective* **1** *(person, feeling, material)* kuat; **2** *(drink, smell)* keras; **3** *(wind)* kencang.

strongly *adverb* **1** betul-betul; **I strongly believe** saya betul-betul percaya; **2** kuat-kuat; **she pulled strongly on the oars** dia menarik dayungnya kuat-kuat.

struggle *noun* **1** perebutan, perjuangan; **the struggle for independence** perjuangan kemerdekaan; **a power struggle** perebutan kekuasaan; **2** perlawanan; **without a struggle** tanpa perlawanan.
verb **1** berusaha keras; **they have struggled to survive** mereka berusaha keras untuk tetap hidup; **I'm struggling to finish this homework** saya berusaha keras untuk menyelesaikan pekerjaan rumah ini; **2** *(physically in order to escape or reach something)* berjuang melawan.

stub *noun* puntung; **a cigarette stub** puntung rokok.
verb menyentuh; **to stub your toe** menyentuh jari kaki.
- **to stub out** *(a cigarette)* mematikan.

stubborn *adjective* bandel, keras kepala.

stubby *noun* kecil, pendek; **a stubby of beer** bir kecil.

stuck *adjective* **1** *(jammed)* **the drawer's stuck** lacinya macet; **2** *(person)* **to get stuck** terperangkap *(in a lift, traffic jam or place).*

a b c d e f g h i j k l m n o p q r s t u v w x y z

stud *noun* **1** *(on a belt or jacket)* kancing; **2** *(earring)* giwang.

student *noun* pelajar, murid *(secondary)*, (maha)siswa *(male)*, (maha)siswi *(female) (tertiary)*.

studio *noun* studio.

study *noun* **1** *(subjects)* pelajaran; **2** penelitian, penyelidikan; **to carry out a study** mengadakan penyelidikan; **3** *(room)* kamar belajar.
verb **1** belajar; **Mishra's studying for his exams** Mishra sedang belajar untuk ujiannya; **2** mempelajari **you should study the customs before you leave** sebaiknya Anda mempelajari adat-istiadatnya sebelum berangkat.

stuff *noun* **1** *(things)* barang(-barang) *(informal)*; **we can throw all that stuff out** kita dapat membuang semua barang-barang itu; **2** *(personal belongings)* barang(-barang) pribadi; **3** *(substance)* bahan; **some antiseptic stuff** bahan antiseptik.
verb **1** *(shove)* memasukkan *(informal)*; **she stuffed some things into a suitcase** dia memasukkan beberapa barang ke dalam koper; **2** *(in cooking)* mengisi; **stuffed eggplant** terong isi.

stuffing *noun (for cooking)* isi.

stuffy *adjective (airless)* pengap, sesak.

stumble *verb (trip)* tersandung, tersuntuk, jatuh.

stunned *adjective (amazed)* tercengang.

stunning *adjective* menakjubkan.

stunt *noun (in a film)* adegan berbahaya.

stuntman *noun* stuntman.

stuntwoman *noun* stuntwoman.

stupid *adjective* bodoh, goblok.

stutter *noun* gagap; **to have a stutter** bicara menggagap.
verb menggagap.

style *noun* **1** gaya; **a style of living** gaya hidup; **your own style** mempunyai gaya sendiri; **2** *(fashion)* mode; **it's the latest style** itu mode terbaru.

subject *noun* **1** pokok, topik; **the subject of my talk** pokok pembicaraan saya; **2** *(at school)* mata pelajaran; **my favourite subject is art** mata pelajaran favorit saya adalah kesenian.

submarine *noun* kapal selam.

a b c d e f g h i j k l m n o p q r s t u v w x y z

subscription *noun* abonemen, langganan; **to take out a subscription** berlangganan.

subsidy *noun* subsidi, tunjangan.

substance *noun* inti, isi pokok.

substitute *noun* pengganti.

subtitled *adjective (film)* disub-judul.

subtitles *plural noun* sub-judul.

subtle *adjective* halus, tidak langsung.

subtract *verb* mengurangi.

suburb *noun* bagian kota, daerah kota; **in the suburbs of Sydney** di daerah kota Sydney.

suburban *adjective* daerah; **suburban area** daerah kota.

subway *noun (underpass)* bawah tanah.

succeed *verb* berhasil, sukses; **we've succeeded in contacting Yusa** kita berhasil menghubungi Yusa.

success *noun* keberhasilan, sukses.

successful *adjective* berhasil baik, sukses; **a successful career** karir yang berhasil.

successfully *adverb* dengan berhasil, dengan sukses.

such *adjective, adverb* **1** amat, begitu, betul-betul, sangat, sekali, sungguh; **they're such nice people** mereka orang yang sangat ramah; **I've had such a busy day** saya amat sibuk hari ini; **it's such a long way** jauh sekali; **2 such a lot of** begitu banyak; **I've got such a lot of things to tell you** begitu banyak yang perlu saya ceritakan kepada Anda; **3 such as** seperti; **in big cities such as Jakarta** di kota-kota besar seperti Jakarta; **4 there's no such thing** tidak ada hal demikian.

suck *verb* menghirup, menghisap.

sudden *adjective* mendadak, tiba-tiba; **all of a sudden** secara tiba-tiba.

suddenly *adverb* mendadak, (dengan) tiba-tiba; **Asrul suddenly started to laugh** Asrul tiba-tiba mulai tertawa; **to die suddenly** meninggal mendadak.

suede *noun* kulit yang agak kasar dan tidak kaku (*definition only*); **a suede jacket** jaket kulit.

suffer *verb* menderita

sufficient *adjective* cukup.

sufficiently *adverb* secukupnya.

sugar *noun* gula; **palm sugar** gula Jawa, gula merah.

suggest *verb* menganjurkan, mengusulkan, menyarankan; **Sari suggested I should speak to you about it** Sari menyarankan supaya saya berbicara kepada Anda mengenai hal itu.

suggestion *noun* saran, usul(an); **to make a suggestion** menyarankan, mengusulkan.

suicide *noun* bunuh diri; **to commit suicide** bunuh diri.

suit *noun* jas.

suitable *adjective (clothing)* cocok, pantas; **I don't have any suitable shoes** saya tidak punya sepatu yang cocok.

suitcase *noun* koper.

sulk *verb* ngambek (*colloquial*), merenggut, bersungut-sungut.

sum *noun* **1** jumlah; **a sum of money** sejumlah uang; **a large sum** sejumlah besar; **2** *(calculation)* penjumlahan, hitungan.

- **to sum up** menyimpulkan, meringkaskan.

summarize *verb* meringkaskan.

summary *noun* ringkasan.

summer *noun* musim panas; **the summer holidays** liburan musim panas; **in summer clothes** berpakaian musim panas.

summertime *noun* musim panas.

summit *noun* puncak.

sun *noun* matahari, surya.

sunbathe *verb* berjemur.

sunblock *noun* salep untuk melindungi kulit dari sinar matahari (*definition only*).

sunburn *noun* kulit terbakar oleh matahari.

sunburned *adjective* terbakar oleh matahari.

Sunday *noun* hari Minggu; **on Sunday** pada hari Minggu; **every Sunday** setiap hari Minggu; **last Sunday** hari Minggu kemarin (*colloquial*), hari Minggu yang lalu; **next Sunday** hari Minggu depan, hari Minggu yang akan datang.

sunflower *noun* bunga matahari; **sunflower oil** minyak bunga matahari.

sunglasses *plural noun* kacamata hitam; kacamata gelap.

sunlight *noun* cahaya matahari, sinar matahari.

sunny *adjective* cerah; **sunny spells** waktu cerah.

sunrise *noun* matahari terbit.

sunroof *noun* atap kaca.

a b c d e f g h i j k l m n o p q r s t u v w x y z

sunscreen *noun* krim untuk melindungi kulit dari sinar matahari (*definition only*).

sunset *noun* matahari terbenam.

sunshine *noun* cahaya matahari, sinar matahari.

sunstroke *noun* sakit akibat terbakar matahari.

suntan *noun* (*there is no concept of this in Indonesian*) warna coklat akibat terbakar matahari.

suntan lotion *noun* (*there is no concept of this in Indonesian*) obat suntan.

suntan oil *noun* (*there is no concept of this in Indonesian*) minyak suntan.

super *adjective* hebat, super.

supermarket *noun* pasar swalayan, supermarket.

supernatural *adjective* gaib, sakti.

superstitious *adjective* bertakhyul, percaya pada hal-hal gaib, percaya takhyul.

supervise *verb* mengamati, mengawasi.

supper *noun* makan malam.

supplement *noun* lampiran, tambahan.

supplies *noun* perbekalan, persediaan.

supply *noun* (*stock*) perbekalan, persediaan; **to be in short supply** kekurangan.
verb menyediakan; **the school supplies the paper** sekolah menyediakan kertas; **we supply them with pencils** kami menyediakan pensil untuk mereka.

support *noun* **1** dukungan (*encouragement*); **he has a lot of support** dia mendapat banyak dukungan; **2** sokongan (*contributions*); **they got support from the government** mereka dapat sokongan dari pemerintah.
verb mendukung, menyokong; **Ralph's teachers have really supported him** guru-guru Ralph betul-betul mendukungnya.

supporter *noun* pendukung.

suppose *verb* mengira, menyangka; **I suppose she's forgotten** saya kira dia sudah lupa.

supposed *adjective* seharusnya; **you're supposed to wear a helmet** orang seharusnya memakai helm.

sure *adjective* **1** pasti, yakin; **are you sure?** Anda yakin?; **2** (*informal*) **'can you shut the door?' – 'sure!'** 'bisakah Anda menutup pintu?' – 'baiklah!'

surely *adverb* **1** pasti, tentu saja; **surely Benny will come** pasti Benny akan datang; **2 surely she couldn't have forgotten!** aneh kenapa dia lupa?

surface *noun* permukaan.

surfboard *noun* papan berselancar.

surfing *noun* **to go surfing** berselancar.

surgeon *noun* ahli bedah.

surgery *noun* **1** operasi, pembedahan; **to have surgery** menjalani pembedahan; **2** *(consulting rooms)* ruang pemeriksaan dokter.

surname *noun* nama keluarga.

surprise *noun* kejutan; **what a surprise!** suatu kejutan!

surprised *adjective* heran; **I was surprised** saya heran.

surprising *adjective* mengherankan.

surround *verb* mengitari, mengelilingi; **to be surrounded by** dikelilingi oleh; **Jasmin's surrounded by friends** Jasmin dikelilingi oleh teman-temannya.

survey *noun* survei.

survival *noun* kelangsungan hidup.

survive *verb* bertahan.

survivor *noun* orang yang terus bertahan.

suspect *noun* orang yang dicurigai, tersangka.
verb mencurigai.

suspend *verb* **1** *(hang)* menggantungkan; **2** *(from school)* mengeluarkan, menskors; **to be suspended** diskors.

suspense *noun* keragu-raguan, kegelisahan, kebimbangan.

suspicion *noun* kecurigaan.

suspicious *adjective* mencurigakan; **a suspicious parcel** bingkisan yang mencurigakan; **a suspicious-looking individual** seseorang yang mencurigakan.

swallow *noun* *(bird)* burung layang-layang.
verb menelan.

swan *noun* angsa berleher panjang, burung undan.

swap *verb* menukar; **do you want to swap?** mau tukar?; **he's swapped his bike for a computer** dia menukar sepedanya dengan sebuah komputer; **to swap seats** tukar tempat.

swear *verb* **1** *(use bad language)* mengutuk; **2** *(an oath)* bersumpah.

swear word *noun* kata kutukan.

a b c d e f g h i j k l m n o p q r s t u v w x y z

sweat *noun* keringat.
verb berkeringat, berpeluh.

sweater *noun* baju hangat, sweater.

Swede *noun* orang Swedia.

Sweden *noun* negeri Swedia.

Swedish *noun* orang Swedia.
adjective Swedia.

sweep *verb* menyapu.

sweet *noun* **1** gula-gula, permen; **2** *(dessert)* makanan pencuci mulut.
adjective **1** *(food)* manis; **sweet things** makanan manis; **2** *(kind)* baik, manis; **Claire's a really sweet person** Claire betul-betul seorang yang manis; **3** *(cute)* manis, mungil; **he looks really sweet in that hat** dia kelihatan manis dengan topinya.

sweetcorn *noun* jagung manis.

swell *noun* *(of a sea tide)* gelombang besar.
verb *(part of the body)* bengkak, membengkak.

swim *noun* renang; **to go for a swim** (pergi) berenang.
verb berenang; **to swim across the lake** berenang ke seberang danau.

swimmer *noun* perenang.

swimming *noun* berenang; **to go swimming** pergi berenang.

swimming cap *noun* topi renang.

swimming costume *noun* baju renang, celana renang *(for men)*, pakaian renang.

swimming pool *noun* kolam renang.

swimming togs *noun* baju renang, celana renang *(for men)*, pakaian renang.

swimming trunks *noun* celana renang.

swimsuit *noun* baju renang, pakaian renang.

swing *noun* ayunan.
verb berayun, mengayunkan.

Swiss *noun* *(person)* **the Swiss** orang Swis.
adjective Swis.

switch *noun* kenop, tombol.
verb *(change)* **to switch places** bertukar tempat.
- **to switch off** mematikan.
- **to switch on** memasang, menghidupkan, menyalakan.

Switzerland *noun* negara Swis.

swollen *adjective* bengkak.

swop *verb* SEE **swap**.

sword *noun* pedang.

syllabus *noun* ikhtisar mata pelajaran, silabus.

symbol *noun* lambang, simbol.

symbolic *adjective* simbolis.

sympathetic *adjective* **1** bersimpati kepada, menunjukkan simpati; **the government was sympathetic towards the flood victims** pemerintah menunjukkan simpatinya kepada para korban banjir; **2** simpatik *(pleasant and agreeable attitude)*; **she's a sympathetic person** dia orang yang simpatik.

sympathize *verb* bersimpati; **I sympathize with them** saya bersimpati kepada mereka.

sympathy *noun* simpati.

symphony *noun* simfoni.

symphony orchestra *noun* orkes simfoni.

symptom *noun* gejala.

synthetic *adjective* buatan, sintetis.

syringe *noun* alat suntik.

system *noun* sistem, susunan.

T t

table *noun* meja; **on the table** di atas meja; **to lay (set) the table** menyiapkan meja; **to clear the table** mengangkat barang-barang dari meja.

tablecloth *noun* taplak meja.

tablespoon *noun* sendok makan; *(in recipes)* **a tablespoon of flour** sesendok makan tepung.

tablet *noun* pil, tablet.

table tennis *noun* pingpong, tenis meja; **to play table tennis** main tenis meja.

tabloid *noun* tabloid.

tackle *verb* **1** *(in football or hockey)* menggasak; **2** melakukan, menangani, mengerjakan; **to tackle a job** melakukan pekerjaan; **3 to tackle a problem** memecahkan suatu persoalan.

tact *noun* kebijaksanaan.

tactful *adjective* bijaksana; **that wasn't very tactful** itu kurang bijaksana.

tadpole *noun* berudu, kecebong.

tail *noun* ekor.

take *verb* **1** mengambil; **who's taken my keys?** siapa yang mengambil kunci saya?; **2** membawa, mengantarkan; *(to accompany a person or thing)* **I'm taking Noto to the doctor** saya akan mengantarkan Noto ke dokter; **I must take the car to the garage** saya harus membawa mobil ke bengkel;

a b c d e f g h i j k l m n o p q r s t u v w x y z

she's taken some work to do at home dia membawa pulang (sebagian dari) pekerjaannya; **3** makan waktu, memerlukan; **it takes two hours** makan waktu dua jam; **4** memegang *(by the hand)*, **take my hand** peganglah tangan saya; **5** menerima; **he took the news badly** dia menerima kabar itu dengan sedih; *(a credit card or a cheque)* **do you take cheques?** apakah Anda dapat menerima cek?; **6** (ada) ujian *(an exam)*; **she's taking her driving test tomorrow** besok dia ujian menyetir mobil; **7** memerlukan; **it takes a lot of courage** diperlukan keberanian besar; **8** memakai; **what size do you take?** Anda memakai ukuran berapa?; **9** naik; **I took the bus** saya naik bis; **10** memuat; **my car can take four more** mobil saya dapat memuat empat orang lagi; **do you take sugar?** Anda mau gula?

- **to take something apart** membongkar.
- **to take something back** membawa kembali, menarik kembali.
- **to take off 1** *(a plane)* lepas landas; **2** *(clothes or shoes)* membuka, menanggalkan; **you have to take off your shoes** Anda harus menanggalkan sepatu Anda; **3** *(money)* memotong; **they took ten dollars off the price** mereka memotong harganya sepuluh dolar, mereka memberikan diskon sepuluh dolar.
- **to take out 1** *(from a bag or pocket)* mengeluarkan; **Yusa took out his wallet** Yusa mengeluarkan dompetnya; **2** membawa pesiar, mengajak; **I'd like to take them out** saya ingin membawa mereka pesiar; **they're taking us out to lunch** mereka mau mengajak kita untuk makan siang; **she took me to the puppet theatre** dia mengajak saya ke pertunjukan wayang golek.

takeaway *noun (a meal)* makanan bungkusan.

take-off *noun (of a plane)* lepas landas.

talent *noun* bakat; **to have a talent for music** mempunyai bakat untuk musik.

talented *adjective* berbakat; **he's really very talented** dia benar-benar berbakat.

talk *noun* **1** *(a chat)* pembicaraan, percakapan; **I had a talk with Armijn about it** saya mengadakan pembicaraan dengan Armijn tentang itu; **2** ceramah; **she's giving a talk on Balinese dance** dia akan mengadakan ceramah tentang tarian Bali.
verb **1** berbicara, memperbincangkan; **I was talking to Bachtiar about football** saya berbicara dengan Bachtiar tentang sepak bola; **what's he talking about?** apa yang dibicarakannya?; **we'll talk about it later** nanti kita akan memperbincangkan soal itu; **2** *(gossip)* mengobrol; **they're always talking** mereka selalu mengobrol.

talkative *adjective* banyak bicara, cerewet, suka bicara; **he's not exactly talkative** dia tidak banyak bicara.

tall *adjective* tinggi; **she's very tall** dia tinggi sekali; **I'm 1.7 metres tall** tinggi saya seratus tujuh puluh centi.

tame *adjective* jinak.

tampon *noun* tampon.

tan *noun* warna coklat; **he got a tan** kulitnya berwarna coklat kemerah-merahan karena sinar matahari.

tank *noun* **1** *(for liquids)* tangki; **2** *(military)* tank.

tanned *adjective* berwarna coklat.

tap *noun* **1** keran; **to turn off the tap** menutup keran; **the hot tap** keran air panas; **2** ketukan, tepukan; **a tap on the table** tekukan pada meja; **a tap on the shoulder** tepukan pada bahu.
verb menepuk, mengetuk.

tap-dancing *noun* dansa tap, tarian dengan mengentak-entak kaki.

tape *noun* **1** kaset; **my tape of Koes Plus** kaset Koes Plus saya; **I've got it on tape** saya sudah merekamnya; **2 sticky tape** selotep.
verb merekam; **I plan to tape the film** saya ada rencana untuk merekam film itu.

tape measure *noun* pita pengukur.

tape recorder *noun* alat perekam, tape recorder.

tapestry *noun* permadani.

target *noun* sasaran, target.

tart *noun* kue tarcis.

tartan *adjective* pola belah ketupat.

task *noun* tugas.

taste *noun* **1** rasa, perasaan; **the taste of durian** rasa

a b c d e f g h i j k l m n o p q r s t u v w x y z

durian; **2 in bad taste** tak berbudi bahasa, tak sopan.
verb **1** mengicipi; **do you want to taste?** apakah Anda mau mengicipi?; **does durian taste wonderful or horrible?** apakah durian enak atau tidak?; **2 to taste of** merasakan seperti; **it tastes of onion** rasanya seperti bawang.

tasty *adjective* enak, gurih, lezat.

tattoo *noun* tato; **he's got a Dayak tattoo** ada tato bermotif Dayak di tubuhnya.

Taurus *noun* Taurus; **Sukma's Taurus** Sukma berbintang Taurus.

tax *noun* **1** pajak; **2** *(on goods)* bea, cukai.

taxi *noun* taksi; **by taxi** dengan taksi, naik taksi; **to take a taxi** naik taksi.

taxi driver *noun* pengemudi taksi; sopir taksi.

taxi rank *noun* pangkalan taksi.

TB *noun* tbc.

tea *noun* **1** teh; **a cup of tea** secangkir teh; **strong tea** teh kental; **weak tea** teh encer; **2** *(evening meal)* makan malam; **to have tea** makan malam.

teabag *noun* teh celup.

teach *verb* **1** mengajar; **he teaches primary school** dia mengajar di sekolah dasar; **she's teaching me Batak language** dia mengajar saya bahasa Batak;
2 mengajarkan; **her mum teaches maths** ibunya mengajar ilmu pasti; **3 to teach yourself** belajar sendiri; **Hikmah taught herself to cook** Hikmah belajar memasak sendiri;
I told you not to eat at that foodstall. That'll teach you! saya sudah bilang jangan makan di warung itu. Ini pelajaran bagi Anda!

teacher *noun* guru; **my mother's a teacher** ibu saya seorang guru; **our biology teacher** guru ilmu hayat (biologi) kami.

teaching *noun* pengajaran.

team *noun* regu, tim; **a football team** kesebelasan, regu sepak bola; **our team won** kesebelasan kita menang.

teapot *noun* teko teh.

tear[1] *noun* *(a rip)* sobekan; **I've got a tear in my jeans** celana jeans saya sobek.
verb **1** menyobek, merobek; **she tore up the letter** dia merobek surat itu; **you've torn your shirt** kemeja Anda sobek; **2 be careful, it tears**

easily hati-hati, itu gampang sobek.

- **to tear off** melepaskan, merobek.
- **to tear open** membuka.

tear[2] *noun (when you cry)* air mata; **to be in tears** menangis; **to burst into tears** menangis mendadak.

tease *verb* menggoda, mengusik.

teaspoon *noun* sendok teh; **a teaspoonful of salt** sesendok teh garam.

teatime *noun (evening meal)* waktu makan malam.

tea towel *noun* lap piring.

technical *adjective* teknis.

technical college *noun* sekolah kejuruan, sekolah teknik.

technician *noun* teknisi.

technique *noun* teknik.

techno *noun (music)* musik tekno.

technological *adjective* teknologi.

technology *noun* teknologi; **information technology** teknologi informasi.

teddy bear *noun* beruang-beruangan.

teenage *adjective* remaja; **they have a teenage son** mereka mempunyai anak laki-laki remaja; **Hai is a teenage magazine** Hai adalah majalah remaja.

teenager *noun* anak belasan tahun, anak tanggung, anak remaja; **teenager group** kelompok remaja.

teens *noun* umur belasan tahun; **he's in his teens** dia berumur belasan tahun.

tee-shirt *noun* baju kaos, kaos oblong.

telephone *noun*, telepon, telpon; **on the telephone** sedang berbicara di telepon. *verb* menelepon, menelpon; **I'll telephone the airline** saya akan menelepon kantor penerbangan.

telephone box *noun* gardu telepon.

telephone call *noun* panggilan telepon.

telephone directory *noun* buku (petunjuk) telepon.

telephone number *noun* nomor telepon.

telescope *noun* teropong.

televise *verb* menyiarkan melalui televisi; **they're televising his speech** pidatonya akan disiarkan melalui televisi.

television *noun* televisi; **she was watching television** dia nonton televisi; **I saw it on television** saya melihat itu di televisi.

a b c d e f g h i j k l m n o p q r s t u v w x y z

television program *noun* acara televisi.

tell *verb* **1** memberitahukan; **that's what she told me** itu yang diberitahukannya kepada saya; **have you told Sara?** apakah Anda sudah memberitahu Sara?; **2** *(instruct)* menyuruh; **he told me to do it myself** dia menyuruh saya mengerjakannya sendiri; **she told me to wait** dia menyuruh saya menunggu; **she told me not to wait** katanya saya tidak usah menunggu; **3** *(explain)* menerangkan; **can you tell me how to do it?** tolong terangkan kepada saya bagaimana melakukannya; **4** mengatakan; **I told him it was important** saya mengatakan kepadanya bahwa hal itu penting; **5** *(a story)* menceritakan; **tell me about your holiday** ceritakan tentang liburan Anda; **6** membedakan; **I can't tell them apart** saya tidak dapat membedakan mereka.

telly *noun* televisi; **to watch telly** menonton televisi; **I saw her on the telly** saya melihat dia di televisi.

temp *noun* *(temporary help)* pekerja sementara.

temper *noun* kemarahan, perangai, tabiat; **to be in a temper** marah; **to lose your temper** menjadi marah, hilang kesabaran; **Diana has a bad temper** Diana mempunyai perangai yang buruk.

temperature *noun* **1** suhu; **the oven temperature** suhu oven; **2 to have a temperature** badannya panas demam.

temple *noun* **1** candi, kelenteng, kuil; **2** pelipis.

temporary *adjective* sementara.

temptation *noun* godaan.

tempted *adjective* tergoda, tertarik; **I'm really tempted to go with them** saya betul-betul tertarik untuk pergi dengan mereka.

tempting *adjective* menarik, menggoda.

ten *number* sepuluh; **Harry's ten** Harry berumur sepuluh tahun.

tend *verb* **to tend to do** cenderung; **he tends to talk a lot** dia cenderung untuk berbicara banyak.

tender *adjective* empuk, lembut.

tennis *noun* tenis; **to play tennis** main tenis.

tennis ball *noun* bola tenis.

tennis court *noun* lapangan tenis.

tennis player *noun* pemain tenis, petenis.

tennis racket *noun* raket tenis.

tenor *noun* suara laki-laki yang tinggi, tenor; **a tenor voice** suara tenor.

ten-pin bowling *noun* tenpin boling.

tense *noun* masa, waktu; **the present tense** masa kini. *adjective* tegang.

tent *noun* kemah, tenda.

tenth *adjective* kesepuluh, sepuluh; **on the tenth floor** di lantai sepuluh; **the tenth of April** tanggal sepuluh April.

term *noun* **1** *(in school)* kwartal, masa; **the school term** masa sekolah selama satu kwartal atau satu semester; **2** hubungan; **to be on good terms with** berhubungan baik dengan.

terminal *noun* **1** *(at an airport, ferry, etc.)* terminal; **terminal two** terminal dua; **2** *(train, bus)* stasiun; **3** *(a computer terminal)* terminal komputer.

terrace *noun* **1** *(of a house or hotel)* teras, tingkat; **2 the terraces** *(at a stadium)* teras; **3** petak, tingkat; **the rice terraces** sawah bertingkat.

terrible *adjective* buruk sekali, mengerikan; **the weather was terrible** cuacanya buruk sekali.

terribly *adverb* **1** *(very)* amat, sangat; **terribly dirty** sangat kotor; **2** *(badly)* buruk sekali; **I played terribly** saya bermain dengan buruk sekali; **3** *(not good or well)* kurang; **not terribly clean** kurang bersih.

terrific *adjective* **1** sekali; **a terrific amount** banyak sekali; **2 terrific!** hebat!; **at a terrific speed** dengan kecepatan yang sangat tinggi.

terrified *adjective* merasa takut sekali.

terrorism *noun* terorisme.

terrorist *noun* perusuh, teroris.

test *noun* **1** *(in school)* ujian; **we've got a maths test tomorrow** besok kami akan ujian matematika; **a driving test** ujian mengendarai mobil; **he passed his driving test** dia lulus ujian mengendarai mobil; **2** *(medical)* pemeriksaan; **a blood test** pemeriksaan darah.

verb **1** *(in school)* menguji; **2** mencoba.

test tube *noun* tabung pengetes.

text *noun* isi, naskah, teks.

textbook *noun* buku pelajaran.

than *preposition, conjunction* dari, daripada; **his new book's better than his last one** bukunya yang baru lebih baik daripada bukunya yang terakhir; **they have more money than we do** mereka punya lebih banyak uang daripada kami; **more than forty** lebih dari empat puluh; **more than twenty years** lebih dari dua puluh tahun.

thank *verb* terima kasih.

thanks *plural noun* **1** terima kasih; **no thanks** terima kasih; *(note that in Indonesian saying* 'terima kasih' *accompanied with appropriate body language after an offer always indicates a refusal)* **'would you like a cup of coffee?' – 'no thanks'** 'Anda mau minum kopi?' – 'terima kasih'; **thanks a lot** terima kasih banyak, **thanks for your help** terima kasih atas bantuan Anda; **with thanks for** terima kasih atas; **2 thanks to** berkat; **thanks to the Soehartos** berkat keluarga Soeharto.

thank you *adverb* terima kasih; **thank you very much for the cheque** terima kasih banyak atas cek itu; **no, thank you** terima kasih *(with appropriate body language)*; **a thank-you letter** surat pernyataan terima kasih.

that *adjective* **1** itu; **that dog** anjing itu; **that man** orang laki-laki itu; **that blue car** mobil biru itu; **2 'which cake would you like?' – 'that one, please'** 'Andi ingin kue yang mana?' – 'yang itu'; **I like all the shirts but I'm going to buy that one** saya suka semua kemejanya tetapi saya ingin membeli yang itu.
adverb begitu *(meaning 'so')*; **it's not that funny** itu tidak begitu lucu; **their house isn't that big** rumahnya tidak begitu besar; **it was that high I couldn't reach it** sebegitu tinggi sehingga saya tidak bisa sampai.
pronoun **1** itu; **that's not true** itu tidak benar; **that's not what you told me** itu bukan yang Anda katakan kepada saya; **what's that?** apa itu?; **who's that?** siapa itu?; **where's that?** di mana itu?; **is that Mustafa?** apakah itu Mustafa?; **did you see that?** apakah Anda melihat itu?;

that's my bedroom itu kamar tidur saya; **2** yang; **the book that's on the table** buku yang di atas meja; **the book that I lent you** buku yang saya pinjamkan kepada Anda.
conjunction bahwa; **I knew that he was wrong** saya tahu bahwa dia salah.

the *definite article (There is no definite article in Indonesian. If you want to indicate a specific one, you can use* itu. SEE **that**.*)* **the cat is an animal** kucing adalah binatang; **the cat** kucing itu; **the tree** pohon itu.

theatre *noun* bioskop, teater; **movie theatre** gedung bioskop; **to go to the theatre** pergi menonton, pergi ke bioskop.

theft *noun* pencurian.

their *adjective* mereka; **their house** rumah mereka; **their mother** ibu mereka, ibunya; **their gifts** hadiah mereka, kado mereka.

theirs *pronoun* (kepunyaan) mereka; **our garden's smaller than theirs** kebun kami lebih kecil daripada kebun mereka; **the yellow car's theirs** mobil kuning itu kepunyaan mereka; **it's theirs** itu kepunyaan mereka.

them *pronoun* mereka; **I know them** saya kenal (akan) mereka; **I don't know them** saya tidak kenal mereka; **listen to them!** dengarkanlah mereka!

theme *noun* motif, tema.

theme park *noun* taman impian.

themselves *pronoun* mereka sendiri; **they've helped themselves** mereka sudah mengambil sendiri; **they can do it themselves** mereka dapat melakukannya sendiri.

then *adverb* **1** *(next)* kemudian, lalu; **I take a bath and then I make the bed** saya mandi lalu saya merapikan tempat tidur; **I went to the bank and then the post office** saya ke bank kemudian ke kantor pos; **2** *(at that time)* waktu itu; **we were living in Kupang then** pada waktu itu kami tinggal di Kupang; **by then it was too late** pada waktu itu sudah terlambat; **3** *(in that case)* kalau begitu, lalu; **then why worry?** lalu kenapa khawatir?; **that's all right then** kalau begitu semuanya beres; **4 between now and then** sementara itu; **5 since then** sejak itu.

theory *noun* teori.

a b c d e f g h i j k l m n o p q r s t u v w x y z

there *adverb* **1** di sana, di situ; **put it there** letakkan di sana, taruh di sana; **they're in there** mereka ada di situ; **she's over there buying some fruit** dia di sana sedang membeli buah-buahan; **2 up there** di atas; **look up there!** lihatlah ke atas!; **3 down there** di bawah; **4** ke sana; **I've seen photos of Mt Bromo but I've never been there** saya pernah melihat foto gunung Bromo tetapi saya belum pernah ke sana; **5 there is** ada; **there's a mouse in the kitchen** ada tikus di dapur; **there was no bread** tidak ada roti; **yes, there's enough** ya, ada cukup; **there are plenty of seats** ada banyak tempat duduk; **6 there they are!** itu mereka!; **there she is!** itu dia!; **7 there's the bus coming** itu bisnya sudah datang.

therefore *adverb* oleh karena itu, oleh sebab itu.

thermometer *noun* alat pengukur panas, termometer.

these *adjective* ini; **these people** orang-orang ini; **these days** dewasa ini.

they *pronoun* **1** mereka; **they're not home** mereka tidak ada di rumah; **2 'where are the knives?' – 'they're in the drawer'** 'di mana pisaunya?' – 'di laci'; **I bought some guavas but they're not very nice** saya membeli beberapa buah jambu klutuk tetapi buah itu kurang enak.

thick *adjective* tebal; **a thick layer of butter** lapisan mentega yang tebal.

thief *noun* maling, pencuri.

thigh *noun* paha.

thin *adjective* **1** *(a slice)* tipis; **2** *(a person)* kurus; **she's got terribly thin** dia menjadi kurus sekali.

thing *noun* **1** *(an object)* barang; **the shops are full of pretty things** toko-toko penuh dengan barang-barang yang menarik; **2** *(a whatsit)* benda; **you can use that thing to open it** Anda dapat memakai benda itu untuk membukanya; **that thing next to the hammer** benda yang di sebelah martil; **3** *(belongings)* **things** barang-barang; **you can put your things in my room** letakkan barang-barang Anda di kamar saya; **4** hal-hal; **oho told me some surprising things** dia memberitahukan hal-hal yang aneh kepada saya; **5 the best thing to do is...**

sebaiknya...; **6 the thing is, I've lost her address** soalnya, alamatnya hilang; **7 how are things with you?** apa kabar?

think *verb* **1** *(believe)* kira; **do you think they'll come?** apakah Anda kira mereka akan datang?; **no, I don't think so** saya kira tidak; **I think he's already left** saya kira dia sudah berangkat; **2** memikirkan; **I'm thinking about you** saya sedang memikirkan Anda; **3** menganggap; **Carmel thinks it's silly** Carmel menganggapnya aneh; **4** *(to think carefully)* berpikir (tentang); **he thought for a moment** dia berpikir sebentar; **I've thought it over carefully** saya sudah mempertimbangkan hal itu; **5 what do you think of this dog?** bagaimana pendapat Anda tentang anjing ini?; **6** menduga; *(imagine)* **just think! we'll soon be in Irian!** siapa yang menduga bahwa tak lama lagi kita akan berada di Irian!; **I never thought it would be like this!** saya tak menduga akan terjadi begini!

third *noun* pertiga; **a third of the population** sepertiga (dari) jumlah penduduk. *adjective* **1** ketiga; **on the third floor** di lantai ketiga; **the third row** barisan yang ketiga; **2** tiga; **the third of May** tanggal tiga Mei; **third class** kelas tiga.

thirdly *adverb* (yang) ketiga.

Third World *noun* Dunia Ketiga.

thirst *noun* kehausan.

thirsty *adjective* **to be thirsty** haus; **I'm thirsty** saya haus.

thirteen *number* tiga belas; **Ahmed's thirteen** Ahmed berumur tiga belas tahun.

thirty *number* tiga puluh.

this *adjective* **1** ini; **this paintbrush** kuas ini; **this plant** tanaman ini; **this morning** pagi ini; **this one** yang ini; **you can use this one** Anda boleh memakai yang ini; **you can borrow this one** Anda boleh pinjam yang ini; **this afternoon** sore ini; **this evening** malam ini; **2** *(already past)* tadi; **they left this morning** mereka berangkat tadi pagi; **this afternoon** tadi sore; **this evening** tadi malam; **3** *(yet to come)* nanti; **this evening** nanti malam; **this afternoon** nanti sore; **she promised to come this afternoon** dia berjanji akan datang nanti sore.
pronoun **1** ini; **can you hold this for a moment?** apakah Anda dapat memegang ini

a b c d e f g h i j k l m n o p q r s t u v w x y z

sebentar?; **what's this?** apa ini?; *(on the phone)* **this is Sukra speaking** ini Sukra; **this is my sister** ini adik saya.

thistle *noun* tumbuhan kecil berduri.

thorn *noun* duri.

those *adjective* itu; **those books** buku-buku itu. *pronoun* (yang) itu; **if you want some forks you can take those** kalau Anda perlu garpu boleh ambil yang itu.

though *conjunction* **1** meskipun, walaupun; **though it's cold** meskipun dingin; **though Amir's older than Tuti is** walaupun Amir lebih tua daripada Tuti; **2** bagaimana pun; **it was a good idea though** bagaimana pun itu ide yang bagus.

thought *noun* gagasan, ide, pikiran.

thoughtful *adjective* **1** *(considerate)* selalu memikirkan orang lain, penuh perhatian; **it was really thoughtful of you** Anda benar-benar penuh perhatian; **2** *(brooding)* termenung.

thoughtless *adjective* alpa, lalai, kurang pikir.

thousand *number* **1** ribu; **a thousand** seribu; **five thousand** lima ribu; **the Thousand Islands** Pulau Seribu; **2 thousands of** ribuan; **there were thousands of tourists in Bali** ada ribuan wisatawan di Bali.

thread *noun* benang.

threat *noun* ancaman.

threaten *verb* mengancam; **to threaten to scream** mengancam akan berteriak.

three *number* tiga; **Oto's three** Oto berumur tiga tahun.

three-quarters *noun* tiga perempat; **three-quarters full** tiga perempat penuh.

thrilled *adjective* gentar, menggetarkan, terharu; **I was thrilled to hear from you** saya terharu mendapat kabar dari Anda.

thriller *noun* ceritera atau film yang mengerikan.

throat *noun* tenggorokan; **to have a sore throat** sakit tenggorokan.

through *preposition* **1** *(across)* melewati; **through the jungle** melewati hutan; **the water went right through** air itu menyusup; **the police let us through** polisi itu mengijinkan kami lewat; **2** *(via)* lewat, melalui, **the train goes through Sukabumi** kereta api itu lewat Sukabumi; **through the**

window melalui jendela; **I know them through my cousins** saya berkenalan dengan mereka melalui saudara sepupu saya; **3 to go through** memeriksa; **I caught him going through Dani's papers** saya memergokinya memeriksa surat-surat Dani; **4 right through the day** sepanjang hari.
adjective (a train or flight) langsung; **a through train** kereta api langsung.

throw *verb* melemparkan, membuang; **I threw the rotten tomato into the garden** saya membuang tomat yang busuk itu ke kebun; **he threw the book on the floor** dia melemparkan buku itu ke lantai; **throw me the ball!** lemparkan bola itu ke saya!
- **to throw away** membuang; **I've thrown away the old newspapers** saya sudah membuang koran-koran yang lama itu.
- **to throw somebody out** mengusir orang.
- **to throw out** *(rubbish)* membuang.
- **to throw up** muntah.

thumb *noun* ibu jari, jempol.

thump *noun* bunyi yang keras.

thunder *noun* geledek, guntur, guruh, petir; **a peal of thunder** gemuruh petir.

thunderstorm *noun* hujan angin ribut disertai petir dan guruh.

thundery *adjective* banyak guntur.

Thursday *noun* hari Kamis; **on Thursday** pada hari Kamis; **see you on Thursday!** sampai hari Kamis!; **every Thursday** setiap hari Kamis; **last Thursday** hari Kamis yang lalu; **next Thursday** hari Kamis depan, hari Kamis yang akan datang.

thyme *noun* semacam rempah yang baunya harum *(definition only)*.

tick *noun* **1** *(on dogs)* caplak, kutu (anjing); **2** *(on paper)* tanda coret.
verb memberi tanda; **to tick the box** memberi tanda pada kotak.

ticket *noun* **1** karcis; **a bus ticket** karcis bis; **2** denda; **a parking ticket** denda parkir.

ticket collector *noun* pemeriksa karcis.

ticket window *noun (at a station)* loket penjualan karcis.

tickle *verb* menggelitik.

ticklish *adjective* geli.

tide *noun* air pasang, air surut; **high tide** pasang naik; **the tide is out** air sedang surut; **at low tide** ketika air sedang surut.

tidy *adjective* necis, rapi, teratur.
verb membereskan, mengatur, merapikan; **I'll tidy up the living room** saya akan merapikan ruang duduk.

tie *noun* **1** dasi; **a red tie** dasi merah; **2** *(in a match)* seri.
verb **1** mengikat; **to tie your shoelaces** mengikat tali sepatu; **2** *(in a match)* berakhir seri; **we tied two–all** kami seri dua dua.

tiger *noun* harimau, macan.

tight *adjective* ketat, sempit; **this skirt's a bit tight** rok ini sedikit ketat; **these shoes are too tight** sepatu ini terlalu sempit; **they wear tight trousers** mereka pakai celana ketat.

tighten *verb* mengeratkan, mengetatkan.

tightly *adverb* rapat sekali.

tights *noun* celana ketat; **a pair of purple tights** celana ketat berwarna ungu.

tile *noun* **1** *(on a floor or wall)* ubin; **2** *(on a roof)* genting.

till[1] *adverb* sampai; **they're here till Sunday** mereka di sini sampai hari Minggu; **till then** sampai waktu itu; **till now** sampai sekarang; **we won't know till Monday** kami tidak akan tahu sampai hari Senen.

till[2] *noun* kasa; **pay at the till** bayar di kasa.

time *noun* **1** *(on the clock)* jam, pukul; **what time is it?** jam berapa?; **2** waktu, tempo; **on time** tepat pada waktunya; **it's time for lunch** sudah waktunya makan siang; **ten o'clock Eastern Standard Time** jam sepuluh Waktu Bagian Timur; **we've got lots of time** kami ada banyak waktu; **there's not much time left** tidak ada banyak waktu lagi; **is this a good time to phone?** apakah ini waktu yang baik untuk menelepon?; **3** lama; **I haven't seen her for a long time** sudah lama saya tidak bertemu dengan dia; **4** *(in a series)* kali; **six times** enam kali; **the first time I ate durian** pertama kali saya makan durian; **three times a year** tiga kali setahun; **five times two is ten** lima kali dua adalah sepuluh; **5 from time to time, at times** kadang-kadang, sekali-sekali; **6 for the time being** untuk sementara; **7 any time now**

kapan saja sekarang; **8 to have a good time** bersenang-senang; **we really had a good time** kami betul-betul senang sekali; **have a good time!** semoga senang!

time off *noun* **1** *(free time)* waktu tidak bekerja; **2** *(leave)* berlibur.

timetable *noun* **1** *(in school)* daftar (jam) pelajaran; **2** *(for trains or buses)* jadwal; **the train timetable** jadwal kereta api.

tin *noun* **1** *(the metal)* timah; **2** *(a container)* kaleng; **a tin of lychees** sekaleng buah leci.

tinned *adjective* kalengan; **tinned sardines** sardencis kalengan.

tin opener *noun* pembuka kaleng.

tinted *adjective* diwarnai.

tiny *adjective* kecil sekali.

tip *noun* **1** *(the end)* ujung; **the tip of my finger** ujung jari saya; **2** *(money)* uang persen, uang rokok, uang tip; **3** *(a useful hint)* petunjuk.
verb **1** *(to give money)* memberi tip, memberi uang persen; **we tipped the waiter** kami memberi uang tip kepada pelayan; **2** *(liquid)* menumpahkan.

tiptoe *noun* ujung jari kaki; **to walk on tiptoes** berjalan berjingkat-jingkat.

tired *adjective* **1** capai, lelah, letih; **I'm tired** saya merasa lelah; **you look tired** Anda kelihatannya letih; **2 to be tired of** bosan; **I'm tired of living in Jakarta** saya sudah bosan tinggal di Jakarta; **I'm tired of watching TV** saya sudah bosan menonton televisi.

tiring *adjective* melelahkan, meletihkan.

tissue *noun* *(a paper hanky)* lap kertas, serbet kertas, tisu; **do you have a tissue?** ada tisu?

tissue paper *noun* kertas tisu.

title *noun* judul *(of a book, play, etc.)*.

to *preposition* **1** *(to a place or person)* ke; **to go to Medan** pergi ke Medan; **I'm going to school** saya mau ke sekolah; **a letter to parents** surat ke(pada) orang tua; **to the dentist's** ke dokter gigi; **2** kepada; **give the book to Leila** berikan buku itu kepada Leila; **3** *(in order to)* untuk; **he gave me some money to buy rice** dia memberi saya uang untuk membeli beras; **4** sampai;

from Monday to Friday dari hari Senin sampai hari Jumat; **5** *(with time)* kurang; **it's ten to nine** sekarang jam sembilan kurang sepuluh (menit); **twenty to six** jam enam kurang dua puluh menit; **6 I have nothing to do** tak ada sesuatu yang harus saya lakukan; **I have a lot of homework to do** saya harus mengerjakan banyak pekerjaan rumah; **it's easy to do** itu gampang dilakukan.

toad *noun* katak, kodok.

toadstool *noun* cendawan, jamur payung; **poisonous toadstool** cendawan yang beracun.

toast *noun* roti panggang; **two slices of toast** dua potong roti panggang.

toaster *noun* pemanggang roti.

tobacco *noun* tembakau.

tobacconist's *noun* kios rokok.

today *noun* hari ini; **today's her birthday** hari ini adalah hari ulang tahunnya.

toe *noun* jari kaki.

together *adverb* **1** bersama-sama; **Totok and Wawuk always swim together** Totok dan Wawuk selalu berenang bersama-sama; **Subekti went to the library together with Hendrik** Subekti ke perpustakaan bersama-sama Hendrik; **2** *(at the same time)* sekaligus; **they all left together** mereka semua berangkat sekaligus.

toilet *noun* kamar kecil, kloset, WC; **where's the toilet?** di mana kamar kecil?; **is there a toilet near here?** ada WC dekat sini?

toilet paper *noun* kertas kloset, tisu kloset.

token *noun* tanda, pernyataan.

tolerant *adjective* bersikap toleran, sabar.

toll *noun* bea (cukai), tol; **toll road** jalan tol.

toll-free *adjective* bebas dari bea, bebas pulsa.

tomato *noun* tomat; **a tomato salad** lalap tomat; **tomato sauce** saus tomat.

tomorrow *noun* besok; **I'll do it tomorrow** besok saya akan melakukannya; **tomorrow afternoon** besok siang, besok sore; **tomorrow morning** besok pagi, besok siang; **tomorrow night** besok malam; **the day after tomorrow** lusa.

tone *noun* **1** *(on an answer phone)* nada; **speak after the tone** bicara sesudah mendengar nada; **2** *(of a voice or a letter)* nada.

tongue *noun* lidah; **to stick your tongue out** mengeluarkan lidah; **it's on the tip of my tongue** hampir-hampir teringat oleh saya *(approximate translation only).*

tonight *noun* malam ini, nanti malam; **I'm going out with my mates tonight** saya akan pergi bersama teman-teman nanti malam.

tonsillitis *noun* radang amandel, radang tonsil.

too *adverb* **1** terlalu; **it's too expensive** itu terlalu mahal; **it's too hot** terlalu panas *(the weather)*; **2 too much, too many** terlalu banyak; **it takes too much time** makan terlalu banyak waktu; **he eats too much** dia makan terlalu banyak; **there are too many accidents** terlalu banyak kecelakaan; **3** *(as well)* juga; **Ngatimin's coming too** Ngatimin akan datang juga; **me too!** saya juga!

tool *noun* alat, perkakas.

tool box *noun* peti perkakas.

tool kit *noun* perlengkapan perkakas.

tooth *noun* gigi; **to brush your teeth** menyikat gigi.

toothache *noun* sakit gigi.

toothbrush *noun* sikat gigi.

toothpaste *noun* obat gosok gigi, odol, pasta gigi, tapal gigi.

top *noun* **1** *(of a page, a ladder, the stairs)* (paling) atas; **at the top of the stairs** di tangga paling atas; **2** *(of a container or box)* atas; **on top of the cupboard** di atas lemari; **3** *(of a mountain)* puncak; **4** *(a lid)* tutup *(of a pen, bottle)*; **5** juara; **to be at the top of the class** juara kelas.
adjective **1** paling atas, teratas; **the office is on the top floor** kantor itu ada di lantai teratas; **on the top shelf** di rak yang paling atas; **in the top left-hand corner** di bagian paling atas sebelah kiri; **2** *(of prices, honours)* paling tinggi, tertinggi; **and on top of all that I lost my wallet** tambahan pula dompet saya hilang; **it was a bit over the top** agak keterlaluan.

topic *noun* pokok (pembicaraan), topik.

torch *noun* lampu senter, obor.

torn *adjective* sobek.

tortoise *noun* kura-kura.

torture *noun* penyiksaan, siksaan.
verb menyiksa.

a b c d e f g h i j k l m n o p q r s t u v w x y z

total *noun* jumlah, total. *adjective* **1** jumlah, seluruhnya; **total cost** harga seluruhnya; **2** mutlak, total; **total failure** kegagalan mutlak.

totally *adverb* sama sekali.

touch *noun* **1** *(physical contact)* sentuhan; **a soft touch** sentuhan lembut; **2** *(contact)* berhubungan; **to get in touch with** berhubungan dengan; **we've lost touch** kami sudah tidak berhubungan; **3** *(a little bit)* sedikit; **a touch of pink** sedikit warna merah muda; **it was a touch embarrassing** agak memalukan. *verb* memegang, menyentuh; **don't touch it!** jangan sentuh itu!

touched *adjective* terharu.

touching *adjective* mengharukan.

tough *adjective* **1** alot, keras; **the meat's a bit tough** daging ini sedikit keras; **2** kasar; **Bruce is a tough guy** Bruce adalah orang yang kasar; **it's a tough area** daerah yang sifat penduduknya kasar; **3** berat, sukar, sulit; **things are a bit tough at the moment** hidup saya sedikit berat sekarang; **4** kuat; **you need to be tough to survive in today's world** harus kuat untuk hidup di masa sekarang; **a tough fabric** kain yang kuat; **5** *(tough luck)* **tough, you're too late** sayang sekali, Anda terlambat.

tour *noun* **1** perjalanan (keliling); **we did the tour of the temple** kami berkeliling melihat-lihat candi itu; **a tour of the city** perjalanan keliling kota; **a package tour** paket perjalanan; **2** *(by a band or a theatre group)* **to go on tour** berkeliling. *verb* *(performers)* berkeliling; **they're touring the United States** mereka sedang berkeliling di Amerika Serikat.

tourism *noun* kepariwisataan, turisme.

tourist *noun* wisatawan, turis; **there were thousands of tourists in Bali** ada ribuan wisatawan di Bali.

tourist information office *noun* biro wisata.

tournament *noun* pertandingan, turnamen; **a badminton tournament** pertandingan bulu tangkis.

tow *verb* *(by a breakdown truck)* menarik, menghela, menyeret; **to be towed away** ditarik.

towards *adverb* ke arah; **she went off towards the lake** dia pergi ke arah danau.

towel *noun* handuk.

tower *noun* menara; **the Eiffel tower** menara Eiffel.

tower block *noun* gedung menara.

town *noun* kota; **to go into town** masuk kota.

town centre *noun* pusat kota.

town hall *noun* balai kota.

toy *noun* permainan; **a toy car** mobil-mobilan.

toyshop *noun* toko permainan.

trace *noun* bekas, jejak; **there was no trace of it** tidak ada bekasnya.

track *noun* **1** *(for sport)* olahraga; **a track event** perlombaan olahraga; **a racing track** lapangan balapan; **2** *(a path)* jalan kecil.

track suit *noun* track suit.

tractor *noun* traktor.

trade *noun* perdagangan, perniagaan.

trade union *noun* serikat buruh.

tradition *noun* adat-istiadat, tradisi.

traditional *adjective* tradisional.

traffic *noun* lalu lintas.

traffic island *noun* pemisah jalan.

traffic jam *noun* kemacetan lalu lintas.

traffic lights *plural noun* lampu lalu lintas.

traffic warden *noun* petugas lalu lintas, polisi lalu lintas.

tragedy *noun* tragedi, peristiwa sedih.

tragic *adjective* tragis.

trail *noun* bekas, jalan kecil (di hutan), jejak; **a nature trail** jalan alam.

trailer *noun* gerobak gandengan, kereta gandengan.

train *noun* kereta api; **he's coming by train** dia akan datang naik kereta api; **the train for Jogja** kereta api ke Jogja.
verb **1** *(a person)* melatih; **2** belajar; **he's training to be a nurse** dia belajar untuk menjadi jururawat; **3** *(in sport)* berlatih; **the team trains on Saturdays** regu itu berlatih pada hari Sabtu.

train ticket *noun* karcis kereta api

train timetable *noun* jadwal kereta api.

a b c d e f g h i j k l m n o p q r s t u v w x y z

trainee *noun* murid, pengikut latihan.

trainer *noun* **1** *(of an athlete or a horse)* pelatih; **2** *(shoes)* sepatu olahraga.

training *noun* **1** *(for a career)* pendidikan; **2** *(for sport)* latihan.

tram *noun* trem.

tramp *noun* orang gelandangan, petualang.

transfer *verb* memindahkan, mengirimkan, menyerahkan.

transform *verb* mengubah.

transistor *noun* transistor.

translate *verb* men(t)erjemahkan; **to translate a novel into Indonesian** menerjemahkan sebuah novel ke dalam bahasa Indonesia.

translation *noun* terjemahan.

translator *noun* alih bahasa, penerjemah; **I'd like to be a translator** saya ingin menjadi penerjemah.

transparent *adjective* jernih, tembus pandang, transparan.

transport *noun* angkutan; **air transport** angkutan udara; **public transport** angkutan umum.

trap *noun* perangkap.

travel *noun* perjalanan; **foreign travel** perjalanan ke luar negeri; **a travel brochure** brosur perjalanan.

travel agency *noun* biro perjalanan, biro wisata.

travel agent *noun* agen perjalanan.

traveller *noun* pelancong, pengembara, wisatawan.

traveller's cheque *noun* cek wisatawan, cek traveller.

travelling *noun* bepergian, perjalanan; **I like travelling** saya suka sekali bepergian.

travel-sick *noun* mabuk dalam kendaraan, mabuk darat; **to be travel-sick, to get travel-sick** merasa mabuk di dalam kendaraan.

tray *noun* baki, dulang, nampan, talam.

tread *verb* menginjak; **to tread on a nail** menginjak paku.

treasure *noun* harta benda.

treat *noun* **1** traktir; **I took them to the circus as a treat** saya mentraktir mereka ke sirkus; **2 it's a little treat for you** sesuatu untuk menyenangkan Anda.
verb **1** memperlakukan; **he treats his animals well** dia memperlakukan hewannya dengan baik; **2** mentraktir **I'll treat you to a drink** saya akan mentraktir Anda minum; **I treated myself to a**

new outfit saya membeli baju baru; **3** mengobati; **the doctor who treated you** dokter yang mengobati Anda.

treatment *noun* **1** perlakuan; **special treatment** perlakuan khusus; **2** *(medical)* pengobatan, perawatan.

tree *noun* pohon.

tree trunk *noun* batang pohon.

tremble *verb* gemetar.

trend *noun* **1** *(a fashion)* gaya, mode; **2** *(a tendency)* gejala kecenderungan.

trendy *adjective* yang gaya, trendi.

trial *noun* pemeriksaan, pengadilan.

triangle *noun* segitiga.

trick *noun* **1** *(by a conjurer or as a joke)* akal, tipu muslihat; **that's a good trick** itu akal yang baik; **to play a trick on** memperdayakan; **2** *(a knack)* cara; **it doesn't work, there must be a trick to it** ini tidak mau jalan, harus ada cara untuk melakukannya.
verb memperdayakan, menipu; **he tricked me!** dia memperdayakan saya!

tricky *adjective* memerlukan penanganan yang baik; **it's a tricky situation** situasi yang memerlukan penanganan yang baik.

tricycle *noun* kendaraan beroda tiga, sepeda beroda tiga.

trim *verb* **1** *(hair)* memangkas; **2** *(nails)* memotong.

trip *noun* perjalanan; **a trip to Flores** perjalanan ke Flores; **a day trip to Puncak** perjalanan pulang pergi ke Puncak; **he's on a business trip** dia sedang pergi untuk urusan dagang.
verb tersandung; **Lina tripped over a rock** Lina tersandung (pada) batu.

triumph *noun* kejayaan, kemenangan.

trolley *noun* kendaraan beroda dua, troli.

trombone *noun* trombone.

troops *noun* pasukan (tentara).

tropical *adjective* tropis.

trot *verb* berlari-lari menderap.

trouble *noun* **1** *(personal problems)* kesukaran; **Steph's in trouble** Steph mengalami kesukaran; **what's the trouble?** apa kesukarannya?; **2** *(difficulty)* kesulitan, masalah; **I had trouble getting a ticket** saya mendapat kesulitan membeli karcis; **the trouble is, I've**

a b c d e f g h i j k l m n o p q r s t u v w x y z

a b c d e f g h i j k l m n o p q r s t u v w x y z

forgotten the number masalahnya ialah saya sudah lupa nomornya; **we've had trouble with the car** mobil kami rewel; **3 it's not worth the trouble** tak ada gunanya lagi; **it's no trouble!** tidak apa apa!

trousers *plural noun* celana panjang; **a new pair of trousers** sebuah celana (panjang) baru.

truck *noun* truk.

true *adjective* benar, betul, nyata; **a true story** cerita benar, kisah benar; **is that true?** benarkah?; **it's true she's absent-minded** memang betul dia pelupa.

trump *noun* truf; **spades are trumps** sekop adalah truf.

trumpet *noun* terompet.

trunk *noun* **1** *(of a tree)* batang; **2** *(of an elephant)* belalai; **3** *(suitcase)* kopor, peti.

trunks *noun* celana pendek; **swimming trunks** celana renang.

trust *noun* kepercayaan. *verb* mempercayai, percaya kepada; **I trust her** saya mempercayainya, saya percaya kepadanya.

truth *noun* kebenaran; **to tell the truth, I'd completely forgotten** sebenarnya, saya sudah lupa sama-sekali.

try *noun* percobaan, usaha; **it's my first try** ini percobaan pertama saya; **to have a try** berusaha, mencoba; **you should give it a try** Anda harus mencoba; *(in football)* berusaha mencetak gol. *verb* mencoba, berusaha; **to try to do** berusaha melakukan; **I'm trying to open the door** saya sedang berusaha membuka pintu.

- **to try something on** *(a garment)* mencoba memakai, memgepas.

T-shirt *noun* baju kaos, kaos oblong.

tube *noun* pembuluh, pipa, tube.

tuberculosis *noun* tbc.

Tuesday *noun* Selasa; **on Tuesday** pada hari Selasa; **I'm going back on Tuesday** saya akan pulang pada hari Selasa; **every Tuesday** (se)tiap hari Selasa; **last Tuesday** hari Selasa yang lalu; **next Tuesday** hari Selasa depan, hari Selasa yang akan datang.

tug *verb* menarik, menggeret, menghela.

tuition *noun* kuliah, les; **piano tuition** les piano; **private tuition** les privat.

tulip *noun* bunga tulip.

tumble-drier *noun*.alat pengering pakaian.

tumbler *noun* gelas minum.

tuna *noun* ikan tongkol.

tune *noun* lagu.

tunnel *noun* terowongan.

turf *noun* rumput.

Turk *noun* orang Turki.

turkey[1] *noun* ayam belanda, ayam kalkun.

Turkey[2] *noun* negeri Turki.

Turkish *noun (language)* bahasa Turki.
adjective Turki.

turn *noun* **1** *(in a game)* giliran; **it's your turn** giliran Anda; **whose turn is it?** giliran siapa?; **it's Suryo's turn to play** sekarang giliran Suryo untuk bermain; **to take turns driving** bergiliran mengemudikan mobil; **2** *(in a road)* belok.
verb **1** membalik; **turn the page** membalik halaman; **2** berbelok; **turn left at the next set of lights** belok kiri di lampu lalu lintas yang berikut; **3** *(become)* menjadi; **she turned red** mukanya memerah.

- **to turn back** memutar kembali; **we turned back** kami memutar kembali.
- **to turn down** *(the volume)* mengecilkan.
- **to turn off 1** *(from a road)* membelok dari; **2** *(switch off)* mematikan.
- **to turn on** *(switch on)* memasang, menyalakan.
- **to turn out 1** berakhir; **to turn out well** berakhir dengan baik; **the holiday turned out badly** liburan itu berakhir dengan buruk; **it all turned out all right in the end** semuanya berakhir dengan baik; **2** ternyata; **it turned out that I was wrong** ternyata saya salah.
- **to turn over 1** *(roll over)* berguling; **2** *(a page)* membalik.
- **to turn up 1** *(to arrive)* muncul, tiba; **they turned up an hour later** mereka tiba satu jam kemudian; **2** *(the gas or the heating)* membesarkan; **3** *(make louder)* mengeraskan; **can you turn up the volume?** tolong keraskan suaranya.

turquoise *adjective* warna biru-hijau.

turtle *noun* kura-kura laut, penyu.

TV *noun* televisi, teve; **I saw her on TV** saya melihat dia di layar televisi.

tweezers *noun* jepitan; penjepit, tang.

a b c d e f g h i j k l m n o p q r s t u v w x y z

twelfth *number* dua belas, yang keduabelas; **on the twelfth floor** di lantai dua belas; **the twelfth of May** tanggal dua belas Mei.

twelve *number* dua belas; **Achmad's twelve** Achmad berumur dua belas tahun; **at twelve o'clock** pada jam dua belas tengah hari *(midday)*; pada jam dua belas tengah malam *(midnight)*.

twenty *number* dua puluh; **Ayesha's twenty** Ayesha berumur dua puluh tahun; **twenty-one** dua puluh satu.

twice *adverb* dua kali; **I've asked him twice** saya sudah dua kali bertanya kepada dia; **twice as much** dua kali banyaknya.

twig *noun* ranting.

twin *noun* kembar; **Tina and Nina are twins** Tina dan Nina kembar; **her twin sister** saudara kembarnya.
verb kembar; **Ambon is twinned with Darwin** Ambon adalah kota kembar Darwin.

twist *verb* memintal, memutarkan.

two *number* dua; **Ben's two** Ben berumur dua tahun; **two by two** berdua-dua.

type *noun* **1** *(sort)* jenis, macam; **a type of banana** sejenis pisang; **a type of musical instrument** sejenis alat musik; **2** *(brand)* cap, mer(e)k; **what type of computer is it?** komputer merk apa itu?
verb (on a typewriter or keyboard) mengetik; **I'm learning to type** saya sedang belajar mengetik; **I was busy typing some letters** saya sedang sibuk mengetik surat-surat.

typewriter *noun* mesin tik.

typical *adjective* khas.

tyre *noun* ban.

U u

ugly *adjective* buruk, jelek.

UK [United Kingdom] *noun* Kerajaan Inggris Raya.

umbrella *noun* payung.

umpire *noun* wasit.

UN [United Nations] *noun* Perserikatan Bangsa-Bangsa, PBB.

unable *adjective* **to be unable to do** tidak dapat, tidak sanggup; **he's unable to come** dia tidak dapat datang.

unanimous *adjective* dengan suara bulat, sepakat.

unattractive *adjective* *(person, place)* buruk, jelek, kurang menarik.

unavoidable *adjective* tidak dapat dihindarkan.

unbearable *adjective* tidak tertahan.

unbelievable *adjective* bukan main, luar biasa, tak dapat dipercaya.

uncertain *adjective* **1** *(not sure)* ragu-ragu, tak pasti, tak tentu; **2** *(unpredictable)* berubah-ubah, tidak menentu *(weather, for instance)*.

unchanged *adjective* tanpa perubahan, tidak berubah.

uncivilized *adjective* biadab, tidak beradab.

uncle *noun* oom, paman; **Uncle Sugi** Oom Sugi.

uncomfortable *adjective* **1** *(shoes or a chair)* merasa tidak enak; **2** *(a journey or a situation)* gelisah, tidak tenang.

uncommon *adjective* luar biasa, tak biasa, tak lazim.

unconscious *adjective* *(out cold)* pingsan, tidak sadar; **Mytha's still unconscious** Mytha masih tidak sadar, Mytha masih belum sadar.

under *preposition*
1 *(underneath)* di bawah; **under the bed** di bawah tempat tidur; **perhaps it's under the cupboard** mungkin di bawah lemari; **children under five** anak-anak di bawah umur lima tahun; **2** *(less than)* kurang dari; **under one million Rupiah** kurang dari satu juta rupiah.

under-age *adjective* **to be under-age** di bawah umur.

underclothes *plural noun* pakaian dalam.

undercooked *adjective* belum masak, kurang masak, setengah masak.

underestimate *verb* meremehkan.

underground *adjective* di bawah tanah; **an underground carpark** tempat parkir di bawah tanah; **an underground railway** jalan kereta api di bawah tanah.

underline *verb* menggarisbawahi.

underneath *preposition* di bawah; **it's underneath all that rubbish** di bawah sampah itu.
adverb di sebelah bawah; **look underneath** lihat di bawah.

a b c d e f g h i j k l m n o p q r s t u v w x y z

a b c d e f g h i j k l m n o p q r s t u v w x y z

underpants *plural noun* celana dalam.

underpass *noun* **1** *(for pedestrians)* terowongan; **2** *(for traffic)* jalan melintang di bawah jalan lain.

understand *verb* mengerti; **I don't understand** saya tidak mengerti; **did you understand what he was saying?** apakah Anda mengerti apa yang dikatakannya?

understandable *adjective* dapat dimengerti; **that's understandable** itu dapat dimengerti.

understanding *noun* pengertian.
adjective penuh pengertian; **he was very understanding** dia betul-betul penuh pengertian.

underwear *noun* pakaian dalam.

undo *verb* membuka, melepaskan, meniadakan.

undone *adjective* terlepas, tak dikerjakan.

undress *verb* menanggalkan pakaian, menanggalkan pakaian; **get undressed** menanggalkan pakaian; **I got undressed** saya menanggalkan pakaian.

unemployed *noun* menganggur, tunakarya; **work for the unemployed** pekerjaan untuk yang tunakarya; **the unemployed** para penganggur.
adjective menganggur; **she's unemployed** dia menganggur.

unemployment *noun* pengangguran.

uneven *adjective* **1** *(of a surface)* tidak rata; **2** *(of a number)* ganjil, tidak genap.

unexpected *adjective* tidak diduga-duga, tidak disangka-sangka.

unexpectedly *adverb* dengan tidak diduga-duga.

unfair *adjective* tidak adil, tidak jujur, tidak wajar; **it's unfair to young people** tidak adil terhadap orang muda.

unfashionable *adjective* tidak sesuai dengan mode atau kebiasaan.

unfasten *verb* membuka.

unfit *adjective* **1** *(health)* tidak bugar, tidak sehat; **I'm terribly unfit** saya sangat tidak sehat; **2** *(to do something)* tidak patut.

unfold *verb* membentangkan, membuka lipatan.

unfortunate *adjective* celaka, malang, sial.

unfortunately *adverb* sayang, sial sekali.

unfriendly *adjective* tidak ramah.

unfurnished *adjective* tidak berperabot.

ungrateful *adjective* tidak berterima kasih.

unhappy *adjective* tidak bahagia, tidak senang.

unhealthy *adjective* tidak sehat.

uniform *noun* pakaian seragam; **in school uniform** berpakaian seragam sekolah.

union *noun* gabungan, perhimpunan, perserikatan, uni.

Union Jack *noun* **the Union Jack** bendera negeri Inggris.

unique *adjective* tunggal, unik.

unit *noun* **1** *(for measuring, for example)* satuan; **2** *(a hospital department)* bagian, unit.

United Kingdom *noun* Kerajaan Inggris Raya.

United Nations *noun* Perserikatan Bangsa-Bangsa.

United States (of America) *plural noun* Amerika Serikat (AS).

universe *noun* alam semesta.

university *noun* universitas; **to go to university** masuk universitas.

unkind *adjective* kejam, tanpa belas kasihan, tanpa kasih sayang.

unknown *adjective* tidak dikenal, tidak diketahui.

unleaded petrol *noun* bensin bebas timah.

unless *conjunction* jika tidak, kecuali kalau; **unless he does it** kecuali kalau dia melakukannya; **unless you tell her/him** kecuali kalau Anda memberitahu dia.

unlike *adjective* **1** tidak biasanya; **it's unlike her to be late** dia tidak biasanya terlambat; **2** tidak seperti; **unlike me, she hates dogs** tidak seperti saya, dia benci akan anjing.

unlikely *adjective* tidak mungkin; **it's unlikely** tidak mungkin.

unlimited *adjective* tidak terbatas.

unload *verb* membongkar.

unlock *verb* membuka kunci; **the car's unlocked** mobil itu tidak dikunci.

unlucky *adjective* **1** malang, sial, celaka; **thirteen is an unlucky number** tiga belas adalah angka yang sial; **2** *(a person)* **to be unlucky** tidak beruntung, tidak mujur.

a b c d e f g h i j k l m n o p q r s t u v w x y z

a b c d e f g h i j k l m n o p q r s t u v w x y z

unmarried *adjective* tidak kawin, tidak nikah, tidak bersuami, tidak beristri.

unnatural *adjective* tidak wajar.

unnecessary *adjective* tidak perlu; **it's unnecessary to book a ticket** tidak perlu memesan tiket.

unpack *verb* membongkar, membuka, mengeluarkan; **I'll just unpack and then come over** saya akan datang sesudah mengeluarkan barang-barang dari koper.

unpaid *adverb* **1** *(a bill)* belum dibayar; **2** *(work)* tidak dibayar, bekerja tanpa upah.

unpleasant *adjective* tidak enak, tidak menyenangkan.

unplug *verb* mencabut steker.

unpopular *adjective* tidak disenangi, tidak disukai, tidak populer.

unreasonable *adjective* tidak masuk akal.

unrecognizable *adjective* tidak dapat dikenal lagi.

unreliable *adjective* tak dapat diandalkan, tidak dapat dipercaya; **he's extremely unreliable** dia sama sekali tidak dapat dipercaya.

unroll *verb* membuka gulungan.

unsafe *adjective* membahayakan, tidak aman *(wiring, for instance)*; tidak selamat.

unsatisfactory *adjective* tidak memuaskan.

unscrew *verb* melepaskan, membuka sekrup.

unshaven *adjective* tidak dicukur.

unsuccessful *adjective* gagal, tidak berhasil, tidak sukses; **I tried but I was unsuccessful** saya berusaha tetapi gagal; **an unsuccessful attempt** percobaan yang gagal, usaha yang gagal.

unsuitable *adjective* tidak cocok, tidak sesuai.

untidy *adjective* tidak teratur, tidak rapi; **the house is always untidy** rumah itu selalu tidak rapi.

until *preposition* **1** hingga, sampai; **until Monday** sampai hari Senin; **until the tenth** sampai tanggal sepuluh; **until now** hingga saat ini, sampai sekarang; **until then** hingga waktu itu; **2 not until** sebelum; **not until September** sebelum bulan September; **it won't be finished until Friday** tidak dapat diselesaikan sebelum hari Jumat.

unusual *adjective* aneh, tidak biasa; **an unusual beetle** kumbang yang aneh; **rain is unusual at this time of year** hujan tidak biasa pada saat ini.

unwilling *adjective* segan, tidak bersedia, tidak mau, tidak sudi; **I'm unwilling to wait** tidak bersedia menunggu.

unwrap *verb* membuka bungkusan.

up *preposition, adverb* **1** *(out of bed)* bangun; **to be up** sudah bangun; **I don't think Yos is up yet** saya rasa Yos belum bangun; **to get up** bangun; **we usually get up at five** biasanya kami bangun jam lima; **I was up late last night** semalam saya tidak tidur sampai jauh malam; **2** *(higher up)* di atas, ke atas; **up on the roof** di atas genteng; **up here** di sini (di atas); **up there** di sana (di atas); **3** naik **to go up the stairs** naik tangga; **4** *(wrong)* **what's up?** ada apa? apa yang terjadi?; **what's up with him?** dia kenapa?; **what's she up to?** apa yang dilakukannya?; **5 up to** sampai; **up to here** sampai di sini; **up to fifty people** sampai lima puluh orang; **6 we went up the road** kami jalan sepanjang jalan; **it's just up the road** ada di jalan ini; **up in Broome** di Broome; **she came up to me** dia datang kepada saya; **it's up to you** terserah kepada Anda; **hands up!** angkat tangan!; **time's up!** waktu sudah habis!

update *noun* **here's an update on the delays** ini adalah berita terakhir tentang keterlambatan. *verb* **1** *(revise) (timetables or information)* pemberitahuan, informasi; **2** *(styles or furnishings)* memperbaharui.

upheaval *noun* kehebohan, pergolakan.

upright *adjective* tegak lurus; **put it upright** memasangnya tegak lurus, mendirikan tegak lurus; **to stand upright** berdiri tegak lurus.

upset *noun* gangguan; **a stomach upset** sakit perut. *adjective* bingung, kacau, marah; **he's upset** dia bingung, dia marah. *verb* membuat marah, mengecewakan, mengganggu.

upside down *adjective* terbalik.

upstairs *adverb* tingkat atas; **my study is upstairs** ruang belajar saya ada di (tingkat)

a b c d e f g h i j k l m n o p q r s t u v w x y z

atas; **to go upstairs** naik ke atas (ke loteng).

up-to-date *adjective* moderen, yang terbaru.

upwards *adjective* ke atas.

urgent *adjective* mendesak, penting, urgen.

US *noun* Amerika Serikat (AS).

us *pronoun* **1** *(excluding the listener)* kami; **why don't you come with us?** mengapa tidak ikut kami?; **2** *(including the listener)* kita; **all five of us** kita berlima; **she knows us** dia kenal kita; **they've seen us** mereka sudah melihat kita.

USA *noun* Amerika Serikat (AS).

use *noun* **1** pakai; **the instructions for use** peraturan pakai; **2** gunanya; **it's no use** tak ada gunanya; **it's no use phoning** tak ada gunanya menelepon.
verb mempergunakan, memakai, menggunakan; **we used the dictionary** kami menggunakan kamus; **I used a knife to open the parcel** saya menggunakan pisau untuk membuka paket itu.
• **to use up** menghabiskan.

used *adjective* **1** biasa, terbiasa; **to be used to** biasa dengan; **I'm not used to the climate** saya belum biasa dengan iklim ini; **I'm not used to eating spicy food** saya tidak biasa makan makanan yang pedas; **2 to get used to** menjadi biasa; sudah biasa; **I've got used to living here** saya sudah biasa tinggal di sini; **you'll get used to it!** Anda pasti akan terbiasa!
verb dahulu, dulu; **they used to live in Surabaya** dahulu mereka tinggal di Surabaya; **she used to smoke** dulu dia merokok.

useful *adjective* berguna, bermanfaat.

useless *adjective* tidak berguna, tidak bermanfaat; **this knife's useless** pisau ini tidak bermanfaat; **you're completely useless!** Anda betul-betul tak berguna!

user-friendly *adjective* mudah dipakai.

usual *adjective* yang biasa; **it's the usual problem** masalah yang biasa; **as usual** seperti biasa; **it's hotter than usual** lebih panas dari biasa.

usually *adverb* biasanya; **I usually leave before six** biasanya saya berangkat sebelum jam enam.

V v

vacancy *noun* **1** *(in a hotel)* **'no vacancies'** 'penuh', 'tidak ada kamar kosong'; **2 a job vacancy** lowongan kerja.

vacant *adjective* **1** *(of a house, building)* kosong; **2** *(of a job)* lowongan.

vaccinate *verb* menyuntik vaksinasi.

vaccination *noun* suntikan, vaksinasi.

vacuum *verb* membersihkan dengan alat penghisap debu; **I'm going to vacuum the car** saya akan membersihkan bagian dalam mobil.

vacuum cleaner *noun* alat penghisap debu.

vague *adjective* kabur, samar, tidak jelas.

vaguely *adverb* samar-samar, tidak jelas.

vain *adjective* suka berlagak, suka menonjolkan diri.

Valentine's Day *noun* Hari Valentin (tanggal 14 Februari).

valley *noun* lembah.

valuable *adjective* **1** berharga; **to be valuable** berharga; **that ring is very valuable** cincin itu berharga sekali; **he gave us some valuable information** dia memberi kami informasi yang berharga; **2** *(appreciated)* dihargai; **your advice is always appreciated** nasihat Anda selalu saya hargai.

value *noun* nilai.
verb (somebody's help, opinion or friendship) menghargai.

van *noun* mobil gerbong.

vandal *noun* perusak, vandal.

vandalism *noun* perusakan, vandalisme.

vanilla *noun* panili; **vanilla ice-cream** es krim panili.

vanish *verb* lenyap, menghilang.

variety *noun* macam.

various *adjective* bermacam-macam, pelbagai; **there are various ways of doing it** ada bermacam-macam cara untuk melakukannya.

vary *verb* berubah-ubah; **the price often varies** harganya sering berubah-ubah.

vase *noun* jambang, tempat bunga.

vast *adjective* besar, luas sekali.

a b c d e f g h i j k l m n o p q r s t u v w x y z

a b c d e f g h i j k l m n o p q r s t u v w x y z

Vatican *noun* Vatikan (tempat tinggal Sri Paus).

vaunt *verb* membual, menyombongkan diri.

veal *noun* daging anak lembu.

vegan *noun* orang yang tidak makan atau memanfaatkan apapun yang diambil dari binatang *(definition only)*.

vegetables *plural noun* sayur, sayuran, sayur-mayur.

vegetarian *adjective* vegetarian, vegetaris; **he's vegetarian** dia seorang vegetarian.

vehicle *noun* kendaraan.

vein *noun* urat, pembuluh darah halus.

velvet *noun* beludru.

vending machine *noun* mesin penjual rokok, minuman atau gula-gula*(definition only)*.

verb *noun* kata kerja.

verdict *noun* keputusan hakim.

verge *noun* **1** *(the roadside)* pinggir, tepi (jalan); **2 to be on the verge of** hampir-hampir; **I was on the verge of leaving** saya hampir saja berangkat.

version *noun* versi.

versus *preposition* berhadapan, melawan, versus.

vertical *adjective* tegak lurus.

vertigo *noun* pusing, vertigo.

very *adverb* sekali, amat, sangat; **it's very difficult** amat sulit, sangat sulit; **very well** *(healthy)* sehat sekali; **very much** banyak sekali. *adjective* **1 the very person I need!** orang yang saya perlukan!; **the very thing for the job!** alat yang tepat untuk pekerjaan ini!; **2 in the very middle** persis di tengah; **at the very end** di ujung sekali; **at the very front** di depan sekali.

vest *noun* rompi.

vet *noun* dokter hewan; **she's a vet** dia dokter hewan.

via *preposition* lewat, melalui; **to go via** pergi lewat, pergi melalui; **we're going via Malang** kami akan pergi melalui Malang; **we'll go via the bank** kami akan lewat bank.

vicar *noun* paderi, pendeta.

vicious *adjective* **1** *(an animal)* buas, galak, ganas; **2** *(an attack)* buruk, kejam.

victim *noun* korban.

victory *noun* kemenangan.

video *noun* **1** *(film)* **to watch a video** menonton video; **I've recorded it on video** saya merekamnya di video; **I bought a video** saya membeli

video; **2** *(cassette)* kaset video; **3** *(video recorder)* VCR.
verb merekam; **I'll video it for you** saya akan merekam itu untuk Anda.

video cassette *noun* pita video.

video game *noun* mainan video.

video recorder *noun* VCR.

video shop *noun* toko video.

Vietnam *noun* Vietnam.

view *noun* **1** pemandangan; **a room with a view of the lake** kamar dengan pemandangan danau; **2** *(opinion)* pandangan, pendapat; **in my view** menurut pendapat saya; **a point of view** pandangan, pendapat.

viewer *noun (person)* pemirsa, penonton.

viewpoint *noun* pandangan, pendapat.

vigorous *adjective* giat, penuh semangat.

vile *adjective* amat buruk, hina, keji.

villa *noun* vila.

village *noun* desa, dusun.

vine *noun* tumbuh-tumbuhan yang merambat.

vinegar *noun* cuka.

vineyard *noun* kebun anggur.

violence *noun* kekerasan.

violent *adjective* **1** *(temper)* bengis, garang; **2** *(storm)* hebat; **3** *(exercise, a blow)* kejam, keras.

violin *noun* biola; **to play the violin** main biola.

violinist *noun* pemain biola.

virgin *noun* anak dara, perawan.

Virgo *noun* bintang Virgo.

virus *noun* virus.

visa *noun* visa.

visible *adjective* kelihatan, tampak.

visit *noun* **1** *(stay)* kunjungan; **a visit to Lombok** kunjungan ke Lombok; **2** *(to a house)* bertamu.
verb **1** *(museum, temple, town)* mengunjungi; **2** *(person)* bertamu; **we visited Auntie Koh at Christmas** kami bertamu ke rumah Tante Koh pada hari Natal.

visitor *noun* **1** tamu; **2** *(a tourist)* turis, wisatawan.

visual *adjective* berhubungan dengan penglihatan, visual.

vital *adjective* sangat penting, vital; **it's vital to book** sangat penting memesan sebelumnya.

vitamin *noun* vitamin.

vivid *adjective* bersemangat, hidup, ramai; **to have a vivid**

a b c d e f g h i j k l m n o p q r s t u v w x y z

a b c d e f g h i j k l m n o p q r s t u v w x y z

imagination mempunyai daya khayal yang hidup.

vocabulary *noun* perbendaharaan kata.

vocational *adjective* kejuruan, pekerjaan.

vodka *noun* vodka, semacam minuman keras.

voice *noun* suara.

volcano *noun* gunung (ber)api.

volleyball *noun* bola voli; **to play volleyball** main bola voli.

volume *noun* kekuatan suara, bunyi; **could you turn down the volume please?** tolong kecilkan suaranya.

voluntary *adjective* **1** *(not compulsory)* sukarela; **voluntary work** kerja bakti, kerja sukarela.

volunteer *noun* **1** *(female)* sukarelawati; **2** *(male)* sukarelawan.

vomit *verb* muntah.

vote *noun* **1** suara; **2** pemilihan; **popular vote** pemilihan oleh semua orang yang berhak memilih.
verb **1** memberikan suara; **2 to vote for, to vote in** memilih.

voter *noun* pemilih.

voucher *noun* voucher.

vowel *noun* huruf hidup.

vulgar *adjective* kasar, kotor.

W w

waffle *noun (to eat)* kue wafel.

wages *plural noun* gaji, upah.

waist *noun* pinggang.

waistcoat *noun* baju rompi.

waist measurement *noun* ukuran pinggang.

wait *noun* waktu menunggu; **an hour's wait** menunggu sejam.
verb **1** menunggu; **they're waiting in the car** mereka sedang menunggu di dalam mobil; **she kept me waiting** dia membiarkan saya menunggu lama; **to wait for** menunggu; **wait for me!** tunggu saya!; **wait for the signal** tunggu tanda; **2 to wait on** melayani; **3 I can't wait to open it!** saya ingin sekali membukanya!

waiter *noun* pelayan.

waiting list *noun* daftar antrian.

waiting room *noun* kamar tunggu.

waitress *noun* pelayan wanita.

wake *verb* **1** *(somebody else)* membangunkan; **the dog woke me** anjing itu membangunkan saya; **2 I woke (up) at six** saya bangun jam enam; **wake up!** bangun!

walk *noun (a little stroll)* jalan-jalan; **to go for a walk** berjalan-jalan; **we went for a walk in the park** kami berjalan-jalan di taman; **it's about five minutes' walk from here** berjalan dari sini makan waktu kira-kira lima menit.
verb **1 I like walking** saya suka berjalan kaki; **2** *(walk around)* berjalan-jalan; **we walked around the temple** kami berjalan-jalan didalam pura; **3** *(go)* mengantar; **I'll walk to the bus stop with you** saya akan mengantar Anda ke halte bis; **4** jalan kaki; **it's not far, we can walk** tidak jauh, kita bisa jalan kaki (ke sana).

walkie-talkie *noun* woki-toki.

walking *noun (hiking)* berjalan kaki; **we're going walking in the tea plantation** kami mau berjalan kaki di kebun teh.

walking distance *noun* tidak jauh; **it's within walking distance of the sea** itu tidak jauh dari laut, orang bisa berjalan kaki ke sana.

walking stick *noun* tongkat.

Walkman™ *noun* walkman.

wall *noun* **1** *(inside)* dinding; **2** *(brick)* tembok.

wallet *noun* dompet.

wallpaper *noun* kertas dinding.

walnut *noun* semacam kenari.

wander *verb* **1** berkelana, berkeliling, mengembara; **to wander around town** berkeliling-keliling kota; **2 to wander off** mengembara.

want *noun* kebutuhan; **all our wants** semua kebutuhan kami.
verb ingin, mau; **do you want some coffee?** apakah Anda mau minum kopi?; **what do you want to do?** Anda ingin berbuat apa?; **I don't want to bother him** saya tidak mau mengganggu dia; **you are wanted on the phone** ada telepon untuk Anda.

war *noun* perang.

ward *noun* ruangan.

wardrobe *noun* lemari pakaian.

warm *adjective* **1** hangat; **a warm drink** minuman

hangat; **are you warm enough?** apakah Anda cukup hangat?; *(friendly)* hangat; **a warm welcome** sambutan hangat; **2** panas; **I am warm** saya panas; **it's warm today** hari ini panas; **I'll keep your dinner warm** makanan Anda tidak akan dibiarkan dingin.
verb menghangatkan; **he warmed the plates** dia menghangatkan piring-piring itu.
- **to warm up 1** *(the weather)* mulai panas; **2** memanaskan; *(an athlete)* memanaskan badan; *(food)* memanaskan; **I'll warm up some soup for you** saya mau memanaskan sop untuk Anda.

warmth *noun* kehangatan.

warn *verb* memperingatkan; **I warn you, it's expensive** saya memperingatkan Anda bahwa itu mahal; **he warned me to lock the car** dia memperingatkan saya supaya mobil dikunci.

warning *noun* peringatan.

wart *noun* kutil.

wash *noun* cucian; **to give the shirt a wash** mencuci baju.
verb **1** mencuci; **I've washed your jeans** saya sudah mencuci celana jeans Anda; **to wash your hands** mencuci tangan; **to wash your hair** keramas, mencuci rambut; **to wash the dishes** mencuci piring; **2** memandikan; **to wash the dog** memandikan anjing; **to get washed** mandi.
- **to wash up** mencuci piring.

washbasin *noun* baskom, tempat cuci tangan, wastafel.

washing *noun* cucian.

washing machine *noun* mesin cuci.

washing powder *noun* sabun cuci.

washing-up *noun* pencucian piring.

washing-up liquid *noun* deterjen.

wasp *noun* tawon.

waste *noun* pemborosan; **it's a waste of time** membuang-buang waktu saja.
verb **1** *(money, paper)* memboroskan; **2** *(time)* membuang-buang; **you're wasting your time** Anda membuang-buang waktu saja.

waste bin *noun* tempat sampah.

wastepaper bin *noun* keranjang sampah.

watch *noun* arloji, jam tangan; **my watch is slow** arloji saya lambat.
verb **1** *(to look at)* menonton; **I was watching TV** saya tadi menonton televisi; **2** *(keep a check on)* mengamati; **3** *(be careful)* berhati-hati; **watch you don't spill it** hati-hati supaya tidak tumpah; **watch out for the monkeys** awas monyet itu; **watch out!** awas! hati-hati!

water *noun* air; **drinking water** air minum.
verb menyirami; **to water the plants** menyirami tanaman.

waterfall *noun* air terjun.

watering can *noun* cerek penyiram (bunga).

watermelon *noun* semangka.

waterproof *adjective* tahan air.

water-skiing *noun* ski air.

water sports *noun* olahraga air.

wave *noun* **1** *(in the sea)* ombak; **2** *(with your hand)* lambaian tangan; **she gave us a wave from the bus** dia melambaikan tangan kepada kami dari bis.
verb **1** *(your hand, a flag)* melambaikan; **2** *(hair)* berombak.

wax *noun* lilin.

way *noun* **1** *(a route or road)* jalan; **the way to Kaliurang** jalan ke Kaliurang; **we asked the way to the station** kami bertanya tentang jalan ke stasiun kereta api; **on the way back** dalam perjalanan kembali; **on the way** dalam perjalanan; **to be in the way** menghalangi; **'way in'** 'masuk'; **'way out'** 'keluar'; **2** *(direction)* arah, jurusan; **which way did they go?** mereka menuju ke arah mana?; **come this way** kemarilah; **3** *(side)* **the right way up** tidak terbalik; **the wrong way round** terbalik; **4** *(distance)* jauh; **it's a long way** jauh sekali; **5** *(manner)* cara; **a way of talking** cara berbicara; **he does it his way** dia mengerjakannya dengan caranya sendiri; **either way** dengan cara apa saja; **she's wrong to do it this way** dia salah melakukannya begini; **6 Terry went all the way to the top** Terry mencapai puncak; **7 no way!** sama sekali tidak, tidak mungkin! **8 by the way** omong-omong *(colloquial)*.

we *pronoun* **1** *(excluding the listener)* kami; **we live in Sumbawa** kami tinggal di Sumbawa; **we won't be home** kami tidak akan ada di rumah; **2** *(including the*

a b c d e f g h i j k l m n o p q r s t u v w x y z

listener) kita; **we're late!** kita terlambat!; **I hope we don't miss the plane** mudah-mudahan kita tidak ketinggalan pesawat.

weak *adjective* lemah; **her voice was weak** suaranya lemah.

wealthy *adjective* berada, kaya, kaya raya.

weapon *noun* senjata.

wear *noun* pakaian; **children's wear** pakaian anak-anak; **sports wear** pakaian olahraga.
verb memakai; **Tamsin's wearing her sneakers** Tamsin memakai sepatu olahraganya; **she often wears red** dia sering berpakaian merah; **to wear make-up** berdandan.

weather *noun* **1** cuaca; **what's the weather like?** bagaimana cuacanya?; **in fine weather** dalam cuaca bagus; **the weather there is terrible** cuaca di sana buruk; **2** hawa; **the weather was cold** hawanya dingin.

weather forecast *noun* prakiraan cuaca, ramalan cuaca; **the weather forecast says it will rain** menurut prakiraan cuaca akan hujan.

wedding *noun* perkawinan, pernikahan.

Wednesday *noun* Rabu; **on Wednesday** pada hari Rabu; **see you on Wednesday!** sampai hari Rabu!; **that shop is closed on Wednesdays** toko itu tutup pada hari Rabu; **every Wednesday** setiap hari Rabu; **last Wednesday** hari Rabu yang lalu; **next Wednesday** hari Rabu depan.

weed *noun* rumput liar.

week *noun* minggu; **last week** minggu lalu; **next week** minggu depan; **this week** minggu ini; **for weeks** berminggu-minggu; **a week today** seminggu dari hari ini.

weekday *noun* hari kerja; **on weekdays** pada hari-hari kerja.

weekend *noun* akhir minggu, akhir pekan; **last weekend** akhir minggu yang lalu; **next weekend** akhir minggu yang akan datang; **for the weekend** selama akhir minggu; **at the weekend** pada akhir minggu; **have a nice weekend!** selamat berakhir minggu!

weigh *verb* menimbang; **to weigh yourself** menimbang badan sendiri; **how much do you weigh?** berapa berat badan Anda?; **I weigh 55**

kilos berat badan saya lima puluh lima kilo.

weight *noun* berat; **to put on weight** menjadi gemuk; **to lose weight** menjadi lebih kurus.

weird *adjective* aneh.

welcome *noun* sambutan; **to receive a warm welcome** mendapat sambutan hangat; **Welcome to Bali!** Selamat Datang di Bali!
adjective boleh saja; **you're welcome any time** Anda boleh datang kapan saja; **'thank you' – 'you're welcome!'** 'terima kasih' – 'kembali', 'sama-sama', 'terima kasih kembali'.
verb menyambut, menerima dengan senang hati.

well¹ *noun* sumur.

well² *adverb* **1** sehat; **to feel well** merasa sehat; **I'm very well thank you** saya baik-baik saja, terima kasih; **2** dengan baik; **Sukra played well** Sukra bermain dengan baik; **the operation went well** pembedahan itu berjalan dengan baik; **well done!** baik sekali!; **3 as well** juga; **Sri's coming as well** Sri akan datang juga; **4 well!** baiklah!; **well then, what's the problem?** baiklah, apa masalahnya?; **very well then, you can go** baiklah, Anda boleh pergi.

well-behaved *adjective* berkelakuan baik.

well-done *adjective (a steak)* dimasak matang-matang.

well-known *adjective* terkenal, termashyur, ternama.

well-off *adjective* kaya, berada, mampu.

west *noun* barat; **in the west** di sebelah barat, bagian barat.
adjective **the west side** sebelah barat; **a west wind** angin barat; **west of Sumbawa** di sebelah barat Sumbawa.

western *noun (a film)* film koboi.

West Indies *noun* Hindia Barat.

wet *adjective* **1** basah; **the grass is wet** rumput itu basah; **2 wet weather** banyak hujan; **we got wet** kami kehujanan.

whale *noun* ikan paus.

what *pronoun, adjective* **1** apa; **what did you say?** Anda berkata apa?; **what did you buy?** apa yang Anda beli?; **what is it?** apa itu?; **what's the matter?** ada apa sih? (*colloquial*), ada masalah apa?; **what's happening?** apa

a b c d e f g h i j k l m n o p q r s t u v w x y z

yang terjadi?; **what make is it?** merk apa itu?; **what's she doing?** dia sedang apa?; **2** siapa; **what's her name?** siapa namanya?; **3** berapa; **what's the fare?** berapa ongkosnya?; **what's the price of?** berapa harganya?; **4** apa yang; **tell me what you bought** apa yang Anda beli?; **she told me what had happened** dia memberitahu saya apa yang terjadi; **5** bagaimana; **what if it rains?** bagaimana kalau hujan?; **what if there's a bus strike?** bagaimana kalau ada pemogokan bis?; **6 what's your address?** di mana alamat Anda?

wheat *noun* gandum, terigu.

wheel *noun* roda; **the spare wheel** roda serep; **the steering wheel** setir.

wheelbarrow *noun* kereta sorong (beroda satu).

wheelchair *noun* kursi roda.

when *adverb, conjunction* **1** kapan; **when is she arriving?** kapan dia akan tiba?; **when's your birthday?** kapan hari ulang tahun Anda?; **2** *(past time)* ketika; **it was raining when I left** hari sedang hujan ketika saya berangkat; **3** kalau, bilamana; **give Lina this message when she comes** tolong sampaikan pesan ini kepada Lina kalau dia datang; **say when** katakan kalau sudah cukup.

where *adverb, conjunction* **1** di mana; **where are the children?** di mana anak-anak?; **where do you live?** Anda tinggal di mana?; **I don't know where they live** saya tidak tahu mereka tinggal di mana; **2** dari mana; **where do you come from?** Anda berasal dari mana?; **3** ke mana; **where are you going?** Anda mau ke mana?

whether *conjunction* apa(kah); **I don't know whether he's back or not** saya tidak tahu apakah dia sudah kembali atau belum.

which *adjective* yang mana, apa; **which CD did you buy?** CD apa yang Anda beli? *pronoun* **1** yang mana; **'I saw your brother' – 'which one?'** 'saya melihat saudara Anda' – 'yang mana?'; **which of these jackets is yours?** jas yang mana milik Anda?; **2** yang; **the lamp which is on the table** lampu yang di meja itu; **the book which you borrowed from me** buku yang Anda pinjam dari saya.

while *noun* **1** saat, waktu; **after a while** beberapa waktu

kemudian; **2** sebentar; **she worked here for a while** dia bekerja di sini beberapa lama; **wait a while** tunggu sebentar.
conjunction **1** ketika, sementara; **you can make some tea while I'm finishing my homework** bagaimana kalau Anda membuat teh sementara saya menyelesaikan pekerjaan rumah saya; **2** sedangkan, walaupun; **while I like the style I don't like the price** walaupun saya suka modenya saya tidak suka harganya; **that bed is expensive while this one is cheap** tempat tidur itu mahal sedangkan yang ini murah.

whip *noun (for a horse)* cambuk, cemeti.
verb **1** *(a person)* mencambuk; **2** mengocok; **whipped cream** krem yang dikocok.

whiskers *plural noun* kumis (kucing).

whisky *noun* wiski.

whisper *noun* bisikan; **speak in a whisper** berbisik-bisik.
verb berbisik, membisikkan.

whistle *noun* peluit.
verb **1** *(by a person, bird)* bersiul; **2** *(by a conductor, referee)* membunyikan peluit.

white *noun* putih; **an egg white** putih telur.
adjective putih; **a white shirt** kemeja putih.

white coffee *noun* kopi susu.

Whitsun *noun* hari Pantekosta.

who *pronoun* **1** siapa; **who wants some hot chocolate?** siapa yang mau minum susu coklat panas?; **2** yang; **my friend who lives in Ujung Pandang** teman saya yang tinggal di Ujung Pandang; **the friends who we invited** teman-teman yang kita undang.

whole *noun* keseluruhan; **on the whole** secara keseluruhan, pada umumnya; **the whole of the class** seluruh kelas.
adjective seluruh; **the whole family** seluruh keluarga; **the whole morning** seluruh pagi, sepanjang pagi; **the whole time** seluruh waktu; **the whole world** seluruh dunia.

wholemeal *adjective* tepung terigu yang terdiri dari biji-biji gandum yang utuh *(definition only)*; **wholemeal bread** roti.

whom *pronoun* yang; **the person whom I saw** orang yang saya lihat; **the person to whom I wrote** orang yang

a b c d e f g h i j k l m n o p q r s t u v w x y z

saya surati, orang yang saya kirimi surat.

whose *pronoun, adjective* **1** siapa (punya); **whose is this jacket?** jaket siapa ini?; **whose shoes are these?** sepatu siapa ini?; **whose is it?** ini milik siapa?; **I know whose it is** saya tahu siapa pemiliknya; **2** yang –nya; **the man whose car was stolen** orang yang mobilnya dicuri.

why *adverb* apa sebabnya, kenapa, mengapa; **why did she phone?** mengapa dia menelepon?; **nobody knows why he did it** tidak ada yang tahu mengapa dia melakukannya.

wicked *adjective* **1** *(bad, a person)* jahat; **2** *(a smile)* nakal; **3** *(brilliant)* hebat.

wide *adjective* **1** lebar; **a piece of paper 20 cm wide** selembar kertas yang lebarnya dua puluh senti; **the door was wide open** pintu itu terbuka lebar; **2** luas; **the river is very wide here** sungai itu lebar sekali di sini; **3** bermacam-macam; **a wide range of goods** bermacam-macam barang.

wide awake *adjective* mata terbuka lebar.

widow *noun* janda.

widower *noun* duda.

width *noun* lebar; **what's the width of this fabric?** berapa lebar kain ini?

wife *noun* istri.

wig *noun* rambut palsu, wig.

wild *adjective* **1** *(an animal or plant)* liar; **wild birds** burung liar; **2** *(crazy)* gila *(idea, party, person)*; **3** gemar sekali; **to be wild about sports** gemar sekali akan olahraga.

wildlife *noun* binatang liar, margasatwa; **a program about wildlife in Kalimantan** program tentang binatang-binatang liar di Kalimantan.

wildlife park *noun* taman margasatwa.

will[1] *noun* surat wasiat.

will[2] *verb* **1** akan; **I'll see you soon** sampai jumpa, sampai nanti; **he'll be pleased to see you** dia akan senang berjumpa dengan Anda; **there won't be a problem** tidak akan ada masalah; **2** mau; **I'll phone them at once** saya akan menelepon mereka dengan segera; **it won't rain** tidak akan hujan; **will you have a drink?** apakah Anda mau minum?; **will you help me?** apakah Anda mau menolong saya?; **'will you write to me?' – 'of course I will!'** 'apakah Anda mau menulis surat kepada

a b c d e f g h i j k l m n o p q r s t u v w x y z

saya?' – 'tentu saja!'; **he won't open the door** dia tidak mau membuka pintu; **the car won't start** mesin mobil tidak mau jalan; **3** dapat; **the drawer won't open** laci ini tidak dapat dibuka; **it will hold about two litres** tempat itu dapat memuat kira-kira dua liter.

willing *adjective* bersedia, mau; **to be willing to do** mau mengerjakan, bersedia mengerjakan; **I'm willing to pay** saya bersedia, mau membayar.

willingly *adverb* dengan senang hati.

willow *noun* semacam pohon.

win *noun* kemenangan; **our win over the Crows** kemenangan regu kita terhadap regu Crows. *verb* menang; **we won!** kami menang!; **Bulldogs won by two goals** regu Bulldogs menang dengan dua gol.

wind[1] *noun* angin; **the South wind** angin dari Selatan.

wind[2] *verb* **1** *(a wire or a rope, for example)* menggulung; **2** *(a clock)* memutar.

wind instrument *noun* alat musik yang ditiup.

window *noun* jendela; **to look out of the window** melihat ke luar jendela.

windscreen *noun* kaca depan (pada mobil).

windscreen wipers *plural noun* weper.

windy *adjective* banyak angin; **it's windy today** ada banyak angin hari ini.

wine *noun* anggur; **a glass of white wine** segelas anggur putih.

wing *noun* sayap.

wink *verb* mengedipkan mata; **to wink at** mengedipkan mata kepada.

winner *noun* pemenang.

winning *adjective* yang menang.

winnings *plural noun* hasil kemenangan.

winter *noun* musim dingin.

wipe *verb* mengelap, membersihkan, menghapus, menyeka; **I'll just wipe the table** saya mau mengelap meja dulu; **to wipe your nose** menyeka hidung.

- **to wipe up** *(dishes)* mengelap.

wire *noun* kawat; **an electric wire** kawat listrik.

wire netting *noun* kawat kasa.

wise *adjective* bijaksana.

wish *noun* **1** hasrat, kehendak, keinginan; **2** pujian, ucapan selamat;

I sent them my best wishes saya mengirimi mereka ucapan selamat. **best wishes on your birthday** ucapan selamat ulang tahun.
verb **1** menginginkan; **wish you were here** ingin Anda ada di sini; **2** mengucapkan; **I wished him happy birthday** saya mengucapkan selamat hari ulang tahun kepadanya.

with *preposition* **1** dengan; **with pleasure** dengan senang hati; **beat the eggs with a fork** mengocok telur dengan garpu; **he took his umbrella with him** dia membawa payungnya; **2** *(at the house of)* di; **we're staying the night with Rendra** kami akan menginap di rumah Rendra; **3** pada; **with Gede** pada Gede; **have you got the keys with you?** apakah kunci-kunci itu ada pada Anda?; **4** *(in descriptions)* yang; **a girl with red hair** anak perempuan yang berambut merah; **the boy with the broken arm** anak laki-laki yang lengannya patah; **4 filled with water** berisi air; **covered with blood** berlumuran darah; **red with rage** merah karena marah.

without *preposition* tanpa; **without you** tanpa Anda; **without sugar** tanpa gula; **without a sweater** tanpa sweater; **without looking** tanpa melihat.

witness *noun* saksi.
verb menyaksikan.

witty *adjective* pintar lucu, pandai berkelakar.

wolf *noun* anjing hutan, serigala.

woman *noun* perempuan, wanita; **a woman friend** teman perempuan; **a woman reporter** wartawati.

wonder *noun* **1** keajaiban; **2** heran, mengherankan; **it's no wonder you're tired** tidak mengherankan Anda lelah.
verb ingin tahu; **I wonder why** saya ingin tahu mengapa; **I wonder where the dog is** di mana anjing itu.

wonderful *adjective* sangat bagus, sangat hebat.

wood *noun* kayu; **the lamp base is made of wood** dasar lampu itu dibuat dari kayu.

wooden *adjective* dari kayu.

woodwork *noun* **1** bagian rumah yang terbuat dari kayu; **2** ketrampilan perkayuan.

wool *noun* bulu domba, wol.

word *noun* **1** kata; **a long word** kata yang panjang; **what's the Indonesian word for 'control'?** apa kata

Indonesianya untuk 'control'?; **in other words** dengan kata lain; **the words of a song** kata-kata lagu; **word for word** kata demi kata; **to have a word with** berbicara dengan; **2** *(promise)* janji; **to give somebody your word** berjanji, menjamin; **he broke his word** dia melanggar janjinya.

word processing *noun* pemrosesan kata.

word processor *noun* komputer, pemroses kata.

work *noun* pekerjaan; **I've got some work to do** ada pekerjaan yang harus saya lakukan; **he's out of work** dia tunakarya (tidak ada pekerjaan) sekarang; **Bawuk's off work** *(sick)* Bawuk sedang cuti sakit; *(on holiday)* Bawuk sedang cuti; **Tun's at work** Tun sedang bekerja; **public works** pekerjaan umum.
verb **1** bekerja; **she works in an office** dia bekerja di kantor; **Dad works from home** Bapak punya kantor di rumah; **Supri works in advertising** Supri bekerja di kantor reklame; **Choon works nights** Choon bekerja malam; **2** *(to operate)* menjalankan; **can you work the video?** apakah Anda bisa menjalankan video ini?; **3** *(function)* berjalan; **the TV's not working** televisi tidak jalan, televisi rusak; **that worked really well!** itu berjalan dengan baik sekali!
- **to work out** **1** *(understand)* mengerti; **I can't work out why** saya tidak mengerti mengapa; **2** *(exercise)* berlatih; **3** *(to go well)* berhasil baik; **4** *(calculate)* menghitung; **I'll work out how much it would cost** saya akan menghitung ongkosnya.

worked up *adjective* **to get worked up** meningkatkan semangat.

worker *noun* buruh, karyawan, pekerja.

work experience *noun* pengalaman kerja; **to do work experience, to be on work experience** bekerja mencari pengalaman.

working-class *adjective* kaum buruh, kelas buruh; **a working-class background** latar belakang kelas buruh.

work of art *noun* karya seni.

workshop *noun* **1** bengkel; **garage, repair shop** bengkel mobil; **2** lokakarya; **there's a management workshop next week** minggu depan ada lokakarya manajemen; **3** ruang kerja.

world *noun* dunia; **the best in the world** yang terbaik (paling baik) di dunia; **the Western world** dunia barat.

World Cup *noun* Piala Dunia.

world war *noun* perang dunia; **the Second World War** Perang Dunia Kedua.

worm *noun* cacing, ulat.

worn out *adjective* **1** *(a person)* kecapaian, kelelahan; **2** *(clothes or shoes)* usang.

worried *adjective* cemas, khawatir; **they're worried** mereka khawatir; **to be worried about** cemas, khawatir; **we're worried about Putri** kami merasa cemas tentang Putri.

worry *noun* kekhawatiran, rasa cemas, rasa khawatir. *verb* khawatir, merasa cemas; **don't worry** jangan khawatir, jangan susah; **there's nothing to worry about** tidak ada yang perlu dicemaskan; **you worry too much** Anda terlalu khawatir.

worse *adjective* lebih buruk, lebih jelek; **it was even worse than the last time** lebih buruk dari yang terakhir; **to get worse** bertambah, semakin buruk, jelek; **the weather's getting worse** cuacanya bertambah buruk; **things are getting worse and worse** keadaan menjadi makin buruk.

worst *adjective* yang paling buruk, yang terburuk; **it was the worst day of my life** itu hari yang terburuk dalam hidup saya; **if the worst comes to the worst** kalau keadaan sampai buruk sekali.

worth *adjective* **1** harga; **to be worth** berharga; **how much is it worth?** berapa harganya?; **2** berguna; **to be worth doing** berguna untuk dilakukan; **it's worth trying** berguna untuk dicoba; **it's not worth the effort** itu memboroskan, membuang-buang tenaga saja.

would *verb* **1** mau; **would you like something to eat?** apakah Anda mau makan?; **2 would not** tidak mau; **he wouldn't answer** dia tidak mau menjawab; **the car wouldn't start** mobil itu tidak mau jalan; **3** ingin; **I would like an omelette** saya ingin makan telur dadar; **I'd like to go to the zoo** saya ingin ke kebun binatang; **if we asked her she would help us** kalau kami minta tentu dia akan membantu;

that would be a good idea itu ide yang baik.

wound *noun* luka.

wrap *verb* membungkus; **I'm going to wrap up this gift** saya akan membungkus kado ini; **could you wrap it for me please?** tolong bungkuskan barang ini.

wrapping paper *noun* kertas kado, kertas pembungkus.

wreck *noun* **1** *(of a crashed car or plane)* puing-puing, rongsokan; **2 I feel a wreck** saya merasa capai sekali.
verb menghancurkan, merusak; **because he was drunk he completely wrecked my evening** karena dia mabuk dia merusak waktu saya semalam.

wrestler *noun* pegulat.

wrestling *noun* gulat.

wrinkled *adjective* **1** *(of skin)* berkerut, kisut; **2** *(of clothing)* kusut.

wrist *noun* pergelangan tangan.

write *verb* **1** menulis; **I wrote to Heather yesterday** saya menulis surat kepada Heather kemarin.
- **to write down** mencatat, menuliskan; **I wrote down her name** saya mencatat namanya.

writer *noun* pengarang, penulis.

writing *noun* karangan, tulisan.

wrong *adjective* **1** salah; **the wrong answer** jawaban yang salah; **it's the wrong address** alamatnya salah; **I've brought the wrong file** saya membawa map yang salah; **you've got the number wrong** nomor itu salah; **to be wrong** salah; **I was wrong** saya salah; **the information was wrong** informasi itu salah; **2 what's wrong?** apa salahnya? ada apa?; **3 the wrong way** cara yang keliru, jalan yang salah.

X x

xerox *noun* mesin fotokopi, mesin xerox.
verb membuat fotokopi, memfotokopi.

X-ray *noun* sinar X, ronsen.
verb menyinar X, meronsen; **they X-rayed her ankle** pergelangan kakinya dironsen.

Y y

yacht *noun* **1** *(sailing boat)* kapal pesiar, perahu; **2** *(large luxury ship)* kapal.

yap *verb* menggonggong, menyalak *(a pup).*

yard *noun* halaman; **school yard** halaman sekolah.

yawn *verb* menguap.

year *noun* **1** tahun; **six years ago** enam tahun yang lalu; **the whole year** sepanjang tahun; **they lived in Kupang for years** mereka tinggal di Kupang selama bertahun-tahun; **a two-year-old child** anak berumur dua tahun; **2** kelas; **I'm in year ten** saya di kelas sepuluh.

yearbook *noun* buku tahunan.

yell *verb* memekik, menjerit.

yellow *adjective* kuning.

yes *adverb* **1** ya; **yes, I know** ya, saya tahu; **'is the cat inside?' – 'yes, it is'** 'apakah kucing itu ada di dalam?' – 'ya, ada'; **2** *(answering an invitation, offer)* **'would you like to have some more' – 'yes, please'** 'apakah Anda mau tambah?' – '(ya) mau'; **3** *(answering a negative)* **'you haven't finished, have you?' – 'yes, I have'** 'Anda belum selesai, bukan?' – 'sudah'.

yesterday *adverb* kemarin; **I saw her yesterday** kemarin saya melihat dia; **yesterday afternoon** kemarin sore; **yesterday morning** kemarin pagi; **the day before yesterday** kemarin dulu.

yet *adverb* **not yet** belum; **it's not ready yet** belum siap, belum selesai.

yoghurt *noun* susu masam kental, yogut; **a banana yoghurt** yogut pisang.

yolk *noun* merah telur.

you *pronoun* Anda, engkau, kamu, kau, saudara. *(Many terms of address are used for 'you' in Indonesian. For example, you can use the person's name or if they are older you should use a title like 'Ibu' or 'Bapak'.)*

young *adjective* muda; **Tutut's two years younger than I am** Tutut dua tahun lebih muda daripada saya; **young people** kaum muda.

your *adjective* *(property)* Anda, kamu, mu, saudara, tuan; **your book** buku Anda, bukumu; **your income** pendapatan Anda, penghasilan Anda.

yours *pronoun* kepunyaan Anda, milik Anda; **is this pen yours?** apakah pena ini kepunyaan Anda?; **my brother's younger than yours** adik saya lebih muda daripada adik Anda.

yourself *pronoun* dirinya, sendiri; **did you do it yourself?** apakah Anda melakukan itu sendiri?; **all by yourself** sendirian; **careful, you'll hurt yourself** hati-hati nanti Anda cedera.

yourselves *pronoun* sendiri; **help yourselves** ambil sendiri; **did you do it yourselves?** apakah saudara melakukannya sendiri?

youth *noun* orang muda, remaja.

youth hostel *noun* hostel, losmen, pesanggrahan muda-mudi.

Yugoslavia *noun* Yugoslavia; **the former Yugoslavia** bekasYugoslavia.

yummy *adjective (slang)* enak, lezat, sedap.

Z z

zany *adjective* amat jenaka, sangat lucu.

zebra *noun* kuda zebra.

zebra crossing *noun* penyeberangan zebra.

zero *noun* nol.

zigzag *verb (of a road)* berliku-liku.

zip *noun* ritsleting.

zodiac *noun* zodiak.

zone *noun* daerah, lingkungan, zona.

zoo *noun* kebun binatang.

zoology *noun* ilmu hewan, zoologi.

zoom lens *noun* lensa zoom.

Map of Indonesia
N
PILIPINA
MALAYSIA
SINGAPURA
SULAWESI
HALMAHERA
PAPUA
BARAT
SUMATRA
Jakarta
KEPULAUAN
MALUKU
INDONESIA
TIMOR TIMUR
JAWA
NUSA
TENGGARA
TIMOR BARAT
Samudra
Hindia
AUSTRALIA

World Map

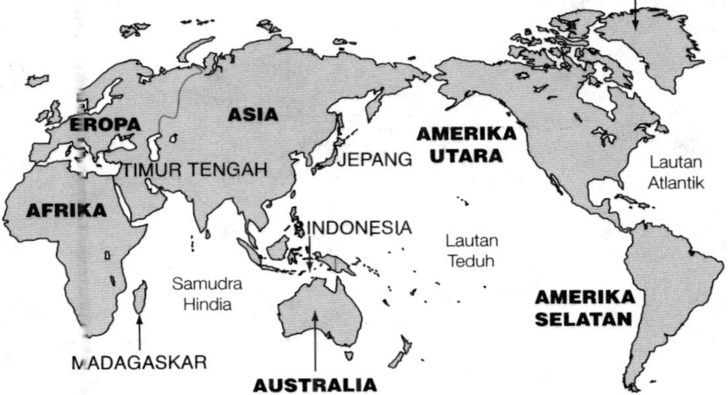
TANAH
HIJAU
EROPA
ASIA
AMERIKA
UTARA
JEPANG
TIMUR TENGAH
Lautan
Atlantik
AFRIKA
INDONESIA
Lautan
Teduh
Samudra
Hindia
AMERIKA
SELATAN
MADAGASKAR
AUSTRALIA